# Problem Solving in Data Structures & Algorithms using Java

Fourth Edition

By Hemant Jain

Problems Solving in Data Structures & Algorithms Using Java
Hemant Jain

**ACKNOWLEDGMENT**

The author is very grateful to GOD ALMIGHTY for his grace and blessing.

I would like to express profound gratitude to my family and friends for their invaluable encouragement, supervision and useful suggestions throughout this book writing work. Their support and continuous guidance enable me to complete my work successfully.

Hemant Jain

# Table of Contents

# Table of Contents

# CHAPTER 0: ABOUT THIS BOOK

## What this book is about

This book will take you through basic to advanced data structures and algorithms. Data structures define how data is arranged in memory for fast and efficient access. An algorithm is a finite set of unambiguous instructions to solve problems by manipulating various data structures.

Designing an efficient algorithm is a very important skill that all software companies pursue. Most of the interviews for software companies are focused on knowledge of data structures and algorithms. Apart from knowing a programming language, you also need to have a good command of these key computer fundamentals to not only crack the interview but also excel in your jobs as a software engineer.

## Prerequisites

You should have a working knowledge of Java programming language. You are not an expert in the Java language, but you are well familiar with concepts of classes, functions, references, and recursion.

## Who should take this course ?

If you're planning to pursue a career in the Java language, get better at it and apply for a job, this book is best for you. If you can put a reasonable amount of time into this book by reading various concepts and solving the various problems on data structures, you can become an expert in data structures and algorithms.

## Code downloads

You can download the code of solved examples in the book from the author's GitHub repositories at ***https://GitHub.com/Hemant-Jain-Author/.*** Hear the author had solved examples in various programming languages like C, C++, C#, Java, Python, JavaScript, Swift, GoLang, Ruby, etc.

## End

It is highly recommended that you should read the problem statement, try to solve the problems by yourself and then only you should look into the solution to find the approach of this book. Practising more and more problems will increase your thinking capacity, and you will be able to handle unseen problems in an interview. We recommend you to practice all the problems given in this book, then solve more and more problems from online resources like www.topcoder.com, www.careercup.com, https://leetcode.com/ etc.

# CHAPTER 1: ALGORITHMS ANALYSIS

## Introduction

An **Algorithm** is a finite set of unambiguous steps or instructions to solve a given problem. Knowledge of algorithms helps us to get desired results faster by applying the appropriate algorithm. We learn by experience. With experience, it becomes easy to solve new problems. By looking into various problem-solving algorithms or techniques, we begin to develop a pattern that will help us in solving similar problems.

The properties of an algorithm are:
1. It takes **zero or more inputs**.
2. It should produce **one or more output**.
3. It should be **Deterministic**. It produces the same output if the same input is provided again.
4. It should be **Correct**. It should be correct and able to process all the given inputs and provide the correct output.
5. It should **Terminate** in a finite time**.**
6. It should be **Efficient**. The algorithm should be efficient in solving problems.

The **complexity** of an algorithm is the amount of Time or Space required by the algorithm to process the input and produce the output.

There are two **types of Complexity**:
1. First is **Time-Complexity**, how much time is required by an algorithm to produce output for an input of size 'n'.

   Time-Complexity is represented by function T(n) - time required versus the input size n.
2. Second is **Space-Complexity**, how much RAM or memory that an algorithm is going to consume to produce output for an input of size 'n'.

   Space-Complexity is represented by function S(n) - memory used versus the input size n.

## Asymptotic Analysis or Asymptotic Notations

Calculating the running time of any algorithm in mathematical units of computation is known as Asymptotic Analysis. The efficiency of algorithms is calculated using asymptotic analysis, independent of the given data set or programming language.

In most cases, we are interested in the order of growth of the algorithm instead of the exact time required for running an algorithm. This time is also known as Asymptotic Running Time.

## Big-O Notation

Definition: "f(n) is big-O of g(n)" or f(n) = O(g(n)), if there are two +ve constants c and n1 such that $f(n) \leq c\, g(n)$ for all $n \geq n1$,

In other words, c g(n) is an upper bound for f(n) for all $n \geq n0$. The function f(n) growth is slower than c g(n). For a sufficiently large value of input n, the (c.g(n)) will always be greater than f(n).

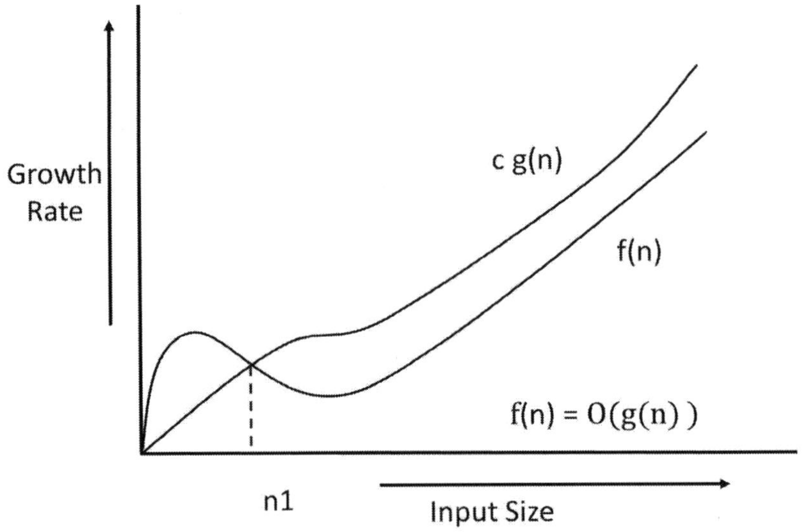


Example : n^2 + n = O(n^2)

## Omega-Ω Notation

Definition: "f(n) is omega of g(n)" or $f(n)=\Omega(g(n))$ if there are two +ve constants c and n1 such that $c\,g(n) \leq f(n)$ for all $n \geq n1$

In other words, c g(n) is the lower bound for f(n). Function f(n) growth is faster than c g(n)

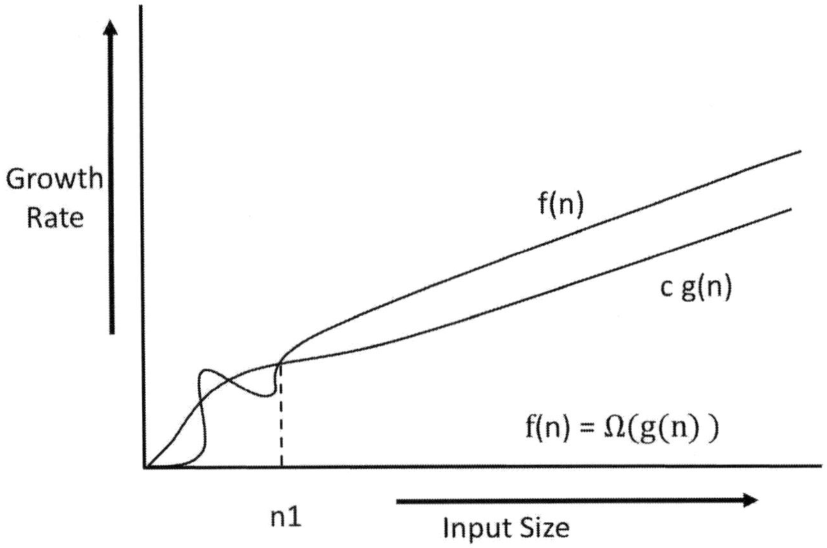


Find relationship of $f(n) = n^c$ and $g(n) = c^n$

$f(n) = \Omega(g(n))$

## Theta-Θ Notation

Definition: "f(n) is theta of g(n)." or f(n) = Θ(g(n)) if there are three +ve constants c1, c2 and n1 such that $c1\ g(n) \leq f(n) \leq c2\ g(n)$ for all $n \geq n1$

Function g(n) is an asymptotically tight bound on f(n). Function f(n) grows at the same rate as g(n).

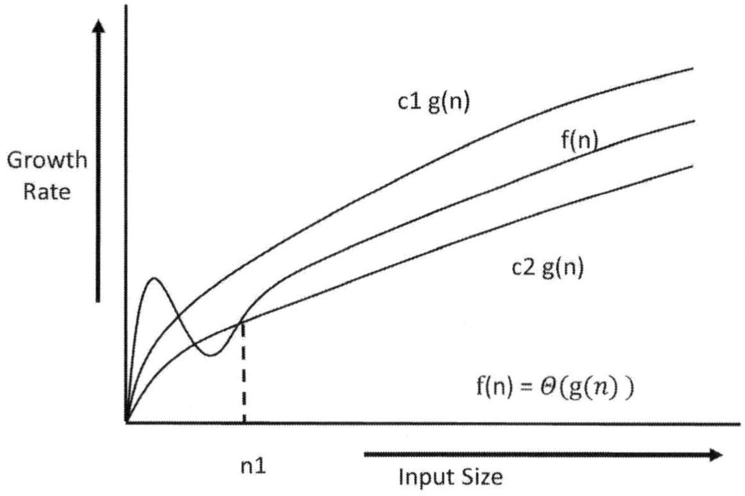


Example: n^3 + n^2 + n = Θ(n^3)

Example: n^2 + n = Θ(n^2)

Find relationship of f(n) = 2n^2 + n and g(n) = n^2

f(n) = O(g(n))

f(n) = Θ(g(n))

f(n) = Ω(g(n))

## Complexity analysis of algorithms

The complexity of an algorithm are analysed in three categories:

- **Worst-Case Complexity:** The worst-case complexity represents the maximum number of steps required to execute an algorithm. It provides us with the upper bound of an algorithm. Usually, we use this complexity to judge algorithm performance.
- **Best-Case Complexity**:The best-case complexity represents the minimum number of steps required to execute an algorithm. It provides us with the lower bound of an algorithm.
- **Average-Case Complexity**:The average-case complexity represents the average number of steps required to execute an algorithm. We take the average of the steps executed in all the cases to calculate average-case complexity.

**Note**: Worst-case complexity is used to find the guarantee in how much time some particular algorithm will finish. This is the most important time complexity. If the type of complexity is not mentioned, then always consider Worst-Case time complexity.

# Growth of functions

Let's look at these growth rates of various functions. The size of the input is n.

## Constant Time, O(1)

An algorithm is said to run in constant time if the output is produced in constant time, regardless of the input size.

Examples:

1. Accessing an $n^{th}$ element of an Array
2. Push and pop of a stack.
3. Add and remove from a queue.
4. Accessing an element of Hash-Table.

## Linear Time, O(n)

An algorithm is said to run in linear time if the execution time of the algorithm is directly proportional to the input size.

Examples:

1. Array operations like search element, find min, find max etc.
2. Linked list operations like traversal, find min, find max etc.

**Note**: If we need to traverse all the nodes of a data structure for some task, then complexity cant be less than O(n)

## Logarithmic Time, O(log(n))

An algorithm is said to run in logarithmic time if the execution time of the algorithm is proportional to the logarithm of the input size. In each step of an algorithm, a significant portion (e.g. half portion) of the input is pruned/rejected out without traversing it.

An example is the Binary search algorithm. We will read about this algorithm in this book.

## n.log(n) Time, O(n.log(n))

An algorithm is said to run in n*log(n) time if the execution time of an algorithm is proportional to the product of input size and logarithm of the input size. In these algorithms, each time the input is divided into half (or some proportion) and each portion is processed independently.

Examples are Merge-Sort, Quick-Sort (average case), Heap-Sort etc.

## Quadratic Time, O(n^2)

An algorithm is said to run in quadratic time if the execution time of an algorithm is proportional to the square of the input size. In these algorithms, each element is compared with all the other elements.

Examples are Bubble-Sort, Selection-Sort, Insertion-Sort

## Exponential Time O(2^n)

In these algorithms, all possible subsets of elements of input data are generated. Its common example is the power set.

## Factorial Time O(n!)

In these algorithms, all possible permutations of the elements of input data are generated. Finding permutations is a common example of factorial time.

A list of commonly occurring algorithm Time Complexity in increasing order:

| Name | Notation |
|---|---|
| Constant | O(1) |
| Logarithmic | O(log(n)) |
| Linear | O(n) |
| N.Log(N) | O(n.log(n)) |
| Quadratic | O(n^2) |
| Polynomial | O(n^c) c is a constant & c>1 |
| Exponential | O(c^m) c is a constant & c>1 |
| Factorial | O(n!) |
| N-Power-N | O(n^n) |

The time taken by certain algorithms to run varies dramatically with the size of the input. Some algorithms take minutes or even seconds to run on huge input, whereas others may take days to complete their execution. To understand how the rate of growth changes with the size of the input in different functions, the following table presents the approximate number of steps required to run an algorithm:

| | Function Growth Rate (Approximate) | | | | | | |
|---|---|---|---|---|---|---|---|
| **N** | **O(1)** | **O(log(n))** | **O(n)** | **O(n.log(n))** | **O(n^2)** | **O(n^3)** | **O(2^n)** |
| 10 | 1 | 3 | 10 | 30 | $10^2$ | $10^3$ | $10^3$ |
| $10^2$ | 1 | 6 | $10^2$ | $6x10^2$ | $10^4$ | $10^6$ | $10^{30}$ |
| $10^3$ | 1 | 9 | $10^3$ | $9x10^3$ | $10^6$ | $10^9$ | $10^{300}$ |
| $10^4$ | 1 | 13 | $10^4$ | $13x10^4$ | $10^8$ | $10^{12}$ | $10^{3000}$ |
| $10^5$ | 1 | 16 | $10^5$ | $16x10^5$ | $10^{10}$ | $10^{15}$ | $10^{30000}$ |
| $10^6$ | 1 | 19 | $10^6$ | $19x10^6$ | $10^{12}$ | $10^{18}$ | $10^{300000}$ |

# Deriving an Algorithm's Runtime Function

## Constants

If any line of code is a statement with basic operations, e.g., comparisons, assignments, or reading a variable, they take constant time each. Thus, the time complexity of each statement is O(1).

## Loops

In loop, a repetition of a particular code for n times, where n is the size of the loop. Every statement inside the loop has a runtime of O(1). The running time of a loop is a product of the running time of the statement inside a loop and the number of iterations in the loop. Time Complexity is O(n)

## Nested Loops

The running time of a nested loops is a product of the running time of the statements inside the loop multiplied by a product of the size of all the loops. Time Complexity is O(n^c). Where c is the number of loops. For two loops, it will be O(n^2)

## Consecutive Statements

In this case, we add the running time of all the consecutive lines of code.

## If-Else Statement

In this case, either "if" will run or "else" will run. So, the block with larger runtime will be considered.

## Logarithmic Statement

In this case, each iteration will cut the input size into b pieces and consider one of the pieces for the next iteration. Time complexity in this situation will be $O(\log_b(n))$.

# Time Complexity Examples

**Example 1.1: Single loop**

```
int fun1(int n) {
    int m = 0;
    for (int i = 0; i < n; i++) {
        m += 1;
    }
    return m;
}

// Testing code.
public static void main(String[] args) {
    Analysis a = new Analysis();
    System.out.println("N = 100, Number of instructions in O(n)::" + a.fun1(100));
}
```

**Output:**

```
N = 100, Number of instructions in O(n)::100
```

**Time Complexity:** O(n), single loop takes linear time.

**Example 1.2: Nested loops**

```
int fun2(int n) {
    int i, j, m = 0;
    for (i = 0; i < n; i++) {
        for (j = 0; j < n; j++) {
            m += 1;
        }
    }
    return m;
}

// Testing code.
public static void main(String[] args) {
    Analysis a = new Analysis();
    System.out.println("N = 100, Number of instructions in O(n^2)::" +
a.fun2(100));
}
```

**Output:**

```
N = 100, Number of instructions in O(n^2)::10000
```

**Time Complexity:** O(n^2), two nested for loop, takes quadratic time. Both the "for" loop is executed n number of times, so the internal statement executed n^2 number of times.

**Example 1.3: Triple nested loops**

```
int fun3(int n) {
    int i, j, k, m = 0;
    for (i = 0; i < n; i++) {
        for (j = 0; j < n; j++) {
            for (k = 0; k < n; k++) {
                m += 1;
            }
        }
    }
    return m;
}

// Testing code.
public static void main(String[] args) {
    Analysis a = new Analysis();
    System.out.println("N = 100, Number of instructions in O(n^3)::" +
a.fun3(100));
}
```

**Output:**

```
N = 100, Number of instructions in O(n^3)::1000000
```

**Time Complexity:** O(n^3), All the three nested loops run for n number of iterations. So the statement inside the innermost loop will run for n^3 number of times.

**Example 1.4: Triple nested loops**

```
int fun4(int n) {
    int i, j, k, m = 0;
```

```
    for (i = 0; i < n; i++) {
        for (j = i; j < n; j++) {
            for (k = j + 1; k < n; k++) {
                m += 1;
            }
        }
    }
    return m;
}

// Testing code.
public static void main(String[] args) {
    Analysis a = new Analysis();
    System.out.println("N=100, Number of instructions in O(n^3)::" + a.fun4(100));
}
```

**Output:**

```
N = 100, Number of instructions in O(n^3)::166650
```

**Time Complexity:** Three nested loops each run for n number of times. The innermost statement will run for n^3 number of times. Time complexity is O(n^3)

**Example 1.5: Arithmetic Progression**

```
int fun5(int n) {
    int i, j, m = 0;

    for (i = 1; i <= n; i++) {
        for (j = 0; j < i; j++) {
            m += 1;
        }
    }
    return m;
}

// Testing code.
public static void main(String[] args) {
    Analysis a = new Analysis();
    System.out.println("N = 100, Number of instructions in O(n^2)::" +
a.fun5(100));
}
```

**Output:**

```
N = 100, Number of instructions in O(n^2)::4950
```

**Time Complexity:** Statement inside inner loop executes for 1 time in first iteration then 2 times then 3 times and so on for n iterations. Total number of times the inner statement is executed = 1 + 2+ 3 +..... + n. This series is an arithmetic progression, which sums to n(n+1)/2. So the final time complexity is O(n(n+1)/2) ignoring the constant factors, time complexity will be O(n^2).

**Example 1.6: Arithmetic Progression**

```
int fun6(int n) {
    int i, j, m = 0;
    for (i = 0; i < n; i++) {
        for (j = i; j > 0; j--) {
            m += 1;
```

```
        }
    }
    return m;
}

// Testing code.
public static void main(String[] args) {
    Analysis a = new Analysis();
    System.out.println("N = 100, Number of instructions in O(n^2)::" +
a.fun6(100));
}
```

**Output:**

```
N = 100, Number of instructions in O(n^2)::4950
```

**Time Complexity**: The inner loop will run 1 time in the first iteration, then 2 times in the second iteration and so on. It is an arithmetic progression, so time complexity will be O(n^2).

**Example 1.7: Nested loops / Geometric Progression**

```
int fun7(int n) {
    int i, j, m = 0;
    for (i = n; i > 0; i /= 2) {
        for (j = 0; j < i; j++) {
            m += 1;
        }
    }
    return m;
}

// Testing code.
public static void main(String[] args) {
    Analysis a = new Analysis();
    System.out.println("N = 100, Number of instructions in O(n)::" + a.fun7(100));
}
```

**Output:**

```
N = 100, Number of instructions in O(n)::197
```

For nested loops, look for inner loop iterations. Time complexity will be calculated by looking into the inner loop. First, it will run for n number of times then n/2 and so on. (n+n/2 +n/4+n/8+n/16 ……)

**Time Complexity:** O(n)

**Example 1.8: Geometric Progression**

```
int fun8(int n) {
    int i, j = 0, m = 0;

    for (i = 1; i <= n; i *= 2) {
        for (j = 0; j <= i; j++) {
            m += 1;
        }
    }
    return m;
}
```

```
// Testing code.
public static void main(String[] args) {
    Analysis a = new Analysis();
    System.out.println("N = 100, Number of instructions in O(n)::" + a.fun8(100));
}
```

**Output:**

```
N = 100, Number of instructions in O(n)::134
```

**Time Complexity:** The inner loop will run for 1, 2, 4, 8,... n times in successive iteration of the outer loop. T(n) = O(1+ 2+ 4+ ....+n/2+n) = O(n)

**Example 1.9: Double the iteration variable**

```
int fun9(int n) {
    int i = 1, m = 0;
    while (i < n) {
        m += 1;
        i = i * 2;
    }
    return m;
}

// Testing code.
public static void main(String[] args) {
    Analysis a = new Analysis();
    System.out.println("N = 100, Number of inst in O(log(n))::" + a.fun9(100));
}
```

**Output:**

```
N = 100, Number of inst in O(log(n))::7
```

In each iteration, i value is doubled. So the value of i after k iterations will be 2^k.

2^k = n ...Will be the condition at the time of exit.

log(2^k) = log(n) ....Taking log both sides.

k = log(n)

**Time Complexity:** O(log(n))

**Example 1.10: Half the iteration variable**

```
int fun10(int n) {
    int m = 0, i = n;
    while (i > 0) {
        m += 1;
        i = i / 2;
    }
    return m;
}

// Testing code.
public static void main(String[] args) {
    Analysis a = new Analysis();
    System.out.println("N = 100, Number of instructions in O(log(n))::" +
a.fun10(100));
}
```

**Output:**
```
N = 100, Number of instructions in O(log(n))::7
```

The initial value of i is n. In each iteration, the value of "i" is halved.

So the value of i after k iterations will be n/2^k.

At the time of exit, n/ 2^k = 1

n = 2^k // At the time of exit.

log(2^k) = log(n) // Taking log both sides.

k = log(n)

**Time Complexity:** O(log(n))

**Example 1.11: Consecutive Statements**
```
int fun11(int n) {
    int i, j, k, m = 0;
    for (i = 0; i < n; i++) {
        for (j = 0; j < n; j++) {
            m += 1;
        }
    }

    for (i = 0; i < n; i++) {
        for (k = 0; k < n; k++) {
            m += 1;
        }
    }
    return m;
}

// Testing code.
public static void main(String[] args) {
    Analysis a = new Analysis();
    System.out.println("N = 100, Number of instructions in O(n^2)::" +
a.fun11(100));
}
```

**Output:**
```
N = 100, Number of instructions in O(n^2)::20000
```

These two groups of loops are consecutive, so their complexity will add up to form the final complexity of the program.

**Time Complexity:** O(n^2) + O(n^2) = O(n^2)

**Example 1.12:**
```
int fun12(int n) {
    int i, j, m = 0;
    for (i = 0; i < n; i++) {
        for (j = 0; j < Math.sqrt(n); j++) {
            m += 1;
        }
    }
    return m;
}
```

```
// Testing code.
public static void main(String[] args) {
    Analysis a = new Analysis();
    System.out.println("N = 100, Number of instructions in O(n^(3/2))::" +
a.fun12(100));
}
```

**Output:**
```
N = 100, Number of instructions in O(n^(3/2))::1000
```

**Time Complexity:** Inner loop always runs for √n times. O(n * √n ) = O(n^3/2)

**Example 1.13: Multiple loops in O(n)**
```
int fun13(int n) {
    int i = 0, j = 0, m = 0;

    for (i = 0; i < n; i++) {
        for (; j < n; j++)
            m += 1;
    }
    return m;
}

// Testing code.
public static void main(String[] args) {
    Analysis a = new Analysis();
    System.out.println("N = 100, Number of instructions in O(n)::" + a.fun13(100));
}
```

**Output:**
```
N = 100, Number of instructions in O(n)::100
```

**Time Complexity**: In this example, j is not initialised for every iteration. For i=0, the loop of j executes completely, making the value of j as n. But for the remaining values of i, the loop of j does not execute. So the time complexity in this case is O(n).

## Recursive Function

Recursion: A recursive function is a function that calls itself, directly or indirectly. A recursive method consists of two parts: Termination Condition and Body (which includes recursive expansion).

1 **Termination Condition:** A recursive method always contains one or more terminating conditions. A condition in which a recursive method processes a simple case and does not call itself.

2 **Body** (including recursive expansion): The main logic of the recursive method is contained in the body of the method. It also contains the recursion expansion statement that, in turn, calls the method itself.

Three important properties of the recursive algorithm are:

1. A recursive algorithm must have a termination condition.
2. A recursive algorithm must change its state, and shift state towards the termination condition.
3. A recursive algorithm must be capable of calling itself.

**Note:** The speed of a recursive program is slower because of stack overheads. If the same problem can be solved using an iterative solution (using loops), then we should prefer an iterative solution in place of recursion to avoid stack overhead.

**Note**: Without termination conditions, the recursive method may run forever and consume full-stack memory.

## Factorial

**Problem:** Given a value N find N!. Where N! = N* (N-1).... 2*1. Use recursion to solve the problem.

**Example 1. 14**: Factorial Calculation.

```
public static int factorial(int i) {
    // Termination Condition
    if (i <= 1) {
        return 1;
    }

    // Body, Recursive Expansion
    return i * factorial(i - 1);
}

// Testing code.
public static void main(String[] args) {
    System.out.println("Factorial:" + factorial(5));
}
```

**Output:**

```
Factorial:120
```

**Analysis**: We calculate factorial(i) as i*factorial(i-1) recursively.

Function F(n) calls F(n-1)
$T(n) = T(n-1) + 1$
$T(n-1) = T(n-2) + 1$
$T(n-2) = T(n-3) + 1$
$T(n) = T(n-1) + 1 = (T(n-2) + 1) + 1 = T(n-2) + 2 = (T(n-3) + 1) + 2 = T(n-3) + 3$
Similarly, for $k^{th}$ term $T(n) = T(n-k) + k$
for base case $(n-k) = 1$ or $n - 1 = k$
$T(n) = T(1) + n - 1 = n$
Time Complexity is **O(n)**

## Print Base 16 Integers

**Problem:** Given an integer in decimal form, print its hexadecimal form. Use recursion to solve the problem.

**Example 1.15**: Generic print to some specific base method.

```
public static void printInt(int number, int base) {
    String conversion = "0123456789ABCDEF";
```

```
    char digit = (char) (number % base);
    number = number / base;
    if (number != 0) {
        printInt(number, base);
    }
    System.out.print(conversion.charAt(digit));
}

// Testing code.
public static void main(String[] args) {
    printInt(500, 16);
    System.out.println();
}
```

**Output:**

```
1F4
```

**Analysis**:

1 The base value is provided along with the number in the function parameter.
2 The remainder of the number is calculated and stored in digits.
3 If the number is greater than the base, then the number divided by the base is passed recursively as an argument to the print() method.
4 The number will be printed higher-ordered first, then the lower order digits.

Time Complexity is O(n), Where n is the number of digits.

## Tower of Hanoi

**Problem:** In the **Tower of Hanoi**, we are given three rods and N number of disks, initially all the disks are added to the first rod (the leftmost one) such that no smaller disk is under the larger one. The objective is to transfer the entire stack of disks from the first tower to the third tower (the rightmost one), moving only one disk at a time. Moving a larger disk onto a smaller one is not allowed.

**Solution:** If we want to transfer N disks from source to destination tower. Let's consider the bottom-most disk, it is the largest disk so can not be placed to any other tower except the destination tower. Also, all the disks above the largest disk need to be placed in the temporary tower, then only the largest disk can be moved to the destination tower. So we move N-1 disks from source to temporary tower and then move the lowest Nth disk from source to destination. Then we will move N-1 disks from the temporary tower to the destination tower.

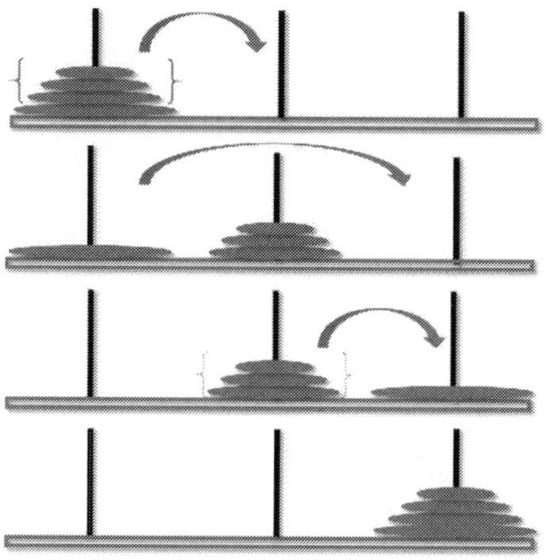

**Example 1.16**:
```
public static void towerOfHanoi(int num, char src, char dst, char temp) {
    if (num < 1)
        return;

    towerOfHanoi(num - 1, src, temp, dst);
    System.out.println("Move " + num + " disk from peg " + src + " to peg "+ dst);
    towerOfHanoi(num - 1, temp, dst, src);
}

// Testing code.
public static void main(String[] args) {
    int num = 3;
    System.out.println("Moves involved in the Tower of Hanoi are:");
    towerOfHanoi(num, 'A', 'C', 'B');
}
```

**Output:**
```
Moves involved in the Tower of Hanoi are:
Move 1 disk  from peg A to peg C
Move 2 disk  from peg A to peg B
Move 1 disk  from peg C to peg B
Move 3 disk  from peg A to peg C
Move 1 disk  from peg B to peg A
Move 2 disk  from peg B to peg C
Move 1 disk  from peg A to peg C
```

**Analysis:**

Recurrence Relation: $T(n) = 1 + 2T(n-1)$

$T(n-1) = 1 + 2*T(n-2)$

$T(n-2) = 1 + 2*T(n-3)$

$T(n) = 1 + 2*( 1 + 2*T(n-2)) = 1 + 2 + 4*T(n-2) = 1 + 2 + 4*( 1 + 2*(T(n-3)) = 1 + 2+ 2^2+ 2^3T(n-3)$

$= 1 + 2 + 2^2 \ldots. + 2^nT(0) = 1(2^{n+1} - 1)/2 - 1 = 2^{n+1} - 1$ // Geometric progression sum

Time complexity will be O(2^n) ignoring the constants.

## Greatest Common Divisor (GCD)

**Problem:** Find the greatest common divisor of two numbers using recursion.

**Solution**: There are many ways to find the greatest common divisor (GCD). We are using Euclid's algorithm to find the GCD. The following are steps of Euclid's algorithm:

1. If n = 0 then GCD(n, m) = m, and this is a termination condition.
2. If m = 0 then GCD(n, m) = n, and this is a termination condition.
3. Write n in the form of a quotient remainder n = mq + q. q is the quotient, and r is the remainder.
4. Since GCD(n, m) = GCD(m, r), use the Euclidean Algorithm to find GCD(m , r).

**Example 1.17**:

```
public static int gcd(int m, int n) {
    if (n == 0)
        return m;

    if (m == 0)
        return n;

    return (gcd(n, m % n));
}

// Testing code.
public static void main(String[] args) {
    System.out.println("Gcd is:: " + gcd(5, 2));
}
```

**Output:**

```
Gcd is:: 1
```

**Time-Complexity**: O(Max(log(m), log(n))), Each step input is reduced by nearly half or more.

## Fibonacci number

**Problem:** Given N,, find the Nth number in the Fibonacci series.

**Solution**: Fibonacci numbers are calculated by adding the sum of the previous two numbers.

**Example 1.18**:

```
public static int fibonacci(int n) {
    if (n < 2)
        return n;

    return fibonacci(n-1) + fibonacci(n-2);
}

// Testing code.
public static void main(String[] args) {
    System.out.print(fibonacci(10));
}
```

**Output:**

```
55
```

**Analysis**: Recurrence Relation: T(n) = 1 + T(n-1) + T(n-2)

T(n) = 1 + 2T(n-1) // Approximately

T(n) = 1 + 2T(n-1)

T(n-1) = 1 + 2T(n-2)

T(n-2) = 1 + 2T(n-3)

T(n) = 1 + 2( 1 + 2T(n-2)) = 1 + 2 + 4T(n-2) = 1 + 2 + 4 ( 1 + 2(T(n-3)) = 1 + 2+ $2^2$+ $2^3$T(n-3)

= 1 + 2 + $2^2$ .... + $2^n$T(0) = 1($2^{n+1}$ – 1)/2 – 1 = $2^{n+1}$ – 1 // Geometric progression sum

Time complexity is O(2^n), ignoring the constants.

**Note**: - There is an inefficiency in the solution. We will look for a better solution in the coming chapters.

## Complexities from Recurrence Relation

**Example 1.19:** Find complexity of the function with the following recurrence relation.

$$T(n) = \begin{cases} 1 & if\, n=0 \\ T(n-1)+1 & if\, n>0 \end{cases}$$

**Solution:**

T(n) = T(n-1) + 1

T(n-1) = T(n-2) + 1

T(n-2) = T(n-3) + 1

T(n) = ( T(n-2) + 1) + 1 = T(n-2) + 2 = (T(n-3) + 1) + 2 = T(n-3) + 3

T(n) = T(n-k) + k

base case when T(0) = 1, n-k = 0 => n = k

T(n) = T(0) + n = 1 + n

Time Complexity is O(n)

**Example 1.20:** Find complexity of the function with the following recurrence relation.

$$T(n) = \begin{cases} 1 & if\, n=0 \\ T(n-1)+n & if\, n>0 \end{cases}$$

**Solution:**

T(n) = T(n-1) + n

T(n-1) = T(n-2) + n

T(n-2) = T(n-3) + n

T(n) = ( T(n-2) + n) + n = T(n-2) + 2n = (T(n-3) + n) + 2n = T(n-3) + 3n

T(n) = T(n-k) + kn

base case when T(0) = 1, n-k = 0 => n = k

T(n) = T(0) + n*n = 1 + n^2

Time Complexity is O(n^2)

**Example 1.21:** Find complexity of the function with the following recurrence relation.

$$T(n) = \begin{cases} 1 & if\, n=0 \\ T(n-1)+\log(n) & if\, n>0 \end{cases}$$

**Solution**:

T(n) = T(n-1) + log(n)

T(n-1) = T(n-2) + log(n) // for simplicity make log(n-1) as log(n)

T(n-2) = T(n-3) + log(n)

T(n) = ( T(n-2) + log(n)) + log(n) = T(n-2) + 2log(n) = (T(n-3) + log(n)) + 2log(n) = T(n-3) + 3log(n)

T(n) = T(n-k) + klog(n)

base case when T(0) = 1, n-k = 0 => n = k

T(n) = T(0) + n*log(n) = 1 + n.log(n)

Time Complexity is O(n.log(n))

| **Recurrence Relation** | **Time-Complexity** |
|---|---|
| T(n) = T(n-1) + 1 | O(n) |
| T(n) = T(n-1) + n | O(n^2) |
| T(n) = T(n-1) + log(n) | O(n.log(n)) |
| T(n) = T(n-c) + 1 , c is a constant | O(n) , complicity is not changed by c. |
| T(n) = T(n-c) + b , c is a constant and b is a polynomial | O(n*b), generalised above 4 cases. |

**Example 1.22:** Find complexity of the function with the following recurrence relation.

$$T(n) = \begin{cases} 1 & if\, n=1 \\ T(n/2)+n & if\, n>1 \end{cases}$$

**Solution**:

T(n) = T(n/2) + n

T(n/2) = T(n/$2^2$) + (n/2) // substituting n as n/2

T(n/$2^2$) = T(n/$2^3$) + (n/$2^2$) // substituting n as n/$2^2$

T(n) = ( T(n/$2^2$) + (n/2) ) + n = T(n/$2^2$) + n/2 + n

T(n) = ( T(n/$2^3$) + (n/$2^2$) ) + n/2 + n = T(n/$2^3$) + n/$2^2$ + n/2 + n

T(n) = T(n/2^k) + n/2^(k-1) + …… + n/$2^2$ + n/2 + n

base case when n = 2^k

T(n) = T(1) + n/2^k-1 + …… + n/$2^2$ + n/2 + n

T(n) = T(1) + n * ( 1/2^(k-1) + …… + 1/$2^2$ + 1/2 + 1 )

T(n) = 1 + n*2

Time Complexity is O(n)

**Example 1.23:** Find complexity of the function with the following recurrence relation.

$$T(n) = \begin{cases} 1 & if\, n=1 \\ 2 * T(n/2)+n & if\, n>1 \end{cases}$$

**Solution**:

T(n) = 2 T(n/2) + n

T(n/2) = 2 T(n/$2^2$) + (n/2) // substituting n as n/2

T(n/$2^2$) = 2 T(n/$2^3$) + (n/$2^2$) // substituting n as n/$2^2$

T(n) = 2 ( 2 T(n/$2^2$) + (n/2) ) + n = $2^2$ T(n/$2^2$) + 2n

T(n) = $2^2$ ( 2 T(n/$2^3$) + (n/$2^2$) ) + 2n = $2^3$T(n/$2^3$) + 3n

T(n) = 2^k T(n/2^k) + kn

base case when n = 2^k

k = log(n)

T(n) = n*T(1) + k*n

T(n) = n + k*n = n + n*log(n)

Time Complexity is O(n.log(n))

**Example 1.24:** Find complexity of the function with the following recurrence relation.

$$T(n) = \begin{cases} 1 & if\, n=0 \\ 2 * T(n-1)+1 & if\, n>0 \end{cases}$$

**Solution:**

T(n) = 2 T(n-1) + 1

T(n-1) = 2T(n-2) + 1

T(n-2) = 2T(n-3) + 1

T(n) = 2( 2T(n-2) + 1) + 1 = $2^2$T(n-2) + 2 + 1 = $2^2$ (2T(n-3) + 1) + 2 + 1 = $2^3$T(n-3) + $2^2$ + 2 + 1

T(n) = $2^k$T(n-k) + $2^{(k-1)}$ + ….. + $2^2$ + 2 + 1

base case when T(0) = 1, n-k = 0 => n = k

T(n) = $2^n$T(0) + $2^{(n-1)}$ + ….. + $2^2$ + 2 + 1 = $2^n$ + $2^{(n-1)}$ + ….. + $2^2$ + 2 + 1 = $2^{(n+1)}$ – 1 // GP

Time Complexity O(2^n)

**Example 1.25:** Find complexity of the function with the following recurrence relation.

$$T(n) = \begin{cases} 1 & if\, n \leq 2 \\ T(\sqrt{n})+1 & if\, n>2 \end{cases}$$

**Solution:**

$T(n) = T(n^{1/2}) + 1$

$T(n^{1/2}) = T( n^{1/4}) + 1$

$T(n^{1/4}) = T( n^{1/8}) + 1$

$T(n) = T(n^{1/2}) + 1 = (T( n^{1/4}) + 1) + 1 = T( n^{1/4}) + 2 = (T( n^{1/8}) + 1) + 2 = T( n^{1/8}) + 3$

$T(n) = T(n^{1/2k}) + k$

for base case $n,^{1/2k} = 2$

(1/(2^k) ) * log(n)= log2 = 1 // taking log.

log(n) = 2^k

log(log(n)) = k log(2) = k // taking log again.

**Time Complexity** is O(log(log(n)))

## Master Theorem

The master theorem solves recurrence relations of the form: $T(n) = a T(n/b) + f(n)$, Where $a \geq 1$ and $b>1$. In this relation, "n" is the size of the input. "a" is the number of sub-problems in the recursion. "n/b" is the size of each sub-problem. "f(n)" is the cost of the division of the problem into sub-problems and merging the individual solutions of the sub-problems into the solution.

It is possible to determine an asymptotic tight bound in these three cases:

Case 1: When $f(n) = O(n^{\log_b a-\varepsilon})$ and constant $\epsilon > 1$, then the final time complexity is $T(n) = O(n^{\log_b a})$

Case 2: When $f(n) = \Theta(n^{\log_b a} \log^k n)$ and constant $k \geq 0$, then the final time complexity is

$T(n) = \Theta(n^{\log_b a} \log^{k+1} n)$

Case 3: When $f(n) = \Omega(n^{\log_b a+\varepsilon})$ and constant $\epsilon > 1$, then the final time complexity is $T(n) = \Theta(f(n))$

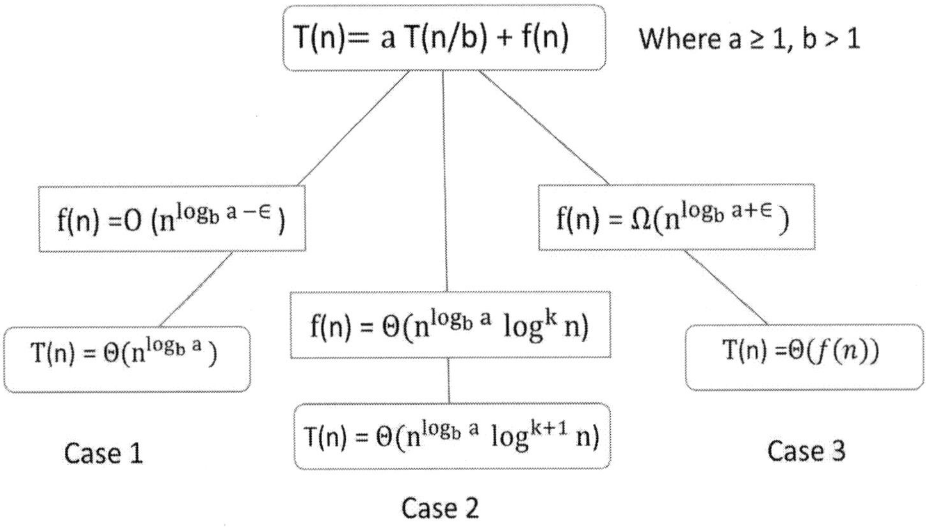


Master theorem flow diagram

**Example 1.26:** In the case of Merge Sort. Its time complexity is T(n) = 2 T(n/2) + n

**Solution:** In this example, a and b both equal to 2. So, $\log_b a = \log_2 2 = 1$.

Which means, $f(n) = n = \Theta(n^{\log_2 2} \log^0 n)$. That means case 2 is applied and $T(n) = \Theta(n^{\log_2 2} \log^{0+1} n)$.

So, its final time complexity will be T(n) = Θ(n.log(n))

**Example 1.27:** It is the case of Binary Search, Its time complexity is T(n) = T(n/2) + 1

**Solution:** In this example, a is equal to 1 and b is equal to 2. So, $\log_b a = \log_2 1 = 0$

Which means, $f(n) = 1 = \Theta(n^{\log_2 1} \log^0 n)$. That means case 2 is applied and $T(n) = \Theta(n^{\log_2 1} \log^{0+1} n)$.

So, its final time complexity will be T(n) = Θ(log(n))

**Example 1.28:** In the case of binary tree traversal, Its time complexity is T(n) = 2T(n/2) + 1

**Solution:** In this example, a is equal to 2 and b is also equal to 2. So, $\log_b a = \log_2 2 = 1$

Which means, $f(n) = 1 = O(n^{\log_2 2 - 1})$. That means case 1 is applied and $T(n) = \Theta(n^{\log_2 2})$.

So, its final time complexity will be T(n) = Θ(n)

**Example 1.29:** T(n) = 2 T(n/2) + n^2

**Solution:** In this example, a is equal to 2 and b is also equal to 2. So, $\log_b a = \log_2 2 = 1$

Which means, $f(n) = n^2 = \Omega(n^{\log_2 2 + 1})$. That means case 3 is applied and T(n) = Θ(f(n)).

So, its final time complexity will be T(n) = Θ(n^2)

**Example 1.30:** T(n) = 4 T(n/2) + n^2

**Solution:** In this example, a is equal to 4 and b is equal to 2. So, $\log_b a = \log_2 4 = 2$.

Which means, $f(n) = n^2 = \Theta(n^{\log_2 4} \log^0 n)$. That means case 2 is applied and $T(n) = \Theta(n^{\log_2 4} \log^{0+1} n)$.

So, its final time complexity will be T(n) = Θ(n^2 * log n)

**Example 1.31:** T(n) = T(n/2) + 2n

**Solution:** In this example, a is equal to 1 and b is equal to 2. So, $\log_b a = \log_2 1 = 0$

Which means, $f(n) = 2n = \Omega(n^{\log_2 1 + 1})$. That means case 3 is applied and T(n) = Θ(f(n)).

So, its final time complexity will be T(n)= Θ(n)

**Example 1.32:** T (n) = 16T (n/4) + n

**Solution:** In this example, a is equal to 16 and b is equal to 4. So, $\log_b a = \log_4 16 = 2$.

Which means, $f(n) = n = O(n^{\log_4 16 - 1})$. That means case 1 is applied and $T(n) = \Theta(n^{\log_4 16})$.

So, its final time complexity will be T(n)= Θ(n^2)

**Example 1.33:** T (n) = 2T (n/2) + n log n

**Solution:** In this example, a is equal to 2 and b is also equal to 2. So, $\log_b a = \log_2 2 = 1$

Which means, $f(n) = n.\log(n) = \Theta(n^{\log_2 2}\log^1 n)$. That means case 2 is applied and $T(n) = \Theta(n^{\log_2 2}\log^{1+1} n)$.
So, its final time complexity will be $T(n) = \Theta(n \log^2(n))$

**Example 1.34:** $T(n) = 2\,T(n/4) + n^{0.5}$
**Solution:** In this example, a is equal to 2 and b is equal to 4. So, $\log_b a = \log_4 2 = 0.5$
Which means, $f(n) = n^{0.5} = \Theta(n^{\log_4 2}\log^0 n)$. That means case 2 is applied and $T(n) = \Theta(n^{\log_4 2}\log^{0+1} n)$.
So, its final time complexity will be $T(n) = \Theta(n^{0.5} \log(n))$

**Example 1.35:** $T(n) = 2\,T(n/4) + n^{0.49}$
**Solution:** In this example, a is equal to 2 and b is equal to 4. So, $\log_b a = \log_4 2 = 0.5$
Which means, $f(n) = n^{0.49} = O(n^{\log_4 2 - 0.01})$. That means case 1 is applied and $T(n) = \Theta(n^{\log_4 2})$.
So its final time complexity will be $T(n) = \Theta(n^{0.5})$

**Example 1.36:** $T(n) = 3T(n/3) + \sqrt{n}$
**Solution:** In this example, a is equal to 3 and b is also equal to 3. So, $\log_b a = \log_3 3 = 1$
Which means, $f(n) = n = O(n^{\log_3 3 - 1/2})$. That means case 1 is applied and $T(n) = \Theta(f(n))$
So, its final time complexity will be $T(n) = \Theta(n)$

**Example 1.37:** $T(n) = 3T(n/3) + n/2$
**Solution:** In this example, a is equal to 3 and b is also equal to 3. So, $\log_b a = \log_3 3 = 1$
Which means, $f(n) = n = \Theta(n^{\log_3 3}\log^0 n)$. That means case 2 is applied and $T(n) = \Theta(n^{\log_3 3}\log^{0+1} n)$
So, final time complexity will be $T(n) = \Theta(n.\log(n))$

## Exercise

1 True or false
   - 5 n + 10 n^2= O(n^2)
   - n.log(n) + 4 n = O(n)
   - log(n^2) + 4 log(log(n)) = O(log(n))
   - $12.n^{1/2}$+ 3 = O(n^2)
   - 3^n + 11.n^2 + n^$2^0$= O(2^n)

2 What is the best-case runtime complexity of searching an Array?

3 What is the average-case runtime complexity of searching an Array?

4 Given an array of positive numbers, you need to find the maximum sum under the constraint that no two elements should be adjacent.

# CHAPTER 2: APPROACH TO SOLVE PROBLEMS

## Introduction

Theoretical knowledge of the algorithm is essential, but it is insufficient. When an interviewer asks the interviewee to solve a problem, then the interviewee can use our five-step approach to solve problems. If you master this technique, you will outperform the majority of applicants in interviews.

Five steps for solving algorithm design questions are:

1. Constraints
2. Ideas Generation
3. Complexities analysis
4. Coding
5. Testing

## Constraints

Solving a technical question is not just about knowing the algorithms and designing a good software system. The interviewer is interested in seeing your approach to any given problem. Often, people make mistakes by failing to ask clarifying follow-up questions about a given problem. They make a lot of assumptions at once and start working with them. Before you start solving a problem, you need to collect a lot of missing information from your interviewer.

In this step, you will write down all the problem's constraints. Never attempt to solve a problem that isn't completely defined. Interview questions are not like exam paper questions, where all the details about a problem are well-defined. The interviewer wants you to ask questions and clarify the problem during the interview.

Suppose, when the interviewer says to write an algorithm to sort numbers. You need to ask the following clarifying question:

1. The first thing you need to know is what sort of data is being given. Assume the interviewer gives you the answer Integer.
2. The size of the data is the second piece of information you need to know. If the input data is 100 integers or 1 billion integers, the algorithm is different.

The basic guideline for the Constraints for an array of numbers:

1. How many numbers of elements are there in an array?
2. What is the range of value in each element? What is the min and max value?
3. What is the kind of data in each element? Is it an integer or a floating point?
4. Does the array contain unique data or not?

The basic guideline for the Constraints for an array of strings:

1. How many total numbers of elements are there in the array?
2. What is the length of each string? What is the min and max length?
3. Does the array contain unique data or not?

The basic guideline for the Constraints for a Graph

1. How many nodes are there in the graph?
2. How many edges are there in the graph?
3. Is it a weighted graph? What is the range of weights?
4. Does the graph have directed edges, or undirected edges?
5. Does the graph have a loop?
6. Does the graph have a negative sum loop?
7. Are there any self-loops in the graph?

We will see in the graph chapter that depending upon the constraints the algorithm applied changes and so is the complexity of the solution.

## Idea Generation

We will cover a lot of theoretical knowledge in this book. It is impossible to cover all the questions, as new questions are created every day. Therefore, you should know how to handle new problems. Even if you know the solution to the problem asked by the interviewer, then also you need to have a discussion with the interviewer and try to reach the solution. You need to analyse the problem also because the interviewer may modify a question a bit, so the approach to solve it will vary.

How to solve an unseen problem? The solution to this problem is to learn a lot, and the more you practice, the more you will be able to answer any unseen problem. When you've solved enough problems, you'll see a pattern in the questions and be able to answer unseen problems with ease.

Following is the strategy that you need to follow to solve an unknown problem:

1. Try to simplify the task at hand.
2. Try a few examples
3. Think of a suitable data structure.
4. Think about similar problems that you have already solved.

## Try to simplify the task at hand

Let's look into the following problem: Husbands and wives are standing at random in a line. Husbands have been numbered, H1, H2, H3 and so on. Wives have been numbered, W1, W2, W3 and so on. You need to arrange them so that H1 will stand first, followed by W1, then H2 followed by W2 and so on.

At first look, it looks complicated, but it is a simple problem. Try to find a relation to the final position.

P(Hi) = i * 2 – 1 and P(Wi) = i * 2

We are leaving an exercise for you to do something like Insertion-Sort for the rest of the algorithm, and you are done.

## Try a few examples

In the above problem, if you try the above problem with an example of three husband-wife pairs then you can get the same formula as shown in the previous section. Using more examples will also assist in solving the problem.

## Think of a suitable data-structure

It's simple to figure out which data structure would be more appropriate for some specific problems. Throughout this book, we will see a variety of data structures. We must determine which data structure would best meet our requirements.

**Problem 1**: If we want to find the minimum and maximum of a given sequence.
**Analysis**: The heap is most likely the data structure we're searching for.

**Problem 2**: We are given a stream of data, at any time, we can be asked to tell the median value of the data, and maybe we can be asked to pop median data.
**Analysis**: We may visualise a tree, maybe a balanced tree with the median at the root. Wait a minute! It's not straightforward to ensure that the tree root is a median. We can't get the median from a heap, although it can give us the minimum or maximum. What if we use two heaps, a max-heap and a min-heap? The max heap will hold the smaller values, while the min-heap will have the larger values. Furthermore, we will keep track of how many elements are in the heaps. It would help if you came up with the rest of the algorithm on your own.

For every unseen problem, think about the data structures you know, and maybe one of them or some combination of them will solve your problem. Think about similar problems you have already solved.

**Problem 3**: Given head pointers of two linked lists that intersect at some point. Find the point of intersection. However, in place of the end of the linked list to be a null pointer, there is a loop.
**Analysis**: You know how to find the intersection point of two intersecting linked lists, and you know how to find if a linked list has a loop (three-pointer solution). Therefore, you can combine both solutions to solve the problem at hand.

# Complexities

Solving a problem is not just finding a correct solution. The solution should be fast and should have reasonable memory requirements. In the previous chapters, you learned about big-O notation. You should be able to perform Big-O analysis. If you believe the solution you have provided is not optimal and there is a better solution, then try to figure it out.

Most interviewers expect that you should be able to find the Time and Space Complexity of the algorithms. You should be able to calculate the Time and Space Complexity quickly. Whenever you are solving any problem, you should find the complexity associated with it. From this, you would be able to choose the best solutions. In some problems there are some trade-offs between Space and Time Complexity, so you should know these trade-offs. Taking a little extra space will save you a lot of time and make your algorithm much faster.

## Coding

At this stage, you have already captured all the constraints of the problem, suggested a few solutions, evaluated the complexities of those solutions and selected the one for final coding. Never begin coding without first discussing with the interviewer about constraints, Idea generation and complexity.

We are used to writing code in an IDE like a Visual Studio. So several people struggle when asked to write code on a whiteboard or some blank sheet. Therefore, you should do some practice coding on a sheet of paper. You should think before coding because there is no back button on the sheet of paper. Always try to write modular code. Small functions need to be created so that the code is clean and managed. If there is a requirement for a swap function, just use this function and tell the interviewer that you will write it later. Everybody knows that you can write a swap function.

## Testing

You're not done even if the code is written. It is essential to validate the code using a variety of small test cases. It shows that you understand the importance of testing. It also gives the interviewer confidence that you would not write a bug-ridden program. Once you have finished coding, you should go over the code line-by-line for some small test cases. This is to ensure that the code is functioning as intended.

Following are some test cases to check:

- **Normal test cases**: These are the positive test cases, which contain the most common scenario, and the emphasis is on the functioning of the code's base logic.

  For example, if we are solving some problems for a linked list, then this test may contain, what happens when a linked list with three or four nodes is given as input. Before declaring the code complete, you should always think about these test cases.
- **Edge cases**: These are the test cases, which are used to test the boundaries of the code. Edge cases can help to make your code more robust. We must add checks in the code to handle edge cases.

  For example, we can generate edge cases with the same linked list algorithm to see how the code reacts when an empty list or only one node liar is passed.

**Note**: Always follow these five steps, never jump to coding before doing constraint analysis, idea generation, and complexity analysis: At last, never miss the testing step.

## Example

Let us suppose the interviewer asks you to give the best sorting algorithm.

Some interviewees will directly jump to Quick-Sort **O(n.log(n))**. Oops, mistake! You need to ask many questions before beginning to solve this problem.

Let's look at these questions one by one.

Question 1: What is the kind of data? Are they integers?

Answer: Yes, they are integers.

Question 2: How much data are we going to sort?

Answer: Maybe thousands.

Question 3: What exactly is this data about?

Answer: They store a person's age

Question 4: What kind of data structure is used to hold this data?

Answer: Data are given in the form of a list

Question 5: Can we modify the given data structure? And many, many more questions...

Answer: No, you cannot modify the data structure provided

So, we are all set to use the given information to make a perfect solution. From the first answer, we will know the type of data we are going to get is an integer. From the second answer, we can conclude that data size is limited. It's only in some thousands. From the next answer, we can conclude that it's age-related data. So we can assume that a person's age will be between 1 to 150. And lastly, we know that data is in the form of a list and cannot change it.

To summarise, we can use bucket sort to sort the data. Since the range is only 1-150, we only need an integer list of 150 elements. We don't have to think about data overflow because the data is in thousands, and we get the solution in linear time.

## Summary

At this point, you know the process of handling unseen problems very well. In the coming chapter, we will be looking into various data structures and the problems they solve. It may be possible that the user cannot understand some portion of this chapter as knowledge of the rest of the book is needed, so they can reread this chapter after reading the rest of the data structures portion. A huge number of problems are solved in this book. However, it is recommended that you first try to solve them yourself and then look for the solution. Always think about the complexity of the problem. In the interview, interaction is the key to get the problem described completely and discuss your approach with the interviewer.

# CHAPTER 3: ABSTRACT DATA TYPE

## Abstract Data Type (ADT)

An abstract data type (ADT) is a logical description of the data and its operations. An ADT is known as a user's point of view of data. An ADT is concerned about the possible values of data and interfaces exposed by it. An ADT is not concerned about the actual implementation of the data structure.

For example, a user wants to store some integers and find their mean value. ADT for this data structure would have two functions, one for adding integers and another to get the mean value. ADT for this data structure does not talk about how exactly it will be implemented.

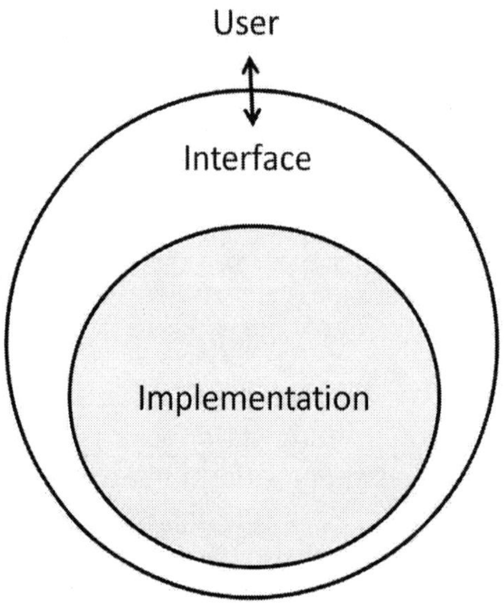


Abstract Data Type

## Data-Structure

Data structures are concrete representations of data that are defined from the perspective of a programmer. The data structure represents how data can be stored in memory. Each data structure has its own set of advantages and disadvantages. Depending on the type of problem, we choose the most appropriate data structure.

For example, according to the question, we can store data in arrays, stack, queue, linked list, and many more.

**Note**: - In this chapter, we will be studying various data structures and their API. So that the user can use them without knowing their internal implementation.

## Java Collection Framework

Java programming language provides a Java Collection Framework, which is a set of high quality, high-performance & reusable data structures and algorithms.

The following advantages of using a Java collection framework:

1. Programmers do not have to implement basic data structures and algorithms repeatedly. Thereby, it prevents the reinvention of the wheel. Thus, the programmer can devote more effort to business logic
2. The Java Collection Framework code is a well-tested, high quality, high-performance code. Using them increases the quality of the programs.
3. Development cost is reduced as basic data structures and algorithms are implemented in the Collections framework.
4. Easy to review and understand programs written by other developers, as most Java developers use the Collection framework. In addition, the collection framework is well documented.

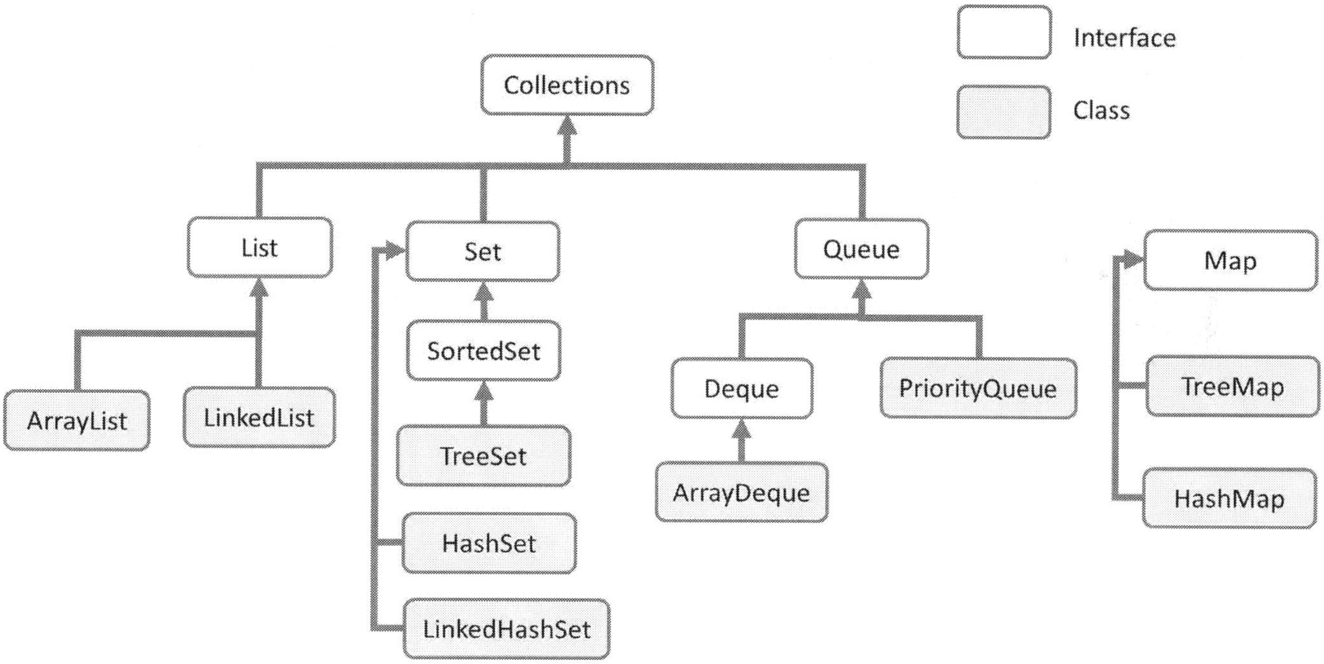


## Array

Arrays are the simplest data structures that store items of the same data type.

### Array ADT Operations

Below is the API of an array:

1. Adds an element at the kth position. Value can be stored in an array at the kth position in **O(1)** constant time. We just need to store value at arr[k].

2. Reading the value stored at the kth position. Accessing the value stored at some index in the array is also **O(1)** constant time. We just need to read the value stored at arr[k].
3. Substitution of value stored in kth position with a new value.
4. **Time complexity: O(1)** constant time.

**Example 3.1:**

```
public class ArrayDemo {
    public static void main(String[] args) {
        int[] arr = new int[10];

        for (int i = 0; i < 10; i++) {
            arr[i] = i;
        }

        for (int i = 0; i < 10; i++) {
            System.out.print(arr[i] + " ");
        }
    }
}
```

**Output:**

```
0 1 2 3 4 5 6 7 8 9
```

## Application of Arrays

Applications of Arrays are:

1. Storing data in tabular format.
2. Used in the creation of Matrices. Online ticket booking system in which seats are represented in the form of Matrices.
3. Used in the creation of various higher level data structures like Stacks, Queues, Heaps, HashTables etc.

**Note:** Problems based on array data structure are discussed throughout this book, especially in the Sorting and Searching chapters.

Java standard arrays are of fixed length. Sometimes we do not know how much memory we need, so we create a bigger size array. Thereby wasting space. If an array is already full, and we want to add more values to it then we need to create a new array, which has sufficient space and then copy the old array to the new array. To avoid this manual reallocation and copy, the Java Collection framework has implemented ArrayList<T> to solve this problem.

## ArrayList implementation in Java Collections

ArrayList<E> in Java Collections is a data structure that implements the List<E> interface, which means that it can have duplicate elements in it. ArrayList is an implementation of a dynamic array that can grow or shrink as needed. (Internally the array is used when it is full, a bigger array is allocated and the old array values are copied to it.)

**Example 3.2:**

```
import java.util.ArrayList;

public class ArrayListDemo {
    public static void main(String[] args) {
        ArrayList<Integer> al = new ArrayList<Integer>();
        al.add(1); // add 1 to the end of the list
        al.add(2); // add 2 to the end of the list

        System.out.println("Contents of Array : " + al);
        System.out.println("Array Size : " + al.size());
        System.out.println("Array IsEmpty : " + al.isEmpty());

        al.remove(al.size() -1); // last element of array is removed.
        al.removeAll(al); // all the elements of the array are removed.
        System.out.println("Array IsEmpty : " + al.isEmpty());
    }
}
```

**Output:**

```
Contents of Array : [1, 2]
Array Size : 2
Array IsEmpty : false
Array IsEmpty : true
```

## Linked List

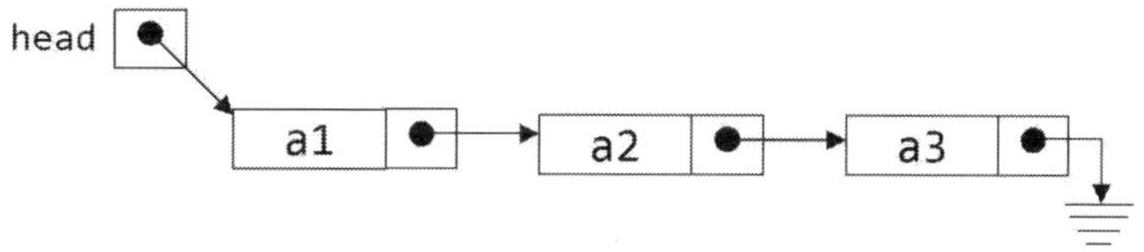


Linked list is a dynamic data structure and memory is allocated at run time. The concept of linked list is not to store data contiguously. Nodes of linked list contain links that point to the next elements in the list.

Performance-wise, linked lists are slower than arrays because there is no direct access to linked list elements. A linked list is a useful data structure when we do not know the number of elements to be stored ahead of time. There are many types of linked lists: linear, circular, doubly, doubly circular etc.

### Linked list ADT Operations

Below is the API of the Linked list:

1. **Insert(k)** will insert an element at the start of the list. Just create a new element and move pointers. So that this new element becomes the first element of the list. This operation will take **O(1)** constant time.
2. **Delete()** will delete an element at the start of the list. We just need to move one pointer. This operation will also take **O(1)** constant time.

3. **Print()** will display all the elements of the list. Start with the first element and then follow the pointers. This operation will take **O(N)** time.
4. **Find(k)** will find the position of the element with the value k. Start with the first element and follow the pointer until we get the value we are looking for or reach the end of the list. This operation will take **O(N)** time.
5. **IsEmpty()** will check if the number of elements in the list is zero. Just check the head pointer of the list, if it is Null then the list is empty, otherwise not empty. This operation will take **O(1)** time.

## LinkedList implementation in Java Collections

LinkedList<E> in by Java Collections is a data structure that also implements the List<E> interface.

**Example 3.3:**

```
import java.util.LinkedList;

public class LinkedListDemo {
    public static void main(String[] args) {
        LinkedList<Integer> ll = new LinkedList<Integer>();
        ll.addFirst(1);
        ll.addLast(3);
        ll.addFirst(2);
        ll.addLast(4);
        System.out.println("Linked List: " + ll);
        ll.removeFirst();
        ll.removeLast();
        System.out.println("Linked List: " + ll);
    }
}
```

**Output:**

```
Linked List: [2, 1, 3, 4]
Linked List: [1, 3]
```

**Analysis:** Values are added to the back and front of the linked list. Then the values stored in the linked list are printed. Then values are removed from the linked list from the front and back and again linked list content is printed to the screen.

## Stack

Stack is a data structure that follows the Last-In-First-Out (LIFO) principle. This means that the element that is added last will be removed first.

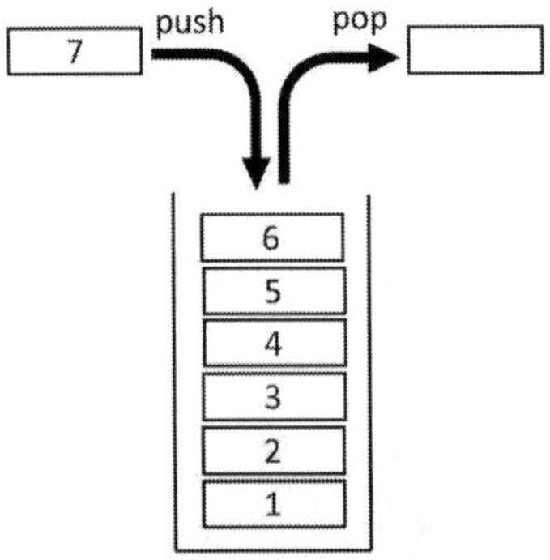

## Stack ADT Operations

Below is the API of the Stack:

1. **Push(k)** will add value k on the top of the stack.
2. **Pop()** will remove an element from the top of the stack and return its value.
3. **Top()** will return the value of the element on top of the stack.
4. **Size()** will return the number of elements in the stack.
5. **IsEmpty()** will tell us whether the stack is empty or not. It returns 1 if the stack is empty, else return 0.

**Note:** All the above stack operations are implemented in **O(1)** time Complexity.

## Stack implementation in Java Collection

Stack is implemented by calling push and pop methods of the Stack <T> class.

**Example 3.4:**
```
import java.util.*;

public class StackDemo {
    public static void main(String[] args) {
        Stack<Integer> stack = new Stack<Integer>();
        stack.push(1);
        stack.push(2);
        stack.push(3);

        System.out.println("Stack size : " + stack.size());
        System.out.println("Stack pop : " + stack.pop());
        System.out.println("Stack top : " + stack.top());
        System.out.println("Stack isEmpty : " + stack.isEmpty());
    }
}
```

**Output:**
```
Stack size : 3
Stack pop : 3
Stack top : 2
Stack isEmpty : false
```

Stack is also implemented by calling push and pop methods of the ArrayDeque<T> class.

JDK provides both ArrayDeque<T> and Stack<T>. We can use both classes. But there are some advantages of ArrayDeque<T>.

1. The first reason is that Stack<T> does not drive from the Collection interface.
2. Second Stack<T> drives from Vector<T> so random access is possible, so it breaks the abstraction of a stack.
3. Third ArrayDeque is more efficient as compared to Stack<T>.

## Queue

A queue is a data structure that follows the First-In-First-Out (FIFO) principle. The first element added to the queue first would be the first to be removed, and vice versa.

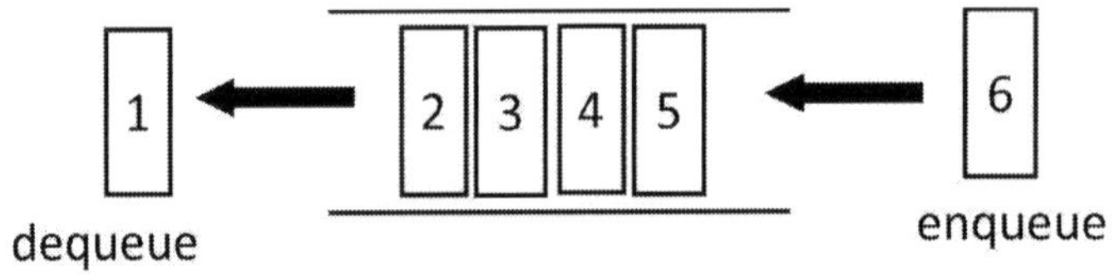


### Queue ADT Operations:

Below is the API of the Queue:

1. **Add(K)** will add element k at the end of the queue.
2. **Remove()** will remove the first element at the front of the queue and return its value.
3. **Front()** will return the value of the element at the front of the queue.
4. **Size()** will return the number of elements in the queue.
5. **IsEmpty()** will check whether the queue is empty or not. If it is empty then return 1, else return 0.

**Note**: All the above queue operations are implemented in **O(1)** Time Complexity.

### Queue implementation in Java Collection

ArrayDeque<T> is the class implementation of a doubly ended queue. If we use add(), remove() and peek () it will behave as a queue. (Moreover, if we use push(), pop() and peekLast() it behaves as a stack.)

**Example 3.5:**

```
import java.util.ArrayDeque;

public class QueueDemo {
    public static void main(String[] args) {
        ArrayDeque<Integer> que = new ArrayDeque<Integer>();
        que.add(1);
        que.add(2);
        que.add(3);

        System.out.println("Queue : " + que);
        System.out.println("Queue size : " + que.size());
        System.out.println("Queue peek : " + que.peek());
        System.out.println("Queue remove : " + que.remove());
        System.out.println("Queue isEmpty : " + que.isEmpty());
    }
}
```

**Output:**
```
Queue : [1, 2, 3]
Queue size : 3
Queue peek : 1
Queue remove : 1
Queue isEmpty : false
```

**Analysis**: Values are added to the queue and printed to the screen. Since the queue is first-in-first-out, the values that are added first are the first to come out of the queue.

## Tree

A tree is a data structure that is organised in a hierarchy. Each element of the tree data structure is called a node. The top node of the tree is called the root node. Each node in a tree, except the root, has a parent node and zero or more child nodes. In the case of the last level of nodes, they have no child. They are called leaf nodes. Where you need to store hierarchical records, the tree is the most appropriate data structure to use.

A binary tree is a type of tree in which each node has at most two children ( 0, 1, or 2 ) which are referred to as left child and right child.

## Binary Search Tree (BST)

A binary search tree (BST) is a binary tree in which nodes are ordered in the following way:

1. The key in the left subtree is less than or equal to the key in its parent node.
2. The key in the right subtree is greater than the key in its parent node.

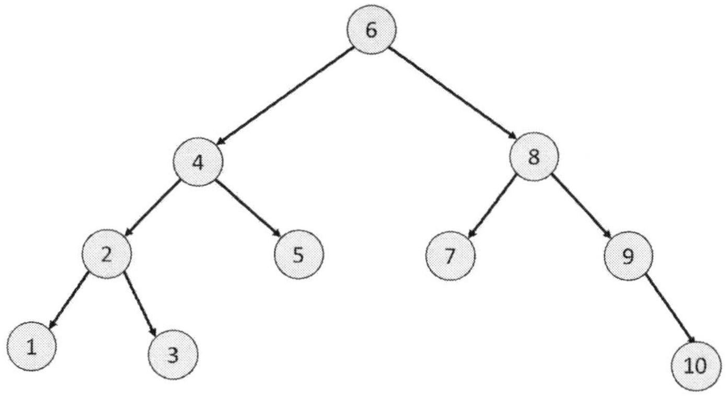


## Binary Search Tree ADT Operations

Below is the API of the BST:

1. **Insert(k)** will insert an element k into the tree.
2. **Delete(k)** will delete an element k from the tree.
3. **Search(k)** will search a value k into the tree if it is present or not.
4. **FindMax()** will find the maximum value stored in the tree.
5. **FindMin()** will find the minimum value stored in the tree.

The average time complexity of all the above operations on a binary search tree is O(log(n)), the case when the tree is balanced. The worst-case time complexity is **O(n)** when the tree is not balanced.

## Balanced Binary search tree

There are few binary search trees, which always keep themselves balanced. Most important among them are Red-Black Tree (RB-Tree) and the AVL tree.

## TreeSet implementation in Java Collections

TreeSet<> is a class that implements the Set<> interface, which means that it stores unique elements. TreeSet<> is implemented using a red-black balanced binary search tree in Java Collections. Since TreeSet<> is implemented using a binary search tree, its elements are stored in sequential order.

**Example 3.6:**

```
import java.util.TreeSet;

public class TreeSetDemo {

    public static void main(String[] args) {
        // Create a tree set.
        TreeSet<String> ts = new TreeSet<String>();

        // Add elements to the hash set.
        ts.add("Banana");
        ts.add("Apple");
        ts.add("Mango");
        System.out.println(ts);
        System.out.println("Apple present : " + ts.contains("Apple"));
        System.out.println("Grapes present : " + ts.contains("Grapes"));
        ts.remove("Apple");
        System.out.println(ts);
        System.out.println("Apple present : " + ts.contains("Apple"));
    }
}
```

**Output:**

```
[Apple, Banana, Mango]
Apple present : true
Grapes present : false
[Banana, Mango]
Apple present : false
```

**Note:** TreeSet is implemented using a binary search tree so add, remove, and contain methods have logarithmic time complexity O(log(n)), where n is the number of elements in the set.

## TreeMap implementation in Java Collection

A Map<> is an interface that maps keys to values. A TreeMap<> is an implementation of Map<> and is implemented using a red-black balanced binary tree so the key-value pairs are stored in sorted order.

**Example 3.7:**

```java
import java.util.TreeMap;

public class TreeMapDemo {
    public static void main(String[] args) {
        // create a tree map.
        TreeMap<String, Integer> tm = new TreeMap<String, Integer>();

        // Put elements into the map
        tm.put("Apple", 40);
        tm.put("Banana", 10);
        tm.put("Mango", 20);

        System.out.println("Size :: " + tm.size());
        for(String key : tm.keySet())
            System.out.println(key + " cost :" + tm.get(key));

        System.out.println("Apple present ::" + tm.containsKey("Apple"));
        System.out.println("Grapes present :: " + tm.containsKey("Grapes"));
    }
}
```

**Output:**

```
Size :: 3
Apple cost :40
Banana cost :10
Mango cost :20
Apple present ::true
Grapes present :: false
```

## Heap / Priority Queue

Heap is a data structure used to implement the priority queue. In a heap, the data is logically organised as a complete binary tree. A complete binary tree is a binary tree that is filled at all possible levels except the last level. The parent value of each node in a heap is greater (or smaller) than the value of its child nodes.

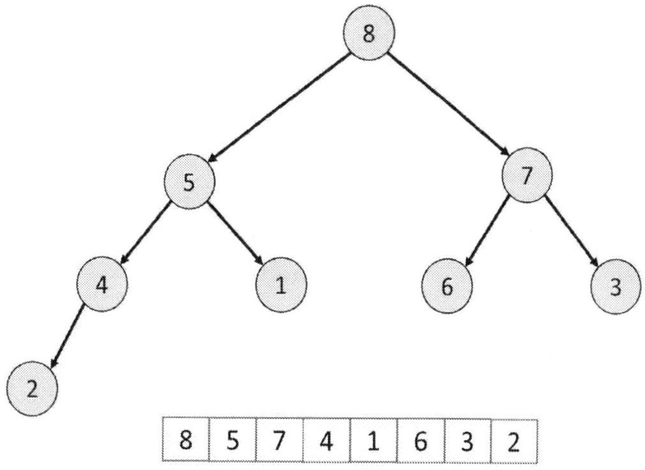


Max Heap

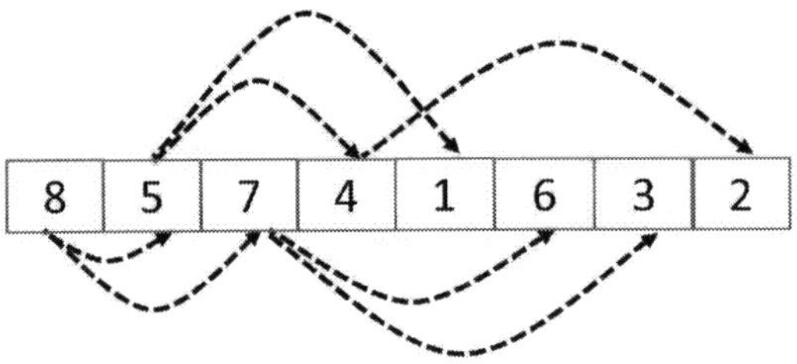


There are two types of heap data structure:

1. Max heap: Each node's value should be less than or equal to the values of its children.
2. Min heap: Each node's value should be greater than or equal to the values of its children.

## Heap ADT Operations

Below is the API of the Heap:

1. **Insert(k)** will add a new element k to the heap. The time complexity of this operation is O(log(n))
2. **Remove()** will extract max for max heap case (or min for min heap case). The time complexity of this operation is O(log(n))
3. **Heapify()** will convert an array of numbers into a heap. This operation has a time complexity **O(n)**

## PriorityQueue implementation in Java Collection

Min heap implementation of Priority Queue

**Example 3.8:**

```
import java.util.PriorityQueue;

public class PriorityQueueDemo {
    public static void main(String[] args) {
        PriorityQueue<Integer> pq = new PriorityQueue<Integer>();
        int[] arr = { 1, 2, 10, 8, 7, 3, 4, 6, 5, 9 };
        for (int i : arr)
            pq.add(i);

        System.out.println("Heap Array: " + pq);
        while (pq.isEmpty() == false)
            System.out.print(pq.remove() + " ");
    }
}
```

**Output**

```
Heap Array: [1, 2, 3, 5, 7, 10, 4, 8, 6, 9]
1 2 3 4 5 6 7 8 9 10
```

Max heap implementation of Priority Queue.

**Example 3.9:**

```
PriorityQueue<Integer> pq=new priorityQueue<Integer> (Collections.reverseOrder());
```

**Output**

```
Heap Array: [10, 9, 4, 6, 8, 2, 3, 1, 5, 7]
10 9 8 7 6 5 4 3 2 1
```

## Hash Table

A Hash-Table is a data structure that maps keys to values. The hash table calculates the index of data in an array using a hash function. We use the Hash-Table when the number of key-value pairs stored is small relative to the number of possible keys.

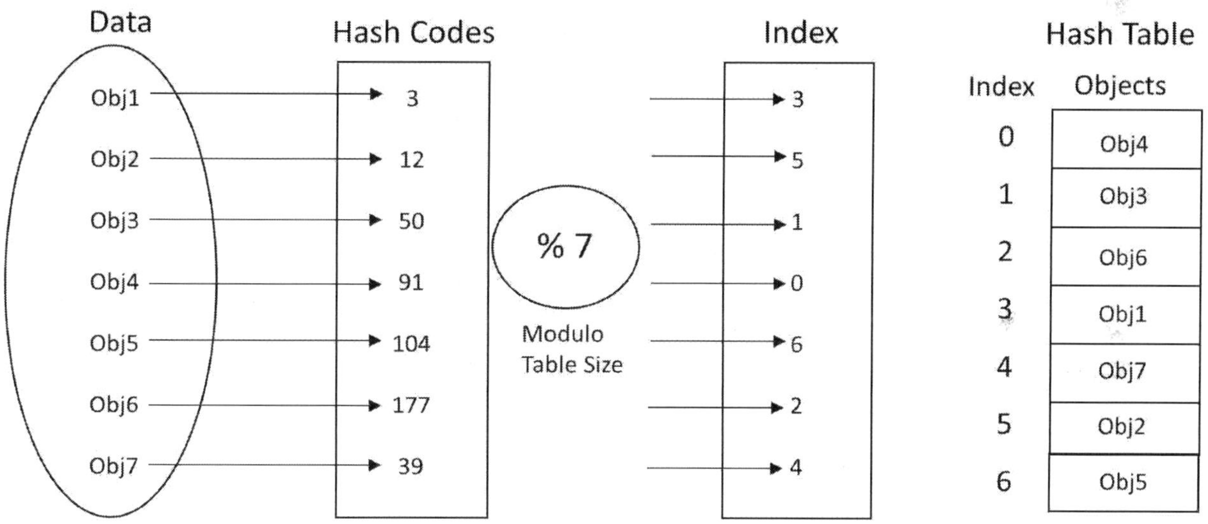


The process of storing data using a hash function is as follows:

1. To store data, create an array of size M, referred to as a Hash-Table.
2. Find a hash code of a key using a hash function.
3. Take a module of hashcode by the size of Hash-Table to get the index where data will be stored.
4. Finally, store this data in the appropriate index.

The process of searching data in a Hash-Table using a hash function is as follows:

1. Using a hash function, we can generate a hash code for the key we're looking for.
2. Take a modulo of hashcode by the hash table size to get the index of the table where data is stored.
3. Finally, get the value from the index you calculated.

## Hash-Table Abstract Data Type (ADT)

Below is the API of the Hash-Table:

1. **Insert(x)** will add x to the hash table.
2. **Delete(x)** will delete x from the hash table.
3. **Search(x)** will search x in the hash table.

The Hash-Table is a useful data structure for implementing a dictionary. The average time to search for an element in a Hash-Table is **O(1)**.

## HashSet implementation of Java Collections

HashSet <> is a class that implements the Set<> interface, which means that it stores unique elements. HashSet <> is implemented using a hash table. Since HashSet<> is implemented using a hash table, its elements are not stored in sequential order.

**Example 3.10:**

```
import java.util.HashSet;

public class HashSetDemo {
    public static void main(String[] args) {
        // Create a hash set.
        HashSet<String> hs = new HashSet<String>();

        // Add elements to the hash set.
        hs.add("Banana");
        hs.add("Apple");
        hs.add("Mango");
        System.out.println(hs);

        System.out.println("Apple present: " + hs.contains("Apple"));
        System.out.println("Grapes present: " + hs.contains("Grapes"));

        hs.remove("Apple");
        System.out.println(hs);
        System.out.println("Apple present: " + hs.contains("Apple"));
    }
}
```

**Output**

```
[Apple, Mango, Banana]
Apple present: true
Grapes present: false
[Mango, Banana]
Apple present: false
```

## LinkedHashSet implementation of Java Collections

LinkedHashSet<> is a class that implements Set<> interface, which means that it stores unique elements. LinkedHashSet<> is implemented using a hash table and a linked list. A LinkedList is used to preserve the order of elements based on insertion. Traversing the elements of the hash table is done in order of insertion.

**Example 3.11:**
```
import java.util.HashSet;
import java.util.LinkedHashSet;

public class LinkedHashSetDemo {
    public static void main(String[] args) {
        // Create a hash set.
        HashSet<String> hs = new HashSet<String>();

        // Add elements to the hash set.
        hs.add("Banana");
        hs.add("Apple");
        hs.add("Mango");

        System.out.println("HashSet:: " + hs);

        // Create a linked hash set.
        LinkedHashSet<String> lhs = new LinkedHashSet<String>();

        // Add elements to the linked hash set.
        lhs.add("Banana");
        lhs.add("Apple");
        lhs.add("Mango");

        System.out.println("LinkedHashSet:: " + lhs);
    }
}
```

**Output**
```
HashSet:: [Apple, Mango, Banana]
LinkedHashSet:: [Banana, Apple, Mango]
```

Comparison of various Set classes.

| | **TreeSet** | **HashSet** | **LinkedHashSet** |
|---|---|---|---|
| **Storage** | Red-Black Tree | Hash Table | Hash Table with Linked List. |
| **Performance** | Slower than HashSet, O(log(N)) | Fastest, constant time | More expensive than HashSet, must maintain a linked list. |
| **Order of Iteration** | Increasing Order | No order guarantee | Order of insertion |

## HashMap implementation in Java Collection

A Map<> is a data structure that maps keys to values. A HashMap<> is an implementation of Map<> and is implemented using a hash table so the key-value pairs are not stored in sorted order. Map<>

does not allow duplicate keys but values can be duplicated.

**Example 3.12:**

```
import java.util.HashMap;

public class HashMapDemo {
    public static void main(String[] args) {
        // Create a hash map.
        HashMap<String, Integer> hm = new HashMap<String, Integer>();

        // Put elements into the map
        hm.put("Apple", 40);
        hm.put("Banana", 10);
        hm.put("Mango", 20);

        System.out.println("Size :: " + hm.size());
        for(String key : hm.keySet())
            System.out.println(key + " cost :" + hm.get(key));

        System.out.println("Apple present ::" + hm.containsKey("Apple"));
        System.out.println("Grapes present :: " + hm.containsKey("Grapes"));
    }
}
```

**Output**

```
Size :: 3
Apple cost :40
Mango cost :20
Banana cost :10
Apple present ::true
Grapes present :: false
```

Comparison of various Set classes.

| | **TreeMap** | **HashMap** | **LinkedHashMap** |
|---|---|---|---|
| **Storage** | Red-Black Tree | Hash Table | Hash Table with Linked List. |
| **Performance** | Slower than HashMap, O(log(N)) | Fastest, constant time | More expensive than HashMap, must maintain a linked list. |
| **Order of Iteration** | Increasing Order of key | No order guarantee | Order of insertion |

## Endnote

This chapter has provided a brief introduction of the various data structures and their complexities. In the next chapters, we will study all these data structures in detail. If you know the interface of a data structure, you can use it to solve other problems without knowing its internal implementation.

# CHAPTER 4: SORTING

## Introduction

Sorting is the process of arranging elements in ascending or descending order. For example, when we play cards, we sort cards by value so that we can find the required card easily.

Another example, When we visit a library, the books are arranged into streams (Algorithms, Operating systems, Networking and so on). Sorting arranges data elements in a logical order to make searching simpler. It's much easier to find a book we're seeking when the books are arranged in appropriate indexing order.

Sorting algorithms like Bubble-Sort, Insertion-Sort and Selection-Sort are easy to implement and work well with small input sets. However, they are inefficient for large datasets. Sorting algorithms like Merge-Sort, Quick-Sort and Heap-Sort are appropriate for sorting large datasets. However, they are overkill if we want to sort a small dataset. Some other algorithms are there to sort a huge data set that cannot be stored in memory completely, for which an external sorting technique is developed.

## Types of Sorting

Internal Sorting: All the elements can be read into memory at the same time, and sorting is performed in memory.

1. Selection-Sort
2. Insertion-Sort
3. Bubble-Sort
4. Quick-Sort
5. Merge-Sort

External Sorting: In this type of sorting, the dataset is so big that it is impossible to load the whole dataset into memory, so sorting is done in chunks.

1. Merge-Sort

## Comparison Function

Before we start a discussion of the various algorithms one by one. First, we should look at a comparison function that is used to compare two values.

**Less function** will return true if value1 is less than value2, otherwise it will return false.

```
boolean less(int value1, int value2) {
    return value1 < value2;
}
```

**Greater function** will return true if value1 is greater than value2, otherwise it will return false.

```
boolean greater(int value1, int value2) {
    return value1 > value2;
}
```

The value in various sorting algorithms is compared using one of the above functions, and it will be swapped depending upon the return value of these functions. If greater() comparison function is used, then sorted output will be in increasing order. On the other hand, if less() comparison function is used, then the resulting output will be in descending order.

## Bubble Sort

Bubble-Sort is the slowest algorithm for sorting used when the data set is small. It is easy to implement and use. In Bubble-Sort, we compare each pair of adjacent values. We want to sort values in increasing order, so if the second value is less than the first value, we swap these two values. Otherwise, we will go to the next pair. Thus, the largest value bubble to the end of the array.

After the first pass, the largest value will be in the rightmost position. We will have N number of passes to get the array completely sorted.

| | | | | | | | |
|---|---|---|---|---|---|---|---|
| 5 | 1 | 2 | 4 | 3 | 7 | 6 | Swap |
| 1 | 5 | 2 | 4 | 3 | 7 | 6 | Swap |
| 1 | 2 | 5 | 4 | 3 | 7 | 6 | Swap |
| 1 | 2 | 4 | 5 | 3 | 7 | 6 | Swap |
| 1 | 2 | 4 | 3 | 5 | 7 | 6 | No Swap |
| 1 | 2 | 4 | 3 | 5 | 7 | 6 | Swap |
| 1 | 2 | 4 | 3 | 5 | 6 | 7 | |

**Example 4.1:**

```
public class BubbleSort {
    public void sort(int[] arr) {
        int size = arr.length, temp;

        for (int i = 0; i < (size - 1); i++) {
            for (int j = 0; j < size - i - 1; j++) {
                if (greater(arr[j], arr[j + 1])) {
                    /* Swapping */
                    temp = arr[j];
                    arr[j] = arr[j + 1];
                    arr[j + 1] = temp;
                }
            }
        }
    }
```

```
    // Testing code.
    public static void main(String[] args) {
        int[] array = { 9, 1, 8, 2, 7, 3, 6, 4, 5 };
        BubbleSort b = new BubbleSort();
        b.sort(array);
        for (int i = 0; i < array.length; i++) {
            System.out.print(array[i] + " ");
        }
    }
}
```

**Output:**
```
1 2 3 4 5 6 7 8 9
```

**Analysis:**

1. The outer loop represents the number of swaps that are done for the comparison of data.
2. The inner loop is used for the comparison of data. In the first iteration, the largest value will be moved to the end of the array, in the second iteration the second-largest value will be moved before the largest value and so on.
3. The greater() function is used for comparison, which means when the value of the first argument is greater than the value of the second argument then performs a swap. With this, we are sorting in increasing order. If we have, the less() function in place of greater() then the array will be sorted in decreasing order.

**Complexity Analysis:**

Each time the inner loop execute for (n-1), (n-2), (n-3) +..... + 3 + 2 + 1 = O(n^2) Worst-case

## Modified (improved) Bubble-Sort

When there is no more swap in one pass of the outer loop, the array is already sorted. At this point, we should stop sorting. This sorting improvement in Bubble-Sort is particularly useful when we know that, except for a few elements, the rest of the array is already sorted.

**Example 4.2:**
```
public void sort2(int[] arr) {
    int size = arr.length;
    int i, j, temp, swapped = 1;

    for (i = 0; i < (size - 1) && swapped == 1; i++) {
        swapped = 0;
        for (j = 0; j < size - i - 1; j++) {
            if (greater(arr[j], arr[j + 1])) {
                temp = arr[j];
                arr[j] = arr[j + 1];
                arr[j + 1] = temp;
                swapped = 1;
            }
```

```
        }
    }
}
```

By applying this improvement, the best-case performance of this algorithm is improved when an array is nearly sorted. In this case, we just need a single pass and the best-case complexity is **O(n)**

**Complexity Analysis:**

| | |
|---|---|
| Worst-case performance | O(n^2) |
| Average-Case performance | O(n^2) |
| Space Complexity | O(1) |
| Modified: When the array is nearly sorted | O(n) |
| Stable Sorting | Yes |

## Insertion Sort

Insertion sort works similar to how we organise a deck of cards. We keep a sorted subarray. Each value is placed in the sorted subarray in its proper position so that the subarray remains sorted. Insertion-Sort Time Complexity is **O(n^2)** which is the same as Bubble-Sort but performs a better than bubble sort.

Let's look at the diagram of insertion sort and check how it works.

| | | | | | | | |
|---|---|---|---|---|---|---|---|
| 5 | 6 | 2 | 4 | 7 | 3 | 1 | Insert 5 |
| 5 | 6 | 2 | 4 | 7 | 3 | 1 | Insert 6 |
| 2 | 5 | 6 | 4 | 7 | 3 | 1 | Insert 2 |
| 2 | 4 | 5 | 6 | 7 | 3 | 1 | Insert 4 |
| 2 | 4 | 5 | 6 | 7 | 3 | 1 | Insert 7 |
| 2 | 3 | 4 | 5 | 6 | 7 | 1 | Insert 3 |
| 1 | 2 | 3 | 4 | 5 | 6 | 7 | Insert 1 |

**Example 4.3:**
```java
public class InsertionSort {
    public void sort(int[] arr) {
        int size = arr.length;
        int temp, j;

        for (int i = 1; i < size; i++) {
            temp = arr[i];
            for (j = i; j > 0 && greater(arr[j - 1], temp); j--) {
                arr[j] = arr[j - 1];
            }
            arr[j] = temp;
        }
    }

    // Testing code.
    public static void main(String[] args) {
        int[] array = { 9, 1, 8, 2, 7, 3, 6, 4, 5 };
        InsertionSort srt = new InsertionSort();
        srt.sort(array);

        for (int i = 0; i < array.length; i++) {
            System.out.print(array[i] + " ");
        }
    }
}
```

**Output:**
```
1 2 3 4 5 6 7 8 9
```

**Analysis:**

1. The outer loop is used to choose the value to be inserted into the sorted array on the left.
2. The chosen value we want to insert is saved in a temp variable.
3. The inner loop is doing the comparison using the greater() function. The values are shifted to the right until we find the proper position of the temp value, for which this iteration is performed.
4. Finally, temp's value is placed in its proper position. In each iteration of the outer loop, the length of the sorted array increases by one. When we exit the outer loop, the array is sorted.

**Complexity Analysis:**

| | |
|---|---|
| Worst-case time complexity | O(n^2) |
| Best-Case time complexity | O(n) |
| Average-Case time complexity | O(n^2) |
| Space Complexity | O(1) |
| Stable sorting | Yes |

## Selection Sort

Selection sort algorithm traverses the unsorted array and puts the largest value at the end. This process is repeated n-1 times. This algorithm also has quadratic time complexity, but it performs better than both bubble sort and insertion sort as fewer swaps are required in this approach. The sorted array is created backward in selection sort.

Let's look at the diagram of selection sort and check how it works.

| | | | | | | | |
|---|---|---|---|---|---|---|---|
| 5 | 6 | 2 | 4 | 7 | 3 | 1 | Swap |
| 5 | 6 | 2 | 4 | 1 | 3 | 7 | Swap |
| 5 | 3 | 2 | 4 | 1 | 6 | 7 | Swap |
| 1 | 3 | 2 | 4 | 5 | 6 | 7 | No Swap |
| 1 | 3 | 2 | 4 | 5 | 6 | 7 | Swap |
| 1 | 2 | 3 | 4 | 5 | 6 | 7 | No Swap |
| 1 | 2 | 3 | 4 | 5 | 6 | 7 | |

**Example 4.4:**
```
public class SelectionSort {
    public void sort(int[] arr) { // sorted array created in reverse order.
        int size = arr.length, i, j, max, temp;
        for (i = 0; i < size - 1; i++) {
            max = 0;
            for (j = 1; j < size - i; j++) {
                if (arr[j] > arr[max]) {
                    max = j;
                }
            }
            temp = arr[size - 1 - i];
            arr[size - 1 - i] = arr[max];
            arr[max] = temp;
        }
    }

    // Testing code.
    public static void main(String[] args) {
        int[] array = { 9, 1, 8, 2, 7, 3, 6, 4, 5 };
        SelectionSort srt = new SelectionSort();
        srt.sort(array);
        for (int i = 0; i < array.length; i++) {
            System.out.print(array[i] + " ");
        }
    }
}
```

**Output:**
```
1 2 3 4 5 6 7 8 9
```

**Analysis:**

1. The outer loop decides the number of times the inner loop will iterate. For an input of N elements, the outer loop will iterate the N number of times.
2. The largest value is placed at the end of the array after each inner loop iteration.
3. After all the iterations the array is sorted. The sorted array is created backwards.

**Complexity Analysis:**

| | |
|---|---|
| Worst-Case time complexity | O(n^2) |
| Best-Case time complexity | O(n^2) |
| Average-Case time complexity | O(n^2) |
| Space Complexity | O(1) |
| Stable Sorting | No |

We can implement the same algorithm by creating the sorted array in the front of the array. Let's look at the second algorithm by which we can implement selection sort.

**Example 4.5:**
```
public void sort2(int[] arr) { // sorted array created in forward direction.
    int i, j, min, temp, size = arr.length;
    for (i = 0; i < size - 1; i++) {
        min = i;
        for (j = i + 1; j < size; j++) {
            if (arr[j] < arr[min]) {
                min = j;
            }
        }
        temp = arr[i];
        arr[i] = arr[min];
        arr[min] = temp;
    }
}
```

## Merge Sort

Merge-Sort uses Divide & Conquer technique to sort the input array. Merge sort recursively divides the input into two halves. The two halves are then sorted separately and finally combine the result into the final sorted output. The recursive step keeps on dividing the input into smaller pieces until the length of each piece becomes one.

Let's look at the diagram of merge sort.

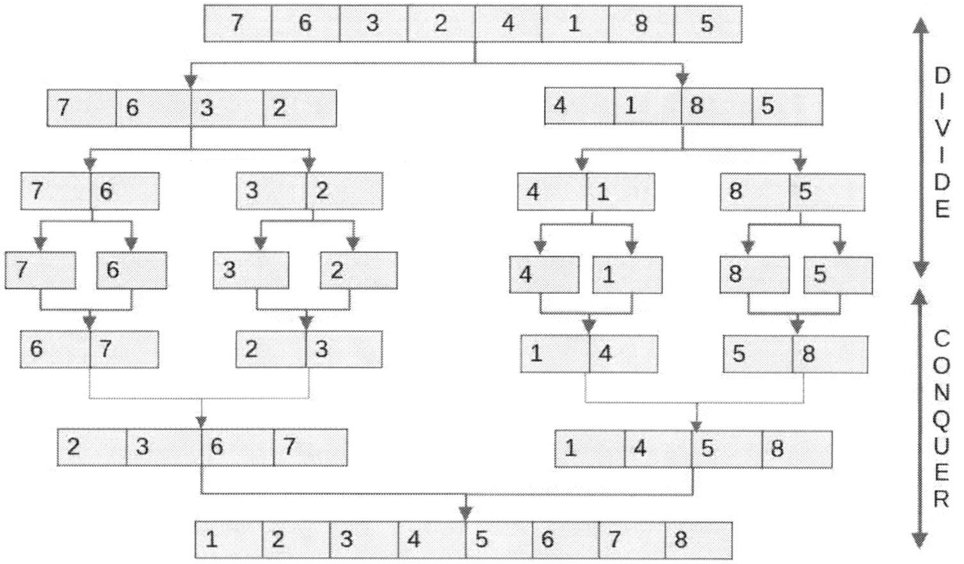

**Example 4.6:**

```
public class MergeSort {
    private void merge(int[] arr, int[] tempArray, int lowerIndex, int middleIndex,
int upperIndex) {
        int lowerStart = lowerIndex;
        int lowerStop = middleIndex;
        int upperStart = middleIndex + 1;
        int upperStop = upperIndex;
        int count = lowerIndex;

        while (lowerStart <= lowerStop && upperStart <= upperStop) {
            if (arr[lowerStart] < arr[upperStart]) {
                tempArray[count++] = arr[lowerStart++];
            } else {
                tempArray[count++] = arr[upperStart++];
            }
        }

        while (lowerStart <= lowerStop) {
            tempArray[count++] = arr[lowerStart++];
        }

        while (upperStart <= upperStop) {
            tempArray[count++] = arr[upperStart++];
        }

        for (int i = lowerIndex; i <= upperIndex; i++) {
            arr[i] = tempArray[i];
        }
    }

    private void mergeSrt(int[] arr, int[] tempArray, int lowerIndex, int
upperIndex) {
        if (lowerIndex >= upperIndex) {
            return;
        }

        int middleIndex = (lowerIndex + upperIndex) / 2;
        mergeSrt(arr, tempArray, lowerIndex, middleIndex);
        mergeSrt(arr, tempArray, middleIndex + 1, upperIndex);
        merge(arr, tempArray, lowerIndex, middleIndex, upperIndex);
    }

    public void sort(int[] arr) {
        int size = arr.length;
        int[] tempArray = new int[size];
        mergeSrt(arr, tempArray, 0, size - 1);
    }

    // Testing code.
    public static void main(String[] args) {
        int[] array = { 3, 4, 2, 1, 6, 5, 7, 8};
        MergeSort m = new MergeSort();
        m.sort(array);

        for (int i = 0; i < array.length; i++)
            System.out.print(array[i] + " ");
    }
}
```

**Output:**
```
1 2 3 4 5 6 7 8
```

**Analysis:**

1. Time complexity of merge sort is O(n.log(n)) in all three cases (best, average, and worst) since it always divides the array into two halves and merges them in linear time.
2. It requires an equal amount of additional space as the unsorted array. Hence, it is not at all recommended for searching large unsorted arrays.

**Complexity Analysis:**

| | |
|---|---|
| Worst-Case time complexity | O(n.log(n)) |
| Best-Case time complexity | O(n.log(n)) |
| Average-Case time complexity | O(n.log(n)) |
| Space Complexity | O(n) |
| Stable Sorting | Yes |

## Pros and Cons of Merge-sort Algorithm

| **Pros of Merge-sort Algorithm** | **Cons of Merge-sort Algorithm** |
|---|---|
| 1) Can be used to sort large-size arrays.<br>2) Can be used to sort linked-lists<br>2) Used in External sorting.<br>4) Merge-sort is stable sorting. | 1) Consumes extra space. Not an in-place sorting algorithm.<br>2) Even if the list is already sorted it will always take O(n.log(n)) time.<br>3) Recursive algorithms are slower than iterative ones. |

## External Sort (External Merge-Sort)

When data needs to be sorted is huge, and it is not possible to load it completely in memory (RAM), for such a dataset we use external sorting. Such data is sorted using the external Merge-Sort algorithm.

1. First data is picked in chunks, and it is sorted in memory. Then this sorted data is written back to disk. The whole data is sorted in chunks using Merge-Sort. Now we need to combine these sorted chunks into final sorted data.
2. We create queues for the data, which will read from the sorted chunks. Each chunk will have its queue. We will pop from these queues, and these queues are responsible for reading from the sorted chunks. Let us suppose we have K different chunks of sorted data, each of length M.
3. The third step is using a Min-Heap, which will take input data from each of these queues. It will take one element from each queue. The minimum value is taken from the Heap and added to the final output. Then the queue from which this minimum value element is added to the heap will again be popped and one more element from this queue is added to the Heap.
4. When the data is exhausted from some queue, that queue is removed from the input list. Finally, we will get sorted data coming out from the heap. We can optimise this process further by adding an output buffer, which will store data coming out of Heap and will do a limited number of the write operation in the final Disk space.

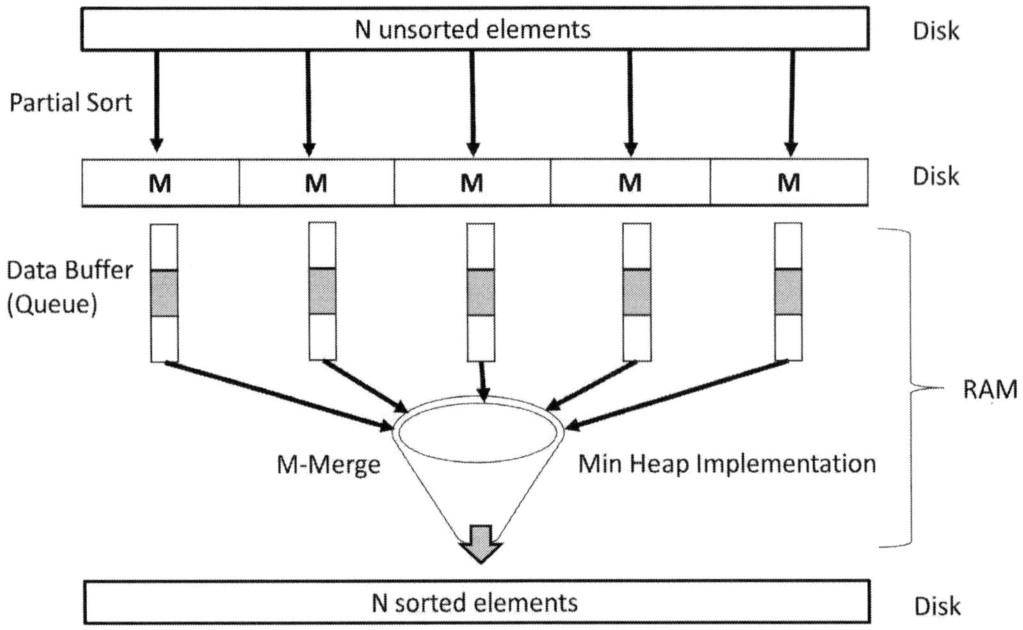


**Note**: No one will be asked to implement external sorting in an interview, but it is good to know about it.

## Quick Sort

Let's look at the working of a quicksort algorithm.

1. Quick Sort is a recursive algorithm. In each step, we select a pivot (let us say the first element of the array).
2. Partition the array into two pieces, with all elements smaller than the pivot are moved to the left side and all elements larger than the pivot are moved to the right side of the array. To do this, we will follow the following steps.
   a) Select pivot as the first element in the array.
   b) Use two index variables, lower and upper.
   c) Set the lower index as the second element in the array and the upper index as the last element of the array.
   d) Increase lower index till value at lower index is less than the pivot.
   e) Then decrement the upper index till the value at the upper index is greater than the pivot.
   f) Then swap the value at lower and upper index.
   g) Repeat the above 3 steps till the upper index is greater than the lower index.
   h) In the end, swap value at pivot and upper index.
3. Then we sort the left and right sub-array separately using recursion.
4. When the algorithm returns, the whole array is sorted.

The below diagram demonstrates the partition step in quickSort.

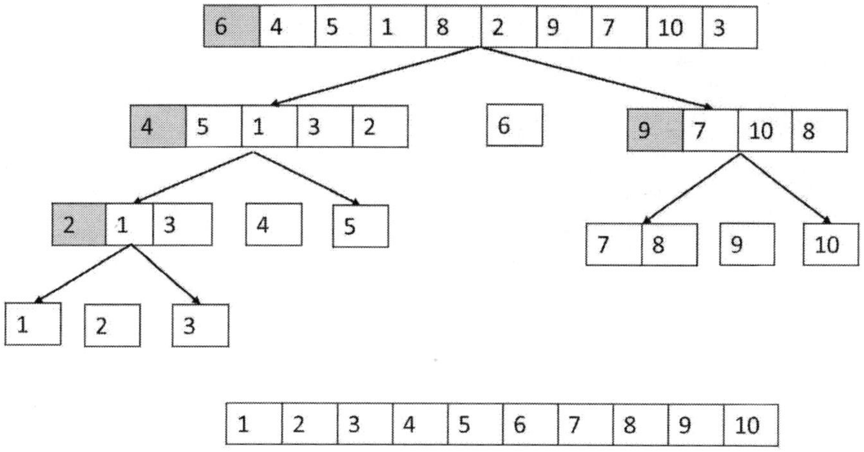


**Example 4.7:**

```
public class QuickSort {

    private void quickSort(int arr[], int lower, int upper) {
        if (upper <= lower)
            return;

        int pivot = arr[lower];
        int start = lower;
        int stop = upper;

        while (lower < upper) {
            while (arr[lower] <= pivot && lower < upper) {
                lower++;
            }

            while (arr[upper] > pivot && lower <= upper) {
                upper--;
            }

            if (lower < upper) {
                swap(arr, upper, lower);
            }
        }
        swap(arr, upper, start); // upper is the pivot position
        quickSort(arr, start, upper - 1);
        quickSort(arr, upper + 1, stop);
    }

    public void sort(int[] arr) {
        int size = arr.length;
        quickSort(arr, 0, size - 1);
    }

    private void swap(int arr[], int first, int second) {
        int temp = arr[first];
        arr[first] = arr[second];
        arr[second] = temp;
    }
```

```
    // Testing code.
    public static void main(String[] args) {
        int[] array = { 3, 4, 2, 1, 6, 5, 7, 8, 10, 9 };
        QuickSort srt = new QuickSort();
        srt.sort(array);
        for (int i = 0; i < array.length; i++) {
            System.out.print(array[i] + " ");
        }
    }
}
```

**Output:**

```
1 2 3 4 5 6 7 8 9 10
```

**Analysis:**

1. The space required by Quick-Sort is very less, only O(n.log(n)) additional space is required.
2. quickSort is not a stable sorting technique. It can reorder elements with identical keys.

**Complexity Analysis:**

| | |
|---|---|
| Worst-Case time complexity | O(n^2) |
| Best-Case time complexity | O(n.log(n)) |
| Average-Case time complexity | O(n.log(n)) |
| Space Complexity | O(n.log(n)) |
| Stable Sorting | No |

Best Case Analysis: The best case occurs when the partition process picks the median element as pivot which divides the array into two equal parts.

Recurrence relation for the best case: T(n) = 2T(n/2) +O(n)

The solution of the above recurrence is O(n.log(n)).

Worst Case Analysis: The worst case occurs when the pivot is not able to divide the array and each iteration it will just reduce the size of the array to be sorted by 1. This happens when all the elements in the array have values either greater or smaller than the pivot value.

The worst occurs in the following cases.

1) Array is already sorted in increasing order.

2) Array is already sorted in decreasing order.

Recurrence relation for the best case: T(n) = T(n-1) +O(n)

The solution of the above recurrence is O(n^2).

## Quick Select

The quick select algorithm is used to find the element in an array that will be at the kth position if the array would have been sorted. Quick select is very similar to Quick-Sort in place of sorting the entire array, at each step of the algorithm, we concentrate on the part where the kth element is located and ignore the other half of the array.

**Example 4.8:**

```
public class QuickSelect {
    public static void quickSelect(int arr[], int lower, int upper, int k) {
        if (upper <= lower)
            return;

        int pivot = arr[lower];
        int start = lower;
        int stop = upper;
        while (lower < upper) {
            while (arr[lower] <= pivot && lower < upper) {
                lower++;
            }
            while (arr[upper] > pivot && lower <= upper) {
                upper--;
            }
            if (lower < upper) {
                swap(arr, upper, lower);
            }
        }

        swap(arr, upper, start); // upper is the pivot position

        if (k < upper)
            quickSelect(arr, start, upper - 1, k); // pivot -1 is the upper for
                                                   // left sub array.
        if (k > upper)
            quickSelect(arr, upper + 1, stop, k); // pivot + 1 is the lower for
                                                  // right sub array.
    }

    public static void swap(int arr[], int first, int second) {
        int temp = arr[first];
        arr[first] = arr[second];
        arr[second] = temp;
    }

    public static int get(int arr[], int k) {
        quickSelect(arr, 0, arr.length - 1, k);
        return arr[k-1];
    }

    // Testing code.
    public static void main(String[] args) {
        int[] array = { 3, 4, 2, 1, 6, 5, 7, 8 };
        System.out.print("value at index 5 is : " + QuickSelect.get(array, 5));
    }
}
```

**Output:**

```
value at index 5 is : 5
```

**Complexity Analysis:**

| | |
|---|---|
| Worst-Case time complexity | O(n^2) |
| Best-Case time complexity | O(log(n)) |
| Average-Case time complexity | O(log(n)) |
| Space Complexity | O(n.log(n)) |

## Counting Sort

Counting sort is the simplest and most efficient type of sorting. Counting sort has a strict requirement of a predefined range of data. For example, we want to sort the number of people in each age group. We know that the age of people can vary between 0 and 130. We can directly store counts in an array of size 130. If we know the range of input, then sorting can be done using counting sort in O(n+k). Where n is the number of elements and k is the possible range, in the above example it is 130.

Let's look at the diagram of counting-sort.

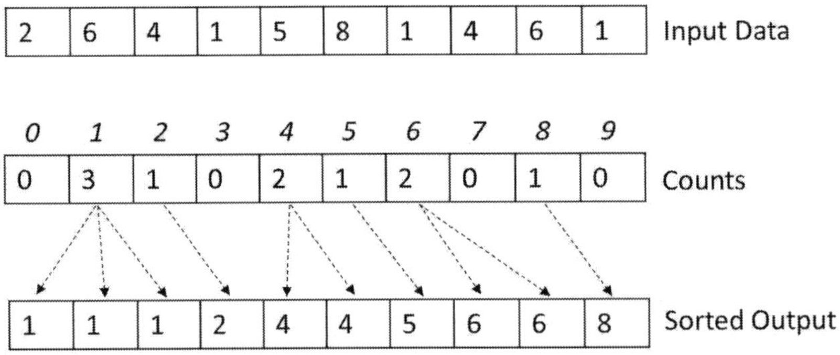


**Example 4.9:**
```
public class CountSort {
    public void sort(int[] arr, int lowerRange, int upperRange) {
        int size = arr.length;
        int range = upperRange - lowerRange;
        int[] count = new int[range];

        for (int i = 0; i < size; i++) {
            count[arr[i] - lowerRange]++;
        }

        int j = 0;
        for (int i = 0; i < range; i++) {
            for (; count[i] > 0; (count[i])--) {
                arr[j++] = i + lowerRange;
            }
        }
    }

    // Testing code.
    public static void main(String[] args) {
        int[] array = { 23, 24, 22, 21, 26, 25, 27, 28, 21, 21 };
        CountSort b = new CountSort();
        b.sort(array, 20, 30);
```

```
        for (int i = 0; i < array.length; i++) {
            System.out.print(array[i] + " ");
        }
    }
}
```

**Output:**

```
21 21 21 22 23 24 25 26 27 28
```

**Analysis:**

1. To store counts, we made a count array.
2. The elements of the count array are set to 0.
3. The index associated with the input array is increased.
4. Finally, the information stored in the count array is saved in the array.

**Complexity Analysis:**

| | |
|---|---|
| Data structure | Array |
| Worst-Case performance | O(n+k) |
| Average-Case performance | O(n+k) |
| Worst-Case Space Complexity | O(k) |

k - Number of distinct elements
n - Total number of elements in the array.

## Radix Sort

Unlike merge-sort or quick-sort etc., Radix sort is a non-comparative sorting algorithm. The lower bound for the Comparison based sorting algorithm (Merge Sort, Quick-Sort etc.) is O(n.log(n)). If the range of values that need to be sorted is fairly small then Counting sort can be used.

Counting sort is a linear time sorting algorithm that sorts in O(n+k) time when elements are in the range from 1 to k. If the range is not small then Radix sort can be used. Radix Sort is used when there is a constant 'd' such that all values are max d digit numbers.

In Radix sort a list of integers are sorted based on digits of numbers. Sorting is performed digit by digit, sort starting from least significant digit to most significant digit. Radix sort uses counting sort as a subroutine to sort according to a single digit.

Input, unsorted Array: 100, 49, 65, 91, 702, 29, 4, 55

Sorting by least significant digit (1s place): 10**0**, 09**1**, 70**2**, 00**4**, 06**5**, 05**5**, 04**9**, 02**9**

Sorting by next digit (10s place): 1**0**0, 7**0**2, 0**0**4, 0**2**9, 0**4**9, 0**5**5, 0**6**5, 0**9**1

Sorting by the most significant digit (100s place): **0**04, **0**29, **0**49, **0**55, **0**65, **0**91, **1**00, **7**02

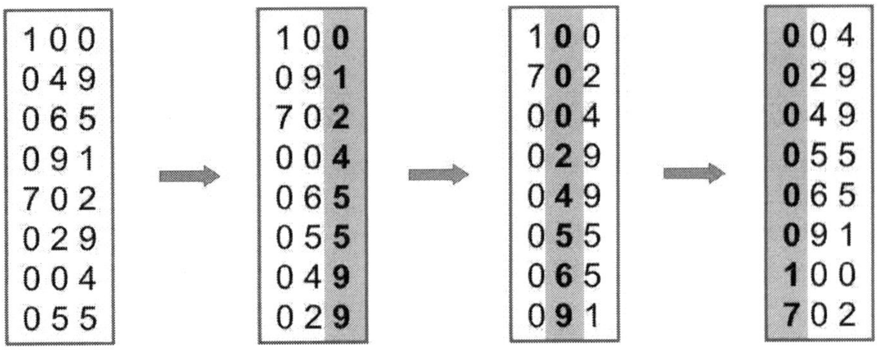


Diagram demonstrates various steps of Radix Sort.

**Example 4.10:**

```
public class RadixSort {
    static int getMax(int arr[], int n) {
        int max = arr[0];
        for (int i = 1; i < n; i++)
            if (max < arr[i])
                max = arr[i];
        return max;
    }

    static void countSort(int arr[], int n, int dividend) {
        int temp[] = arr.clone();
        int count[] = new int[10];
        Arrays.fill(count, 0);

        // Store count of occurrences in count array.
        // (number / dividend) % 10 is used to find the working digit.

        for (int i = 0; i < n; i++)
            count[(temp[i] / dividend) % 10]++;

        // Change count[i] so that count[i] contains
        // number of elements till index i in output.

        for (int i = 1; i < 10; i++)
            count[i] += count[i - 1];

        // Copy content to input arr.
        for (int i = n-1; i >= 0; i--) {
            arr[count[(temp[i] / dividend) % 10] - 1] = temp[i];
            count[(temp[i] / dividend) % 10]--;
        }
    }

    public void sort(int[] arr) {
        int n = arr.length;
        int m = getMax(arr, n);

        // Counting sort for every digit.
        // The dividend passed is used to calculate the current working digit.
        for (int div = 1; m / div > 0; div *= 10) {
            countSort(arr, n, div);
            printArray(arr);
        }
    }
```

```
    public void printArray(int[] arr) {
        for (int i = 0; i < arr.length; i++) {
            System.out.print(arr[i] + " ");
        }
        System.out.println();
    }

    // Testing code.
    public static void main(String[] args) {
        int[] array = { 100, 49, 65, 91, 702, 29, 4, 55 };
        RadixSort b = new RadixSort();
        b.sort(array);
    }
}
```

**Output:**

```
4 29 49 55 65 91 100 702
```

**Complexity Analysis:**

Let us suppose the total number of elements that need to be sorted is n, the largest value is k and the number is of base b. The total number of iterations will be the number of digits in the largest value which is $\log_b(k)$. The numbers are sorted according to digits in each iteration using counting sort. Each iteration cost will be O(n+b). Total complexity of algorithm is $O((n+b) * \log_b(k))$.

Considering the number of digits is 64 for an integer and the base is 10. These two values become constant. Time complexity will be O((n + 10)*64) so ignoring constant time complexity will be O(n).

| | |
|---|---|
| Data structure | Array |
| Best-Case performance | O(n) |
| Worst-Case performance | O(n) |
| Average-Case performance | O(n) |
| Space Complexity | O(n) |

n - Total number of elements in the array.

## Heap Sort

In Heap-Sort we will store data in Heap data structure which will always give data in sorted order. Heap-Sort we will study in the Heap chapter.

**Complexity Analysis:**

| | |
|---|---|
| Data structure | Array |
| Worst-Case performance | O(n.log(n)) |
| Average-Case performance | O(n.log(n)) |
| Worst-Case Space Complexity | O(1) |

## Tree Sorting

In Tree-Sorting data is stored in a Binary Search Tree data structure. An In-Order traversal of the Binary Search Tree produces data in increasing order. We will study the Binary Search Tree in Tree chapter.

**Complexity Analysis:**

| | |
|---|---|
| Worst-Case time complexity | O(n^2) |
| Best-Case time complexity | O(n.log(n)) |
| Average-Case time complexity | O(n.log(n)) |
| Space Complexity | O(n) |
| Stable Sorting | Yes |

## Shell Sort

Shell sort is an improvement on insertion sort. Insertion sort is not efficient when elements of the unsorted array are widely placed, which means they are far from their sorted position (e.g. reverse sorted array). In a widely placed array, the number of shifts are more.
Shell sort reduces the number of shifts by dividing the array into sub-arrays of intervals/gaps. Then performing insertion sort on the sub-array. The process is repeated by reducing the gap size by half till the gap size is zero. By doing this change, the number of comparisons increases but the number of shifts decreases.

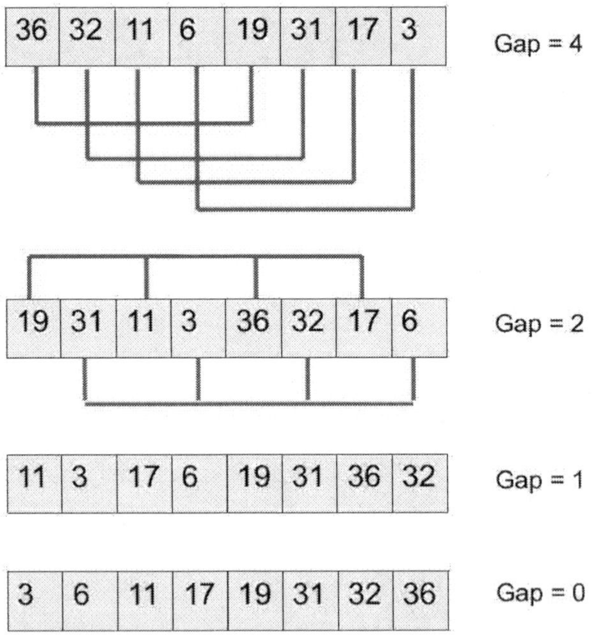


**Example 4.11:**
```
public class ShellSort {
    private boolean greater(int value1, int value2) {
        return value1 > value2;
    }
```

```
    public void sort(int[] arr) {
        int n = arr.length;

        // Gap starts with n/2 and half in each iteration.
        for (int gap = n/2; gap > 0; gap /= 2)
        {
            // Do a gapped insertion sort.
            for (int i = gap; i < n; i += 1)
            {
                int curr = arr[i];
                // Shift elements of already sorted list
                // to find the right position for curr value.
                int j;
                for (j = i; j >= gap && greater(arr[j - gap], curr); j -= gap)
                    arr[j] = arr[j - gap];
                // Put current value in its correct location
                arr[j] = curr;
            }
        }
    }

    // Testing code.
    public static void main(String[] args) {
        int[] array = { 36, 32, 11, 6, 19, 31, 17, 3 };
        ShellSort ss = new ShellSort();
        ss.sort(array);
        for (int i = 0; i < array.length; i++) {
            System.out.print(array[i] + " ");
        }
    }
}
```

**Output:**

```
3 6 11 17 19 31 32 36
```

**Time Complexity:**

| | |
|---|---|
| Data structure | Array |
| Best-Case performance | O(n.log(n)) |
| Worst-Case performance | O(n^2) |
| Average-Case performance | O(n.log(n)) |
| Space Complexity | O(1) |

## Bucket Sort

Bucket sort is mainly useful when input is uniformly distributed over a range. In Bucket Sort, the input array elements are divided into several groups called buckets. Each bucket is filled with a specific range of elements. The elements inside each bucket are sorted separately using any other sorting algorithm. Finally, the elements of the buckets are combined to get a final sorted array.

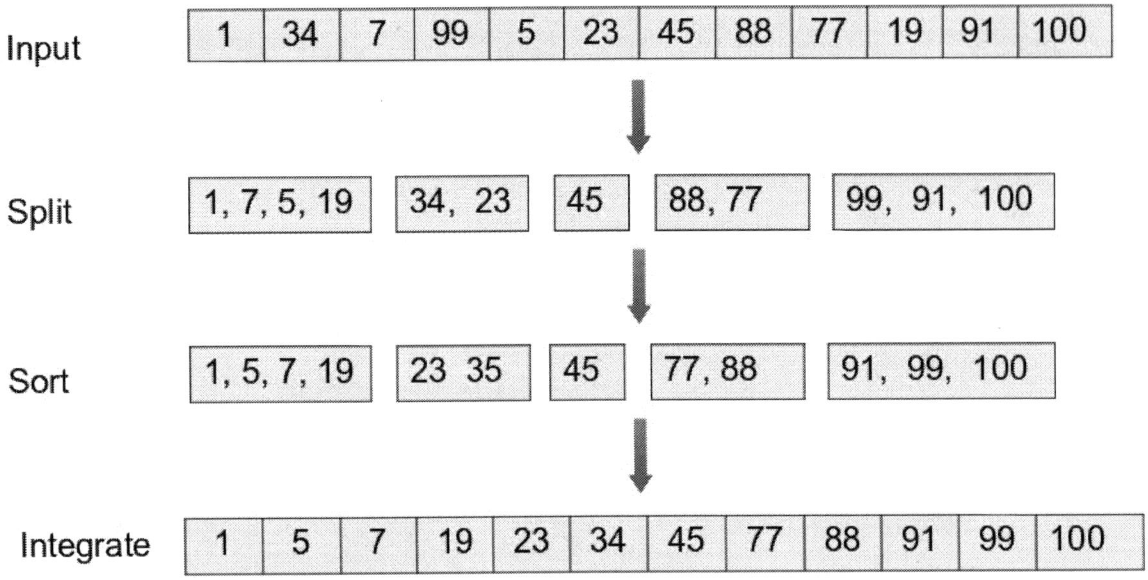


**Example 4.12:**

```
public class BucketSort {
    // Allowed values from 0 to maxValue.
    public void sort(int[] arr, int maxValue) {
        int numBucket = 5;
        sort(arr, maxValue, numBucket);
    }

    public void sort(int[] arr, int maxValue, int numBucket) {
        int length = arr.length;
        if (length == 0)
            return;

        ArrayList<ArrayList<Integer> > bucket =
                  new ArrayList<ArrayList<Integer> >(numBucket);

        // Create empty buckets
        for (int i = 0; i < numBucket; i++)
            bucket.add(new ArrayList<Integer>());


        int div = (int)Math.ceil((double)maxValue / (numBucket));

        // Add elements into the buckets
        for (int i = 0; i < length; i++) {
            if(arr[i] < 0  || arr[i] > maxValue){
                System.out.println("Value out of range.");
                return;
            }

            int bucketIndex = (arr[i]/div);
            // Maximum value will be assigned to the last bucket.
            if(bucketIndex >= numBucket)
                bucketIndex = numBucket - 1;

            bucket.get(bucketIndex).add(arr[i]);
        }
```

```
        // Sort the elements of each bucket.
        for (int i = 0; i < numBucket; i++) {
            Collections.sort(bucket.get(i));
        }

        // Populate output from the sorted subarray.
        int index = 0, count;
        for (int i = 0; i < numBucket; i++) {
            ArrayList<Integer> temp = bucket.get(i);
            count = temp.size();
            for (int j = 0; j < count; j++) {
                arr[index++] = temp.get(j);
            }
        }
    }

    public static void main(String[] args) {
        int[] array = { 1, 34, 7, 99, 5, 23, 45, 88, 77, 19, 91, 100 };
        int maxValue = 100;
        BucketSort b = new BucketSort();
        b.sort(array, maxValue);
        for (int i = 0; i < array.length; i++) {
            System.out.print(array[i] + " ");
        }
    }
}
```

**Output:**

```
1 5 7 19 23 34 45 77 88 91 99 100
```

## Generalised Bucket Sort

There are cases when the elements falling into a bucket are not unique but are in the same range. When we want to sort an index of a name, we can use the pointer bucket to store names.

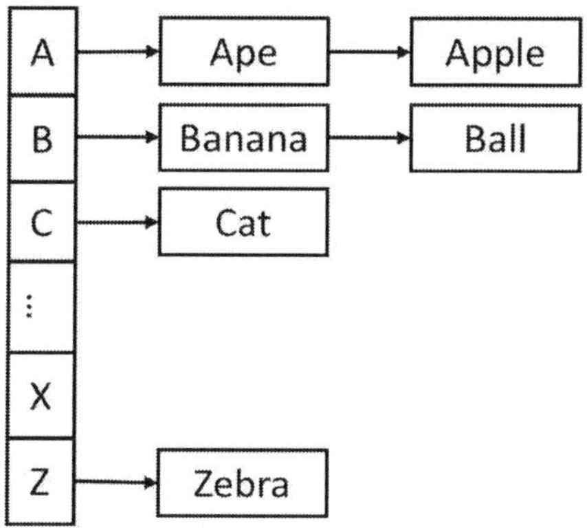


The buckets are already sorted, and the elements inside each bucket can be kept sorted by using an Insertion-Sort algorithm. We are leaving this generalised bucket sort implementation to the reader of this book. A similar data structure will be defined in the coming chapter of Hash-Table using separate chaining.

## Stable Sorting

A sorting algorithm is stable if two elements with identical key values appear in the same order in sorted output as they do in unsorted input. Stable sorting algorithms guarantee that elements with identical keys will not be reordered.

## Comparisons of the various sorting algorithms.

Below is the comparison of various sorting algorithms:

| Sort | Average Time | Best Time | Worst Time | Space | Stable |
|---|---|---|---|---|---|
| **Bubble Sort** | O(n^2) | O(n^2) | O(n^2) | O(1) | Yes |
| **Modified Bubble Sort** | O(n^2) | O(n) | O(n^2) | O(1) | Yes |
| **Selection Sort** | O(n^2) | O(n^2) | O(n^2) | O(1) | No |
| **Insertion Sort** | O(n^2) | O(n) | O(n^2) | O(1) | Yes |
| **Heap Sort** | O(n.log(n)) | O(n.log(n)) | O(n.log(n)) | O(1) | No |
| **Merge Sort** | O(n.log(n)) | O(n.log(n)) | O(n.log(n)) | O(n) | Yes |
| **Quick Sort** | O(n.log(n)) | O(n.log(n)) | O(n^2) | O(n) Worst-Case O(log(n))average case | No |
| **Counting Sort** | O(n) | O(n) | O(n) | O(k) | Yes |
| **Bucket Sort** | O(n+k) | O(n+k) | O(n^2) | O(n+k) | Yes, if the underlying sort is stable. |
| **Radix Sort** | O(n) | O(n) | O(n) | O(n) | No |
| **Shell Sort** | O(n.log(n)) | O(n.log(n)) | O(n^2) | O(1) | No |

## Selection of Best Sorting Algorithm

No sorting algorithm is perfect. Each of them has its own pros and cons. Let us discuss them one by one:

**Quick-Sort:** This algorithm is used when a stable sort isn't required, and average-case performance is more important than worst-case performance. We choose quick sort when the data is random. The Average-Case time complexity of Quick-Sort is O(n.log(n)) and the worst-case time complexity is O(n^2). Space Complexity of Quick-Sort is O(log(n)) auxiliary storage, which is stack space used in recursion.

**Merge-Sort**: Merge-Sort is used when you need a stable sort and a time complexity of **O(n.log(n))**. Merge-Sort is slower than Quick-Sort because a lot of copy is involved in the merge step. There are two uses of merge-sort:

- First to merge two sorted linked lists
- Second merge-sort is used in external sorting.

**Heap-Sort**: When you do not need a stable sort, and you care more about worst-case performance than average-case performance. It is guaranteed to be **O(n.log(n))**, and using **O(1)** auxiliary space, means you will not unpredictably run out of memory on very large inputs.

**Insertion-Sort**: When we need a stable sort and input size is guaranteed to be small, such as the base case of a Quick-Sort or Merge-Sort. The worst-case time complexity is **O(n^2)**. It has a very small constant factor multiplied to calculate the actual time taken. Therefore, for smaller input sizes, it performs better than Merge-Sort or Quick-Sort. It is also useful when the data is already sorted. In this case, its running time is **O(n)**.

**Bubble-Sort**: Where we know the data is nearly sorted. Say only two elements are out of place. Then in one pass, Bubble Sort will make the data sorted and in the second pass, it will see everything is sorted and then exit. Only takes 2 passes of the array.

**Selection-Sort**: Best, Worst & Average Case running time all are **O(n^2)**. It is only useful when you want to do something quickly. They can be used when you are just doing some prototyping.

**Counting-Sort**: When you are sorting data within a limited range.

**Radix-Sort**: When log(N) is significantly larger than K, where K is the number of radix digits.

**Bucket-Sort**: When your input is more or less uniformly distributed.

## Problems based on sorting

### Partition 0 and 1

**Problem:** Given an array containing 0s and 1s. Write an algorithm to sort the array so that 0s come first, followed by 1s. Also, find the minimum number of swaps required to sort the array.

**First solution:** Start from both ends, the left will store the start index and the right will store the end index. Traverse left forward till we have 0s value in the array. Then traverse right backwards till we have 1s in the end. Then swap the two and follow the same process till left is less than right.

**Example 4.13:**
```
public static int partition01(int[] arr, int size) {
    int left = 0;
    int right = size - 1;
    int count = 0;

    while (left < right) {
        while (arr[left] == 0)
            left += 1;

        while (arr[right] == 1)
            right -= 1;
```

```
        if (left < right) {
            swap(arr, left, right);
            count += 1;
        }
    }
    return count;
}

// Testing code.
public static void main(String[] args) {
    int arr[] = { 0, 1, 1, 0, 1, 0, 1, 1, 0, 0, 0, 1 };
    partition01(arr, arr.length);
    printArray(arr, arr.length);
}
```

**Output:**

```
[ 0 0 0 0 0 0 1 1 1 1 1 1 ]
```

Time complexity looks like a quadratic (loop inside a loop) but it is linear or O(n). As at each iteration of the inner loop, either the left is increasing or the right is decreasing. Once left is equal or greater than right, the loops stop. Therefore, in total, the inner loops combined run for N number of times.

## Partition 0, 1 and 2

**Problem:** Given an array containing 0s, 1s and 2s. Write an algorithm to sort the array so that 0s come first, followed by 1s and then 2s in the end.

**First solution:** You can use a counter for 0s, 1s and 2s. Then replace the values in the array. This will take two passes. What if we want to do this in a single pass?

**Example 4.14:**

```
public static void partition012_(int[] arr, int size) {
    int zero = 0, one = 0, two = 0;

    for (int i =0; i < size;i++) {
        if (arr[i] == 0) {
            zero += 1;
        } else if (arr[i] == 1) {
            one += 1;
        } else {
            two += 1;
        }
    }

    int index = 0;
    while(zero > 0){
        arr[index++] = 0;
        zero -= 1;
    }

    while(one > 0){
        arr[index++] = 1;
        one -= 1;
    }
```

```
    while(two > 0){
        arr[index++] = 2;
        two -= 1;
    }
}

// Testing code.
public static void main(String[] args) {
    int arr2[] = { 0, 1, 1, 0, 1, 2, 1, 2, 0, 0, 0, 1 };
    partition012_(arr2, arr2.length);
    printArray(arr2, arr2.length);
}
```

**Output:**
```
[ 0 0 0 0 0 1 1 1 1 1 2 2 ]
```

**Second solution:** The basic approach is to use three indices. First left, second right and third to traverse the array. Index left starts from 0, Index right starts from N-1. We traverse the array whenever we find a 0 we swap it with the value at start and increment start. And whenever we find a 2 we swap this value with right and decrement right. When traversal is complete, and we reach the right, then the array is sorted.

**Example 4.15:**
```
public static void partition012(int[] arr, int size) {
    int left = 0;
    int right = size - 1;
    int i = 0;

    while (i <= right) {
        if (arr[i] == 0) {
            swap(arr, i, left);
            i += 1;
            left += 1;
        } else if (arr[i] == 2) {
            swap(arr, i, right);
            right -= 1;
        } else {
            i += 1;
        }
    }
}
```

Time complexity is linear or O(n).

## Range Partition

**Problem:** Given an array of integers and a range. Write an algorithm to partition the array so that values smaller than the range come to the left, then values under the range follow with values greater than the range.

**First solution:** The basic approach is to use three indices. First left, second right and third to traverse the array. Index left starts from 0, Index right starts from N-1. We traverse the array whenever we find a value lower than range, we swap it with the value at start and increment start. And whenever we find a value greater than range, we swap this value with right and decrement right. When traversal is complete, we have the array partitioned about range.

**Example 4.16:**
```
public static void rangePartition(int[] arr, int size, int lower, int higher) {
    int start = 0, end = size - 1;
    int i = 0;
    while (i <= end) {
        if (arr[i] < lower) {
            swap(arr, i, start);
            i += 1;
            start += 1;
        } else if (arr[i] > higher) {
            swap(arr, i, end);
            end -= 1;
        } else {
            i += 1;
        }
    }
}

// Testing code.
public static void main(String[] args) {
    int arr[] = { 1, 2, 3, 4, 18, 5, 17, 6, 16, 7, 15, 8, 14, 9, 13, 10, 12, 11 };
    rangePartition(arr, arr.length, 9, 12);
    printArray(arr, arr.length);
}
```

**Output:**
```
[ 1 2 3 4 5 6 7 8 10 12 9 11 14 13 15 16 17 18 ]
```

Time complexity is linear or O(n).

## Minimum swaps

**Problem:** Find the minimum number of swaps required to bring all elements less than the given value together at the start of the array.

**First solution:** Use a quick sort technique by taking two indexes, one from the start and another from the end and try to use the given value as a key. Count the number of swaps, that is the answer.

**Example 4.17:**
```
public static int minSwaps(int arr[], int size, int val) {
    int swapCount = 0;
    int first = 0;
    int second = size - 1;
    int temp;
    while (first < second) {
        if (arr[first] <= val)
            first += 1;
        else if (arr[second] > val)
            second -= 1;
        else {
            temp = arr[first];
            arr[first] = arr[second];
```

```
                arr[second] = temp;
                swapCount += 1;
            }
        }
        return swapCount;
}

//Testing code
public static void main(String[] args) {
 int array[] = { 2, 7, 5, 6, 1, 3, 4, 9, 10, 8 };
 System.out.println("minSwaps: " + minSwaps(array, array.length, 10));
}
```

**Output:**

```
minSwaps:: 2
```

Time complexity is linear or O(n).

## Absolute Sort

**Problem:** Sort array according to the absolute difference from the given value.

**Solution:** Any sorting algorithms can be used to solve this problem. We are using BubbleSort. The only change is comparing functions more. Which will take another field ref.

**Example 4.18:**

```
public static boolean absGreater(int value1, int value2, int ref) {
    return (Math.abs(value1 - ref) > Math.abs(value2 - ref));
}

public static void absBubbleSort(int[] arr, int size, int ref) {
    for (int i = 0; i < (size - 1); i++) {
        for (int j = 0; j < (size - i - 1); j++) {
            if (absGreater(arr[j], arr[j + 1], ref)) {
                swap(arr, j, j + 1);
            }
        }
    }
}

// Testing code.
public static void main(String[] args) {
    int array[] = { 9, 1, 8, 2, 7, 3, 6, 4, 5 };
    int ref = 5;
    absBubbleSort(array, array.length, ref);
    printArray(array, array.length);
}
```

**Output:**

```
[ 5 6 4 7 3 8 2 9 1 ]
```

Time complexity is linear or O(n).

## Equation Sort

**Problem:** Sort array according to the equation $A.X^2$.

**Solution:** Any sorting algorithms can be used to solve this problem also. The only change is comparing functions more. Which will take another field A.

**Example 4.19:**
```
public static boolean eqGreater(int value1, int value2, int A) {
    value1 = A * value1 * value1;
    value2 = A * value2 * value2;
    return value1 > value2;
}
```

## Separate even and odd numbers in List

**Problem:** Given an array of even and odd numbers, write a program to separate even numbers from odd numbers.

**First solution:** allocate a separate list, then scan through the given list, and fill even numbers from the start and odd numbers from the end.

**Example 4.20:**
```
public static void separateEvenAndOdd(int data[], int size) {
    int left = 0, right = size - 1;
    int[] aux = new int[size];

    for (int i=0;i< size;i++) {
        if (data[i] % 2 == 0) {
            aux[left] = data[i];
            left++;
        } else if (data[i] % 2 == 1) {
            aux[right] = data[i];
            right--;
        }
    }

    for (int i=0;i< size;i++)
        data[i] = aux[i];
}

// Testing code.
public static void main(String[] args) {
    int array[] = { 9, 1, 8, 2, 7, 3, 6, 4, 5 };
    separateEvenAndOdd(array, array.length);
    printArray(array, array.length);
}
```

**Output:**
```
[ 8 2 6 4 5 3 7 1 9 ]
```

**Second solution:** The algorithm is as follows.

1. Initialise the two variables, left and right. Variable left=0 and right= size-1.
2. Keep increasing the left index until the element at that index is even.
3. Keep decreasing the right index until the element at that index is odd.
4. Swap the number at the left and right index.
5. Repeat steps 2 to 4 until the left is less than the right.

**Example 4.21:**
```
public static void separateEvenAndOdd2(int data[], int size) {
    int left = 0, right = size - 1;

    while (left < right) {
        if (data[left] % 2 == 0)
            left++;
        else if (data[right] % 2 == 1)
            right--;
        else {
            swap(data, left, right);
            left++;
            right--;
        }
    }
}
```

Time complexity is linear or O(n).

## Array Reduction

**Problem:** Given an array of positive elements. You need to perform a reduction operation. In each reduction operation, the smallest positive element value is picked and all the elements are subtracted by that value. You need to print the number of elements left after each reduction process.
Input: [5, 1, 1, 1, 2, 3, 5]
Output: 4

**Solution**: Sort the input array. The total number of reductions is equal to the number of distinct elements. Every index of the input array on which the value of the element is increasing will give the number of elements after each reduction operation, which is (size - index) value.

**Example 4.22:**
```
public static void arrayReduction(int[] arr, int size) {
    Arrays.sort(arr);
    int count = 1;
    int reduction = arr[0];
    for (int i = 0; i < size; i++) {
        if (arr[i] - reduction > 0) {
            reduction = arr[i];
            count += 1;
        }
    }
    System.out.println("Total number of reductions: " + count);
}

// Testing code.
public static void main(String[] args) {
    int arr[] = { 5, 1, 1, 1, 2, 3, 5 };
    arrayReduction(arr, arr.length);
}
```

**Output:**
```
Total number of reductions 4
```

**Time complexity:** O(n.log(n)). O(n.log(n)) required for sorting.

## Merge Array

**Problem:** Given two sorted arrays. Sort the elements of these arrays so that the first half of sorted elements will lie in the first array and the second half lies in the second array. Extra space allowed is O(1).

**Solution:** The first array will contain a smaller part of the sorted output. We traverse the first array. Always compare the value of the first array with the first element of the second array. If the first array value is smaller than the first element of the second array, we iterate further. If the first array value is greater than the first element of the second array. Then copy the value of the first element of the second array into the first array. And insert the value of the first array into the second array in sorted order. The second array is always kept sorted, so we need to compare only its first element.

Time complexity is O(M*N) where M is the length of the first array and N is the length of the second array.

**Example 4.23:**
```
public static void merge(int[] arr1, int size1, int[] arr2, int size2) {
    int index = 0;
    int temp;
    while (index < size1) {
        if (arr1[index] <= arr2[0]) {
            index += 1;
        } else {
            // always the first element of arr2 is compared.
            temp = arr1[index];
            arr1[index] = arr2[0];
            arr2[0] = temp;
            index += 1;
            // After swap arr2 may be unsorted.
            // Insertion of the element in proper sorted position.
            for (int i = 0; i < (size2 - 1); i++) {
                if (arr2[i] < arr2[i + 1])
                    break;
                temp = arr2[i];
                arr2[i] = arr2[i + 1];
                arr2[i + 1] = temp;
            }
        }
    }
}

// Testing code.
public static void main(String[] args) {
    int arr1[] = { 1, 5, 9, 10, 15, 20 };
    int arr2[] = { 2, 3, 8, 13 };
    merge(arr1, arr1.length, arr2, arr2.length);
    printArray(arr1, arr1.length);
    printArray(arr2, arr2.length);
}
```

**Output:**
```
[ 1 2 3 5 8 9 ]
[ 10 13 15 20 ]
```

## Check Reverse

**Problem:** Given an array of integers, find if reversing a sub-array makes the array sorted.

**Solution:** In this algorithm start and stop are the boundaries of a reversed subarray whose reversal makes the whole array sorted. Find the starting index from which the sub-array is reversed. Then check if the sub-array when reversed will fit properly in the array. The subarray end has a value greater than the value before the sub-array. Subarray start has a value less than the value of the element after sub-array. Check if the rest of the array after the sub-array is sorted.

**Example 4.24:**

```
public static boolean checkReverse(int[] arr, int size) {
    int start = -1;
    int stop = -1;
    for (int i = 0; i < (size - 1); i++) {
        if (arr[i] > arr[i + 1]) {
            start = i;
            break;
        }
    }

    if (start == -1) // already sorted.
        return true;

    for (int i = start; i < (size - 1); i++) {
        if (arr[i] < arr[i + 1]) {
            stop = i;
            break;
        }
    }

    if (stop == -1) // reversed subarray stop till the end.
        return true;

    // Increasing property
    // After reversal, the sub array should fit in the array.
    if (arr[start - 1] > arr[stop] || arr[stop + 1] < arr[start])
        return false;

    for (int i = stop + 1; i < size - 1; i++) {
        if (arr[i] > arr[i + 1]) {
            return false;
        }
    }
    return true;
}

// Testing code.
public static void main(String[] args) {
    int arr1[] = { 1, 2, 6, 5, 4, 7};
    System.out.println(checkReverse(arr1, arr1.length));
}
```

**Output:**

```
true
```

Time complexity is linear or O(n).

## Union Intersection Sorted

**Problem:** Given two unsorted arrays, find the union and intersection of these two arrays.

**Solution:** Sort both the arrays. Then traverse both the array, when we have common elements, we add it to intersection list and union list, when we have uncommon elements then we add it only to the union list.

**Example 4.25:**

```
public static void unionIntersectionSorted(int arr1[], int size1, int arr2[], int
size2) {
    int first = 0, second = 0;
    int[] unionArr = new int[size1 + size2];
    int[] interArr = new int[min(size1, size2)];
    int uIndex = 0;
    int iIndex = 0;

    while (first < size1 && second < size2) {
        if (arr1[first] == arr2[second]) {
            unionArr[uIndex++] = arr1[first];
            interArr[iIndex++] = arr1[first];
            first += 1;
            second += 1;
        } else if (arr1[first] < arr2[second]) {
            unionArr[uIndex++] = arr1[first];
            first += 1;
        } else {
            unionArr[uIndex++] = arr2[second];
            second += 1;
        }
    }

    while (first < size1) {
        unionArr[uIndex++] = arr1[first];
        first += 1;
    }

    while (second < size2) {
        unionArr[uIndex++] = arr2[second];
        second += 1;
    }

    printArray(unionArr, uIndex);
    printArray(interArr, iIndex);
}

public static void unionIntersectionUnsorted(int arr1[], int size1, int arr2[], int
size2) {
    Arrays.sort(arr1);
    Arrays.sort(arr2);
    unionIntersectionSorted(arr1, size1, arr2, size2);
}
```

```
// Testing code.
public static void main(String[] args) {
    int arr1[] = { 1, 11, 2, 3, 14, 5, 6, 8, 9 };
    int arr2[] = { 2, 4, 5, 12, 7, 8, 13, 10 };
    unionIntersectionUnsorted(arr1, arr1.length, arr2, arr2.length);
}
```

**Output:**
```
[ 1 2 3 4 5 6 7 8 9 10 11 12 13 14 ]
[ 2 5 8 ]
```

Time complexity is O(n.log(n)). O(n.log(n)) required for sorting.

## Rotating an array by K positions.

**Problem:** Given an Array, you need to rotate its elements K number of times. For example, an Array [10,20,30,40,50,60] rotate by 2 positions to [30,40,50,60,10,20]

**Example 4.26:**
```
public static void rotateArray(int[] a, int n, int k) {
    reverseArray(a, 0, k-1);
    reverseArray(a, k, n-1);
    reverseArray(a, 0, n-1);
}

public static void reverseArray(int[] a, int start, int end) {
    for (int i = start, j = end; i < j; i++, j--) {
        int temp = a[i];
        a[i] = a[j];
        a[j] = temp;
    }
}

// Testing code.
public static void main(String[] args) {
    int[] arr = { 1, 2, 3, 4, 5, 6 };
    rotateArray(arr, arr.length, 2);
    printArray(arr, arr.length);
}
```

**Output:**
```
[ 3 4 5 6 1 2 ]
```

**Analysis:**
1. The rotating list is done in two parts. In the first part, we first reverse elements of the list first half and then the second half.
   1,2,3,4,5,6,7,8,9,10 => 5,6,7,8,9,10,1,2,3,4
   1,2,3,4,5,6,7,8,9,10 => 4,3,2,1,10,9,8,7,6,5 => 5,6,7,8,9,10,1,2,3,4
2. Then we reverse the whole list there by completing the whole rotation.
3. First reversal of the two parts of list is done in O(n) time and the final list reversal is also done in O(n) so the total time complexity of this algorithms is O(n)

## Array wave form

**Problem:** Given an array, arrange its elements in wave form such that odd elements are lesser than its neighbouring even elements.

**First solution:** Compare even index values with their neighbour odd index values and swap if the odd index is not smaller than the even index. By doing this we will create local minima at various odd indexes at positions 1, 3, 5 etc.

**Example 4.27:**
```
public static void waveArray2(int[] arr) {
    int size = arr.length;

    /* Odd elements are lesser than even elements.*/
    for (int i = 1; i < size; i += 2) {
        if ((i - 1) >= 0 && arr[i] > arr[i - 1]) {
            swap(arr, i, i - 1);
        }
        if ((i + 1) < size && arr[i] > arr[i + 1]) {
            swap(arr, i, i + 1);
        }
    }
}

// Testing code.
public static void main(String[] args) {
    int[] arr2 = { 8, 1, 2, 3, 4, 5, 6, 4, 2 };
    waveArray2(arr2);
    printArray(arr2, arr2.length);
}
```

**Output:**
```
[ 8 1 3 2 5 4 6 2 4 ]
```

**Time Complexity:** O(n)

**Second solution:** Sort the array, then swap ith and i+1th index value, so the array will form a wave. Since the array is sorted in increasing order. Swapping indexes (0&1), (2&3), (4&5) etc. will make local minima at 1, 3, 5 etc.

**Example 4.28:**
```
public static void waveArray(int[] arr)
{
    int size = arr.length;
    Arrays.sort(arr);
    for(int i = 0 ; i < size -1 ; i+= 2) {
        swap(arr, i, i+1);
    }
}
```

**Time Complexity:** O(n)

## Index Array

**Problem:** Given an array of size N, containing elements from 0 to N-1. All values from 0 to N-1 are present in the array and if they are not there then -1 is there to take its place. Arrange values of the array so that value i is stored at arr[i].
Input: [8, -1, 6, 1, 9, 3, 2, 7, 4, -1]
Output: [-1, 1, 2, 3, 4, -1, 6, 7, 8, 9]

**First solution:** For each index value, pick the element and then put it into its proper destination index position. If some other value is stored in the destination index, then those values are also kept at the proper position. When all the indexes are processed, then we will get an index array.

**Example 4.29:**
```
public static void indexArray(int[] arr, int size) {
    for (int i = 0; i < size; i++) {
        int curr = i;
        int value = -1;

        /* swaps to move elements in the proper position. */
        while (arr[curr] != -1 && arr[curr] != curr) {
            int temp = arr[curr];
            arr[curr] = value;
            value = curr = temp;
        }

        /* check if some swaps happened. */
        if (value != -1) {
            arr[curr] = value;
        }
    }
}

// Testing code.
public static void main(String[] args) {
    int[] arr = { 8, -1, 6, 1, 9, 3, 2, 7, 4, -1 };
    size = arr.length;
    indexArray(arr, size);
    printArray(arr, size);
}
```

**Output:**
```
[ -1 1 2 3 4 -1 6 7 8 9 ]
```

**Time Complexity:** O(n), it looks like quadratic time complexity, but the inner loop traverses elements only once. Once inner loop elements are processed, then the elements at that position will be either that index value or it will contain -1.

**Second solution:** For each index, we will pick the value at an index. If the value is not at its proper position, then we replace it with the element which is at its proper position. When we repeat this for all the indexes, we get an index array.

**Example 4.30:**
```
public static void indexArray2(int[] arr, int size) {
    for (int i = 0; i < size; i++) {
        while (arr[i] != -1 && arr[i] != i) {
            /* swap arr[i] and arr[arr[i]] */
            int temp = arr[i];
            arr[i] = arr[temp];
            arr[temp] = temp;
        }
    }
}
```

**Time Complexity:** O(n), it looks like quadratic time complexity, but the inner loop swaps elements once no matter how many times the outer loop runs. Once inner loop elements are processed, then the elements at that position will be either that index value or it will contain -1.

## Sort 1toN

**Problem:** Given an array of length N. It contains unique elements from 1 to N. Sort the elements of the array.

**First solution:** For each index value, pick the element stored at that index. If the value stored in the index is in its proper position, then process for another index. If the value stored at the index is not at its proper position, then put it into its proper position. If some other element is in its destination position, then pick it and repeat the process.

**Example 4.31:**
```
public static void sort1toN(int[] arr, int size) {
    int curr, value, next;

    for (int i = 0; i < size; i++) {
        curr = i;
        value = -1;

        /* swaps to move elements in the proper position. */
        while (curr >= 0 && curr < size && arr[curr] != curr + 1) {
            next = arr[curr];
            arr[curr] = value;
            value = next;
            curr = next - 1;
        }
    }
}

// Testing code.
public static void main(String[] args) {
    int[] arr = { 8, 5, 6, 1, 9, 3, 2, 7, 4, 10 };
    int size = arr.length;
    sort1toN2(arr, size);
    printArray(arr, size);
}
```

**Output:**
```
[ 1 2 3 4 5 6 7 8 9 10 ]
```

**Time Complexity:** O(n), it looks like quadratic time complexity, but the inner loop traverses elements only one. Once inner loop elements are processed, then the elements at that position will be either that index value or it will contain -1.

**Second solution:** For each index, we will pick the value at that index and swap it with the element which is stored at its position of the index value.

**Example 4.32:** Swapping the elements
```
public static void sort1toN2(int[] arr, int size) {
    int temp;

    for (int i = 0; i < size; i++) {
        while (arr[i] != i + 1 && arr[i] > 1) {
            temp = arr[i];
            arr[i] = arr[temp - 1];
            arr[temp - 1] = temp;
        }
    }
}
```

**Time Complexity:** O(n), it looks like quadratic time complexity, but the inner loop swaps elements once no matter how many times the outer loop runs. Once inner loop elements are processed, then the elements at that position will be either that index value or it will contain -1.

## Maximum Minimum Array

**Problem:** Given a sorted array, rearrange it in maximum-minimum form.
Input: [1, 2, 3, 4, 5, 6, 7], Output: [7, 1, 6, 2, 5, 3, 4]

**First solution:** Using an auxiliary array, create a copy of the input array. The auxiliary array is also sorted in increasing order. Traverse from start and end of the auxiliary array, and put these values in the input array in alternate order.

**Example 4.33:**
```
public static void maxMinArr(int arr[], int size) {
    int[] aux = Arrays.copyOf(arr, size);
    int start = 0;
    int stop = size - 1;

    for (int i = 0; i < size; i++) {
        if (i % 2 == 0) {
            arr[i] = aux[stop];
            stop -= 1;
        } else {
            arr[i] = aux[start];
            start += 1;
        }
    }
}

// Testing code.
public static void main(String[] args) {
    int[] arr = { 1, 2, 3, 4, 5, 6, 7 };
    int size = arr.length;
```

```
    maxMinArr(arr, size);
    printArray(arr, size);
}
```

**Output:**

```
[ 7 1 6 2 5 3 4 ]
```

**Time Complexity:** O(n), **Space Complexity:** O(n).

**Second solution:** Without using any auxiliary array. Reverse the array from index 0 to N, by this largest value will come at the front. Then reverse the array from index 1 to N. Then reverse the array from index 2 to N and so on. Use reverse array operation on the array and change the array as follows:
1, 2, 3, 4, 5, 6, 7
7, 6, 5, 4, 3, 2, 1
7, 1, 2, 3, 4, 5, 6
7, 1, 6, 5, 4, 3, 2
7, 1, 6, 2, 3, 4, 5
7, 1, 6, 2, 5, 4, 3
7, 1, 6, 2, 5, 3, 4

**Example 4.34:**

```
public static void reverseArr(int arr[], int start, int stop) {
    while (start < stop) {
        swap(arr, start, stop);
        start += 1;
        stop -= 1;
    }
}

public static void maxMinArr2(int arr[], int size) {
    for (int i = 0; i < (size - 1); i++) {
        reverseArr(arr, i, size - 1);
    }
}
```

**Time Complexity:** O(n^2), **Space Complexity:** O(1).

## Max Circular Sum

**Problem:** Given an array, you need to find the maximum sum of arr[i]* i for all elements such that you can rotate the array.

**Solution**: We will find sum currValue = Σarr[i]*i & sumAll = Σarr[i] for all the elements. Then if we want to make a rotation by making the last element as first. So the new value of the currValue can be obtained by adding sumAll to it and then subtracting the last value arr[n-1]*(n-1) from it. The maximum currValue is stored as the final maxValue.

**Example 4.35:**

```
public static int maxCircularSum(int[] arr, int size) {
    int sumAll = 0;
    int currVal = 0;
    int maxVal;
```

```
    for (int i = 0; i < size; i++) {
        sumAll += arr[i];
        currVal += (i * arr[i]);
    }

    maxVal = currVal;
    for (int i = 1; i < size; i++) {
        currVal = (currVal + sumAll) - (size * arr[size - i]);
        if (currVal > maxVal) {
            maxVal = currVal;
        }
    }

    return maxVal;
}

// Testing code.
public static void main(String[] args) {
    int[] arr = { 10, 9, 8, 7, 6, 5, 4, 3, 2, 1 };
    System.out.println("MaxCirculrSum: " + maxCircularSum(arr, arr.length));
}
```

**Output:**

```
MaxCirculrSum: 290
```

**Time Complexity:** O(n), **Space Complexity:** O(1).

## Exercise

1. In a given text file, print the words with their frequency. Now print the kth word in terms of frequency.

   Hint:
   - ➢ The first solution maybe you can use the sorting and return the kth element.
   - ➢ The second solution: You can use the kth element quick select algorithm.
   - ➢ Third solution: You can use Hashtable or Trie to keep track of the frequency. Use Heap to get the Kth element.

2. In given K input streams of numbers in sorted order. You need to make a single output stream, which contains all the elements of the K streams in sorted order. The input streams support ReadNumber() operation and output streams support WriteNumber() operation.

   Hint:
   - ➢ Read the first number from all the K input streams and add them to a Priority Queue. (Nodes should keep track of the input stream; data added to the PQ is value & stream id.)
   - ➢ Dequeue one element at a time from PQ and put that element to the output stream, Read the input stream number and from the same input stream add another element to PQ.
   - ➢ If the stream is empty, just continue
   - ➢ Repeat until PQ is empty.

3. In given K sorted Lists of fixed length M. Also, given a final output list of length M*K. Give an efficient algorithm to merge all the arrays into the final list, without using any extra space.

   Hint: You can use the end of the final list to make PQ.

4. How will you sort 1 PB numbers? 1 PB = 1000 TB.

5. What will be the complexity of the above solution?

6. Any other improvement can be done on the question 3 solution if the number of CPU cores is eight.

7. In a given integer list that supports three functions findMin(), findMax(), findMedian(). Sort the array.

8. In a given pile of patient files of High, mid and low priority. Sort these files such that higher priority comes first, then mid and last low priority.
   Hint: Use Bucket sort.

9. Write pros and cons of Heap-Sort, Merge-Sort and Quick-Sort.

10. In a given rotated-sorted list of N integers. (The array was sorted, then it was rotated some arbitrary number of times.) If all the elements in the array were unique, find the index of some value.
    Hint: Modified binary search

11. In problem 9, what if there are repetitions allowed, and you need to find the index of the first occurrence of the element in the rotated-sorted list.

12. Merge two sorted lists into a single sorted list.
    Hint: Use the merge method of Merge-Sort.

13. Given an array containing 0's and 1's, sort the array such that all the 0's come before 1's.

14. Given an array of English characters, sort the array in linear time.

15. Write a method to sort an array of strings so that all the anagrams are next to each other.

    Hint:-
    - Loop through the array. For each word, sort the characters and add them to the hashtable with keys as sorted words and values as the original words. At the end of the loop, you will get all anagrams as the value to a key (which is sorted by its constituent chars).
    - Iterate over the hashmap, print all values of a key together, and then move to the next key.
    - Space Complexity: O(n), Time Complexity: O(n)

16. Given an array, sort elements in the order of their frequency.

    Hint: First, the frequency of various elements of the array is calculated by adding it to a HashTable. Then sorting of the new data structures with value and key is done. The sorting function first gives preference to frequency, then value.

# CHAPTER 5: SEARCHING

## Introduction

Searching is the process of finding an item in a collection of items. The item may be a keyword in a file, a record in a database, a node in a tree or a value in an array etc.

## Why Searching?

Imagine you are in a library with millions of books. You want to get a specific book with a specific title. How will you find it? You will search the book in the section of the library, which contains the books whose name starts with the initial letter of the desired book. Then you continue matching with a whole book title until you find your book. (By doing this small heuristic method, you have reduced the search space by a factor of 26, considering we have an equal number of books whose titles begin with a particular char.)

Similarly, computers store lots of information and to retrieve this information efficiently, we need very efficient searching algorithms. To make searching efficient, we keep the data in some proper order. If you keep the data organised in proper order, it is easy to search for the required value or key. For example, keeping the data in sorted order is one of the ways to organise data.

## Different Searching Algorithms

1. Linear Search – Unsorted Input
2. Linear Search – Sorted Input
3. Binary Search (Sorted Input)
4. String Search: Tries, Suffix Trees, Ternary Search.
5. Hashing and Symbol Tables

## Linear Search or Sequential Search – Unsorted Input

When elements of an array are not ordered or sorted, and we want to search for a value, we need to scan the full list until we find the desired value. This kind of algorithm is known as an unordered linear search. The major problem with this algorithm is less performance or high Time Complexity in the Worst-Case.

**Example 5.1:**

```
public static boolean linearSearchUnsorted(int[] arr, int size, int value) {
    for (int i = 0; i < size; i++) {
        if (value == arr[i]) {
            return true;
        }
    }
    return false;
}
```

```
// Testing code.
public static void main(String[] args) {
    int[] first = { 1, 3, 5, 7, 9, 25, 30 };
    System.out.println(linearSearchUnsorted(first, 7, 8));
    System.out.println(linearSearchUnsorted(first, 7, 25));
}
```

**Output:**

```
false
true
```

**Analysis:**

1. Since we have no idea about the data stored in the array, or if the data is not sorted, then we must sequentially search the array one by one.
2. If we find the value which we are looking for, we return true.
3. Else, we return the index false in the end, as we did not find the value we are looking for.
4. The first element may be the one we are looking for, so the Best-Case time complexity is O(1)
5. The element which we are searching for maybe the last one, so time complexity will be O(n). In the average case, the middle element will be the one which we are searching for, so also the time complexity will be O(n/2) ignoring the constant term. Average-Case time complexity will be O(n)

**Time Complexity**: O(n). As we need to traverse the complete list in the Worst-Case. Worst-Case is when your desired element is at the last position of the array. Here, 'n' is the size of the array.

**Space Complexity**: O(1). No extra memory is used to allocate the array.

## Linear Search – Sorted

If elements of the array are sorted either in increasing order or in decreasing order, searching for the desired element will be much more efficient than an unordered linear search. In many cases, we do not need to traverse the complete list. If the array is sorted in increasing order. We can traverse it from the beginning and when we encounter a value greater than the key, we stop searching further and declare that the key is not present in the array. This is how this algorithm saves time and improves performance.

**Example 5.2:**

```
public static boolean linearSearchSorted(int[] arr, int size, int value) {
    for (int i = 0; i < size; i++) {
        if (value == arr[i]) {
            return true;
        } else if (value < arr[i]) {
            return false;
        }
    }
    return false;
}
```

**Time Complexity**: O(n). As we need to traverse the complete list in the Worst-Case. Worst-Case is when your desired element is at the last position of the sorted list. However, in the average case, this algorithm is more efficient even though the growth rate is the same as unsorted.

**Space Complexity**: O(1). No extra memory is used to allocate the array.

## Binary Search

How do we search for a word in a dictionary? In general, we go to some approximate page (mostly middle) and start searching from that word. If we see the word that we are searching is on the same page, then we are done with the search. Else, if we see that alphabetically the word we are searching for is in the first half, then we reject the second half and vice versa. We apply the same procedure repeatedly until we find the desired keyword. The Binary Search algorithm also works in the same way.

The binary search algorithm is used to find a specific value in the **sorted array**. At each step, we look at the middle index. If the item at the middle index is the same as the desired one, it is returned. Otherwise, the middle value is larger or smaller than the value we are looking for. If our desired value is smaller, we confine our search space to the left half of the array and ignore the right half and vice versa. We will be pruning half of the search space at each stage, making this algorithm more efficient than the linear search algorithm.

**Note**: Binary search requires the array to be sorted, otherwise binary search cannot be applied.

**Example 5.3**: Binary Search Algorithm - Iterative Way

```
public static boolean binarySearch(int[] arr, int size, int value) {
    int low = 0;
    int high = size - 1;
    int mid;

    while (low <= high) {
        mid = (low + high) / 2;
        if (arr[mid] == value) {
            return true;
        } else if (arr[mid] < value) {
            low = mid + 1;
        } else {
            high = mid - 1;
        }
    }

    return false;
}

// Testing code.
public static void main(String[] args)  {
    int[] first = { 1, 3, 5, 7, 9, 25, 30 };
    System.out.println(binarySearch(first, 7, 8));
    System.out.println(binarySearch(first, 7, 25));
}
```

**Output:**

```
false
true
```

**Analysis:**

1. Since we have data sorted in increasing order, we can search efficiently by applying binary search. At each step, we reduce our search space by half.
2. At each step, we compare the middle value with the value we are searching for. If the mid-value is equal to the value we are searching for, then we return the middle index.
3. If the value is smaller than the middle value, we search the left half of the array.
4. If the value is greater than the middle value, then we search the right half of the array.
5. If we find the value we are looking for then true is returned, otherwise false is returned.
6. Best-Case time complexity will be O(1).
7. The Worst-Case and Average-Case Time complexity of this algorithm is O(log(n)).

**Time Complexity:**

Recurrence Relation: T(n) = T(n/2) + 1 for n > 1

T(n)= 1 if n <= 1

T(n/2) = T(n/$2^2$) + 1 // Substitution

T(n/22) = T(n/$2^3$) + 1 // Substitution

T(n) => T(n/2) + 1 => (T(n/$2^2$) + 1 ) + 1 = T(n/$2^2$) + 2 => (T(n/$2^3$) + 1) + 2 => T(n/$2^3$) + 3

Similarly T(n) = T(n/2^k) + k

for base case n/2^k = 1

2^k = n

k = log(n) // Taking log both sides to find k total number of steps.

T(n) = T(1) + k = 1 + log(n)

Time complexity : O(log(n))

**Space Complexity:** O(1)

## Binary Search implementation using recursion

**Problem**: Given an array of integers in increasing order, you need to find if some value is present in the array using recursion.

**Example 5.4:** Binary search implementation using recursion.

```
public static boolean binarySearchRec(int[] arr, int size, int value) {
    int low = 0;
    int high = size - 1;
    return binarySearchRecUtil(arr, low, high, value);
}
```

```
public static boolean binarySearchRecUtil(int[] arr, int low, int high, int value)
{
    if (low > high) {
        return false;
    }

    int mid = (low + high) / 2;

    if (arr[mid] == value) {
        return true;
    } else if (arr[mid] < value) {
        return binarySearchRecUtil(arr, mid + 1, high, value);
    } else {
        return binarySearchRecUtil(arr, low, mid - 1, value);
    }
}
```

**Analysis**: Similar iterative solution we have already seen. Now let us look into the recursive solution of the same problem. In this solution, we are dividing the search space in half and discarding the rest. This solution is very efficient as at each step we are rejecting half the search space/list.

**Time Complexity**: O(log(n)). Space Complexity: O(log(n)) for system stack in recursion.

## Fibonacci Search

Given a sorted array arr[], we need to find if some element x is present in the array or not.

**Fibonacci Search** is a comparison-based algorithm that uses Fibonacci numbers to search an element in a sorted array. Fibonacci Numbers are recursively defined as F(n) = F(n-1) + F(n-2), F(0) = 0, and F(1) = 1.

Fibonacci Search is just like Binary Search but in place of dividing the interval using division by 2. Fibonacci Search uses addition and subtraction. The division operation may be costly on some computers.

**Algorithm**: Let us suppose we are searching x in a sorted array arr[].

1. We first find the smallest Fibonacci number which is greater than the size of the array arr[].
2. Let us call that fibonacci number as fibN and the fibonacci numbers before it as fibNMn2 (fibN minus 2) and fibNMn1(fibN minus 1). Such that fib0+fib1 = fib2.
3. We use the fibNMn2 index for the comparison.
4. If the value in arr[] at index fibNMn2 is the same as x, then we will return true.
5. If the value in arr[] at index fibNMn2 is greater than x, then we search in the left part. This step is performed by moving the three Fibonacci variables two Fibonacci down. By doing this, the search space is reduced to approximately one-third of the previous search space.
6. Else if the value in arr[] at index fibNMn2 is less than x, then we search in the right part. This step is performed by moving the three Fibonacci variables one Fibonacci down. The lower

index of the search is moved to fibNMn2. By doing this, the search space is reduced to approximately two-third of the previous search space.

7. There might be a single element remaining for comparison. Check if arr[low + fibNMn2] is equal to x.

**Example 5.5:**
```
public static boolean fibonacciSearch(int[] arr, int size, int value) {
    /* Initialize fibonacci numbers */
    int fibNMn2 = 0, fibNMn1 = 1;
    int fibN = fibNMn2 + fibNMn1;

    while (fibN < size) {
        fibNMn2 = fibNMn1;
        fibNMn1 = fibN;
        fibN = fibNMn2 + fibNMn1;
    }

    int low = 0;
    while (fibN > 1) { // fibonacci series start with 0, 1, 1, 2
        int i = Math.min(low + fibNMn2, size - 1);
        if (arr[i] == value)
            return true;
        else if (arr[i] < value) {
            fibN = fibNMn1;
            fibNMn1 = fibNMn2;
            fibNMn2 = fibN - fibNMn1;
            low = i;
        } else { // for feb2 <= 1, these will be invalid.
            fibN = fibNMn2;
            fibNMn1 = fibNMn1 - fibNMn2;
            fibNMn2 = fibN - fibNMn1;
        }
    }
    if (arr[low + fibNMn2] == value)// above loop does not check when fibNMn2 = 0
        return true;
    return false;
}
```

**Time complexity**: O(log(n)), either 1/3 or 2/3 of the search space is ignored in each iteration.

## Bit Manipulation

Some of the important bit manipulation operations that are useful in various algorithms:

| Operation | Code | Example |
|---|---|---|
| Bitwise And operator | `int andEx(int a, int b) { return a & b; }` | A = 4 = 00000100<br>B = 8 = 00001000<br>A & B = 00000000 |
| Bitwise Or operator | `int orEx(int a, int b) { return a \| b; }` | A = 4 = 00000100<br>B = 8 = 00001000<br>A \| B = 00001100 = 12 |

| | | |
|---|---|---|
| Bitwise XoR operator | int xorEx(int a, int b) {<br>    return a ^ b;<br>} | A = 12 = 00001100<br>B = 8 = 00001000<br>A^B = 00001000 = 8 |
| Multiply number by 2 | int leftShiftEx(int a) { // multiply by 2<br>    return a << 1;<br>} | A = 4 = 00000100<br>A<<1 = 00001000 = 8 |
| Divide number by 2 | int rightShiftEx(int a) { // divide by 2<br>    return a >> 1;<br>} | A = 4 = 00000100<br>A>>1 = 00000010 = 2 |
| Once complement of a number. | int bitReversalEx(int a) {<br>    return ~a;<br>} | A = 00000100<br>~A = 11111011 |
| Two's complement of a number. | int twoComplementEx(int a) {<br>    return -a;<br>} | A = 00000100<br>-A = 11111100 |
| Check if Kth Bit is set. | int kthBitCheck(int a, int k) {<br>    return (a & 1 << (k - 1)) > 0;<br>} | A = 12 = 00001100, K = 4<br>1<<(k-1) = 00001000<br>(A & 1<<(k-1)) = 00001000 |
| Set kth bit in a number. | int kthBitSet(int a, int k) {<br>    return (a \| 1 << (k - 1));<br>} | A = 4 = 00000100, K = 4<br>1<<(k-1) = 00001000<br>(A \| 1<<(k-1)) = 00001100 = 12 |
| Reset the Kth bit in a number. | int kthBitReset(int a, int k) {<br>    return (a & ~(1 << (k - 1)));<br>} | A = 12 = 00001100, K = 4<br>1<<(k-1) = 00001000<br>~(1<<(k-1)) = 11110111<br>a & ~(1<<(k-1)) = 00000100 = 4 |
| Rightmost set bit of a number. | int rightMostBit(int a) {<br>    return a & -a;<br>} | A = 00001100<br>-A = 11110100<br>A & -A = 00000100 |
| Reset the rightmost set bit of a given number. | int resetRightMostBit(int a) {<br>    return a & (a - 1);<br>} | A = 00001100<br>A - 1 = 00001011<br>A & (A - 1) = 00001000 |
| Find if a number is a power of 2 | int isPowerOf2(int a) {<br>    if ((a & (a - 1)) == 0) {<br>        return 1;<br>    } else {<br>        return 0;<br>    }<br>} | A = 00001000<br>A - 1 = 00000111<br>A & (A - 1) = 00000000 |
| Count the set bits in a number. | int countBits(int a) {<br>    int count = 0;<br>    while (a > 0) {<br>        count += 1;<br>        a = a & (a - 1); // reset least significant bit.<br>    }<br>    return count;<br>} | Reset the rightmost set bit in a loop and count the number of iterations. |

## How is sorting useful in Selection Algorithms?

Selection problems can be converted into sorting problems. Once the array is sorted, it is easy to find the minimum / maximum (or desired element) from the sorted list. The method 'Sorting and then selecting' is inefficient for selecting a single element, but it is efficient when many selections need to be made from the array. It is because only one initial expensive sort is needed, followed by many cheap selection operations.

For example, if we want to get the maximum element from an array. After sorting the array, we can simply return the last element from the array. What if we want to get the second maximum? Now, we do not have to sort the array again, and can return the second last element from the sorted list. Similarly, we can return the kth maximum element by just one scan of the sorted list.

So, with the above discussion, sorting is used to improve performance. In general, this method requires O(n.log(n)) (for sorting) time.

## Problems in Searching

### Sum Array

**Problem:** Write a method that will return the sum of all the integer array elements, given array as an input argument.

**Example 5.6:**
```
public static int sumArray(int[] arr) {
    int size = arr.length;
    int total = 0;
    for (int index = 0; index < size; index++) {
        total = total + arr[index];
    }
    return total;
}

// Testing code.
public static void main(String[] args) {
    int[] arr = { 1, 2, 3, 4, 5, 6, 7, 8, 9 };
    System.out.println("Sum of all the values in array: " + sumArray(arr));
}
```

**Output:**
```
Sum of all the values in array: 45
```

**Analysis**: All the elements of the array are traversed and added. Finally, the result is returned.
Since all the elements are required to be traversed at least once. So Best Case, Average Case, and Worst-Case all have the same time complexity of O(n).

## First Repeated element in the array

**Problem**: Given an unsorted list of n elements, find the first element, which is repeated.

**First solution**: Exhaustive search or Brute force; for each element in the list, find if there is some other element with the same value. This is done using two loops, the first loop to select the elements and the second loop to find their duplicate entries.

**Time Complexity** is O(n^2) and **Space Complexity** is O(1)

**Example 5.7:**

```
public static int firstRepeated(int[] arr, int size) {
    for (int i = 0; i < size; i++) {
        for (int j = i + 1; j < size; j++) {
            if (arr[i] == arr[j]) {
                return arr[i];
            }
        }
    }
    return 0;
}

// Testing code.
public static void main(String[] args)  {
    int[] first = { 1, 3, 5, 3, 9, 1, 30 };
    System.out.println(firstRepeated(first, first.length));
}
```

**Output:**

```
1
```

**Second solution**: Using Hash-Table, we can keep track of the number of times an element came into the array. The first scan just populates the Hashtable. The second scan just looks at the occurrence of the elements in the Hashtable. If the occurrence is more than one for some element, then we have our solution, which is the first repeated element.

**Example 5.8:**

```
public static int firstRepeated2(int[] arr, int size) {
    HashMap<Integer, Integer> hm = new HashMap<Integer, Integer>();

    for (int i = 0; i < size; i++) {
        if (hm.containsKey(arr[i]))
            hm.put(arr[i], 2);
        else
            hm.put(arr[i], 1);
    }

    for (int i = 0; i < size; i++) {
        if (hm.get(arr[i]) == 2) {
            return arr[i];
```

```
        }
    }
    return 0;
}
```

Hash-Table insertion and finding take constant time O(1) so the total time complexity of the algorithm is O(n) time. Space Complexity is also O(n) for maintaining hash.

## Print duplicates in an array

**Problem**: Given an array of n numbers, print the duplicate elements in the array.

**First solution**: Exhaustive search or Brute force; for each element in the list, find if there is some other element with the same value. This is done using two loops, the first loop to select the element and the second loop to find its duplicate entry.

**Example 5.9:**

```
public static void printRepeating(int[] arr, int size) {
    System.out.print("Repeating elements are ");
    for (int i = 0; i < size; i++) {
        for (int j = i + 1; j < size; j++) {
            if (arr[i] == arr[j]) {
                System.out.print(" " + arr[i]);
            }
        }
    }
}

// Testing code.
public static void main(String[] args)  {
    int[] first = { 1, 3, 5, 3, 9, 1, 30 };
    printRepeating(first, first.length);
}
```

**Output:**

```
Repeating elements are :  1 3
```

**Time Complexity** is O(n^2) and **Space Complexity** is O(1)

**Second solution**: Sorting; Sort all the elements in the array and after this in a single scan, we can find the duplicates.

**Example 5.10:**

```
public static void printRepeating2(int[] arr, int size) {
    Arrays.sort(arr);
    System.out.print("Repeating elements are ");
    for (int i = 1; i < size; i++) {
        if (arr[i] == arr[i - 1]) {
            System.out.print(" " + arr[i]);
```

```
        }
    }
}
```

Sorting algorithms take O(n.log(n)) time, and a single scan takes O(n) time.

**Time Complexity** is O(n.log(n)) and **Space Complexity** is O(1)

**Third solution**: Using Hash-Table, we can keep track of the elements we have already seen, and we can find the duplicates in just one scan.

**Example 5.11:**

```
public static void printRepeating3(int[] arr, int size) {
    HashSet<Integer> hs = new HashSet<Integer>();
    System.out.print("Repeating elements are ");
    for (int i = 0; i < size; i++) {
        if (hs.contains(arr[i])) {
            System.out.print(" " + arr[i]);
        } else {
            hs.add(arr[i]);
        }
    }
}
```

Hash-Table insert and find operations take constant time O(1) so the total time complexity of the algorithm is O(n) time. Space Complexity is also O(n)

**Fourth solution**: Counting, this solution is only possible if we know the range of the input. If we know that, the elements in the array are in the range 0 to n-1. We can reserve an array of length n call it counter and when we see an element, we can increase its corresponding count. In just one single scan, we know the duplicates. If we know the range of the elements, then this is the fastest way to find the duplicates.

**Example 5.12:**

```
public static void printRepeating4(int[] arr, int size, int range) {
    int[] count = new int[range];
    int i;
    for (i = 0; i < range; i++) {
        count[i] = 0;
    }
    System.out.print("Repeating elements are ");
    for (i = 0; i < size; i++) {
        if (count[arr[i]] == 1) {
            System.out.print(" " + arr[i]);
        } else {
            count[arr[i]]++;
        }
    }
}
```

```
// Testing code.
public static void main(String[] args)  {
    int[] first = { 1, 3, 5, 3, 9, 1, 30 };
    printRepeating4(first, first.length, 50);
}
```

**Output:**

```
Repeating elements are :  1 3
```

The counting solution just uses an array so inserting and finding takes constant time O(1) so the total time complexity of the algorithm is O(n) time. Space Complexity for creating a count list is also O(n)

## Remove duplicates in an integer list

**Problem:** Remove duplicate in an integer list.

**First solution:** Sorting, Steps are as follows:

1. Sort the array.
2. Take two references. A subarray will be created with all unique elements starting from 0 to the first reference (The first reference points to the last index of the subarray). The second reference iterates through the array from 1 to the end. Unique numbers will be copied from the second reference location to the first reference location, and the same elements are ignored.

Time Complexity calculation:
Time to sort the array = **O(n.log(n))**. Time to remove duplicates = **O(n).**
Overall Time Complexity = **O(n.log(n))**.
No additional space is required, so Space Complexity is **O(1)**.

**Example 5.13:**

```
public static int[] removeDuplicates(int[] array, int size) {
    int j = 0;
    Arrays.sort(array);
    for (int i = 1; i < size; i++) {
        if (array[i] != array[j]) {
            j++;
            array[j] = array[i];
        }
    }
    return Arrays.copyOf(array, j + 1);
}

// Testing code.
public static void main(String[] args)  {
    int[] first = { 1, 3, 5, 3, 9, 1, 30 };
    int[] ret = removeDuplicates(first, first.length);
    for (int i = 0; i < ret.length; i++) {
        System.out.print(ret[i] + " ");
    }
}
```

**Output:**

```
1 3 5 9 30
```

**Second solution:** Use a Hash Table to keep track of the elements already visited. Create an output array and add unique elements to it and also add that value to the hash table.

Time Complexity is **O(n)** and Space Complexity is **O(n)** for a hash table.

**Example 5.14:**
```
public static int[] removeDuplicates2(int[] arr, int size) {
    HashMap<Integer, Integer> hm = new HashMap<Integer, Integer>();
    int j = 0;
    for (int i = 0; i < size; i++) {
        if (!hm.containsKey(arr[i])) {
            arr[j] = arr[i];
            j++;
            hm.put(arr[i], 1);
        }
    }

    int[] ret = Arrays.copyOf(arr, j);
    return ret;
}
```

Other solutions to the previous problems can also be used to solve this problem.

## Find the missing number in an array

**Problem:** In a given list of n-1 elements, which are in the range of 1 to n. There are no duplicates in the array. One of the integers is missing. Find the missing element.

**First solution:** Exhaustive search or Brute force, for each value in the range 1 to n, find if there is an element in the range that is not present in the list. This is done using two loops, the first loop to select values in the range 1 to n and the second loop to find if this element is in the array or not. If we do not find the value, then this is the missing value.

Time Complexity is O(n^2) and Space Complexity is O(1)

**Example 5.15:**
```
public static int findMissingNumber(int[] arr, int size) {
    int i, j, found = 0;
    for (i = 1; i <= size; i++) {
        found = 0;
        for (j = 0; j < size; j++) {
            if (arr[j] == i) {
                found = 1;
                break;
            }
        }

        if (found == 0) {
            return i;
        }
    }
    return Integer.MAX_VALUE;
}
```

```
// Testing code.
public static void main(String[] args)  {
    int[] first = { 1, 5, 4, 3, 2, 7, 8, 9 };
    System.out.println(findMissingNumber(first, first.length));
}
```

**Output:**

```
6
```

**Second solution:** Sorting; Sort all the elements in the array and after this in a single scan, we can find the duplicates.

Sorting algorithms takes O(n.log(n)) time and a single scan takes O(n) time.
Time Complexity is O(n.log(n)) and Space Complexity is O(1)

**Example 5.16:**

```
public static int findMissingNumber2(int[] arr, int size) {
    Arrays.sort(arr);
    for (int i = 0; i < size; i++) {
        if (arr[i] != i + 1)
            return i + 1;
    }

    return size;
}
```

**Third solution:** Using Hash-Table Set; we can keep track of the elements we have already seen, and we can find the missing element in just one scan.

Set insertion and finding take constant time O(1) so the total time complexity of the algorithm is O(n) time. Space Complexity is also O(n)

**Example 5.17:**

```
public static int findMissingNumber3(int[] arr, int size) {
    HashMap<Integer, Integer> hm = new HashMap<Integer, Integer>();
    for (int i = 0; i < size; i++)
        hm.put(arr[i], 1);

    for (int i = 1; i <= size; i++)
        if (!hm.containsKey(i))
            return i;

    return Integer.MAX_VALUE;
}
```

**Fourth solution:** Counting, we know the range of the input, so counting will work. As we know that, the elements in the array are in the range 0 to n. We can reserve an array of length n and when we see an element, we can increase its count. In just one single scan, we know the missing element.

Counting solution just uses an array so insertion and finding take constant time O(1) so the total time complexity of the algorithm is O(n) time. Space Complexity for creating a count list is also O(n)

**Example 5.18:**

```
public static int findMissingNumber4(int[] arr, int size) {
    int[] count = new int[size + 1];
    Arrays.fill(count, -1);
    for (int i = 0; i < size; i++)
        count[arr[i] - 1] = 1;

    for (int i = 0; i <= size; i++)
        if (count[i] == -1)
            return i + 1;

    return Integer.MAX_VALUE;
}
```

**Fifth solution:** You can modify the given input list. Modify the given input list in such a way that in the next scan you can find the missing element.

When you scan through the array. When at index “index”, the value stored in the array will be arr[index] so add the number “n + 1” to arr[ arr[ index]]. Always read the value from the array using a reminder operator “%”. When you scan the array for the first time and modify all the values. Then in one single scan you can see if there is some value in the array which is smaller than “n+1” that index is the missing number.

In this solution, the array is scanned two times. The Time Complexity of this algorithm is O(n). Space Complexity is O(1)

**Example 5.19:**

```
public static int findMissingNumber6(int[] arr, int size) {
    for (int i = 0; i < size; i++) {
        // len(arr)+1 value should be ignored.
        if (arr[i] != size + 1 && arr[i] != size * 3 + 1) {
            // 1 should not become (len(arr)+1) so multiplied by 2
            arr[(arr[i] - 1) % size] += size * 2;
        }
    }

    for (int i = 0; i < size; i++)
        if (arr[i] < (size * 2))
            return i + 1;
    return Integer.MAX_VALUE;
}
```

**Sixth solution:** Summation formula to find the sum of n numbers from 1 to n. Subtract the values stored in the array, and you will have your missing number.
The Time Complexity of this algorithm is O(n). Space Complexity is O(1)

**Example 5.20:**

```
public static int findMissingNumber5(int[] arr, int size) {
    int sum = 0;
    // Element value range is from 1 to size+1.
    for (int i = 1; i < (size + 2); i++)
        sum += i;
```

```
    for (int i = 0; i < size; i++)
        sum -= arr[i];

    return sum;
}
```

**Seventh solution:** XOR approach to find the sum of n numbers from 1 to n. XOR the values stored in the array, and you will have your missing number.
The Time Complexity of this algorithm is O(n). Space Complexity is O(1)

**Example 5.21:**

```
public static int findMissingNumber7(int[] arr, int size) {
    int i;
    int xorSum = 0;
    // Element value range is from 1 to size+1.
    for (i = 1; i < (size + 2); i++) {
        xorSum ^= i;
    }
    // loop through the array and get the XOR of elements
    for (i = 0; i < size; i++) {
        xorSum ^= arr[i];
    }
    return xorSum;
}
```

**Note:** The same problem can be asked in many forms (sometimes you must perform xor of the range):

1 There are numbers in the range of 1-n out of which all appear a single time, but there is one that appears two times.
2 All the elements in the range 1-n are appearing 16 times, and one element appears 17 times. Find the element that appears 17 times.

## Missing Values

**Problem:** Given an array, find the maximum and minimum value in the array, and also find the values in range minimum and maximum that are absent in the array.

**First solution:** Brute force approach, traverse the array, find the minimum and maximum value. Then find values from minimum to maximum in the array. The time complexity of this solution will be O(n^2)

**Example 5.22:**

```
public static void missingValues(int[] arr, int size) {
    int max = arr[0];
    int min = arr[0];
    for (int i = 1; i < size; i++) {
        if (max < arr[i])
            max = arr[i];

        if (min > arr[i])
            min = arr[i];
    }
    boolean found;
    for (int i = min + 1; i < max; i++) {
        found = false;
```

```
        for (int j = 0; j < size; j++) {
            if (arr[j] == i) {
                found = true;
                break;
            }
        }
        if (!found)
            System.out.print(i + " ");
    }
}

// Testing code.
public static void main(String[] args)  {
    int[] arr = { 11, 14, 13, 17, 21, 18, 19, 23, 24 };
    int size = arr.length;
    missingValues(arr, size);
}
```

**Output:**

```
12 15 16 20 22
```

**Second solution:** Sorting approach, we can sort the given array. Then traverse the whole array and print the missing values. The time complexity of this solution will be O(n.log(n)) for sorting and traversal will take O(n) so the overall time complexity is O(n.log(n)).

**Example 5.23:**

```
public static void missingValues2(int[] arr, int size) {
    Arrays.sort(arr);
    int value = arr[0];

    int i = 0;
    while (i < size) {
        if (value == arr[i]) {
            value += 1;
            i += 1;
        } else {
            System.out.print(value + " ");
            value += 1;
        }
    }
}
```

**Third solution:** Hashtable approach, we can traverse the array and insert its elements in a hashtable. Also, in this single traversal, we can find the smallest and largest value in the array. Now find if the values between minimum and maximum are present in the hashtable. If such values are not present, then print those values.

The time complexity of this algorithm is O(n). Space complexity is O(n) for a hashtable.

**Example 5.24:**

```
public static void missingValues3(int[] arr, int size) {
    HashSet<Integer> ht = new HashSet<Integer>();
    int minVal = 999999;
    int maxVal = -999999;
```

```
    for (int i = 0; i < size; i++) {
        ht.add(arr[i]);
        if (minVal > arr[i])
            minVal = arr[i];
        if (maxVal < arr[i])
            maxVal = arr[i];
    }

    for (int i = minVal; i < maxVal + 1; i++) {
        if (ht.contains(i) == false) {
            System.out.print(i + " ");
        }
    }
}
```

## Odd Count Element

**Problem:** Given an array in which all the elements appear an even number of times except one, which appears an odd number of times. Find the element which appears an odd number of times.

**First solution:** XOR approach, XOR all the elements of the array the elements which appear even number of times will cancel themselves. Finally, we will get the number we are searching for.
The Time Complexity of this algorithm is O(n). Space Complexity is O(1)

**Example 5.25:**

```
public static void oddCount(int[] arr, int size) {
    int xorSum = 0;
    for (int i = 0; i < size; i++) {
        xorSum ^= arr[i];
    }
    System.out.println("Odd values: " + xorSum);
}

// Testing code.
public static void main(String[] args)  {
    int[] arr = { 10, 25, 30, 10, 15, 25, 15 };
    int size = arr.length;
    oddCount(arr, size);
}
```

**Output:**

```
Odd values: 30
```

**Second solution:** Use a Hashtable to keep track of frequency. Then traverse the Hashtable to find the odd number of times the element appears.
The Time Complexity of this algorithm is O(n). Space Complexity is O(n)

**Example 5.26:**

```
public static void oddCount2(int[] arr, int size) {
    HashMap<Integer, Integer> hm = new HashMap<Integer, Integer>();

    for (int i = 0; i < size; i++) {
        if (hm.containsKey(arr[i]))
            hm.remove(arr[i]);
```

```java
        else
            hm.put(arr[i], 1);
    }
    System.out.print("Odd values: ");
    for (Integer key : hm.keySet())
        System.out.print(key + " ");
    System.out.println();
    System.out.println("Odd count is :: " + hm.size());
}
```

## Odd Count Elements

**Problem:** Given an array in which all the elements appear an even number of times except two, which appear an odd number of times. Find the elements which appear an odd number of times in O(n) time complexity and O(1) space complexity.

**Solution**:

1. Since the space complexity required is O(1) so we cannot use Hashtable.
2. We know that when we xor all the elements of an array, then the even number of appearing elements will cancel themselves out. So, we have the sum of the two values we are searching for.
3. If we can divide the array elements into two groups such that these two values go in different groups and then xor the values in these groups, then we can get these values separately.
4. As shown in the algorithm below, the rightmost set bit is used to separate these two elements.

**Example 5.27:**

```java
public static void oddCount3(int[] arr, int size) {
    int xorSum = 0;
    int first = 0;
    int second = 0;
    int setBit;
    /*
     * xor of all elements in arr[] even occurrence will cancel each other. sum
     * will contain sum of two odd elements.
     */
    for (int i = 0; i < size; i++)
        xorSum = xorSum ^ arr[i];

    /* Rightmost set bit. */
    setBit = xorSum & ~(xorSum - 1);

    /*
     * Dividing elements in two group: Elements having setBit bit as 1. Elements
     * having setBit bit as 0. Even elements cancelled themselves if group and we
     * get our numbers.
     */
    for (int i = 0; i < size; i++) {
        if ((arr[i] & setBit) != 0)
            first ^= arr[i];
        else
            second ^= arr[i];
    }
    System.out.println("Odd values: " + first + " " + second);
}
```

```
// Testing code.
public static void main(String[] args)  {
    int[] arr2 = { 10, 25, 30, 10, 15, 25, 15, 40 };
    int size2 = arr2.length;
    oddCount3(arr2, size2);
}
```

**Output:**

```
Odd values: 30 40
```

## Sum Distinct

**Problem:** Given an array of size N, the elements in the array may be repeated. You need to find the sum of distinct elements of the array. If there is some value repeated continuously, then they should be added once.

**Example 5.28:**

```
public static void sumDistinct(int[] arr, int size) {
    int sum = 0;
    Arrays.sort(arr);
    for (int i = 0; i < (size - 1); i++) {
        if (arr[i] != arr[i + 1])
            sum += arr[i];
    }
    sum += arr[size - 1];
    System.out.println("sum : " + sum);
}

// Testing code.
public static void main(String[] args)  {
    int[] arr = { 1, 2, 3, 1, 1, 4, 5, 6 };
    int size = arr.length;
    sumDistinct(arr, size);
}
```

**Output:**

```
sum : 21
```

**Analysis:** Sort the input array. Duplicate values will come adjacent. Create a sum variable and add only those values to it which are not equal to its next value.

The Time Complexity of this algorithm is O(n). Space Complexity is O(1)

## Min Absolute Sum

**Problem:** In the given list of integers, both +ve and -ve. You need to find the two elements such that their sum is closest to zero.

**First solution:** Exhaustive search or Brute force; for each element in the array, find the other element whose value when added will give minimum absolute value. This is done using two loops, the first loop to select the element and the second loop to find the element that should be added to it so that the absolute of the sum will be minimum or close to zero.

Time Complexity is O(n^2) and Space Complexity is O(1)

**Example 5.29:**
```
public static void minAbsSumPair(int[] arr, int size) {
    int l, r, minSum, sum, minFirst, minSecond;
    // Array should have at least two elements
    if (size < 2) {
        System.out.println("Invalid Input");
        return;
    }
    // Initialisation of values
    minFirst = 0;
    minSecond = 1;
    minSum = Math.abs(arr[0] + arr[1]);
    for (l = 0; l < size - 1; l++) {
        for (r = l + 1; r < size; r++) {
            sum = Math.abs(arr[l] + arr[r]);
            if (sum < minSum) {
                minSum = sum;
                minFirst = l;
                minSecond = r;
            }
        }
    }
    System.out.println("Minimum sum elements are : " + arr[minFirst] + " , " +
arr[minSecond]);
}

// Testing code.
public static void main(String[] args)  {
    int[] first = { 1, 5, -10, 3, 2, -6, 8, 9, 6 };
    minAbsSumPair2(first, first.length);
}
```

**Output:**
```
Minimum sum elements are : -6 , 6
```

**Second solution:** Sorting is used.

The steps are as follows:

1. Sort all the elements in the array.
2. Take two variable firstIndex = 0 and secondIndex = size -1
3. Compute sum = arr[firstIndex]+arr[secondIndex]
4. If the sum is equal to 0 then we have the solution
5. If the sum is less than 0 then we will increase first
6. If the sum is greater than 0 then we will decrease the second
7. We repeat the above process 3 to 6 until we get the desired pair or we get first >= second

Time complexity is O(n.log(n)) for sorting and O(n) for comparison.

**Total time complexity:** O(n.log(n))

**Example 5.30:**

```
public static void minAbsSumPair2(int[] arr, int size) {
    int l, r, minSum, sum, minFirst, minSecond;
    // Array should have at least two elements
    if (size < 2) {
        System.out.println("Invalid Input");
        return;
    }
    Arrays.sort(arr);

    // Initialisation of values
    minFirst = 0;
    minSecond = size - 1;
    minSum = Math.abs(arr[minFirst] + arr[minSecond]);

    for (l = 0, r = size - 1; l < r;) {
        sum = (arr[l] + arr[r]);
        if (Math.abs(sum) < minSum) {
            minSum = Math.abs(sum);
            minFirst = l;
            minSecond = r;
        }
        if (sum < 0) {
            l++;
        } else if (sum > 0) {
            r--;
        } else {
            break;
        }
    }
    System.out.println("Minimum sum elements are : " + arr[minFirst] + " , " +
arr[minSecond]);
}
```

Time Complexity is O(n.log(n)) and Space Complexity is O(1)

## Find Pair in an array

**Problem:** Given an array of n numbers, find two elements such that their sum is equal to “value”

**First solution:** Exhaustive search or Brute force, for each element in the list find if there is some other element, which sums up to the desired value. This is done using two loops, the first loop is to select the element and the second loop is to find another element.

Time Complexity is O(n^2) and Space Complexity is O(1)

**Example 5.31:**

```
public static boolean findPair(int[] arr, int size, int value) {
    for (int i = 0; i < size; i++) {
        for (int j = i + 1; j < size; j++) {
            if ((arr[i] + arr[j]) == value) {
                System.out.println("The pair is:" + arr[i] + ", " + arr[j]);
                return true;
            }
        }
```

```
    }
    return false;
}

// Testing code.
public static void main(String[] args)  {
    int[] first = { 1, 5, 4, 3, 2, 7, 8, 9, 6 };
    findPair(first, first.length, 8);
}
```

**Output:**

```
The pair is : 1, 7
```

**Second solution:** Sorting, Steps are as follows:

1. Sort all the elements in the array.
2. Take two variables, first and second. Variable first= 0 and second = size -1
3. Compute sum = arr[first]+arr[second]
4. If the sum is equal to the desired value, then we have the solution
5. If the sum is less than the desired value, then we will increase the first
6. If the sum is greater than the desired value, then we will decrease the second
7. We repeat the above process until we get the desired pair or we get first >= second

Sorting algorithms takes O(n.log(n)) time and a single scan takes O(n) time.
Time Complexity is O(n.log(n)) and Space Complexity is O(1)

**Example 5.32:**

```
public static boolean findPair2(int[] arr, int size, int value) {
    int first = 0, second = size - 1;
    int curr;
    Arrays.sort(arr);
    while (first < second) {
        curr = arr[first] + arr[second];
        if (curr == value) {
            System.out.println("The pair is " + arr[first] + ", " + arr[second]);
            return true;
        } else if (curr < value) {
            first++;
        } else {
            second--;
        }
    }
    return false;
}
```

**Third solution:** Using Hash-Table; we can keep track of the elements we have already seen, and we can find the pair in just one scan.

1. For each element, insert the value in Hashtable. Let's say the current value is arr[index]
2. If value - arr[index] is in the Hashtable then we have the desired pair.
3. Else, proceed to the next entry in the array.

Hash-Table insertion and finding take constant time O(1) so the total time complexity of the algorithm is O(n) time. Space Complexity is also O(n)

**Example 5.33:**
```
public static boolean findPair3(int[] arr, int size, int value) {
    HashSet<Integer> hs = new HashSet<Integer>();
    for (int i = 0; i < size; i++) {
        if (hs.contains(value - arr[i])) {
            System.out.println("The pair is : " + arr[i] + ", " + (value -
arr[i]));
            return true;
        }
        hs.add(arr[i]);
    }
    return false;
}
```

**Fourth solution:** Counting approach, this approach is only possible if we know the range of the input. If we know that, the elements in the array are in the range 0 to n. We can reserve an array of length n and when we see an element, we can increase its count. In place of the Hashtable in the above approach, we will use an array and will find out the pair.

The counting approach just uses an array so insertion and finding take constant time O(1) so the total time complexity of the algorithm is O(n) time. Space Complexity for creating a count list is also O(n)

**Example 5.34:**
```
public static boolean findPair4(int[] arr, int size, int range, int value) {
    int[] count = new int[range + 1];
    Arrays.fill(count, 0);

    for (int i = 0; i < size; i++) {
        if (count[value - arr[i]] > 0) {
            System.out.println("The pair is : " + arr[i] + ", " + (value -
arr[i]));
            return true;
        }
        count[arr[i]] += 1;
    }
    return false;
}
```

## Find the Pair in two Lists

**Problem:** Given two lists X and Y. Find a pair of elements (xi, yi) such that $xi \in X$ and $yi \in Y$ where xi+yi = value.

**First solution:** Exhaustive search or Brute force search; loop through element xi of X and see if you can find (value – xi) in Y. This is done using two loops, the first loop is to select an element from X and the second loop is to find its corresponding value in Y.

Time Complexity is O(n^2) and Space Complexity is O(1)

**Example 5.35:**
```
public static boolean findPairTwoLists(int[] arr1, int size1, int[] arr2, int
size2, int value) {
    for (int i = 0; i < size1; i++) {
        for (int j = 0; j < size2; j++) {
```

```
            if ((arr1[i] + arr2[j]) == value) {
                System.out.println("The pair is : " + arr1[i] + ", " +arr2[j]);
                return true;
            }
        }
    }
    return false;
}

// Testing code.
public static void main(String[] args)  {
    int[] first = { 1, 5, 4, 3, 2, 7, 8, 9, 6 };
    int[] second = { 1, 5, 4, 3, 2, 7, 8, 9, 6 };
    System.out.println(findPairTwoLists(first, first.length, second, second.length,
8));
}
```

**Output:**

```
The pair is : 1, 7
```

**Second solution:** Sorting; Sort all the elements in the second list Y. For each element of X, you can see if that element is there in Y by using binary search.

Sorting algorithms take O(m.logm) and searching will take O(n.logm) time. Time Complexity is O(n.logm) or O(m.logm) and Space Complexity is O(1)

**Example 5.36:**

```
public static boolean findPairTwoLists2(int[] arr1, int size1, int[] arr2, int
size2, int value) {
    Arrays.sort(arr2);
    for (int i = 0; i < size1; i++) {
        if (binarySearch(arr2, size2, value - arr1[i])){
            System.out.println("The pair is " + arr1[i] + ", " + (value -
arr1[i]));
            return true;
        }
    }
    return false;
}
```

**Third solution:** Sorting, Steps are as follows:

1. Sort the elements of both X and Y in increasing order.
2. Take the sum of the smallest element of X and the largest element of Y.
3. If the sum is equal to the value, we got our pair.
4. If the sum is smaller than the value, take the next element of X
5. If the sum is greater than the value, take the previous element of Y

Sorting algorithms take O(n.log(n)) + O(m.logm) for sorting and searching will take O(n+m) time.
Time Complexity is O(n.log(n)) and Space Complexity is O(1)

**Example 5.37:**

```
public static boolean findPairTwoLists3(int[] arr1, int size1, int[] arr2, int
size2, int value) {
    int first = 0, second = size2 - 1, curr = 0;
```

```
    Arrays.sort(arr1);
    Arrays.sort(arr2);
    while (first < size1 && second >= 0) {
        curr = arr1[first] + arr2[second];
        if (curr == value) {
            System.out.println("The pair is " + arr1[first] + ", " + arr2[second]);
            return true;
        } else if (curr < value) {
            first++;
        } else {
            second--;
        }
    }
    return false;
}
```

**Fourth solution:** Using Hash-Table, Steps are as follows:

1. Scan through all the elements in the array Y and insert them into Hashtable.
2. Now scan through all the elements of list X, let us suppose the current element is xi to see if you can find (value - xi) in the Hashtable.
3. If you find the value, you got your pair.
4. If not, then go to the next value in the array X.

Hash-Table insertion and finding take constant time O(1) so the total time complexity of the algorithm is O(n) time. Space Complexity is also O(n)

**Example 5.38:**

```
public static boolean findPairTwoLists4(int[] arr1, int size1, int[] arr2, int
size2, int value) {
    HashSet<Integer> hs = new HashSet<Integer>();
    for (int i = 0; i < size2; i++)
        hs.add(arr2[i]);

    for (int i = 0; i < size1; i++) {
        if (hs.contains(value - arr1[i])) {
            System.out.println("The pair is : " + arr1[i] + ", " + (value -
arr1[i]));
            return true;
        }
    }
    return false;
}
```

**Fifth solution:** Counting; this approach is only possible if we know the range of the input. Same as Hashtable implementation, just use a simple list in place of Hashtable and you are done.
The counting approach just uses an array so insertion and finding take constant time O(1) so the total time complexity of the algorithm is O(n) time. Space Complexity for creating a count list is also O(n)

**Example 5.39:**

```
public static boolean findPairTwoLists5(int[] arr1, int size1, int[] arr2, int
size2, int range, int value) {
    int[] count = new int[range + 1];
    Arrays.fill(count, 0);
```

```
    for (int i = 0; i < size2; i++)
        count[arr2[i]] = 1;

    for (int i = 0; i < size1; i++) {
        if (count[value - arr1[i]] != 0) {
            System.out.println("The pair is: " + arr1[i] + ", " + (value-arr1[i]));
            return true;
        }
    }
    return false;
}
```

## Find Difference Pair

**Problem:** In an array of positive integers, find a pair whose absolute value of the difference is equal to a given value.

**First solution:** Brute force, find all the possible pairs and find if the absolute value of their difference is equal to the given value. Time complexity will O(n^2)

**Example 5.40:**

```
public static boolean findDifference(int arr[], int size, int value) {
    for (int i = 0; i < size; i++) {
        for (int j = i + 1; j < size; j++) {
            if (Math.abs(arr[i] - arr[j]) == value) {
                System.out.println("The pair is:: " + arr[i] + " & " + arr[j]);
                return true;
            }
        }
    }

    return false;
}

// Testing code.
public static void main(String[] args)  {
    int[] first = { 1, 5, 4, 3, 2, 7, 8, 9, 6 };
    System.out.println(findDifference(first, first.length, 6));
}
```

**Output:**

```
The pair is:: 1 & 7
```

**Second solution: Using sorting,** the performance can be improved by sorting the array. We take two indexes from the start of the array at index 0, call them first and second. When the difference of values is less than the desired value then we increase the second index or if the difference is greater than the desired value then increase the first index. Time complexity is O(n.log(n)) which is for sorting operations.

**Example 5.41:**

```
public static boolean findDifference2(int arr[], int size, int value) {
    int first = 0;
    int second = 0;
    int diff;
```

```
    Arrays.sort(arr);

    while (first < size && second < size) {
        diff = Math.abs(arr[first] - arr[second]);
        if (diff == value) {
            System.out.println("The pair is::" + arr[first] + " & " + arr[second]);
            return true;
        } else if (diff > value)
            first += 1;
        else
            second += 1;
    }
    return false;
}
```

## Find Min Diff

**Problem:** Given an array of integers, find the element pair with minimum difference.

**First solution:** you can always pick two elements, find differences between them, and find the elements with a minimum difference using two loops and comparing each pair. Time complexity is O(n^2)

**Example 5.42:**

```
public static int findMinDiff(int arr[], int size) {
    int diff = Integer.MAX_VALUE;

    for (int i = 0; i < size; i++) {
        for (int j = i + 1; j < size; j++) {
            int value = Math.abs(arr[i] - arr[j]);
            if (diff > value)
                diff = value;
        }
    }

    return diff;
}

// Testing code.
public static void main(String[] args)  {
    int[] second = { 1, 6, 4, 19, 17, 20 };
    System.out.println("findMinDiff : " + findMinDiff(second, second.length));
}
```

**Output:**

```
findMinDiff : 1
```

**Second solution:** This performance can be improved by sorting the array. Since we need a minimum sum, the pair which we are searching for is adjacent to each other. Time complexity is O(n.log(n))

**Example 5.43:**

```
public static int findMinDiff2(int[] arr, int size) {
    Arrays.sort(arr);
    int diff = Integer.MAX_VALUE;
```

```
    for (int i = 0; i < (size - 1); i++) {
        if ((arr[i + 1] - arr[i]) < diff)
            diff = arr[i + 1] - arr[i];
    }
    return diff;
}
```

## Minimum Difference Pair

**Problem:** Given two arrays, find a minimum difference pair such that it should take one element from each array.

**First solution:** Brute force solution, you can always pick two elements, one from the first array and another from the second array. Then find their difference to find the minimum difference. Time complexity is O(nm)

**Example 5.44:**

```
public static int minDiffPair(int arr1[], int size1, int arr2[], int size2) {
    int diff = Integer.MAX_VALUE;
    int first = 0;
    int second = 0;

    for (int i = 0; i < size1; i++) {
        for (int j = 0; j < size2; j++) {
            int value = Math.abs(arr1[i] - arr2[j]);
            if (diff > value) {
                diff = value;
                first = arr1[i];
                second = arr2[j];
            }
        }
    }

    System.out.println("The pair is :: " + first + " & " + second);
    System.out.println("Minimum difference is :: " + diff);
    return diff;
}

// Testing code.
public static void main(String[] args)  {
    int[] first = { 1, 5, 4, 3, 2, 7, 8, 9, 6 };
    int[] second = { 6, 4, 19, 17, 20 };
    minDiffPair(first, first.length, second, second.length);
}
```

**Output:**

```
The pair is :: 4 & 4
Minimum difference is :: 0
```

**Second solution:** This performance can be improved by sorting the arrays. Since we need a minimum difference pair. We will pick one element from the first array and find its difference from one element from the second array. If the difference is negative then we will increase the index of the first array and if the difference is positive then we will increase the index of the second array. Time Complexity is O(n.log(n) + mlogm) for sorting and O(n+m) for comparison.

**Total time complexity:** O(n.log(n) + mlogm)

**Example 5.45:**
```
public static int minDiffPair2(int arr1[], int size1, int arr2[], int size2) {
    int minDiff = Integer.MAX_VALUE;
    int i = 0;
    int j = 0;
    int first = 0, second = 0, diff;
    Arrays.sort(arr1);
    Arrays.sort(arr2);
    while (i < size1 && j < size2) {
        diff = Math.abs(arr1[i] - arr2[j]);
        if (minDiff > diff) {
            minDiff = diff;
            first = arr1[i];
            second = arr2[j];
        }
        if (arr1[i] < arr2[j])
            i += 1;
        else
            j += 1;
    }
    System.out.println("The pair is :: " + first + " & " + second);
    System.out.println("Minimum difference is :: " + minDiff);
    return minDiff;
}
```

## Closest Pair

**Problem:** Given an array of positive integers and a number. You need to find a pair in an array whose sum is closest to the given number.

**First solution:** Brute force, for each pair find their sum and get its absolute difference from the given value. This can be done using two loops. Time complexity is O(n^2)

**Example 5.46:**
```
public static void closestPair(int arr[], int size, int value) {
    int diff = 999999;
    int first = -1, second = -1, curr;
    for (int i = 0; i < size; i++) {
        for (int j = i + 1; j < size; j++) {
            curr = Math.abs(value - (arr[i] + arr[j]));
            if (curr < diff) {
                diff = curr;
                first = arr[i];
                second = arr[j];
            }
        }
    }
    System.out.println("closest pair is :: " + first + " " + second);
}

// Testing code.
public static void main(String[] args)  {
    int[] first = { 10, 20, 3, 4, 50, 80 };
    closestPair(first, first.length, 47);
}
```

**Output:**
```
closest pair is :: 3 50
```

**Second solution:** Sorting, the performance of the above solution can be improved by sorting the array. Since we need a pair whose sum is closest to the given value. We start two indexes, one from the start and the other from the end. Add these two index values and call it current. If the current sum is greater than the given value then decreases the end index and if the current sum is smaller than the value then we increase the start index.

Time complexity is O(n.log(n)) for sorting and O(n) for searching pairs. So overall Time complexity is O(n.log(n))

**Example 5.47:**
```java
public static void closestPair2(int arr[], int size, int value) {
    int first = 0, second = 0;
    int start = 0;
    int stop = size - 1;
    int diff, curr;
    Arrays.sort(arr);
    diff = 9999999;

    while (start < stop) {
        curr = (value - (arr[start] + arr[stop]));
        if (Math.abs(curr) < diff) {
            diff = Math.abs(curr);
            first = arr[start];
            second = arr[stop];
        }

        if (curr == 0) {
            break;
        } else if (curr > 0) {
            start += 1;
        } else {
            stop -= 1;
        }
    }

    System.out.println("closest pair is :: " + first + " " + second);
}
```

## Sum of Pair Equal to Rest Array

**Problem:** Given an array, find if there is a pair whose sum is equal to the sum of the rest of the elements of the array.

**Solution:** Sort the array. Sum all the elements of the array, called this value total. Find a pair in the sorted array whose sum is total/2. Total time complexity is O(n.log(n)).

**Example 5.48:**
```java
public static boolean sumPairRestArray(int[] arr, int size) {
    int total, low, high, curr, value;
```

```
    Arrays.sort(arr);
    total = 0;
    for (int i = 0; i < size; i++)
        total += arr[i];
    value = total / 2;
    low = 0;
    high = size - 1;
    while (low < high) {
        curr = arr[low] + arr[high];
        if (curr == value) {
            System.out.println("Pair is :: " + arr[low] + " " + arr[high]);
            return true;
        } else if (curr < value)
            low += 1;
        else
            high -= 1;
    }
    return false;
}

// Testing code.
public static void main(String[] args)  {
    int[] first = { 1, 2, 4, 8, 16, 15 };
    System.out.println(sumPairRestArray(first, first.length));
}
```

**Output:**

```
Pair is :: 8 15
true
```

## Zero-Sum Triplets

**Problem:** Given an array of integers, you need to find a triplet whose sum is 0.

**First solution:** Brute force, for each triplet find their sum. This can be done using three loops. Time complexity is O(n^3)

**Example 5.49:**

```
public static void zeroSumTriplets(int[] arr, int size) {
    for (int i = 0; i < (size - 2); i++) {
        for (int j = i + 1; j < (size - 1); j++) {
            for (int k = j + 1; k < size; k++) {
                if (arr[i] + arr[j] + arr[k] == 0)
                    System.out.println("Triplet:: " + arr[i] + " " + arr[j] + " " +
arr[k]);
            }
        }
    }
}

// Testing code.
public static void main(String[] args)  {
    int[] first = { 0, -1, 2, -3, 1 };
    zeroSumTriplets(first, first.length);
}
```

**Output:**
```
Triplet:: 0 -1 1
Triplet:: 2 -3 1
```

**Second solution:** We can increase performance by sorting. Sort the given array. Select an element from the array in a loop, and then find the other two values such that their sum is negative of the first value.
Time complexity is O(n^2)

**Example 5.50:**
```
public static void zeroSumTriplets2(int[] arr, int size) {
    int start, stop;
    Arrays.sort(arr);
    for (int i = 0; i < (size - 2); i++) {
        start = i + 1;
        stop = size - 1;

        while (start < stop) {
            if (arr[i] + arr[start] + arr[stop] == 0) {
                System.out.println("Triplet :: " + arr[i] + " " + arr[start] + " "
+ arr[stop]);
                start += 1;
                stop -= 1;
            } else if (arr[i] + arr[start] + arr[stop] > 0)
                stop -= 1;
            else
                start += 1;
        }
    }
}
```

## Find Triplet

**Problem:** Given an array of integers, you need to find a triplet whose sum is equal to the given value.

**First solution:** Brute force, for each triplet find their sum. This can be done using three loops. Time complexity is O(n^3)

**Example 5.51:**
```
public static void findTriplet(int arr[], int size, int value) {
    for (int i = 0; i < (size - 2); i++)
        for (int j = i + 1; j < (size - 1); j++)
            for (int k = j + 1; k < size; k++) {
                if ((arr[i] + arr[j] + arr[k]) == value)
                    System.out.println("Triplet :: " + arr[i] + " " + arr[j] + " "
+ arr[k]);
            }
}

// Testing code.
public static void main(String[] args)  {
    int[] first = { 1, 5, 15, 6, 9, 8 };
    findTriplet(first, first.length, 22);
}
```

**Output:**
```
Triplet :: 1 15 6
Triplet :: 5 9 8
```

**Second solution:** We can increase performance by sorting. Sort the given array. Select the first element from the array in a loop, and then find two other values such that the sum of all three is equal to the given value. Time complexity is O(n^2)

**Example 5.52:**
```
public static void findTriplet2(int arr[], int size, int value) {
    int start, stop;
    Arrays.sort(arr);
    for (int i = 0; i < size - 2; i++) {
        start = i + 1;
        stop = size - 1;
        while (start < stop) {
            if (arr[i] + arr[start] + arr[stop] == value) {
                System.out.println("Triplet ::" + arr[i] + " " + arr[start] + " " +
arr[stop]);
                start += 1;
                stop -= 1;
            } else if (arr[i] + arr[start] + arr[stop] > value)
                stop -= 1;
            else
                start += 1;
        }
    }
}
```

## A+B = C Triplet

**Problem:** Given an array of integers, you need to find a triplet such that the sum of two elements of the triplet is equal to the third value. We need to find a triplet (A, B, C) such that A+B = C.

**First solution:** Brute force approach, for each triplet, find if constraint A+B=C satisfies. This can be done using three loops. Time complexity is O(n^3)

**Example 5.53:**
```
public static void abcTriplet(int[] arr, int size) {
    for (int i = 0; i < size - 1; i++)
        for (int j = i + 1; j < size; j++)
            for (int k = 0; k < size; k++) {
                if (k != i && k != j && arr[i] + arr[j] == arr[k])
                    System.out.println("abcTriplet:: " + arr[i] + " " + arr[j] + "
" + arr[k]);
            }
}

// Testing code.
public static void main(String[] args)  {
    int[] first = { 1, 5, 15, 6, 9, 8 };
    abcTriplet(first, first.length);
}
```

**Output:**

```
abcTriplet:: 1 5 6
abcTriplet:: 1 8 9
abcTriplet:: 6 9 15
```

**Second solution:** We can increase performance by sorting. Sort the given array in decreasing order. Select the first element from the array in a loop, and then find the other two values such that the sum of these two is equal to the first value.
Time complexity is O(n^2)

**Example 5.54:**

```
public static void abcTriplet2(int[] arr, int size) {
    int start, stop;
    Arrays.sort(arr);
    for (int i = 0; i < size; i++) {
        start = 0;
        stop = size - 1;
        while (start < stop) {
            if (arr[i] == arr[start] + arr[stop]) {
                System.out.println("abcTriplet:: " + arr[start] + " " + arr[stop] +
" " + arr[i]);
                start += 1;
                stop -= 1;
            } else if (arr[i] < arr[start] + arr[stop])
                stop -= 1;
            else
                start += 1;
        }
    }
}
```

## Smaller than triplets Count

**Problem:** Given an array of integers, you need to find a triplet such that the sum of elements of the triplet is less than the value. We need to find triplets (A, B, C) such that A+B+C < value.

**First solution:** Brute force, for each triplet find if constraint A+B+C < value satisfies. This can be done using three loops. Time complexity is O(n^3)

**Example 5.55:**

```
public static void smallerThenTripletCount(int arr[], int size, int value) {
    int count = 0;
    for (int i = 0; i < size - 1; i++)
        for (int j = i + 1; j < size; j++)
            for (int k = j + 1; k < size; k++)
                if (arr[i] + arr[j] + arr[k] < value)
                    count += 1;

    System.out.println("smallerThenTripletCount:: " + count);
}

// Testing code.
public static void main(String[] args)  {
    int[] first = { -2, -1, 0, 1 };
```

```
    smallerThenTripletCount(first, first.length, 2);
}
```

**Output:**

```
smallerThenTripletCount:: 4
```

**Second solution:** We can increase performance by sorting. Sort the given array. Select the first element from the array in a loop, and then find two other values such that the sum of all three is less than the given value. Time complexity is O(n^2)

**Example 5.56:**

```
public static void smallerThenTripletCount2(int arr[], int size, int value) {
    int start, stop;
    int count = 0;
    Arrays.sort(arr);

    for (int i = 0; i < (size - 2); i++) {
        start = i + 1;
        stop = size - 1;
        while (start < stop) {
            if (arr[i] + arr[start] + arr[stop] >= value)
                stop -= 1;
            else {
                count += stop - start;
                start += 1;
            }
        }
    }

    System.out.println("smallerThenTripletCount:: " + count);
}
```

## Arithmetic progression triplet

**Problem:** Given a sorted array, find all Arithmetic progression triplets possible.

**Solution**: The input array is sorted. We will traverse the array from index 1 to n-2 this will be the middle element of the AP. Then we will find the first and third elements of the AP, which are at the left and right of the middle value. Time complexity O(n^2)

**Example 5.57:**

```
public static void apTriplets(int[] arr, int size) {
    int i, j, k;
    for (i = 1; i < size - 1; i++) {
        j = i - 1;
        k = i + 1;

        while (j >= 0 && k < size) {
            if (arr[j] + arr[k] == 2 * arr[i]) {
                System.out.println("AP Triplet:: " + arr[j] + " " + arr[i] + " " +
arr[k]);
                k += 1;
                j -= 1;
            } else if (arr[j] + arr[k] < 2 * arr[i])
```

```
                k += 1;
            else
                j -= 1;
        }
    }
}

// Testing code.
public static void main(String[] args)  {
    int[] arr = { 2, 4, 10, 12, 14, 18, 36 };
    apTriplets(arr, arr.length);
}
```

**Output:**

```
AP Triplet:: 2 10 18
AP Triplet:: 10 12 14
AP Triplet:: 10 14 18
```

## Geometric Progression Triplet

**Problem:** Given a sorted array, find all geometric progression triplets possible.

**Solution**: The input array is sorted. We will traverse the array from index 1 to n-2 this will be the middle element of the GP. Then we will find the first and third elements of the GP, which are at the left and right of the middle value. Time complexity O(n^2)

**Example 5.58:**

```
public static void gpTriplets(int[] arr, int size) {
    int i, j, k;

    for (i = 1; i < size - 1; i++) {
        j = i - 1;
        k = i + 1;

        while (j >= 0 && k < size) {
            if (arr[j] * arr[k] == arr[i] * arr[i]) {
                System.out.println("GP Triplet:: " + arr[j] + " " + arr[i] + " " +
arr[k]);
                k += 1;
                j -= 1;
            } else if (arr[j] + arr[k] < 2 * arr[i])
                k += 1;
            else
                j -= 1;
        }
    }
}

// Testing code.
public static void main(String[] args)  {
    int[] arr = { 1, 2, 4, 8, 16 };
    gpTriplets(arr, arr.length);
}
```

**Output:**

```
GP Triplet:: 1 2 4
```

```
GP Triplet:: 2 4 8
GP Triplet:: 1 4 16
GP Triplet:: 4 8 16
```

## Number of Triangles

**Problem:** Given an array of positive integers representing edges of triangles. Find the number of triangles that can be formed from these elements representing sides of triangles. For a triangle, the sum of two edges is always greater than the third edge.

Input: [1, 2, 3, 4, 5]
Output: 3, Corresponds to (2, 3, 4) (2, 4, 5) (3, 4, 5)

**First solution:** Brute force solution, by picking all the triplets and then checking if the triangle property holds. Time Complexity is O(n^3)

**Example 5.59:**

```
public static int numberOfTriangles(int[] arr, int size) {
    int i, j, k, count = 0;
    for (i = 0; i < (size - 2); i++) {
        for (j = i + 1; j < (size - 1); j++) {
            for (k = j + 1; k < size; k++) {
                if (arr[i] + arr[j] > arr[k])
                    count += 1;
            }
        }
    }
    return count;
}

// Testing code.
public static void main(String[] args)  {
    int[] arr = { 1, 2, 3, 4, 5 };
    System.out.println(numberOfTriangles(arr, arr.length));
}
```

**Output:**

```
3
```

**Second solution:** This solution takes advantage of one simple property. In a sorted array, If the sum of arr[i] & arr[j] is greater than arr[k] then the sum of arr[i] & arr[j+1] is also greater than arr[k]. This improvement makes the time complexity of this algorithm as O(n^2)

**Example 5.60:**

```
public static int numberOfTriangles2(int[] arr, int size) {
    int i, j, k, count = 0;
    Arrays.sort(arr);

    for (i = 0; i < (size - 2); i++) {
        k = i + 2;
        for (j = i + 1; j < (size - 1); j++) {
            /*
             if sum of arr[i] & arr[j] is greater arr[k] then sum of arr[i] &
             arr[j + 1]is also greater than arr[k] this improvement make algo O(n2)
```

```
            */
            while (k < size && arr[i] + arr[j] > arr[k])
                k += 1;

            count += k - j - 1;
        }
    }
    return count;
}
```

## Find max, appearing element in an array

**Problem:** In a given list of n numbers, find the element, which appears the maximum number of times.

**First solution:** Exhaustive search or Brute force; for each element in the array, find how many times this value appears in the array. Keep track of the maxCount and when some element count is greater than maxCount then update the maxCount. This is done using two loops, the first loop to select the element and the second loop to count the occurrence of that element.

Time Complexity is O(n^2) and Space Complexity is O(1)

**Example 5.61:**

```
public static int getMax(int[] arr, int size) {
    int max = arr[0], count = 1, maxCount = 1;

    for (int i = 0; i < size; i++) {
        count = 1;
        for (int j = i + 1; j < size; j++) {
            if (arr[i] == arr[j]) {
                count++;
            }
        }
        if (count > maxCount) {
            max = arr[i];
            maxCount = count;
        }
    }

    return max;
}

// Testing code.
public static void main(String[] args)  {
    int[] first = { 1, 30, 5, 13, 9, 31, 5 };
    System.out.println(getMax(first, first.length));
}
```

**Output:**

```
5
```

**Second solution:** Sorting; Sort all the elements in the array. In a single scan, we can find the counts. Sorting algorithms takes O(n.log(n)) time and a single scan takes O(n) time.

Time Complexity is O(n.log(n)) and Space Complexity is O(1)

**Example 5.62:**
```
public static int getMax2(int[] arr, int size) {
    Arrays.sort(arr); // Sort(arr,size);
    int max = arr[0], maxCount = 1;
    int curr = arr[0], currCount = 1;
    for (int i = 1; i < size; i++) {
        if (arr[i] == arr[i - 1]) {
            currCount++;
        } else {
            currCount = 1;
            curr = arr[i];
        }
        if (currCount > maxCount) {
            maxCount = currCount;
            max = curr;
        }
    }
    return max;
}
```

**Third solution:** Counting, this approach is possible only if we know the range of the input. If we know that, the elements in the array are in the range 0 to n-1. We can traverse an array of length n and when we see an element, we can increase its count. In just one single scan, we know the duplicates. If we know the range of the elements, then this is the fastest way to find the max count.

The counting approach just uses a list so to increase count takes constant time O(1) so the total time complexity of the algorithm is O(n) time. Space Complexity for creating a count list is also O(n)

**Example 5.63:**
```
public static int getMax3(int[] arr, int size, int range) {
    int max = arr[0], maxCount = 1;
    int[] count = new int[range];
    for (int i = 0; i < size; i++) {
        count[arr[i]]++;
        if (count[arr[i]] > maxCount) {
            maxCount = count[arr[i]];
            max = arr[i];
        }
    }
    return max;
}
```

## Majority element in an array

**Problem:** In a given array of n elements. Find the majority element, which appears more than n/2 times. Return 0 in case there is no majority element.

**First solution:** Exhaustive search or Brute force, for each element in the array, find how many times its value appears in the array. Keep track of the maxCount and when some element count is greater than maxCount then update the maxCount. This is done using two loops, the first loop to select the element and the second loop to count the occurrence of that element. If the final maxCount is greater than n/2 we have a majority, otherwise we do not have any majority.

Time Complexity is O(n^2) + O(1) = O(n^2) and Space Complexity is O(1)

**Example 5.64:**

```
public static int getMajority(int[] arr, int size) {
    int max = 0, count = 0, maxCount = 0;

    for (int i = 0; i < size; i++) {
        for (int j = i + 1; j < size; j++) {
            if (arr[i] == arr[j]) {
                count++;
            }
        }
        if (count > maxCount) {
            max = arr[i];
            maxCount = count;
        }
    }

    if (maxCount > size / 2) {
        return max;
    } else {
        return 0;
    }
}

// Testing code.
public static void main(String[] args)  {
    int[] first = { 1, 5, 5, 13, 5, 31, 5 };
    System.out.println(getMajority(first, first.length));
}
```

**Output:**

```
5
```

**Second solution:** Sorting all the elements in the array. If there is a majority, then the middle element at the index n/2 must be the majority number. So, just a single scan can be used to find its count and see if the majority is there or not.

Sorting algorithms take O(n.log(n)) time and single scans take O(n) time.
Time Complexity is O(n.log(n)) and Space Complexity is O(1)

**Example 5.65:**

```
public static int getMajority2(int[] arr, int size) {
    int majIndex = size / 2, count = 1;
    int candidate;
    Arrays.sort(arr);
    candidate = arr[majIndex];
    count = 0;
    for (int i = 0; i < size; i++) {
        if (arr[i] == candidate) {
            count++;
        }
    }
    if (count > size / 2) {
        return arr[majIndex];
    } else {
        return Integer.MIN_VALUE;
```

```
    }
}
```

**Third solution:** This is a cancellation approach (Moore's Voting Algorithm) if all the elements stand against the majority and each element is cancelled with one element of majority, if there is a majority the majority prevails.

1. Set the first element of the array as the majority candidate and Initialise the count to be 1.
2. Start scanning the array.
   - If we get some element whose value is the same as a majority candidate, then we increase the count.
   - If we get an element whose value is different from the majority candidate, then we decrement the count.
   - If the count becomes 0, that means we have a new majority candidate. Make the current candidate as majority candidate and reset the count to 1.
   - In the end, we will have the only probable majority candidate.
3. Now scan through the array once again to see if that candidate we found above has appeared more than n/2 times.

The counting approach just scans the throw list two times. Time Complexity is O(n) time. Space Complexity for creating a count list is also O(1)

**Example 5.66:**

```
public static int getMajority3(int[] arr, int size) {
    int majIndex = 0, count = 1;
    int i;
    int candidate;
    for (i = 1; i < size; i++) {
        if (arr[majIndex] == arr[i]) {
            count++;
        } else {
            count--;
        }
        if (count == 0) {
            majIndex = i;
            count = 1;
        }
    }

    candidate = arr[majIndex];
    count = 0;

    for (i = 0; i < size; i++) {
        if (arr[i] == candidate) {
            count++;
        }
    }
    if (count > size / 2) {
        return arr[majIndex];
    } else {
        return 0;
    }
}
```

## Is Majority

**Problem:** Given a sorted array, find if there is a majority and find the majority element.

**First solution:** Using brute force traversal of the array, we can find the number of occurrences of the middle element in the array. If the number of occurrences is not greater than or equal to the ceiling of count/2 then there is no majority.
Time complexity is O(N)

**Example 5.67:**
```
public static boolean isMajority(int arr[], int size) {
    int count = 0;
    int mid = arr[size / 2];
    for (int i = 0; i < size; i++)
        if (arr[i] == mid)
            count += 1;

    if (count > size / 2)
        return true;
    return false;
}

// Testing code.
public static void main(String[] args)  {
    int[] arr = { 3, 3, 3, 3, 4, 5, 10 };
    System.out.println(isMajority(arr, arr.length));
}
```

**Output:**
```
true
```

**Second solution:** Since the array is sorted, our first thought should be binary search. We can find the probable majority of the candidates at the size/2 location. Then we need to find its first occurrence in the sorted array, say it index i. Then once we have index i then if the majority exists then the element at index i+n/2 also has a value the same as the majority candidate.
Time complexity is O(log(n))

**Example 5.68:** Using binary search method.
```
public static int firstIndex(int arr[], int size, int low, int high, int value) {
    int mid = 0;
    if (high >= low)
        mid = (low + high) / 2;

    /*
    Find first occurrence of value, either it should be the first element
    of the array or the value before it is smaller than it.
    */
    if ((mid == 0 || arr[mid - 1] < value) && (arr[mid] == value))
        return mid;
    else if (arr[mid] < value)
        return firstIndex(arr, size, mid + 1, high, value);
    else
        return firstIndex(arr, size, low, mid - 1, value);
}
```

```
public static boolean isMajority2(int arr[], int size) {
    int majority = arr[size / 2];
    int i = firstIndex(arr, size, 0, size - 1, majority);
    /*
     * we are using majority element form array so we will get some valid index
     * always.
     */
    if (((i + size / 2) <= (size - 1)) && arr[i + size / 2] == majority)
        return true;
    else
        return false;
}
```

## Find a median of an array

**Problem:** In an unsorted list of numbers of size n, if all the elements of the array are sorted, then find the element, which lies at the index n/2.

**First solution:** Sort the array and return the element in the middle.
Sorting algorithms takes O(n.log(n)).
Time Complexity is O(n.log(n)) and Space Complexity is O(1)

**Example 5.69:**

```
public static int getMedian(int[] arr, int size) {
    Arrays.sort(arr);
    return arr[size / 2];
}

// Testing code.
public static void main(String[] args)  {
    int[] first = { 1, 5, 6, 6, 6, 6, 6, 6, 7, 8, 10, 13, 20, 30 };
    System.out.println(getMedian(first, first.length));
}
```

**Output:**

```
6
```

**Second solution:** Use the quickSelect algorithm. Find the n/2 element using the quickSelect algorithm.

**Example 5.70:**

```
public static int getMedian2(int[] arr, int size) {
    quickSelectUtil(arr, 0, size - 1, size / 2);
    return arr[size / 2];
}
```

The Average-Case time complexity of this algorithm will be O(n)

## Find maxima in a bitonic list

**Problem:** A bitonic list comprises an increasing sequence of integers immediately followed by a decreasing sequence of integers.

**First solution:** Sequential search, traverse through the array and find a point at which the next value is less than the current value. This is the maxima and returns this value.

**Example 5.71:**
```
public static int searchBitonicArrayMax(int[] arr, int size) {
    for (int i = 0; i < size - 2; i++) {
        if (arr[i] > arr[i + 1])
            return arr[i];
    }
    System.out.println("error not a bitonic array");
    return 0;
}

// Testing code.
public static void main(String[] args)  {
    int[] first = { 1, 5, 10, 13, 20, 30, 8, 7, 6 };
    System.out.println(searchBitonicArrayMax(first, first.length));
}
```

**Output:**
```
30
```

**Second solution:** Binary search method, since the elements are sorted in some order, we should go for an algorithm similar to binary search. The steps are as follows:

1. Take two variables for storing start and end indexes. Variable start=0 and end=size-1
2. Find the middle element of the array.
3. See if the middle element is the maxima. If yes, return the middle element.
4. Alternatively, if the middle element is in the increasing part, then we need to look at mid+1 and end.
5. Alternatively, if the middle element is in the decreasing part, then we need to look at the start and mid-1.
6. Repeat steps 2 to 5 until we get the maxima.

**Example 5.72:**
```
public static int searchBitonicArrayMax2(int[] arr, int size) {
    int start = 0, end = size - 1;
    int mid = (start + end) / 2;
    int maximaFound = 0;
    if (size < 3) {
        System.out.println("error");
        return 0;
    }
    while (start <= end) {
        mid = (start + end) / 2;
        if (arr[mid-1] < arr[mid] && arr[mid+1] < arr[mid]) // maxima
        {
            maximaFound = 1;
            break;
        } else if (arr[mid-1] < arr[mid] && arr[mid] < arr[mid+1]) // increasing
        {
            start = mid + 1;
        } else if (arr[mid-1] > arr[mid] && arr[mid] > arr[mid+1]) // decreasing
        {
            end = mid - 1;
```

```
        } else {
            break;
        }
    }
    if (maximaFound == 0) {
        System.out.println("error not a bitonic array");
        return 0;
    }
    return arr[mid];
}
```

**Note**: - This algorithm works with strictly increasing then decreasing bitonic array. If there are repetitive values then this algorithm will fail.

## Search element in a bitonic list

**Problem:** A bitonic list comprises an increasing sequence of integers immediately followed by a decreasing sequence of integers. Find an element in a bitonic list.

**Solution:** To search an element in a bitonic list:

1. Find the index or maximum element in the array. By finding the end of increasing part of the array, using binary search.
2. Once we have the maximum element, search the given value in increasing part of the array using binary search.
3. If the value is not found in the increasing part, search the same value in the decreasing part of the array using binary search.

**Example 5.73:**

```
public static int searchBitonicArray(int[] arr, int size, int key) {
    int max = findMaxBitonicArray(arr, size);
    int k = binarySearch(arr, 0, max, key, true);
    if (k != -1) {
        return k;
    } else {
        return binarySearch(arr, max + 1, size - 1, key, false);
    }
}

public static int findMaxBitonicArray(int[] arr, int size) {
    int start = 0, end = size - 1, mid;
    if (size < 3) {
        System.out.println("error");
        return -1;
    }

    while (start <= end) {
        mid = (start + end) / 2;
        if (arr[mid - 1] < arr[mid] && arr[mid + 1] < arr[mid])// maxima
        {
            return mid;
        } else if (arr[mid - 1] < arr[mid] && arr[mid] < arr[mid + 1])// increasing
        {
            start = mid + 1;
        } else if (arr[mid - 1] > arr[mid] && arr[mid] > arr[mid + 1])// decreasing
        {
```

```
            end = mid - 1;
        } else {
            break;
        }
    }

    System.out.println("error");
    return -1;
}

// Testing code.
public static void main(String[] args)  {
    int[] first = { 1, 5, 10, 13, 20, 30, 8, 7, 6 };
    System.out.println(searchBitonicArray(first, first.length, 7));
}
```

**Output:**

```
7
```

## Occurrence counts in sorted List

**Problem:** Given a sorted list arr[] find the number of occurrences of a number.

**First solution:** Brute force, Traverse the array and in linear time we will get the occurrence count of the number. This is done using one loop.

Time Complexity is O(n) and Space Complexity is O(1)

**Example 5.74:**

```
public static int findKeyCount(int[] arr, int size, int key) {
    int count = 0;
    for (int i = 0; i < size; i++) {
        if (arr[i] == key) {
            count++;
        }
    }

    return count;
}

// Testing code.
public static void main(String[] args)  {
    int[] first = { 1, 5, 10, 13, 20, 30, 8, 7, 6 };
    System.out.println(findKeyCount(first, first.length, 6));
}
```

**Output:**

```
1
```

**Second solution:** Since we have a sorted list, we should think about some binary search.

1. First, we should find the first occurrence of the key.
2. Then we should find the last occurrence of the key.
3. Take the difference between these two values and you will have the solution.

**Example 5.75:**
```java
public static int findFirstIndex(int[] arr, int start, int end, int key) {
    int mid;
    if (end < start) {
        return -1;
    }

    mid = (start + end) / 2;
    if (key == arr[mid] && (mid == start || arr[mid - 1] != key)) {
        return mid;
    }
    if (key <= arr[mid]) {
        return findFirstIndex(arr, start, mid - 1, key);
    } else {
        return findFirstIndex(arr, mid + 1, end, key);
    }
}

public static int findLastIndex(int[] arr, int start, int end, int key) {
    if (end < start) {
        return -1;
    }

    int mid = (start + end) / 2;
    if (key == arr[mid] && (mid == end || arr[mid + 1] != key)) {
        return mid;
    }

    if (key < arr[mid]) {
        return findLastIndex(arr, start, mid - 1, key);
    } else {
        return findLastIndex(arr, mid + 1, end, key);
    }
}

public static int findKeyCount2(int[] arr, int size, int key) {
    int firstIndex, lastIndex;
    firstIndex = findFirstIndex(arr, 0, size - 1, key);
    lastIndex = findLastIndex(arr, 0, size - 1, key);
    return (lastIndex - firstIndex + 1);
}
```

## Stock purchase-sell

**Problem:** In a given list, in which nth element is the price of the stock on an nth day. You are asked to buy once and sell once, on what date you will be buying and at what date you will be selling to get maximum profit.

Or

In a given list of numbers, you need to maximise the difference between two numbers, such that you can subtract the number, which appears before from the number that appears after it.

**First solution:** Brute force; for each element in the array, find another element whose difference is maximum or for which profit is maximum. This is done using two loops, the first loop to select by date index and the second loop to find its selling date entry.

**Example 5.76:**
```
public static int maxProfit(int stocks[], int size) {
    int maxProfit = 0;
    int buy = 0, sell = 0;

    for (int i = 0; i < size - 1; i++) {
        for (int j = i + 1; j < size; j++) {
            if (maxProfit < stocks[j] - stocks[i]) {
                maxProfit = stocks[j] - stocks[i];
                buy = i;
                sell = j;
            }
        }
    }

    System.out.println("Purchase day is " + buy + " at price " + stocks[buy]);
    System.out.println("Sell day is " + sell + " at price " + stocks[sell]);
    return maxProfit;
}

// Testing code.
public static void main(String[] args)  {
    int[] first = { 10, 150, 6, 67, 61, 16, 86, 6, 67, 78, 150, 3, 28, 143 };
    System.out.println("Profit : " + maxProfit(first, first.length));
}
```

**Output:**
```
Purchase day is 2 at price 6
Sell day is 10 at price 150
Profit is 144
```

Time Complexity is O(n^2) and Space Complexity is O(1)

**Second solution:** Another clever solution is to keep track of the smallest value seen so far from the start. At each point, we can find the difference and keep track of the maximum profit. This is a linear solution.
Time Complexity is O(n) time. Space Complexity for creating a count list is also O(1)

**Example 5.77:**
```
public static int maxProfit2(int stocks[], int size) {
    int buy = 0, sell = 0;
    int curMin = 0;
    int currProfit = 0;
    int maxProfit = 0;
    for (int i = 0; i < size; i++) {
        if (stocks[i] < stocks[curMin]) {
            curMin = i;
        }
        currProfit = stocks[i] - stocks[curMin];
        if (currProfit > maxProfit) {
            buy = curMin;
            sell = i;
            maxProfit = currProfit;
        }
    }
```

```
    System.out.println("Purchase day is " + buy + " at price " + stocks[buy]);
    System.out.println("Sell day is " + sell + " at price " + stocks[sell]);
    return maxProfit;
}
```

## Find the median of two sorted Lists.

**Problem:** Given two sorted lists. Find the median of the arrays if they are combined to form a bigger list.

**First solution:** We need to Keep track of the index of both the arrays, say the indexes are i and j. Keep increasing the index of the array whichever has a smaller value. Use a counter to keep track of the elements that we have already traced. Once the count is equal to half of the combined length of two lists, we have our median.

Time Complexity is O(n) and Space Complexity is O(1)

**Example 5.78:**

```
public static int findMedian(int[] arrFirst, int sizeFirst, int[] arrSecond, int
sizeSecond) {
    int medianIndex = ((sizeFirst + sizeSecond) + (sizeFirst + sizeSecond) % 2) /
2; // ceiling function.
    int i = 0, j = 0;
    int count = 0;
    while (count < medianIndex - 1) {
        if (i < sizeFirst - 1 && arrFirst[i] < arrSecond[j]) {
            i++;
        } else {
            j++;
        }
        count++;
    }
    if (arrFirst[i] < arrSecond[j]) {
        return arrFirst[i];
    } else {
        return arrSecond[j];
    }
}

// Testing code.
public static void main(String[] args)  {
    int[] first = { 1, 5, 6, 6, 6, 6, 6, 6, 7, 8, 10, 13, 20, 30 };
    int[] second = { 1, 5, 6, 6, 6, 6, 6, 6, 7, 8, 10, 13, 20, 30 };
    System.out.println(findMedian(first, first.length, second, second.length));
}
```

**Output:**

```
6
```

## Search 01 List

**Problem:** In the given list of 0's and 1's in which all the 0's come before 1's. Write an algorithm to find the index of the first 1.

Or

You are given an array which contains either 0 or 1, and they are in sorted order Ex. a [] = {0, 0, 0, 1, 1, 1, 1}, How will you count no of 1's and 0's?

**First solution:** Linear Search, we can always find the index of the first 1 in the array using traversal. Time Complexity is O(n) and Space Complexity is O(1)

**Example 5.79:**
```
public static int search01(int[] arr, int size) {
    for (int i = 0; i < size; i++)
        if (arr[i] == 1)
            return i;

    return -1;
}

// Testing code.
public static void main(String[] args)  {
    int[] first = { 0, 0, 0, 0, 0, 0, 0, 0, 1, 1, 1, 1 };
    System.out.println(search01(first, first.length));
}
```

**Output:**
```
8
```

**Second solution:** Binary Search, since the array is sorted using binary search to find the desired index.
Time Complexity is O(log(n)) and Space Complexity is O(1)

**Example 5.80:**
```
public static int binarySearch01(int[] arr, int size) {
    if (size == 1 && arr[0] == 1) {
        return 0;
    }

    return binarySearch01Util(arr, 0, size - 1);
}

public static int binarySearch01Util(int[] arr, int start, int end) {
    if (end < start) {
        return -1;
    }

    int mid = (start + end) / 2;
    if (1 == arr[mid] && 0 == arr[mid - 1]) {
        return mid;
    }

    if (0 == arr[mid]) {
        return binarySearch01Util(arr, mid + 1, end);
    } else {
        return binarySearch01Util(arr, start, mid - 1);
    }
}
```

## Find the index of max value in a Rotated array

**Problem:** Given a sorted list S of N integer. S is rotated an unknown number of times. Find the index of the largest element in the array.

**First solution:** Linear Search, we can always find the index of the first 1 in the array using traversal. Time Complexity is O(n) and Space Complexity is O(1)

**Example 5.81:**
```
public static int rotationMax(int[] arr, int size) {
    for (int i = 0; i < size - 1; i++)
        if (arr[i] > arr[i + 1])
            return arr[i];

    return -1;
}

// Testing code.
public static void main(String[] args)  {
    int[] first = { 34, 56, 77, 1, 5, 6, 6, 8, 10, 20, 30, 34 };
    System.out.println(rotationMax(first, first.length));
}
```

**Output:**
```
77
```

**Second solution:** Since the array is sorted, we can use a modified binary search to find the element. Time Complexity is O(log(n)) and Space Complexity is O(1)

**Example 5.82:**
```
public static int rotationMaxUtil(int arr[], int start, int end) {
    if (end <= start) {
        return arr[start];
    }

    int mid = (start + end) / 2;
    if (arr[mid] > arr[mid + 1])
        return arr[mid];

    if (arr[start] <= arr[mid]) /* increasing part. */
        return rotationMaxUtil(arr, mid + 1, end);
    else
        return rotationMaxUtil(arr, start, mid - 1);
}

public static int rotationMax2(int[] arr, int size) {
    return rotationMaxUtil(arr, 0, size - 1);
}
```

## Count Rotation

**Problem:** Given a rotated array, find the count of rotation.

**Solution**: Find the index of the max value in the rotated array. **(maxIndex + 1) % size** is the number of rotations.

**Example 5.83:**
```
public static int countRotation(int[] arr, int size) {
    int maxIndex = findRotationMaxUtil(arr, 0, size - 1);
    return (maxIndex + 1) % size;
}

// Testing code.
public static void main(String[] args)  {
    int[] first = { 34, 56, 77, 1, 5, 6, 6, 8, 10, 20, 30, 34 };
    System.out.println(countRotation(first, first.length));
}
```

**Output:**
```
3
```

## Search in sorted rotated List

**Problem:** Given a sorted list S of N integer. S is rotated an unknown number of times. Find an element in the array.

**First solution:** Linear Search, we can always find the value in the array using traversal.
Time Complexity is O(n) and Space Complexity is O(1)

**Example 5.84:**
```
public static int searchRotateArray(int[] arr, int size, int key) {
    for (int i = 0; i < size - 1; i++)
        if (arr[i] == key)
            return i;
    return -1;
}

// Testing code.
public static void main(String[] args)  {
    int[] first = { 34, 56, 77, 1, 5, 6, 6, 6, 6, 6, 6, 7, 8, 10, 13, 20, 30 };
    System.out.println(searchRotateArray(first, first.length, 20));
}
```

**Output:**
```
15
```

**Second solution:** Since the array is sorted, we can use a modified binary search to find the element.
Time Complexity is O(log(n)) and Space Complexity is O(1)

**Example 5.85:**
```
public static int binarySearchRotateArrayUtil(int[] arr, int start, int end, int key) {
    if (end < start) {
        return -1;
    }

    int mid = (start + end) / 2;
```

```
    if (key == arr[mid]) {
        return mid;
    }

    if (arr[mid] > arr[start]) {
        if (arr[start] <= key && key < arr[mid]) {
            return binarySearchRotateArrayUtil(arr, start, mid - 1, key);
        } else {
            return binarySearchRotateArrayUtil(arr, mid + 1, end, key);
        }
    } else {
        if (arr[mid] < key && key <= arr[end]) {
            return binarySearchRotateArrayUtil(arr, mid + 1, end, key);
        } else {
            return binarySearchRotateArrayUtil(arr, start, mid - 1, key);
        }
    }
}

public static int binarySearchRotateArray(int[] arr, int size, int key) {
    return binarySearchRotateArrayUtil(arr, 0, size - 1, key);
}
```

## Minimum Absolute Difference Adjacent Circular Array

**Problem:** Given an array of integers, find the minimum absolute difference of adjacent elements in this array, considering this is a circular array in which the last and first elements are also adjacent.

**Solution**: Traverse the array and find the difference of the adjacent elements, and use a modular operator to consider the first element and last element as adjacent.

**Example 5.86:**

```
public static int minAbsDiffAdjCircular(int[] arr, int size) {
    int diff = 9999999;
    if (size < 2)
        return -1;

    for (int i = 0; i < size; i++)
        diff = Math.min(diff, Math.abs(arr[i] - arr[(i + 1) % size]));

    return diff;
}

// Testing code.
public static void main(String[] args)  {
    int[] arr = { 5, 29, 18, 51, 11 };
    System.out.println(minAbsDiffAdjCircular(arr, arr.length));
}
```

**Output:**

```
6
```

## Transform List

**Problem:** How would you swap elements of an array like [a1 a2 a3 a4 b1 b2 b3 b4] to convert it into [a1 b1 a2 b2 a3 b3 a4 b4]?

**Solution**:

1. First swap elements in the middle pair
2. Next swap elements in the middle two pairs
3. Next swap elements in the middle three pairs
4. Iterate n-1 steps.

**Example 5.87:**
```
public static void swapch(char[] arr, int first, int second) {
    char temp = arr[first];
    arr[first] = arr[second];
    arr[second] = temp;
}

public static void transformArrayAB1(char[] arr, int size) {
    int N = size / 2, i, j;

    for (i = 1; i < N; i++) {
        for (j = 0; j < i; j++) {
            swapch(arr, N - i + 2 * j, N - i + 2 * j + 1);
        }
    }
}

//Testing Code
public static void main(String[] args)  {
    char[] str = "aaaabbbb".toCharArray();
    transformArrayAB1(str, str.length);
    System.out.println(str);
}
```

**Output:**
```
abababab
```

## Check if two Lists are permutation of each other

**Problem:** In given two integer lists; You must check whether they are permutations of each other.

**First solution:** Sorting; Sort all the elements of both the arrays and compare each element of both the arrays from beginning to end. If there is no mismatch, return true. Otherwise, false.
Sorting algorithms takes O(n.log(n)) time and comparison takes O(n) time.
Time Complexity is O(n.log(n)) and Space Complexity is O(1)

**Example 5.88:**
```
public static boolean checkPermutation(char[] array1, int size1, char[] array2, int
size2) {
    if (size1 != size2) {
        return false;
    }

    Arrays.sort(array1);
    Arrays.sort(array2);
    for (int i = 0; i < size1; i++) {
        if (array1[i] != array2[i]) {
            return false;
```

```
        }
    }
    return true;
}

// Testing code.
public static void main(String[] args)  {
    char[] str1 = "aaaabbbb".toCharArray();
    char[] str2 = "bbaaaabb".toCharArray();
    System.out.println(checkPermutation(str1, str1.length, str2, str2.length));
}
```

**Output:**

```
true
```

**Second solution:** Hash-Table (Assumption: No duplicates).

1. Create a Hash-Table for all the elements of the first list.
2. Traverse the other list from beginning to end and search for each element in the Hash-Table.
3. If all the elements are found in, the Hash-Table returns true, otherwise returns false.

**Example 5.89:**

```
public static boolean checkPermutation2(char[] arr1, int size1, char[] arr2, int
size2) {
    if (size1 != size2)
        return false;

    HashMap<Character, Integer> hm = new HashMap<Character, Integer>();
    for (int i = 0; i < size1; i++) {
        if (hm.containsKey(arr1[i])) {
            hm.put(arr1[i], hm.get(arr1[i]) + 1);
        } else
            hm.put(arr1[i], 1);
    }

    for (int i = 0; i < size2; i++) {
        if (hm.containsKey(arr2[i]) && hm.get(arr2[i]) != 0) {
            hm.put(arr2[i], hm.get(arr2[i]) - 1);
        } else
            return false;
    }
    return true;
}
```

Hash-Table insert and find take constant time O(1) so the total time complexity of the algorithm is O(n) time. Space Complexity is also O(n)
Time Complexity = O(n) (For creation of Hash-Table and look-up),
Space Complexity = O(n) (For creation of Hash-Table).

**Third Solution**: If they are permutations, then their length should be the same. Create a count[] array of length 256(Different characters possible). For characters of the first string, increment its corresponding ASCII location. And for characters of the second string, decrement their corresponding ASCII location. If both the strings are permutations of each other, all the entries of the count[] array should be 0.

**Example 5.90:**

```java
public static boolean checkPermutation3(char[] array1, int size1, char[] array2,
int size2) {
    if (size1 != size2) {
        return false;
    }
    int[] count = new int[256];
    for (int i = 0; i < size1; i++) {
        count[array1[i]]++;
        count[array2[i]]--;
    }

    for (int i = 0; i < size1; i++) {
        if (count[i] != 0) {
            return false;
        }
    }
    return true;
}
```

**Time complexity:** O(n), where n is the number of characters in the text.

## Searching for an element in a 2d sorted array

**Problem:** In a given 2-dimensional list. Each row and column is sorted in ascending order. How would you find an element in it?

**Solution:** The algorithm works as:

1. Start with the element at the last column and the first row
2. If the element is the value we are looking for, return true.
3. If the element is greater than the value we are looking for, go to the element in the previous column but in the same row.
4. If the element is less than the value we are looking for, go to the element in the next row but in the same column.
5. Return false, if the element is not found after reaching the element of the last row of the first column. Condition (row < r && column >= 0) is false.

**Example 5.91:**

```java
public static boolean findElementIn2DArray(int[] arr[], int r, int c, int value) {
    int row = 0;
    int column = c - 1;
    while (row < r && column >= 0) {
        if (arr[row][column] == value) {
            return true;
        } else if (arr[row][column] > value) {
            column--;
        } else {
            row++;
        }
    }
    return false;
}
```

Time-Complexity O(N).

## Arithmetic progression

**Problem:** Given an array of N integers, you need to find if array elements can form an Arithmetic progression.

**First solution:** Arithmetic relations can be found only by sorting the elements. Then traversing that AP exists. Time complexity will O(n.log(n)) for sorting

**Example 5.92:**
```
public static boolean isAP(int[] arr, int size) {
    if (size <= 1)
        return true;

    Arrays.sort(arr);
    int diff = arr[1] - arr[0];
    for (int i = 2; i < size; i++) {
        if (arr[i] - arr[i - 1] != diff)
            return false;
    }
    return true;
}

// Testing code.
public static void main(String[] args)  {
    int[] arr = { 20, 25, 15, 5, 0, 10, 35, 30 };
    System.out.println(isAP(arr, arr.length));
}
```

**Output:**
```
true
```

**Second solution:** We can find the first and second-lowest elements of the array in a single traversal. By this, we can find the first value of AP and the increment value of AP. We traverse values in the input array and add them to the hashtable. Finally, we have the first element of AP and difference, so we can test that all the elements are in HashTable.

Time complexity is O(n) and space complexity is O(n) for a hashtable.

**Example 5.93:**
```
public static boolean isAP2(int[] arr, int size) {
    int first = 9999999;
    int second = 9999999;
    int value;
    HashSet<Integer> hs = new HashSet<Integer>();

    for (int i = 0; i < size; i++) {
        if (arr[i] < first) {
            second = first;
            first = arr[i];
        } else if (arr[i] < second)
            second = arr[i];
    }
```

```
    int diff = second - first;

    for (int i = 0; i < size; i++) {
        if (hs.contains(arr[i]))
            return false;
        hs.add(arr[i]);
    }

    for (int i = 0; i < size; i++) {
        value = first + i * diff;
        if (!hs.contains(value))
            return false;
    }

    return true;
}
```

**Third solution:** We can solve this problem in O(n) time and O(1) space. We find the first and second-lowest elements of the array in a single traversal. Now we will traverse the array again and will put each element into its proper position by swapping. Index of each element will be (value – first) / diff. We will keep the count also so that we can find duplicate values too.

**Example 5.94:**

```
public static boolean isAP3(int[] arr, int size) {
    int first = 9999999;
    int second = 9999999;
    int[] count = new int[size];
    int index = -1;
    for (int i = 0; i < size; i++) {
        if (arr[i] < first) {
            second = first;
            first = arr[i];
        } else if (arr[i] < second)
            second = arr[i];
    }

    int diff = second - first;
    for (int i = 0; i < size; i++) {
        index = (arr[i] - first) / diff;
        if (index > size - 1 || count[index] != 0)
            return false;
        count[index] = 1;
    }

    for (int i = 0; i < size; i++) {
        if (count[i] != 1)
            return false;
    }
    return true;
}
```

## Balance Point

**Problem:** Given an array, you need to find a balance point or balance index. An index is a balanced index if the element in the left of it and elements in the right of it have the same sum.

**Solution:** Create two sets first and second. Sum all the elements from index 1 to size-1 in seconds. One by one add elements to the first set and remove them from the second set.
Time complexity is O(n)

**Example 5.95:**
```
public static int findBalancedPoint(int[] arr, int size) {
    int first = 0;
    int second = 0;
    for (int i = 1; i < size; i++)
        second += arr[i];

    for (int i = 0; i < size; i++) {
        if (first == second) {
            return i;
        }
        if (i < size - 1) {
            first += arr[i];
            second -= arr[i + 1];
        }
    }
    return -1;
}

// Testing code.
public static void main(String[] args)  {
    int[] arr = { -7, 1, 5, 2, -4, 3, 0 };
    System.out.println(findBalancedPoint(arr, arr.length));
}
```

**Output:**
```
3
```

## Find Floor and Ceil

**Problem:** Given a sorted array, you need to find the ceiling or floor of an input value. A Ceil is the value in an array that is just greater than the given input value. A floor is a value in an array that is just smaller than the given input value.

**Solution:** Since the array is sorted, the floor and ceiling can be found by binary search type algorithm. Time complexity will be O(log(n)) Using binary search we try to find the value if the value is found then it is floor and ceil both. If the value is not found, then we try to find the number which is just smaller than the given key for the floor. And will try to find the number which is just greater than the given key to find the ceil.

**Example 5.96:**
```
public static int findFloor(int arr[], int size, int value) {
    int start = 0;
    int stop = size - 1;
    int mid;
    while (start <= stop) {
        mid = (start + stop) / 2;
        /*
        * search value is equal to arr[mid] value.. search value is greater
```

```
         * than mid index value and less than mid+1 index value. value is greater
         * than arr[size-1] then floor is arr[size-1]
         */
        if (arr[mid] == value || (arr[mid] < value &&
                (mid == size - 1 || arr[mid + 1] > value)))
            return arr[mid];
        else if (arr[mid] < value)
            start = mid + 1;
        else
            stop = mid - 1;
    }
    return -1;
}

public static int findCeil(int arr[], int size, int value) {
    int start = 0;
    int stop = size - 1;
    int mid;

    while (start <= stop) {
        mid = (start + stop) / 2;
        /*
         * search value is equal to arr[mid] value.. search value is less than
           mid index value and greater than mid-1 index value. value is less than
           arr[0] then ceil is arr[0]
         */
        if (arr[mid] == value || (arr[mid] > value &&
                (mid == 0 || arr[mid - 1] < value)))
            return arr[mid];
        else if (arr[mid] < value)
            start = mid + 1;
        else
            stop = mid - 1;
    }
    return -1;
}

//Testing Code
public static void main(String[] args)  {
    int[] arr = { 2, 4, 8, 16 };
    System.out.println("Floor :  " + findFloor(arr, arr.length, 5));
    System.out.println("Ceil :  " + findCeil(arr, arr.length, 5));
}
```

**Output:**

```
Floor :  4
Ceil :  8
```

## Closest Number

**Problem:** Given a sorted array and a number. You need to find the element in the array which is closest to the given number.

**Solution:** Since the array is sorted, we can perform a binary search.

**Example 5.97:**
```
public static int closestNumber(int arr[], int size, int num) {
    int start = 0;
    int stop = size - 1;
    int output = -1;
    int minDist = Integer.MAX_VALUE;
    int mid;
    while (start <= stop) {
        mid = (start + stop) / 2;
        if (minDist > Math.abs(arr[mid] - num)) {
            minDist = Math.abs(arr[mid] - num);
            output = arr[mid];
        }

        if (arr[mid] == num)
            break;
        else if (arr[mid] > num)
            stop = mid - 1;
        else
            start = mid + 1;
    }
    return output;
}

//Testing Code
public static void main(String[] args)  {
    int[] arr = { 2, 4, 8, 16 };
    System.out.println(closestNumber(arr, arr.length, 9));
}
```

**Output:**
```
8
```

## Frequency Counts

**Problem:** Given an array of size N, which contain integers from 1 to N. Elements can appear any number of times. Print frequency of all elements in the array also print the frequency of the missing elements as 0

Input: [1, 2, 2, 2, 1]
Output: (1 : 2) (2 : 3)

**First solution:** Use a Hashtable to keep track of the value and its frequency. Traverse in the range and keep on printing the values.

**Example 5.98:**
```
public static void frequencyCounts(int[] arr, int size) {
    HashMap<Integer, Integer> hm = new HashMap<Integer, Integer>();
    for (int i = 0; i < size; i++) {
        if (hm.containsKey(arr[i])) {
            hm.put(arr[i], hm.get(arr[i]) + 1);
        } else {
            hm.put(arr[i], 1);
        }
    }
```

```
    for (Integer key : hm.keySet())
        System.out.print("(" + key + " : " + hm.get(key) + ") ");
}

// Testing code.
public static void main(String[] args)  {
    int[] arr = { 1, 2, 2, 2, 1 };
    frequencyCounts(arr, arr.length);
}
```

**Output:**

```
(1 : 2) (2 : 3)
```

**Second solution:** Using sorting, we can sort the array first, then we can traverse the array and print the element and its frequency.

**Example 5.99:**

```
public static void frequencyCounts2(int[] arr, int size) {
    Arrays.sort(arr);
    int count = 1;

    for (int i = 1; i < size; i++) {
        if (arr[i] == arr[i - 1])
            count++;
        else {
            System.out.print("(" + arr[i - 1] + " : " + count + ") ");
            count = 1;
        }
    }
    System.out.print("(" + arr[size - 1] + " : " + count + ") ");
}
```

**Third solution:** Using an auxiliary array, now since we have data in the range 1 to N, so an extra auxiliary array can be used to keep track of frequency. While traversing the input array, we found a value V then its corresponding index in the auxiliary array will be (V-1), since array indexing starts from 0.

**Example 5.100:**

```
public static void frequencyCounts3(int[] arr, int size) {
    int[] aux = new int[size + 1];
    for (int i = 0; i < size; i++) {
        aux[arr[i]] += 1;
    }
    for (int i = 0; i < size + 1; i++) {
        if (aux[i] > 0) {
            System.out.print("(" + i + " : " + aux[i] + ") ");
        }
    }
}
```

**Fourth solution:** Now solve this problem in linear time, without using any extra space. We have to look carefully to see if this problem provides us with extra information regarding the range of values from 1 to N.

Traverse the input array if we find a value V, its corresponding index value in the array is (V - 1). If the value at index (V-1) has a valid value in the range (1 to N), then we copy that value to our traversal index and then mark the value at index (V-1) as -1. If the value of the array at index (V-1) is not in range, then we decrease it by 1. Now we can print the absolute value to the output.

**Example 5.101:**
```
public static void frequencyCounts4(int[] arr, int size) {
    int index;
    for (int i = 0; i < size; i++) {
        while (arr[i] > 0) {
            index = arr[i] - 1;
            if (arr[index] > 0) {
                arr[i] = arr[index];
                arr[index] = -1;
            } else {
                arr[index] -= 1;
                arr[i] = 0;
            }
        }
    }
    for (int i = 0; i < size; i++)
        if (arr[i] != 0)
            System.out.print("(" + (i + 1) + " : " + Math.abs(arr[i]) + ") ");
}
```

## K Largest Elements

**Problem:** Given an array of integers of size N, you need to print k largest elements in the array in the order in which they appear in the array.

**First solution:** Sort the array and again find the kth largest element. Scan the array and print all the elements which have values greater than or equal to the kth largest element.

**Example 5.102:**
```
public static void kLargestElements(int arrIn[], int size, int k) {
    int[] arr = new int[size];
    for (int i = 0; i < size; i++)
        arr[i] = arrIn[i];

    Arrays.sort(arr);
    for (int i = 0; i < size; i++) {
        if (arrIn[i] >= arr[size - k]) {
            System.out.print(arrIn[i] + " ");
        }
    }
}

// Testing code.
public static void main(String[] args)  {
    int[] arr = { 10, 50, 30, 60, 15 };
    kLargestElements(arr, arr.length, 2);
}
```

**Output:**
```
50 60
```

**Second solution:**
First, copy the array into another array. Then using quick-select find the Kth elements in the array. Then scan the original array and print all the elements which have values greater than or equal to k. O(N) for quick-select and O(N) for a scan.

**Example 5.103:**
```
public static void kLargestElements2(int arrIn[], int size, int k) {
    int[] arr = new int[size];
    for (int i = 0; i < size; i++)
        arr[i] = arrIn[i];

    quickSelectUtil(arr, 0, size - 1, size - k);
    for (int i = 0; i < size; i++) {
        if (arrIn[i] >= arr[size - k]) {
            System.out.print(arrIn[i] + " ");
        }
    }
}
```

**Note**: Quick Select algorithms, closely related to quick sort, both of these algorithms we had seen in the sorting chapter.

**Note**: There is a catch in the above solutions. The number of values printed may be more than K so make sure they are exactly k.

## Fix Point

**Problem:** Given a sorted array of integers, you need to find the fix point. Fix point is an index of an array in which the index and value are the same.

**First solution:** Brute force approach, traverse the array to find a fixed point. Time complexity is O(n)

**Example 5.104 : linear search method**
```
public static int fixPoint(int[] arr, int size) {
    for (int i = 0; i < size; i++) {
        if (arr[i] == i)
            return i;
    }
    return -1; /* fix point not found so return invalid index */
}

// Testing code.
public static void main(String[] args)  {
    int[] arr = { -10, -2, 0, 3, 11, 12, 35, 51, 200 };
    System.out.println(fixPoint(arr, arr.length));
}
```

**Output:**
```
3
```

**Second solution:** Since the array is sorted, we should think about a binary sort algorithm.

**Example 5.105** : Binary search method

```
public static int fixPoint2(int[] arr, int size) {
    int low = 0;
    int high = size - 1;
    int mid;

    while (low <= high) {
        mid = (low + high) / 2;
        if (arr[mid] == mid)
            return mid;
        else if (arr[mid] < mid)
            low = mid + 1;
        else
            high = mid - 1;
    }

    return -1; /* fix point not found so return invalid index */
}
```

## Subarray Sums

**Problem:** Given an array of positive integers, you need to find if there is some range in the array such that if we add all the elements in that range, then it becomes equal to the given value.

**Solution**: We will keep two indexes start and end indicating the start and end of the subarray whose sum we will compare with the given value. If the subarray sum is larger than the given value, then we will ignore the first element pointed by the start index. If the subarray sum is smaller than the given value, then we will include one more element to it.

**Example 5.106:**

```
public static void subArraySums(int arr[], int size, int value) {
    int start = 0, end = 0, sum = 0;

    while (start < size && end < size) {
        if (sum < value) {
            sum += arr[end];
            end += 1;
        } else {
            sum -= arr[start];
            start += 1;
        }

        if (sum == value) {
            System.out.print("(" + start + " to " + (end - 1) + ") ");
        }
    }
}

//Testing Code
public static void main(String[] args)  {
    int[] arr = { 15, 5, 5, 20, 10, 5, 5, 20, 10, 10 };
    subArraySums(arr, arr.length, 20);
}
```

**Output:**
```
(0 to 1) (3 to 3) (4 to 6) (7 to 7) (8 to 9)
```

**Time complexity:** O(n)

## Maximum contiguous subarray sum

**Problem:** Given an array of positive and negative integers, find the contiguous subarray whose sum is maximum..

**Solution: Kadane's Algorithm,** traverse the array and keep track of the sum of all positive contiguous segments of the array. For each element, we will find if adding this element to the subarray sum will give a positive or a negative value. If the subarray sum becomes negative, then we will ignore this element and make the subarray sum 0. Repeat this process till all the elements are observed. We will keep track of the maximum and finally return it.

**Example 5.107:** find maximum contiguous subarray sum.
```
public static int maxConSub(int[] arr, int size) {
    int currMax = 0, maximum = 0;
    for (int i = 0; i < size; i++) {
        currMax += arr[i];
        if (currMax < 0)
            currMax = 0;
        if (maximum < currMax)
            maximum = currMax;
    }
    System.out.println(maximum);
    return maximum;
}

// Testing code.
public static void main(String[] args)  {
    int[] arr = { 1, 2, -3, 4, 5, -10, 6, 7 };
    maxConSub(arr, arr.length);
}
```

**Output:**
```
13
```

## Maximum contiguous subarray sum (A-B)

**Problem:** Given an array A of integers and an array B of integers, find the maximum contiguous subarray in A, such that it does not contain elements in B.

**First Solution: Kadane's Algorithm** is modified by using a HashTable to solve this problem. All the elements of B in the hashtable and while making the sub-array keep track that those values are not in the hash-table.

**Example 5.108:**
```
public static int maxConSubArr(int[] A, int sizeA, int[] B, int sizeB) {
    int currMax = 0;
    int maximum = 0;
    HashSet<Integer> hs = new HashSet<Integer>();
```

```
    for (int i = 0; i < sizeB; i++)
        hs.add(B[i]);

    for (int i = 0; i < sizeA; i++)
        if (hs.contains(A[i]))
            currMax = 0;
        else {
            currMax = currMax + A[i];
            if (currMax < 0)
                currMax = 0;
            if (maximum < currMax)
                maximum = currMax;
        }

    System.out.println(maximum);
    return maximum;
}

// Testing code.
public static void main(String[] args)  {
    int[] arr2 = { 1, 2, 3, 4, 5, -10, 6, 7, 3 };
    int[] arr3 = { 1, 3 };
    maxConSubArr(arr2, arr2.length, arr3, arr3.length);
}
```

**Output:**

```
13
```

**Time complexity:** O(M + N).

**Second Solution:** Sort array B. Binary search is used to find if some element is present in B.

**Example 5.109:**

```
public static int maxConSubArr2(int A[], int sizeA, int B[], int sizeB) {
    Arrays.sort(B);
    int currMax = 0;
    int maximum = 0;

    for (int i = 0; i < sizeA; i++) {
        if (binarySearch(B, sizeB, A[i]))
            currMax = 0;
        else {
            currMax = currMax + A[i];
            if (currMax < 0)
                currMax = 0;
            if (maximum < currMax)
                maximum = currMax;
        }
    }
    System.out.println(maximum);
    return maximum;
}
```

**Time complexity:** O(MlogM + NlogM) For sorting and then for searching each element.

## Rain Water

**Problem:** Given an array of N non-negative integers. Each element of the array represents a bar of histogram. Considering that each bar is one unit wide. You need to find how much water can be accommodated in the structure.

For example: [4, 0, 1, 5] will contain 7 units of water.

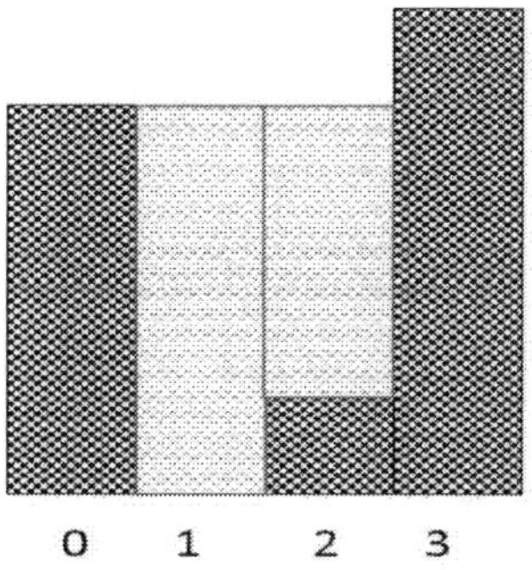


**Solution:** This problem can be solved very easily if we can find how much water a particular bar of unit width can contain. Water contained at $i^{th}$ index = minimum (maximum length in left, maximum length in right) – length $i^{th}$ bar.

**Example 5.110:**
```
public static int rainWater(int[] arr, int size) {
    int[] leftHigh = new int[size];
    int[] rightHigh = new int[size];

    int max = arr[0];
    leftHigh[0] = arr[0];
    for (int i = 1; i < size; i++) {
        if (max < arr[i])
            max = arr[i];
        leftHigh[i] = max;
    }

    max = arr[size - 1];
    rightHigh[size - 1] = arr[size - 1];
    for (int i = (size - 2); i >= 0; i--) {
        if (max < arr[i])
            max = arr[i];
        rightHigh[i] = max;
    }

    int water = 0;
    for (int i = 0; i < size; i++)
        water += Math.min(leftHigh[i], rightHigh[i]) - arr[i];

    System.out.println("Water : " + water);
    return water;
}

// Testing code.
public static void main(String[] args)  {
    int[] arr = { 0, 1, 0, 2, 1, 0, 1, 3, 2, 1, 2, 1 };
    rainWater(arr, arr.length);
}
```

**Output:**
```
Water: 6
```

**Time complexity:** O(N)

Further optimization on the above problem in a single iteration, the water is calculated along with leftMax and rightMax calculation.

**Example 5.111:**
```
public static int rainWater2(int[] arr, int size) {
    int water = 0;
    int leftMax = 0, rightMax = 0;
    int left = 0;
    int right = size - 1;

    while (left <= right) {
        if (arr[left] < arr[right]) {
            if (arr[left] > leftMax)
                leftMax = arr[left];
            else
                water += leftMax - arr[left];
            left += 1;
        } else {
            if (arr[right] > rightMax)
                rightMax = arr[right];
            else
                water += rightMax - arr[right];
            right -= 1;
        }
    }

    System.out.println("Water : " + water);
    return water;
}
```

## Array Index Max Diff

**Problem:** Given an array arr[], find maximum distance of index j and i, such that arr[j] > arr[i]

**First solution:** Brute force, for each index call it i find index j such that arr[j] > arr[i]. We will need two loops, one to select index i and another to traverse index i+1 to the size of the array.

**Example 5.112:**
```
public static int arrayIndexMaxDiff(int[] arr, int size) {
    int maxDiff = -1;
    int j;
    for (int i = 0; i < size; i++) {
        j = size - 1;
        while (i < j) {
            if (arr[i] <= arr[j]) {
                maxDiff = Math.max(maxDiff, j - i);
                break;
            }
```

```
            j -= 1;
        }
    }
    return maxDiff;
}

// Testing code.
public static void main(String[] args)  {
    int[] arr = { 33, 9, 10, 3, 2, 60, 30, 33, 1 };
    System.out.println("ArrayIndexMaxDiff : " + arrayIndexMaxDiff(arr, 
arr.length));
}
```

**Output:**

```
ArrayIndexMaxDiff : 7
```

**Time Complexity:** O(n^2), **Space Complexity:** O(1).

**Second solution:** Pre-processing and creating an auxiliary array. Array rightMax[] will store the maximum value to the right of the given index. Start traversing the input arrays arr[] for each index i we try to find the maximum value of index j such arr[i] <= rightMax[j]. For all values of i and j, till arr[i] <= rightMax[j] we will increase the value of j. When arr[i] > rightMax[j] then increases the value of i since we will not get any other solution from the current position of i. Also, with the increase in the value of i, we don't need to reconsider the value of j less than the current value of j as we are searching for a better solution. If some better solution exists, then it must be with some bigger value of j. In each iteration, either i is increasing or j is increasing, so we will get a solution in linear time.

**Example 5.113:**

```
public static int arrayIndexMaxDiff2(int arr[], int size) {
    int[] rightMax = new int[size];
    rightMax[size - 1] = arr[size - 1];

    for (int i = size - 2; i >= 0; i--)
        rightMax[i] = Math.max(rightMax[i + 1], arr[i]);

    int maxDiff = -1;
    for(int i=0, j=1; i < size && j < size;) {
        if (arr[i] <= rightMax[j]) {
            if(i < j)
                maxDiff = Math.max(maxDiff, j - i);
            j = j + 1;
        } else {
            i = i + 1;
        }
    }

    return maxDiff;
}
```

**Time Complexity:** O(n), **Space Complexity:** O(n).

## Find the largest sum contiguous subarray.

**Problem:** Given an array of positive and negative integers, find a contiguous sub-array. Whose sum (sum of elements) is maximum.

**Example 5.114:**
```
public static int maxSubArraySum(int[] a, int size) {
    int maxSoFar = 0, maxEndingHere = 0;

    for (int i = 0; i < size; i++) {
        maxEndingHere = maxEndingHere + a[i];
        if (maxEndingHere < 0) {
            maxEndingHere = 0;
        }

        if (maxSoFar < maxEndingHere) {
            maxSoFar = maxEndingHere;
        }
    }

    return maxSoFar;
}

// Testing code.
public static void main(String[] args)  {
    int[] arr = { 1, -2, 3, 4, -4, 6, -4, 3, 2 };
    System.out.println("Max sub array sum :" + maxSubArraySum(arr, 9));
}
```

**Output:**
```
Max sub array sum :10
```

**Analysis:**
1. Maximum subarray in an Array is found in a single scan. We keep track of the global maximum sum so far and the maximum sum, which include the current element.
2. When we find that the global maximum value so far is less than the maximum value containing the current value, we update the global maximum value.
3. Finally, return the global maximum value.
4. Time complexity is O(n).

## Max Path Sum

**Problem:** Given two arrays in increasing order, you need to find the maximum sum by choosing a few consecutive elements from one array then a few elements from another array. The element switching can happen at transition points only when the element value is the same in both arrays.
arr1 = [12, 13, **18**, 20, 22, **26**, 70]
arr2 = [11, 15, **18**, 19, 20, **26**, 30, 31]
Max Sum elements: 11, 15, 18, 19, 20, 22, 26, 70
Max Sum: 201

**Solution**: We will traverse both the array arr1[] and arr2[] using index variables i and j respectively. We will store the sum of arr1[] elements in the sum1 variable and store the sum of arr2[] elements in sum2 till we reach the transition point. At the transition point, we will keep the bigger value among sum1 and sum2 and add it to the final result. At the transition point, both sum1 and sum2 are reset to 0. We will follow this process till both the arrays are traversed completely.

**Example 5.115:**
```
public static int maxPathSum(int[] arr1, int size1, int[] arr2, int size2) {
    int i = 0, j = 0, result = 0, sum1 = 0, sum2 = 0;
    while (i < size1 && j < size2) {
        if (arr1[i] < arr2[j]) {
            sum1 += arr1[i];
            i += 1;
        } else if (arr1[i] > arr2[j]) {
            sum2 += arr2[j];
            j += 1;
        } else {
            result += Math.max(sum1, sum2);
            result = result + arr1[i];
            sum1 = 0;
            sum2 = 0;
            i += 1;
            j += 1;
        }
    }

    while (i < size1) {
        sum1 += arr1[i];
        i += 1;
    }

    while (j < size2) {
        sum2 += arr2[j];
        j += 1;
    }

    result += Math.max(sum1, sum2);
    return result;
}

// Testing code.
public static void main(String[] args)  {
    int[] arr1 = { 12, 13, 18, 20, 22, 26, 70 };
    int[] arr2 = { 11, 15, 18, 19, 20, 26, 30, 31 };
    System.out.println("Max Path Sum:: " + maxPathSum(arr1, arr1.length, arr2, 
arr2.length));
}
```

**Output:**
```
Max Path Sum:: 201
```

**Time Complexity:** O(n), **Space Complexity:** O(n).

## Exercise

1. In a given list of n elements, write an algorithm to find three elements in an array whose sum is a given value.

Hint: Try to do this problem using a brute force approach. Then try to apply the sorting approach along with a brute force approach. Time Complexity is O(n^2)

2. In a given list of –ve and +ve numbers, write a program to separate –ve numbers from the +ve numbers.

3. In a given list of 1's and 0's, write a program to separate 0's from 1's.

4. In a given list of 0's, 1's and 2's, write a program to separate 0's, 1's and 2's.

5. In a given list whose elements are monotonically increasing with both negative and positive numbers. Write an algorithm to find the point at which the list becomes positive.

6. In a sorted list, find a number. If found then return the index if not found then insert it into the array.

7. Find max and min in the sorted & rotated list.

8. Find kth Smallest Element in the Union of Two Sorted Lists

9. Find the 2nd largest number in an array with minimum comparisons. Suppose you are given an unsorted list of n distinct elements. How will you identify the second-largest element with the minimum number of comparisons?

10.

Hint:

- First solution: Find the largest element in the array. Then replace the last element with the largest element. Then search the second-largest element in the remaining n-1 elements.
  The total number of comparisons is: (n-1) + (n-2)
- Second solution: Sort the array and then give the (n-1) element. This approach is still more inefficient.
- Third solution: Using priority queue / Heap; in this approach, we will study the heap chapter. Use the buildHeap() function to build a heap from the array. This is done in n comparisons. Arr[0] is the largest number, and the greater among arr[1] and arr[2] is the second largest.
- The total number of comparisons are: (n-1) + 1 = n

11. In a given list of n elements, we need to find the first repeated element. Which of the following methods will work for us? If a method works, then implement it.

12.

Hint: When the order in which elements appear in input is important, we cannot use sorting.

- Brute force exhaustive search.
- Use Hash-Table to keep an index of the elements and use the second scan to find the element.
- Sorting the elements.
- If we know the range of the element then we can use counting techniques.

# CHAPTER 6: LINKED LIST

## Introduction

Let us suppose we have an array that contains the following five elements 1, 2, 4, 5, 6. We want to insert a new element with the value "3" in-between "2" and "4". In the array, we cannot do it so easily. We need to create another array that is long enough to store the current values and one more space for "3". Then we need to copy these elements in the new space. This copy operation is inefficient. To remove this inefficiency in addition, a new data linked list is used.

## Linked List

The linked list is a list of items, called nodes. Nodes have two parts, the value part and the link part. The value part is used to store the data. The value part of the node can be a basic data type as an integer, or it can be some other data type like a structure. The link part is a pointer, which is used to store the addresses of the next element in the list.

Linked list node

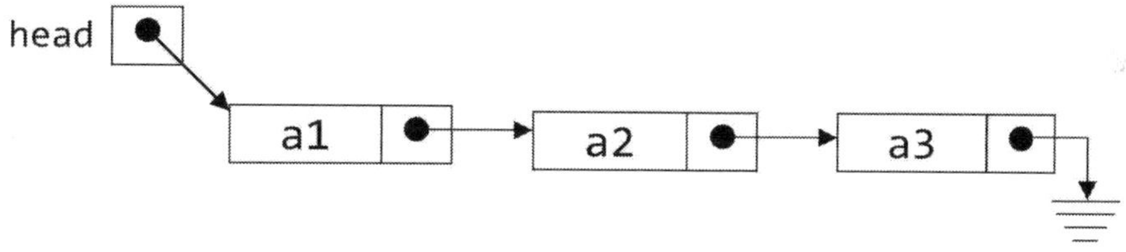


Linked list

The various parts of the linked list:

1 **Head**: Head is a pointer that holds the address of the first node in the linked list.

2 **Nodes**: Items in the linked list are called nodes.

3 **Value**: The data that is stored in each node of the linked list.

4 **Link**: The link part of the node is used to store the reference of another node. We will use "next" and "prev" to store addresses of next or previous nodes.

## Types of Linked list

There are different types of linked lists. The main difference among them is how their nodes are connected. We will discuss singly linked list, doubly linked list, circular linked list and doubly circular linked list.

## Singly Linked List

A singly linked list is made up of nodes. Each node has two parts, the first part is the data and the second part is the link that has a reference to the next node in the linked list. The link portion of the last node contains the value null. The beginning of the list is called “Head” which points to the first node of the linked list.

**Note**: In a singly linked list we can only traverse in a single direction as each node has reference to the next node.

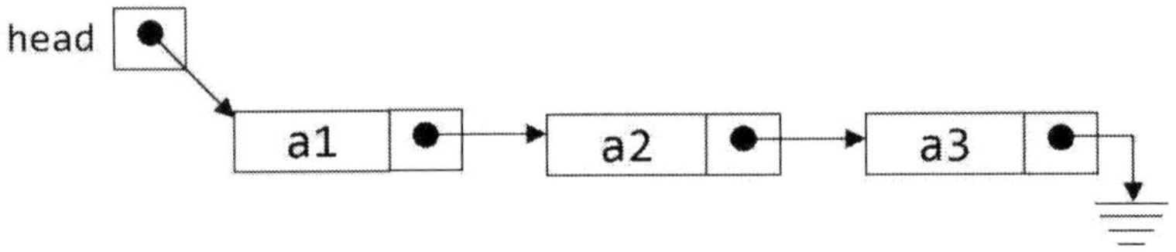


Let us look at the Node. The Value part of the node is of type integer, but it can be some other data type. The link part of the node is named as Link in the below diagram.

**Example 6.1**: Singly Linked List class

```
public class LinkedList {
    private static class Node {
        private int value;
        private Node next;

        public Node(int v, Node n) {
            value = v;
            next = n;
        }
    }

    private Node head;
    private int size = 0;

    public int size() {
        return size;
    }

    public boolean isEmpty() {
        return size == 0;
    }

    public int peek() throws IllegalStateException {
        if (isEmpty())
            throw new IllegalStateException("EmptyListException");
        return head.value;
    }
    // Other Methods.
}
```

The various basic operations that we can perform on linked lists:

1. Insert an element in the list, this operation is used to create a linked list.
2. Print various elements of the list.
3. Search for an element in the list.
4. Delete an element from the list.
5. Reverse a linked list.

For a singly linked list, we should always test these three test cases:

1. Zero element / Empty linked list.
2. One element / Single node case.
3. General case.

One node and zero node cases are used to test boundary cases. It is always mandatory to take care of these cases before submitting code.

## Insert element in a linked list

An element can be inserted into a linked list in various orders. Some example cases are mentioned below:

1 Insertion of an element at the start of linked list
2 Insertion of an element at the end of linked list
3 Insertion of an element at the Nth position in a linked list
4 Insert element in sorted order in a linked list

## Insert an element at the Head

**Problem**: Insert an element at the start of the linked list.

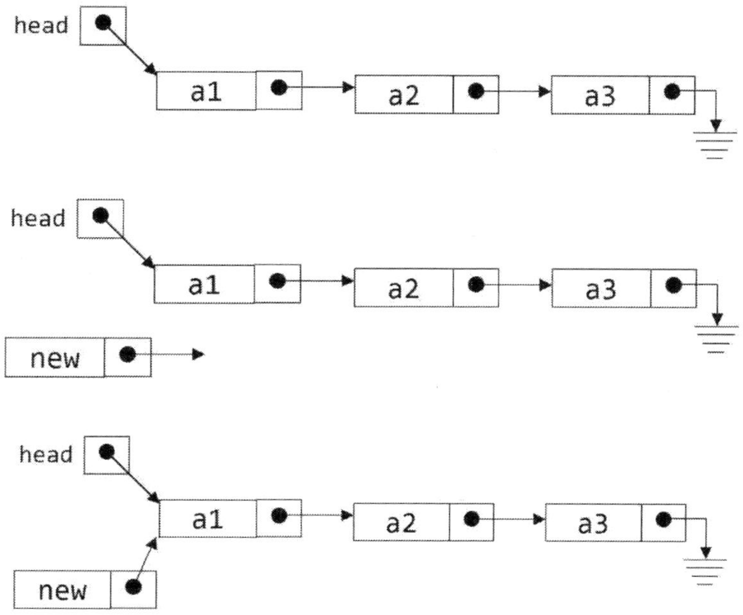

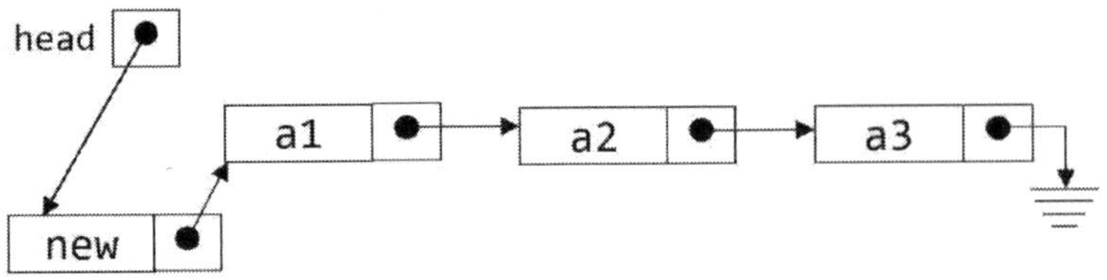


**Example 6.2:**

```
public void addHead(int value) {
    head = new Node(value, head);
    size++;
}
```

**Analysis:**

1. We need to create a new node with the value passed to the function as an argument.
2. The next pointer of the new node will point to the head of the linked list or null in case the list is empty.
3. The newly created node will become the head of the linked list.

**Time Complexity**: O(1).

## Insertion of an element at the end

**Problem**: Insertion of an element at the end of linked list

**Example 6.3:**

```
public void addTail(int value) {
    Node newNode = new Node(value, null);
    Node curr = head;

    if (head == null) {
        head = newNode;
    }

    while (curr.next != null) {
        curr = curr.next;
    }
    curr.next = newNode;
}
```

**Analysis:**

1. A new node is created, and the value is stored inside it and stores the null value to its next pointer.
2. If the list is empty, then this new node will become the head of the linked list.
3. If the list is not empty, then we must traverse to the end of the list.
4. Finally, a new node is added to the end of the list.

**Time Complexity**: O(n).

**Note**: This operation is inefficient as each time you want to insert an element you have to traverse to the end of the list. Therefore, the complexity of the creation of the list is O(n^2). So to make it efficient, we must keep track of the last element by keeping a tail pointer. Therefore, if it is required to insert an element at the end of the linked list, then we will keep track of the tail reference also.

## Traversing Linked List

**Problem**: Print various elements of a linked list

**Example 6.4:**
```
public void print() {
    Node temp = head;
    while (temp != null) {
        System.out.print(temp.value + " ");
        temp = temp.next;
    }
    System.out.println();
}
```

**Analysis**: We will traverse the list and print the value stored in nodes. The list is traversed by making head pointing to its next.

**Time Complexity**: O(n).

## Testing code for list creation and printing the list.

**Example 6.5**: Test code for linked list creation, adding value at head and printing elements.
```
public static void main(String[] args)  {
    LinkedList ll = new LinkedList();
    ll.addHead(1);
    ll.addHead(2);
    ll.addHead(3);
    ll.print();
    System.out.println("Size : " + ll.size());
    System.out.println("Is empty : " + ll.isEmpty());
    System.out.println("Peek : " + ll.peek());
}
```

**Output:**
```
3 2 1
Size : 3
Is empty : false
Peek : 3
```

**Analysis:**

- A new instance of the linked list is created. Elements are added to the start of the list by calling the addHead() function.
- Finally, all the content of the list is printed to screen by calling the print() function.

## Sorted Insert

**Problem**: Insert an element in sorted order in the linked list given head pointer

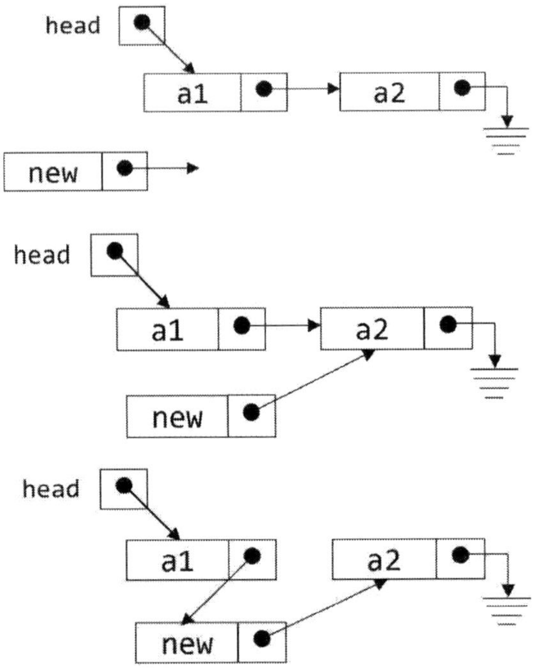


**Example 6.6:**

```
public void sortedInsert(int value) {
    Node newNode = new Node(value, null);
    Node curr = head;

    if (curr == null || curr.value > value) {
        newNode.next = head;
        head = newNode;
        return;
    }
    while (curr.next != null && curr.next.value < value) {
        curr = curr.next;
    }

    newNode.next = curr.next;
    curr.next = newNode;
}

// Testing code.
public static void main(String[] args) {
    LinkedList ll = new LinkedList();
    ll.sortedInsert(1);
    ll.sortedInsert(2);
    ll.sortedInsert(3);
    ll.sortedInsert(1);
    ll.sortedInsert(2);
    ll.sortedInsert(3);
    ll.print();
}
```

**Output:**

```
1 1 2 2 3 3
```

**Analysis:**

1. A new empty node of the linked list is created. And initialised by storing an argument value into its value. Next of the node will point to null.
2. If the list is empty or if the value stored in the first node is greater than the newly created node value. Then this newly created node will be added to the start of the list. And the head needs to be modified.
3. In all other cases, we iterate through the list to find the proper position where the node can be inserted to keep the list sorted.
4. Finally, the node will be added to the list.

**Time Complexity**: O(n).

## Search Element in a Linked-List

**Problem**: Search element in a linked list. Given a head pointer and value. Returns 1 if the value found in the list, else returns 0.

**Example 6.7:**

```
public boolean search(int data) {
    Node temp = head;
    while (temp != null) {
        if (temp.value == data)
            return true;
        temp = temp.next;
    }
    return false;
}
```

**Analysis:**

1. We will iterate through the list using a loop.
2. The value of each element of the list is compared with the given value. If a value is found, then the function will return true.
3. If the value is not found, then false will be returned from the function in the end.

**Time Complexity**: O(n).

**Note**: Search in a single linked list can only be done in one direction. Since all elements in the list have reference to the next item in the list. Therefore, the traversal of linked lists is linear.

## Delete the First element in a linked list.

**Problem**: Delete element at the head of the linked list.

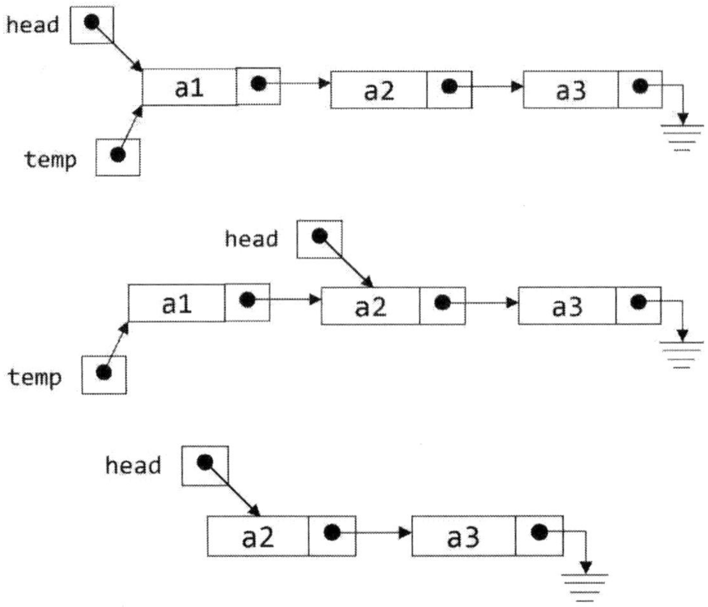


**Example 6.8:**

```
public int removeHead() throws IllegalStateException {
    if (isEmpty())
        throw new IllegalStateException("EmptyListException");

    int value = head.value;
    head = head.next;
    size--;
    return value;
}
```

**Analysis:**

- First, we need to check if the list is already empty. If empty, then return.
- If the list is not empty, then the head of the list will store the reference of the next node of the current head.

**Time Complexity**: O(1).

## Delete a node from the linked list given its value.

**Problem**: Delete the first node whose value is equal to the given value.

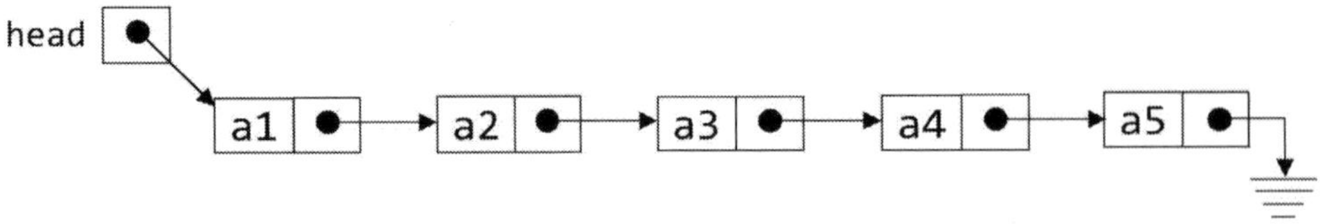

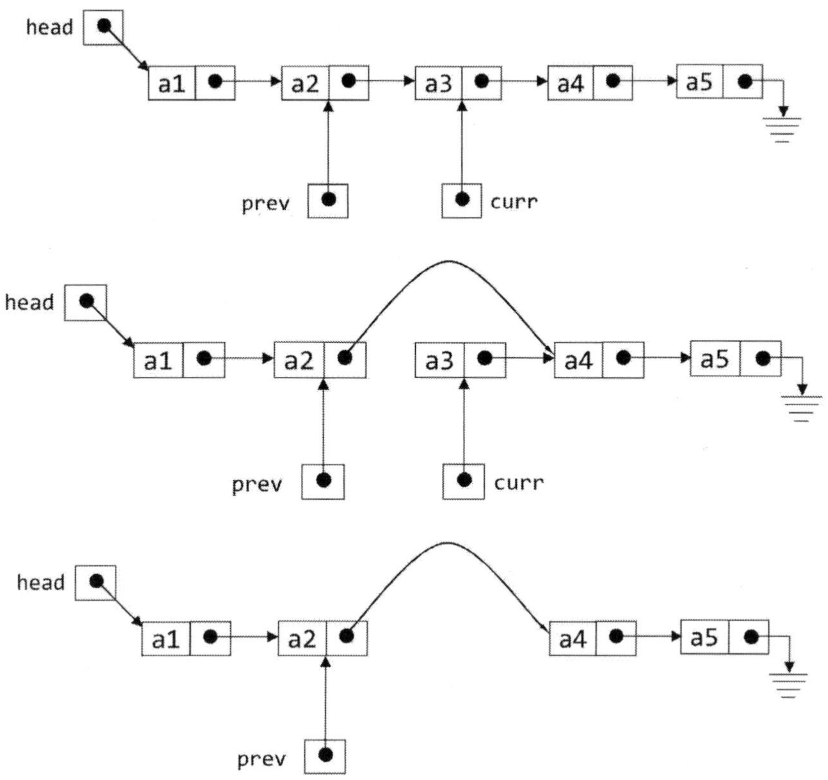


**Example 6.9:**

```
public boolean deleteNode(int delValue) {
    Node temp = head;
    if (isEmpty())
        return false;
    if (delValue == head.value) {
        head = head.next;
        size--;
        return true;
    }
    while (temp.next != null) {
        if (temp.next.value == delValue) {
            temp.next = temp.next.next;
            size--;
            return true;
        }
        temp = temp.next;
    }
    return false;
}

// Testing code.
public static void main(String[] args) {
    LinkedList ll = new LinkedList();
    ll.addHead(1);
    ll.addHead(2);
    ll.addHead(1);
    ll.addHead(2);
    ll.addHead(1);
    ll.addHead(3);
    ll.print();
```

```
    System.out.println("deleteNode : " + ll.deleteNode(2));
    ll.print();
}
```

**Output:**

```
3 1 2 1 2 1
deleteNode : true
3 1 1 2 1
```

**Analysis:**

1. There are two cases, the first case when the node that needs to be deleted is the first node and the second case when the node that needs to be deleted is not the first node in the list. When the node that needs to be deleted is the first node, then the head of the linked list will be modified. In other cases, it will not modify.
2. First, we check if the first node is the node with the value we are searching for, then the head of the list will point to the next reference of the current head.
3. In other cases, we will traverse the link list using a while loop and try to find the node that needs to be deleted. If the node is found then, we will point its previous node next points to the node next to the node we want to remove.

**Time Complexity**: O(n).

## Delete all occurrences of a particular value in the linked list.

**Problem**: Delete all the nodes whose value is equal to the given value.

**Example 6.10:**

```
public boolean deleteNodes(int delValue) {
    Node currNode = head;
    Node nextNode;
    boolean found = false;
    while (currNode != null && currNode.value == delValue) {  /* first node */
        head = currNode.next;
        currNode = head;
        found = true;
    }

    while (currNode != null) {
        nextNode = currNode.next;
        if (nextNode != null && nextNode.value == delValue) {
            currNode.next = nextNode.next;
            found = true;
        } else {
            currNode = nextNode;
        }
    }

    return found;
}
```

```
// Testing code.
public static void main(String[] args) {
    LinkedList ll = new LinkedList();
    ll.addHead(1);
    ll.addHead(2);
    ll.addHead(1);
    ll.addHead(1);
    ll.addHead(3);
    ll.print();
    System.out.println("deleteNodes : " + ll.deleteNodes(1));
    ll.print();
}
```

**Output:**

```
3 1 1 2 1
deleteNodes : true
3 2
```

**Analysis:**

- In the first while loop, we will remove all the nodes that are at the front of the list, which have values equal to the value we want to delete. In this, we need to update the head of the list.
- In the second while loop, we will remove all the nodes that are not at the beginning of the list and have a value equal to the value we want to delete. Remember that we are not returning; we traverse till the end of the list.

**Time Complexity**: O(n).

## Delete a single linked list

**Problem**: Given a linked list, delete all the elements of list.

**Example 6.11:**

```
public void deleteList() {
    head = null;
    size = 0;
}
```

**Analysis**: We just need to mark the head of the list as null. The list nodes will be freed by the garbage collector. Also set the size of list as 0.

**Time Complexity**: O(n).

## Reverse a linked list.

**Problem**: Reverse a singly linked List iteratively using three Pointers

**Example 6.12:**

```
public void reverse() {
    Node curr = head;
    Node prev = null;
    Node next = null;

    while (curr != null) {
        next = curr.next;
        curr.next = prev;
        prev = curr;
        curr = next;
    }
    head = prev;
}

// Testing code.
public static void main(String[] args) {
    LinkedList ll = new LinkedList();
    ll.addHead(1);
    ll.addHead(2);
    ll.addHead(3);
    ll.print();
    ll.reverse();
    ll.print();
}
```

**Output:**

```
3 2 1
1 2 3
```

**Analysis**: The list is iterated. Make the next variable point to the next of the current node. Make the next of the current node point to the previous node. Make prev as the current node and curr as the next node.

**Time Complexity**: O(n).

## Recursively Reverse a singly linked list

**Problem:** Reverse a singly linked list using Recursion.

**Example 6.13:**

```
public Node reverseRecurseUtil(Node currentNode, Node nextNode) {
    Node ret;
    if (currentNode == null)
        return null;

    if (currentNode.next == null) {
        currentNode.next = nextNode;
        return currentNode;
    }

    ret = reverseRecurseUtil(currentNode.next, currentNode);
```

```
    currentNode.next = nextNode;
    return ret;
}

public void reverseRecurse() {
    head = reverseRecurseUtil(head, null);
}
```

**Analysis:**

1. ReverseRecurse() function will call a reverseRecurseUtil() function to reverse the list and the pointer returned by the reverseRecurseUtil will be the head of the reversed list.
2. The current node will point to the nextNode that is the previous node of the old list.

**Time Complexity:** O(n).

**Note**: A linked list can be reversed using two solutions, the First solution is by using three-pointers. The Second solution is using recursion; both are linear solutions, but a three-pointer solution is more efficient.

## Remove duplicates from the linked list

**Problem:** Remove duplicate values from the linked list. The linked list is sorted, and it contains some duplicate values, you need to remove those duplicate values. (You can create the required linked list using SortedInsert() function)

**Example 6.14:**

```
public void removeDuplicate() {
    Node curr = head;
    while (curr != null) {
        if (curr.next != null && curr.value == curr.next.value) {
            curr.next = curr.next.next;
        } else {
            curr = curr.next;
        }
    }
}

// Testing code.
public static void main(String[] args) {
    LinkedList ll = new LinkedList();
    ll.sortedInsert(1);
    ll.sortedInsert(2);
    ll.sortedInsert(3);
    ll.sortedInsert(1);
    ll.sortedInsert(2);
    ll.sortedInsert(3);
    ll.print();
    ll.removeDuplicate();;
    ll.print();
}
```

**Output:**

```
1 1 2 2 3 3
1 2 3
```

**Analysis:** Traverse the list, if there is a node whose value is equal to its next node's value, then the current node next will point to the next of next node. The whole list is processed, and the repeated values are removed from the list.

**Time Complexity:** O(n).

## Copy List Reversed

**Problem:** Copy the content of the linked list in another linked list in reverse order. If the original linked list contains elements in order 1,2,3,4, the new list should contain the elements in order 4,3,2,1.

**Example 6.15:**
```
public LinkedList copyListReversed() {
    Node tempNode = null;
    Node tempNode2 = null;
    Node curr = head;
    while (curr != null) {
        tempNode2 = new Node(curr.value, tempNode);
        curr = curr.next;
        tempNode = tempNode2;
    }
    LinkedList ll2 = new LinkedList();
    ll2.head = tempNode;
    return ll2;
}

// Testing code.
public static void main(String[] args) {
    LinkedList ll = new LinkedList();
    ll.addHead(1);
    ll.addHead(2);
    ll.addHead(3);
    ll.print();
    LinkedList l3 = ll.copyListReversed();
    l3.print();
}
```

**Output:**
```
3 2 1
1 2 3
```

**Analysis**: Traverse the list and add the node value to the head of the new list. Since the list is traversed in the forward direction and each node is added to the head of the new list, the new list is formed in reverse of the original list.

**Time Complexity**: O(n).

## Copy the content of the given linked list into another linked list

**Problem**: Copy the content of the given linked list into another linked list. If the original linked list contains elements in order 1,2,3,4, the new list should contain the elements in order 1,2,3,4.

**Example 6.16:**

```
public LinkedList copyList() {
    Node headNode = null;
    Node tailNode = null;
    Node tempNode = null;
    Node curr = head;

    if (curr == null)
        return null;

    headNode = new Node(curr.value, null);
    tailNode = headNode;
    curr = curr.next;

    while (curr != null) {
        tempNode = new Node(curr.value, null);
        tailNode.next = tempNode;
        tailNode = tempNode;
        curr = curr.next;
    }
    LinkedList ll2 = new LinkedList();
    ll2.head = headNode;
    return ll2;
}

// Testing code.
public static void main(String[] args) {
    LinkedList ll = new LinkedList();
    ll.addHead(1);
    ll.addHead(2);
    ll.addHead(3);
    ll.print();
    LinkedList l2 = ll.copyList();
    l2.print();
}
```

**Output:**

```
3 2 1
3 2 1
```

**Analysis**: Traverse the list and add the node's value to the new list, but this time always at the end of the list. Another pointer tailNode is used to keep track of the end of the list. Since the list is traversed in the forward direction and each node's value is added to the end of the new list. Therefore, the formed list is the same as the given list.

**Time Complexity**: O(n).

## Compare List

**Problem**: Compare the values of two linked lists given their head pointers.

**Example 6.17**: Recursive Solution

```
public boolean compareList(LinkedList ll) {
    return compareList(head, ll.head);
}

public boolean compareList(Node head1, Node head2) {
    if (head1 == null && head2 == null)
        return true;
    else if ((head1 == null) || (head2 == null) || (head1.value != head2.value))
        return false;
    else
        return compareList(head1.next, head2.next);
}

// Testing code.
public static void main(String[] args) {
    LinkedList ll = new LinkedList();
    ll.addHead(1);
    ll.addHead(2);
    ll.addHead(3);
    ll.print();
    LinkedList l2 = ll.copyList();
    l2.print();
    System.out.println("compareList: " + ll.compareList(l2));
}
```

**Output:**

```
3 2 1
3 2 1
compareList: true
```

**Analysis:**

1. The list is compared recursively. Moreover, if we reach the end of the list and both the lists are null. Then both the lists are equal and so return true.
2. The list is compared recursively. If either one of the lists is empty or the value of corresponding nodes is unequal, then the lists are not equal and the compareList() function will return false.
3. Recursively calls a compare list function for the next node of the current nodes.

**Example 6.18**: Iterative Solution

```
public boolean compareList2(LinkedList ll2) {
    Node head1 = head;
    Node head2 = ll2.head;
    while (head1 != null && head2 != null) {
        if (head1.value != head2.value)
            return false;
        head1 = head1.next;
        head2 = head2.next;
    }
    if (head1 == null && head2 == null)
        return true;
    return false;
}
```

**Analysis:**

1. Traverse both the list in a loop and at any point if the values of both the nodes of the list are not equal then return false that they are not equal lists.
2. If in the end, both the lists are completely traversed then return true else return false if any one of them have some untraversed elements.

**Time Complexity**: Both solutions have the same O(n) time complexity.

## Find Length

**Problem**: Find the length of the given linked list.

**Example 6.19:**

```
public int findLength() {
    Node curr = head;
    int count = 0;
    while (curr != null) {
        count++;
        curr = curr.next;
    }
    return count;
}
```

**Analysis**: The length of the linked list is found by traversing the list until we reach the end of the list.

**Time Complexity**: O(n).

## Nth Node from Beginning

**Problem**: Find Nth node from the beginning

**Example 6.20:**

```
public int nthNodeFromBeginning(int index) {
    if (index > size() || index < 1)
        return Integer.MAX_VALUE;

    int count = 0;
    Node curr = head;

    while (curr != null && count < index - 1) {
        count++;
        curr = curr.next;
    }

    return curr.value;
}
```

```
// Testing code.
public static void main(String[] args) {
    LinkedList ll = new LinkedList();
    ll.addHead(1);
    ll.addHead(2);
    ll.addHead(3);
    System.out.println(ll.nthNodeFromBeginning(2));
}
```

**Output:**

```
2
```

**Analysis**: Nth node can be found by traversing the list N-1 number of times and then returning the node. If the list does not have N elements, then the function returns null.

**Time Complexity**: O(K) if we are searching the kth node from start.

## Nth Node from End

**Problem**: Find Nth node from the end in a singly linked list.

**Example 6.21:**

```
public int nthNodeFromEnd(int index) {
    int size = findLength();
    int startIndex;

    if (size != 0 && size < index) {
        return Integer.MAX_VALUE;
    }
    startIndex = size - index + 1;
    return nthNodeFromBeginning(startIndex);
}

// Testing code.
public static void main(String[] args) {
    LinkedList ll = new LinkedList();
    ll.addHead(1);
    ll.addHead(2);
    ll.addHead(3);
    System.out.println(ll.nthNodeFromEnd(2));
}
```

**Output:**

```
2
```

**Analysis**: First, find the length of the list, then the nth node from the end will be (length – nth +1) node from the beginning.

**Time Complexity**: O(n).

**Example 6.22:**

```
public int nthNodeFromEnd2(int index) {
    int count = 1;
    Node forward = head;
    Node curr = head;
    while (forward != null && count <= index) {
        count++;
        forward = forward.next;
    }

    if (forward == null)
        return Integer.MAX_VALUE;

    while (forward != null) {
        forward = forward.next;
        curr = curr.next;
    }

    return curr.value;
}
```

**Analysis**: The second solution is to use two pointers one is N steps/nodes ahead of the other when the forward pointer reaches the end of the list then the backward pointer will point to the desired node.

**Time Complexity**: O(n).

## Loop Detect

**Problem**: Find if there is a loop in a linked list. If there is a loop, then return true and if there is no loop found, then return false.

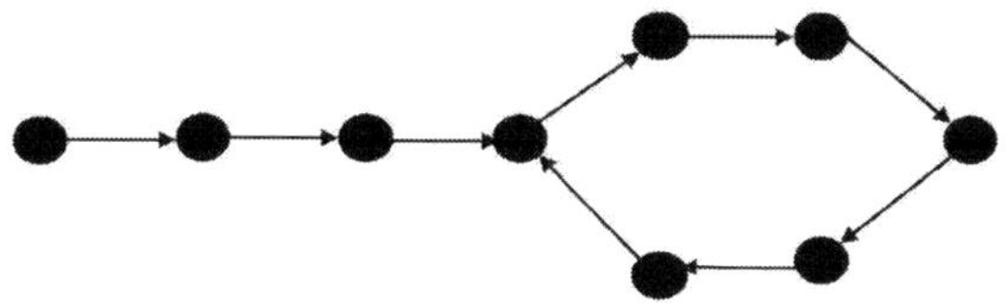

**Solutions:** There are many ways to find if there is a loop in a linked list:

**First solution**: User some map or hash-table

1. Traverse through the list.
2. If the current node is not there in the Hash-Table, then insert it into the Hash-Table.
3. If the current node is already in the Hashtable then we have a loop.

**Example 6.23:**

```
public boolean loopDetect() {
    Node curr = head;
    HashSet<Node> hs = new HashSet<Node>();

    while (curr != null) {
        if(hs.contains(curr)){
            System.out.println("loop found");
```

```
            return true;
        }

        hs.add(curr);
        curr = curr.next;
    }

    System.out.println("loop not found");
    return false;
}
```

**Second solution**: Slow pointer and fast pointer approach (SPFP), we will use two pointers, one will move 2 steps at a time and another will move 1 step at a time. If there is a loop, then both will meet at a point.

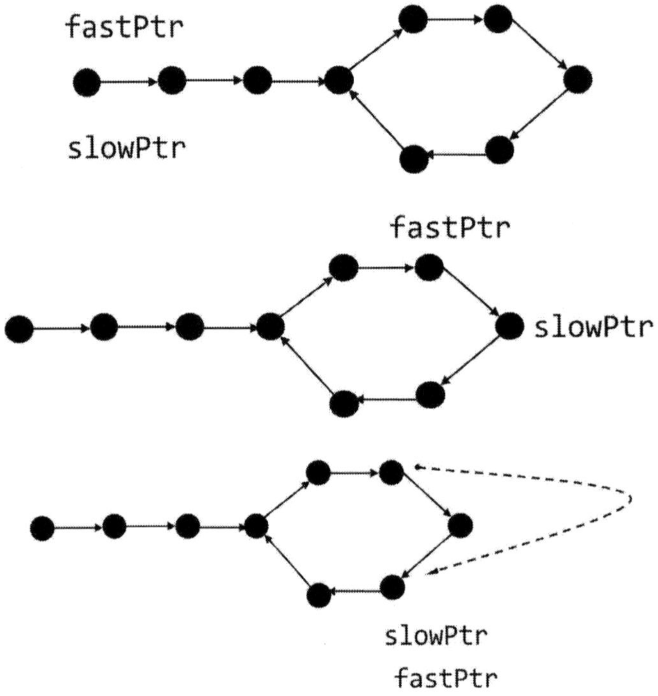


**Example 6.24:**

```
public boolean loopDetect2() {
    Node slowPtr;
    Node fastPtr;
    slowPtr = fastPtr = head;

    while (fastPtr.next != null && fastPtr.next.next != null) {
        slowPtr = slowPtr.next;
        fastPtr = fastPtr.next.next;
        if (slowPtr == fastPtr) {
            System.out.println("loop found");
            return true;
        }
    }

    System.out.println("loop not found");
    return false;
}
```

**Analysis:**

- The list is traversed with two pointers, one is a slow pointer and another is a fast pointer. The slow pointer always moves one step. A fast pointer always moves two steps. If there is no loop, then control will come out of the while loop. So, return false.
- If there is a loop, then there comes a point in a loop where the fast pointer will come and try to pass a slow pointer, and they will meet at a point. When this point arrives, we come to know that there is a loop in the list. So, return true.

**Time Complexity**: O(n).

**Third solution**: Reverse list loop detect approach, if there is a loop in a linked list, then the reverse list function will give the head of the original list as the head of the new list.

**Example 6.25:** Find if there is a loop in a linked list. Use a reverse list approach.

```
public boolean reverseListLoopDetect() {
    Node tempHead = head;
    reverse();

    if (tempHead == head) {
        reverse();
        System.out.println("loop found");
        return true;
    } else {
        reverse();
        System.out.println("loop not found");
        return false;
    }
}
```

**Analysis:**

1. Store pointer of the head of the list in a temp variable.
2. Reverse the list
3. Compare the reversed list head pointer to the current list head pointer.
4. If the head of the reversed list and the original list are the same, then reverse the list back and return true.
5. If the head of the reversed list and the original list are not the same, then reverse the list back and return false. Which means there is no loop.

**Time Complexity**: O(n).

**Note**: Both SPFP and Reverse List approaches are linear, but still in the SPFP approach, we do not require modification of the linked list, so it is preferred.

## Loop Type Detect

**Problem**: Find if there is a loop in a linked list. If there is no loop, then return 0, if there is loop return 1, if the list is circular then 2. Use a slow pointer fast pointer approach.

**Solution**: Modifying the above two-pointer solution. If the loop is not found, then there is no loop. If the loop is found then there are two cases: first, the loop is at the start of the list or second, the loop is at some other node other than the start. We will add one more check to see if the fast pointer is passing through the head node, this will give us the check for the circular list loop case or the start of the list loop case.

**Example 6.26:**

```
public int loopTypeDetect() {
    Node slowPtr;
    Node fastPtr;
    slowPtr = fastPtr = head;

    while (fastPtr.next != null && fastPtr.next.next != null) {
        if (head == fastPtr.next || head == fastPtr.next.next) {
            System.out.println("circular list loop found");
            return 2;
        }

        slowPtr = slowPtr.next;
        fastPtr = fastPtr.next.next;
        if (slowPtr == fastPtr) {
            System.out.println("loop found");
            return 1;
        }
    }

    System.out.println("loop not found");
    return 0;
}
```

**Time Complexity:** O(n).

## Remove Loop

**Problem**: Given there is a loop in the linked list remove the loop.

**Solution**:

1. Loop through the list by two pointers, one fast pointer and one slow pointer. A fast pointer jumps two nodes at a time and a slow pointer jumps one node at a time. The point where these two pointers intersect is a point in the loop.
2. If that intersection point is the head of the list, this is a circular list case, and you need to again traverse through the list and make the node before the head point to null.
3. In the other case, you need to use two pointer variables: one starts from the head and another starts from the intersection point. They both will meet at the point of the loop. (You can mathematically prove it ;) ) Make the next pointer of the node before the intersection point as null.

**Example 6.27:**

```
public Node loopPointDetect() {
    Node slowPtr;
    Node fastPtr;
    slowPtr = fastPtr = head;
    while (fastPtr.next != null && fastPtr.next.next != null) {
        slowPtr = slowPtr.next;
        fastPtr = fastPtr.next.next;
        if (slowPtr == fastPtr) {
            return slowPtr;
        }
    }
    return null;
}

public void removeLoop() {
    Node loopPoint = loopPointDetect();
    if (loopPoint == null)
        return;

    Node firstPtr = head;
    if (loopPoint == head) {
        while (firstPtr.next != head)
            firstPtr = firstPtr.next;
        firstPtr.next = null;
        return;
    }

    Node secondPtr = loopPoint;
    while (firstPtr.next != secondPtr.next) {
        firstPtr = firstPtr.next;
        secondPtr = secondPtr.next;
    }
    secondPtr.next = null;
}

// Testing code.
public static void main(String[] args) {
    LinkedList ll = new LinkedList();
    ll.addHead(1);
    ll.addHead(2);
    ll.addHead(3);
    ll.print();
    ll.makeLoop();
    ll.loopDetect();
    ll.loopTypeDetect();
    ll.removeLoop();
    ll.loopDetect();
}
```

**Output:**

```
3 2 1
loop found
circular list loop found
loop not found
```

**Time Complexity:** O(n), all operations are linear.

## Find Intersection

**Problem**: In a given two-linked list that meets at some point, find that intersection point.

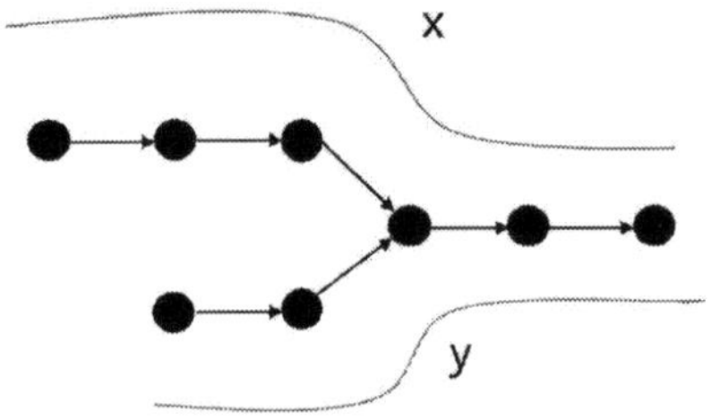


**Solution**: Find the length of both lists. Find the difference in length of both lists. Increment the longer list by diff steps, and then increment both the lists and get the intersection point.

**Example 6.28:**

```
public Node findIntersection(LinkedList lst2) {
    Node head2 = lst2.head;
    int l1 = 0;
    int l2 = 0;
    Node tempHead = this.head;
    Node tempHead2 = head2;
    while (tempHead != null) {
        l1++;
        tempHead = tempHead.next;
    }

    while (tempHead2 != null) {
        l2++;
        tempHead2 = tempHead2.next;
    }

    int diff;
    tempHead = this.head;
    tempHead2 = head2;

    if (l1 < l2) {
        Node temp = tempHead;
        tempHead = tempHead2;
        tempHead2 = temp;
        diff = l2 - l1;
    } else {
        diff = l1 - l2;
    }

    for (; diff > 0; diff--) {
        tempHead = tempHead.next;
    }

    while (tempHead != tempHead2) {
        tempHead = tempHead.next;
        tempHead2 = tempHead2.next;
    }

    return tempHead;
}
```

```
// Testing code.
public static void main(String[] args) {
    LinkedList ll = new LinkedList();
    ll.addHead(1);
    ll.addHead(2);
    LinkedList ll2 = new LinkedList();
    ll2.addHead(3);
    ll2.head.next = ll.head;
    ll.addHead(4);
    ll2.addHead(5);
    ll.print();
    ll2.print();

    Node nd = ll.findIntersection(ll2);
    if(nd != null)
        System.out.println("Intersection:: " + nd.value);
}
```

**Output:**

```
4 2 1
5 3 2 1
Intersection:: 2
```

**Time Complexity**: O(n).

## Adding two polynomials using Linked List

**Problem**: Given two polynomial numbers represented by a linked list with nodes containing coefficient and power. Write a function that adds these lists by adding the coefficients which have the same powers.

6x^2 + 5x^1 + 4  +  3x^3 + 2x^1 + 1  => 3x^3 + 6x^2 + 7x^1 + 5

**Solution**: We will traverse both the lists p1 and p2, there are three cases in which if p1 is null or p1 power is lower than p2 then we will create an another node with p2 power and coefficient add then add it to p1. If p2 is null or p2 power is lower than p1 then we will traverse p1 to next of p1. If p1 and p2 both are not null and their power of the element is the same, then add their coefficient and traverse both of them to their next node.

**Example 6.29:**

```
public class Polynomial {
    public static class Node {
        int coeff, pow;
        Node next;

        Node(int c, int p) {
            coeff = c;
            pow = p;
            next = null;
        }
    }

    Node head, tail;
    Polynomial(int[] coeffs, int[] pows, int size) {
        head = null;
```

```
        tail = null;
        Node temp = null;
        for (int i = 0; i < size; i++) {
            temp = new Node(coeffs[i], pows[i]);
            if (head == null)
                head = tail = temp;
            else {
                tail.next = temp;
                tail = tail.next;
            }
        }
    }

    Polynomial() {
        this(null, null, 0);
    }

    public Polynomial add(Polynomial poly2) {
        Node p1 = head;
        Node p2 = poly2.head;
        Node temp = null;
        Polynomial poly = new Polynomial();
        while (p1 != null || p2 != null) {
            if (p1 == null || (p2 != null && p1.pow < p2.pow)) {
                temp = new Node(p2.coeff, p2.pow);
                p2 = p2.next;
            } else if (p2 == null || p1.pow > p2.pow) {
                temp = new Node(p1.coeff, p1.pow);
                p1 = p1.next;
            } else if (p1.pow == p2.pow) {
                temp = new Node(p1.coeff + p2.coeff, p1.pow);
                p1 = p1.next;
                p2 = p2.next;
            }

            if (poly.head == null)
                poly.head = poly.tail = temp;
            else {
                poly.tail.next = temp;
                poly.tail = poly.tail.next;
            }
        }
        return poly;
    }

    public void print() {
        Node curr = head;
        while (curr != null) {
            System.out.print(curr.coeff + "x^" + curr.pow);
            if (curr.next != null)
                System.out.print(" + ");
            curr = curr.next;
        }
        System.out.println();
    }

    public static void main(String args[]) {
        int[] c1 = { 6, 5, 4 };
```

```
        int[] p1 = { 2, 1, 0 };
        int s1 = c1.length;
        Polynomial first = new Polynomial(c1, p1, s1);

        int[] c2 = { 3, 2, 1 };
        int[] p2 = { 3, 1, 0 };
        int s2 = c2.length;
        Polynomial second = new Polynomial(c2, p2, s2);

        Polynomial sum = first.add(second);
        sum.print();
    }
}
```

**Output:**

```
3x^3 + 6x^2 + 7x^1 + 5x^0
```

## Doubly Linked List

A Doubly Linked list is made up of nodes. Each node in a doubly-linked list is made up of three parts, the first part is data and the other two are references to other nodes of the linked list. These references are called prev and next. The previous pointer of the node will point to the node before it, and the next pointer will point to the node next to the given node. The beginning of the list is called "Head" which points to the first node of the linked list.

**Note**: In a doubly-linked list we can traverse in both directions as we have reference to both previous and next nodes.

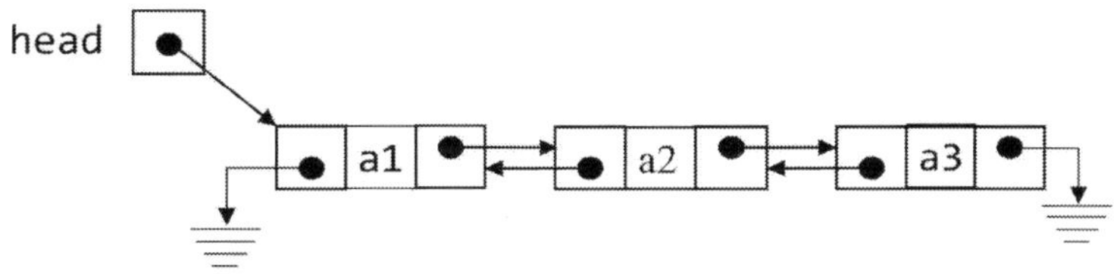


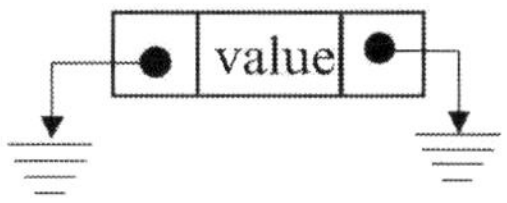


Let us look at the Node. The value part of the node is of type integer, but it can be of some other data type. The two link pointers are prev and next.

**Example 6.30**: Doubly Linked List node struct.

```
public class DoublyLinkedList {
    private Node head =  null;
    private Node tail = null;
    private int size = 0;

    private static class Node {
        private int value;
        private Node next;
        private Node prev;
```

```
        public Node(int v, Node nxt, Node prv) {
            value = v;
            next = nxt;
            prev = prv;
        }
    }

    public int size() {
        return size;
    }

    public boolean isEmpty() {
        return size == 0;
    }
    /* Other methods */
};
```

## Basic operations of Linked List

The basic operation of a linked list requires traversing a linked list. Various operations that we can perform on linked lists, many of these operations require list traversal:

1. Insert an element in the list, this operation is used to create a linked list.
2. Print various elements of the list.
3. Search for an element in the list.
4. Delete an element from the list.
5. Reverse a linked list.

Search in a doubly linked list can only be done in one direction. Since all elements in the list have reference to the next item in the list. Therefore, the traversal of linked lists is linear.

In the doubly linked list, below are a few cases that we need to keep in mind while coding:

1. Zero element case (head will be modified)
2. One element case (head can be modified)
3. The first element (head can be modified)
4. General case

**Note**: Any program that is likely to change head pointer is to be passed as a double reference, which is pointing to head pointer.

## Search List

**Problem:** Search a value in a linked list.
**Solution:** Traverse the list, same as done in the singly linked list.

## Delete List

**Problem:** Free all elements of the linked list
**Solution:** Same as done in singly-linked lists.

## Print list

**Problem:** Print all the elements of the linked list.
**Solution:** Traverse the list and print the value of each node in the doubly linked list is the same as done in the singly linked list.

## Find Length

**Problem:** Find the number of elements in a linked list.
**Solution:** Traverse the list and find its length in a doubly-linked list is the same as done in a singly linked list.

## Compare Lists

**Problem:** Compare two linked lists.
**Solution:** Traverse both the lists and compare in doubly linked lists is the same as done in singly-linked lists.

## Insert at Head

**Problem:** Insert node at the start of the linked list.

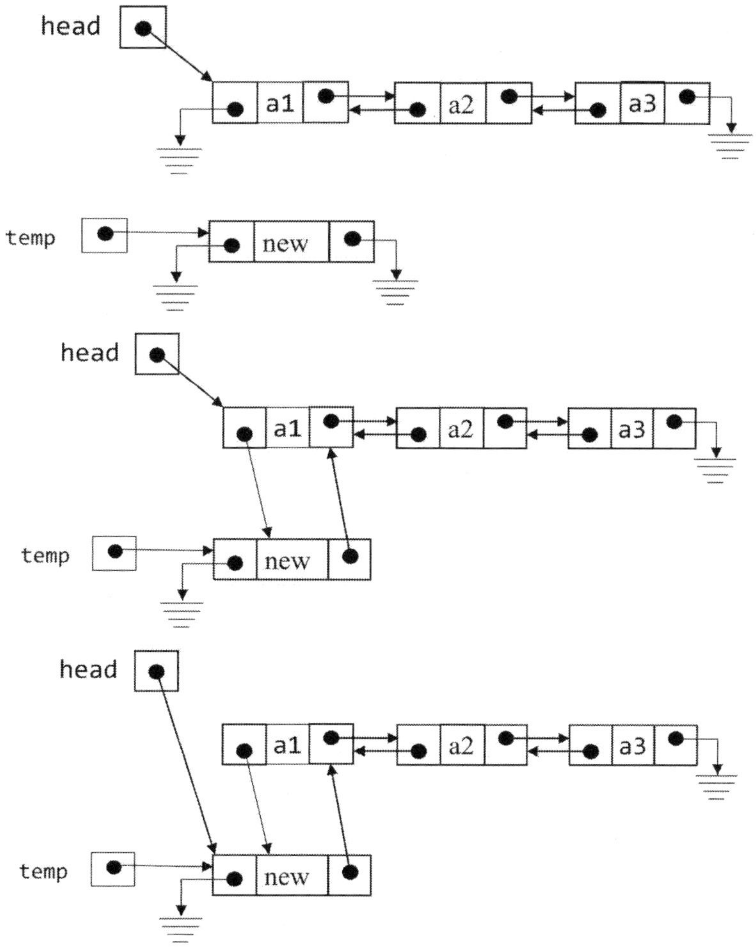

**Example 6.31:**
```
public void addHead(int value) {
    Node newNode = new Node(value, null, null);
    if (size == 0) {
        tail = head = newNode;
    } else {
        head.prev = newNode;
        newNode.next = head;
        head = newNode;
    }
    size++;
}

// Testing code.
public static void main(String[] args)  {
    DoublyLinkedList ll = new DoublyLinkedList();
    ll.addHead(1);
    ll.addHead(2);
    ll.addHead(3);
    ll.print();
    System.out.println("size : " + ll.size());
    System.out.println("isEmpty : " + ll.isEmpty());
}
```

**Output:**
```
3 2 1
size : 3
isEmpty : false
```

**Analysis:** Inserting in a doubly-linked list is similar to inserting in a singly linked list.

1. Create a node and assign null to the prev pointer of the node.
2. If the list is empty, then the tail and head will point to the new node.
3. If the list is not empty, then the prev of the head will point to newNode and the next of newNode will point to head. Then the head will be modified to point to newNode.

**Time Complexity:** O(1).

## Sorted Insert

**Problem:** Insert elements in the linked list in sorted order.

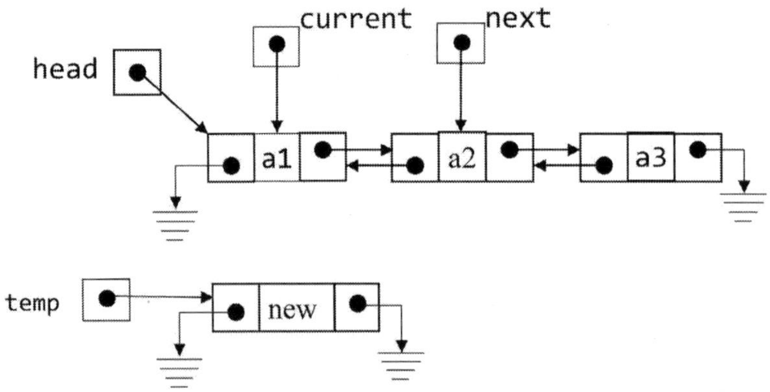

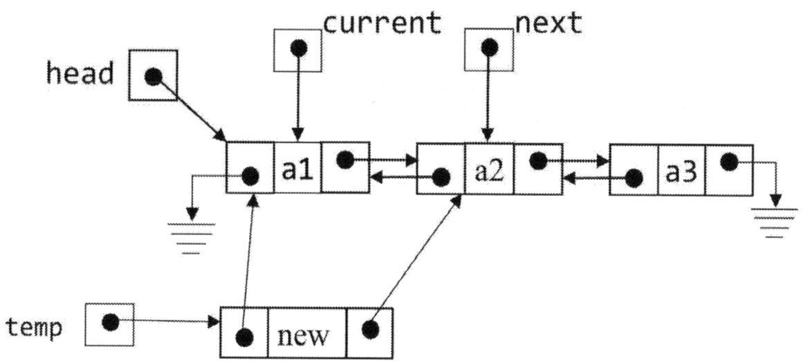


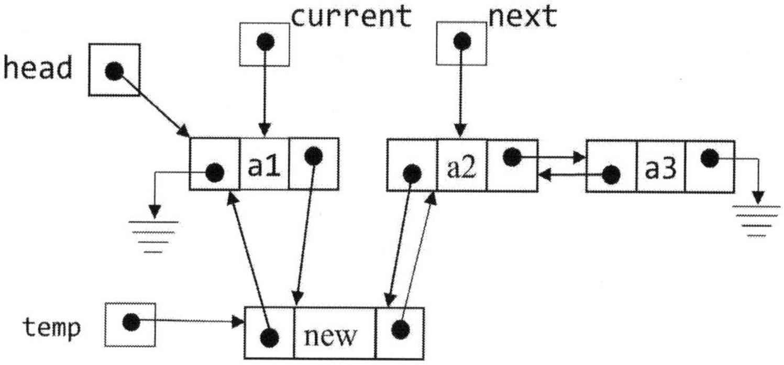


**Example 6.32:**
```java
public void sortedInsert(int value) {
    Node temp = new Node(value, null, null);
    Node curr = head;

    if (curr == null) { // first element
        head = temp;
        tail = temp;
        return;
    }

    if (head.value > value) { // at the beginning
        temp.next = head;
        head.prev = temp;
        head = temp;
        return;
    }

    while (curr.next != null && curr.next.value < value) { // traversal
        curr = curr.next;
    }

    if (curr.next == null) { // at the end
        tail = temp;
        temp.prev = curr;
        curr.next = temp;
    } else { // all other
        temp.next = curr.next;
        temp.prev = curr;
        curr.next = temp;
        temp.next.prev = temp;
    }
}
```

```
// Testing code.
public static void main(String[] args) {
    DoublyLinkedList ll = new DoublyLinkedList();
    ll.sortedInsert(1);
    ll.sortedInsert(2);
    ll.sortedInsert(3);
    ll.print();
}
```

**Output:**

```
1 2 3
```

**Analysis:**

1. We need to consider only the element case first. In this case, both head and tail will modify.
2. Then, we need to consider the case when the head will be modified when a new node is added to the beginning of the list.
3. Then, we need to consider general cases
4. Finally, we need to consider the case when the tail will be modified.

**Time Complexity:** O(n).

## Remove Head

**Problem:** Remove the head node of the linked list.

**Example 6.33:**

```
public int removeHead() {
    if (isEmpty())
        throw new IllegalStateException("EmptyListException");

    int value = head.value;
    head = head.next;

    if (head == null)
        tail = null;
    else
        head.prev = null;

    size--;
    return value;
}

// Testing code.
public static void main(String[] args) {
    DoublyLinkedList ll = new DoublyLinkedList();
    ll.addHead(1);
    ll.addHead(2);
    ll.addHead(3);
    ll.print();

    ll.removeHead();
    ll.print();
}
```

**Output:**
```
3 2 1
2 1
```

**Analysis**:
1. If the list is empty, then we do not do anything.
2. The Head will point to the next of the head. If now the head is not null, then its prev will point to null.
3. Update the list so that its head will point to the second node.

**Time Complexity:** O(1).

## Delete a node

**Problem:** Delete node with the given value in a linked list

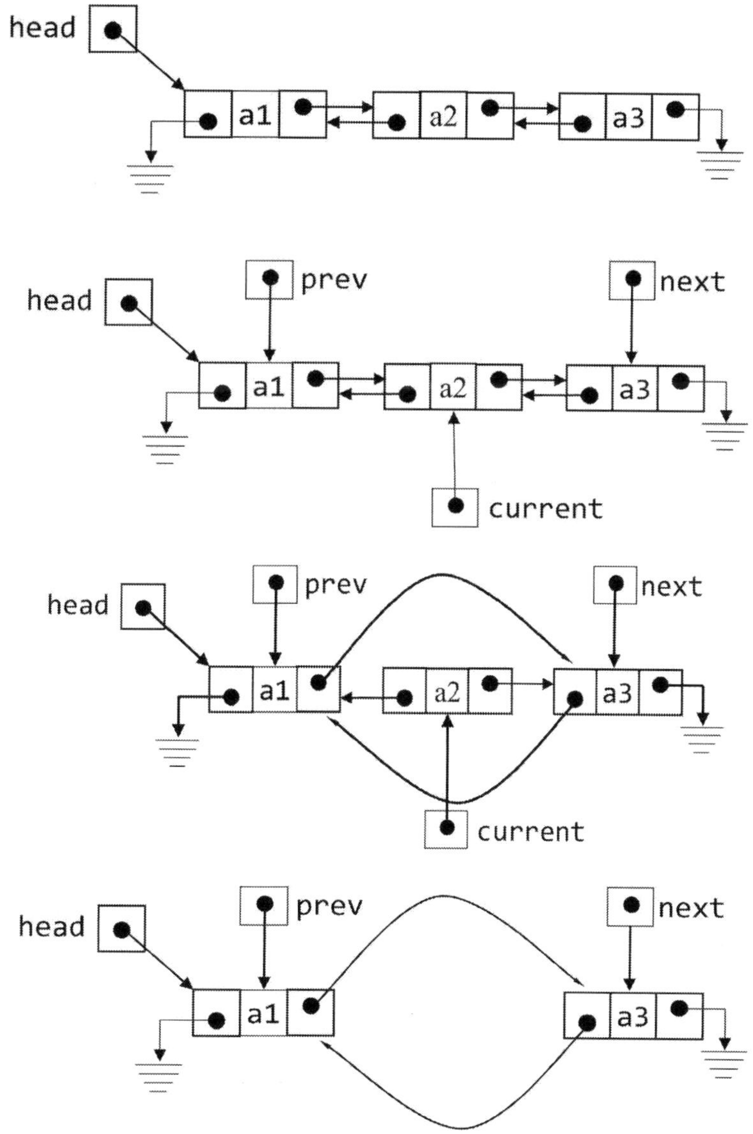

**Example 6.34:**
```
public boolean removeNode(int key) {
    Node curr = head;
    if (curr == null) // empty list
        return false;

    if (curr.value == key) { // head is the node with value key.
        head = head.next;
        size--;
        if (head != null)
            head.prev = null;
        else
            tail = null; // only one element in the list.
        return true;
    }

    while (curr.next != null) {
        if (curr.next.value == key) {
            curr.next = curr.next.next;
            if (curr.next == null) // last element case.
                tail = curr;
            else
                curr.next.prev = curr;
            size--;
            return true;
        }
        curr = curr.next;
    }
    return false;
}

// Testing code.
public static void main(String[] args) {
    DoublyLinkedList ll = new DoublyLinkedList();
    ll.addHead(1);
    ll.addHead(2);
    ll.addHead(3);
    ll.print();
    ll.removeNode(2);
    ll.print();
}
```

**Output:**
```
3 2 1
3 1
```

**Analysis:** Traverse the list and find the node that needs to be removed. Then remove it and adjust the next pointer of the node before it and the prev pointer of the node next to it.

**Time Complexity:** O(n).

## Remove Duplicate

**Problem:** Consider the list is sorted and remove the repeated value nodes of the list.

**Example 6.35:**
```
public void removeDuplicate() {
    Node curr = head;
    while (curr != null) {
        if ((curr.next != null) && curr.value == curr.next.value) {
            curr.next = curr.next.next;

            if(curr.next != null)
                curr.next.prev = curr;
            else
                tail = curr;
        } else {
            curr = curr.next;
        }
    }
}

// Testing code.
public static void main(String[] args) {
    DoublyLinkedList ll = new DoublyLinkedList();
    ll.sortedInsert(1);
    ll.sortedInsert(2);
    ll.sortedInsert(3);
    ll.sortedInsert(1);
    ll.sortedInsert(2);
    ll.sortedInsert(3);
    ll.print();
    ll.removeDuplicate();
    ll.print();
}
```

**Output:**
```
1 1 2 2 3 3
1 2 3
```

**Analysis:**
1. Head can never be modified.
2. Find the node that has the same value as the previous node. Remove this node by pointer adjustment for it.

**Time Complexity:** O(n).

## Reverse a doubly linked List iteratively

**Problem:** Reverse elements of doubly linked list iteratively.

**Example 6.36:**
```
public void reverseList() {
    Node curr = head;
    Node tempNode;

    while (curr != null) {
        tempNode = curr.next;
        curr.next = curr.prev;
        curr.prev = tempNode;
```

```
        if (curr.prev == null) {
            tail = head;
            head = curr;
            return;
        }

        curr = curr.prev;
    }
    return;
}

// Testing code.
public static void main(String[] args) {
    DoublyLinkedList ll = new DoublyLinkedList();
    ll.addHead(1);
    ll.addHead(2);
    ll.addHead(3);
    ll.print();
    ll.reverseList();
    ll.print();
}
```

**Output:**

```
3 2 1
1 2 3
```

**Analysis**: Traverse the list. Swap the next and prev. Then traverse to the direction curr. Prev, which is next before the swap. If you reach the end of the list, then set head and tail.

**Time Complexity:** O(n).

## Copy List Reversed

**Problem:** Copy the content of the list into another list in reverse order.

**Example 6.37:**

```
public DoublyLinkedList copyListReversed() {
    DoublyLinkedList dll = new DoublyLinkedList();
    Node curr = head;
    while (curr != null) {
        dll.addHead(curr.value);
        curr = curr.next;
    }
    return dll;
}

// Testing code.
public static void main(String[] args) {
    DoublyLinkedList ll = new DoublyLinkedList();
    ll.addHead(1);
    ll.addHead(2);
    ll.addHead(3);
    ll.print();
    DoublyLinkedList l3 = ll.copyListReversed();
    l3.print();
}
```

**Output:**
```
3 2 1
1 2 3
```

**Analysis:**
1. Traverse through the list and copy the value of the nodes into another list by calling the addHead() function.
2. Since the new nodes are added to the head of the list, the new list formed has nodes ordered reversed, thereby making a reverse list.

**Time Complexity:** O(n).

## Copy List

**Problem:** Copy the content of the list into another in the same order.

**Example 6.38:**
```
public DoublyLinkedList copyList() {
    DoublyLinkedList dll = new DoublyLinkedList();
    Node curr = head;

    while (curr != null) {
        dll.addTail(curr.value);
        curr = curr.next;
    }
    return dll;
}

// Testing code.
public static void main(String[] args) {
    DoublyLinkedList ll = new DoublyLinkedList();
    ll.addHead(1);
    ll.addHead(2);
    ll.addHead(3);
    ll.print();
    DoublyLinkedList l2 = ll.copyList();
    l2.print();
}
```

**Output:**
```
3 2 1
3 2 1
```

**Analysis:**
1. Traverse through the list and copy the value of the nodes into another list by calling the addTail() function.
2. Since the new nodes are added to the tail of the list, the new list formed has nodes ordered the same as the original list.

**Time Complexity:** O(n).

## Circular Linked List

A circular linked list is made up of nodes. Each node has two parts, the first part is the data and the second part is the link that has a reference to the next node in the linked list. The link portion of the last node contains the address of the first node. A circular linked list is like a singly linked list, except that the last node points to the first node of the list.

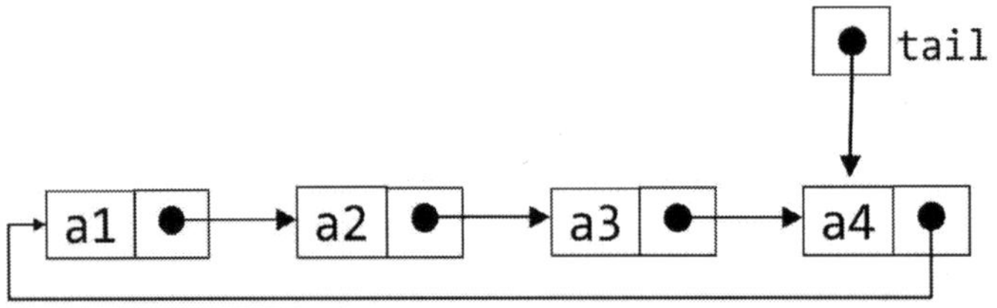


**Note**: In a circular linked list, we can insert at the end and remove nodes at the head in constant time. These two operations efficiencies make it appropriate for use as a queue.

**Example 6.39:** Circular Linked List node.

```
public class CircularLinkedList {
    private Node tail = null;
    private int size = 0;

    private static class Node {
        private int value;
        private Node next;

        public Node(int v, Node n) {
            value = v;
            next = n;
        }
    }

    public int size() {
        return size;
    }

    public boolean isEmpty() {
        return size == 0;
    }

    public int peek() {
        if (isEmpty())
            throw new IllegalStateException("EmptyListException");
        return tail.next.value;
    }
    /* Other methods */
};
```

**Analysis**: In the circular linked list, nodes are just like a singly linked list. The last element node next always points to the first node of the list.

### Insert element in front

**Problem:** Add an element to the head of the circular linked list.

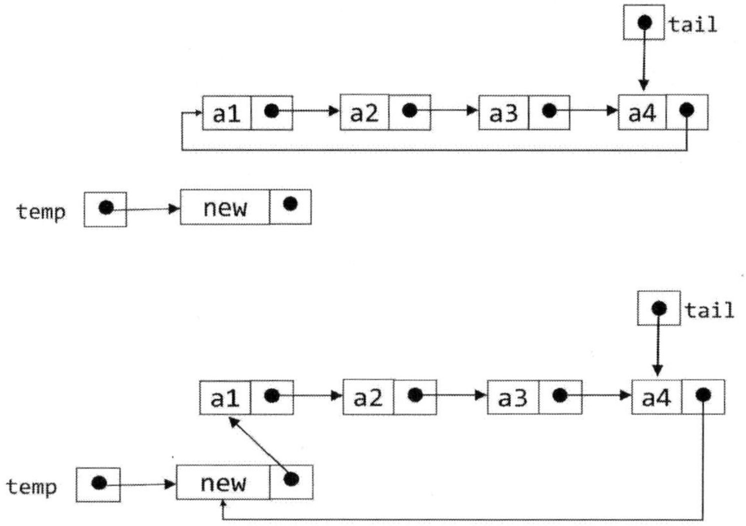


**Example 6.40:**

```
public void addHead(int value) {
    Node temp = new Node(value, null);
    if (isEmpty()) {
        tail = temp;
        temp.next = temp;
    } else {
        temp.next = tail.next;
        tail.next = temp;
    }
    size++;
}

// Testing code.
public static void main(String[] args)  {
    CircularLinkedList ll = new CircularLinkedList();
    ll.addHead(1);
    ll.addHead(2);
    ll.addHead(3);
    ll.print();
}
```

**Output:**

```
3 2 1
```

**Analysis:**

1. First, we create a node with a given value and its next pointing to null.
2. If the list is empty, then the tail of the list will point to it. In addition, the next node will point to itself
3. If the list is not empty, then the next of the new nodes will be next to the tail. In addition, the tail next will start pointing to the new node.
4. Thus, the new node is added to the head of the list.
5. The demo program creates an instance of CircularLinkedList. Then add some value to it and finally print the content of the list.

**Time Complexity:** O(1).

## Print the content of the list

**Problem:** Print all the elements of a circular linked list.

**Example 6.41:**
```
public void print() {
    if (isEmpty()) {
        System.out.println("Empty List.");
        return;
    }
    Node temp = tail.next;
    while (temp != tail) {
        System.out.print(temp.value + " ");
        temp = temp.next;
    }
    System.out.println(temp.value);
}
```

**Analysis:** In a circular list, the end of the list is not there, so we cannot check with null. In place of null, the tail is used to check the end of the list.

**Time Complexity:** O(n).

## Insert an element at the end

**Problem:** Insert an element at the end of the circular linked list.

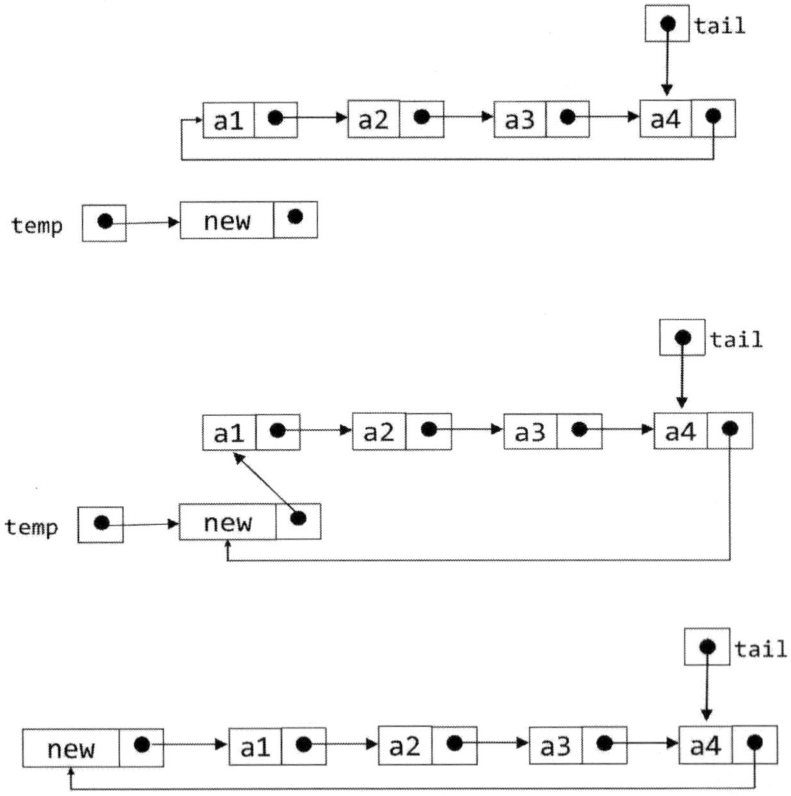

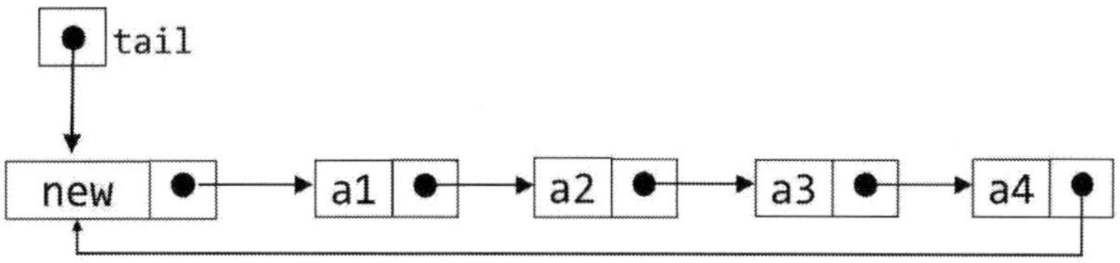


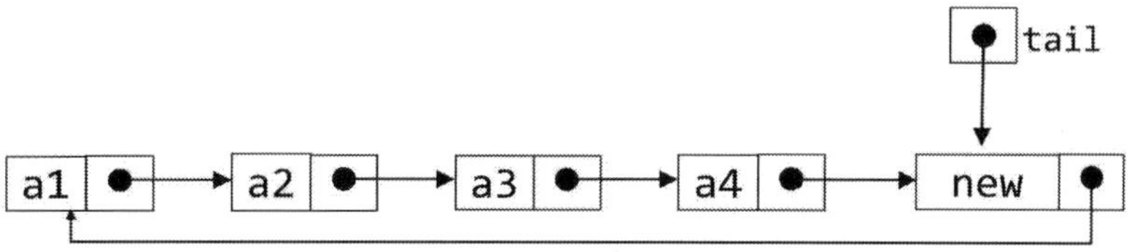


**Example 6.42:**
```
public void addTail(int value) {
    Node temp = new Node(value, null);
    if (isEmpty()) {
        tail = temp;
        temp.next = temp;
    } else {
        temp.next = tail.next;
        tail.next = temp;
        tail = temp;
    }
    size++;
}

// Testing code.
public static void main(String[] args)  {
    CircularLinkedList ll = new CircularLinkedList();
    ll.addTail(1);
    ll.addTail(2);
    ll.addTail(3);
    ll.print();
}
```

**Output:**
```
1 2 3
```

**Analysis:** Adding nodes at the end is the same as adding at the beginning. We just need to modify the tail pointer in place of the head pointer.

**Time Complexity:** O(1).

## Search element in the list

**Problem:** Search value in a circular linked list.

**Example 6.43:**
```
public boolean search(int data) {
    Node temp = tail;
    for (int i = 0; i < size; i++) {
        if (temp.value == data)
            return true;
```

```
        temp = temp.next;
    }
    return false;
}

// Testing code.
public static void main(String[] args)  {
    CircularLinkedList ll = new CircularLinkedList();
    ll.addHead(1);
    ll.addHead(2);
    ll.addHead(3);
    ll.print();
    System.out.println(ll.search(3));
}
```

**Output:**

```
3 2 1
true
```

**Analysis**: Iterate through the list to find if the value is there or not.

**Time Complexity:** O(n).

## Remove element in the front

**Problem:** Remove the first element of the linked list.

**Example 6.44:**

```
public int removeHead() throws IllegalStateException {
    if (isEmpty()) {
        throw new IllegalStateException("EmptyListException");
    }
    int value = tail.next.value;
    if (tail == tail.next)
        tail = null;
    else
        tail.next = tail.next.next;

    size--;
    return value;
}

// Testing code.
public static void main(String[] args)  {
    CircularLinkedList ll = new CircularLinkedList();
    ll.addHead(1);
    ll.addHead(2);
    ll.addHead(3);
    ll.print();
    ll.removeHead();
    ll.print();
}
```

**Output:**

```
3 2 1
2 1
```

**Analysis**:

1. If the list is empty, then return.
2. If the next node of the tail is the same as the tail, then it is a single node case. Mark tail as null.
3. If it is not a single node case, then point the tail node next to the second node from the head.

**Time Complexity:** O(1).

## Remove a node given its value

**Problem:** Delete a node with a given value in a circular linked list

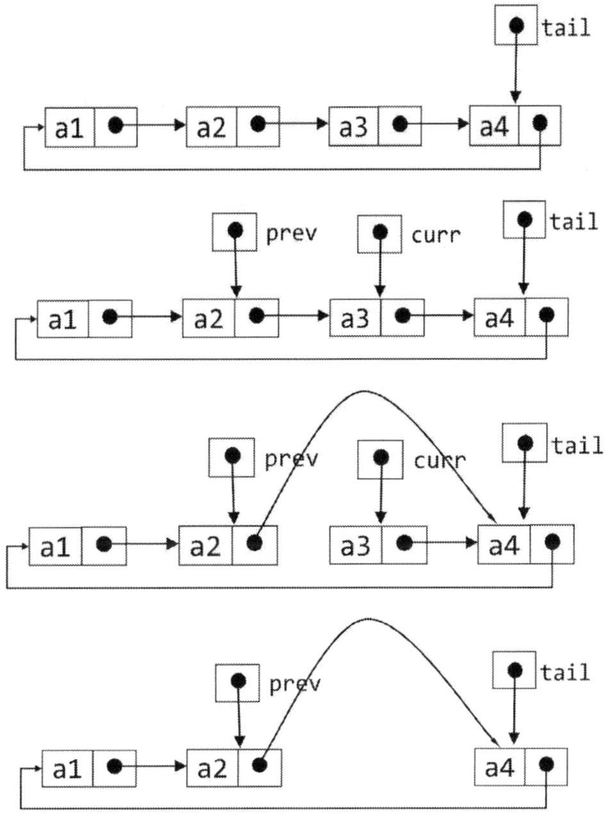


**Example 6.45:**
```
public boolean removeNode(int key) {
    if (isEmpty()) {
        return false;
    }
    Node prev = tail;
    Node curr = tail.next;
    Node head = tail.next;

    if (curr.value == key)// head and single node case.
    {
        if (curr == curr.next)// single node case
            tail = null;
        else // head case
            tail.next = tail.next.next;
        return true;
    }
```

```
    prev = curr;
    curr = curr.next;

    while (curr != head) {
        if (curr.value == key) {
            if (curr == tail)
                tail = prev;
            prev.next = curr.next;
            return true;
        }
        prev = curr;
        curr = curr.next;
    }

    return false;
}

// Testing code.
public static void main(String[] args)  {
    CircularLinkedList ll = new CircularLinkedList();
    ll.addHead(1);
    ll.addHead(2);
    ll.addHead(3);
    ll.print();
    ll.removeNode(2);
    ll.print();
}
```

**Output:**

```
3 2 1
3 1
```

**Analysis:** Find the node that needs to be removed. The only difference is that while traversing the list, the end of the list is tracked by the tail pointer in place of null. If the node that needs to be removed is other than the tail node, then the tail node pointer is not modified. If the node that needs to be removed is a tail node, then the tail node pointer of the list will be modified.

**Time Complexity:** O(n).

## Delete List

**Problem:** Delete a circular linked list.

**Example 6.46:**

```
public void deleteList() {
    tail = null;
    size = 0;
}
```

**Analysis:** The tail of the list is marked as null. The various nodes of list will be free using garbage collection.

**Time Complexity:** O(n).

## Copy circular linked-list reversed

**Problem:** Copy a circular linked list in reversed order.

**Solution**: A new empty circular list is created. The given circular list is traversed and all its elements value is added to the new list by calling the addHead() function. This will create a reverse list.

**Example 6.47:**

```
public CircularLinkedList copyListReversed() {
    CircularLinkedList cl = new CircularLinkedList();
    if (tail == null) {
        return cl;
    }
    Node curr = tail.next;
    Node head = curr;

    if (curr != null) {
        cl.addHead(curr.value);
        curr = curr.next;
    }
    while (curr != head) {
        cl.addHead(curr.value);
        curr = curr.next;
    }
    return cl;
}

// Testing code.
public static void main(String[] args)  {
    CircularLinkedList ll = new CircularLinkedList();
    ll.addHead(1);
    ll.addHead(2);
    ll.addHead(3);
    ll.print();
    CircularLinkedList ll3 = ll.copyListReversed();
    ll3.print();
}
```

**Output:**

```
3 2 1
1 2 3
```

**Time Complexity:** O(n).

## Copy circular linked list

**Problem:** Copy a circular linked list.

**Solution**: A new empty circular linked list is created. The input list is traversed and the value of its various elements are added to the new list by calling the addTail() function. By doing this, a copy of the given list is created.

**Example 6.48:**

```
public CircularLinkedList copyList() {
    CircularLinkedList cl = new CircularLinkedList();
    if (tail == null) {
        return cl;
    }

    Node curr = tail.next;
    Node head = curr;

    if (curr != null) {
        cl.addTail(curr.value);
        curr = curr.next;
    }

    while (curr != head) {
        cl.addTail(curr.value);
        curr = curr.next;
    }

    return cl;
}

// Testing code.
public static void main(String[] args)  {
    CircularLinkedList ll = new CircularLinkedList();
    ll.addHead(1);
    ll.addHead(2);
    ll.addHead(3);
    ll.print();
    CircularLinkedList ll2 = ll.copyList();
    ll2.print();
}
```

**Output:**

```
3 2 1
3 2 1
```

**Time Complexity:** O(n).

## Doubly Circular list

A Doubly Circular Linked list is made up of nodes. Each node in a doubly-linked list is made up of three parts, the first part is data and the other two are references to other nodes of the linked list. These references are called prev and next. The previous pointer of the node will point to the node before the current node, and the next pointer will point to the node next to the current node. The beginning of the list is called "Head" which points to the first node of the linked list. The prev of the first node points to the last node. The next of the last nodes points to the first node.

In the doubly linked list, we have the following cases:

1 Zero element case.
2 Only element.
3 General case
4 Avoid using recursion solutions, it makes life harder

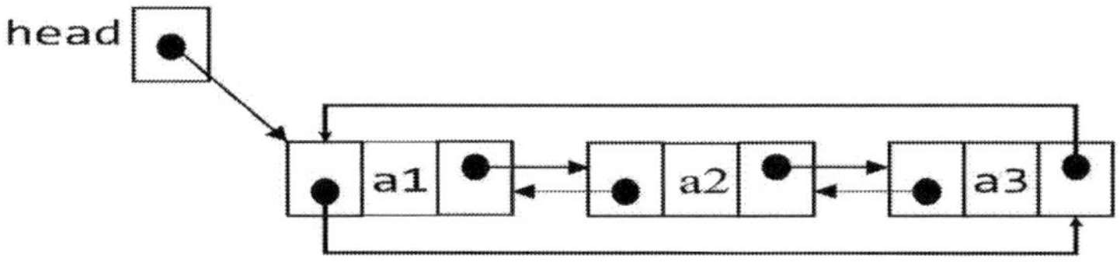


**Example 6.49:** Doubly Circular Linked List class.

```
public class DoublyCircularLinkedList {
    private Node head = null;
    private Node tail = null;
    private int size = 0;

    private static class Node {
        private int value;
        private Node next;
        private Node prev;

        public Node(int v, Node nxt, Node prv) {
            value = v;
            next = nxt;
            prev = prv;
        }
    }

    public int size() {
        return size;
    }

    public boolean isEmpty() {
        return size == 0;
    }

    /* Other methods */
};
```

**Analysis:** The node of the doubly circular linked list is the same as the node of the doubly linked list. The only difference is that the previous pointer of the first node points to the last node of the list, and the next pointer of the last node points to the first node of the list.

## Delete List

**Problem:** Free a linked list.

**Solution:** Delete list is the same as given in the circular linked list.

## Search Value

**Problem:** Search a value in a doubly circular linked list.

**Solution:** The algorithm for searching a value in a doubly circular linked list is the same as a circular linked list.

## Print List

**Problem:** Print all the elements of the linked list.

**Solution:** The algorithm to print the content of the doubly circular list is the same as given in a circular linked list.

## Insert Node at head

**Problem:** Insert value at the front of the list.

**Example 6.50**:
```
public void addHead(int value) {
    Node newNode = new Node(value, null, null);
    if (size == 0) {
        tail = head = newNode;
        newNode.next = newNode;
        newNode.prev = newNode;
    } else {
        newNode.next = head;
        newNode.prev = head.prev;
        head.prev = newNode;
        newNode.prev.next = newNode;
        head = newNode;
    }
    size++;
}

// Testing code.
public static void main(String[] args)  {
    DoublyCircularLinkedList ll = new DoublyCircularLinkedList();
    ll.addHead(1);
    ll.addHead(2);
    ll.addHead(3);
    ll.print();
    System.out.println("size : " + ll.size());
    System.out.println("isEmpty : " + ll.isEmpty());
}
```

**Output:**
```
3 2 1
size : 3
isEmpty : false
```

**Analysis**:
1. A new node is created and if the list is empty then head and tail will point to it. The newly created newNode next and prev also point to newNode.
2. If the list is not empty, then the pointers are adjusted and a new node is added to the front of the list. Only the head needs to be changed in this case.
3. Size of the list has increased by one.

**Time Complexity:** O(1).

## Insert Node at the tail

**Problem:** Insert value at the end of a linked list.

**Example 6.51:**
```
public void addTail(int value) {
    Node newNode = new Node(value, null, null);
    if (size == 0) {
        head = tail = newNode;
        newNode.next = newNode;
        newNode.prev = newNode;
    } else {
        newNode.next = tail.next;
        newNode.prev = tail;
        tail.next = newNode;
        newNode.next.prev = newNode;
        tail = newNode;
    }
    size++;
}

// Testing code.
public static void main(String[] args)  {
    DoublyCircularLinkedList ll = new DoublyCircularLinkedList();
    ll.addTail(1);
    ll.addTail(2);
    ll.addTail(3);
    ll.print();
}
```

**Output:**
```
1 2 3
```

**Analysis**:
1. A new node is created and if the list is empty then head and tail will point to it. The newly created newNode's next and prev also point to newNode.
2. If the list is not empty, then the pointers are adjusted and a new node is added to the end of the list. Only the tail needs to be changed in this case.
3. The size of the list has increased by one.

**Time Complexity:** O(1).

## Remove Head node

**Problem:** Remove node at the head of a doubly circular linked list

**Example 6.52:**
```
public int removeHead() {
    if (size == 0)
        throw new IllegalStateException("EmptyListException");

    int value = head.value;
    size--;

    if (size == 0) {
        head = null;
```

```
        tail = null;
        return value;
    }

    Node next = head.next;
    next.prev = tail;
    tail.next = next;
    head = next;
    return value;
}

// Testing code.
public static void main(String[] args)  {
    DoublyCircularLinkedList ll = new DoublyCircularLinkedList();
    ll.addHead(1);
    ll.addHead(2);
    ll.addHead(3);
    ll.print();

    ll.removeHead();
    ll.print();
}
```

**Output:**

```
3 2 1
2 1
```

**Analysis:** Remove nodes in a doubly circular linked list is just the same as removing nodes in a circular linked list. Just a few extra pointers need to be adjusted.
**Time Complexity:** O(1).

## Remove Tail node

**Problem:** Remove the tail node of a linked list.

**Example 6.53:**

```
public int removeTail() {
    if (size == 0)
        throw new IllegalStateException("EmptyListException");

    int value = tail.value;
    size--;

    if (size == 0) {
        head = null;
        tail = null;
        return value;
    }

    Node prev = tail.prev;
    prev.next = head;
    head.prev = prev;
    tail = prev;
    return value;
}
```

```
// Testing code.
public static void main(String[] args)  {
    DoublyCircularLinkedList ll = new DoublyCircularLinkedList();
    ll.addHead(1);
    ll.addHead(2);
    ll.addHead(3);
    ll.print();

    ll.removeTail();
    ll.print();
}
```

**Output:**
```
3 2 1
3 2
```

**Analysis:** In case of empty list return. In the case of a single node case, the head and tail will store null. In other cases, the next of the second last node will point to the head, the previous of the head will point to the second last node.

**Time Complexity:** O(1).

## Skip List

The worst case search time for a linked list is O(n). Even if the list elements are sorted then also we can only linearly traverse the list. On the other hand if we have a sorted array, we can apply the Binary Search method for searching by reducing the search space by half at each comparison. By using Skip List we can get a similar benefit. We create multiple layers so that we can skip multiple nodes.

The lowest layer of the skip list is a commonly sorted linked list, and the higher layers of the skip list contain less and less elements. The higher layers are like an "express train" where the many stops are skipped. And the lowest layer is like a “Local train” which will stop at each and every station.

Definition: The skip list is a probabilistic data structure which uses probability to build multiple layers over a sorted linked list. Each additional layer of links contains fewer elements, but no new elements.

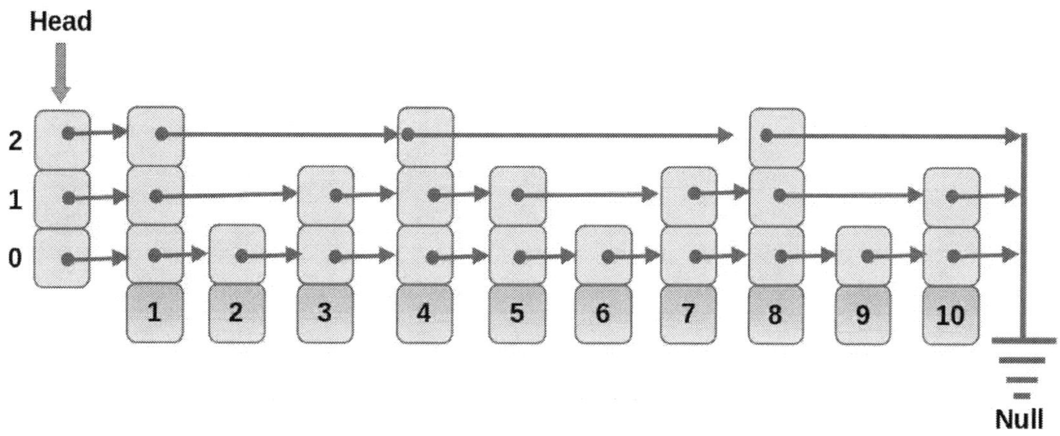

Skip List Basic Operations are: Search, Insert and Delete.

1. **Search** : The search operation is used to search a particular node in a skip list.

```
function Search(list, key)
    p = top-left node in list
    while (p.below != null)       //Scan down
        p = p.below
        while (key >= p.next)      //Scan forward
            p = p.next
    return p
```

2. **Insertion** : It is used to add a new node to a particular location in a specific situation.

```
function Insert(list, key, value)
    // Create update array
    local update[0...MaxLevel+1]
    x = list.header

    // Populate update array to find
    // the position of the new node at each level.
    for i = (list.level - 1) downto 0
        while x.forward[i] != Null and x.forward[i].key < key
            x = x.forward[i]
        update[i] = x

    // Key already present so just update value.
    if x.forward[0] != Null and x.forward[0].key = key
        x.forward[0].value = value
        return;

    // Level of the new node is created. If level is increased then
    // header will be the start of a new level list.
    lvl = randomLevel()
    if lvl > list.level
        for i = list.level to (lvl - 1)
            update[i] = list.header
        list.level = lvl

    // New nodes are created and linked at each level.
    x = makeNode(key, value, lvl)

    for i = 0 to lvl
        x.forward[i] = update[i].forward[i]
        update[i].forward[i] = x
```

3. **Deletion** : It is used to delete a node in a specific situation.

```
function Delete(list, key)
    local update[0..MaxLevel+1]
    x = list.header

    for i = (list.level - 1) downto 0 do
        while x.forward[i] != Null and x.forward[i].key < key
            x = x.forward[i]
        update[i] = x
```

```
x = x.forward[0]
if x.key = key
    for i = 0 to list.level-1
        if update[i].forward[i] ≠ x
            break
        update[i].forward[i] = x.forward[i]
    free(x)
    while list.level > 0 and list.header.forward[list.level] = Null
        list.level = list.level - 1
```

| | Average Case | Worst Case |
|---|---|---|
| **Search** | O(log(n)) | O(n) |
| **Insert** | O(log(n)) | O(n) |
| **Delete** | O(log(n)) | O(n) |

## Uses of Linked List

Applications of Linked List are:

1. Used to implement various data structures like Stack, Queue, Hashtable, Graph etc.
2. Next and Previous function in photo viewer. Doubly linked list is used in photo viewers. We can go from the current picture to previous or next.
3. Next and Previous track in music player. A doubly circular linked list is used in the music player. We can play the previous or next song. And once the whole list of songs is played, it starts again at the beginning.

## Exercise

1 Insert an element at the $k^{th}$ position from the start of the linked list. Return true if success and if the list is not long enough, then return -1.

Hint: Take a pointer of head and then advance it by K steps forward, and inserts the node.

2 Insert an element at the $k^{th}$ position from the end of the linked list. Return true if success and if the list is not long enough, then return -1.

Hint: Take a pointer to the head and then advance it by K steps forward. Take another pointer and then advance both simultaneously, so that when the first pointer reaches the end of a linked list, then the second pointer is at the point where you need to insert the node.

3 Consider there is a loop in a linked list, write a program to remove the loop if there is a loop in this linked list.

4 In the above SearchList program return, the count of how many instances of the same value are found else if the value is not found then return 0. For example, if the value passed is "4". The elements in the list are 1,2,4,3 & 4. The program should return 2.

Hint: In place of return true in the above program, increment a counter and then return its value.

5 Given two linked list head-pointers, they meet at some point and need to find the point of intersection. However, in place of the end of both the linked list to be a null pointer, there is a loop.

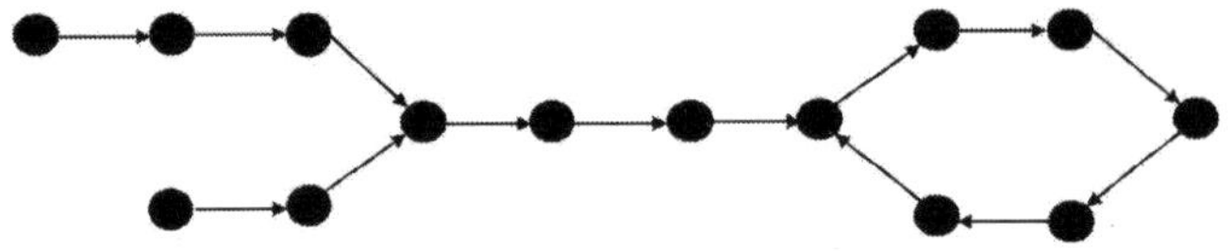

6 If a linked list having a loop is given. Count the number of nodes in the linked list

7 We were supposed to write the complete code for the addition of polynomials using Linked Lists. This takes time if you do not have it by heart, so revise it well.

8 In given two linked lists. We must find whether the data in one is reverse that of data in another. No extra space should be used, and traverse the linked lists only once.

9 Find the middle element in a singly linked list. Tell the complexity of your solution.

Hint:- First solution: Find the length of the linked list. Then find the middle element and return it. Second solution: Use two pointers, one will move fast and another will move slow, make sure you handle border cases properly. (Even length and odd length linked list cases.)

10 Print list in reverse order.

11 In a huge linked list, you are given a pointer to some middle node. Write a program to remove this node.

Hint: Copy the values of the next node to the current node. Then remove the next node.

12 In a linked list, you are given a pointer to some middle node and node next to it. Write a program to remove this middle node.

Hint: Copy the values of the next node to the current node. Then remove the next node.

13 Given a special list, whose nodes have an extra pointer random which points to some other node in the linked list. Create another list that is a copy of the given list. Also, make sure that a random pointer is also allocated to the respective node in the new list.

Hint: Traverse the list and go on adding nodes to the list, which have the same value but have random pointer points to null. Now traverse the modified list again. Let us call the node, which was already present in the list as an old node and the node, which is added as a new node. Find the random pointer node pointed to by the old node, and assign its next node to the random pointer of the new node. Follow this procedure for all the nodes. Finally, separate the old and new nodes. The list formed by new nodes is the desired list.

14 Modify the AddHead() function of LinkedList such that below operation is allowed.

```
LinkedList ll = new LinkedList();
ll.AddHead(1).AddHead(2).AddHead(3);
```

# CHAPTER 7: STACK

## Introduction

Stack is a basic data structure that organises data in a **last-in-first-out(LIFO)** manner. The last element inserted in a stack will be the first to be removed from it.

The real-life analogy of the stack is "stack of plates". Imagine a stack of plates in a dining area. Everybody takes a plate from the top of the stack. As a result, the next plate becomes available to be picked. Stack allows you to access only the top element. The element that is at the bottom of the stack is the one that stays there for the longest time.

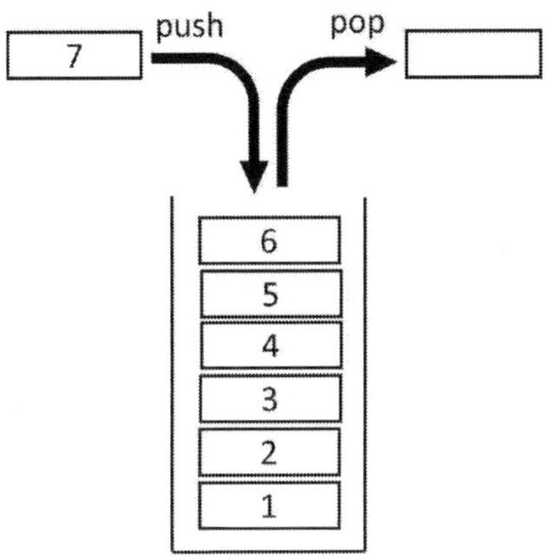


Computer science also has the common example of a stack. A function call stack is a good example of a stack. Function main() calls function foo() and then foo() calls bar(). These function calls are implemented using stack. First, bar() exists, then foo() and then finally main().

As we navigate from web page to web page, the URL of web pages are kept in a stack, with the current page URL at the top. If we click the back button, then each URL entry is popped one by one.

## The Stack Abstract Data Type

Stack abstract data type is defined as a data structure, which follows LIFO or last-in-first-out for the elements added to it.

The stack should support the following operations:

1 Push(): Adds a single element at the top of the stack
2 Pop(): Removes a single element from the top of a stack.
3 Top(): Reads the value of the top element of the stack (does not remove it)
4 isEmpty(): Returns 1 if stack is empty otherwise return 0.
5 Size(): Returns the number of elements in a stack.

Push: Add value to the top of a stack

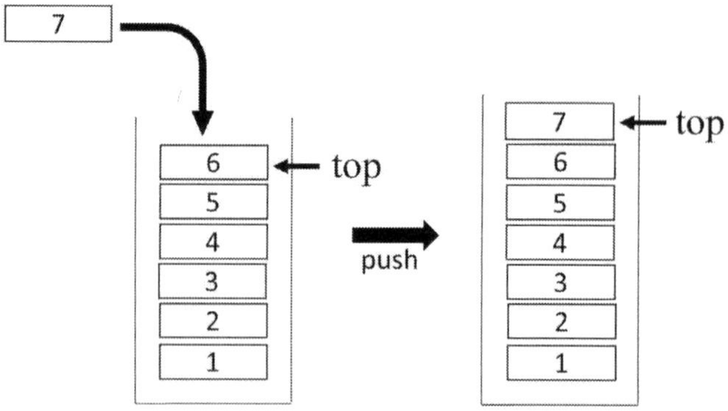


Pop: Remove the top element of the stack and return it to the caller function.

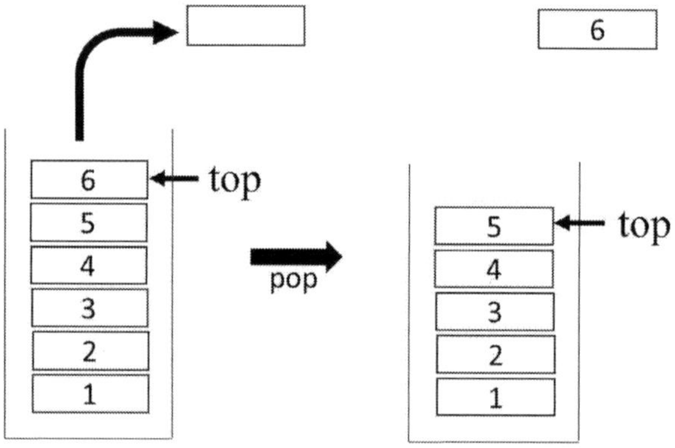


The stack can be implemented using an array or a linked list.

1. When stack is implemented using arrays, its capacity is fixed.
2. In the case of a linked list, there is no such limit on the number of elements it can contain.

When a stack is implemented, using an array, the top of the stack is managed using an index variable called top.

When a stack is implemented using a linked list, push() and pop() are implemented using insert at the head of the linked list and remove from the head of the linked list.

## Stack using array

**Problem:** Implement a stack using a fixed length array.

**Example 7.1**: Stack implementation using array

```
public class Stack {
    private int capacity;
    private int[] data;
    private int top = -1;

    public Stack() {
        this(1000);
    }
```

```
    public Stack(int s) {
        data = new int[s];
        capacity = s;
    }
    /* Other methods */
}
```

**isEmpty**() function returns true if stack is empty or false in all other cases.

```
public boolean isEmpty() {
    return (top == -1);
}
```

**size**() function returns the number of elements in the stack.

```
public int size() {
    return top + 1;
}
```

The **print**() function will print the elements of the array.

```
public void print() {
    for (int i = top; i >= 0; i--) {
        System.out.print(data[i] + " ");
    }
    System.out.println();
}
```

**push**() function to append value to the data.

```
public void push(int value) throws IllegalStateException {
    if (top + 1 == capacity) {
        throw new IllegalStateException("StackOverflowException");
    }
    top++;
    data[top] = value;
}
```

In the **pop**() function, first it will check that the stack is not empty. Then it will pop the value from the data array and return it.

```
public int pop() {
    if (isEmpty()) {
        throw new IllegalStateException("StackEmptyException");
    }
    int topVal = data[top];
    top--;
    return topVal;
}
```

**top**() function returns the value of stored in the top element of stack (does not remove it)

```
public int top() throws IllegalStateException {
    if (isEmpty()) {
        throw new IllegalStateException("StackEmptyException");
    }
    return data[top];
}
```

Testing code for stack.

```
public static void main(String[] args) {
    Stack s = new Stack();
    s.push(1);
    s.push(2);
    s.push(3);
    s.print();
    System.out.println(s.pop());
    System.out.println(s.pop());
}
```

**Output:**

```
3 2 1
3
2
```

**Analysis:**

1. The stack object is declared and initialised.
2. push() and pop() functions are used to add and remove values to the stack.

**Time Complexity**: Push(), Pop(), Top(), Size() and IsEmpty() all these operations have time complexity of O(1).

StackPrint() function has a time complexity of O(n).

## Stack using array with memory management

**Problem:** Create a stack using an array, but the memory of the array needs to be managed. When the stack is full its capacity is doubled. Also, when the number of elements falls below capacity/2, the capacity of the stack is halved. Also, we do not want to let the capacity of the stack below the initially allocated size. We can define min length when the stack is created.

**Analysis:** The Stack struct contains four fields. "Top" which is the index of the topmost element, a pointer "data" that will point to dynamically allocated memory. "Size" which is used to store the size of the stack and "capacity" which is the capacity of the stack.

Push and pop functions are implemented next**.** All the other functions like, isEmpty(), size() and top() will remain the same.

### Push function growing capacity implementation

Implementing push() function of the stack such that when the stack is filled, then double the capacity of the stack.

**Example 7.2:**

```
public void push2(int value) {
    if (top + 1 == capacity) {
        System.out.println("size doubled");
        int[] newData = new int[capacity * 2];
        System.arraycopy(data, 0, newData, 0, capacity);
        data = newData;
```

```
        capacity = capacity * 2;
    }
    top++;
    data[top] = value;
}
```

**Analysis:**

1. We are doubling the max capacity variable of the stack.
2. Size of the memory is reallocated to a bigger value in this line. All the data on the stack is copied into the new location.
3. Finally, the data is pushed into the increased capacity stack.

## Pop function reducing capacity implementation

Implementing pop() function such that when count of elements in stack fall below capacity/2 the capacity of the stack is reduced.

**Example 7.3:**

```
public class Stack {
    private int capacity;
    private int[] data;
    private int top = -1;
    private int minCapacity; // for dynamic stack

    public Stack() {
        this(1000);
    }

    public Stack(int s) {
        data = new int[s];
        capacity = s;
        minCapacity = s; // for dynamic stack
    }

    /* Other methods */
}

public int pop2() {
    if (isEmpty()) {
        throw new IllegalStateException("StackEmptyException");
    }

    int topVal = data[top];
    top--;

    if (top + 1 < (capacity / 2) && capacity > minCapacity) {
        System.out.println("size halved top ");
        capacity = capacity / 2;
        int[] newData = new int[capacity];
        System.arraycopy(data, 0, newData, 0, capacity);
        data = newData;
    }
    return topVal;
}
```

**Analysis:** The size of the stack is checked if it goes below half of the capacity and is greater than the minimum size. The capacity of the stack is divided by 2 and memory is reallocated to point to half size memory.

## Stack using linked list

**Problem:** Stack can be implemented using a linked list. Push() adds elements at the head of the list and Pop() removes elements from the head of the list.

**Example 7.4**: Implement stack using a linked list.

```
public class StackLL {
    private Node head = null;
    private int length = 0;

    private static class Node {
        private int value;
        private Node next;

        public Node(int v, Node n) {
            value = v;
            next = n;
        }
    }

    public int size() {
        return length;
    }

    public boolean isEmpty() {
        return length == 0;
    }

    public int peek() throws IllegalStateException {
        if (isEmpty()) {
            throw new IllegalStateException("StackEmptyException");
        }
        return head.value;
    }

    public void push(int value) {
        head = new Node(value, head);
        length++;
    }

    public int pop() throws IllegalStateException {
        if (isEmpty()) {
            throw new IllegalStateException("StackEmptyException");
        }

        int value = head.value;
        head = head.next;
        length--;
        return value;
    }
```

```
    public void insertAtBottom(int value) {
        if (isEmpty()) {
            push(value);
        } else {
            int temp = pop();
            insertAtBottom(value);
            push(temp);
        }
    }

    public void print() {
        Node temp = head;
        while (temp != null) {
            System.out.print(temp.value + " ");
            temp = temp.next;
        }
        System.out.println();
    }

    // Testing code.
    public static void main(String[] args) {
        StackLL s = new StackLL();
        s.push(1);
        s.push(2);
        s.push(3);
        s.print();
        System.out.println(s.pop());
        System.out.println(s.pop());
    }
}
```

**Output:**

```
3 2 1
3
2
1
```

**Analysis:**

1. Stack implemented using a linked list is simply insertion and deletion at the head of a singly linked list.
2. In the Push() function, memory is created for one node. Then the value is stored into that node. Finally, the node is inserted at the beginning of the list.
3. In the Pop() function, the head of the linked list starts pointing to the second node. And the value of the first node is returned.

**Time Complexity**: Push(), Pop(), and IsEmpty() all these operations have time complexity of O(1). Print() function has a time complexity of O(n).

## Stack implementation in Java Collection

Stack is implemented by calling push and pop methods of Stack<T> class.

**Example 7.5:**

```
import java.util.*;
```

```
public class StackDemo {
    public static void main(String[] args) {
        Stack<Integer> stack = new Stack<Integer>();
        stack.push(1);
        stack.push(2);
        stack.push(3);
        System.out.println("Stack : " + stack);
        System.out.println("Stack size : " + stack.size());
        System.out.println("Stack pop : " + stack.pop());
        System.out.println("Stack top : " + stack.top());
        System.out.println("Stack isEmpty : " + stack.isEmpty());
    }
}
```

**Output:**

```
Stack : [1, 2, 3]
Stack size : 3
Stack pop : 3
Stack top : 2
Stack isEmpty : false
```

**Analysis:**

1. Value 1, 2 and 3 are added to the stack using push() function. Then the stack is printed.
2. Stack top is returned using top() function.
3. Size of stack is returned using size() function.
4. Function is `isEmpty()` return true if stack is empty else return false.
5. Function pop() is used to remove top element of the stack.

## System stack and function Calls

Function calls are implemented using a stack called system stack. When a method is called, the current execution is stopped and the control goes to the called function. After the called function exits / returns, the execution resumes from the point at which the execution was stopped.

To get the exact point at which execution should be resumed, the address of the next instruction is stored in the system stack. When the function call completes, the address at the top of the stack is taken out.

**Example 7.6:** Function call flow

```
public static void function2() {
    System.out.println("fun2 line 1");
}

public static void function1() {
    System.out.println("fun1 line 1");
    function2();
    System.out.println("fun1 line 2");
}
```

```
// Testing code.
public static void main(String[] args)  {
    System.out.println("main line 1");
    function1();
    System.out.println("main line 2");
}
```

**Output:**

```
main line 1
fun1 line 1
fun2 line 1
fun1 line 2
main line 2
```

**Analysis:**

1. This program starts with the main() function.
2. The first statement of main() will be executed. This will print "main line 1" as output.
3. Then statement function1() is called. Before control goes to function1() then the next instruction that is the address of the next line is stored in the system stack.
4. Control goes to function1() function.
5. The first statement inside function1() is executed, this will print "fun1 line 1" to output.
6. function2() is called from function1(). Before control goes to the function2() address of the next instruction, that is the address of the next line is added to the system stack.
7. Control goes to the function2() function.
8. "fun2 line 1" is printed to the screen.
9. When function2() exits, control comes back to function1(). Then the program reads the next instruction from the stack, and the next line is executed and prints "fun1 line 2" to screen.
10. When fun1 exits, control comes back to the main function. Then the program reads the next instruction from the stack and executes it and finally "main line 2" is printed to screen.

**Points to remember:**

1. Functions are implemented using a stack.
2. When a function is called, the address of the next instruction is pushed into the stack.
3. When a function is finished, the address of the execution is taken out of the stack.

## Problems in Stack

### Sorted Insert

**Problem:** Given a stack whose elements are sorted, write a function that will insert elements in sorted order. With highest at the top and lowest at the bottom.

**Solution:** Pop elements from the stack till the top of the stack is greater than the current value. Then add the current value to the stack and then add the popped elements to the stack again. Time complexity O(n)

**Example 7.7:**

```
public static void sortedInsert(Stack<Integer> stk, int element) {
    int temp;
```

```
    if (stk.isEmpty() || element > stk.peek())
        stk.push(element);
    else {
        temp = stk.pop();
        sortedInsert(stk, element);
        stk.push(temp);
    }
}

// Testing code.
public static void main(String[] args)  {
    Stack<Integer> stk = new Stack<Integer>();
    stk.push(1);
    stk.push(3);
    stk.push(4);
    System.out.println(stk);
    sortedInsert(stk, 2);
    System.out.println(stk);
}
```

**Output:**

```
[1, 3, 4]
[1, 2, 3, 4]
```

## Sort Stack

**Problem:** Given a stack, sort elements such that the largest value is at the top.

**First solution:** Recursively call sortStack() function. Then call the sortedInsert() function inside recursion to make the stack sorted. Time complexity is O(n^2).

**Example 7.8:**

```
public static void sortStack(Stack<Integer> stk) {
    if (stk.isEmpty() == false) {
        int temp = stk.pop();
        sortStack(stk);
        sortedInsert(stk, temp);
    }
}

// Testing code.
public static void main(String[] args)  {
    Stack<Integer> stk = new Stack<Integer>();
    stk.push(3);
    stk.push(1);
    stk.push(4);
    stk.push(2);
    System.out.println(stk);

    sortStack(stk);
    System.out.println(stk);
}
```

**Output:**

```
[3, 1, 4, 2]
[1, 2, 3, 4]
```

**Second solution:** Same problem can be solved iteratively by using another stack stk2. We use a stack stk2 which will store elements always in sorted order. Each time, a new element is popped from the original input stack and gets added to the new stack. Time Complexity is O(n^2)

**Example 7.9:**
```
public static void sortStack2(Stack<Integer> stk) {
    int temp;
    Stack<Integer> stk2 = new Stack<Integer>();
    while (stk.isEmpty() == false) {
        temp = stk.pop();
        while ((stk2.isEmpty() == false) && (stk2.peek() < temp))
            stk.push(stk2.pop());
        stk2.push(temp);
    }

    while (stk2.isEmpty() == false)
        stk.push(stk2.pop());
}
```

## Bottom Insert

**Problem:** Given stack, write a function to insert an element at the bottom of the stack.

**Solution:** Pop elements from the stack recursively till it is empty. Once empty then insert the input value in the stack. Then again put the popped values back to the stack. Time complexity is O(n)

**Example 7.10:**
```
public static void bottomInsert(Stack<Integer> stk, int element) {
    int temp;
    if (stk.isEmpty())
        stk.push(element);
    else {
        temp = stk.pop();
        bottomInsert(stk, element);
        stk.push(temp);
    }
}

// Testing code.
public static void main(String[] args)  {
    Stack<Integer> stk = new Stack<Integer>();
    stk.push(1);
    stk.push(2);
    stk.push(3);
    System.out.println(stk);
    bottomInsert(stk, 4);
    System.out.println(stk);
}
```

**Output:**
```
[1, 2, 3]
[4, 1, 2, 3]
```

## Reverse Stack

**Problem:** Given a stack, reverse its elements.

**First solution:** Using recursion, in a recursion pop element from stack and use bottomInsert function to add them at the bottom. Finally, the whole stack will be reversed. Time complexity is O(n^2)

**Example 7.11:**
```
public static <T> void reverseStack(Stack<T> stk) {
    if (stk.isEmpty()) {
        return;
    } else {
        T value = stk.pop();
        reverseStack(stk);
        bottomInsert(stk, value);
    }
}

// Testing code.
public static void main(String[] args)  {
    Stack<Integer> stk = new Stack<Integer>();
    stk.push(1);
    stk.push(2);
    stk.push(3);
    stk.push(4);
    System.out.println(stk);

    reverseStack(stk);
    System.out.println(stk);
}
```

**Output:**
```
[ 1 2 3 4 ]
[ 4 3 2 1 ]
```

**Second solution:** let's solve the problem using a queue. Pop all the elements of the stack and insert them into a queue. Then remove elements from the queue and insert them into the stack. As a result, stack elements will be reversed. Time complexity is O(n).

**Example 7.12:**
```
public static void reverseStack2(Stack<Integer> stk) {
    ArrayDeque<Integer> que = new ArrayDeque<Integer>();

    while (stk.isEmpty() == false)
        que.add(stk.pop());

    while (que.isEmpty() == false)
        stk.push(que.remove());
}
```

## Reverse K Element in a Stack

**Problem:** Given an integer k and a stack, reverse the k elements from the top of the stack.

**Solution:** Create a queue, pop k elements from the stack and add them to the queue. Then remove these elements from the queue and push them back to the stack. Top k elements of the stack will be reversed. Time complexity is O(n)

**Example 7.13:**
```
public static void reverseKElementInStack(Stack<Integer> stk, int k) {
    ArrayDeque<Integer> que = new ArrayDeque<Integer>();
    int i = 0;
    while (stk.isEmpty() == false && i < k) {
        que.add(stk.pop());
        i++;
    }
    while (que.isEmpty() == false)
        stk.push(que.remove());
}

// Testing code.
public static void main(String[] args)  {
    Stack<Integer> stk = new Stack<Integer>();
    stk.push(1);
    stk.push(2);
    stk.push(3);
    stk.push(4);
    System.out.println(stk);
    reverseKElementInStack(stk, 2);
    System.out.println(stk);
}
```

**Output:**
```
[ 1 2 3 4 ]
[ 1 2 4 3 ]
```

## Reverse Queue

**Problem:** Reverse elements of a queue.

**Solution:** Remove all the elements of the queue and push them to the stack till the queue is empty. Then pop elements from the stack and add them to the queue. Finally, all the elements of the queue are reversed. Time complexity is O(n)

**Example 7.14:**
```
public static void reverseQueue(ArrayDeque<Integer> que) {
    Stack<Integer> stk = new Stack<Integer>();
    while (que.isEmpty() == false)
        stk.push(que.remove());

    while (stk.isEmpty() == false)
        que.add(stk.pop());
}

// Testing code.
public static void main(String[] args)  {
    ArrayDeque<Integer> que = new ArrayDeque<Integer>();
    que.add(1);
```

```
    que.add(2);
    que.add(3);
    System.out.println(que);
    reverseQueue(que);
    System.out.println(que);
}
```

**Output:**

```
[ 1 2 3 ]
[ 3 2 1 ]
```

## Reverse K Element in a Queue

**Problem:** Reverse first K elements in a queue.

**Solution:** Use a stack, remove first K elements from the queue and push them into the stack. Then pop the element from the stack and add them to the queue. The K elements are reversed, but they are added to the end of the queue. So, we need to bring those elements at the start of the queue by removing the elements at the front and adding them at the back of the queue. Time complexity is O(n)

**Example 7.15:**

```
public static void reverseKElementInQueue(ArrayDeque<Integer> que, int k) {
    Stack<Integer> stk = new Stack<Integer>();
    int i = 0, diff, temp;
    while (que.isEmpty() == false && i < k) {
        stk.push(que.remove());
        i++;
    }

    while (stk.isEmpty() == false) {
        que.add(stk.pop());
    }

    diff = que.size() - k;
    while (diff > 0) {
        temp = que.remove();
        que.add(temp);
        diff -= 1;
    }
}

// Testing code.
public static void main(String[] args)  {
    ArrayDeque<Integer> que = new ArrayDeque<Integer>();
    que.add(1);
    que.add(2);
    que.add(3);
    System.out.println(que);
    reverseKElementInQueue(que, 2);
    System.out.println(que);
}
```

**Output:**

```
[1, 2, 3]
[2, 1, 3]
```

## Two stacks using single array

**Problem:** How to implement two stacks using one single array.

**Solution:** First stack is used by adding to the left and removing elements from the left. Second stack is used by adding to the right and removing elements from the right. Push and pop of both the stack has a time complexity of O(1).

**Example 7.16:**
```
public class TwoStack {
    private final int MAX_SIZE = 50;
    int top1;
    int top2;
    int[] data;

    public TwoStack() {
        top1 = -1;
        top2 = MAX_SIZE;
        data = new int[MAX_SIZE];
    }

    public void push1(int value) {
        if (top1 < top2 - 1) {
            data[++top1] = value;
        } else {
            System.out.print("Stack is Full!");
        }
    }

    public void push2(int value) {
        if (top1 < top2 - 1) {
            data[--top2] = value;
        } else {
            System.out.print("Stack is Full!");
        }
    }

    public int pop1() {
        if (top1 >= 0) {
            int value = data[top1--];
            return value;
        } else {
            System.out.print("Stack Empty!");
        }
        return -999;
    }

    public int pop2() {
        if (top2 < MAX_SIZE) {
            int value = data[top2++];
            return value;
        } else {
            System.out.print("Stack Empty!");
        }
        return -999;
    }
```

```
    // Testing code.
    public static void main(String[] args) {
        TwoStack st = new TwoStack();
        st.push1(1);
        st.push1(2);
        st.push1(3);
        st.push2(4);
        st.push2(5);
        st.push2(6);
        System.out.println("stk1 pop: " + st.pop1());
        System.out.println("stk1 pop: " + st.pop1());
        System.out.println("stk2 pop: " + st.pop2());
        System.out.println("stk2 pop: " + st.pop2());
    }
}
```

**Output:**

```
stk1 pop: 3
stk1 pop: 2
stk2 pop: 6
stk2 pop: 5
```

**Analysis:** Same list is used to implement two stacks. The first stack is filled from the beginning of the array and the second stack is filled from the end of the array. Overflow and underflow conditions need to be taken care of carefully.

## Balanced Parenthesis

**Problem:** Write a program to check balanced symbols (such as {}, (), []). The closing symbol should be matched with the most recently seen opening symbol. e.g. {()} is legal, {()({})} is legal, but {((} and {(}) are not legal.

**Example 7.17:**

```
public static boolean isBalancedParenthesis(String expn) {
    Stack<Character> stk = new Stack<Character>();
    for (char ch : expn.toCharArray()) {
        switch (ch) {
        case '{':
        case '[':
        case '(':
            stk.push(ch);
            break;
        case '}':
            if (stk.pop() != '{') {
                return false;
            }
            break;
        case ']':
            if (stk.pop() != '[') {
                return false;
            }
            break;
        case ')':
            if (stk.pop() != '(') {
```

```
                return false;
            }
            break;
        }
    }
    return stk.isEmpty();
}

// Testing code.
public static void main(String[] args)  {
    String expn = "{()}[]";
    boolean value = isBalancedParenthesis(expn);
    System.out.println("isBalancedParenthesis: " + value);
}
```

**Output:**

```
isBalancedParenthesis : true
```

**Analysis:**

1. Traverse the input string. When we get an opening parenthesis, we push it into the stack. When we get a closing parenthesis then we pop a parenthesis from the stack and compare if it is the corresponding closing parenthesis.
2. We return false if there is a mismatch of parenthesis.
3. If at the end of the whole string traversal, we reach the end of the string and the stack is empty then we have balanced parenthesis.

## Max Depth Parenthesis

**Problem:** Given a balanced parenthesis expression, you need to find the maximum depth of parenthesis. For example, in (), maximum depth is 1 and in (((()))(), maximum depth is 3.

**First solution:** Create a stack, when we get opening parenthesis then we insert it to the stack and increase depth counter. When we get a closing parenthesis, then we pop the opening parenthesis from the stack and decrease the depth counter. We keep track of depth to find maximum depth.

**Example 7.18:**

```
public static int maxDepthParenthesis(String expn, int size) {
    Stack<Character> stk = new Stack<Character>();
    int maxDepth = 0;
    int depth = 0;
    char ch;
    for (int i = 0; i < size; i++) {
        ch = expn.charAt(i);
        if (ch == '(') {
            stk.push(ch);
            depth += 1;
        } else if (ch == ')') {
            stk.pop();
            depth -= 1;
        }
        if (depth > maxDepth)
            maxDepth = depth;
    }
```

```
    return maxDepth;
}

// Testing code.
public static void main(String[] args)  {
    String expn = "(((A)))((((BBB()))))()()()())";
    int size = expn.length();
    System.out.println("Max depth parenthesis is " + maxDepthParenthesis(expn, 
size));
}
```

**Output:**

```
Max depth parenthesis is 6
```

**Second solution:** We do not need to find if the expression is balanced or not. It is given that it is balanced, so we don't need a stack as shown in the previous solution.

**Example 7.19:**

```
public static int maxDepthParenthesis2(String expn, int size) {
    int maxDepth = 0;
    int depth = 0;
    char ch;
    for (int i = 0; i < size; i++) {
        ch = expn.charAt(i);
        if (ch == '(')
            depth += 1;
        else if (ch == ')')
            depth -= 1;

        if (depth > maxDepth)
            maxDepth = depth;
    }
    return maxDepth;
}
```

## Longest Continuous Balanced Parenthesis

**Problem:** Given a string of opening and closing parentheses, you need to find the length of the longest substring that has balanced parentheses.

**Solution**: Traverse through the list of parentheses and add the current index to the stack when an opening parenthesis is observed. When a closing parenthesis is observed, then pop from the stack. And then find the length of continuous parenthesis by subtracting the popped value with the current index. By doing this we will get balanced parenthesis, but it may not be the largest. Because this method will consider two balanced substrings with equal number of opening parenthesis and closing parenthesis as different strings, even though they are continuous.

To avoid the above issue we will also add -1 to the stack. The lowest value stored in the stack is on an index less than the probable balanced parenthesis. When the number of closing parenthesis is more than the number of the opening parenthesis. Then at that point, the index before the probable longest balanced parenthesis string is the index of the unbalanced closing parenthesis.

**Example 7.20:**
```
public static int longestContBalParen(String string, int size) {
    Stack<Integer> stk = new Stack<Integer>();
    stk.push(-1);
    int length = 0;
    for (int i = 0; i < size; i++) {
        if (string.charAt(i) == '(')
            stk.push(i);
        else {
            stk.pop();
            if (stk.size() != 0)
                length = Math.max(length, i - stk.peek());
            else
                stk.push(i);
        }
    }
    return length;
}

// Testing code.
public static void main(String[] args)  {
    String expn = "())((()))(())()(()";
    int size = expn.length();
    System.out.println("longestContBalParen " + longestContBalParen(expn, size));
}
```

**Output:**
```
longestContBalParen 12
```

## Reverse Parenthesis

**Problem:** How many reversals will be needed to make an unbalanced expression to balanced expression.

Input: ")(())(((“

Output: 3

Input: “)(((“

Output: 3

**Solution**:

1. First, the parenthesis, which is already balanced, doesn't need to be flipped, so they are first removed. If all the parenthesis which are balanced are removed, then we will have the parenthesis of the form ...)))((((....
2. Let's name the total number of open parenthesis as OpenCount and the total number of closed parenthesis as CloseCount.
3. When OpenCount is even, then CloseCount is also even. Their half-element reversal will make the expression balanced.
4. When OpenCount is odd and CloseCount is also odd, then once you have to perform OpenCount/2 and CloseCount/2 reversals. You will be left with )(, which needs 2 more reversals, so the formula is derived from this.
   Total number of reversal = math.ceil (OpenCount / 2.0) + math.ceil(CloseCount/2.0)

**Example 7.21:**
```
public static int reverseParenthesis(String expn, int size) {
    Stack<Character> stk = new Stack<Character>();
    int openCount = 0;
    int closeCount = 0;
    char ch;

    if (size % 2 == 1) {
        System.out.println("Invalid odd length " + size);
        return -1;
    }
    for (int i = 0; i < size; i++) {
        ch = expn.charAt(i);
        if (ch == '(')
            stk.push(ch);
        else if (ch == ')')
            if (stk.size() != 0 && stk.peek() == '(')
                stk.pop();
            else
                stk.push(')');
    }
    while (stk.size() != 0) {
        if (stk.pop() == '(')
            openCount += 1;
        else
            closeCount += 1;
    }
    int reversal = (int) Math.ceil(openCount / 2.0) + (int) Math.ceil(closeCount /
2.0);
    return reversal;
}

// Testing code.
public static void main(String[] args)  {
    String expn2 = ")(())(((";
    int size = expn2.length();
    int value = reverseParenthesis(expn2, size);
    System.out.println("reverse Parenthesis is : " + value);
}
```

**Output:**
```
reverse Parenthesis is : 3
```

## Find Duplicate Parenthesis

**Problem:** Given an expression, you need to find duplicate or redundant parentheses in it. Redundant parentheses are those parenthesis pairs that do not change the outcome of expression.

**Solution:** A parenthesis pair is redundant if it contains 0 or 1 element between them. The algorithm works by adding all the elements except ) to the stack. When we get a ) at that point, we find its corresponding pair and count all the elements between this pair. If the number of elements is 0 or 1, then we have a redundant parenthesis.

**Example 7.22:**
```
public static boolean findDuplicateParenthesis(String expn, int size) {
    Stack<Character> stk = new Stack<Character>();
```

```
    char ch;
    int count;
    for (int i = 0; i < size; i++) {
        ch = expn.charAt(i);

        if (ch == ')') {
            count = 0;
            while (stk.size() != 0 && stk.peek() != '(') {
                stk.pop();
                count += 1;
            }

            if (count <= 1)
                return true;
        } else
            stk.push(ch);
    }
    return false;
}

// Testing code.
public static void main(String[] args)  {
    String expn = "(((a+b))+c)";
    int size = expn.length();
    boolean value = findDuplicateParenthesis(expn, size);
    System.out.println("Duplicate Found : " + value);
}
```

**Output:**

```
Duplicate Found : true
```

## Print Parenthesis Number

**Problem:** Given an expression, number each parenthesis pair such that for each pair, the opening and closing parenthesis have the same number.

Example:

Input: '(((a+(b))+(c+d)))'

Output: [1, 2, 3, 4, 4, 3, 5, 5, 2, 1]

**Solution**: A stack is used to keep track of the parenthesis count. And a count variable is used to keep track of the count of the current opening parenthesis. Traverse the string and when we get an opening parenthesis, then we add the count to the stack and output. And increase count by one. When we get a closing parenthesis, we will pop its corresponding opening parentheses and add it to the output.

**Example 7.23:**

```
public static void printParenthesisNumber(String expn, int size) {
    char ch;
    Stack<Integer> stk = new Stack<Integer>();
    String output = new String();
    int count = 1;
    for (int i = 0; i < size; i++) {
        ch = expn.charAt(i);
        if (ch == '(') {
            stk.push(count);
            output += count;
```

```
                output += " ";
                count += 1;
            } else if (ch == ')') {
                output += stk.pop();
                output += " ";
            }
        }
        System.out.println("Parenthesis Count " + output);
}

// Testing code.
public static void main(String[] args)  {
        String expn1 = "(((a+(b))+(c+d)))";
        printParenthesisNumber(expn1, expn1.length());
}
```

**Output:**

```
Parenthesis Count :: 1 2 3 4 4 3 5 5 2 1
```

## Infix, Prefix, and Postfix Expressions

**Infix Expression** : When we have an algebraic expression like A + B, we know that variable A is added to variable B. This type of expression is called infix expression because the operator + is there between operand A and operand B.

Now consider another infix expression, A + B * C. In the expression, there is a problem of operator precedence. What operation will be performed first: + or *. Are A and B added first, and then the result is multiplied with C? Alternatively, B and C are multiplied first, and then the result is added to A. This makes the expression ambiguous. To deal with this ambiguity, we define the precedence rule or use parentheses to remove ambiguity.

So, if we want to multiply B and C first and then add the result to A. Then the same expression can be written unambiguously using parentheses as A + (B * C). On the other hand, if we want to add A and B first and then the sum will be multiplied by C, we will write it as (A + B) * C. Therefore, we need parenthesis in the infix expression to make the expression unambiguous.

**Infix expression**: In this notation, we place operators in the middle of the operands.
< Operand > < Operator > < Operand >

**Prefix expressions**: In this notation, we place operators at the beginning of the operands.
< Operator > < Operand > < Operand >

**Postfix expression**: In this notation, we place operators at the end of the operands.
< Operand > < Operand > < Operator >

| Infix Expression | Prefix Expression | Postfix Expression |
|---|---|---|
| A + B | + A B | A B + |
| A + (B * C) | + A * B C | A B C * + |
| (A + B) * C | * + ABC | A B + C * |

Why do we need such unnatural prefix or postfix expressions when we already have infix expressions that work for us?

The answer is that infix expressions are ambiguous, and they need parenthesis to make them unambiguous. While postfix and prefix notations do not need any parenthesis.

## Infix-to-Postfix Conversion

**Problem:** Write a function to convert infix expression to postfix expression.

**Solution:**

1. Print operands in the same order as they arrive.
2. If the stack is empty or contains a left parenthesis "(" on top, we should push the incoming operator in the stack.
3. If the incoming symbol is a left parenthesis "(", push left parenthesis in the stack.
4. If the incoming symbol is a right parenthesis ")", pop from the stack and print the operators until you see a left parenthesis "(". Discard the pair of parentheses.
5. If the precedence of the incoming symbol is higher than the precedence of the operator at the top of the stack, then push it to the stack.
6. If the incoming symbol has equal precedence compared to the top of the stack, use association. If the association is left to right, pop and print the symbol at the top of the stack and then push the incoming operator. If the association is right to leave, then push the incoming operator.
7. If the precedence of the incoming symbol is lower than the precedence of the operator on the top of the stack, then pop and print the top operator. Then compare the incoming operator against the new operator at the top of the stack.
8. At the end of the expression, pop and print all operators on the stack.

**Example 7.24:**

```
public static int precedence(char x) {
    if (x == '(') {
        return (0);
    }
    if (x == '+' || x == '-') {
        return (1);
    }
    if (x == '*' || x == '/' || x == '%')
        return (2);
    if (x == '^') {
        return (3);
    }

    return (4);
}

public static String infixToPostfix(String expn) {
    String output = "";
    char[] out = infixToPostfix(expn.toCharArray());

    for (char ch : out) {
        output = output + ch;
    }
    return output;
}
```

```
public static char[] infixToPostfix(char[] expn) {
    Stack<Character> stk = new Stack<Character>();

    String output = "";
    char out;

    for (char ch : expn) {
        if (ch <= '9' && ch >= '0') {
            output = output + ch;
        } else {
            switch (ch) {
            case '+':
            case '-':
            case '*':
            case '/':
            case '%':
            case '^':
                while (stk.isEmpty() == false && precedence(ch) <=
precedence(stk.peek())) {
                    out = stk.pop();
                    output = output + " " + out;
                }
                stk.push(ch);
                output = output + " ";
                break;
            case '(':
                stk.push(ch);
                break;
            case ')':
                while (stk.isEmpty() == false && (out = stk.pop()) != '(') {
                    output = output + " " + out + " ";
                }
                break;
            }
        }
    }

    while (stk.isEmpty() == false) {
        out = stk.pop();
        output = output + out + " ";
    }
    return output.toCharArray();
}

// Testing code.
public static void main(String[] args)  {
    String expn = "10+((3))*5/(16-4)";
    String value = infixToPostfix(expn);
    System.out.println("Infix Expn: " + expn);
    System.out.println("Postfix Expn: " + value);
}
```

**Output:**

```
Infix Expn: 10+((3))*5/(16-4)
Postfix Expn: 10 3 5 * 16 4 - / +
```

## Infix-to-Prefix Conversion

**Problem:** Write a function to convert infix expression to postfix expression.

**Solution:**
1. Reverse the given infix expression.
2. Replace '(' with ')' and ')' with '(' in the reversed expression.
3. Now, apply infix to the postfix subroutine already discussed.
4. Reverse the generated postfix expression, and this will give the required prefix expression.

**Example 7.25:**
```
public static String infixToPrefix(String expn) {
    char[] arr = expn.toCharArray();
    reverseString(arr);
    replaceParenthesis(arr);
    arr = infixToPostfix(arr);
    reverseString(arr);
    expn = new String(arr);
    return expn;
}

public static void replaceParenthesis(char[] a) {
    int lower = 0;
    int upper = a.length - 1;

    while (lower <= upper) {
        if (a[lower] == '(') {
            a[lower] = ')';
        } else if (a[lower] == ')') {
            a[lower] = '(';
        }
        lower++;
    }
}

public static void reverseString(char[] expn) {
    int lower = 0;
    int upper = expn.length - 1;
    char tempChar;

    while (lower < upper) {
        tempChar = expn[lower];
        expn[lower] = expn[upper];
        expn[upper] = tempChar;
        lower++;
        upper--;
    }
}

// Testing code.
public static void main(String[] args)  {
    String expn = "10+((3))*5/(16-4)";
    String value = infixToPrefix(expn);
    System.out.println("Infix Expn: " + expn);
    System.out.println("Prefix Expn: " + value);
}
```

**Output:**
```
Infix Expn: 10+((3))*5/(16-4)
Prefix Expn:  +10 * 3 / 5 - 16 4
```

## Postfix Evaluate

**Problem:** Write a function to evaluate a postfix expression. Such as: expression "1 2 + 3 4 + *" gives output 21

**Example 7.26:**
```
public static int postfixEvaluate(String expn) {
    Stack<Integer> stk = new Stack<Integer>();
    Scanner tokens = new Scanner(expn);

    while (tokens.hasNext()) {
        if (tokens.hasNextInt()) {
            stk.push(tokens.nextInt());
        } else {
            int num1 = stk.pop();
            int num2 = stk.pop();
            char op = tokens.next().charAt(0);
            switch (op) {
            case '+':
                stk.push(num1 + num2);
                break;
            case '-':
                stk.push(num1 - num2);
                break;
            case '*':
                stk.push(num1 * num2);
                break;
            case '/':
                stk.push(num1 / num2);
                break;
            }
        }
    }
    tokens.close();
    return stk.pop();
}

// Testing code.
public static void main(String[] args)  {
    String expn = "6 5 2 3 + 8 * + 3 + *";
    int value = postfixEvaluate(expn);
    System.out.println("Result after Evaluation: " + value);
}
```

**Output:**
```
Result after Evaluation: 288
```

**Analysis**:
1 Create a stack to store values or operands.
2 Scan through the given expression and do the following for each element:
   - If the element is a number, then push it into the stack.

- If the element is an operator, then pop values from the stack. Evaluate the operator over the values and push the result into the stack.

3 When the expression is scanned completely, the number in the stack is the result.

## Stack Based Rejection Method

**Stack Based Rejection** technique is used when processing data following a specific property of rejection. That value at some index can be used to reject some other values that are processed before it. The values that are rejected are those values, which are unimportant for the rest of the processing. Below examples of "Stock Span Problem", "Get Max Rectangular Area in a Histogram" "Stock Analyst Problem" etc. are a few of its examples.

## Stock Span Problem

**Problem:** In a given list of daily stock prices in an array A[i]. Find the span of the stocks for each day. A span of stock is the maximum number of days for which the price of stock was lower than that day.

Or

Given a histogram, find the number of consecutive bars in the left of the current bar that have values less than the current bar.

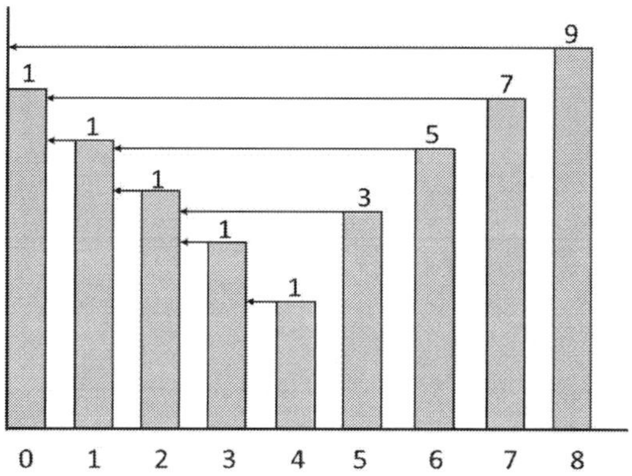


**First solution:** Brute force, two loops are used. Outer loop to select the bar / elements in histogram. The inner loop is used to find the count of consecutive bars smaller to the current bar.

**Example 7.27:**

```
public static int[] stockSpanRange(int[] arr) {
    int[] SR = new int[arr.length];
    SR[0] = 1;
    for (int i = 1; i < arr.length; i++) {
        SR[i] = 1;
        for (int j = i - 1; (j >= 0) && (arr[i] >= arr[j]); j--) {
            SR[i]++;
        }
    }
    return SR;
}

// Testing code.
public static void main(String[] args)  {
    int[] arr = { 6, 5, 4, 3, 2, 4, 5, 7, 9 };
    int[] value = stockSpanRange(arr);
    System.out.print("stockSpanRange : ");
```

```
    for (int val : value)
        System.out.print(val + " ");
}
```

**Output:**
```
StockSpanRange : 1 1 1 1 1 4 6 8 9
```

**Time complexity:** O(n^2), length of each bar, is compared with the bars before it.

**Second solution:** In the above algorithms for each bar, we are comparing the length of bars before it. If somehow, we can get the index of the bar that is before the current bar and is having length greater than the current bar. Let us suppose the index of this hypothetical bar is M and the index of the current bar is N then the stock span range will be (N – M). By using a stack such index can be obtained by doing some bookkeeping.

Let us call the stock input array as "arr". Create a stack to store index value and add value 0 to it. Then traverse the values in the stock input array. Let's call the current index we are analysing as "curr", the index at the top of the stack is "top". For each value of the stock input, arr[curr] is compared with arr[top]. If the value arr[curr] is less than or equal to arr[top] then add curr to the stack. If the value of arr[curr] is greater than arr[top] then start popping values from stack till arr[curr] > arr[top]. Then add curr to the stack. Store stock range to SR[curr] = curr – top. Repeat this process for all the index of input array and SR array will be populated.

**Example 7.28:**
```
public static int[] stockSpanRange2(int[] arr) {
    Stack<Integer> stk = new Stack<Integer>();
    int[] SR = new int[arr.length];
    stk.push(0);
    SR[0] = 1;
    for (int i = 1; i < arr.length; i++) {
        while (!stk.isEmpty() && arr[stk.peek()] <= arr[i]) {
            stk.pop();
        }
        SR[i] = (stk.isEmpty()) ? (i + 1) : (i - stk.peek());
        stk.push(i);
    }
    return SR;
}
```

For each value in the input array, an index is added to the stack only once, and that index can be taken out of the stack only once. Each comparison operation leads to either adding a value to the stack or taking a value out of the stack. Therefore, if there are n elements in an array then at most there will be 2n comparisons, so this algorithm is linear.

Time complexity is O(n), space complexity will also be O(n) for stack.

## Get Max Rectangular Area in a Histogram

**Problem:** In the given histogram of rectangle bars of each one unit wide. Find the maximum area rectangle in the histogram.

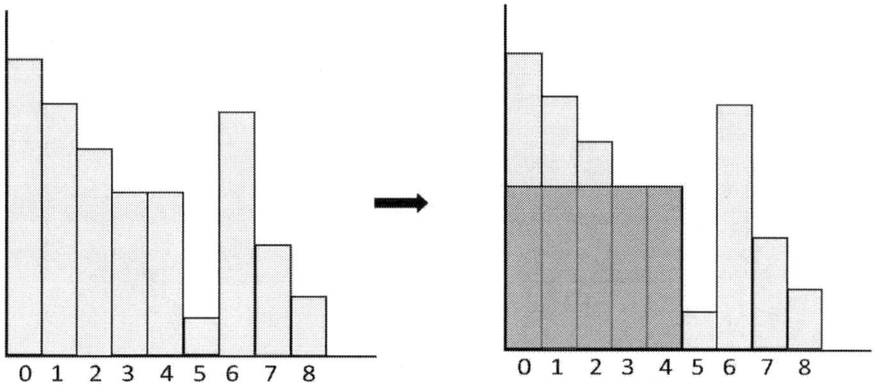


**First solution:** Brute force approach. We use two loops to find the desired greatest area. First loop to find the right boundary of a rectangle and then another inner loop to find the left boundary of the rectangle. This approach has time complexity of O(n^2)

**Example 7.29:**
```
public static int getMaxArea(int[] arr) {
    int size = arr.length;
    int maxArea = -1;
    int currArea;
    int minHeight = 0;
    for (int i = 1; i < size; i++) {
        minHeight = arr[i];
        for (int j = i - 1; j >= 0; j--) {
            if (minHeight > arr[j]) {
                minHeight = arr[j];
            }
            currArea = minHeight * (i - j + 1);
            if (maxArea < currArea) {
                maxArea = currArea;
            }
        }
    }
    return maxArea;
}

// Testing code.
public static void main(String[] args)  {
    int[] arr = { 7, 6, 5, 4, 4, 1, 6, 3, 1 };
    int value = getMaxArea(arr);
    System.out.println("getMaxArea :: " + value);
}
```

**Output:**
```
getMaxArea :: 20
```

**Second solution:** Using Stack
- Create a stack that contains indexes in increasing order.
- When a current index value is smaller than the values at the top of the stack, the current index is added to the stack.
- When a current index value is smaller than the values at the top of the stack, the stack is popped till the top value is less than the current index value.
- The value that is popped out from the stack will contribute to creating a rectangle. The height of rectangle is arr[top] and width will be "i" if stack is empty and is i-stk[-1]-1

Time complexity is O(n)

**Example 7.30:**
```
public static int getMaxArea2(int[] arr) {
    int size = arr.length;
    Stack<Integer> stk = new Stack<Integer>();
    int maxArea = 0;
    int top;
    int topArea;
    int i = 0;
    while (i < size) {
        while ((i < size) && (stk.isEmpty() || arr[stk.peek()] <= arr[i])) {
            stk.push(i);
            i++;
        }
        while (!stk.isEmpty() && (i == size || arr[stk.peek()] > arr[i])) {
            top = stk.peek();
            stk.pop();
            topArea = arr[top] * (stk.isEmpty() ? i : i - stk.peek() - 1);
            if (maxArea < topArea) {
                maxArea = topArea;
            }
        }
    }
    return maxArea;
}
```

## Stock Analyst Problem

**Problem:** A stock analyst had approached you to write a program to find stock hike points in some stocks. A stock hike point is the value of stock that is greater than all its previous values. You are provided stock price in an infinite stream, with the most recent value first (in terms of time, the data is provided in reverse order.).

For example, in stock values are [20, 19, 10, 21, 40, 35, 39, 50, 45, 42], stock hike points values are 20, 21, 40 and 50 but the data is provided in reverse order.

**Solution**:

1 If data is provided in order of old value first then new values. Then this can be done in linear time, just by using a single variable to store the maximum value so far. However, in our problem, data is provided in reverse order.

2 When we are processing some value at that time, we do not know if it will become a hike point.

3 We will use a stack to store the data. We read input from the stream; if the value at the top of the stack is smaller than the input value, then we pop the value from the stack until the value at the top of the stack is smaller than the input value. Then we add the input value to the stack.

4 If the value at the top of the stack is greater than the input value, then we add the input value to the stack. At the end, the content of the stack is stock hike points.

5 Time complexity of this solution is O(n)

**Example 7.31:**
```
public static void stockAnalystAdd(Stack<Integer> stk, int value) {
    while (!stk.isEmpty() && stk.peek() <= value)
```

```
        stk.pop();
    stk.push(value);
}

// Testing code.
public static void main(String[] args)  {
    int[] arr = { 20, 19, 10, 21, 40, 35, 39, 50, 45, 42 };
    Stack<Integer> stk = new Stack<Integer>();
    for (int i = arr.length - 1; i >= 0; i--)
        stockAnalystAdd(stk, arr[i]);
    System.out.println(stk);
}
```

**Output:**

```
[ 50 40 21 20 ]
```

## Next Larger Element

**Problem:** Function to print the next larger element of each element of the array.

**First Solution:** Brute force approach, for each index we can traverse the array indexes right to it to find a larger value. Time complexity is O(n^2)

**Example 7.32:**

```
public static void nextLargerElement(int[] arr, int size) {
    int[] output = new int[size];
    int outIndex = 0;
    int next;

    for (int i = 0; i < size; i++) {
        next = -1;
        for (int j = i + 1; j < size; j++) {
            if (arr[i] < arr[j]) {
                next = arr[j];
                break;
            }
        }
        output[outIndex++] = next;
    }

    for (int val : output)
        System.out.print(val + " ");
    System.out.println();
}

// Testing code.
public static void main(String[] args)  {
    int[] arr = { 13, 21, 3, 6, 20, 3 };
    int size = arr.length;
    nextLargerElement(arr, size);
}
```

**Output:**

```
21 -1 6 20 -1 -1
```

**Second Solution:** Let us suppose we are processing elements of an array. The elements which are less than ith element does not have the largest element on the right of ith index. So, we can say the elements which are left of the ith element and which are less the ith element are independent of the elements at the index higher than ith. So, a stack-based reduction method applies.

1. Create an empty stack. This stack contains index of elements that have value in decreasing order.
2. We will traverse through the input array.
3. If the top of the stack is smaller than the current element, then pop from the stack and mark its next larger element as the current index. We will pop from the stack and repeat this process until the value of the index at the top of the stack is greater than the current value.
4. When we process the input array, then for those indexes for which we have the next largest element is populated.
5. The indexes which are present in the stack do not have any next largest element, so we should mark those indexes in the output array as -1.

**Example 7.33:**
```
public static void nextLargerElement2(int[] arr, int size) {
    Stack<Integer> stk = new Stack<Integer>();
    int[] output = new int[size];
    int index = 0;
    int curr;

    for (int i = 0; i < size; i++) {
        curr = arr[i];
        // stack always have values in decreasing order.
        while (stk.isEmpty() == false && arr[stk.peek()] <= curr) {
            index = stk.pop();
            output[index] = curr;
        }
        stk.push(i);
    }
    // index which don't have any next Larger.
    while (stk.isEmpty() == false) {
        index = stk.pop();
        output[index] = -1;
    }
    for (int val : output)
        System.out.print(val + " ");
    System.out.println();
}
```

## Next Smaller Element

**Problem:** Function to print the next smallest element of each element of the array.

**First Solution:** Brute force approach, for each index we can traverse the array indexes right to it to find a smaller value. Time complexity is O(n^2)

**Example 7.34:**
```
public static void nextSmallerElement(int[] arr, int size) {
    int[] output = new int[size];
    Arrays.fill(output, -1);
```

```
    for (int i = 0; i < size; i++) {
        for (int j = i + 1; j < size; j++) {
            if (arr[j] < arr[i]) {
                output[i] = arr[j];
                break;
            }
        }
    }

    for (int val : output)
        System.out.print(val + " ");
    System.out.println();
}

// Testing code.
public static void main(String[] args)  {
    int[] arr = { 13, 21, 3, 6, 20, 3 };
    int size = arr.length;
    nextSmallerElement(arr, size);
}
```

**Output:**

```
3 3 -1 3 3 -1
```

**Second Solution:** Let us suppose we are processing elements of an array. The elements that are greater than ith element do not have a smaller element on the right of ith index. Therefore, we can say the elements which are left of the ith element and which are greater than the ith element are independent of the elements at the index higher than ith. So, a stack-based reduction method applies.

**Example 7.35:**

```
public static void nextSmallerElement2(int[] arr, int size) {
    Stack<Integer> stk = new Stack<Integer>();
    int[] output = new int[size];
    int curr, index;
    for (int i = 0; i < size; i++) {
        curr = arr[i];
        // stack always have values in increasing order.
        while (stk.isEmpty() == false && arr[stk.peek()] > curr) {
            index = stk.pop();
            output[index] = curr;
        }
        stk.push(i);
    }

    // index which don't have any next Smaller.
    while (stk.isEmpty() == false) {
        index = stk.pop();
        output[index] = -1;
    }

    for (int val : output)
        System.out.print(val + " ");
}
```

## Next Larger Element Circular

**Problem:** Function to print the next larger element of each element of the circular array.
Input: [6, 3, 9, 8, 10, 2, 1, 15, 7]
Output: [9, 9, 10, 10, 15, 15, 15, -1, 9]

**First Solution:** Brute force approach, let us suppose the number of elements in the array is n. For each index, we will traverse the (n-1) number of nodes (in circular manner) to find a larger value. Time complexity is O(n^2)

**Example 7.36:**
```
public static void nextLargerElementCircular(int[] arr, int size) {
    int[] output = new int[size];
    Arrays.fill(output, -1);
    for (int i = 0; i < size; i++) {
        for (int j = 1; j < size; j++) {
            if (arr[i] < arr[(i + j) % size]) {
                output[i] = arr[(i + j) % size];
                break;
            }
        }
    }

    for (int val : output)
        System.out.print(val + " ");
    System.out.println();
}

// Testing code.
public static void main(String[] args)  {
    int arr[] = { 6, 3, 9, 8, 10, 2, 1, 15, 7 };
    nextLargerElementCircular(arr, arr.length);
}
```

**Output:**
```
9 9 10 10 15 15 15 -1 9
```

**Second Solution:** The solution of this problem is the same as the Next Largest Element problem. The only difference is that (2n – 1) nodes are traversed. As for each node, the farthest node that has its effect is at max (n-1) distance apart. Therefore, total (n + n -1) nodes are traversed. Time Complexity of stack-based reduction process is O(n)

**Example 7.37:**
```
public static void nextLargerElementCircular2(int[] arr, int size) {
    Stack<Integer> stk = new Stack<Integer>();
    int curr, index;
    int[] output = new int[size];
    for (int i = 0; i < (2 * size - 1); i++) {
        curr = arr[i % size];
        // stack always have values in decreasing order.
        while (stk.isEmpty() == false && arr[stk.peek()] <= curr) {
            index = stk.pop();
            output[index] = curr;
        }
        stk.push(i % size);
```

```
    }
    // index which don't have any next Larger.
    while (stk.isEmpty() == false) {
        index = stk.pop();
        output[index] = -1;
    }
    for (int val : output)
        System.out.print(val + " ");
    System.out.println();
}
```

## Find Celebrity Problem

**Problem:** At a party, there is a possibility that a celebrity has visited it. A celebrity is a person who does not know anyone in the party, and everyone in the party knows a celebrity. You want to find a celebrity at the party. You can ask only one question DoYouKnow(X, Y), which means to X you can ask only one question" Do you know Y?". X will answer the question as yes or no.

**First solution:** brute force approach, you can traverse the guest one by one and ask them if they know the other guest one by one. If you find a guest who does not know anyone, then you have a probable candidate. If the guest is known to all other guests, then he is a celebrity.
This is an inefficient solution with time complexity of O(n^2)

**Example 7.38:**

```
public static boolean isKnown(int relation[][], int a, int b) {
    if (relation[a][b] == 1)
        return true;
    return false;
}

public static int findCelebrity(int relation[][], int count) {
    int i, j;
    boolean cel = true;
    for (i = 0; i < count; i++) {
        cel = true;
        for (j = 0; j < count; j++) {
            if (i != j && (!isKnown(relation, j, i) || isKnown(relation, i, j))) {
                cel = false;
                break;
            }
        }
        if (cel == true)
            return i;
    }
    return -1;
}

// Testing code.
public static void main(String[] args)  {
    int[][] arr = { { 1, 0, 1, 1, 0 }, { 1, 0, 0, 1, 0 }, { 0, 0, 1, 1, 1 }, { 0,
0, 0, 0, 0 }, { 1, 1, 0, 1, 1 } };
    System.out.println("Celebrity : " + findCelebrity3(arr, 5));
}
```

**Output:**

```
Celebrity : 3
```

**Second solution**: Use stack,

1. We add the entire guest list index from 1 to N in a stack. We take two index values out of the stack and store them in two variables: first and second.
2. If the guest at index first knows the guest at index second, then first is not a celebrity, so copy second to first. Else, if the guest at index first does not know guest second, then second is not a celebrity.
3. In both cases pop another element from the stack and mark it second.
4. In each comparison, one value is rejected.
5. In the end first will contain the probable celebrity.
6. Then we need to check that the celebrity candidate is known by all the other guests.
7. Time-complexity : O(n)

**Example 7.39:**

```
public static int findCelebrity2(int relation[][], int count) {
    Stack<Integer> stk = new Stack<Integer>();
    int first = 0, second = 0;
    for (int i = 0; i < count; i++) {
        stk.push(i);
    }
    first = stk.pop();
    while (stk.size() != 0) {
        second = stk.pop();
        if (isKnown(relation, first, second))
            first = second;
    }
    for (int i = 0; i < count; i++) {
        if (first != i && isKnown(relation, first, i))
            return -1;
        if (first != i && isKnown(relation, i, first) == false)
            return -1;
    }
    return first;
}
```

**Third solution:** let us suppose we have a guest list as [g1, g2, g3, g4 …]. We take two index counters, namely the first and second. The first is assigned 0 value and the second is assigned 1 value.

We will ask the guest at index first if he knows the guest at index second. If the answer is yes, then we make first = second and second = second + 1 (guest at first index is not a celebrity.). If the answer is no, then we make second = second + 1 (guest at index second is not a celebrity.). In the end, we will have a probable celebrity at the first index. Then check that the guest at the first index is known by all the other guests. Time-complexity : O(n)

**Example 7.40:**

```
public static int findCelebrity3(int relation[][], int count) {
    int first = 0;
    int second = 1;

    for (int i = 0; i < (count - 1); i++) {
        if (isKnown(relation, first, second))
            first = second;
```

```
        second = second + 1;
    }
    for (int i = 0; i < count; i++) {
        if (first != i && isKnown(relation, first, i))
            return -1;
        if (first != i && isKnown(relation, i, first) == false)
            return -1;
    }
    return first;
}
```

## Depth-First Search with a Stack

In a depth-first search, we traverse down a path until we get a dead-end; then we backtrack by popping a stack to get an alternative path.

- Create a stack
- Create a start point
- Push the start point onto the stack
- While (value searching is not found and the stack is not empty)
    - Pop the stack
    - Find all possible points after the one which we just tried
    - Push these points onto the stack

## Uses of Stack

1 Where LIFO functionality is required.
2 Undo and Redo functions in a text editor.
3 Back and Forward function in web browser.
4 Grammar checking such as Parenthesis matching
5 Expression conversion (like infix to postfix etc.)
6 Postfix evaluation of an expression.
7 Function calls are implemented using the system stack.
8 Depth-first search of trees and graphs.

## Exercise

1 Find if a given string is a palindrome or not using a stack. A palindrome is a sequence of characters that is the same backwards or forward.
E.g. “AAABBBCCCBBBAAA”, “ABA” & “ABBA”
**Hint**: Push characters to the stack until the half-length of the string. Then pop these characters and then compare. Make sure you take care of the odd length and even length.

2 Min stack Problem: Design a stack in which we can get the minimum value in the stack should also work in O(1) Time Complexity.
**Hint**: Keep two stacks, one will be a general stack, which will just keep the elements. The second will keep the min value.
- Push: Push an element to the top of stack1. Compare the new value with the value at the top of stack2. If the new value is smaller, then push the new value into stack2. Or push the value at the top of the stack2 to itself once more.

- Pop: Pop an element from the top of stack1 and return. Pop an element from the top of stack2 too.
- Min: Reads from the top of the stack2, this value will be the min.

3 Converting Decimal Numbers to Binary Numbers using the stack data structure.
**Hint**: store reminders into the stack and then print the stack.

4 Convert an infix expression to a prefix expression.
**Hint**: Reverse the given expression, apply infix to postfix, and then reverse the expression again.
Step 1. Reverse the infix expression.
    5^E+D*) C^B+A (
Step 2. Make Every '(' as ')' and every ')' as '('
    5^E+D*(C^B+A)
Step 3. Convert an expression to postfix form.
Step 4. Reverse the expression.
    +*+A^BCD^E5

5 Write an HTML opening tag and closing tag-matching program.
**Hint**: parenthesis matching.

6 Write a function that will transform Postfix to Infix Conversion

7 Write a function that will transform Prefix to Infix Conversion

8 Write a palindrome matching function, which ignores characters other than the English alphabet and digits. String "Madam, I'm Adam." should return true.

9 At a party, there is a possibility that a stranger has visited it. A stranger is a person who is not known by anyone and who doesn't know anyone. You want to find a stranger at the party. You can ask only one question DoYouKnow(X, Y), which means to X you can ask only one question" Do you know Y?". X will answer the question as yes or no.

# CHAPTER 8: QUEUE

## Introduction

A **Queue** is a data structure that organises items in a first-in-first-out (FIFO) manner. The first element, added to the queue, will be the first to be removed. It is also known as "first-come-first-served".

The real-life analogy of queue is a typical line in which we all participate from time to time.

1. We waited in a line at the railway reservation counter.
2. We wait in the cafeteria line.
3. We wait in a queue when we call some customer-care.

The elements, which are at the front of the queue, are the ones that stayed in the queue for the longest time.

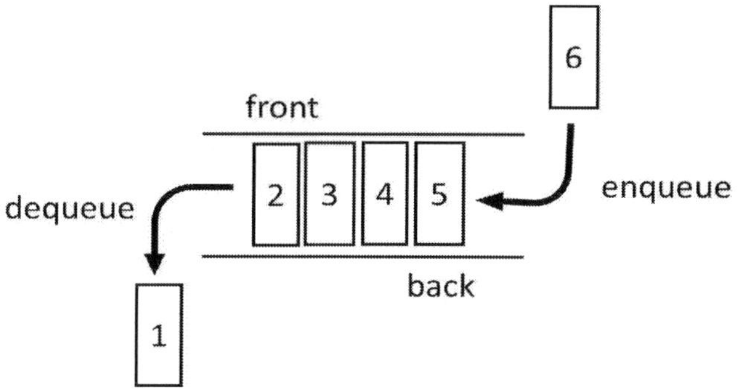


In computer science, some typical examples of queues are:

- Print command: When we issue a print command from our office to a single printer, the print tasks are lined up in a printer queue. The print command that is issued first will be printed before the next commands in line.
- Operating system: The operating system uses different queues to control process scheduling. Processes are added to the processing queue, which is used by an operating system for various scheduling algorithms.
- Graph traversals: The breadth-first traversal of graphs use queue data structure.

## The Queue Abstract Data Type

Queue abstract data type is defined as a data structure whose instance follows FIFO or first-in-first-out for the elements added to it.

The queue should support the following operations:

- queueAdd(): The Add() function adds a single element at the back of a queue.
- queueRemove(): The Remove() function removes a single element from the front of a queue.
- queueIsEmpty(): The isEmpty() function returns 1 if the queue is empty. It returns 0 if the queue is not empty.
- queueSize(): The size() function returns the number of elements in a queue.

## Queue Using Array

To implement a queue using an array, create an array arr of size N and take two variables front and back, both of which are initialised to 0. Initially, the size of the queue is 0. Add() function is used to add an element at the end of the queue using the back variable. The remove() function is used to remove elements from the front of the queue using the front variable. The back variable is incremented when a new value is added to the queue, and the back variable is incremented when the value is deleted from the queue. The modular operator is used to get the next value of the back and front variable to make the array behave like a circular array.

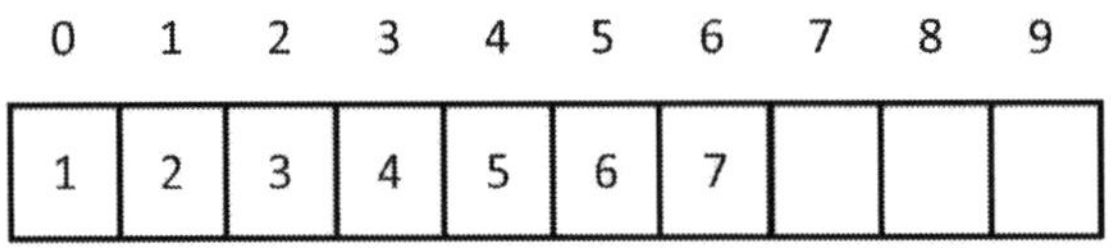


Circular view of arrays.

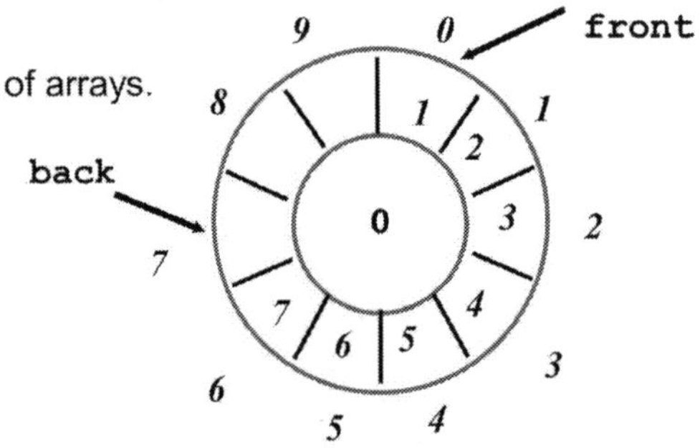


**Example 8.1:**

```
public class Queue {
    private int size;
    private int capacity;
    private int[] data;
    int front = 0;
    int back = 0;

    public Queue(int n) {
        size = 0;
        capacity = n;
        data = new int[n];
    }

    public Queue() {
        this(1000);
    }

    public boolean add(int value) {
        if (size >= capacity) {
            System.out.println("Queue is full.");
            return false;
        } else {
            size++;
            data[back] = value;
            back = (++back) % capacity;
        }
        return true;
    }
```

```
    public int remove() {
        int value;
        if (size <= 0) {
            System.out.println("Queue is empty.");
            return -999;
        } else {
            size--;
            value = data[front];
            front = (++front) % capacity;
        }
        return value;
    }

    boolean isEmpty() {
        return size == 0;
    }

    int size() {
        return size;
    }

    void print(){
        if(size == 0) {
            System.out.print("Queue is empty.");
            return;
        }
        int temp = front;
        int s = size;
        System.out.print("Queue is : ");
        while(s > 0){
            s--;
            System.out.print(data[temp] + " ");
            temp = (++temp) % capacity;
        }
        System.out.println();
    }

    // Testing code.
    public static void main(String[] args) {
        Queue que = new Queue();
        que.add(1);
        que.add(2);
        que.add(3);
        System.out.println("isEmpty : " + que.isEmpty());
        System.out.println("size : " + que.size());
        System.out.println("Queue remove : " + que.remove());
        System.out.println("Queue remove : " + que.remove());
    }
}
```

**Output:**

```
isEmpty : false
size : 3
Queue remove : 1
Queue remove : 2
```

## Queue Using Circular Linked List

A queue is implemented using a circular linked list. The advantage of using a circular linked list is that we can get head and tail nodes in constant time. When we want to insert an element to the queue, we add elements to the tail. When we need to delete an element from a queue, we delete it from the head of the list.

**Example 8.2:**

```
public class QueueLL {
    private Node tail = null;
    private int size = 0;

    private static class Node {
        private int value;
        private Node next;

        public Node(int v, Node n) {
            value = v;
            next = n;
        }
    }

    public int size() {
        return size;
    }

    public boolean isEmpty() {
        return size == 0;
    }

    public int peek() throws IllegalStateException {
        if (isEmpty())
            throw new IllegalStateException("StackEmptyException");
        int value;
        if (tail == tail.next)
            value = tail.value;
        else
            value = tail.next.value;

        return value;
    }

    void print() {
        if (size == 0) {
            System.out.print("Queue is empty.");
            return;
        }
        Node temp = tail.next;
        System.out.print("Queue is : ");
        for (int i = 0; i < size; i++) {
            System.out.print(temp.value + " ");
            temp = temp.next;
        }
        System.out.println();
    }
}
```

## Add

Enqueue into a queue using a circular linked list. Nodes are added to the end of the linked list. The below diagram indicates how a new node is added to the list. The tail is modified whenever a new value is added to the queue.

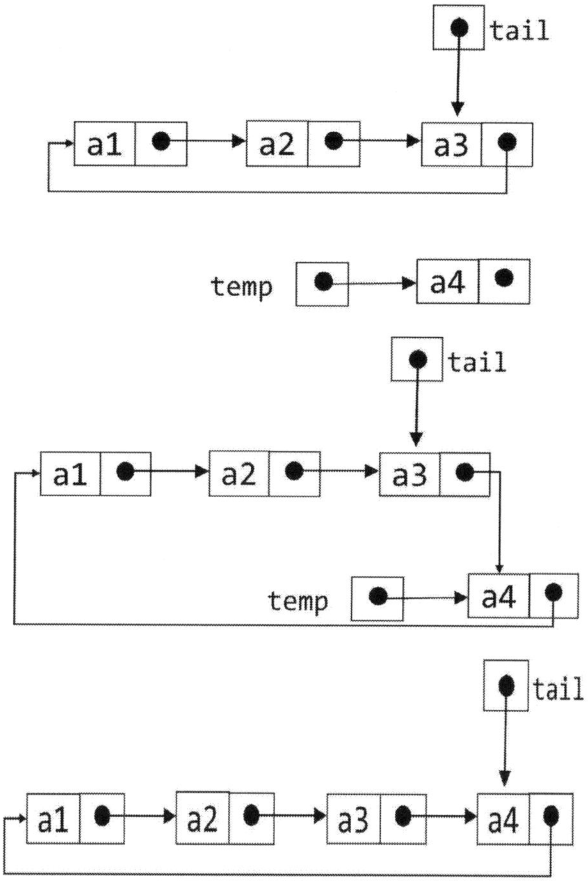


**Example 8.3:**

```
public void add(int value) {
    Node temp = new Node(value, null);
    if (tail == null) {
        tail = temp;
        tail.next = tail;
    } else {
        temp.next = tail.next;
        tail.next = temp;
        tail = temp;
    }
    size++;
}
```

**Analysis:** The add() operation adds one element at the end of the Queue (circular linked list).

## Remove

Dequeue operation is done by deleting the head node. The next node of the tail node is the head node. The tail node next will point to the next of the head nodes. Free memory of the deleted node. And return its value.

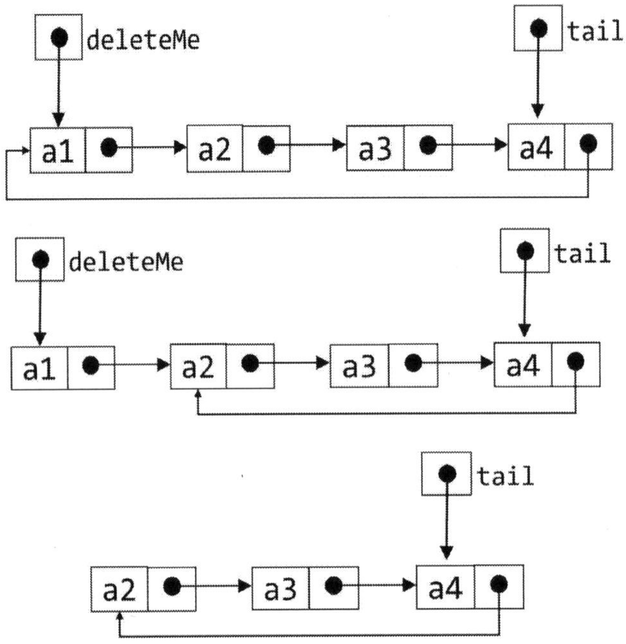


**Example 8.4:**
```
public int remove() throws IllegalStateException {
    if (size == 0)
        throw new IllegalStateException("StackEmptyException");

    int value = 0;
    if (tail == tail.next) {
        value = tail.value;
        tail = null;
    } else {
        value = tail.next.value;
        tail.next = tail.next.next;
    }
    size--;
    return value;
}

// Testing code.
public static void main(String[] args) {
    QueueLL que = new QueueLL();
    que.add(1);
    que.add(2);
    que.add(3);
    System.out.println("isEmpty : " + que.isEmpty());
    System.out.println("size : " + que.size());
    System.out.println("Queue remove : " + que.remove());
    System.out.println("Queue remove : " + que.remove());
}
```

**Output:**
```
isEmpty : false
size : 3
Queue remove : 1
Queue remove : 2
```

**Analysis:** Remove operation removes the first node from the start of the queue (circular linked list).

# Problems in Queue

## Queue using a stack

**Problem:** How to implement a queue using a stack. You can use multiple stacks.

**Solution:** We can use two stacks to implement a queue.

1. **Enqueue Operation**: new elements are added to the top of the first stack.
2. **Dequeue Operation**: elements are popped from the second stack. When the second stack is empty then all the elements of the first stack are popped one by one and pushed into the second stack.

**Example 8.5:**

```
public class QueueUsingStack {
    private Stack<Integer> stk1;
    private Stack<Integer> stk2;

    public QueueUsingStack() {
        stk1 = new Stack<Integer>();
        stk2 = new Stack<Integer>();
    }

    void add(int value) {
        stk1.push(value);
    }

    int remove() {
        int value;
        if (stk2.isEmpty() == false) {
            return stk2.pop();
        }

        while (stk1.isEmpty() == false) {
            value = stk1.pop();
            stk2.push(value);
        }
        return stk2.pop();
    }

    // Testing code.
    public static void main(String[] args) {
        QueueUsingStack que = new QueueUsingStack();
        que.add(1);
        que.add(2);
        que.add(3);
        System.out.println("Queue remove : " + que.remove());
        System.out.println("Queue remove : " + que.remove());
    }
}
```

**Output:**

```
Queue remove : 1
Queue remove : 2
```

**Analysis:** All add() happens to stack 1. When remove() is called, removal happens from stack 2. When stack 2 is empty, then stack 1 is popped and pushed into stack 2. This popping from stack 1 and pushing into stack 2 revert the order of retrieval, thereby making queue behaviour out of two stacks.

Time complexity is O(1) on average, elements are added to the first stack only once. They are taken to the second stack only once and taken out using pop operation.

## Stack using a Queue

**Problem:** Implement stack using a queue.

**First Solution:** use two queues

**Push**: add new elements to queue1.
**Pop**: while the size of queue1 is bigger than 1. Push all items from queue 1 to queue 2 except the last item. Switch the name of queue 1 and queue 2. Then return the last item.

Push operation is **O(1)** and Pop operation is **O(n)**

**Example 8.6:**
```
public class Stack {
    ArrayDeque<Integer> que1 = new ArrayDeque<Integer>();
    ArrayDeque<Integer> que2 = new ArrayDeque<Integer>();
    int size = 0;

    public void push(int value) {
        que1.add(value);
        size += 1;
    }

    public int pop() {
        int value = 0, s = size;
        while (s > 0) {
            value = que1.peek();
            que1.remove();
            if (s > 1)
                que2.add(value);
            s--;
        }
        ArrayDeque<Integer> temp = que1;
        que1 = que2;
        que2 = temp;
        size -= 1;
        return value;
    }

    // Testing code.
    public static void main(String[] args) {
        Stack stk = new Stack();
        stk.push(1);
        stk.push(2);
        stk.push(3);
        System.out.println("Stack pop : " + stk.pop());
        System.out.println("Stack pop : " + stk.pop());
    }
}
```

**Output:**

```
Stack pop : 3
Stack pop : 2
```

**Second Solution:** This same can be done using just one queue.

**Push**: add the element to the queue.
**Pop**: find the size of the queue. If the size is zero, then return an error. Else, if the size is positive, then remove size- 1 elements from the queue and again add to the same queue. At last, remove the next element and return it.
Push operation is **O(1)** and Pop operation is **O(n)**

**Example 8.7:**

```
public void push(int value) {
    que1.add(value);
    size += 1;
}

public int pop2() {
    int value = 0, s = size;
    while (s > 0) {
        value = que1.peek();
        que1.remove();
        if (s > 1)
            que1.add(value);
        s--;
    }
    size -= 1;
    return value;
}
```

## Breadth-First Search with a Queue

In breadth-first search, we explore all the nearest nodes first by finding all possible successors and adding them to a queue.

**Solution:**
1. Create a queue
2. Create a start point
3. Enqueue the start points onto the queue
4. while (value searching not found, and the queue is not empty)
   - Dequeue from the queue
   - Find all possible paths from the dequeued point.
   - Enqueue these paths in the queue

## Josephus problem

**Problem:** N people are standing in a queue waiting to be executed. The counting begins at the front of the queue. In each step, k number of people are removed and again added one by one from the queue. Then the next person is executed. The execution proceeds around the circle until only the last person remains, who will be free. Find that position where you want to stand and gain your freedom.

**Solution:**

- Just insert an integer for 1 to k in a queue. (corresponds to k people)
- Define a Kpop() function such that it will remove and add the queue k-1 times and then remove one more time. (This man is dead.)
- Repeat the second step until the size of the queue is 1.
- Print the value in the last element. This is the solution.

**Example 8.8:**
```
static int josephus(int n, int k) {
    ArrayDeque<Integer> que = new ArrayDeque<Integer>();
    for (int i = 0; i < n; i++)
        que.add(i + 1);

    while (que.size() > 1) {
        for (int i = 0; i < k - 1; i++) {
            que.add(que.peek());
            que.remove();
        }
        que.remove();// Kth person executed.
    }
    return que.peek();
}

// Testing code.
public static void main(String[] args)  {
    System.out.println("Position : " + josephus(11, 5));
}
```

**Output**:
```
Position : 8
```

## Circular tour

**Problem:** There are N number of petrol pumps in a circular path. Each petrol pump has a limited amount of petrol. You are given the amount of petrol each petrol pump has and the distance from the next petrol pump. Find if there is a circular tour possible to visit all the petrol pumps.

**First Solution:** Find all the possible paths starting from different petrol pumps.
For each petrol pump, we will add (net petrol available – net petrol needed to reach its next petrol pump.). While iterating the pumps if we can find a path with petrol value always positive then it is the path which we are searching. Otherwise, find another path by selecting another starting point.

Time complexity is O(n^2)

**Example 8.9:**
```
public static int CircularTour(int[][] arr, int n) {
    for (int i = 0; i < n; i++) {
        int total = 0;
        boolean found = true;
        for (int j = 0; j < n; j++) {
            total += (arr[(i + j) % n][0] - arr[(i + j) % n][1]);
            if (total < 0) {
                found = false;
                break;
```

```
            }
        }
        if (found)
            return i;
    }
    return -1;
}

// Testing code.
public static void main(String[] args)  {
    int tour[][] = { { 8, 6 }, { 1, 4 }, { 7, 6 } };
    System.out.println("Circular Tour : " + CircularTour(tour, 3));
}
```

**Output:**

```
Circular Tour : 2
```

**Second Solution:** There is inefficiency in the above problem. Net petrol calculations are done repeatedly for the same node. If we had started from the $i^{th}$ pump and got a negative value of net petrol after visiting $k^{th}$ petrol pump. Then we can find the net petrol value starting from the $i+1^{th}$ pump and ending to the kth pump in constant time by subtracting the petrol value of the $i^{th}$ pump.

So, when we are traversing the array of pumps, we go on adding an index of pumps to the array. When we get a positive value of net petrol, then we go on adding the next petrol pump and keep track of net petrol. When we get a negative net petrol value, then we remove the starting pump ID from the queue and do the needed calculation on the net petrol. Once a value is added to the queue, we don't need to do more calculations for it. So, this solution is linear. Time complexity is O(N).

**Example 8.10:**

```
public static int CircularTour2(int[][] arr, int n) {
    ArrayDeque<Integer> que = new ArrayDeque<Integer>();
    int nextPump = 0, prevPump;
    int count = 0;
    int petrol = 0;

    while (que.size() != n) {
        while (petrol >= 0 && que.size() != n) {
            que.add(nextPump);
            petrol += (arr[nextPump][0] - arr[nextPump][1]);
            nextPump = (nextPump + 1) % n;
        }
        while (petrol < 0 && que.size() > 0) {
            prevPump = que.remove();
            petrol -= (arr[prevPump][0] - arr[prevPump][1]);
        }
        count += 1;
        if (count == n)
            return -1;
    }
    if (petrol >= 0)
        return que.remove();
    else
        return -1;
}
```

## Convert XY

**Problem:** Given two values X and Y. You need to convert X to Y by performing various steps. In a step, we can either multiply 2 on the value or subtract 1 from it.

**Solution:** Breadth-first traversal (BFS) of the possible values that can be generated from the source value is done. The various values that can be generated are added to the queue for BFS. In addition, the various values are added to the map to keep track of the values already processed. Each value is added to the queue only once so the time complexity of this algorithm is O(n).

**Example 8.11:**

```
public static int convertXY(int src, int dst) {
    ArrayDeque<Integer> que = new ArrayDeque<Integer>();
    int arr[] = new int[100];
    int steps = 0;
    int index = 0;
    int value;

    que.add(src);
    while (que.size() != 0) {
        value = que.remove();
        arr[index++] = value;

        if (value == dst) {
            return steps;
        }
        steps++;
        if (value < dst)
            que.add(value * 2);
        else
            que.add(value - 1);
    }
    return -1;
}

// Testing code.
public static void main(String[] args)  {
    System.out.println("Steps count :: " + convertXY(2, 7));
}
```

**Output:**

```
Steps count :: 3
```

## The maximum value in Sliding Windows

**Problem:** Given an array of integers, find the maximum value in all the sliding windows of length k.
Input: 11, 2, 75, 92, 59, 90, 55 and k = 3
Output: 75, 92, 92, 92, 90

**First Solution:** Brute force approach, run loop for all the indexes of an array. Inside a loop run another loop of length k, find the maximum of this inner loop and display it to the screen. This time complexity is O(NK).

**Example 8.12:**
```
public static void maxSlidingWindows(int arr[], int size, int k) {
    for (int i = 0; i < size - k + 1; i++) {
        int max = arr[i];
        for (int j = 1; j < k; j++) {
            max = Math.max(max, arr[i + j]);
        }
        System.out.print(max + " ");
    }
}

// Testing code.
public static void main(String[] args)  {
    int arr[] = { 11, 2, 75, 92, 59, 90, 55 };
    maxSlidingWindows(arr, 7, 3);
}
```

**Output**
```
75 92 92 92 90
```

**Second Solution**:
1. We traverse the input array and add the index values to a queue.
2. When the index added to the queue is out of range, then we remove them from the queue.
3. We are searching for maximum value so those values which are in the queue and which are less than the value of the current index will be of no use, so we will pop them from the queue.
4. So the maximum value of the window is always present at the index que[0] so they will be displayed.

**Note**: Problems that involve sliding windows are solved efficiently using a doubly ended queue.

**Example 8.13:**
```
public static void maxSlidingWindows2(int arr[], int size, int k) {
    ArrayDeque<Integer> que = new ArrayDeque<Integer>();
    for (int i = 0; i < size; i++) {
        // Remove out of range elements
        if (que.size() > 0 && que.peek() <= i - k)
            que.remove();

        // Remove smaller values at left.
        while (que.size() > 0 && arr[que.peekLast()] <= arr[i])
            que.removeLast();

        que.add(i);
        // Largest value in window of size k is at index que[0]
        // It is displayed to the screen.
        if (i >= (k - 1))
            System.out.print(arr[que.peek()] + " ");
    }
    System.out.println();
}
```

## Minimum of Maximum Values in Sliding Windows

**Problem:** Given an array of integers, find the minimum of all the maximum values in the sliding windows of length k.
Input: 11, 2, 75, 92, 59, 90, 55 and k = 3

Output: 75

**Solution:** Same as the above problem. You will keep track of the minimum of all the maximum values in sliding windows too.

**Example 8.14:**
```
public static int minOfMaxSlidingWindows(int arr[], int size, int k) {
    ArrayDeque<Integer> que = new ArrayDeque<Integer>();
    int minVal = 999999;
    for (int i = 0; i < size; i++) {
        // Remove out of range elements
        if (que.size() > 0 && que.peek() <= i - k)
            que.remove();

        // Remove smaller values at left.
        while (que.size() > 0 && arr[que.peekLast()] <= arr[i])
            que.removeLast();

        que.add(i);
        // window of size k
        if (i >= (k - 1) && minVal > arr[que.peek()])
            minVal = arr[que.peek()];
    }
    System.out.println("Min of max is :: " + minVal);
    return minVal;
}

// Testing code.
public static void main(String[] args)  {
    int arr[] = { 11, 2, 75, 92, 59, 90, 55 };
    minOfMaxSlidingWindows(arr, 7, 3);
}
```

**Output**
```
Min of max is :: 75
```

## Maximum of Minimum Values in Sliding Windows

**Problem:** Given an array of integers, find the maximum of all the minimum values in the sliding windows of length k.
Input: 11, 2, 75, 92, 59, 90, 55 and k = 3
Output: 59, as minimum values in sliding windows are [2, 2, 59, 59, 55]

**Solution:** Same as the above problem. You will keep track of the minimum of all the maximum values in sliding windows too.

**Example 8.15:**
```
public static void maxOfMinSlidingWindows(int arr[], int size, int k) {
    ArrayDeque<Integer> que = new ArrayDeque<Integer>();
    int maxVal = -999999;

    for (int i = 0; i < size; i++) {
        // Remove out of range elements
        if (que.size() > 0 && que.peek() <= i - k)
            que.remove();
```

```
        // Remove smaller values at left.
        while (que.size() > 0 && arr[que.peekLast()] >= arr[i])
            que.removeLast ();

        que.add(i);
        // window of size k
        if (i >= (k - 1) && maxVal < arr[que.peek()])
            maxVal = arr[que.peek()];
    }
    System.out.println("Max of min is :: " + maxVal);
}

// Testing code.
public static void main(String[] args)  {
    int arr[] = { 11, 2, 75, 92, 59, 90, 55 };
    maxOfMinSlidingWindows(arr, 7, 3);
}
```

**Output:**

```
Max of min is :: 59
```

## First Negative Sliding Windows

**Problem:** Given an array of integers, find the first negative of all the values in the sliding windows of length k.

Input: Arr = [13, -2, -6, 10, -14, 50, 14, 21], k = 3

Output: [-2, -2, -6, -14, -14, NAN]

**Solution:** We will create a queue. Only those indices are added to the queue which has negative values. Pop those values which are out of the range of the window.

**Example 8.16:**

```
public static void firstNegSlidingWindows(int arr[], int size, int k) {
    ArrayDeque<Integer> que = new ArrayDeque<Integer>();
    for (int i = 0; i < size; i++) {
        // Remove out of range elements
        if (que.size() > 0 && que.peek() <= i - k)
            que.remove();
        if (arr[i] < 0)
            que.add(i);
        // window of size k
        if (i >= (k - 1)) {
            if (que.size() > 0)
                System.out.print(arr[que.peek()] + " ");
            else
                System.out.print("NAN");
        }
    }
}

// Testing code.
public static void main(String[] args)  {
    int arr[] = { 3, -2, -6, 10, -14, 50, 14, 21 };
    firstNegSlidingWindows(arr, 8, 3);
}
```

**Output:**
```
-2 -2 -6 -14 -14 NAN
```

## Rotten Fruit

**Problem:** Given that, fruits are arranged in a 2-dimensional grid. Among which few fruits are rotten. The empty slots are represented by 0, fresh fruits are represented by 1 and the rotten fruits are represented by 2. In one day, a rotten fruit rotates adjacent fruits that come to its contact. You need to find the maximum number of days in which the fruits of the whole grid will rot.

**First solution:** Using DFS / Recursion**,** each fruit can rot at max 4 other fruits that are adjacent to it. Traverse all the elements that are in the input grid. If the element is rotten fruit with value 2 then process that element. Check all the four adjacent elements, if those elements are not empty slots and are in the range of the grid. Keep track of how many days it takes to rot some fruit, starting from the rotten fruit. If we get a better day's solution then we will process the node further, else we backtrack.

Time-complexity is O(T * 4^RC), T is the total number of rotten fruits at the start, 4 is the branching factor and from each branch, we will explore all the cells of the crate which are in total RC. The total number of nodes of a tree with 4 branching factors and height will be ($4^{RC+1}$ -1) ignoring the constants we will get (4^RC). This is an exponential time complexity solution.

**Example 8.17:**
```
public static void rottenFruitUtil(int[][] arr, int maxCol, int maxRow, int
currCol, int currRow, int[][] traversed,
        int day) {
    int[][] dir = { { -1, 0 }, { 1, 0 }, { 0, -1 }, { 0, 1 } };
    int x, y;
    for (int i = 0; i < 4; i++) {
        x = currCol + dir[i][0];
        y = currRow + dir[i][1];
        if (x >= 0 && x < maxCol && y >= 0 && y < maxRow
                            && traversed[x][y] > day + 1 && arr[x][y] == 1) {
            traversed[x][y] = day + 1;
            rottenFruitUtil(arr, maxCol, maxRow, x, y, traversed, day + 1);
        }
    }
}

public static int rottenFruit(int[][] arr, int maxCol, int maxRow) {
    int[][] traversed = new int[maxCol][maxRow];
    for (int i = 0; i < maxCol; i++) {
        for (int j = 0; j < maxRow; j++) {
            traversed[i][j] = Integer.MAX_VALUE;
        }
    }

    for (int i = 0; i < maxCol; i++) {
        for (int j = 0; j < maxRow; j++) {
            if (arr[i][j] == 2) {
                traversed[i][j] = 0;
                rottenFruitUtil(arr, maxCol, maxRow, i, j, traversed, 0);
            }
        }
```

```
    }

    int maxDay = 0;
    for (int i = 0; i < maxCol; i++) {
        for (int j = 0; j < maxRow; j++) {
            if (arr[i][j] == 1) {
                if (traversed[i][j] == Integer.MAX_VALUE)
                    return -1;
                if (maxDay < traversed[i][j])
                    maxDay = traversed[i][j];
            }
        }
    }
    return maxDay;
}

// Testing code.
public static void main(String[] args)  {
    int arr[][] = { { 1, 0, 1, 1, 0 }, { 2, 1, 0, 1, 0 }, { 0, 0, 0, 2, 1 }, { 0,
2, 0, 0, 1 }, { 1, 1, 0, 0, 1 } };
    System.out.println(rottenFruit(arr, 5, 5));
}
```

**Output:**

```
rottenFruit :3
```

**Second solution:** Using BFS, We had a queue to store all the locations of rotten fruits. Then we will perform BFS by taking one element out of the queue and processing it. When processing an element taken out of the queue, all its branches or adjacent fruit locations are again inserted at the end of the queue. By doing this, those nodes which are closer to the rotten fruits are processed before the far nodes. This is an efficient algorithm with time complexity O(RC).

**Example 8.18:**

```
public static class Fruit {
    int x, y;
    int day;
    Fruit(int a, int b, int d) {
        x = a;
        y = b;
        day = d;
    }
}

public static int rottenFruit2(int[][] arr, int maxCol, int maxRow) {
    boolean[][] traversed = new boolean[maxCol][maxRow];
    int[][] dir = { { -1, 0 }, { 1, 0 }, { 0, -1 }, { 0, 1 } };
    ArrayDeque<Fruit> que = new ArrayDeque<Fruit>();
    for (int i = 0; i < maxCol; i++) {
        for (int j = 0; j < maxRow; j++) {
            traversed[i][j] = false;
            if (arr[i][j] == 2) {
                que.add(new Fruit(i, j, 0));
                traversed[i][j] = true;
            }
        }
    }
```

```
    int max = 0, x, y, day;
    Fruit temp;
    while (!que.isEmpty()) {
        temp = que.peek();
        que.pop();
        for (int i = 0; i < 4; i++) {
            x = temp.x + dir[i][0];
            y = temp.y + dir[i][1];
            day = temp.day + 1;
            if (x >= 0 && x < maxCol && y >= 0 && y < maxRow && arr[x][y] != 0 &&
traversed[x][y] == false) {
                que.add(new Fruit(x, y, day));
                max = Math.max(max, day);
                traversed[x][y] = true;
            }
        }
    }
    for (int i = 0; i < maxCol; i++) {
        for (int j = 0; j < maxRow; j++) {
            if (arr[i][j] == 1 && traversed[i][j] == false) {
                return -1;
            }
        }
    }
    return max;
}
```

## Steps of Knight

**Problem:** Given a chessboard and a knight start position. You need to find the minimum number of steps required to move a knight from the start position to the final position.

**First Solution**: DFS, Each knight can go to 8 other positions. Find the positions which are not already visited with less number of steps and are in the range of the chessboard. Perform DFS traversal of the chessboard. If we get a better solution for some nodes then only we process it further, if we already have a better solution then we backtrack.

Time-complexity will be O(8^(n^2)) since 8 is the branching factor and from each branch, we will explore all the cells of the board which are in total n^2. This is an exponential time complexity solution.

**Example 8.19:**

```
public static void stepsOfKnightUtil(int size, int currCol, int currRow, int[][]
traversed, int dist) {
    int[][] dir = { { -2, -1 }, { -2, 1 }, { 2, -1 }, { 2, 1 },
                    { -1, -2 }, { 1, -2 }, { -1, 2 }, { 1, 2 } };
    int x, y;
    for (int i = 0; i < 8; i++) {
        x = currCol + dir[i][0];
        y = currRow + dir[i][1];
        if (x >= 0 && x < size && y >= 0 && y < size && traversed[x][y] > dist+1){
            traversed[x][y] = dist + 1;
            stepsOfKnightUtil(size, x, y, traversed, dist + 1);
        }
    }
}
```

```
public static int stepsOfKnight(int size, int srcX, int srcY, int dstX, int dstY) {
    int[][] traversed = new int[size][size];
    for (int i = 0; i < size; i++) {
        for (int j = 0; j < size; j++) {
            traversed[i][j] = Integer.MAX_VALUE;
        }
    }
    traversed[srcX - 1][srcY - 1] = 0;
    stepsOfKnightUtil(size, srcX - 1, srcY - 1, traversed, 0);
    return traversed[dstX - 1][dstY - 1];
}

// Testing code.
public static void main(String[] args)  {
    System.out.println(stepsOfKnight(20, 10, 10, 20, 20));
}
```

**Output:**

```
8
```

**Second Solution**: BFS, We had taken a queue to store the start location of the knight. Then we will perform BFS by taking one element out of the queue and processing it. When processing an element taken out of the queue, all its branches or 8 different cells are inserted at the end of the queue. By doing this, those nodes which are closer to the starting location of the knight are processed before the far cells. This is an efficient algorithm with time complexity O(N^2), where N is the size of the board.

**Example 8.20:**

```
public static class Knight {
    int x, y;
    int cost;
    Knight(int a, int b, int c) {
        x = a;
        y = b;
        cost = c;
    }
}

public static int stepsOfKnight2(int size, int srcX, int srcY, int dstX, int dstY)
{
    int[][] traversed = new int[size][size];
    int[][] dir = {{-2,-1},{-2,1},{2,-1},{2,1},{-1,-2},{1,-2},{-1,2},{1,2 }};
    ArrayDeque<Knight> que = new ArrayDeque<Knight>();

    for (int i = 0; i < size; i++) {
        for (int j = 0; j < size; j++) {
            traversed[i][j] = Integer.MAX_VALUE;
        }
    }
    que.add(new Knight(srcX - 1, srcY - 1, 0));
    traversed[srcX - 1][srcY - 1] = 0;

    int x, y, cost;
    Knight temp;
    while (!que.isEmpty()) {
        temp = que.peek();
        que.pop();
```

```
        for (int i = 0; i < 8; i++) {
            x = temp.x + dir[i][0];
            y = temp.y + dir[i][1];
            cost = temp.cost + 1;
            if (x>=0 && x < size && y>=0 && y<size && traversed[x][y] > cost) {
                que.add(new Knight(x, y, cost));
                traversed[x][y] = cost;
            }
        }
    }
    return traversed[dstX - 1][dstY - 1];
}
```

## Distance nearest fill

**Problem:** Given a matrix 2D array, with some cells filled by 1 and other 0. You need to create a 2D array that will contain the minimum distance of each 0 elements to any one of the cells with a value of 1. Manhattan distance is considered.

**First Solution**: DFS, Grid-based traversal using DFS is performed to find the nearest fill. We create a 2-dimensional traversed array to keep track of distance. For each node traverse all nodes accessible from it. A node is traversed if it is in the range of the grid and has a distance less than the previous distance.

Time-complexity will be O(4^RC) since 4 is the branching factor and from each branch, we will explore all the elements of the crate which are in total RC. This is an exponential time complexity solution.

**Example 8.21:**

```
public static void distNearestFillUtil(int[][] arr, int maxCol, int maxRow,
                        int currCol, int currRow, int[][] traversed, int dist) {
    int x, y;
    int[][] dir = { { -1, 0 }, { 1, 0 }, { 0, -1 }, { 0, 1 } };
    for (int i = 0; i < 4; i++) {
        x = currCol + dir[i][0];
        y = currRow + dir[i][1];
        if (x>=0 && x<maxCol && y>=0 && y < maxRow && traversed[x][y] > dist + 1) {
            traversed[x][y] = dist + 1;
            distNearestFillUtil(arr, maxCol, maxRow, x, y, traversed, dist + 1);
        }
    }
}

public static void distNearestFill(int[][] arr, int maxCol, int maxRow) {
    int[][] traversed = new int[maxCol][maxRow];
    for (int i = 0; i < maxCol; i++) {
        for (int j = 0; j < maxRow; j++) {
            traversed[i][j] = Integer.MAX_VALUE;
        }
    }

    for (int i = 0; i < maxCol; i++) {
        for (int j = 0; j < maxRow; j++) {
            if (arr[i][j] == 1) {
                traversed[i][j] = 0;
                distNearestFillUtil(arr, maxCol, maxRow, i, j, traversed, 0);
```

```
            }
        }
    }

    for (int i = 0; i < maxCol; i++) {
        for (int j = 0; j < maxRow; j++) {
            System.out.print(traversed[i][j] + " ");
        }
        System.out.println();
    }
}

// Testing code.
public static void main(String[] args)  {
    int arr[][] = { { 1, 0, 1, 1, 0 }, { 1, 1, 0, 1, 0 }, { 0, 0, 0, 0, 1 }, { 0,
0, 0, 0, 1 }, { 0, 0, 0, 0, 1 } };
    distNearestFill(arr, 5, 5);
}
```

**Output:**

```
0 1 0 0 1
0 0 1 0 1
1 1 2 1 0
2 2 2 1 0
3 3 2 1 0
```

**Second Solution**: BFS, We had taken a queue to store all the cells with 1 value. Then we will perform BFS by taking one element out of the queue and processing it. When processing an element taken out of the queue, all its branches or adjacent cells are again inserted at the end of the queue. By doing this, those nodes which are closer to the nodes with 1 are processed before the far nodes. This is an efficient algorithm with time complexity O(RC), where R is the number of rows and C is the number of columns.

**Example 8.22:**

```
public static class Node {
    int x, y;
    int dist;

    Node(int a, int b, int d) {
        x = a;
        y = b;
        dist = d;
    }
}

public static void distNearestFill2(int[][] arr, int maxCol, int maxRow) {
    int[][] traversed = new int[maxCol][maxRow];
    int[][] dir = { { -1, 0 }, { 1, 0 }, { 0, -1 }, { 0, 1 } };
    ArrayDeque<Node> que = new ArrayDeque<Node>();
    for (int i = 0; i < maxCol; i++) {
        for (int j = 0; j < maxRow; j++) {
            traversed[i][j] = Integer.MAX_VALUE;
            if (arr[i][j] == 1) {
                que.add(new Node(i, j, 0));
                traversed[i][j] = 0;
            }
```

```
        }
    }
    int x, y, dist;
    Node temp;
    while (!que.isEmpty()) {
        temp = que.peek();
        que.pop();
        for (int i = 0; i < 4; i++) {
            x = temp.x + dir[i][0];
            y = temp.y + dir[i][1];
            dist = temp.dist + 1;
            if (x>=0 && x<maxCol && y>=0 && y<maxRow && traversed[x][y] > dist) {
                que.add(new Node(x, y, dist));
                traversed[x][y] = dist;
            }
        }
    }
    for (int i = 0; i < maxCol; i++) {
        for (int j = 0; j < maxRow; j++) {
            System.out.print(traversed[i][j] + " ");
        }
        System.out.println();
    }
}
```

## Largest island

**Problem:** Given a map represented by a 2D array. 1s are land and 0s are water. You need to find the largest landmass. The largest landmass has the largest number of 1s.

**Solution**: The largest island is found by doing DFS traversal of neighbouring nodes of a current node. The largest island of the current node is the sum of the largest island of all the neighbouring nodes + 1 (for the current node).

Time-complexity will be O(RC), we will explore all the cells of the grid and once a cell is traversed then it will not be traversed again.

**Example 8.23:**

```
public static int findLargestIslandUtil(int[][] arr, int maxCol, int maxRow, int
currCol, int currRow, boolean[][] traversed) {
    int[][] dir = {{-1,-1}, {-1,0}, {-1,1 }, {0,-1}, {0,1}, {1,-1}, {1,0}, {1,1}};
    int x, y, sum = 1;

    for (int i = 0; i < 8; i++) {
        x = currCol + dir[i][0];
        y = currRow + dir[i][1];
        if (x >= 0 && x < maxCol && y >= 0 && y < maxRow
                    && traversed[x][y] == false && arr[x][y] == 1) {
            traversed[x][y] = true;
            sum += findLargestIslandUtil(arr, maxCol, maxRow, x, y, traversed);
        }
    }
    return sum;
}
```

```
public static int findLargestIsland(int[][] arr, int maxCol, int maxRow) {
    int maxVal = 0;
    int currVal = 0;
    boolean[][] traversed = new boolean[maxCol][maxRow];
    for (int i = 0; i < maxCol; i++) {
        for (int j = 0; j < maxRow; j++) {
            traversed[i][j] = false;
        }
    }

    for (int i = 0; i < maxCol; i++) {
        for (int j = 0; j < maxRow; j++) {
            if (arr[i][j] == 1) {
                traversed[i][j] = true;
                currVal = findLargestIslandUtil(arr, maxCol, maxRow, i, j,
traversed);
                if (currVal > maxVal)
                    maxVal = currVal;
            }
        }
    }
    return maxVal;
}

// Testing code.
public static void main(String[] args)  {
    int arr[][] = { { 1, 0, 1, 1, 0 }, { 1, 0, 0, 1, 0 }, { 0, 1, 1, 1, 1 }, { 0,
1, 0, 0, 0 }, { 1, 1, 0, 0, 1 } };
    System.out.println("Largest Island : " + findLargestIsland(arr, 5, 5));
}
```

**Output:**

```
Largest Island : 12
```

## Uses of Queue

Applications of Queue are:

1. Where FIFO functionality is required
2. Printer has its queue to schedule various print commands.
3. Scheduling of shared resources in the operating system.
4. Multiprogramming tasks.
5. Message queue of a messaging service.
6. Breadth-first search (BFS) of trees and graphs.

## Exercise

1. Implement a queue using dynamic memory allocation, such that the implementation should follow the following constraints.
   - The user should use memory allocation from the heap using a new operator. In this, you need to take care of the max value in the queue.

- Once you are done with the above exercise, you can test your queue. Then you can add some more complexity to your code. In the add() function when the queue is full, in place of printing, "Queue is full" you should allocate more space using a new operator.
- Once you are done with the above exercise. Now in the remove function, once you are below half of the capacity of the queue, you need to decrease the size of the queue by half. You should add one more variable "min" to the queue so that you can track what is the original value capacity passed to the initialization() function. Moreover, the capacity of the queue will not go below the value passed in the initialization.

2. Implement the below function for the queue:
   - IsEmpty: This is left as an exercise for the user. Take a variable, which will take care of the size of a queue if the value of that variable is zero, isEmpty should return true. If the queue is not empty, then it should return false.
   - Size: Use the size variable to be used under the size function call. The size() function should return the number of elements in the queue.

3. Implement stack using a queue. Write a program for this problem. You can use just one queue.

4. Write a program to Reverse a stack using queue

5. Write a program to Reverse a queue using stack

6. Write a CompStack() function which takes a pointer to two stacks as an argument and returns true or false depending upon whether all the elements of the stack are equal or not. You are given isEqual(int, int) which will compare and return true if both values are equal and 0 if they are different.

7. Given two values X and Y. You need to convert X to Y by performing various steps. In a step, we can either multiply 2 to the value or subtract 1 from it. You need to display the number of steps and the path. To reach 3 from 1, the path will be [1, 2, 4, 3] and the number of steps will be 3.

   Hint: Create an array to keep track of the number of steps and another array to keep track of parent value.

8. The number of islands: Given a map represented by a 2D array. 1s are land and 0s are water. You need to find several islands. An island is a landmass formed by a group of connected 1s.

   Hint: Solve this problem in the same way you had solved the above largest island problem.

9. Snake and Ladder Problem: Given a snake and ladder board, which starts with 1 and ends at 100. You need to find the minimum number of dice throws required to reach the 100th cell from the 1st cell. There is a list of snakes' coordinates provided and a list of ladder coordinates provided as pairs.

   Hint: create a dice count array of length 100. Processing each cell starts from 1st to 100th. Each cell has 6 outcomes. Which changes with the presence of snakes and ladders. Use BFS or DFS and reach your destination.

10. Rat in Maze: Given a maze, NxN matrix of 0's and 1's. A rat has to find a path from source maze[0][0] to destination maze[N-1][N-1]. A rat can move in any direction ( left, right, up and down). A rat can move only in unblocked cells with cell value 1. Return the shortest path and its length.

# CHAPTER 9: TREE

## Introduction

A tree is a **non-linear** data structure, which is used to represent the **hierarchical** relationship between a parent node and a child node. Each node in the tree is connected to another node by **directed edges**.

Why do we use trees? Linear data structures like an array, linked list etc. have a drawback of linear time for searching an element.

Example 1: Tree in a team of some manager

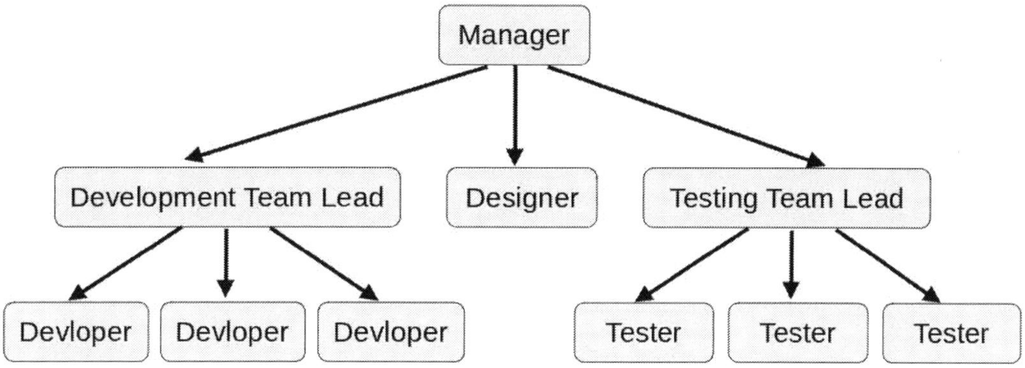


Example 2: Tree in a file system

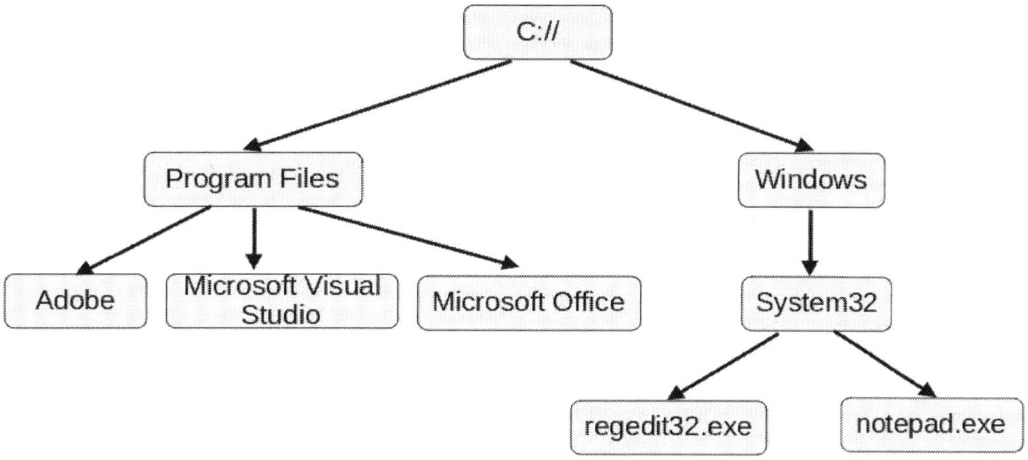


## Terminology in tree

The basic tree terminologies are as follows:

**Node:** It is a fundamental element of a tree. Each node has data and two pointers that may point to null or its children.

**Edge**: It is also a fundamental part of a tree, which is used to connect two nodes.

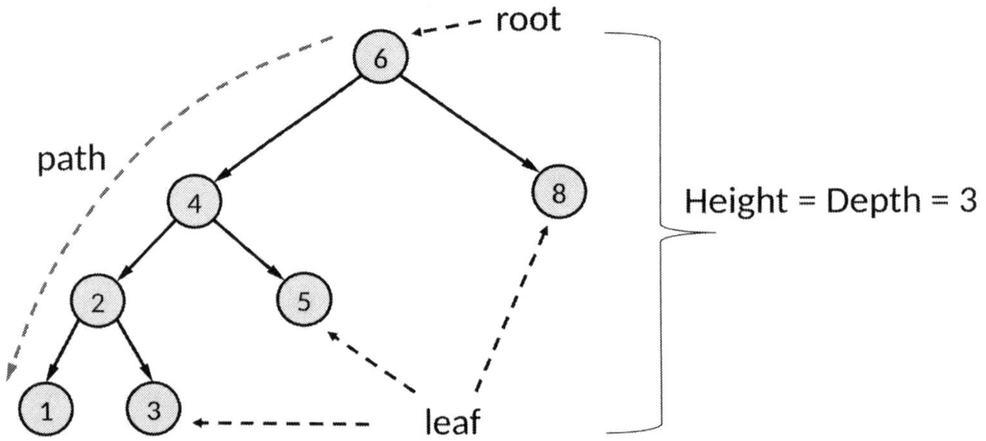


**Root**: The root of the tree is the only node without incoming edges. It is the top node of a tree.

**Leaf**: A leaf node is a node that has no children.

**Path**: A path is an ordered list of nodes that are connected by edges.

**Height of node**: It is the number of edges on the longest path between the node to a leaf node.

**Height of tree**: It is the number of edges on the longest path between the root and a leaf node.

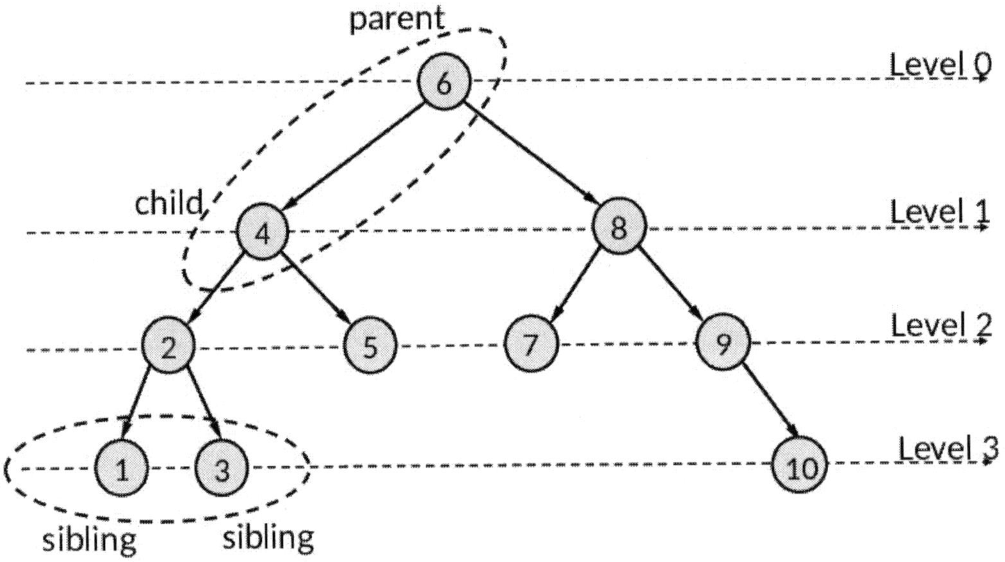


**Parent**: A node is said to be a parent node if it has outgoing edges to other nodes.

**Child**: A node that has incoming edges from some other node is said to be the child of that node.

**Sibling**: Nodes that are children of the same parent are called sibling nodes.

**Ancestor**: A node is said to be an ancestor node if it is reachable while moving from child to parent.

**`Level or Depth of a node`**: The level of a node is the number of edges on the path from the root node to that node. For example, the level of root is 0 and levels of left and right children of root is 1.

## Binary Tree

A binary tree is a type tree in which each node has at most two children (0, 1 or 2), which are referred to as the left child and the right child. Below is a node of the binary tree with "a" stored as data and whose left child (lChild) and whose right child (rchild) both points to null.

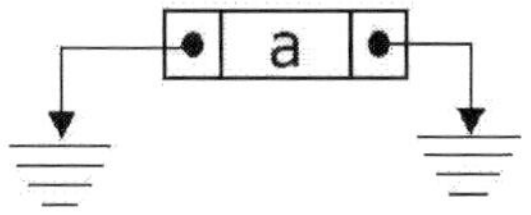


**Example 9.1**: Binary tree class and its methods.

```
public class Tree {
    private Node root;

    private static class Node {
        private int value;
        private Node left;
        private Node right;

        public Node(int v, Node l, Node r) {
            value = v;
            left = l;
            right = r;
        }

        public Node(int v) {
            value = v;
            left = null;
            right = null;
        }
    }

    public Tree() {
        root = null;
    }
    /* Other methods */
}
```

A binary tree whose nodes contain data from 1 to 10 is given below:

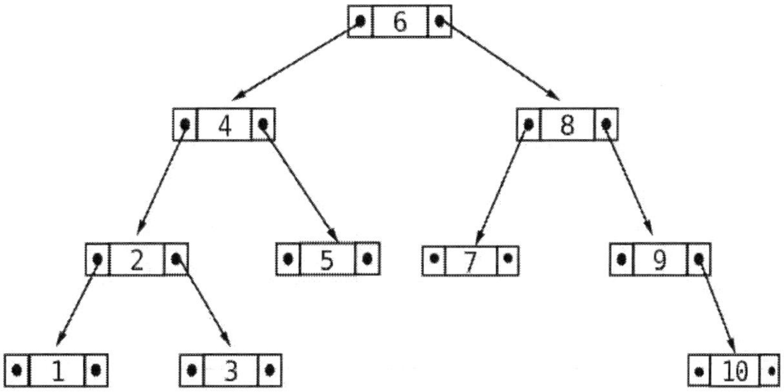


6, 4, 2, 5, 1, 3, 8, 7, 9, 10

In the rest of the book, the binary tree will be represented as below:

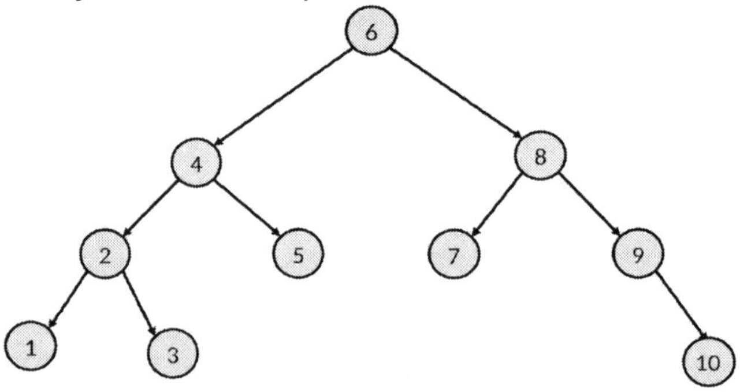

The properties of a binary tree are as follows:

1. The maximum number of nodes on level i of a binary tree is $2^i$, where i >= 0
2. The maximum number of nodes in a binary tree of height k is 2^(k+1) - 1, where k >= 0
3. There is exactly one path from the root to any nodes in a tree.
4. A tree with N nodes has exactly N-1 edges connecting these nodes.
5. The height of a complete binary tree of N nodes is $\log_2 N$.

## Types of Binary trees

### Complete binary tree

In a complete binary tree, every level except the last one is completely filled. All nodes on the left are filled first, then the right one. A binary heap is an example of a complete binary tree.

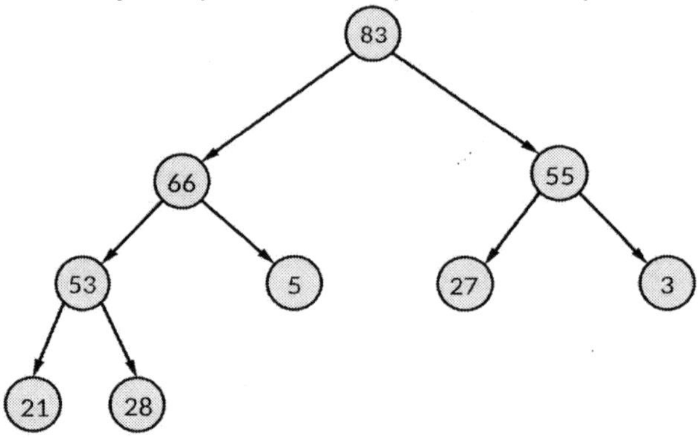

### Full (Strictly or Proper) binary tree

The full binary tree is a binary tree in which each node has exactly zero or two children.

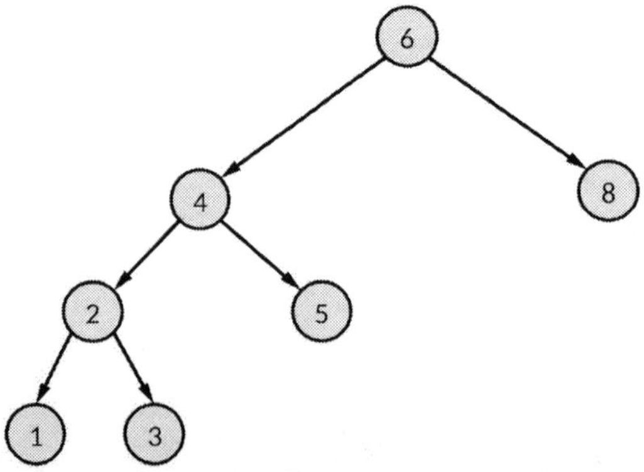

## Perfect binary tree

The perfect binary tree is a type of full binary tree in which each non-leaf node has exactly two child nodes. All leaf nodes have identical path lengths and all possible node slots are occupied

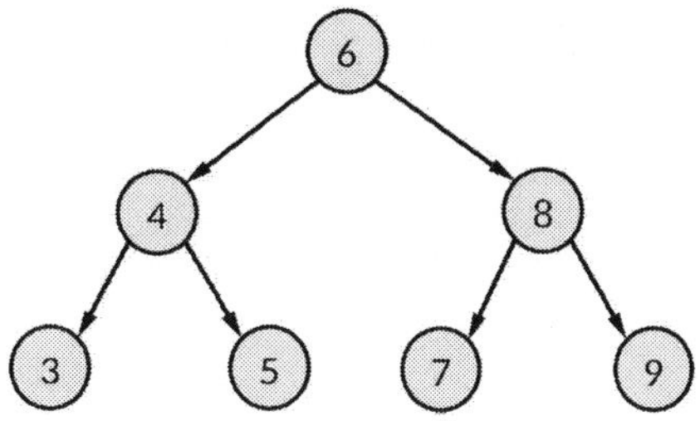


## Right skewed binary tree

A binary tree in which either each node is has a right child or no child (leaf) is called a right-skewed binary tree

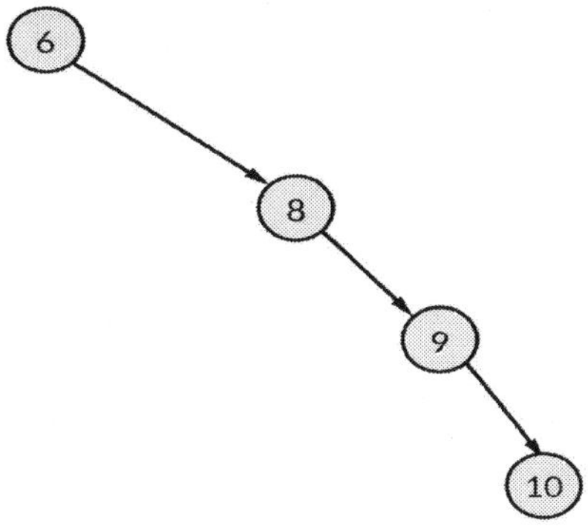


## Left skewed binary tree

A binary tree in which either each node is has a left child or no child (leaf) is called a Left skewed binary tree

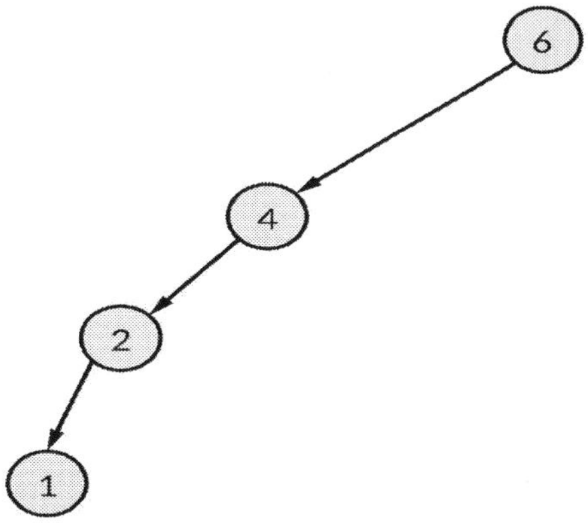


## Height-balanced Binary Tree

A height-balanced binary tree is a binary tree such that the left & right subtrees for any given node differ in height by max one. AVL tree and RB tree are examples of height-balanced trees.

**Note**: Each complete binary tree is a height-balanced binary tree

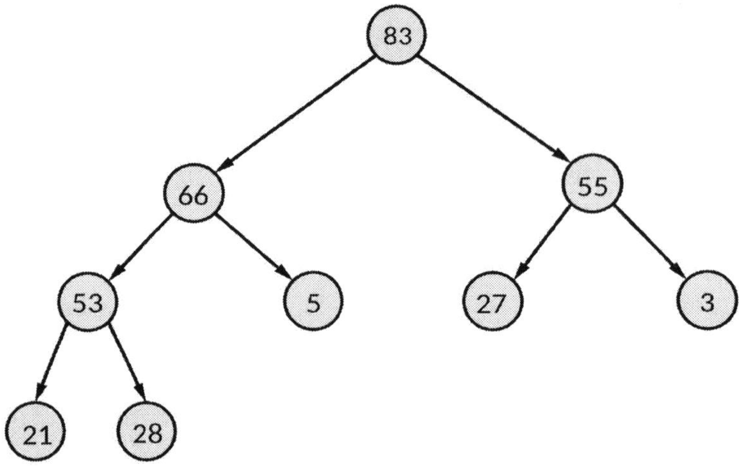


## Problems in Binary Tree

### Create a Complete binary tree

**Problem:** Create a complete binary tree from values given as an array.

**Solution:** To create a complete binary tree, we will fill the elements in the tree level-wise starting from level 0.

The steps of creating a complete binary tree are as follows:

- Insert the first element present in the array (index i = 0) as the root node at level 0 of the tree.
- Calculate left child as 2 * i + 1 and add it in the left subtree of the root.
- Calculate right child as 2 * i + 2 and add it in the right subtree of the root.
- Recursively, apply these steps for left and right subtree nodes.

**Example 9.2:**

```
public void createCompleteBinaryTree(int[] arr) {
    root = createCompleteBinaryTree(arr, 0);
}

public Node createCompleteBinaryTree(int[] arr, int start) {
    int size = arr.length;
    Node curr = new Node(arr[start]);
    int leftIndex = 2 * start + 1;
    int rightIndex = 2 * start + 2;

    if (leftIndex < size)
        curr.left = createCompleteBinaryTree(arr, leftIndex);
    if (rightIndex < size)
        curr.right = createCompleteBinaryTree(arr, rightIndex);

    return curr;
}

// Testing code.
public static void main(String[] args)  {
    Tree t = new Tree();
    int[] arr = { 1, 2, 3, 4, 5, 6, 7, 8, 9, 10 };
    t.createCompleteBinaryTree(arr);
```

```
    t.printPreOrder();
}
```

**Output:**
```
1 2 4 8 9 5 10 3 6 7
```

**Complexity Analysis:** This is an efficient algorithm for creating a complete binary tree.

**Time Complexity:** O(n), **Space Complexity:** O(n)

## Pre-Order Traversal

**Problem:** Perform Pre-Order Traversal of a binary tree.

**Solution:** In pre-order traversal, the **node** is visited / traversed first, then its **left child** (or left subtree), and then its **right child** (or right subtree) are printed. This approach is followed recursively for each node in the tree until we reach the leaf node.

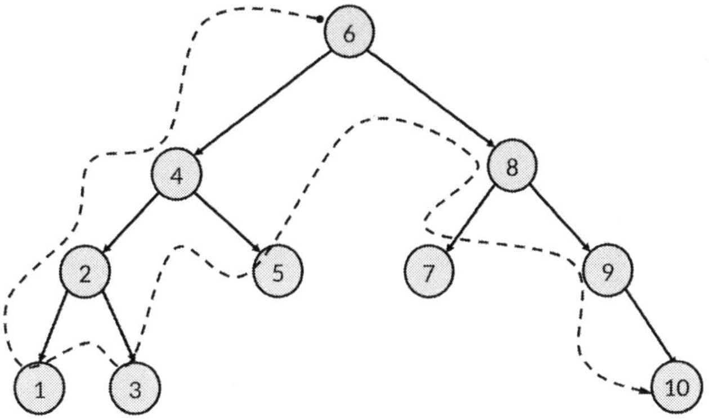


**Example 9.3:**
```
public void printPreOrder() {
    printPreOrder(root);
    System.out.println();
}

private void printPreOrder(Node node) { /* pre order */
    if (node != null) {
        System.out.print(node.value + " ");
        printPreOrder(node.left);
        printPreOrder(node.right);
    }
}

// Testing code.
public static void main(String[] args)  {
    Tree t = new Tree();
    int[] arr = { 1, 2, 3, 4, 5, 6, 7, 8, 9, 10 };
    t.createCompleteBinaryTree(arr);
    t.printPreOrder();
}
```

**Output:**
```
1 2 4 8 9 5 10 3 6 7
```

**Time Complexity:** O(n), **Space Complexity:** O(n)

**Note**: If there is an algorithm, in which all nodes are traversed, then complexity cannot be less than O(n). When there is a large portion of the tree, which is not traversed, then complexity reduces.

## Post-Order Traversal

**Problem:** Perform Post-Order Traversal of a binary tree.

**Solution:** In post-order traversal, a node's **left child** is visited / traversed first, then its **right child**, and then the value stored in the current **node** is printed. This approach is followed recursively for each node in the tree until we reach the leaf node.

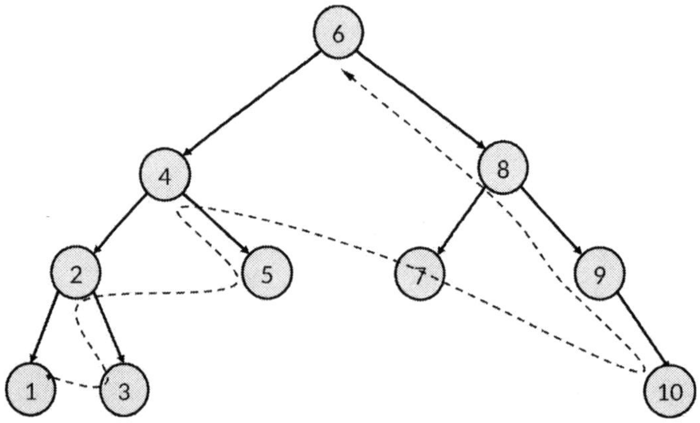


**Example 9.4:**
```
public void printPostOrder() {
    printPostOrder(root);
    System.out.println();
}

private void printPostOrder(Node node) { /* post order */
    if (node != null) {
        printPostOrder(node.left);
        printPostOrder(node.right);
        System.out.print(node.value + " ");
    }
}

// Testing code.
public static void main(String[] args)  {
    Tree t = new Tree();
    int[] arr = { 1, 2, 3, 4, 5, 6, 7, 8, 9, 10 };
    t.createCompleteBinaryTree(arr);
    t.printPostOrder();
}
```

**Output**:
```
8 9 4 10 5 2 6 7 3 1
```

**Time Complexity:** O(n), **Space Complexity:** O(n)

## In-Order Traversal

**Problem:** Perform In-Order Traversal of a binary tree.

**Solution:** In In-Order traversal, the left child (or left subtree) of a node is visited / traversed first, then the node itself, and then finally its right child (or right subtree) is traversed. This approach is followed recursively for each node in the tree until we reach the leaf node.

**Note:** The output of the In-Order traversal of BST is a sorted list in increasing order.

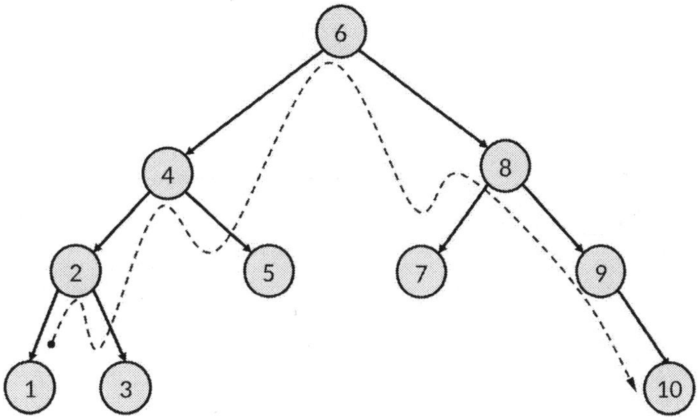


**Example 9.5:**
```
public void printInOrder() {
    printInOrder(root);
    System.out.println();
}

private void printInOrder(Node node) { /* In order */
    if (node != null) {
        printInOrder(node.left);
        System.out.print(node.value + " ");
        printInOrder(node.right);
    }
}

// Testing code.
public static void main(String[] args)  {
    Tree t = new Tree();
    int[] arr = { 1, 2, 3, 4, 5, 6, 7, 8, 9, 10 };
    t.createCompleteBinaryTree(arr);
    t.printInOrder();
}
```

**Output**:
```
8 4 9 2 10 5 1 6 3 7
```

**Time Complexity:** O(n), **Space Complexity:** O(n)

**Note**: Pre-Order, Post-Order, and In-Order traversal are meant for all binary trees. They can be used to traverse any kind of binary tree.

## Level order traversal / Breadth First traversal

**Problem:** Write code to implement level order traversal of a tree. Such that nodes at depth k are printed before nodes at depth k+1.

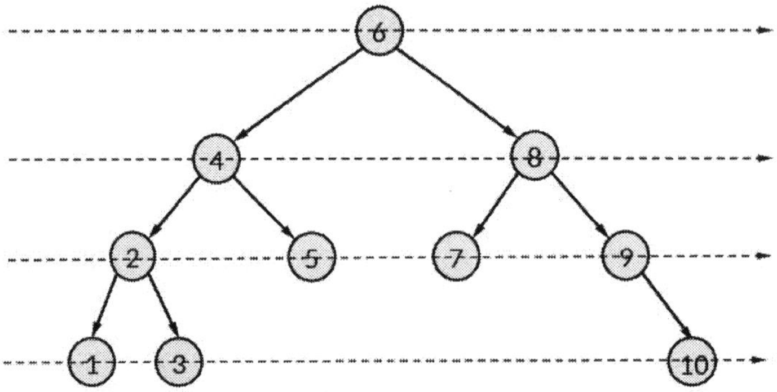


**Solution:** Level order traversal or Breadth-First traversal of a tree is done using a queue. At first, the root node pointer is added to a queue. The traversal of the tree is done until the queue is empty. When we traverse the tree, we first remove an element from the queue, print the value stored in that node and then its left child and right child will be added to the queue.

**Example 9.6:**
```
public void printBreadthFirst() {
    ArrayDeque<Node> que = new ArrayDeque<Node>();
    Node temp;
    if (root != null)
        que.add(root);

    while (que.isEmpty() == false) {
        temp = que.remove();
        System.out.print(temp.value + " ");

        if (temp.left != null)
            que.add(temp.left);
        if (temp.right != null)
            que.add(temp.right);
    }
}

// Testing code.
public static void main(String[] args)  {
    Tree t = new Tree();
    int[] arr = { 1, 2, 3, 4, 5, 6, 7, 8, 9, 10 };
    t.createCompleteBinaryTree(arr);
    t.printBreadthFirst();
}
```

**Output:**
```
1 2 3 4 5 6 7 8 9 10
```

**Time Complexity:** O(n), **Space Complexity:** O(n)

## Print Depth First without using the recursion/system stack.

**Problem:** Perform a depth-first search of a binary tree without using recursion.

**Solution:** Depth-first traversal of the tree is done by using the system stack recursion. However, the same can be implemented by using a stack data structure as well. In the beginning, root node reference is added to the stack. The whole tree is traversed until the stack is empty. In each iteration, an element is popped from the stack, its value is printed to the screen. Then the right child and then the left child of the node is added to the stack. The following code demonstrates the latter approach.

**Example 9.7:**
```
public void printDepthFirst() {
    Stack<Node> stk = new Stack<Node>();
    Node temp;

    if (root != null)
        stk.push(root);

    while (stk.isEmpty() == false) {
        temp = stk.pop();
        System.out.print(temp.value + " ");

        if (temp.left != null)
            stk.push(temp.left);
        if (temp.right != null)
            stk.push(temp.right);
    }
}

// Testing code.
public static void main(String[] args)  {
    Tree t = new Tree();
    int[] arr = { 1, 2, 3, 4, 5, 6, 7, 8, 9, 10 };
    t.createCompleteBinaryTree(arr);
    t.printDepthFirst();
}
```

**Output:**
```
1 3 7 6 2 5 10 4 9 8
```

**Time Complexity:** O(n), **Space Complexity:** O(n)

## Print Level Order Line by Line

**Problem:** Perform level order traversal of a binary tree, such that the levels are printed line by line.

**First Solution:** We will use two queues to perform level order traversal. Alternatively, we will process queues and put the children of elements of the queue into another queue so that when each level is processed, we can print the output in different lines.

**Example 9.8:**
```
void printLevelOrderLineByLine() {
    ArrayDeque<Node> que1 = new ArrayDeque<Node>();
    ArrayDeque<Node> que2 = new ArrayDeque<Node>();
    Node temp = null;
    if (root != null)
        que1.add(root);
```

```
    while (que1.size() != 0 || que2.size() != 0) {
        while (que1.size() != 0) {
            temp = que1.remove();
            System.out.print(temp.value + " ");
            if (temp.left != null)
                que2.add(temp.left);
            if (temp.right != null)
                que2.add(temp.right);
        }
        System.out.println();

        while (que2.size() != 0) {
            temp = que2.remove();
            System.out.print(temp.value + " ");
            if (temp.left != null)
                que1.add(temp.left);
            if (temp.right != null)
                que1.add(temp.right);
        }
        System.out.println();
    }
}

// Testing code.
public static void main(String[] args)  {
    Tree t = new Tree();
    int[] arr = { 1, 2, 3, 4, 5, 6, 7, 8, 9, 10 };
    t.createCompleteBinaryTree(arr);
    t.printLevelOrderLineByLine();
}
```

**Output:**

```
1
2 3
4 5 6 7
8 9 10
```

**Second solution:** We can solve this problem using a single queue. Let us suppose at any time we have all the nodes of the kth level present in a queue. We can find the count of these elements. We can process elements from the queue count number of times and add their children to the queue. Then we can print a new line. At this point, we have all the nodes at the k+1 level. Start with adding root nodes as the first level to the queue and follow the steps mentioned above.

**Example 9.9:**

```
void printLevelOrderLineByLine2() {
    ArrayDeque<Node> que = new ArrayDeque<Node>();
    Node temp = null;
    int count = 0;

    if (root != null)
        que.add(root);
    while (que.size() != 0) {
        count = que.size();
        while (count > 0) {
            temp = que.remove();
            System.out.print(temp.value + " ");
```

```
            if (temp.left != null)
                que.add(temp.left);
            if (temp.right != null)
                que.add(temp.right);
            count -= 1;
        }
        System.out.println();
    }
}
```

## Print Spiral Tree

**Problem:** Given a binary tree, print the nodes breadth-first in spiral order.

**Solution:** Stacks are last in first out, so two stacks are used to process each level alternatively. The nodes are added and processed in such an order that nodes are printed in spiral order.

**Example 9.10:**

```
void printSpiralTree() {
    Stack<Node> stk1 = new Stack<Node>();
    Stack<Node> stk2 = new Stack<Node>();

    Node temp;
    if (root != null)
        stk1.push(root);

    while (stk1.size() != 0 || stk2.size() != 0) {
        while (stk1.size() != 0) {
            temp = stk1.pop();
            System.out.print(temp.value + " ");
            if (temp.right != null)
                stk2.push(temp.right);
            if (temp.left != null)
                stk2.push(temp.left);
        }

        while (stk2.size() != 0) {
            temp = stk2.pop();
            System.out.print(temp.value + " ");
            if (temp.left != null)
                stk1.push(temp.left);
            if (temp.right != null)
                stk1.push(temp.right);
        }
    }
    System.out.println();
}

// Testing code.
public static void main(String[] args)  {
    Tree t = new Tree();
    int[] arr = { 1, 2, 3, 4, 5, 6, 7, 8, 9, 10 };
    t.createCompleteBinaryTree(arr);
    t.printSpiralTree();
}
```

**Output:**
```
1 2 3 7 6 5 4 8 9 10
```

## Nth Pre-Order

**Problem:** Given a binary tree, print the value of nodes that will be at the nth index when the tree is traversed in pre-order.

**Solution:** We keep track of our indexes using a counter. Since we want to print the node that is at the nth index when we traverse the tree in pre-order, therefore, we will increment the counter as soon as we find a non-empty node. When the counter becomes equal to the index, we print the value and return the nth pre-order index node.

**Example 9.11:**
```
public void nthPreOrder(int index) {
    int[] counter = { 0 };
    nthPreOrder(root, index, counter);
}

private void nthPreOrder(Node node, int index, int[] counter) { /* pre order */
    if (node != null) {
        counter[0]++;
        if (counter[0] == index) {
            System.out.println(node.value);
        }

        nthPreOrder(node.left, index, counter);
        nthPreOrder(node.right, index, counter);
    }
}

// Testing code.
public static void main(String[] args)  {
    Tree t = new Tree();
    int[] arr = { 1, 2, 3, 4, 5, 6, 7, 8, 9, 10 };
    t.createCompleteBinaryTree(arr);
    t.nthPreOrder(2);
}
```

**Output:**
```
2
```

**Time Complexity:** O(n), **Space Complexity:** O(n)

## Nth Post-Order

**Problem:** Given a binary tree, print the value of nodes that will be at the nth index when the tree is traversed in post-order.

**Solution:** We keep track of index using a counter. Since we want to print the node that is at the nth index when we traverse the tree in post-order, we will increment the counter after the left child and the right child traversals. When the counter becomes equal to the index, we print the value and return the nth post-order index node.

**Example 9.12:**
```
public void nthPostOrder(int index) {
    int[] counter = { 0 };
    nthPostOrder(root, index, counter);
}

private void nthPostOrder(Node node, int index, int[] counter) { /* post order */
    if (node != null) {
        nthPostOrder(node.left, index, counter);
        nthPostOrder(node.right, index, counter);
        counter[0]++;
        if (counter[0] == index) {
            System.out.println(node.value);
        }
    }
}

// Testing code.
public static void main(String[] args)  {
    Tree t = new Tree();
    int[] arr = { 1, 2, 3, 4, 5, 6, 7, 8, 9, 10 };
    t.createCompleteBinaryTree(arr);
    t.nthPostOrder(2);
}
```

**Output:**
```
9
```

**Time Complexity:** O(n), **Space Complexity:** O(n)

## Nth In Order

**Problem:** Given a binary tree, print the value of nodes that will be at the nth index when the tree is traversed in In-order.

**Solution:** We keep track of our index using a counter. Since we want to print the node that is at the nth index when we traverse the tree in in-order, therefore, we will increment the counter after the left child traversal but before the right child traversal. When the counter becomes equal to the index, we print the value and return the nth in-order index node.

**Example 9.13:**
```
public void nthInOrder(int index) {
    int[] counter = { 0 };
    nthInOrder(root, index, counter);
}

private void nthInOrder(Node node, int index, int[] counter) {

    if (node != null) {
        nthInOrder(node.left, index, counter);
        counter[0]++;
```

```
        if (counter[0] == index) {
            System.out.println(node.value);
        }
        nthInOrder(node.right, index, counter);
    }
}

// Testing code.
public static void main(String[] args)  {
    Tree t = new Tree();
    int[] arr = { 1, 2, 3, 4, 5, 6, 7, 8, 9, 10 };
    t.createCompleteBinaryTree(arr);
    t.nthInOrder(2);
}
```

**Output:**

```
4
```

**Time Complexity:** O(n), **Space Complexity:** O(1)

## Print all the paths

**Problem:** Given a binary tree, print all the paths from the roots to the leaf.

**Solution:** We will use a stack and follow the depth-first approach. Whenever we traverse a node, we add that node to the stack. When we reach a leaf, we print the whole stack (from the root node to that leaf node). When we return from the function, we remove the element that was added to the stack when we entered this function.

**Example 9.14:**

```
public void printAllPath() {
    Stack<Integer> stk = new Stack<Integer>();
    printAllPathUtil(root, stk);
}

private void printAllPathUtil(Node curr, Stack<Integer> stk) {
    if (curr == null)
        return;

    stk.push(curr.value);
    if (curr.left == null && curr.right == null) {
        System.out.println(stk);
        stk.pop();
        return;
    }

    printAllPathUtil(curr.right, stk);
    printAllPathUtil(curr.left, stk);
    stk.pop();
}

// Testing code.
public static void main(String[] args)  {
    Tree t = new Tree();
    int[] arr = { 1, 2, 3, 4, 5, 6, 7, 8, 9, 10 };
    t.createCompleteBinaryTree(arr);
```

```
    t.printAllPath();
}
```

**Output:**
```
[1, 3, 7]
[1, 3, 6]
[1, 2, 5, 10]
[1, 2, 4, 9]
[1, 2, 4, 8]
```

**Time Complexity:** O(n), **Space Complexity:** O(n)

## Number of Nodes

**Problem:** Find the total number of nodes in a binary tree.

**Solution:** We find the number of nodes in a binary tree by summing, the number of nodes in the right child / subtree, and the number of nodes in the left child/ subtree. And adding `1` to this sum.

**Example 9.15:**
```
public int numNodes() {
    return numNodes(root);
}

public int numNodes(Node curr) {
    if (curr == null)
        return 0;
    else
        return (1 + numNodes(curr.right) + numNodes(curr.left));
}

// Testing code.
public static void main(String[] args)  {
    Tree t = new Tree();
    int[] arr = { 1, 2, 3, 4, 5, 6, 7, 8, 9, 10 };
    t.createCompleteBinaryTree(arr);
    System.out.println(t.numNodes());
}
```

**Output:**
```
10
```

**Time Complexity:** O(n), **Space Complexity:** O(n)

## Sum of All nodes in a BT

**Problem:** Given a binary tree, find the sum of values of all the nodes of it.

**Solution:** We will calculate the sum of nodes by recursion. First, the `sumAllBT()` function will return the sum of all the nodes in the left subtree and then the nodes in the right subtree. Finally, we will add the value of the current node to this sum and return the final sum.

**Example 9.16:**

```
public int sumAllBT() {
    return sumAllBT(root);
}

private int sumAllBT(Node curr) {
    if (curr == null)
        return 0;

    return (curr.value + sumAllBT(curr.left) + sumAllBT(curr.right));
}

// Testing code.
public static void main(String[] args)  {
    Tree t = new Tree();
    int[] arr = { 1, 2, 3, 4, 5, 6, 7, 8, 9, 10 };
    t.createCompleteBinaryTree(arr);
    System.out.println(t.sumAllBT());
}
```

**Output:**

```
55
```

## Number of Leaf nodes

**Problem:** Given a binary tree, find the number of leaf nodes in it.

**Solution:** We will calculate the total number of leaf nodes in the tree by adding the number of leaf nodes in the right child/subtree with the number of leaf nodes in the left child/subtree.

**Example 9.17:**

```
public int numLeafNodes() {
    return numLeafNodes(root);
}

private int numLeafNodes(Node curr) {
    if (curr == null)
        return 0;

    if (curr.left == null && curr.right == null)
        return 1;
    else
        return (numLeafNodes(curr.right) + numLeafNodes(curr.left));
}

// Testing code.
public static void main(String[] args)  {
    Tree t = new Tree();
    int[] arr = { 1, 2, 3, 4, 5, 6, 7, 8, 9, 10 };
    t.createCompleteBinaryTree(arr);
    System.out.println(t.numLeafNodes());
}
```

**Output:**

```
5
```

**Time Complexity:** O(n), **Space Complexity:** O(n)

## Number of Full Nodes in a BT

**Problem:** Given a binary tree, find the count of full nodes in it. A full node has non-null left and right children.

**Solution:** A full node is a node that has both left and right children. We will recursively traverse the whole tree and will increase the count of full nodes as we find them.

**Example 9.18:**
```
public int numFullNodesBT() {
    return numFullNodesBT(root);
}

public int numFullNodesBT(Node curr) {
    if (curr == null)
        return 0;

    int count = numFullNodesBT(curr.right) + numFullNodesBT(curr.left);
    if (curr.right != null && curr.left != null)
        count++;

    return count;
}

// Testing code.
public static void main(String[] args)  {
    Tree t = new Tree();
    int[] arr = { 1, 2, 3, 4, 5, 6, 7, 8, 9, 10 };
    t.createCompleteBinaryTree(arr);
    System.out.println(t.numFullNodesBT());
}
```

**Output:**
```
4
```

## Search value in a Binary Tree

**Problem:** Search for a particular value in the binary tree.

**Solution:** To find if a value exists in a binary tree, we use the exhaustive search algorithm. First, the value in the current node is compared with our key. If it matches, we end our search. If it doesn't, we recursively look for the key in the left and right subtrees. We stop when we find our desired key in the tree or if the tree is traversed completely without finding the key then return 0.

**Example 9.19:**
```
public boolean searchBT(int value) {
    return searchBTUtil(root, value);
}

public boolean searchBTUtil(Node curr, int value) {
    if (curr == null)
        return false;
```

```
    if ((curr.value == value) || searchBTUtil(curr.left, value) ||
                        searchBTUtil(curr.right, value))
        return true;

    return false;
}

// Testing code.
public static void main(String[] args)  {
    Tree t = new Tree();
    int[] arr = { 1, 2, 3, 4, 5, 6, 7, 8, 9, 10 };
    t.createCompleteBinaryTree(arr);
    System.out.println(t.searchBT(9));
}
```

**Output:**

```
true
```

## Find Max in Binary Tree

**Problem:** Given a binary tree, find the maximum value in it.

**Solution:** We will solve this problem by recursively traversing the nodes of the binary tree. First, we will find the respective maximum values in the left and right subtree of a node then we will compare these values with the value of the current node. Finally, we will return the largest of these three values.

**Example 9.20:**

```
public int findMaxBT() {
    int ans = findMaxBT(root);
    return ans;
}

private int findMaxBT(Node curr) {
    int leftmax, rightmax;

    if (curr == null)
        return Integer.MIN_VALUE;

    int max = curr.value;

    leftmax = findMaxBT(curr.left);
    rightmax = findMaxBT(curr.right);

    if (leftmax > max)
        max = leftmax;
    if (rightmax > max)
        max = rightmax;

    return max;
}

// Testing code.
public static void main(String[] args)  {
    Tree t = new Tree();
```

```
    int[] arr = { 1, 2, 3, 4, 5, 6, 7, 8, 9, 10 };
    t.createCompleteBinaryTree(arr);
    System.out.println(t.findMaxBT());
}
```

**Output:**

```
10
```

## Tree Depth

**Problem:** Given a binary tree, find its depth.

**Solution:** We find the depth of a tree by recursively traversing the left and right child of the root. At each level of traversal, the depth of both left and right children is calculated. The greater depth among the left and right children is added by one (which is the depth of the current node). Finally, this value is returned.

**Example 9.21:**

```
public int treeDepth() {
    return treeDepth(root);
}

private int treeDepth(Node curr) {
    if (curr == null)
        return 0;
    else {
        int lDepth = treeDepth(curr.left);
        int rDepth = treeDepth(curr.right);

        if (lDepth > rDepth)
            return lDepth + 1;
        else
            return rDepth + 1;
    }
}

// Testing code.
public static void main(String[] args)  {
    Tree t = new Tree();
    int[] arr = { 1, 2, 3, 4, 5, 6, 7, 8, 9, 10 };
    t.createCompleteBinaryTree(arr);
    System.out.println(t.treeDepth());
}
```

**Output:**

```
4
```

**Time Complexity:** O(n), **Space Complexity:** O(n)

## Maximum Length Path in a BT/ Diameter of BT

**Problem:** Given a binary tree, find the maximum length path in it.

**Solution:** To find the diameter of the binary tree, we need to find the depth of the left child and right child. Then these two depth values are added and incremented by one to get the maximum length path (diameter candidate) which contains the current node. Then we will find the max length path in the left child subtree. We will also find the max length path in the right child subtree. Finally, we will compare the three values and return the maximum value among them. This value will be the diameter of the Binary tree.

**Example 9.22:**
```
public int maxLengthPathBT() {
    return maxLengthPathBT(root);
}

private int maxLengthPathBT(Node curr) { // diameter
    int max;
    int leftPath, rightPath;
    int leftMax, rightMax;

    if (curr == null)
        return 0;

    leftPath = treeDepth(curr.left);
    rightPath = treeDepth(curr.right);

    max = leftPath + rightPath + 1;

    leftMax = maxLengthPathBT(curr.left);
    rightMax = maxLengthPathBT(curr.right);

    if (leftMax > max)
        max = leftMax;

    if (rightMax > max)
        max = rightMax;

    return max;
}

// Testing code.
public static void main(String[] args)  {
    Tree t = new Tree();
    int[] arr = { 1, 2, 3, 4, 5, 6, 7, 8, 9, 10 };
    t.createCompleteBinaryTree(arr);
    System.out.println(t.maxLengthPathBT());
}
```

**Output:**
```
6
```

## Copy Tree

**Problem:** Given a binary tree, copy its value in another binary tree.

**Solution:** The copy of a tree is generated by copying the nodes of the input tree, at each level of traversal, to the output tree. At each level of traversal, a new node is created and in this node, the value of the input tree node is copied. The left subtree is copied recursively and then a pointer to a new subtree is returned, which will then be assigned to the left child pointer of the current new node. Similarly, this process is followed for the right subtree. This way, the tree is copied at the end.

**Example 9.23:**
```
public Tree copyTree() {
    Tree tree2 = new Tree();
    tree2.root = copyTree(root);
    return tree2;
}

private Node copyTree(Node curr) {
    Node temp;
    if (curr != null) {
        temp = new Node(curr.value);
        temp.left = copyTree(curr.left);
        temp.right = copyTree(curr.right);
        return temp;
    } else
        return null;
}

// Testing code.
public static void main(String[] args)  {
    Tree t = new Tree();
    int[] arr = { 1, 2, 3, 4, 5, 6, 7, 8, 9, 10 };
    t.createCompleteBinaryTree(arr);
    Tree t1 = t.copyTree();
    t.printInOrder();
    t1.printInOrder();
}
```

**Output:**
```
8 4 9 2 10 5 1 6 3 7
8 4 9 2 10 5 1 6 3 7
```

**Time Complexity:** O(n), **Space Complexity:** O(n)

## Copy Mirror Tree

**Problem:** Given a binary tree, copy its value to create another tree, which is a mirror image of the original tree.

**Solution:** A mirror image copy of a tree is created the same way as the copy of a tree is created. The only difference here is that in place of the left child pointing to the tree that is formed by the left child traversal of the input tree, this time the left child points to the tree formed by the right child traversal of the input tree. Similarly, the right child points to the tree formed by the traversal of the left child of the input tree.

**Example 9.24:**
```
public Tree copyMirrorTree() {
    Tree tree2 = new Tree();
    tree2.root = copyMirrorTree(root);
    return tree2;
}
```

```
private Node copyMirrorTree(Node curr) {
    Node temp;

    if (curr != null) {
        temp = new Node(curr.value);
        temp.right = copyMirrorTree(curr.left);
        temp.left = copyMirrorTree(curr.right);
        return temp;
    } else
        return null;
}

// Testing code.
public static void main(String[] args)  {
    Tree t = new Tree();
    int[] arr = { 1, 2, 3, 4, 5, 6, 7, 8, 9, 10 };
    t.createCompleteBinaryTree(arr);
    Tree t3 = t.copyMirrorTree();
    t3.printInOrder();
}
```

**Output:**

```
7 3 6 1 5 10 2 9 4 8
```

**Time Complexity:** O(n), **Space Complexity:** O(n)

## Identical

**Problem:** The two trees are said to be identical if, at each level, the value in the respective node is equal.

**Example 9.25:**

```
public boolean isEqual(Tree T2) {
    return isEqualUtil(root, T2.root);
}

private boolean isEqualUtil(Node node1, Node node2) {
    if (node1 == null && node2 == null)
        return true;
    else if (node1 == null || node2 == null)
        return false;
    else
        return (isEqualUtil(node1.left, node2.left) && isEqualUtil(node1.right,
node2.right) && (node1.value == node2.value));
}

// Testing code.
public static void main(String[] args)  {
    Tree t = new Tree();
    int[] arr = { 1, 2, 3, 4, 5, 6, 7, 8, 9, 10 };
    t.createCompleteBinaryTree(arr);
    Tree t2 = t.copyTree();
    System.out.println(t.isEqual(t2));
}
```

**Output:**
```
true
```

**Time Complexity:** O(n), **Space Complexity:** O(n)

## Free Tree

**Problem:** Given a binary tree, free all its nodes.

**Solution**: Root will be assigned to null. The tree nodes will be removed by garbage collector.

**Example 9.26:**
```
public void free() {
    root = null;
}
```

**Time Complexity:** O(n), **Space Complexity:** O(logn), for recursion.

## Is Complete Tree

**Problem:** Given a binary tree, find if it is a complete tree. The tree is complete if it is filled at all possible levels except the last level. The last level is filled from left to right.

**First Solution:** We will perform breadth-first traversal of the tree using a queue. Since in a complete tree, if we get a node that does not have a left child then it cannot have a right child too. And, if we find a node that does not have any child, then no other node in breadth-first traversal can have any child.

**Example 9.27:**
```
boolean isCompleteTree() {
    ArrayDeque<Node> que = new ArrayDeque<Node>();
    Node temp = null;
    int noChild = 0;

    if (root != null)
        que.add(root);

    while (que.size() != 0) {
        temp = que.remove();
        if (temp.left != null) {
            if (noChild == 1)
                return false;
            que.add(temp.left);
        } else
            noChild = 1;

        if (temp.right != null) {
            if (noChild == 1)
                return false;
            que.add(temp.right);
        } else
            noChild = 1;
    }
    return true;
}
```

```
// Testing code.
public static void main(String[] args)  {
    Tree t = new Tree();
    int[] arr = { 1, 2, 3, 4, 5, 6, 7, 8, 9, 10 };
    t.createCompleteBinaryTree(arr);
    System.out.println(t.isCompleteTree());
}
```

**Output:**

```
true
```

**Second Solution:** We can solve this problem through recursion by treating the given tree like a heap. If we consider that parent's location is `index` then the left child location should be at `2*index+1` and the right child location should be at `2*index+2`. If it is true for every node then we have a complete tree.

**Example 9.28:**

```
boolean isCompleteTreeUtil(Node curr, int index, int count) {
    if (curr == null)
        return true;
    if (index > count)
        return false;
    return isCompleteTreeUtil(curr.left, index * 2 + 1, count)
            && isCompleteTreeUtil(curr.right, index * 2 + 2, count);
}

boolean isCompleteTree2() {
    int count = numNodes();
    return isCompleteTreeUtil(root, 0, count);
}
```

## Is a Heap

**Problem:** Given a binary tree, find if it represents a Min-Heap.

To see if a tree is a heap, we need to check two conditions:
1) It is a complete tree.
2) The Value of a parent node is smaller than or equal to its left and right child.

**First Solution:** We need to find if the given tree is complete and heap parent-child property is followed (parent nodes have a value less than or equal to its children) then this tree represents a Min Heap.

The isComleteTree() function call takes linear time, so is the isHeap() function. Therefore, the total time complexity is O(n). The whole tree is traversed three times, first to find the total number of elements in the tree, second to find if it is a complete tree and finally for testing the heap property.

**Example 9.29:**

```
boolean isHeapUtil(Node curr, int parentValue) {
    if (curr == null)
        return true;
```

```
    if (curr.value < parentValue)
        return false;

    return (isHeapUtil(curr.left, curr.value) && isHeapUtil(curr.right,
curr.value));
}

boolean isHeap() {
    int infinite = -9999999;
    return (isCompleteTree() && isHeapUtil(root, infinite));
}

// Testing code.
public static void main(String[] args)  {
    Tree t = new Tree();
    int[] arr = { 1, 2, 3, 4, 5, 6, 7, 8, 9, 10 };
    t.createCompleteBinaryTree(arr);
    System.out.println(t.isHeap());
}
```

**Output:**

```
true
```

**Second Solution:** We can combine isCompleteTree and isHeapUtil function inside a single function.

**Example 9.30:**

```
boolean isHeapUtil2(Node curr, int index, int count, int parentValue) {
    if (curr == null)
        return true;
    if (index > count)
        return false;
    if (curr.value < parentValue)
        return false;
    return isHeapUtil2(curr.left, index * 2 + 1, count, curr.value)
            && isHeapUtil2(curr.right, index * 2 + 2, count, curr.value);
}

boolean isHeap2() {
    int count = numNodes();
    int parentValue = -9999999;
    return isHeapUtil2(root, 0, count, parentValue);
}
```

## Iterative Pre-order

**Problem:** Given a binary tree, without using recursion, perform pre-order traversal of the tree.

**Solution:** In place of using the system stack in recursion, we can traverse the tree using the stack data structure.

**Example 9.31:**

```
public void iterativePreOrder() {
    Stack<Node> stk = new Stack<Node>();
    Node curr;
```

```
    if (root != null)
        stk.add(root);

    while (stk.isEmpty() == false) {
        curr = stk.pop();

        System.out.print(curr.value + " ");

        if (curr.right != null)
            stk.push(curr.right);

        if (curr.left != null)
            stk.push(curr.left);
    }
    System.out.println();
}

// Testing code.
public static void main(String[] args)  {
    Tree t = new Tree();
    int[] arr = { 1, 2, 3, 4, 5, 6, 7, 8, 9, 10 };
    t.createCompleteBinaryTree(arr);
    t.iterativePreOrder();
}
```

**Output:**

```
1 2 4 8 9 5 10 3 6 7
```

**Time Complexity:** O(n), **Space Complexity:** O(n)

## Tree to List Recursively

**Problem:** Given a binary tree, create a doubly linked list from this such that the elements are in the order of in-order traversal of the tree.

**Solution:** The tree to the list conversion is done recursively. At each node, we must assume that the `treeToListRec()` function will do its job for the left child and right child. Then we will combine the result of the left child and right child traversal. We need a head and tail pointer of the left list and right list to combine them with the current node. In the process of integration, the current node will be added to the tail of the left list and the current node will be added to the head to the right list. The head of the left list will become the head of the newly created list and the tail of the right list will become the tail of the newly created list.

**Example 9.32:**

```
public Node treeToListRec() {
    return treeToListRec(root);
}

private Node treeToListRec(Node curr) {
    Node Head = null, Tail = null;
    if (curr == null)
        return null;
```

```
    if (curr.left == null && curr.right == null) {
        curr.left = curr;
        curr.right = curr;
        return curr;
    }

    if (curr.left != null) {
        Head = treeToListRec(curr.left);
        Tail = Head.left;

        curr.left = Tail;
        Tail.right = curr;
    } else
        Head = curr;

    if (curr.right != null) {
        Node tempHead = treeToListRec(curr.right);
        Tail = tempHead.left;
        curr.right = tempHead;
        tempHead.left = curr;
    } else
        Tail = curr;

    Head.left = Tail;
    Tail.right = Head;
    return Head;
}
```

**Time Complexity:** O(n), **Space Complexity:** O(n)

## Binary Search Tree (BST)

A binary search tree (BST) is a binary tree in which nodes are ordered in the following way:

- The key in the left subtree is less than the key in its parent node.
- The key in the right subtree is greater than the key in its parent node.
- No duplicate key is allowed.

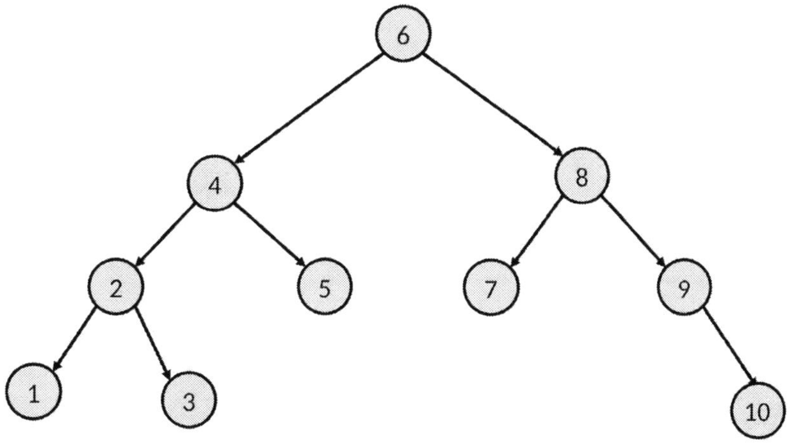

Before moving forward, let us keep the following points in our mind.

1. There can be two separate key and value fields in the tree node. However, for simplicity, we are considering value as the key. All problems in the binary search tree are solved using this supposition that the value in the node is key for the tree.
2. Since a binary search tree is a binary tree, therefore, all the algorithms of a binary tree (covered in the previous chapter) are applicable to a binary search tree.

## Problems in Binary Search Tree (BST)

### Create a binary search tree from a sorted array

**Problem:** Create a binary tree from an array of values in sorted order.

**Solution:** Since the elements in the array are in sorted order, we want to create a binary search tree in which left subtree nodes have values less than the current node, and right subtree nodes have values greater than the value of the current node. We will have to find the middle node to create a current node and send the rest of the array to construct the left and right subtree.

**Example 9.33:**
```
public void createBinarySearchTree(int[] arr) {
    root = createBinarySearchTree(arr, 0, arr.length - 1);
}

private Node createBinarySearchTree(int[] arr, int start, int end) {
    Node curr = null;
    if (start > end)
        return null;

    int mid = (start + end) / 2;
    curr = new Node(arr[mid]);
    curr.left = createBinarySearchTree(arr, start, mid - 1);
    curr.right = createBinarySearchTree(arr, mid + 1, end);
    return curr;
}

// Testing code.
public static void main(String[] args)  {
    Tree t = new Tree();
    int[] arr = { 1, 2, 3, 4, 5, 6, 7, 8, 9, 10 };
    t.createBinarySearchTree(arr);
    t.printInOrder();
}
```

**Output:**
```
1 2 3 4 5 6 7 8 9 10
```

### Insertion

Below is a step by step tree after inserting nodes in the order. Nodes with keys 6,4,2,5,1,3,8,7,9,10 are inserted in a tree.

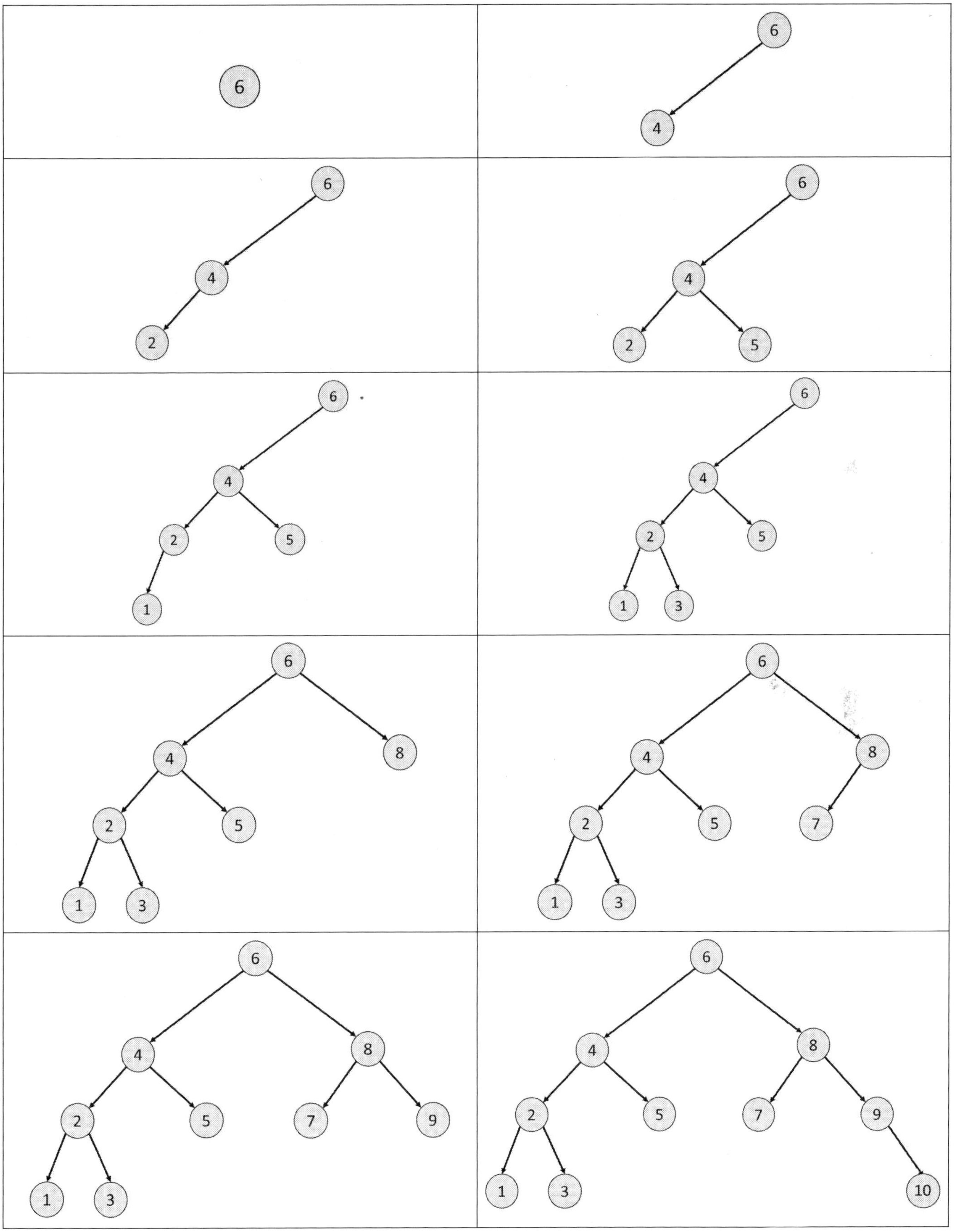
6
6 4
6 4 2
6 4 2 5
6 4 2 5 1
6 4 2 5 1 3
6 4 8 2 5 1 3
6 4 8 2 5 7 1 3
6 4 8 2 5 7 9 1 3
6 4 8 2 5 7 9 1 3 10

**Solution:** The smaller values are added to the left child subtree of the current node, and greater values are added to the right child subtree of the current node.

**Example 9.34:**
```
public void insert(int value) {
    root = insert(root, value);
}

private Node insert(Node node, int value) {
    if (node == null) {
        node = new Node(value, null, null);
    } else {
        if (node.value > value) {
            node.left = insert(node.left, value);
        } else {
            node.right = insert(node.right, value);
        }
    }
    return node;
}

// Testing code.
public static void main(String[] args)  {
    Tree t = new Tree();
    t.insert(6);
    t.insert(4);
    t.insert(2);
    t.insert(5);
    t.insert(1);
    t.insert(3);
    t.insert(8);
    t.insert(7);
    t.insert(9);
    t.insert(10);
    t.printInOrder();
}
```

**Output:**
```
1 2 3 4 5 6 7 8 9 10
```

**Time Complexity:** O(n), **Space Complexity:** O(n)

## Find Node

**Problem:** Find the node with the value given.

**Solution:** In a BST, the value greater than the current node value will always be present in the right subtree, and the value smaller than the current node will always be present in the left subtree. Therefore, we can find our desired key value by traversing the left and right subtree iteratively.

**Example 9.35:**
```
public boolean find(int value) {
    Node curr = root;
```

```
    while (curr != null) {
        if (curr.value == value) {
            return true;
        } else if (curr.value > value) {
            curr = curr.left;
        } else {
            curr = curr.right;
        }
    }
    return false;
}

// Testing code.
public static void main(String[] args)  {
    Tree t = new Tree();
    int[] arr = { 1, 2, 3, 4, 5, 6, 7, 8, 9, 10 };
    t.createBinarySearchTree(arr);
    System.out.println(t.find(3));
    System.out.println(t.find(16));
}
```

**Output:**

```
true
false
```

**Time Complexity:** O(n), **Space Complexity:** O(1)

## Find Min

**Problem:** Find the node with the minimum value.

**Solution:** The leftmost child of the tree will be the node with the minimum value. We will iteratively traverse from root to its left child until we hit the leftmost node.

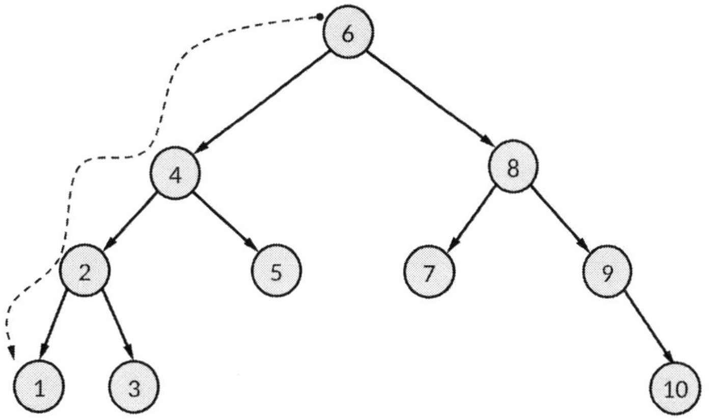


**Example 9.36:**

```
public int findMin() {
    Node node = root;
    if (node == null) {
        return Integer.MAX_VALUE;
    }

    while (node.left != null) {
        node = node.left;
    }
```

```
    return node.value;
}

// Testing code.
public static void main(String[] args)  {
    Tree t = new Tree();
    int[] arr = { 1, 2, 3, 4, 5, 6, 7, 8, 9, 10 };
    t.createBinarySearchTree(arr);
    System.out.println(t.findMin());
}
```

**Output:**

```
1
```

**Example 9.37:**

```
public Node findMinNode(Node curr) {
    Node node = curr;
    if (node == null) {
        return null;
    }

    while (node.left != null) {
        node = node.left;
    }
    return node;
}
```

**Time Complexity:** O(n), **Space Complexity:** O(1)

## Find Max

**Problem:** Find the node in the tree with the maximum value.

**Solution:** Rightmost node of the tree will be the node with the maximum value.

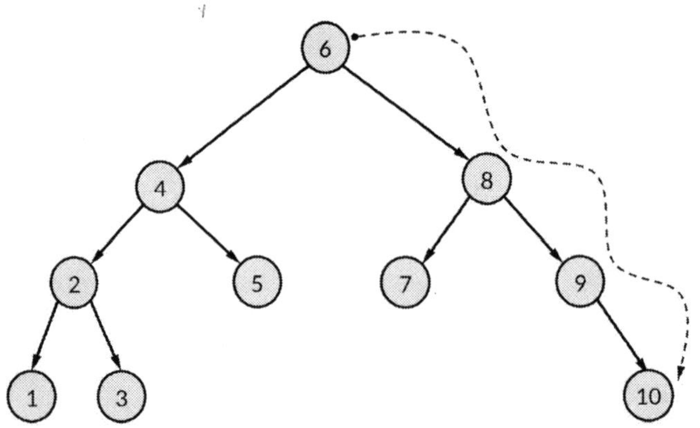


**Example 9.38:**

```
public int findMax() {
    Node node = root;
    if (node == null) {
        return Integer.MIN_VALUE;
    }
```

```
    while (node.right != null) {
        node = node.right;
    }
    return node.value;
}

// Testing code.
public static void main(String[] args)  {
    Tree t = new Tree();
    int[] arr = { 1, 2, 3, 4, 5, 6, 7, 8, 9, 10 };
    t.createBinarySearchTree(arr);
    System.out.println(t.findMax());
}
```

**Output:**

```
10
```

**Example 9.39:**

```
public Node findMaxNode(Node curr) {
    Node node = curr;
    if (node == null) {
        return null;
    }

    while (node.right != null) {
        node = node.right;
    }
    return node;
}
```

**Time Complexity:** O(n), **Space Complexity:** O(1)

## Is tree a BST

**Problem:** Find is a given binary tree is a binary search tree.

**First solution**: At each node, we will check whether the max value of the left subtree is smaller than the value of the current node and the min value of the right subtree is greater than the current node. If these conditions are fulfilled, then the given binary tree is a BST.

**Example 9.40:**

```
public boolean isBST3() {
    return isBST3(root);
}

private boolean isBST3(Node root) {
    if (root == null)
        return true;
    if (root.left != null && findMaxNode(root.left).value > root.value)
        return false;
    if (root.right != null && findMinNode(root.right).value <= root.value)
        return false;
    return (isBST3(root.left) && isBST3(root.right));
}
```

```
// Testing code.
public static void main(String[] args)  {
    Tree t = new Tree();
    int[] arr = { 1, 2, 3, 4, 5, 6, 7, 8, 9, 10 };
    t.createBinarySearchTree(arr);
    System.out.println(t.isBST3());
}
```

**Output:**

```
true
```

**Time Complexity:** O(n), **Space Complexity:** O(n)

Although the above solution is correct, it is inefficient, as the same tree nodes are traversed many times.

**Second solution:** A better solution will be the one in which we will traverse each node only once. This can be done by narrowing the range. To do so, we will use the IsBST() function, which takes the max and min range of the values of the nodes. The initial value of min and max would be the minimum and maximum values of the integer(for simplicity, we are taking -999999 and 999999).

**Example 9.41:**

```
public boolean isBST() {
    return isBST(root, Integer.MIN_VALUE, Integer.MAX_VALUE);
}

private boolean isBST(Node curr, int min, int max) {
    if (curr == null)
        return true;

    if (curr.value < min || curr.value > max)
        return false;

    return isBST(curr.left, min, curr.value) && isBST(curr.right, curr.value, max);
}
```

**Time Complexity:** O(n), **Space Complexity:** O(n) for stack.

**Third solution:** Yet another easier approach for the above-mentioned method will be the in-order traversal of nodes and see if we are getting a strictly increasing sequence.

**Example 9.42:**

```
public boolean isBST2() {
    int[] count = new int[1];
    return isBST2(root, count);
}

private boolean isBST2(Node root, int[] count) { /* in order traversal */
    boolean ret;
    if (root != null) {
        ret = isBST2(root.left, count);

        if (!ret)
            return false;
```

```
        if (count[0] > root.value)
            return false;

        count[0] = root.value;
        ret = isBST2(root.right, count);

        if (!ret)
            return false;
    }
    return true;
}
```

**Time Complexity:** O(n), **Space Complexity:** O(n) for stack

## Delete Node

**Problem:** Remove the node x from the binary search tree, reorganise nodes of the binary search tree to maintain its necessary properties.

We have three cases for deleting a node. For simplicity the node that needs to be deleted is x.

Case 1: node x has no children. Just delete it (i.e. Change parent node so that it does not point to x)
Case 2: node x has one child. Splice out x by linking x's parent to x's child
Case 3: node x has two children. Splice out the x's successor and replace x with x's successor

**When the node to be deleted has no children**
This is a trivial case, in which we directly remove the node by returning null.

**When the node to be deleted has only one child.**
In this case, we return the child of the node.

| | |
|---|---|
| 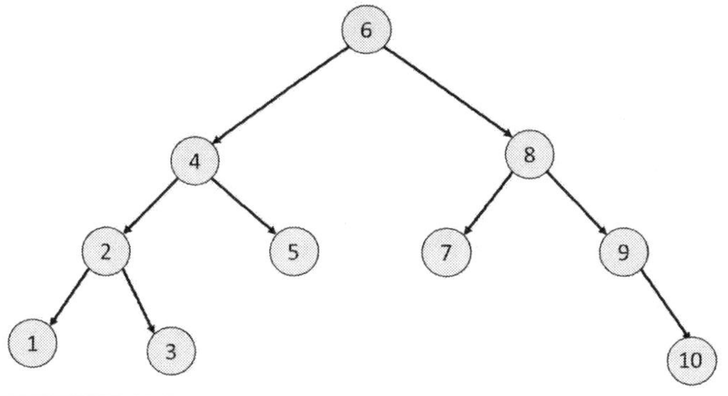 | We want to remove nodes with a value of 9. The node has only one child. |
| 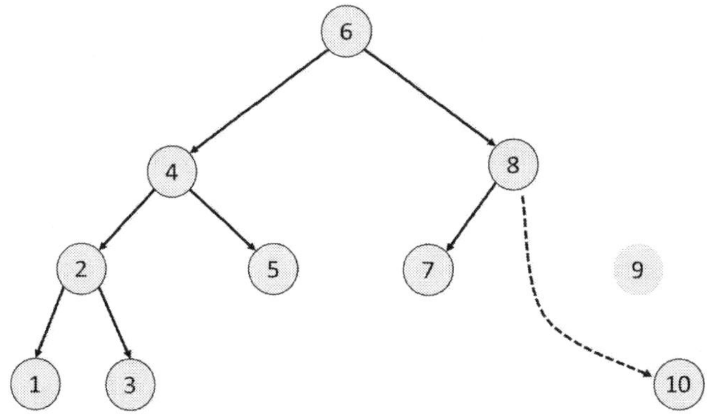 | The right child of the parent of a node with value 9 that is the node with value 8 will point to the child node of the node with value 9. i.e. node with value 10. |

| | |
|---|---|
| 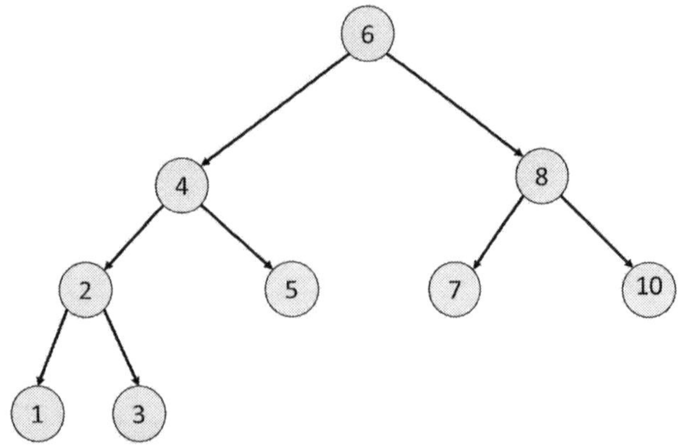 | Finally, a node with the value of 9 is removed from the tree. |

**When the node to be deleted has two children.**

| | |
|---|---|
| 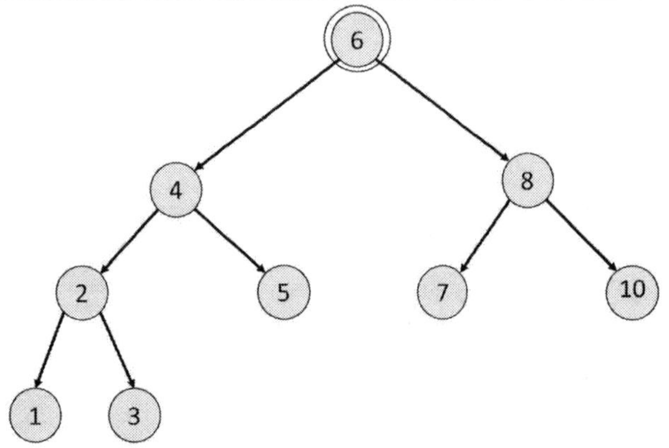 | We want to delete nodes with value 6, which have two children. |
| 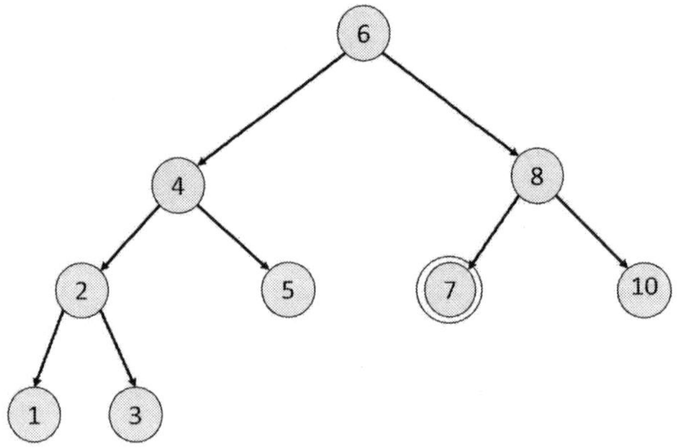 | We have found the minimum value node of the right subtree of the node with a value of 6. |
| 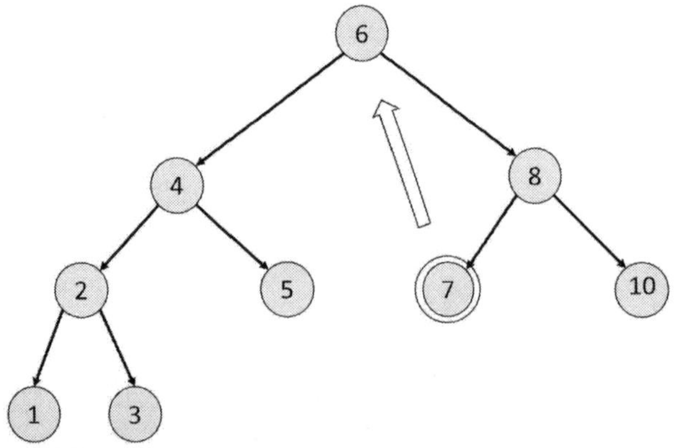 | The minimum of  value is copied to the node with a value of 6. |

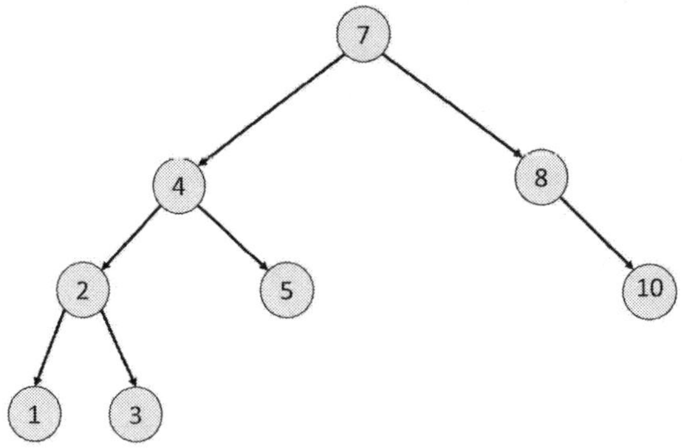


Delete node with minimum value 7 is called over the right subtree of the node.

Finally, the value 6 is removed from the tree.

**Example 9.43:**
```
public void deleteNode(int value) {
    root = deleteNode(root, value);
}

private Node deleteNode(Node node, int value) {
    if (node != null) {
        if (node.value == value) {
            if (node.left == null && node.right == null) {
                return null;
            } else {
                if (node.left == null) {
                    return node.right;
                }

                if (node.right == null) {
                    return node.left;
                }
                Node minNode = findMinNode(node.right);
                int minValue = minNode.value;
                node.value = minValue;
                node.right = deleteNode(node.right, minValue);
            }
        } else {
            if (node.value > value) {
                node.left = deleteNode(node.left, value);
            } else {
                node.right = deleteNode(node.right, value);
            }
        }
    }
    return node;
}

// Testing code.
public static void main(String[] args)  {
    Tree t = new Tree();
    int[] arr = { 1, 2, 3, 4, 5, 6, 7, 8, 9, 10 };
    t.createBinarySearchTree(arr);
    t.printInOrder();
    t.remove(6);
    t.printInOrder();
}
```

**Output:**
```
1 2 3 4 5 6 7 8 9 10
1 2 3 4 5 7 8 9 10
```

**Time Complexity:** O(n), **Space Complexity:** O(n)

## Least Common Ancestor

**Problem:** In a binary search tree T. The least common ancestor between two nodes n1 and n2 is defined as the lowest node in T that has both n1 and n2 as descendants. Or if n1 is the ancestor of n2, then n1 itself is the least common ancestor. You are given two values and need to find the LCA of both of the values.

**Solution**: Consider the two values are first and second. The first is smaller than the second. Go on traversing the tree till we have one of the following cases:
1. When the first is the ancestor of the second, then the first is the LCA.
2. When the second is the ancestor of the first, then the second is the LCA.
3. Both first and second are on different sides of some node, that node is the LCA.

**Example 9.44:**
```
public int lcaBST(int first, int second) {
    int result;
    if (first > second)
        result = lcaBST(root, second, first);
    else
        result = lcaBST(root, first, second);

    if (result == Integer.MAX_VALUE)
        System.out.println("lca does not exist");
    else
        System.out.println("lca is :" + result);

    return result;
}

private int lcaBST(Node curr, int first, int second) {
    if (curr == null) {
        return Integer.MAX_VALUE;
    }

    if (curr.value > second) {
        return lcaBST(curr.left, first, second);
    }
    if (curr.value < first) {
        return lcaBST(curr.right, first, second);
    }
    if (find(first) && find(second))
        return curr.value;
    return Integer.MAX_VALUE;
}

// Testing code.
public static void main(String[] args)  {
    Tree t = new Tree();
    int[] arr = { 1, 2, 3, 4, 5, 6, 7, 8, 9, 10 };
```

```
    t.createBinarySearchTree(arr);
    t.lcaBST(3, 4);
    t.lcaBST(1, 4);
    t.lcaBST(10, 4);
}
```

**Output:**

```
lca is :3
lca is :2
lca is :5
```

## Print Tree nodes which are in Range

**Problem:** Print only those nodes of the tree whose value is in the given range.

**Solution:** We can print the nodes in the given range by traversing the tree in in-order and checking if the current value is inside the given range.

**Example 9.45:**

```
public void printInRange(int min, int max) {
    printInRange(root, min, max);
    System.out.println();
}

private void printInRange(Node root, int min, int max) {
    if (root == null)
        return;

    printInRange(root.left, min, max);

    if (root.value >= min && root.value <= max)
        System.out.print(root.value + " ");

    printInRange(root.right, min, max);
}

// Testing code.
public static void main(String[] args)  {
    Tree t = new Tree();
    int[] arr = { 1, 2, 3, 4, 5, 6, 7, 8, 9, 10 };
    t.createBinarySearchTree(arr);
    t.printInRange(4, 8);
}
```

**Output:**

```
4 5 6 7 8
```

## Trim the Tree nodes which are Outside Range

**Problem:** Given a binary search tree and a range as min, max. We need to delete all the nodes of the tree that are out of this range.

**Solution:** Traverse the tree post-order, and each node that is having a value outside the range will be deleted. All the deletion will happen from the inside out, so we do not have to care about the children of a node as if they are out of range then they have already deleted themselves.

**Example 9.46:**
```
public void trimOutsideRange(int min, int max) {
    trimOutsideRange(root, min, max);
}

private Node trimOutsideRange(Node curr, int min, int max) {
    if (curr == null)
        return null;

    curr.left = trimOutsideRange(curr.left, min, max);
    curr.right = trimOutsideRange(curr.right, min, max);

    if (curr.value < min) {
        return curr.right;
    }

    if (curr.value > max) {
        return curr.left;
    }

    return curr;
}

// Testing code.
public static void main(String[] args)  {
    Tree t = new Tree();
    int[] arr = { 1, 2, 3, 4, 5, 6, 7, 8, 9, 10 };
    t.createBinarySearchTree(arr);
    t.trimOutsideRange(4, 8);
    t.printInOrder();
}
```

**Output:**
```
4 5 6 7 8
```

## Find Ceil and Floor value inside BST given key

**Problem:** In a given tree and a value, we need to find the floor value in a tree that is smaller than the given value and need to find the ceiling value in the tree which is bigger. For a given value we aim to find ceiling and floor value as close as possible.

**Solution:** We will use search in BST to find the ceil and floor of a value in a BST. When we are searching for ceil, if we find any value greater than the given input, we save this value as a probable value. We narrow down our search for a value much closer to our input value. This algorithm takes O(log(n)) time if BST is balanced. Similarly, we can find a floor too.

**Example 9.47:**
```
public int ceilBST(double val) {
    Node curr = root;
    int ceil = Integer.MIN_VALUE;
```

```
    while (curr != null) {
        if (curr.value == val) {
            ceil = curr.value;
            break;
        } else if (curr.value > val) {
            ceil = curr.value;
            curr = curr.left;
        } else {
            curr = curr.right;
        }
    }
    return ceil;
}

// Testing code.
public static void main(String[] args)  {
    Tree t = new Tree();
    int[] arr = { 1, 2, 3, 4, 5, 6, 7, 8, 9, 10 };
    t.createBinarySearchTree(arr);
    System.out.println(t.ceilBST(5.5));
}
```

**Output:**

```
6
```

**Example 9.48:**

```
public int floorBST(double val) {
    Node curr = root;
    int floor = Integer.MAX_VALUE;

    while (curr != null) {
        if (curr.value == val) {
            floor = curr.value;
            break;
        } else if (curr.value > val) {
            curr = curr.left;
        } else {
            floor = curr.value;
            curr = curr.right;
        }
    }
    return floor;
}

// Testing code.
public static void main(String[] args)  {
    Tree t = new Tree();
    int[] arr = { 1, 2, 3, 4, 5, 6, 7, 8, 9, 10 };
    t.createBinarySearchTree(arr);
    System.out.println(t.floorBST(5.5));
}
```

**Output:**

```
5
```

## Is a BST Array

**Problem:** Given an array of integers, you need to find if it represents a PreOrder traversal of a binary search tree.

**Solution:** In PreOrder traversal <Root><Left child><Right child>. Once we have a value greater than the root value, then we are in the Right child subtree. So, all the nodes that will come will have values greater than the root value.

**Example 9.49:**

```
boolean isBSTArray(int preorder[]) {
    int size = preorder.length;
    Stack<Integer> stk = new Stack<Integer>();
    int value;
    int root = -999999;
    for (int i = 0; i < size; i++) {
        value = preorder[i];
        // If value of the right child is less than root.
        if (value < root)
            return false;

        // First left child values will be popped
        // Last popped value will be the root.
        while (stk.size() > 0 && stk.peek() < value)
            root = stk.pop();

        // add current value to the stack.
        stk.push(value);
    }
    return true;
}

// Testing code.
public static void main(String[] args)  {
    int[] arr1 = { 5, 2, 4, 6, 9, 10 };
    int[] arr2 = { 5, 2, 6, 4, 7, 9, 10 };
    System.out.println(t.isBSTArray(arr1));
    System.out.println(t.isBSTArray(arr2));
}
```

**Output:**

```
true
false
```

## Segment Tree

A segment tree is a binary tree that is used to make multiple range queries and range updates in an array.

Examples of problems for which Segment Tree can be used are:

1. Finding the sum of all the elements of an array in a given range of index
2. Finding the maximum value of the array in a given range of the index.
3. Finding the minimum value of the array in a given range of indexes (also known as Range Minimum Query problem)

Let us consider a simple problem: Given an array of N numbers. You need to perform the following operations:
1. Update any element in the array
2. Find the maximum in any given range (i, j)

**First Solution:**
Updating: Just update the element in the array, a[i] =x. Finding maximum in the range (i, j), by traversing through the elements of the array in that range.
Time Complexity of Update is O(1) and of Finding is O(n)

**Second approach:** Keep another array that will store the prefix sum. Value at "$i^{th}$" index is the sum of the first "I" elements of the input array.

Input array

| | | | | | | | | | | |
|---|---|---|---|---|---|---|---|---|---|---|
| 1 | 2 | 3 | 4 | 5 | 6 | 7 | 8 | 9 | 10 | 11 |

Prefix sum array

| | | | | | | | | | | |
|---|---|---|---|---|---|---|---|---|---|---|
| 1 | 3 | 6 | 10 | 15 | 21 | 28 | 36 | 45 | 55 | 66 |

By this approach, prefix sum will be given in constant O(1) time. But the update of one element at the "$i^{th}$" index will update all the elements after the "ith" index in the prefix sum array. So the update will take O(n) time. This approach will be helpful if the prefix sum calculations are frequent, but an update is rare.

**Third Solution:** The above solutions are good. However, can we have good performance for both update and range queries. The answer is yes. We can do both the operations in O(log(n)) where n is the size of the array. This we can do using a segment tree.

Let us suppose we are given an input array A = {1, 8, 2, 7, 3, 6, 4, 5}. Moreover, the below diagram will represent the segment tree formed corresponding to the input array A.

Properties of Segment Tree:
1. A segment tree is a binary tree.
2. Each node in a segment tree represents an interval in the array.
3. The root of the tree represents the whole array.
4. Each leaf node represents a single element.

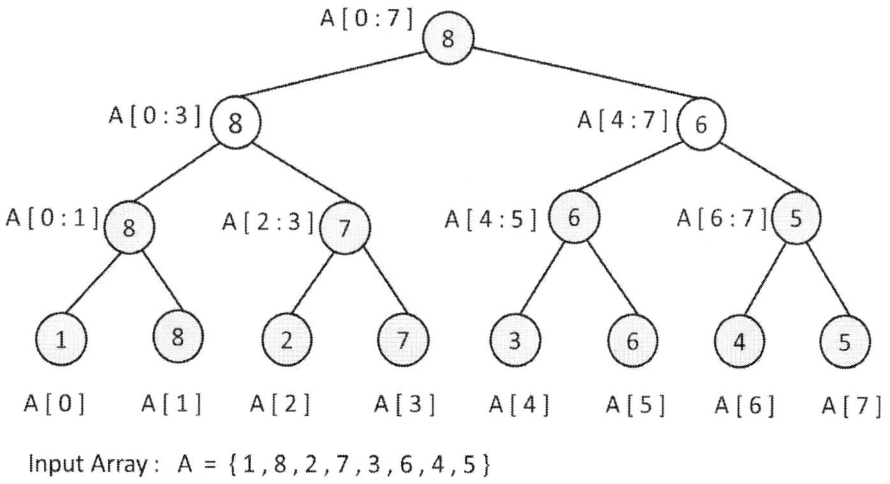

**Example 9.50:**
```
public class rangeMaxST {
    int segArr[];
    int n;

    rangeMaxST(int input[]) {
        n = input.length;
        // Height of segment tree.
        int x = (int) (Math.ceil(Math.log(n) / Math.log(2)));
        //Maximum size of segment tree
        int max_size = 2 * (int) Math.pow(2, x) - 1;
        // Allocate memory for segment tree
        segArr = new int[max_size];
        constructST(input, 0, n - 1, 0);
    }

    int constructST(int input[], int start, int end, int index) {
        // Store it in current node of the segment tree and return
        if (start == end) {
            segArr[index] = input[start];
            return input[start];
        }

        // If there are more than one elements,
        // then traverse left and right subtrees
        // and store the minimum of values in current node.
        int mid = (start + end) / 2;
        segArr[index] = max(constructST(input, start, mid, index * 2 + 1),
                constructST(input, mid + 1, end, index * 2 + 2));
        return segArr[index];
    }

    int max(int first, int second) {
        if (first > second)
            return first;
        else
            return second;
    }
    /* Other methods */
}
```

**Analysis**:
- Segment tree is created using an array. The number of nodes that are required to create a segment tree is (2*n – 1) if n is a power of 2. else it will be 2*(power of 2 bigger than n) – 1/. This is calculated using below steps.
  **int** x = (**int**) (Math.ceil(Math.log(n) / Math.log(2)));
  **int** max_size = 2 * (**int**) Math.pow(2, x) – 1;
- Function **constructST** is used to populate the various elements of the segment tree.

**Example 9.51:**
```
int getMax(int start, int end) {
    // Check for error conditions.
    if (start > end || start < 0 || end > n - 1) {
        System.out.println("Invalid Input.");
        return Integer.MIN_VALUE;
    }
```

```
    return getMaxUtil(0, n - 1, start, end, 0);
}

int getMaxUtil(int segStart, int segEnd, int queryStart, int queryEnd, int index) {
    if (queryStart <= segStart && segEnd <= queryEnd) //complete overlapping case.
        return segArr[index];

    if (segEnd < queryStart || queryEnd < segStart) //no overlapping case.
        return Integer.MIN_VALUE;

    // Segment tree is partly overlaps with the query range.
    int mid = (segStart + segEnd) / 2;
    return max(getMaxUtil(segStart, mid, queryStart, queryEnd, 2 * index + 1),
        getMaxUtil(mid + 1, segEnd, queryStart, queryEnd, 2 * index + 2));
}
```

**Analysis**: Function getMax() is used to perform range query. If the range of nodes segStart and segEnd are inside the query range, then the max of the node is returned. In case of no overlap, MIN Value is returned so that it will not contribute to the final answer. In case of partial overlap, both left and right child queries are performed, and their result is combined to get the final result.

**Example 9.52:**

```
void update(int ind, int val) {
    // Check for error conditions.
    if (ind < 0 || ind > n - 1) {
        System.out.println("Invalid Input.");
        return;
    }

    // Update the values in segment tree
    updateUtil(0, n - 1, ind, val, 0);
}

// Always min inside valid range will be returned.
int updateUtil(int segStart, int segEnd, int ind, int val, int index) {
    // Update index lies outside the range of current segment.
    // So minimum will not change.
    if (ind < segStart || ind > segEnd)
        return segArr[index];

    // If the input index is in range of this node, then update the
    // value of the node and its children
    if (segStart == segEnd) {
        if (segStart == ind) { // Index value need to be updated.
            segArr[index] = val;
            return val;
        } else {
            return segArr[index]; // index value is not changed.
        }
    }

    int mid = (segStart + segEnd) / 2;

    // Current node value is updated with min.
    segArr[index] = max(updateUtil(segStart, mid, ind, val, 2 * index + 1),
            updateUtil(mid + 1, segEnd, ind, val, 2 * index + 2));
```

```
    // Value of diff is propagated to the parent node.
    return segArr[index];
}
```

**Analysis**:

1. If the index which needs to be modified is outside the segStart and segEnd range, then it will not change the segment. And the min value of the segment will be returned.
2. In case the index that needs to be modified is found, then the value of that index is updated.
3. In all the other cases that binary tree both left and right subtree are traversed for modification.

**Example 9.53:** Testing code

```
public static void main(String[] args) {
    int arr[] = { 1, 8, 2, 7, 3, 6, 4, 5 };
    rangeMaxST tree = new rangeMaxST(arr);
    System.out.println("Max value in the range(1, 5): " + tree.getMax(1, 5));
    System.out.println("Max value in the range(2, 7): " + tree.getMax(2, 7));
    System.out.println("Max value of all the elements: " + tree.getMax(0,
arr.length - 1));

    tree.update(2, 9);
    System.out.println("Max value in the range(1, 5): " + tree.getMax(1, 5));
    System.out.println("Max value of all the elements: " + tree.getMax(0,
arr.length - 1));
}
```

**Output:**

```
Max value in the range(1, 5): 8
Max value in the range(2, 7): 7
Max value of all the elements: 8
Max value in the range(1, 5): 9
Max value of all the elements: 9
```

**Analysis:** In the given array the max between index range 1 and 5 is 8. Similarly, the max between index 2 and 7 is 7. Value at the index 2 is modified to 9 so the max in the range 1 and 5 become 9.

## Binary Index Tree / Fenwick Tree

A **Binary Indexed Tree or Fenwick Tree** is a data structure that helps compute prefix sums efficiently.

**Problem statement**: Given an array, you need to find the prefix sum for $i^{th}$ index. The $i^{th}$ *prefix sum* of a given array is the sum of the first "i" elements of the array. Given an array, you should be able to perform updates and calculate prefix sum effectively.

**First approach:** Find the prefix sum by iterating through the various elements of the array and adding them to get the sum. In this naive approach, updating the array will take O(1) time but prefix sum calculation will take O(n) time. This approach will work with a lot of updates but few prefix sum calculations.

**Second approach:** Keep another array that will store the prefix sum. Value at "$i^{th}$" index is the sum of the first "I" elements of the input array.

Input array

| | | | | | | | | | | |
|---|---|---|---|---|---|---|---|---|---|---|
| 1 | 2 | 3 | 4 | 5 | 6 | 7 | 8 | 9 | 10 | 11 |

Prefix sum array

| | | | | | | | | | | |
|---|---|---|---|---|---|---|---|---|---|---|
| 1 | 3 | 6 | 10 | 15 | 21 | 28 | 36 | 45 | 55 | 66 |

By this approach, prefix sum will be given in constant O(1) time. But the update of one element at the "$i^{th}$" index will update all the elements after the "ith" index in the prefix sum array. So the update will take O(n) time. This approach will be helpful if the prefix sum calculations are frequent, but the updates are rare.

**Third approach**: When many updates and many prefix sum calculations are there, then Binary Index Tree or Fenwick Tree are used. (Segment trees can also be used in this scenario, Fenwick trees are easy to implement and consume less space than segment trees). Using Fenwick Tree, both the operations will take O(log(n)) time.

The Binary Index tree is implemented using a one-dimensional array. Let's call the array BIT[]. Each element in a BIT[] stores the sum of some elements of the input array. If the size of the input array is n, then the size of the Fenwick tree array is n+1. Index 0 of BIT[] is a dummy node and does not store any information.
Each index in BIT[] represents a vertex in the tree. Each element of the BIT[] contains a sum of some range of elements in the input array. The prefix sum is calculated by combining the values by moving up from child to parent. The index of the parent vertex is calculated by resetting the least significant set bit of the child index.

Input array Arr[] values stored in Fenwick array BIT[]

| Index | 1 | 2 | 3 | 4 | 5 | 6 | 7 | 8 | 9 | 10 | 11 |
|---|---|---|---|---|---|---|---|---|---|---|---|
| BIT Array | Arr[1] | Arr[1] + Arr[2] | Arr[3] | Sum of Arr[1] to Arr[4] | Arr[5] | Arr[5] + Arr[6] | Arr[7] | Sum of Arr[1] to Arr[8] | Arr[9] | Arr[9] + Arr[10] | Arr[11 ] |

BIT[] array stores a partial sum, but which elements?. Let "i" be the index of the BIT[] array. The least significant set bit of "i" is reset and calls this new number "j". So the BIT[] array at index "I" will store the sum of input array Arr[] from index "j+1" to "I".

Let us suppose we went to find the value stored in BIT[] at index I = 6, Binary representation of 6 is $(0110)_2$. Reset the least significant set bit we will get j = $(0100)_2$ which is j = 4. So BIT[6] will store 5 & 6 index values. BIT[6] = Arr[5] + Arr[6]

Similarly, for an index "i" which is a power of 2. There will be only one set bit. After resetting that set bit we will get 0. So BIT[] at index "i" will store the sum of the first "i" elements of the input array.

We need the least significant set bit to do various updates in the binary index tree. The least significant set bit in a number "i" can be calculated by (i & -i)

Let the binary representation of the number "i" be x1y, where x consists of 0's and 1's. y is all 0's.
-i = 2's complement of index = (x1y)' + 1 = x'0y' + 1 = x'0(0….0)' + 1 = x'0(1...1) + 1 = x'1(0…0) = x'1y

i & (-i) = x1y & x'1y = (0…0)1(0…0), only the least significant set bit of "i" is set. Both x and x` are Complements and y is all zeros. Calculating the prefix sum from BIT[] array. Prefix sum is calculated by adding partial sum at BIT[] at the queried index and all its parent indexes. The parent index is calculated by resetting the least significant set bit.

Prefix sum index 11 or $(1101)_2$
= BIT[$(1101)_2$] + BIT[$(1100)_2$] + BIT[$(1000)_2$]
= BIT[11] + BIT[10] + BIT[8]
= Arr[11] + (Arr[9] + Arr[10]) + (Arr[1] to Arr[8])

The parent index is calculated using bit manipulation.
Each element contains the sum of the values since its parent in the tree. The index of the parent vertex is calculated by resetting the least significant set bit of the child index.

ParentIndex = Index - (Index & (-Index))

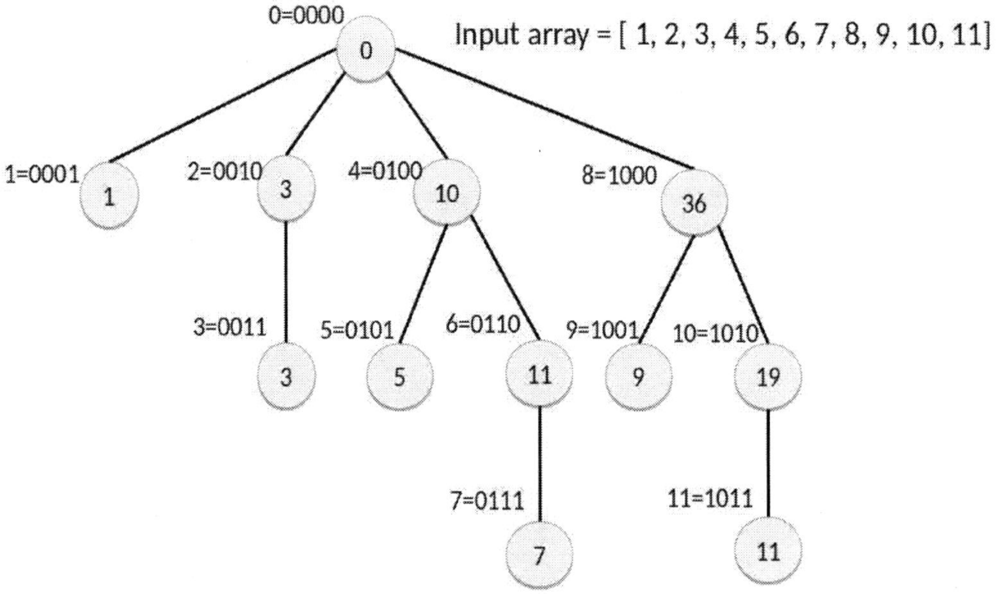


Fenwick Binary Index Tree

**Time complexities**:
- Populating the BIT[] array will take O(n) time.
- Update and prefix sum calculation will take O(log(n)) time. Which is in the worst-case equal to the total number of bits needed to represent the largest index.

**Example 9.54:**
```
public class BinaryIndexTree {
    int BIT[];
    int size;

    BinaryIndexTree(int arr[]) {
        size = arr.length;
        BIT = new int[size + 1];
        Arrays.fill(BIT, 0);
```

```
        // Populating bit.
        for (int i = 0; i < size; i++)
            update(i, arr[i]);
    }

    public void set(int arr[], int index, int val) {
        int diff = val - arr[index];
        arr[index] = val;

        // Difference is propagated.
        update(index, diff);
    }

    private void update(int index, int val) {
        // Index in bit is 1 more than the input array.
        index = index + 1;

        // Traverse to ancestors of nodes.
        while (index <= size) {
            // Add val to current node of Binary Index Tree.
            BIT[index] += val;

            // Next element which need to store val.
            index += index & (-index);
        }
    }

    // Range sum in the range start to end.
    int rangeSum(int start, int end) {
        // Check for error conditions.
        if (start > end || start < 0 || end > size - 1) {
            System.out.println("Invalid Input.");
            return -1;
        }

        return prefixSum(end) - prefixSum(start - 1);
    }

    // Prefix sum in the range 0 to index.
    int prefixSum(int index) {
        int sum = 0;
        index = index + 1;

        // Traverse ancestors of Binary Index Tree nodes.
        while (index > 0) {
            // Add current element to sum.
            sum += BIT[index];

            // Parent index calculation.
            index -= index & (-index);
        }
        return sum;
    }

    // Testing code.
    public static void main(String[] args) {
        int arr[] = { 1, 2, 3, 4, 5, 6, 7, 8, 9, 10, 11 };
        BinaryIndexTree tree = new BinaryIndexTree(arr);
```

```
        System.out.println("Sum of elements in range(0,5):"+ tree.prefixSum(5));
        System.out.println("Sum of elements in range(2,5):"+tree.rangeSum(2,5));
        // Set fourth element to 10.
        tree.set(arr, 3, 10);
        // Find sum after the value is updated
        System.out.println("Sum of elements in range(0,5):"+ tree.prefixSum(5));
    }
}
```

**Output**:

```
Sum of elements in range(0, 5): 21
Sum of elements in range(2, 5): 18
Sum of elements in range(0, 5): 27
```

**Analysis**:

1 Function prefixSum() calculates prefix sum by adding queries index value and all its parent index values.
2 Function update() is used to propagate the changed value to all the nodes which contain that particular element.
3 Function set() is used to update the original Arr[] and also propagate differences to the BIT[] using update() function.
4 Function rangeSum() will calculate range query by calling two prefixSum().

## AVL Tree

An AVL Tree is a height-balanced binary search tree(BST). An AVL tree is a binary search tree (BST) with an additional property that it is a balanced tree. The difference between the height of the left and right subtree of every node differs in height by at most one. The difference between the left and right subtree of every node in the tree is either -1, 0 or +1. In an AVL tree, every node maintains extra information known as **height**.

**Example 9.55:**

```
public class AVLTree {
    private Node root;

    private static class Node {
        private int data;
        private Node left;
        private Node right;
        private int height;

        public Node(int d, Node l, Node r) {
            data = d;
            left = l;
            right = r;
            height = 0;
        }
    }

    public AVLTree() {
        root = null;
    }
```

```
    int height(Node n) {
        if (n == null)
            return -1;
        return n.height;
    }

    int getBalance(Node node) {
        return (node == null) ? 0 : height(node.left) - height(node.right);
    }

    public void printTree() {
        printTree(root, "", false);
        System.out.println();
    }

    private void printTree(Node node, String indent, boolean isLeft) {
        if (node == null)
            return;
        if (isLeft) {
            System.out.print(indent + "L:");
            indent += "|  ";
        } else {
            System.out.print(indent + "R:");
            indent += "   ";
        }

        System.out.println(node.data + "(" + node.height + ")");
        printTree(node.left, indent, true);
        printTree(node.right, indent, false);
    }
}
```

**Analysis:** Adding or removing a node from an AVL tree may make the AVL tree unbalanced. Such violations of AVL balance property are corrected by rotations. Let us assume that the insertion of a new node converts a previously balanced AVL tree into an unbalanced tree. Since the tree is previously balanced and a single new node is added to it, the unbalanced maximum difference in height will be 2.

Therefore, in the bottom-most unbalanced node there are only four cases:
1 Left-Left case, the new node is the left child of its parent, which is the left child of the grandparent.
2 Left-Right case, the new node is the right child of its parent, which is the left child of the grandparent.
3 Right-Left case, the new node is the left child of its parent, which is the right child of the grandparent.
4 Right-Right case, the new node is the right child of its parent, which is the right child of the grandparent.

## Left Rotation to fix Right-Right case

The left rotation is performed by rotating nodes arranged anti-clockwise.
Let us consider the following insertion to understand left rotation. Insert 1, 2 and 3 to the tree.

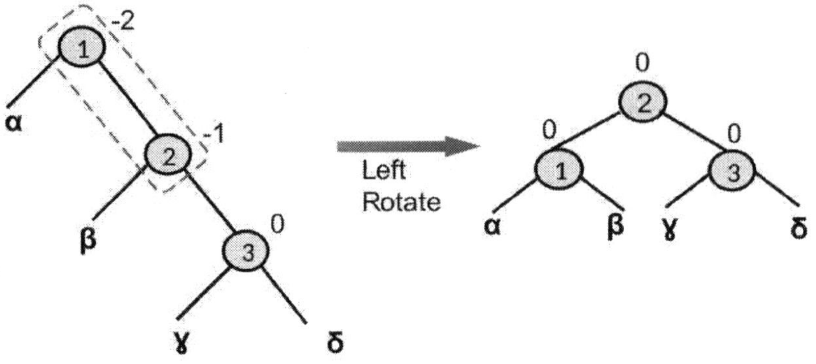


**Example 9.56**
```
// Function to left rotate subtree rooted with x
Node leftRotate(Node x) {
    Node y = x.right;
    Node T = y.left;

    // Rotation
    y.left = x;
    x.right = T;

    // Update heights
    x.height = max(height(x.left), height(x.right)) + 1;
    y.height = max(height(y.left), height(y.right)) + 1;

    // Return new root
    return y;
}
```

## Right Rotation to fix Left-Left case(LL Case)

The right rotation is performed by rotating nodes arranged clockwise.
Let us consider the following insertion to understand left rotation. Insert 3, 2 and 1 to the tree.

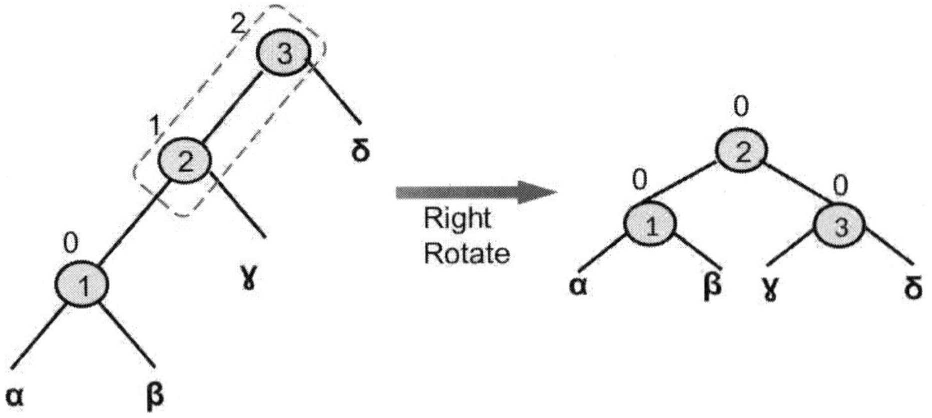


**Example 9.57**
```
// Function to right rotate subtree rooted with x
Node rightRotate(Node x) {
    Node y = x.left;
    Node T = y.right;
```

```
    // Rotation
    y.right = x;
    x.left = T;

    // Update heights
    x.height = max(height(x.left), height(x.right)) + 1;
    y.height = max(height(y.left), height(y.right)) + 1;

    // Return new root
    return y;
}
```

## Left-right rotation to fix Left-Right case

The Left-Right rotation is a left rotation followed by a right rotation. In this rotation, the lower two nodes first perform anti-clockwise left rotation followed by clockwise right rotation for the above two nodes.
Let us consider the following insertion to understand left rotation. Insert 3, 1 and 2

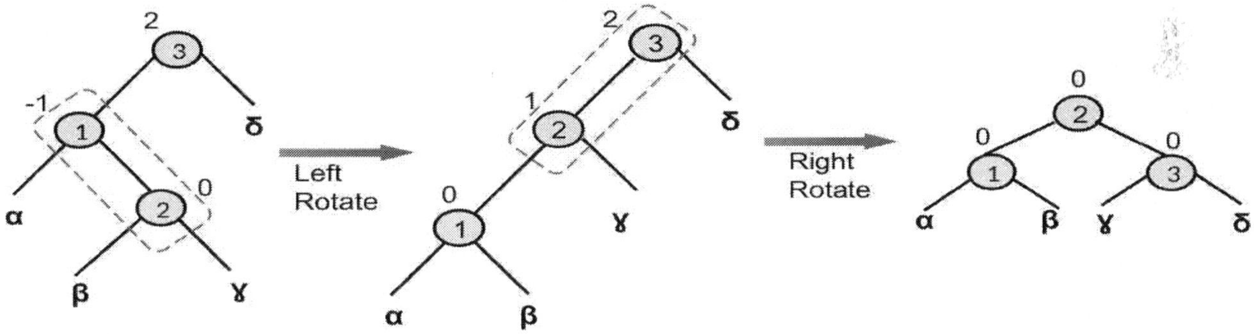


**Example 9.58 :** Function to left then right rotate subtree rooted with x

```
Node leftRightRotate(Node x) {
    x.left = leftRotate(x.left);
    return rightRotate(x);
}
```

## Right-Left rotation to fix Right-Left case(RL case)

The Right-Left rotation is the right rotation followed by the left rotation. In this rotation, the lower two nodes first perform clockwise right rotation followed by anti-clockwise left rotation for the above two nodes.
Let us consider the following insertion to understand left rotation. Insert 1, 3 and 2

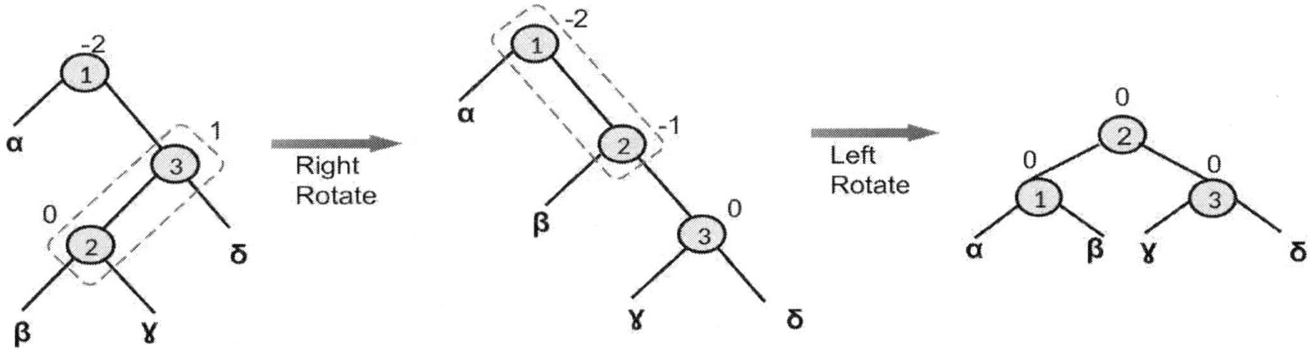

**Example 9.59 :** Function to right then left rotate subtree rooted with x

```
Node rightLeftRotate(Node x) {
    x.right = rightRotate(x.right);
    return leftRotate(x);
}
```

## Operations on AVL Tree

AVL tree is a binary search tree. So all the operations of traversal and search of binary search trees are applicable on the AVL tree; the only difference is in the insert() and delete() operation, which can create the tree unbalanced.

## Insertion in AVL Tree

In an AVL tree, the insertion operation is performed as follows:

- Insert the new element into the tree using Binary Search Tree insertion.
- After insertion, check the **Balance Factor** of every node.
- If the **Balance Factor** of every node is **0 or 1 or -1** then done else go to the next step.
- If the **Balance Factor** of any node is other than **0 or 1 or -1** then that tree is unbalanced. In this case, perform a suitable **Rotation** to make it balanced. There are four cases(LL case, LR case, RL case and RR case) that need to be considered to make it balanced.

In an AVL tree, the insertion operation has **O(log(n))** time complexity.

**Example 9.60:**

```
public void insert(int data) {
    root = insert(root, data);
}

private Node insert(Node node, int data) {
    if (node == null)
        return new Node(data, null, null);

    if (node.data > data) {
        node.left = insert(node.left, data);
    } else if (node.data < data) {
        node.right = insert(node.right, data);
    } else { // Duplicate data not allowed
        return node;
    }

    node.height = max(height(node.left), height(node.right)) + 1;
    int balance = getBalance(node);

    if (balance > 1) {
        if (data < node.left.data) { // Left Left Case
            return rightRotate(node);
        }

        if (data > node.left.data) { // Left Right Case
            return leftRightRotate(node);
        }
    }
```

```
    if (balance < -1) {
        if (data > node.right.data) { // Right Right Case
            return leftRotate(node);
        }

        if (data < node.right.data) { // Right Left Case
            return rightLeftRotate(node);
        }
    }

    return node;
}
```

## Deletion in AVL Tree

In an AVL tree, the deletion operation is performed as follows:

1. Delete an element from the tree is performed using standard Binary Search Tree deletion.
2. After deletion, traverse up and check the **Balance Factor** of every node. If found any unbalanced node then perform the next step.
3. If the **Balance Factor** of any node is other than **0 or 1 or -1** then that tree is unbalanced. In this case, perform a suitable **Rotation** to make it balanced. There are four cases(LL case, LR case, RL case and RR case) that need to be considered to make it balanced.

**Example 9.61:**

```
public void delete(int data) {
    root = delete(root, data);
}

private Node delete(Node node, int data) {
    if (node == null)
        return null;

    if (node.data == data) {
        if (node.left == null && node.right == null) {
            return null;
        } else if (node.left == null) {
            return node.right; // no need to modify height
        } else if (node.right == null) {
            return node.left; // no need to modify height
        } else {
            Node minNode = findMin(node.right);
            node.data = minNode.data;
            node.right = delete(node.right, minNode.data);
        }
    } else {
        if (node.data > data) {
            node.left = delete(node.left, data);
        } else {
            node.right = delete(node.right, data);
        }
    }

    node.height = max(height(node.left), height(node.right)) + 1;
    int balance = getBalance(node);
```

```
    if (balance > 1) {
        if (data >= node.left.data) { // Left Left Case
            return rightRotate(node);
        }

        if (data < node.left.data) { // Left Right Case
            return leftRightRotate(node);
        }
    }

    if (balance < -1) {
        if (data <= node.right.data) { // Right Right Case
            return leftRotate(node);
        }
        if (data > node.right.data) { // Right Left Case
            return rightLeftRotate(node);
        }
    }
    return node;
}
```

Time Complexity of deletion is O(log(n))

**Example 9.62**

```
public static void main(String[] arg) {
    AVLTree t = new AVLTree();
    t.insert(1);
    t.insert(2);
    t.insert(3);
    t.insert(4);
    t.insert(5);
    t.insert(6);
    t.insert(7);
    t.insert(8);
    t.printTree();
    t.delete(5);
    t.printTree();
}
```

**Output:**

```
R:4(3)
   L:2(1)
   |  L:1(0)
   |  R:3(0)
   R:6(2)
      L:5(0)
      R:7(1)
         R:8(0)

R:4(2)
   L:2(1)
   |  L:1(0)
   |  R:3(0)
   R:7(1)
      L:6(0)
      R:8(0)
```

## Red-Black Tree

The Red-Black tree contains its data, left and right children like any other binary tree. In addition to this, its node also contains an extra bit of information that represents colour which can either be red or black. The red-Black tree also contains a specialised type of node called null nodes. Null nodes are pseudo nodes that exist at the leaf of the tree and are black. All internal nodes have their data associated with them.

A red-Black tree has the following properties:

- The root of the tree is black.
- Every leaf node (null node) is black.
- Two red nodes can't have a parent-child relationship.
- Every path from a node to a descendant leaf contains the same number of black nodes.

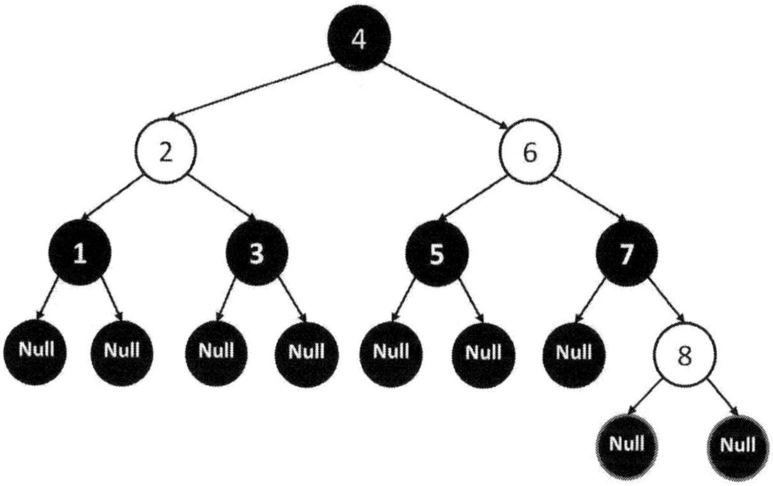


The first three properties are self-explanatory. The fourth property states that, from any node in the tree to any leaf (null node), the number of black nodes must be the same. In the above figure, from the root node to the leaf node (null node) the number of black nodes is always three nodes.

Like the AVL tree, red-black trees are also self-balancing binary search trees. Whereas the balance property of an AVL tree has a direct relationship between the heights of left and right subtrees of each node. In red-black trees, the balancing property is governed by the four rules mentioned above. Adding or removing a node from a red-black tree may violate the properties of a red-black tree. The red-black properties are restored through recolouring and rotation. Insert, delete, and search operations have a time complexity of O(log(n)).

**Example 9.63:**

```
public class RBTree {
    private Node root;
    private Node NullNode;

    private static class Node {
        Node left, right, parent;
        int data;
        boolean colour; // true for red colour, false for black colour
```

```
        Node(int data, Node nullNode) {
            this.data = data;
            left = nullNode;
            right = nullNode;
            colour = true; // New node are red in colour.
            parent = nullNode;
        }
    }

    public RBTree() {
        NullNode = new Node(0, null);
        NullNode.colour = false;
        root = NullNode;

    }

    // To check whether node is of colour red or not.
    boolean isRed(Node node) {
        return (node == null) ? false : (node.colour == true);
    }

    public void printTree() {
        printTree(root, "", false);
        System.out.println();
    }

    private void printTree(Node node, String indent, boolean isLeft) {
        if (node == NullNode)
            return;
        if (isLeft) {
            System.out.print(indent + "L:");
            indent += "|   ";
        } else {
            System.out.print(indent + "R:");
            indent += "    ";
        }

        System.out.println(node.data + "(" + node.colour + ")");
        printTree(node.left, indent, true);
        printTree(node.right, indent, false);
    }
    /* Other methods */
}
```

## Insertion in RED BLACK Tree

In a Red-Black Tree, every new node must be inserted with the colour RED. The insertion operation in Red-Black Tree is similar to the insertion operation in BST. After every insertion operation, we need to check all the properties of the Red-Black Tree. If all the properties are not satisfied, then we perform rotations and recolouring to restore its Red Black Tree properties. The new node inserted is always Red, so the property that is mostly violated is two consecutive reds.

The insertion operation in the Red-Black tree is performed using the following steps:
STEP 1, Insert the new node according to BST insertion with the new node colour as Red.
STEP 2, If the newly inserted node is the root node then colour it black and exit.
STEP 3, If the parent of the new node is Black, then exit.

STEP 4, If the parent of the new node is Red and uncle (sibling of the parent) colour is Red, then perform recolouring. Make grandparent red and both parent and uncle colour as black.
STEP 5, If the parent of the new node is Red and uncle colour is Black or null, then make suitable rotations and recolour it.

The below diagram shows STEP 4, recolouring in a case when the parent and uncle of the new node are Red.

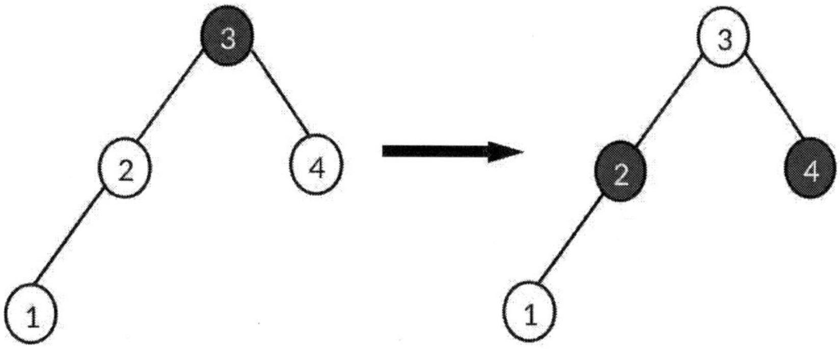


Recolouring in Red-Black tree to correct double red condition.

## Left Rotation to fix Right-Right case (RR Case)

The left rotation is performed by rotating nodes arranged anti-clockwise.

**Example 9.64 :** Function to left rotate subtree rooted with x

```
Node leftRotate(Node x) {
    Node y = x.right;
    Node T = y.left;

    // Rotation
    y.parent = x.parent;
    y.left = x;
    x.parent = y;
    x.right = T;

    if (T != NullNode)
        T.parent = x;

    if (x == root) {
        root = y;
        return y;
    }

    if (y.parent.left == x)
        y.parent.left = y;
    else
        y.parent.right = y;

    // Return new root
    return y;
}
```

## Right Rotation to fix Left-Left case(LL Case)

The right rotation is performed by rotating nodes arranged clockwise.

**Example 9.65 :** Function to right rotate subtree rooted with x

```
Node rightRotate(Node x) {
    Node y = x.left;
    Node T = y.right;

    // Rotation
    y.parent = x.parent;
    y.right = x;
    x.parent = y;
    x.left = T;
    if (T != NullNode)
        T.parent = x;

    if (x == root) {
        root = y;
        return y;
    }

    if (y.parent.left == x)
        y.parent.left = y;
    else
        y.parent.right = y;

    // Return new root
    return y;
}
```

## Left-right rotation to fix Left-Right case(LR Case)

The Left-Right rotation is a left rotation followed by a right rotation. In this rotation, the lower two nodes first perform anti-clockwise left rotation followed by clockwise right rotation for the above two nodes.

**Example 9.66**

```
Node leftRightRotate(Node node) {
    node.left = leftRotate(node.left);
    return rightRotate(node);
}
```

## Right-Left rotation to fix Right-Left case(RL case)

The Right-Left rotation is a right rotation followed by a left rotation. In this rotation, the lower two nodes first perform clockwise right rotation followed by anti-clockwise left rotation for the above two nodes.

**Example 9.67**

```
Node rightLeftRotate(Node node) {
    node.right = rightRotate(node.right);
    return leftRotate(node);
}
```

Below is the diagram to show Step 5, rotation is performed followed by recolouring.

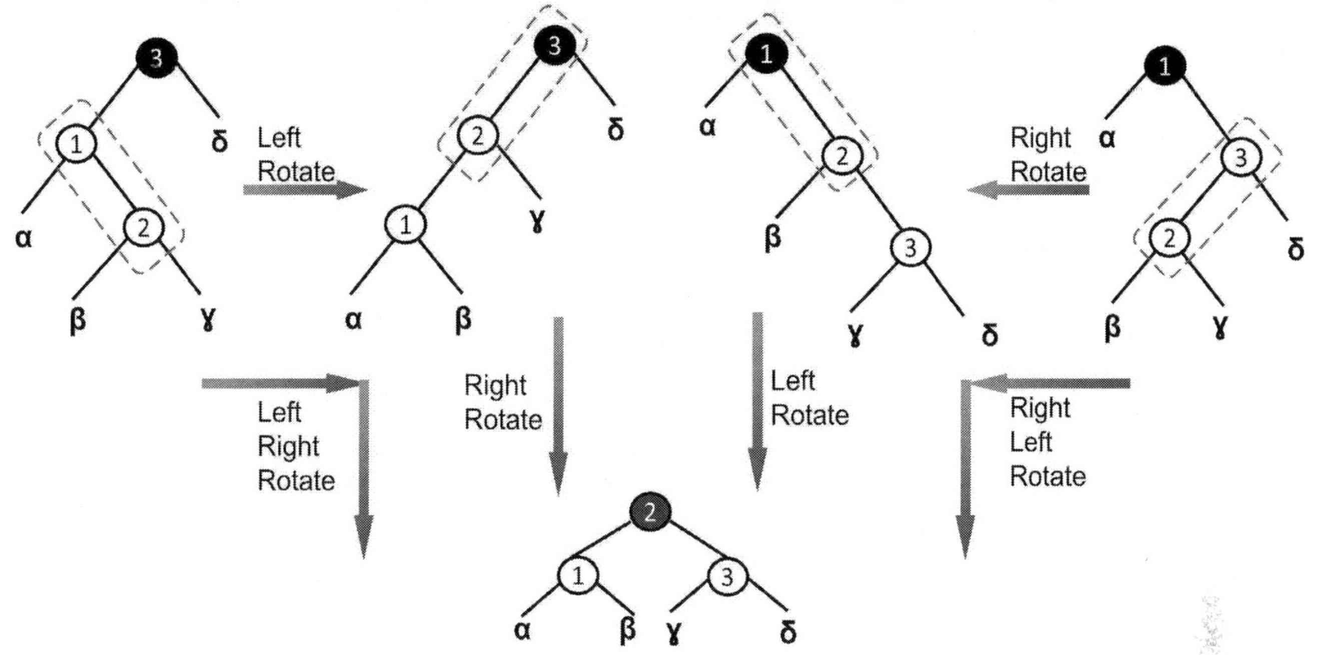


Restructuring in Red-Black tree to correct double red condition.

**Example 9.68:**

```
public void insert(int data) {
    root = insert(root, data);
    Node temp = find(data);
    fixRedRed(temp);
}

private Node insert(Node node, int data) {
    if (node == NullNode) {
        node = new Node(data, NullNode);
    } else if (node.data > data) {
        node.left = insert(node.left, data);
        node.left.parent = node;
    } else if (node.data < data) {
        node.right = insert(node.right, data);
        node.right.parent = node;
    }
    return node;
}

void fixRedRed(Node x) {
    // if x is root colour it black and return
    if (x == root) {
        x.colour = false;
        return;
    }

    if (x.parent == NullNode || x.parent.parent == NullNode) {
        return;
    }
```

```
    // Initialize parent, grandparent, uncle
    Node parent = x.parent, grandparent = parent.parent, uncle = uncle(x);
    Node mid = null;

    if (parent.colour == false) {
        return;
    }

    // parent colour is red. gp is black.
    if (uncle != NullNode && uncle.colour == true) {
        // uncle and parent is red.
        parent.colour = false;
        uncle.colour = false;
        grandparent.colour = true;
        fixRedRed(grandparent);
        return;
    }

    // parent is red, uncle is black and gp is black.
    // Perform LR, LL, RL, RR
    if (parent == grandparent.left && x == parent.left) // LL
    {
        mid = rightRotate(grandparent);
    } else if (parent == grandparent.left && x == parent.right) // LR
    {
        mid = leftRightRotate(grandparent);
    } else if (parent == grandparent.right && x == parent.left) // RL
    {
        mid = rightLeftRotate(grandparent);
    } else if (parent == grandparent.right && x == parent.right) // RR
    {
        mid = leftRotate(grandparent);
    }

    mid.colour = false;
    mid.left.colour = true;
    mid.right.colour = true;
}

private Node uncle(Node node) {
    // If no parent or grandparent, then no uncle
    if (node.parent == NullNode || node.parent.parent == NullNode)
        return null;

    if (node.parent == node.parent.parent.left)
        // uncle on right
        return node.parent.parent.right;
    else
        // uncle on left
        return node.parent.parent.left;
}
```

## Deletion in Red Black Tree

In an RB tree, the deletion operation is performed as follows:

1 Delete an element from the tree using standard Binary Search Tree deletion. In BST deletion, we always delete a leaf node or one child node. As for the 2 child nodes, data of inorder successor is copied, and we recursively call it's delete.
2 If the deleted node is red, then the Red-Black property will not be violated.
3 If the deleted node is black. Then deleted nodes may cause reduced black node count in one of the paths from the root to leaf.
4 To fix violated properties of Red-Black Tree, suitable Rotation and Recolour is performed.

Steps to fix the RB Tree after deletion of black node:

1. Let's call the deleted node "y". Child of the deleted node as "x". Sibling of deleted nodes as "s".
2. Case 1: If the child of the deleted node is red. Make the colour of the child as black and black node count will be restored.

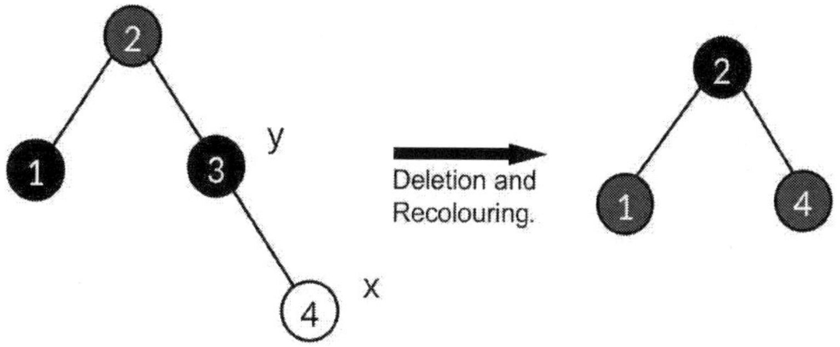


**Case 1:** When deleted node's child colour is red.

3. Case 2: When the sibling of the deleted node is black and at least one of the sibling children is red. In this there are 4 different combinations:
   - Case 2(a): When the sibling "s" of the deleted node "y" is black. Sibling "s" is the left child of the parent, and the sibling's left child is red. This is a Left-Left configuration, so perform right rotation. Then change the colour of the child to black. This case is shown in the below diagram.

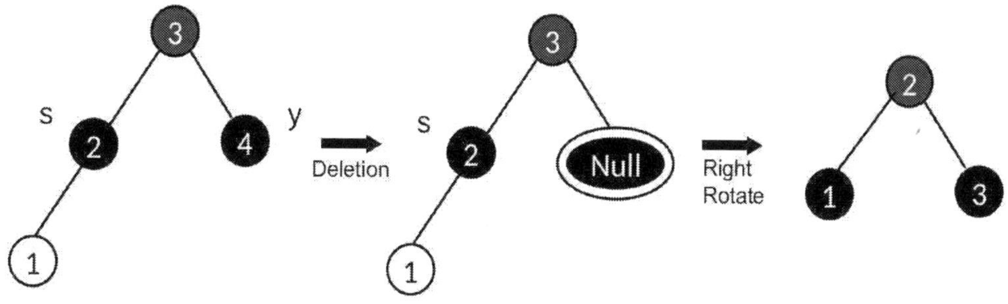


**Case 2(a)**: When sibling of deleted node is black. Sibling is left child of parent and its left child is red. Left Left configuration so right rotation is performed. Child node colour became black.

   - Case 2(b): Mirror image of the above case. Sibling "s" is the right child of its parent and its right child is red. Right-Right configuration so performs the left rotation. Then change the colour of the child to black. Black node count property will be restored.

- Case 2(c): When sibling "s" of deleted node "y" is black. Sibling "s" is the left child of its parent and its right child is red. This is a Left-Right configuration, so left rotation followed by right rotation is performed. The child node is coloured black.

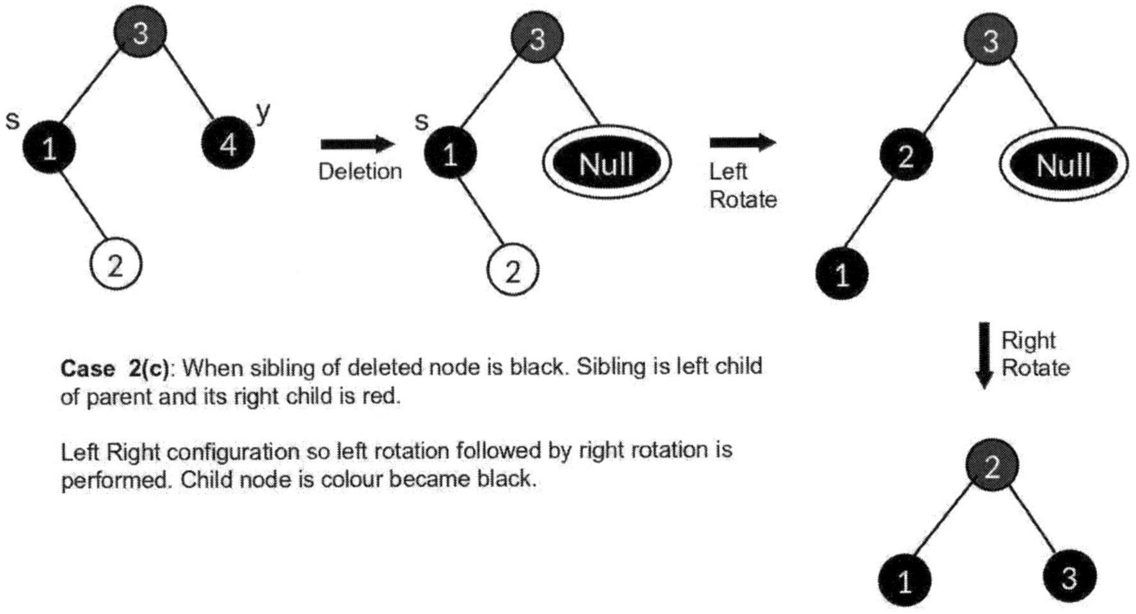


- Case 2(d): When sibling "s" of deleted node "y" is black. Sibling "s" is the right child of its parent and its left child is red. Then Right-Left configuration so right rotation followed by left rotation is performed. Child node colour is changed to black.

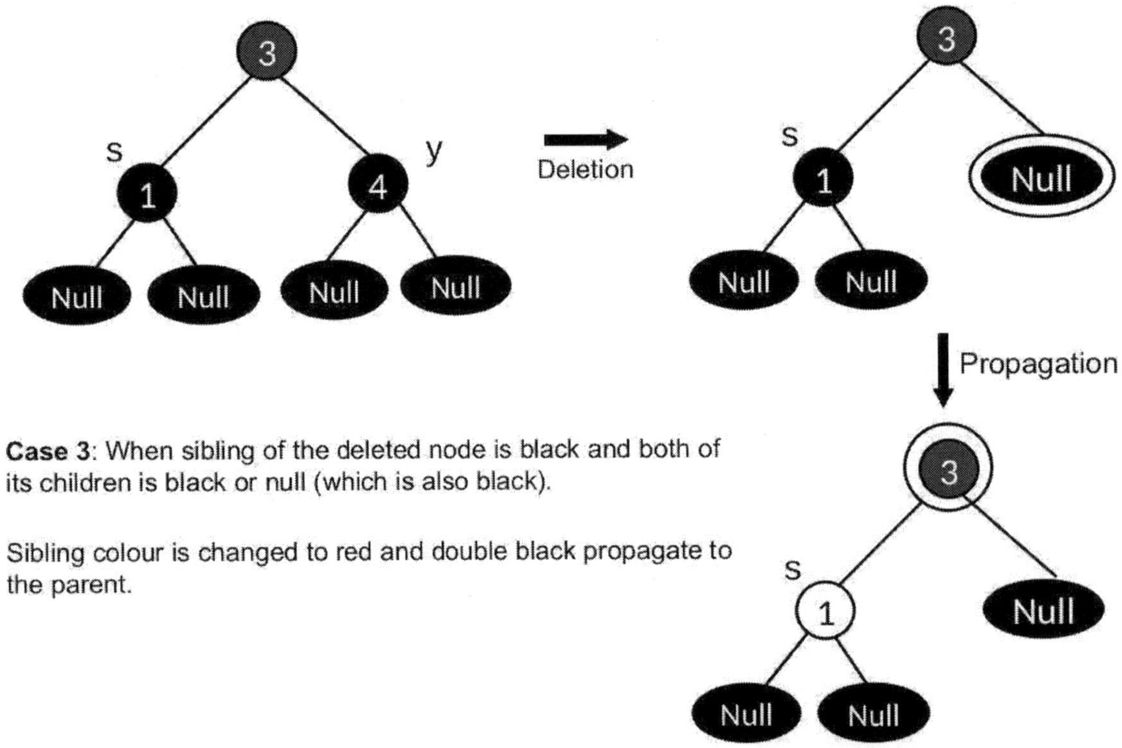

4. Case 3: When the sibling of the deleted node is black and both of its children are black or null node (which is also black). Make siblings red and recursively add black colour to the parent. If the parent was red then it would become black. If the parent was black it would become double black. If the parent is root then we make the root node as black and exit.

5. Case 4: When sibling "s" of deleted node "y" is red. Rotation is performed to bring siblings up. Then recolour the sibling and parent.
   - Sibling "s" is the left child of a parent. This is a Left-Left configuration so perform right rotation.
   - Sibling "s" is the right child of a parent. This is a Right-Right configuration so perform left rotation.
   - Rotation is performed and parent and sibling colours are swapped. After rotation one of Case 2(a), 2(b), 2(c), 2(d) or Case 3 will be applied.
   - In the below diagram case, the sibling is the right child of the parent so left rotation is performed. Parent and sibling colours are swapped. After rotation and recolouring case 3 is applied.

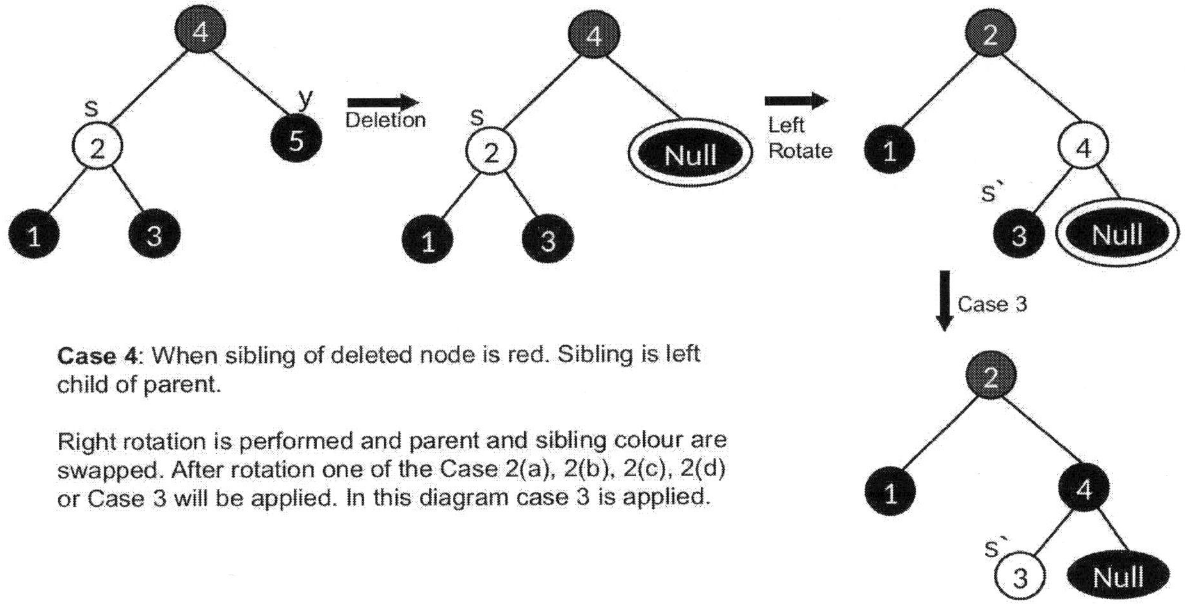


**Example 9.69:**
```
public void delete(int data) {
    delete(this.root, data);
}

private void delete(Node node, int key) {
    Node z = NullNode;
    Node x, y;
    while (node != NullNode) {
        if (node.data == key) {
            z = node;
            break;
        } else if (node.data <= key) {
            node = node.right;
        } else {
            node = node.left;
```

```
        }
    }

    if (z == NullNode) {
        System.out.println("Couldn't find key in the tree");
        return;
    }

    y = z;
    boolean yColour = y.colour;
    if (z.left == NullNode) {
        x = z.right;
        joinParentChild(z, z.right);
    } else if (z.right == NullNode) {
        x = z.left;
        joinParentChild(z, z.left);
    } else {
        y = minimum(z.right);
        yColour = y.colour;
        z.data = y.data;
        joinParentChild(y, y.right);
        x = y.right;
    }

    if (yColour == false) {
        if (x.colour == true) {
            x.colour = false;
            return;
        } else {
            fixDoubleBlack(x);
        }
    }
}

private void fixDoubleBlack(Node x) {
    if (x == root) // Root node.
        return;

    Node sib = sibling(x);
    Node parent = x.parent;
    if (sib == NullNode) {
        // No sibling double black shifted to parent.
        fixDoubleBlack(parent);
    } else {
        if (sib.colour == true) {
            // Sibling colour is red.
            parent.colour = true;
            sib.colour = false;
            if (sib.parent.left == sib) {
                // Sibling is left child.
                rightRotate(parent);
            } else {
                // Sibling is right child.
                leftRotate(parent);
            }
            fixDoubleBlack(x);
        } else {
            // Sibling colour is black
```

```
            // At least one child is red.
            if (sib.left.colour == true || sib.right.colour == true) {
                if (sib.parent.left == sib) {
                    // Sibling is left child.
                    if (sib.left != NullNode && sib.left.colour == true) {
                        // left left case.
                        sib.left.colour = sib.colour;
                        sib.colour = parent.colour;
                        rightRotate(parent);
                    } else {
                        // left right case.
                        sib.right.colour = parent.colour;
                        leftRotate(sib);
                        rightRotate(parent);
                    }
                } else {
                    // Sibling is right child.
                    if (sib.left != NullNode && sib.left.colour == true) {
                        // right left case.
                        sib.left.colour = parent.colour;
                        rightRotate(sib);
                        leftRotate(parent);
                    } else {
                        // right right case.
                        sib.right.colour = sib.colour;
                        sib.colour = parent.colour;
                        leftRotate(parent);
                    }
                }
                parent.colour = false;
            } else {
                // Both children black.
                sib.colour = true;
                if (parent.colour == false)
                    fixDoubleBlack(parent);
                else
                    parent.colour = false;
            }
        }
    }
}

private Node sibling(Node node) {
    // sibling null if no parent
    if (node.parent == NullNode)
        return null;

    if (node.parent.left == node)
        return node.parent.right;

    return node.parent.left;
}

private void joinParentChild(Node u, Node v) {
    if (u.parent == NullNode) {
        root = v;
    } else if (u == u.parent.left) {
        u.parent.left = v;
```

```
    } else {
        u.parent.right = v;
    }
    v.parent = u.parent;
}

private Node minimum(Node node) {
    while (node.left != NullNode) {
        node = node.left;
    }
    return node;
}

// Testing code.
public static void main(String[] arg) {
    RBTree tree = new RBTree();
    tree.insert(1);
    tree.insert(2);
    tree.insert(3);
    tree.insert(4);
    tree.insert(5);
    tree.insert(7);
    tree.insert(6);
    tree.insert(8);
    tree.insert(9);
    tree.printTree();
    tree.delete(4);
    tree.printTree();
}
```

**Output:**

```
R:4(false)
   L:2(true)
   |  L:1(false)
   |  R:3(false)
   R:6(true)
      L:5(false)
      R:8(false)
         L:7(true)
         R:9(true)

R:5(false)
   L:2(true)
   |  L:1(false)
   |  R:3(false)
   R:7(true)
      L:6(false)
      R:8(false)
         R:9(true)
```

## Splay Tree

A **Splay tree** is a self-adjusting binary search tree with the additional property that recently accessed elements are quick to access again. It performs basic operations such as insertion, look-up, and removal in O(log(n)) amortized time.

Elements of the tree are rearranged so that the recently accessed element is placed at the top of the tree. When an element is searched then we use standard BST search and then use rotation to bring the element to the top.

| | Average-Case | Worst Case |
|---|---|---|
| Space complexity | O(n) | O(n) |
| Time complexity search | O(log(n)) | Amortized O(log(n)) |
| Time complexity insert | O(log(n)) | Amortized O(log(n)) |
| Time complexity delete | O(log(n)) | Amortized O(log(n)) |

**Example 9.70:**
```
public class SPLAYTree {
    private Node root;

    private static class Node {
        int data;
        Node left, right, parent;

        public Node(int d, Node l, Node r) {
            data = d;
            left = l;
            right = r;
            parent = null;
        }
    }

    public SPLAYTree() {
        root = null;
    }

    public void printTree() {
        printTree(root, "", false);
        System.out.println();
    }

    private void printTree(Node node, String indent, boolean isLeft) {
        if (node == null)
            return;
        if (isLeft) {
            System.out.print(indent + "L:");
            indent += "|  ";
        } else {
            System.out.print(indent + "R:");
            indent += "   ";
        }

        System.out.println(node.data);
        printTree(node.left, indent, true);
        printTree(node.right, indent, false);
    }

    // Function to right rotate subtree rooted with x
    Node rightRotate(Node x) {
        Node y = x.left;
```

```
        Node T = y.right;

        // Rotation
        y.parent = x.parent;
        y.right = x;
        x.parent = y;
        x.left = T;
        if (T != null)
            T.parent = x;

        if (y.parent != null && y.parent.left == x)
            y.parent.left = y;
        else if (y.parent != null && y.parent.right == x)
            y.parent.right = y;
        // Return new root
        return y;
    }

    // Function to left rotate subtree rooted with x
    Node leftRotate(Node x) {
        Node y = x.right;
        Node T = y.left;

        // Rotation
        y.parent = x.parent;
        y.left = x;
        x.parent = y;
        x.right = T;
        if (T != null)
            T.parent = x;

        if (y.parent != null && y.parent.left == x)
            y.parent.left = y;
        else if (y.parent != null && y.parent.right == x)
            y.parent.right = y;
        // Return new root
        return y;
    }

    Node parent(Node node) {
        if (node == null || node.parent == null)
            return null;
        return node.parent;
    }

    public void splay(Node node) {
        Node parent, grand;
        while (node != root) {
            parent = parent(node);
            grand = parent(parent);
            if (parent == null) { // rotations had created new root, always last
condition.
                root = node;
            } else if (grand == null) { // single rotation case.
                if (parent.left == node) {
                    node = rightRotate(parent);
                } else {
                    node = leftRotate(parent);
```

```
                }
            } else if (grand.left == parent && parent.left == node){//Zig Zig case.
                rightRotate(grand);
                node = rightRotate(parent);
            } else if(grand.right == parent && parent.right == node){//Zag Zag case
                leftRotate(grand);
                node = leftRotate(parent);
            } else if(grand.left == parent && parent.right == node){//Zig Zag case.
                leftRotate(parent);
                node = rightRotate(grand);
            } else if(grand.right == parent && parent.left == node){//Zag Zig case.
                rightRotate(parent);
                node = leftRotate(grand);
            }
        }
    }

    public boolean find(int data) {
        Node curr = root;
        while (curr != null) {
            if (curr.data == data) {
                splay(curr);
                return true;
            } else if (curr.data > data) {
                curr = curr.left;
            } else {
                curr = curr.right;
            }
        }
        return false;
    }

    public void insert(int data) {
        Node newNode = new Node(data, null, null);
        if (root == null) {
            root = newNode;
            return;
        }

        Node node = root;
        Node parent = null;
        while (node != null) {
            parent = node;
            if (node.data > data) {
                node = node.left;
            } else if (node.data < data) {
                node = node.right;
            } else {
                splay(node); // duplicate insertion not allowed but splaying for
it.
                return;
            }
        }

        newNode.parent = parent;

        if (parent.data > data) {
            parent.left = newNode;
```

```
        } else {
            parent.right = newNode;
        }
        splay(newNode);
    }

    public Node findMinNode(Node curr) {
        Node node = curr;
        if (node == null) {
            return null;
        }
        while (node.left != null) {
            node = node.left;
        }
        return node;
    }

    public void delete(int data) {
        Node node = root;
        Node parent = null;
        Node next = null;
        while (node != null) {
            if (node.data == data) {
                parent = node.parent;
                if (node.left == null && node.right == null) {
                    next = null;
                } else if (node.left == null) {
                    next = node.right;
                } else if (node.right == null) {
                    next = node.left;
                }

                if (node.left == null || node.right == null) {
                    if (node == root) {
                        root = next;
                        return;
                    }
                    if (parent.left == node) {
                        parent.left = next;
                    } else {
                        parent.right = next;
                    }
                    if (next != null)
                        next.parent = parent;
                    break;
                }

                Node minNode = findMinNode(node.right);
                data = minNode.data;
                node.data = data;
                node = node.right;

            } else if (node.data > data) {
                parent = node;
                node = node.left;
            } else {
                parent = node;
                node = node.right;
```

```
            }
        }
        splay(parent); // Splaying for the parent of the node deleted.
    }

    // Testing code.
    public static void main(String[] arg) {
        SPLAYTree tree = new SPLAYTree();
        tree.insert(5);
        tree.insert(4);
        tree.insert(6);
        tree.insert(3);
        tree.insert(2);
        tree.insert(1);
        tree.insert(3);
        tree.printTree();
        System.out.println("Value 2 found: " + tree.find(2));
        tree.delete(2);
        tree.delete(5);
        tree.printTree();
    }
}
```

**Output:**

```
R:3
   L:2
   |  L:1
   R:6
      L:4
      |  R:5

Value 2 found: true
R:4
   L:3
   |  L:1
   R:6
```

**Note**: Unlike the AVL tree, the splay tree is not guaranteed to be height-balanced. What is guaranteed is that the total cost of the entire series of accesses will be cheap.

## B Tree

As we had already seen various types of binary trees for searching, insertion and deletion of data in the main memory. However, these data structures are not appropriate for huge data that cannot fit into the main memory, the data that is stored in the disk.

A B-tree is a self-balancing search tree that allows searches, insertions, and deletions in logarithmic time. The B-tree is a tree in which a node can have multiple children. Unlike self-balancing binary search trees, the B-tree is optimised for systems that read and write entire blocks (page) of data. The read-write operation from the disk is very slow as compared with the main memory. The main purpose of B-Tree is to reduce the number of disk accesses. The node in a B-Tree has a huge number of pointers to the children nodes. Thereby reducing the size of the tree. While accessing data from a disk, it makes sense to read an entire block of data and store it into a node of a tree. B-Tree nodes are designed such that the entire block of data (page) fits into it. It is commonly used in databases and file systems.

**B-Tree of minimum degree d** has the following properties:

1. All the leaf nodes must be at the same level.
2. A B-tree defines a degree 'd'. The value of 'd' is the disk size.
3. All nodes except the root must have at least (ceiling)([d-1]/2) keys and a maximum of d-1 keys. The root may contain a minimum of 1 key.
4. If the root node is a non-leaf node, then it must have at least 2 children.
5. A non-leaf node with N keys must have an (N+1) number of children.
6. All the key values within a node must be in Ascending Order.
7. All keys of a node are sorted in ascending order. The child between two keys, K1 and K2 contain all keys in the range from K1 and K2.

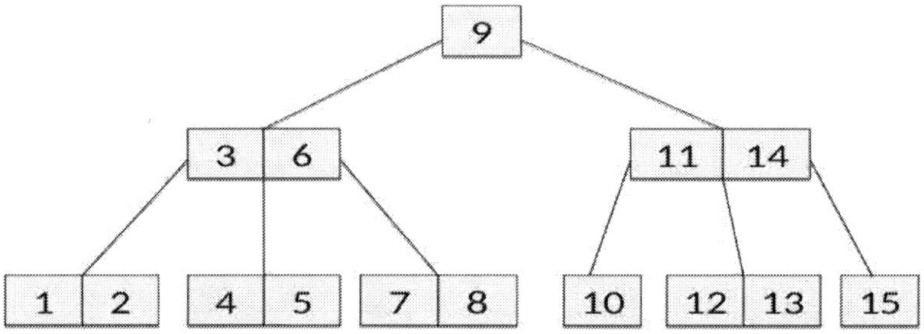


| B-Tree | Average-Case | Worst Case |
|---|---|---|
| Space complexity | O(n) | O(n) |
| Time complexity search | O(log(n)) | O(log(n)) |
| Time complexity insert | O(log(n)) | O(log(n)) |
| Time complexity delete | O(log(n)) | O(log(n)) |

## Insertion

To insert a new value takes the following steps:

1 Use search to find the leaf node on which new value will be added.

2 Add a new value to this node in the appropriate place among the values already present in the node.

3 If the number of values after the addition of the new value is less than max, then we are done.

4 If the number of values after addition is equal to max, then the node is split into three parts. The first median index is calculated. The nodes at the left of the median are made left child. The nodes at the right of the median are added to another node. The median value is added to the parent as a key. Then the newly created node makes another child of the parent by doing the appropriate shifting.

5 If after the median is added to the parent and parent node has less than the max number of allowed keys, then we are done.

6 If after the median is added to the parent and parent node has reached the max number of allowed keys, then again it is split into three. This process is repeated until the root itself has reached the max.

7 If a root has max nodes, then it is again split, and its median will become the new root.

Below are the steps of the creation of B-Tree by adding value from 1 to 7.

| | | | |
|---|---|---|---|
| 1 |  | Insert 1 to the tree. | Stable |
| 2 |  | Insert 2 to the tree. | Stable |
| 3 |  | Insert 3 to the tree. | Intermediate |
| 4 | 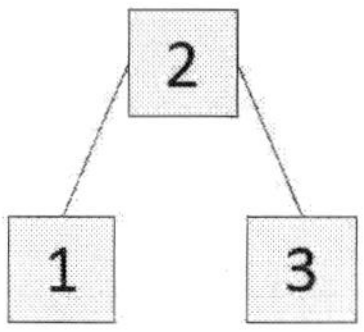 | The new node is created and data is distributed. | Stable |
| 5 | 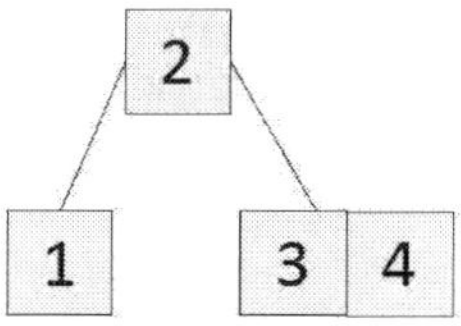 | Insert 4 to the tree. | Stable |
| 6 | 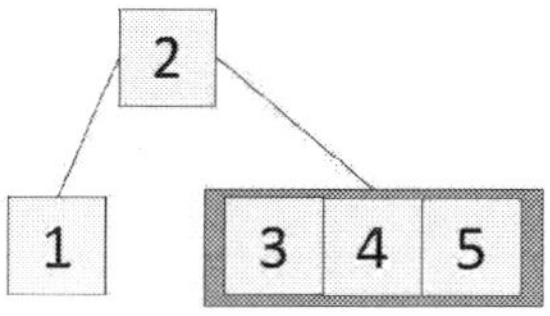 | Insert 5 to the tree. | Intermediate |
| 7 | 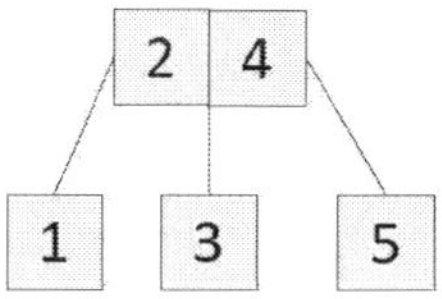 | The node is created and data is distributed. | Stable |
| 8 | 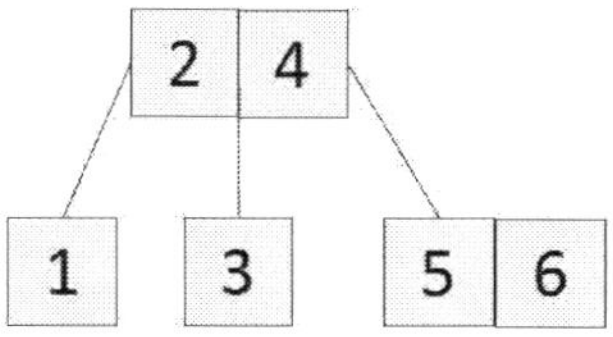 | Insert 6 to the tree. | Stable |
| 9 | 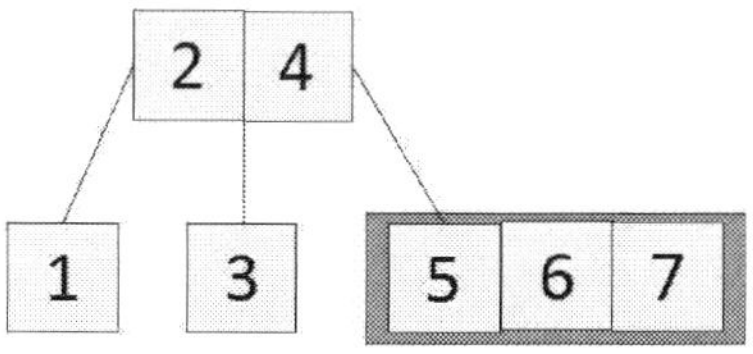 | Insert 7 to the tree. New node is created and data is distributed. | Intermediate |
| 10 | 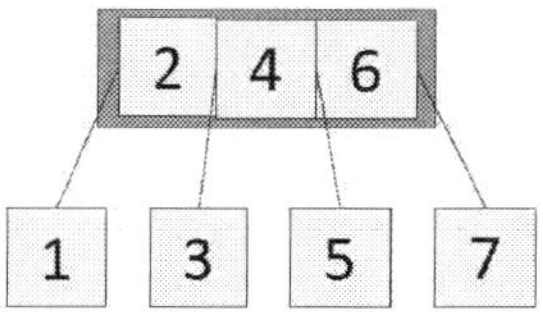 | After rearranging the intermediate node, still, another intermediate node has more keys than the maximum number of allowed keys. | Intermediate |

| | | | |
|---|---|---|---|
| 11 | 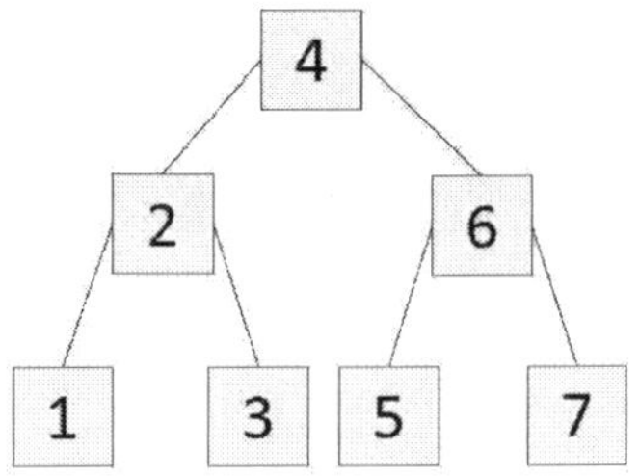 | A new node is created and data is distributed. The height of the tree has increased. | Stable |

**Note**: 2-3 trees is a B-tree of degree three.

## Deletion

To delete a new value takes the following steps:

1 Search for the value that needs to be deleted.

2 If the value is in a leaf node, then delete it from the node.

- If the number of values is less than minimum, then rebalancing is performed.
- If a deficient node's left sibling has extra values, then the value of the parent is added to the deficient node and the last value of the left sibling is added to the parent. This makes the tree balanced.
- If a deficient node's right sibling has extra value, then the value of the parent is added to the deficient node and the first value of the right sibling is added to the parent. This makes the tree balanced.
- If both immediate siblings of a deficient node have a minimum number of elements, then merge with the left or right sibling. This makes the tree balanced.

3 If the deleted value is from an internal node.

- If the left child has more than the minimum number of elements, then copy the last element to the root. This makes the tree balanced.
- If the right child has more than the minimum number of elements, then copy the first element to the root. This makes the tree balanced.
- If both the right and left child have a minimum number of elements. Then merge both the children. This leads to the removal of one of the keys from the parent node. This can make the parent node with the number of elements less than the minimum number of elements.
- If the parent has at least a minimum number of elements, then we are done.
- If the parent has less than the minimum number of elements, so again step 3 will be applied. This merging and rebalancing can continue till the root.
- The merging and rebalancing lead to the root, and if the root has no elements then the root will point to the first child of the root.

| | | |
|---|---|---|
| 1 | 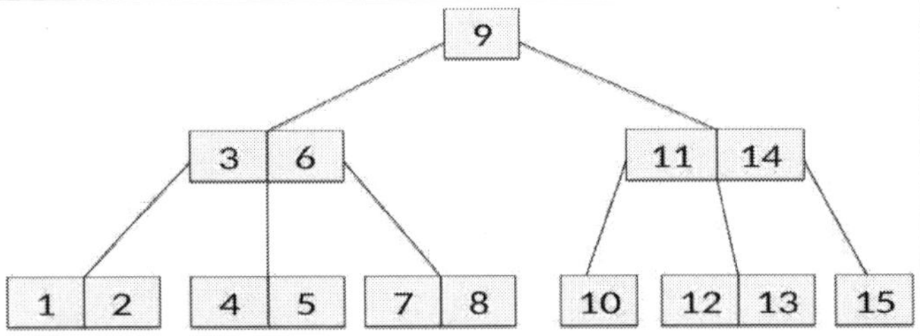 | Node with value 5 is deleted. Node is a leaf node, and it contains more than the minimum number of values in leaf node, so 5 is deleted and done. |

| | | |
|---|---|---|
| 2 | 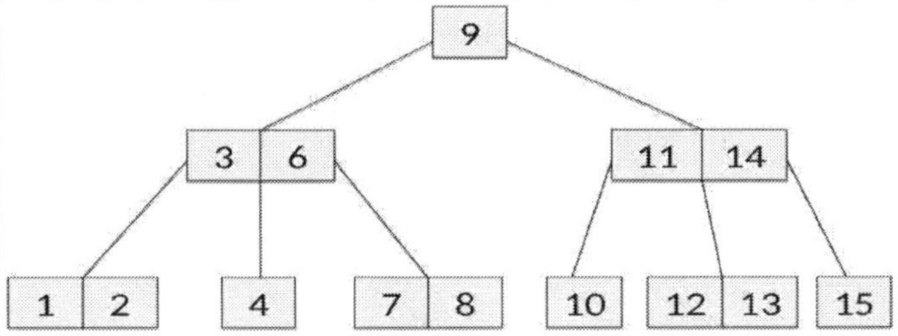 | We want to delete value 4. It is a leaf node but has a minimum number of keys, so it will borrow from the left cousin. |
| 3 | 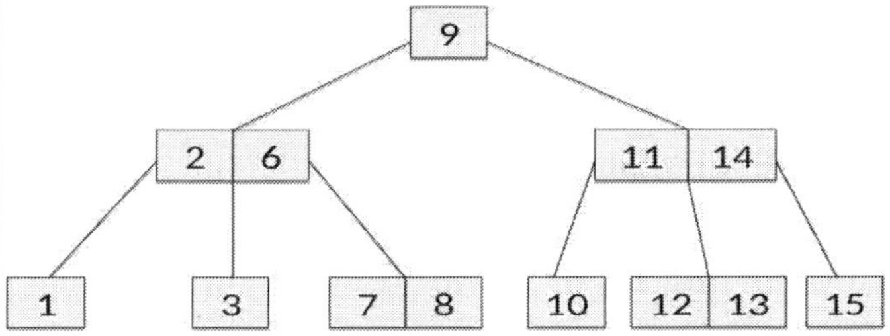 | Now we want to delete 3. It is a leaf node and has a minimum number of keys, so it will borrow from the right cousin. |
| 4 | 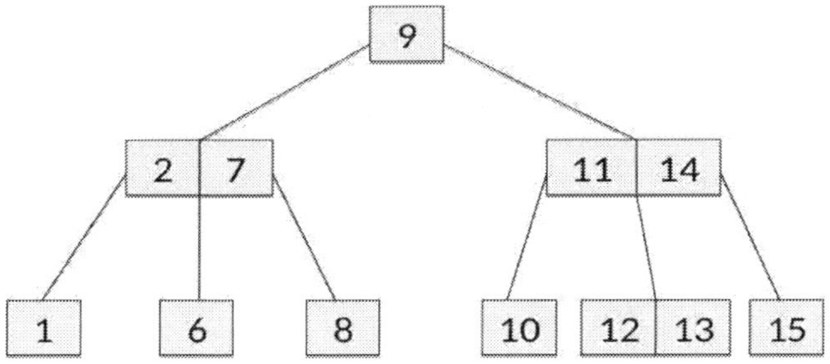 | Now we want to delete 6. It is in leaf nodes, and leaf nodes contain a minimum number of keys. And it can't borrow from its left or right cousin, so it will merge with any of the available cousins. In our case, our cousin left. |
| 5 | 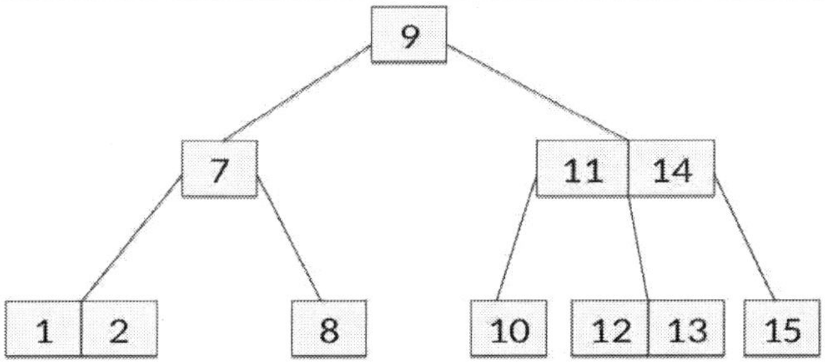 | Now we want to delete 7. It is inside a non-leaf node. Its left child has more than the minimum number of keys, so 7 will be replaced by in-order predecessor 2. And 2 will be deleted from the left sub-tree. |
| 6 | 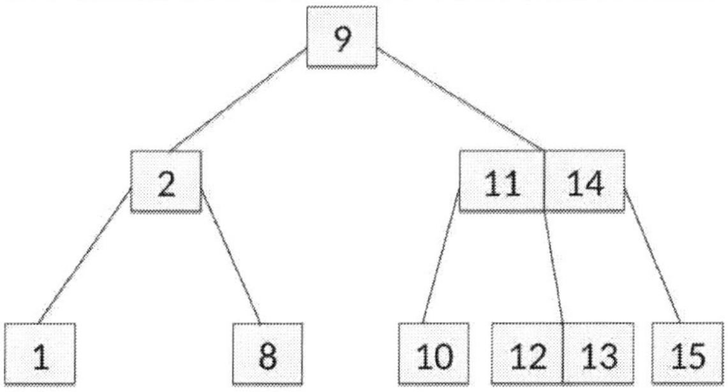 | Now we want to delete 11. It is inside a non-leaf node. Its left child has a minimum number of keys. Its right child has more than the minimum number of keys. So 11 will be replaced by in-order successor 12. And 12 is deleted from the right subtree. |
| 7 | 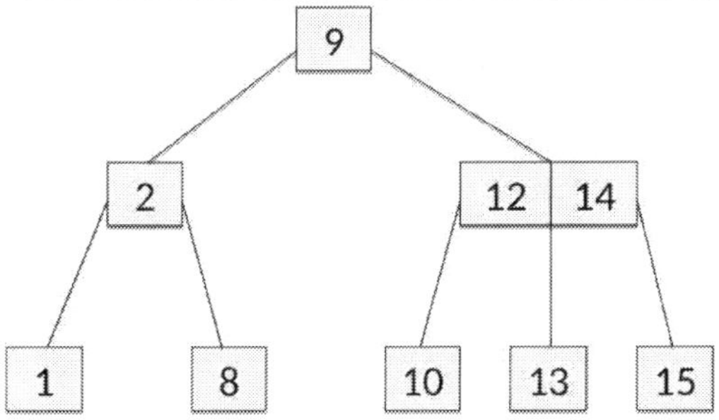 | Now we want to delete 12. The left and right child of 12 contains the minimum number of keys. So they will be merged and then 12 is removed. |

| | | |
|---|---|---|
| 8 | 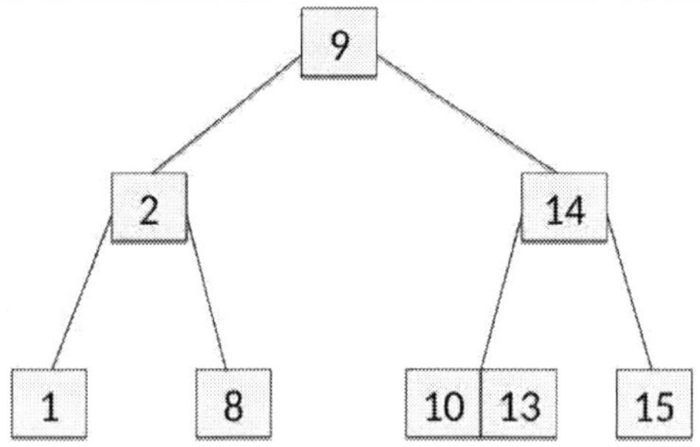 | Now we want to delete 2. The right and left children have a minimum number of keys, so merge will happen. |
| 9 | 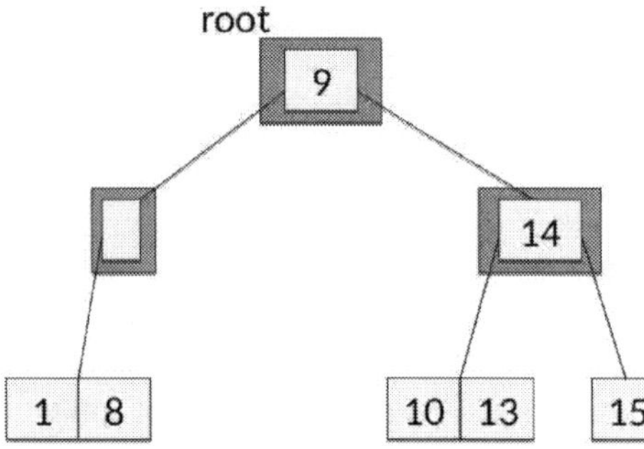 | After the merge, the parent node will have less than the minimum number of keys. Then it will try to borrow a key from its sibling. But siblings also have a minimum number of keys. So the parent will be merged.<br>(Intermediate state) |
| 10 | 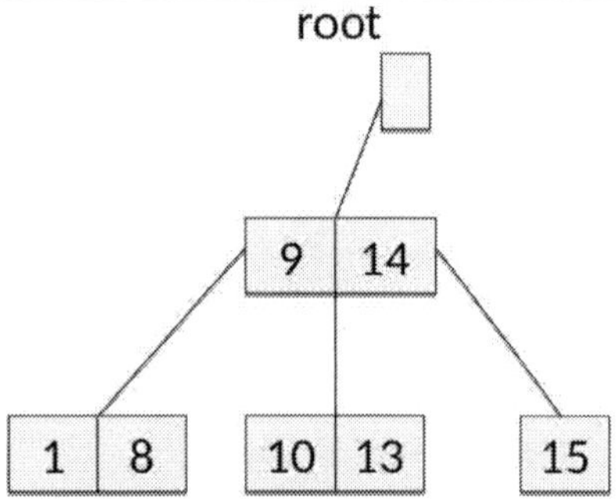 | This creates again an empty root node. So the root will point to the first child of the root node.<br>(Intermediate state) |
| 11 | 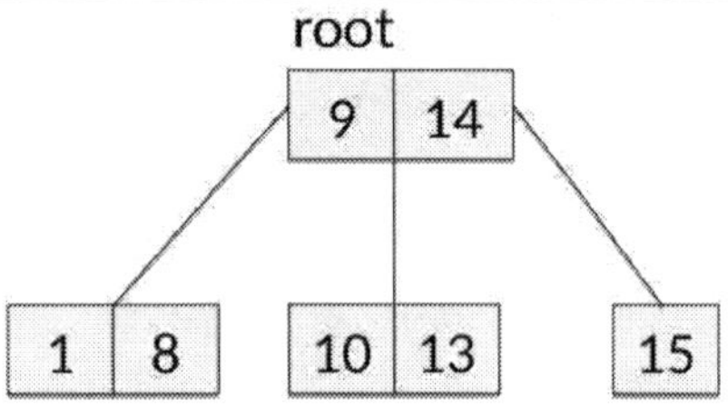 | Btree after root rearrangement. |

## B+ Tree

B+ Tree is a variant of B-Tree. The B+ Tree stores record only at the leaf nodes. The internal nodes store keys. These keys are used for insertion, deletion, and search. The rules of splitting and merging of nodes are the same as B-Tree.

| b-order B+ tree | Average-Case | Worst Case |
|---|---|---|
| Space complexity | $O(n)$ | $O(n)$ |
| Time complexity search | $O(\log_b(n))$ | $O(\log_b(n))$ |
| Time complexity insert | $O(\log_b(n))$ | $O(\log_b(n))$ |
| Time complexity delete | $O(\log_b(n))$ | $O(\log_b(n))$ |

Below is the B+ Tree created by adding value from 1 to 5.

| | | |
|---|---|---|
| 1 |  | Value 1 is inserted into the leaf node. |
| 2 | 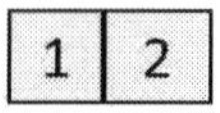 | Value 2 is inserted into the leaf node. |
| 3 | 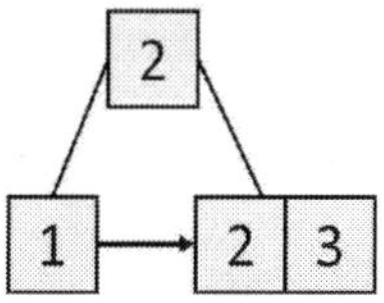 | Value 3 is inserted into the leaf node. Content of the leaf node passed the maximum number of elements. Therefore, the node is split and an intermediate/key node is created. |
| 4 | 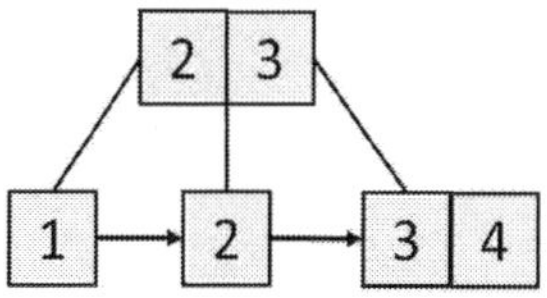 | Value 4 is further inserted into the leaf node. Which further splits the leaf node. |
| 5 | 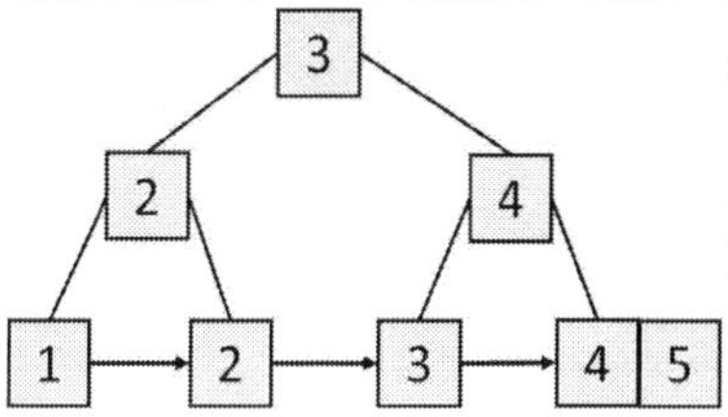 | Value 5 is added to the leaf node. The number of nodes in the leaf passed the maximum number of nodes limit that it could contain, so it is divided into 2. One more key is added to the intermediate node, which also makes it pass the maximum number of nodes it can contain, and finally divided, and a new node is created. |

## Threaded Binary Tree

Binary trees have a lot of wasted space. If the tree has n elements then it will have n+1 null pointers. These null pointers memory can be used to get faster inorder traversal of trees. These pointers store reference to the next node in an inorder traversal. These linkages are called thread in the Threaded Binary Tree. To know if a pointer is an actual link or a thread, a boolean flag is kept for each pointer

**A Threaded Binary Tree** is a binary tree in which every node that does not have a right child has a link (thread) to its inorder successor. And every node that does not have a left child has a link to its inorder predecessor.

**Advantages of using Threaded Binary Tree:**

1 Threading in the TBT makes inorder traversal of trees faster.
2 Inorder traversal of TBT is done using a single loop, It avoids recursion, which uses the system stack and consumes a lot of memory and time.

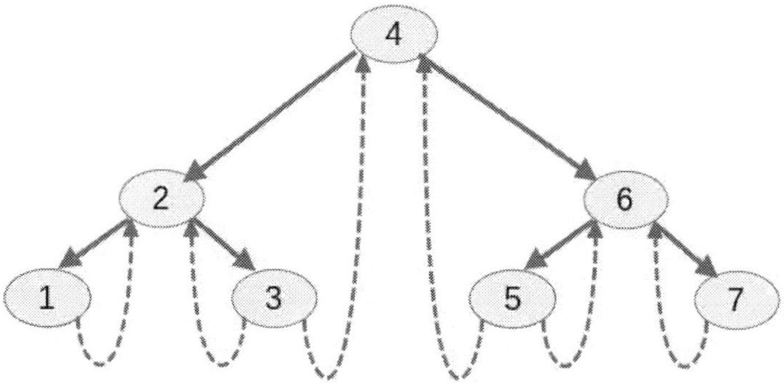

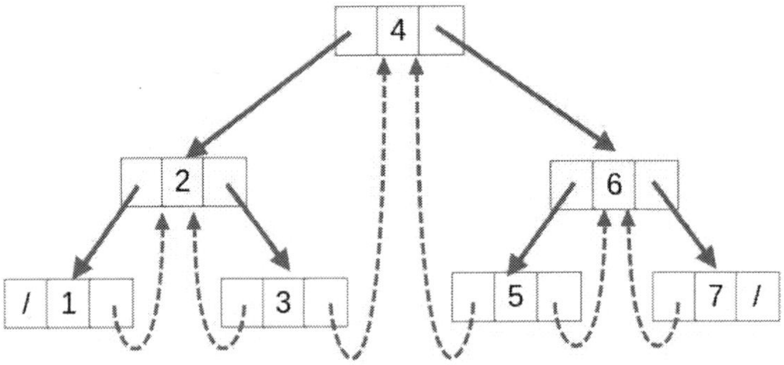


Threaded Tree traversal:

1. Mark the root of the tree as the current node.
2. Traverse to the left most node of the current node. Print it.
3. Follow the right thread of the node. Print it. And continue.
4. Follow the right child of the node. And go to step 2.

```
function inOrder(n)
    cur = leftmost(n)
    while cur != null
        print cur
        if cur.rThread
            cur = cur.right
        else
            cur = leftmost(cur.right)
```

```
function leftMost(cur)
    if cur == null
        return null

    while cur.left != null
        cur = cur.left

    return cur
```

## Uses of Trees

Applications of Trees are:

1. Implementing the directory and file system
2. Used in decision-making in games like chess.
3. Parsing of XML expressions uses trees.
4. Parsing syntax of programming language in compilers.

## Exercise

1. Construct a tree given its in-order and pre-order traversal strings.
   - inorder: 1 2 3 4 5 6 7 8 9 10
   - pre-order: 6 4 2 1 3 5 8 7 9 10

2. Construct a tree given its in-order and post-order traversal strings.
   - inorder: 1 2 3 4 5 6 7 8 9 10
   - post-order: 1 3 2 5 4 7 10 9 8 6

3. Write a delete node function in the Binary tree.

4. Write a function print depth-first in a binary tree without using system stack
   Hint: you may want to keep another element to tree nodes, like the visited flag.

5. Check whether a given Binary Tree is a Perfect binary tree or not. The perfect binary tree- is a type of full binary tree in which each non-leaf node has exactly two child nodes.

6. Isomorphic: two trees are isomorphic if they have the same shape, it does not matter what the value is. Write a program to find if two given trees are isomorphic or not.

7. Check whether a given Binary Tree is Complete or not.In a complete binary tree, every level except the last one is filled. All nodes on the left are filled first, then the right one.

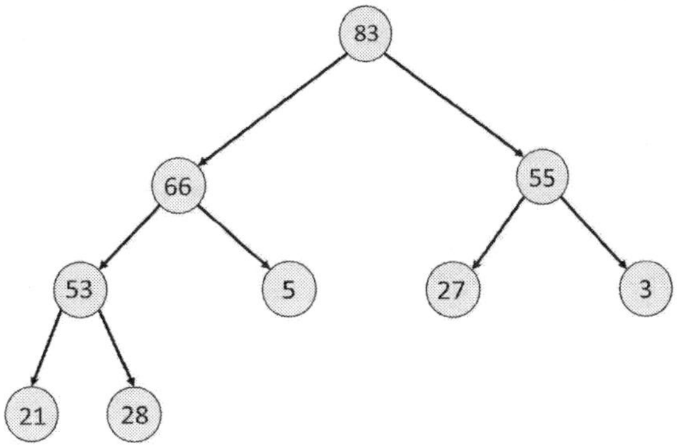


8. Check whether a given Binary Tree is a Full/ Strictly binary tree or not. The full binary tree is a binary tree in which each node has zero or two children.

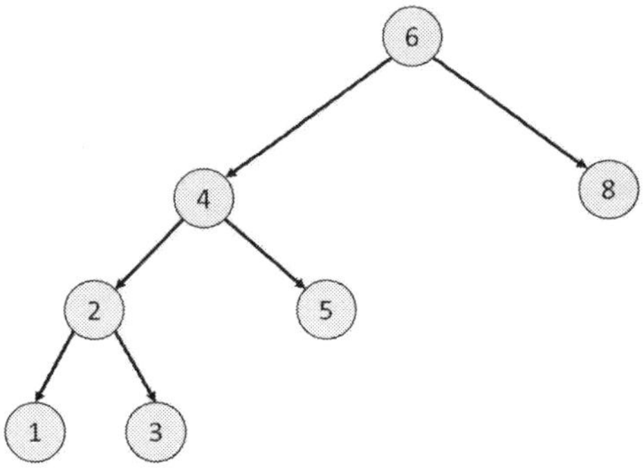


9. Check whether a given Binary Tree is a Height-balanced Binary Tree or not. A height-balanced binary tree is a binary tree such that the left & right subtrees for any given node differ in height by not more than one

10. The worst-case runtime Complexity of building a BST with n nodes
    - O(n^2)
    - O(n * log n)
    - O(n)
    - O(log(n))

11. The worst-case runtime Complexity of insertion into a BST with n nodes is
    - O(n^2)
    - O(n * log n)

- o O(n)
- o O(log(n))

12. The worst-case runtime Complexity of a search of a value in a BST with n nodes is:
    - o O(n^2)
    - o O(n * log n)
    - o O(n)
    - o O(log(n))

13. Which of the following traversals always gives the sorted sequence of the elements in a BST?
    - o Preorder
    - o Ignored
    - o Postorder
    - o Undefined

14. The height of a Binary Search Tree with n nodes in the worst case?
    - o O(n * log n)
    - o O(n)
    - o O(log(n))
    - o O(1)

15. Try to optimise the above solution to give a DFS traversal without recursion using some stack or queue.

16. This is an open exercise for the readers. Every algorithm that is solved using recursion (system stack) can also be solved using a user-defined or library defined stack. So, try to figure out all algorithms that use recursion and try to figure out how you will do this using a user-defined stack.

17. In a binary tree, print the nodes in zigzag order. In the first level, nodes are printed in the left to right order. In the second level, nodes are printed in right to left and the third level again in the order left to right.
    Hint: Use two stacks. Pop from the first stack and push into another stack. Swap the stacks alternatively.

18. Find the nth smallest element in a binary search tree.
    Hint: Nth inorder in a binary tree.

19. Find the floor value of the key that is inside a BST.

20. Find the Ceil value of the key, which is inside a BST.

# CHAPTER 10: PRIORITY QUEUE / HEAPS

## Introduction

A Priority-Queue, also known as heap, is a variant of the queue. Items are removed from the beginning of the queue. However, in a Priority-Queue, the logical ordering of objects is determined by their priority. The highest priority item is at the front of the Priority-Queue. When you add an item to the Priority-Queue, the new item moves to its proper position according to its priority. A Priority-Queue is a very important data structure. Priority-Queue is used in various graph algorithms like Prim's Algorithm and Dijkstra's algorithm. Priority-Queue is also used in the timer implementation etc.

A Priority-Queue is implemented using Heap. A Heap data structure is an array of elements that can be observed as a complete binary tree.

A heap is a binary tree that satisfies the following properties:

1. The tree is a complete binary tree. A heap is a complete binary tree, so the height of the tree with N nodes is always **O(log(n))**.
2. Heap satisfies the heap ordering property. In max-heap, the parent's value is greater than or equal to its children's value. In min-heap, the parent's value is less than or equal to its children's value.

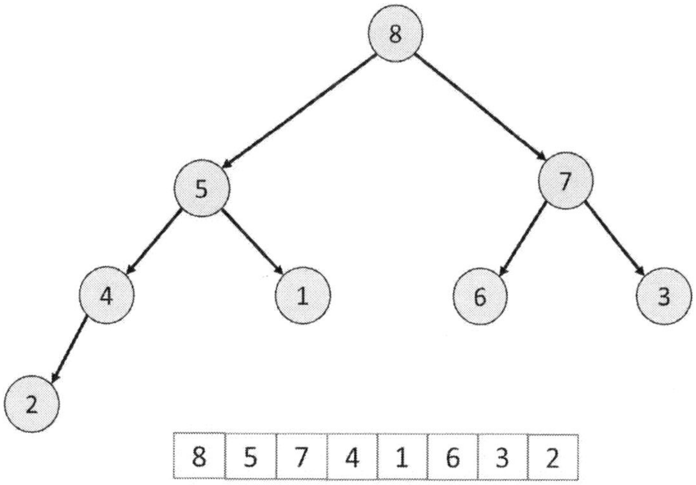


Max Heap

A heap is not a sorted data structure and can be regarded as partially ordered. As you can see in the picture, there is no relationship among nodes at any given level, even among the siblings.

Heap is implemented using an array. Moreover, because the heap is a complete binary tree, the left child of a parent (at position x) is the node that is found in position (2x+1) in the array. Similarly, the right child of the parent is at position (2x+2) in the array. To find the parent of any node in the heap, we can simply divide. In a given index y of a node, the parent index will be (y-1)/2.

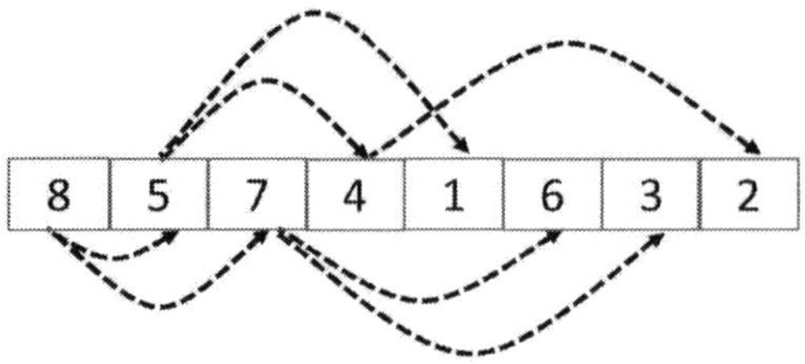


Parent-Child relationship in heap array.

## Types of Heap

There are two types of heap and the type depends on the ordering of the elements. The ordering can be done in two ways: Min-Heap and Max-Heap.

### Max-Heap

Max-Heap: the value of each node is less than or equal to the value of its parent, with the largest-value element at the root.

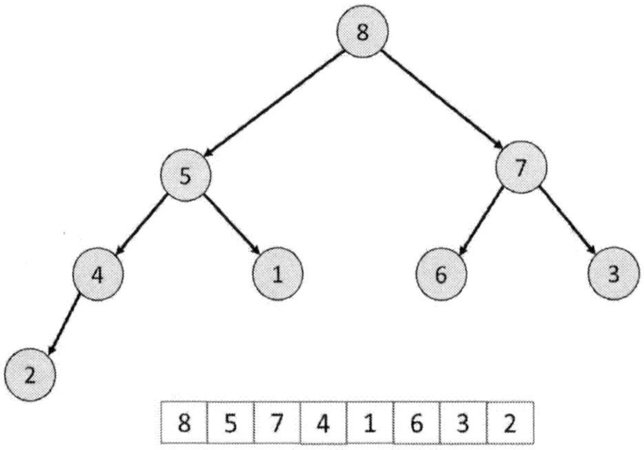


Max Heap

Max-Heap Operations

| | |
|---|---|
| Insert | O(log(n)) |
| DeleteMax | O(log(n)) |
| Remove | O(log(n)) |
| findMax | O(1) |

### Min-Heap

Min-Heap: the value of each node is greater than or equal to the value of its parent, with the minimum-value element at the root.

Use it whenever you need quick access to the smallest item because that item will always be at the root of the tree or the first element in the array. However, the remainder of the array is kept partially sorted. Thus, instant access is only possible for the smallest item.

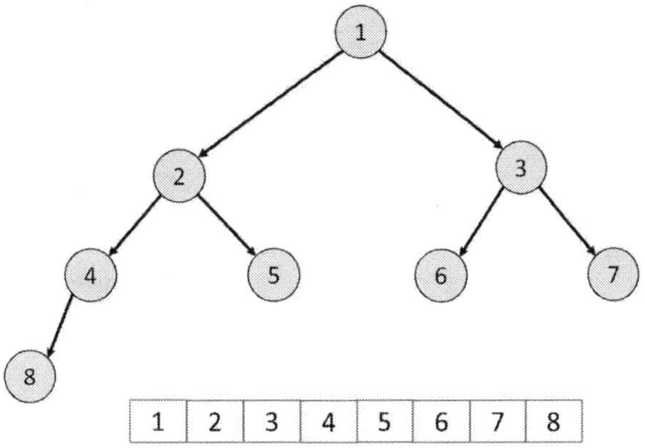


Min Heap

Min-Heap Operations

| | |
|---|---|
| Insert | O(log(n)) |
| DeleteMin | O(log(n)) |
| Remove | O(log(n)) |
| findMin | O(1) |

## Heap ADT Operations

The basic operations of the binary heap are as follows:

| | | |
|---|---|---|
| Binary Heap | Creates a new empty binary heap | O(1) |
| Insert | Adding a new element to the heap | O(log(n)) |
| DeleteMax | Deletes the maximum element from the heap. | O(log(n)) |
| findMax | Finds the maximum element in the heap. | O(1) |
| isEmpty | Returns true if the heap is empty else return false | O(1) |
| Size | Returns the number of elements in the heap. | O(1) |
| BuildHeap | Builds a new heap from the array of elements | O(log(n)) |

## Operation on Heap

Before looking in detail at how to Initialise a heap, add or remove elements into it we need to understand two important operations involved in the heap. These operations are used to restore heap order property when a single element is out of its position.

There are two cases are:

1. When a node (parent node) is not following heap property with its children. This is resolved by the **procolateDown()** operation, in which the parent node value is swapped with one of the child values and heap property is restored recursively.

2. When a node (child node) is not following heap property with its parent. This is resolved by **percolateUp()** or **bubbleUp()** operation, in which child node value is swapped with parent node value and heap property is restored recursively.

**Example 10.1:** Below is the code of percolateUp and percolateDown operation.

```
private void percolateDown(int parent) {
    int lChild = 2 * parent + 1;
    int rChild = lChild + 1;
    int child = -1;
    int temp;
    if (lChild < size) {
        child = lChild;
    }

    if (rChild < size && compare(arr, lChild, rChild)) {
        child = rChild;
    }

    if (child != -1 && compare(arr, parent, child)) {
        temp = arr[parent];
        arr[parent] = arr[child];
        arr[child] = temp;
        percolateDown(child);
    }
}

private void percolateUp(int child) {
    int parent = (child - 1) / 2;
    int temp;

    if (parent >= 0 && compare(arr, parent, child)) {
        temp = arr[child];
        arr[child] = arr[parent];
        arr[parent] = temp;
        percolateUp(parent);
    }
}
```

Heap is represented using a class. The following elements of heap class are:

1. "arr" is used to store heaps.
2. "`size`", which is the number of elements in the heap.
3. "`compare`" will be used to create Min-Heap or Max-Heap

**Example 10.2:**

```
public class Heap {
    private static final int CAPACITY = 32;
    private int size; // Number of elements in Heap
    private int[] arr; // The Heap array
    boolean isMinHeap;

    // Creating empty heap.
    public Heap(boolean isMin) {
        arr = new int[CAPACITY];
        size = 0;
        isMinHeap = isMin;
    }

    boolean compare(int[] arr, int first, int second) {
        if (isMinHeap)
            return (arr[first] - arr[second]) > 0; // Min heap compare
```

```
        else
            return (arr[first] - arr[second]) < 0; // Max heap compare
    }

    public boolean isEmpty() {
        return (size == 0);
    }

    public int length() {
        return size;
    }

    public int peek() {
        if (isEmpty()) {
            throw new IllegalStateException();
        }
        return arr[0];
    }
    // Other Methods.
}
```

**Analysis:** Empty heap is created by creating an empty array. Since the heap is empty, we do not need any heapify operations.

1. isEmpty() function returns true if the heap is empty or else returns false.
2. size() function returns the number of elements in the heap.
3. peek() function will return the highest priority element from the heap without deleting it.

## Create Heap from an array

**Heapify** is an important algorithm for converting an array into heap.

The various steps are:

1. Values are present in the array.
2. Starting from the middle of the array, move down towards the start of the array. At each step, compare parent value with its left child and right child. In addition, restore the heap property by shifting the parent value with its largest-value child. Such that the parent value will always be greater than or equal to the left child and the right child.
3. For all elements from the middle of the array to the start of the array. We make comparisons and shift until we reach the leaf nodes of the heap.

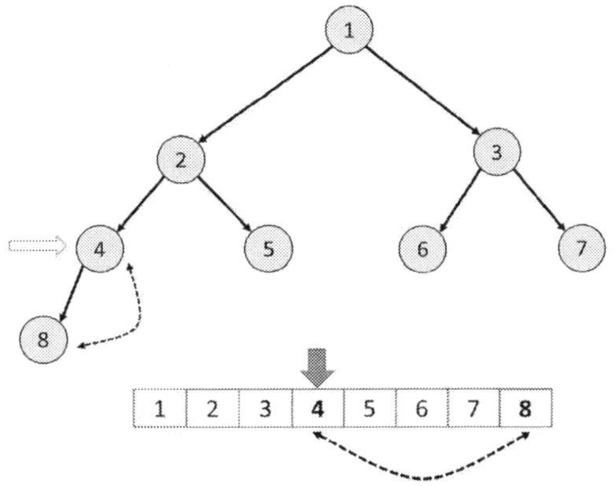


Given an array as input to create a heap function. The value of index i is compared with the value of its children nodes that are at index ( i*2 + 1 ) and ( i*2 + 2 ). Middle of list N/2, that is index 3, is compared with index 7. If the children node value is greater than the parent node, then the value will be swapped.

| | |
|---|---|
| 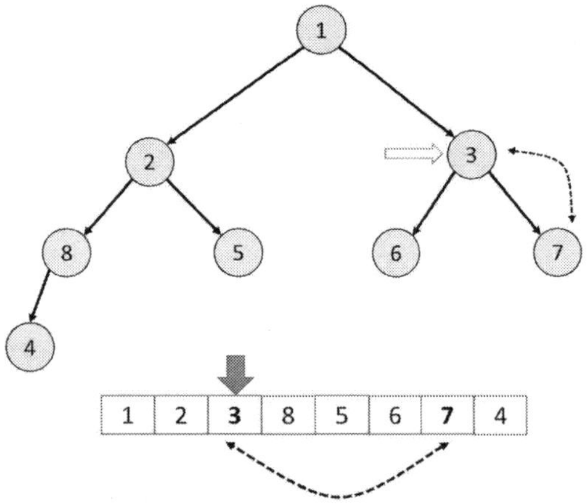 | Similarly, the value of index 2 is compared with indexes 5 and 6. The largest of all the values is 7 and will be swapped with the value at index 2. |
| 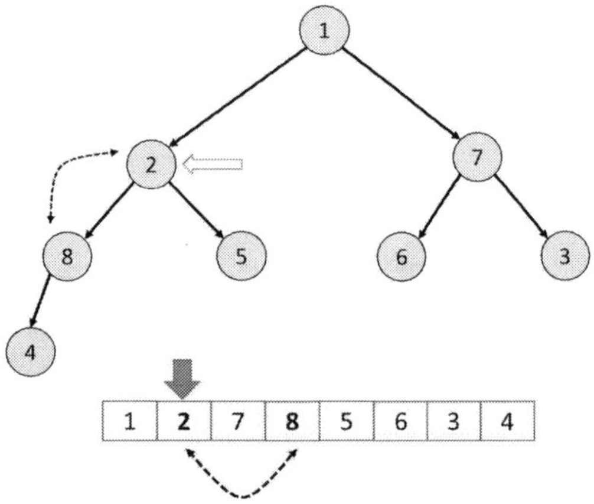 | Similarly, the value of index 1 is compared with index 3 and 4 The largest of all the values is 8 which will be swapped with the value of index 1. |
| 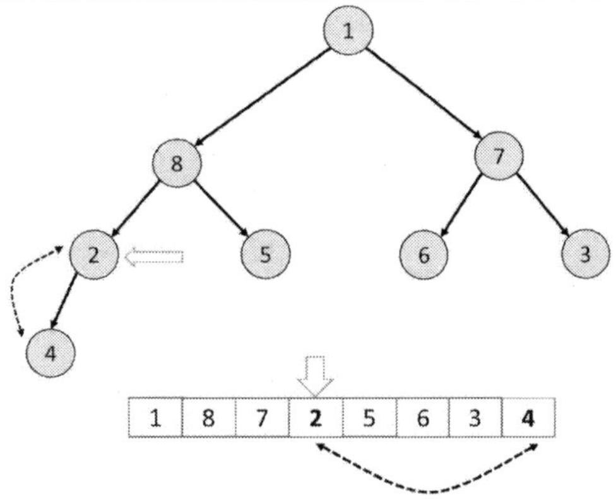 | The percolate down function is used to subsequently adjust the value replaced in the previous step by comparing it with its children nodes. |
| 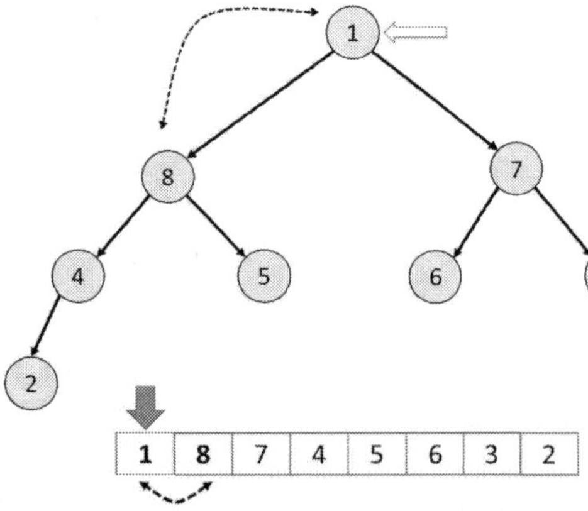 | Now the value of index 0 is compared with index 1 and 2. 8 is the largest value, so it is swapped with the value at index 0. |

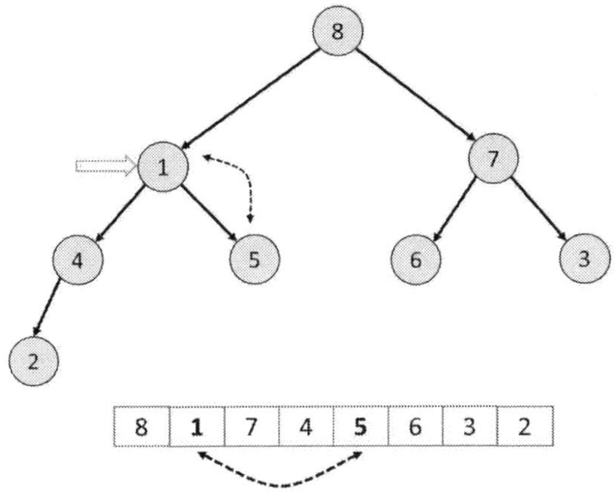


The percolate down function is used to further compare the value at index 1 with its children nodes at index 3 and 4.

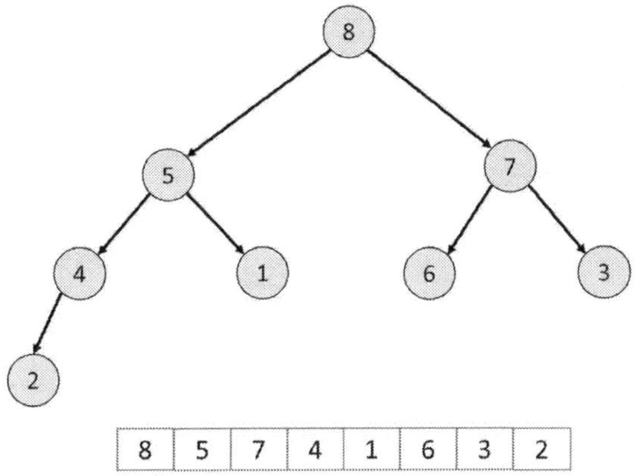


In the end, a Max-Heap is created.

**Example 10.3:** `Creating heap from input array.`

```
public Heap(int[] array, boolean isMin) {
    size = array.length;
    arr = array;
    isMinHeap = isMin;

    // Build Heap operation over array
    for (int i = (size / 2); i >= 0; i--) {
        percolateDown(i);
    }
}
```

**Analysis:** Heap can be initialised by passing an array to it. Heapify() function is called over the array to make it heap.

Time Complexity of the build heap is **O(N)**. The number of comparisons is related to the height of the node. Total number of comparison will be represented as: (1*n/4) + (2*n/8)+ (3*n/16)……((h-1)*1) == N Where "h" is the height of the heap.

## Enqueue / add

1. Add the new element at the end of the array. This keeps the values as a complete binary tree, but it might no longer be a heap, since the new element might have a value greater than its parent's value.
2. Swap the new element with its parent until it has a value greater than its parent's value.

3. Step 2 will be terminated when the new element reaches the root or when the new element's parent has a value greater than or equal to the new element's value.

Let us take an example of the Max-Heap created in the above example.

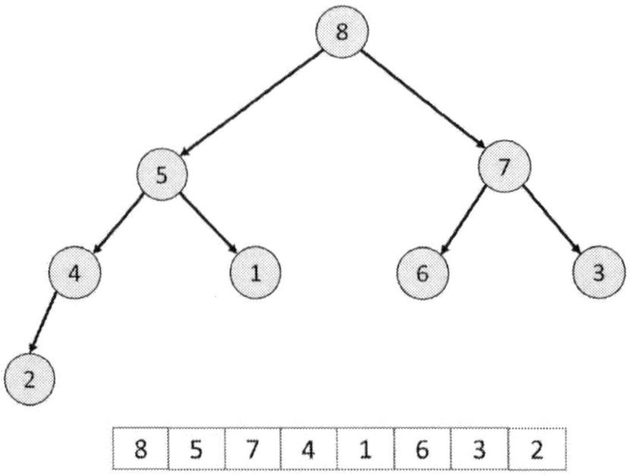


Let us take an example by inserting an element with the value of 9 to the heap. The element is added to the end of the Heap array. Now the value will be percolated up by comparing it with the parent. The value is added to index 8 and its parent will be (N-1)/2 = index 3.

| | |
|---|---|
| 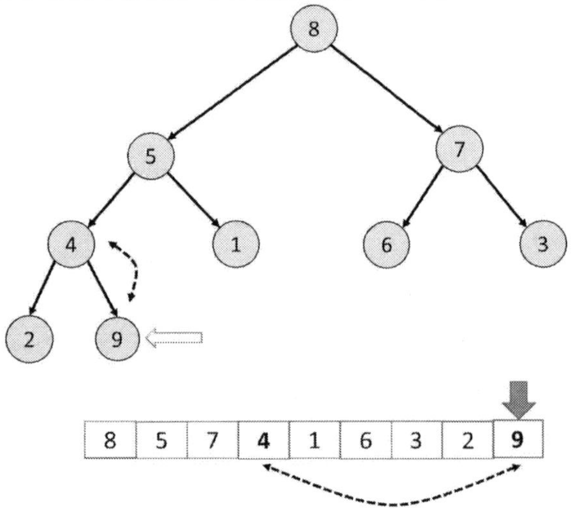 | New value 9 was added to the end of the array. Since the value 9 is greater than 4 it will be swapped with it. |
| 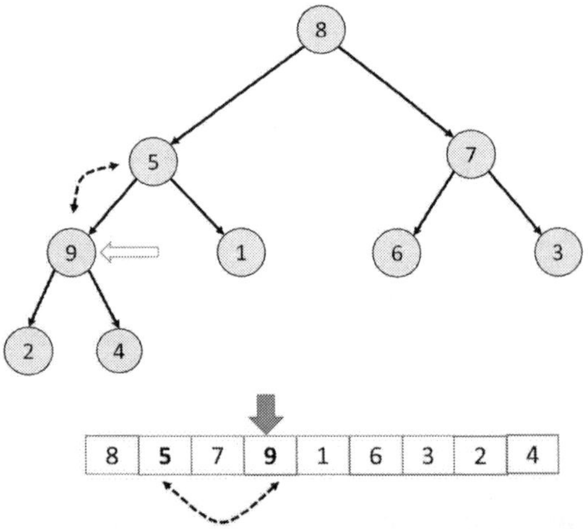 | Percolate up is used, and the value is moved up until heap property is satisfied. |

| | |
|---|---|
| 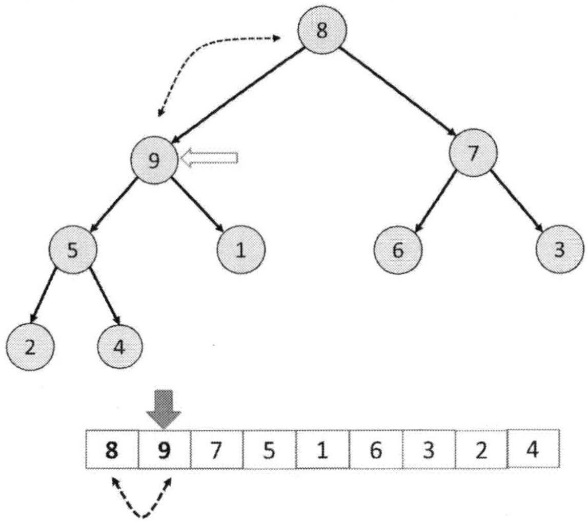 | Now the value of index 1 is compared with index 0 and to satisfy heap property it is further swapped. |
| 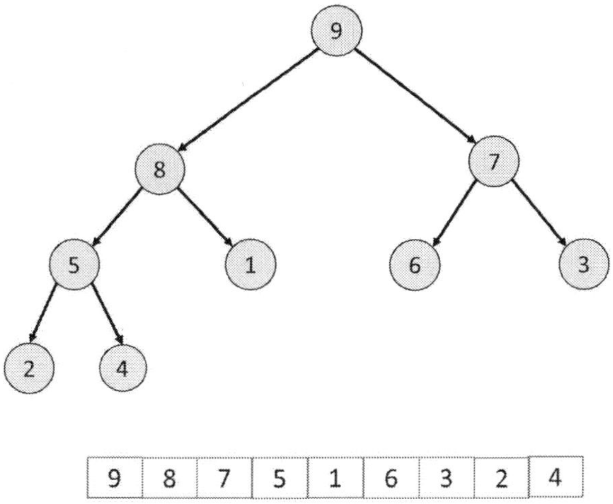 | Now, finally, the Max-Heap is created by inserting a new node. |

**Example 10.4:**

```
public void add(int value) {
    if (size == arr.length) {
        doubleSize();
    }
    arr[size++] = value;
    percolateUp(size - 1);
}

private void doubleSize() {
    int[] old = arr;
    arr = new int[arr.length * 2];
    System.arraycopy(old, 0, arr, 0, size);
}
```

**Analysis:** We check if the heap is full. In case when the heap is already full, then we create another array of twice capacity. Copy the content of the heap into it. Then add the new element to the heap, and then use the percolateUp() operation to restore the heap property.

The time complexity of insertion in heap is O(log(n))

## Dequeue / remove

- Copy the value at the root of the heap to the variable that will be used to return that value.
- Copy the last element of the heap to the root, and then reduce the size of the heap by 1. This element is called the "out-of-place" element.
- Restore heap property by swapping the out-of-place element with its greatest-value child. Repeat this process until the out-of-place element reaches a leaf, or it has a value that is greater or equal to all its children.
- Return the answer that was saved in Step 1.

| | |
|---|---|
| 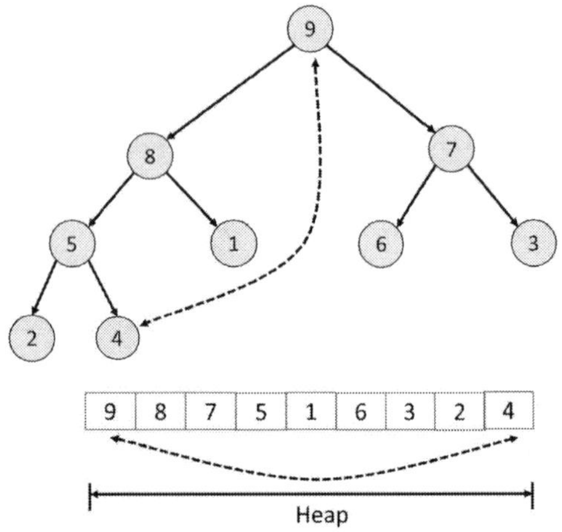 | Value at the start and end of the heap are swapped. Heap size is reduced by one. Heap property is disturbed, so we need to percolate down by comparing nodes with its children nodes and restoring heap property. |
| 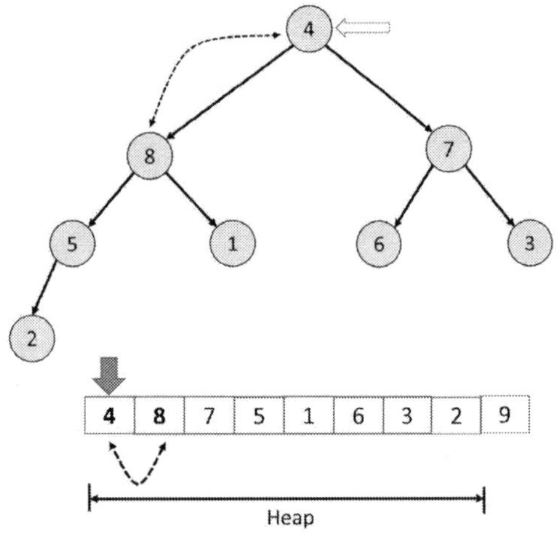 | Percolate down is continued by comparing with its children nodes. |
| 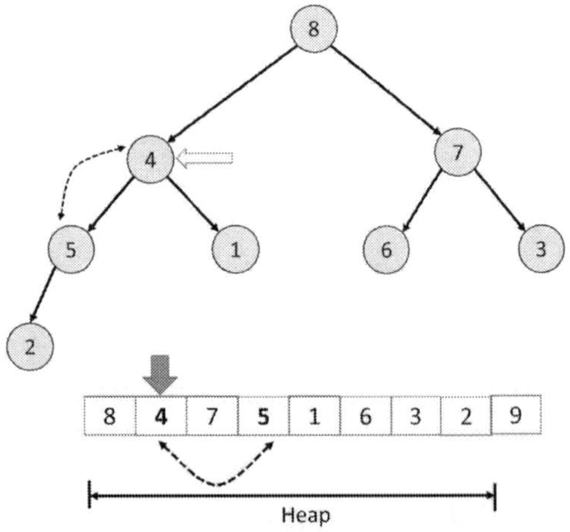 | Percolate down |

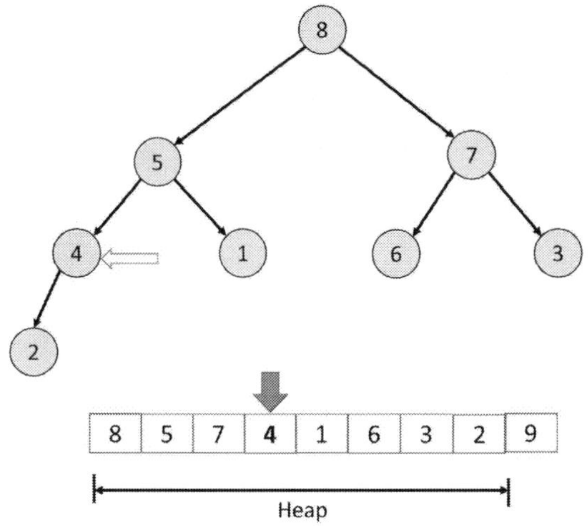


Percolate down Complete

**Example 10.5:**
```
public int remove() {
    if (isEmpty()) {
        throw new IllegalStateException();
    }

    int value = arr[0];
    arr[0] = arr[size - 1];
    size--;
    percolateDown(0);
    return value;
}
```

**Analysis:** the Value at the top of the heap is swapped with the value at the end of the heap array. The size of the heap is reduced by one and percolateDown is called to restore heap property.
The time complexity of removing elements from the heap is O(log(n)).

## Traversal in Heap

Heaps are not designed to traverse (to find some element) or print content of heap,. They are made to get min or max elements quickly. Still, if you want to traverse a heap, just traverse the array sequentially. Time Complexity of traversal is linear O(n).

**Example 10.6:**
```
public void print() {
    System.out.print("Heap : ");
    for (int i = 0; i < size; i++) {
        System.out.print(arr[i] + " ");
    }
    System.out.println();
}

// Testing code.
public static void main(String[] args)  {
    Heap hp = new Heap(true);
    hp.add(1);
    hp.add(6);
    hp.add(5);
```

```
        hp.add(7);
        hp.add(3);
        hp.add(4);
        hp.add(2);
        hp.print();

        while (!hp.isEmpty())
            System.out.print(hp.remove() + " ");
}
```

**Output:**

```
Heap : 1 3 2 7 6 5 4
1 2 3 4 5 6 7
```

## Deleting Arbiter element from Min-Heap

Again, the heap is not designed to delete an arbitrary element, still if you want to do so. Find the element by linear search in the Heap array. Replace it with the value stored at the end of the Heap value. Reduce the size of the heap by one. Compare the newly inserted value with its parent. If its value is smaller than the parent value, then percolate up. Else if its value is greater than its left and right child then percolate down. Time Complexity is **O(n)**, for searching.

**Example 10.7:**

```
public boolean delete(int value) {
    for (int i = 0; i < size; i++) {
        if (arr[i] == value) {
            arr[i] = arr[size - 1];
            size -= 1;
            percolateUp(i);
            percolateDown(i);
            return true;
        }
    }
    return false;
}
```

## PriorityQueue implementation in Java Collection

Min heap implementation of Priority Queue

**Example 10.8:**

```
import java.util.PriorityQueue;

public class PriorityQueueDemo {
    public static void main(String[] args) {
        PriorityQueue<Integer> pq = new PriorityQueue<Integer>();
        int[] arr = { 1, 2, 10, 8, 7, 3, 4, 6, 5, 9 };
        for (int i : arr)
            pq.add(i);

        System.out.println("Heap Array: " + pq);
        while (pq.isEmpty() == false)
            System.out.print(pq.remove() + " ");
    }
}
```

**Output**
```
Heap Array: [1, 2, 3, 5, 7, 10, 4, 8, 6, 9]
1 2 3 4 5 6 7 8 9 10
```

Max heap implementation of Priority Queue.

**Example 10.9:**
```
PriorityQueue<Integer> pq=new priorityQueue<Integer> (Collections.reverseOrder());
```

**Output**
```
Heap Array: [10, 9, 4, 6, 8, 2, 3, 1, 5, 7]
10 9 8 7 6 5 4 3 2 1
```

## Heap Sort

1. Use the create heap function to build a Max-Heap from the given list of elements. This operation will take O(N) time.
2. Swap the max value at the root of the heap and the value to the end of the heap at location arr[size-1]. Reduce the heap size by 1.
3. Restoration, this element at the root of the heap is "out-of-place" element. Restore heap property by swapping the out-of-place element with its greatest-value child. Repeat this process until the out-of-place element reaches a leaf, or it has a value that is greater or equal to all its children
4. Repeat this operation 2 and 3 until there is just one element in the heap.

Let us take an example of the heap that we had already created at the start of the chapter. Heapsort is an algorithm that starts by creating a heap of the given list, which is done in linear time. Then at each step, the head of the heap is swapped with the end of the heap and the heap size is reduced by 1. Then percolate down is used to restore the heap property. Moreover, the same is done multiple times until the heap contains just one element. Total Time-complexity **O(n.log(n))**

| | |
|---|---|
| 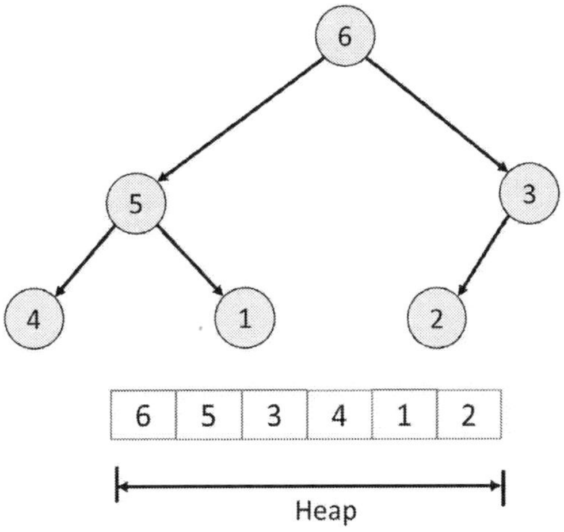 | Max-Heap is created from the input array. |

<table>
<tr>
<td>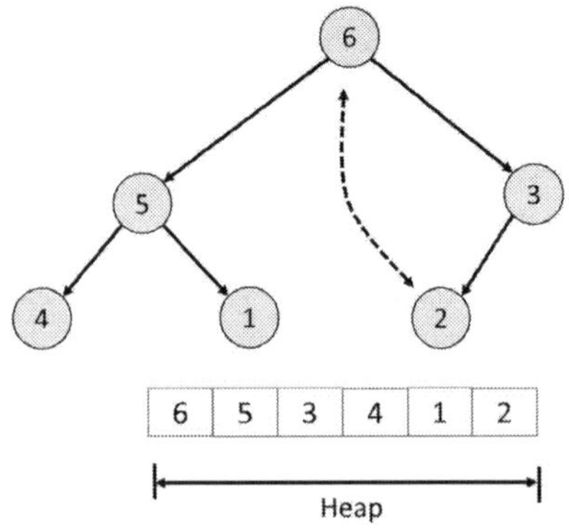
</td>
<td>The maximum value, which is the first element of the Heap array, is swapped with the last element of the array. Now the largest value is at the end of the array. Then we will reduce the size of the heap by one.</td>
</tr>
<tr>
<td>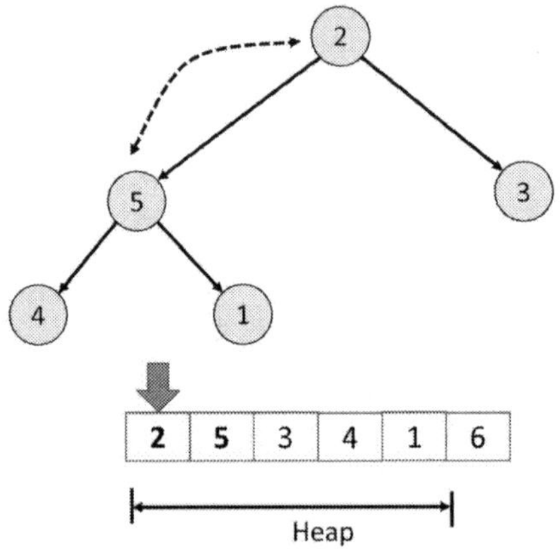
</td>
<td>Since 2 is at the top of the heap. Its heap property is lost. We will use the Percolate down function to regain the heap property.</td>
</tr>
<tr>
<td>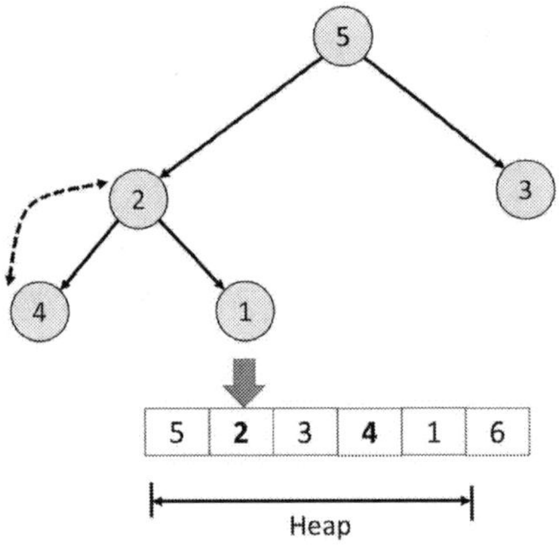
</td>
<td>Percolate down continued.</td>
</tr>
<tr>
<td>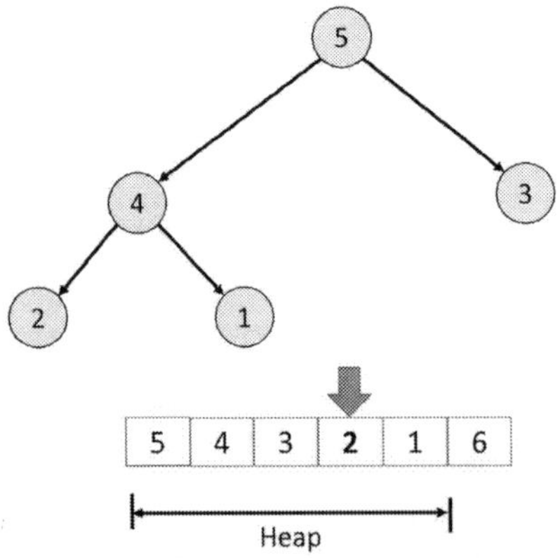
</td>
<td>Heap property is regained.</td>
</tr>
</table>

| | |
|---|---|
| 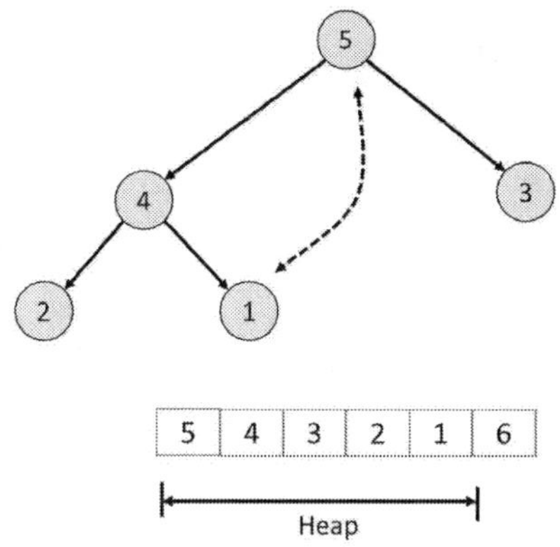 | We will copy the first element of the heap array to the second last position. The size of the heap is further reduced by one. |
| 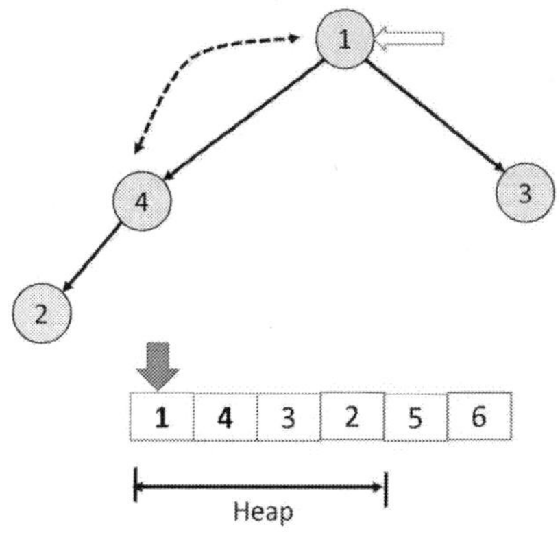 | Heap property is lost. Perform percolate down to regain heap property. |
| 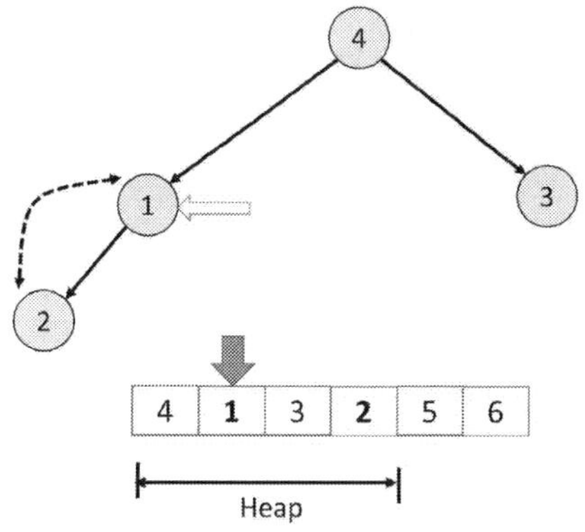 | Percolate down continued. |
| 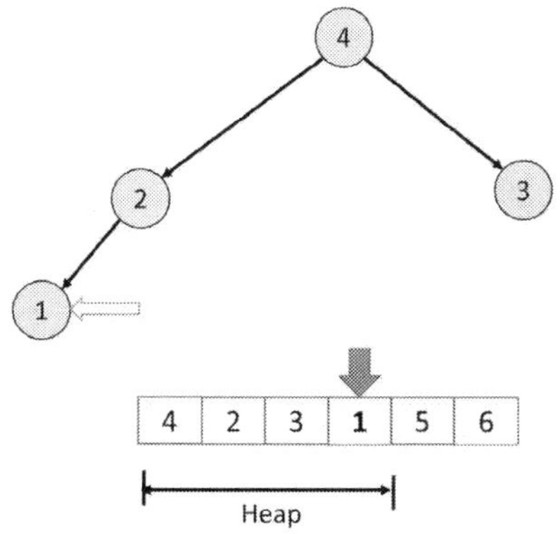 | Heap property regained. |

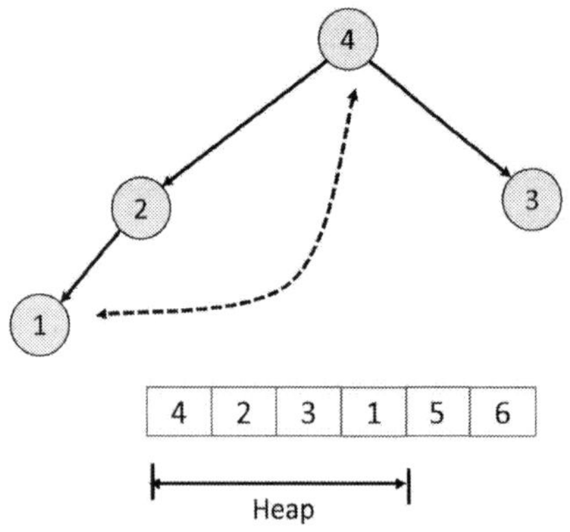


Swap first and the last value in the heap array. Reduce the size of the heap.

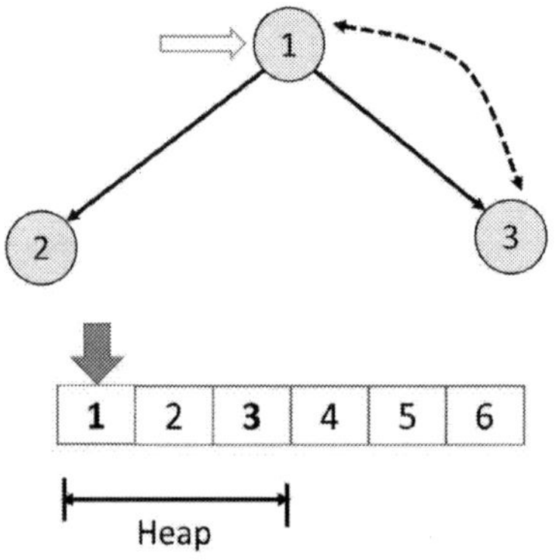


Percolate down.

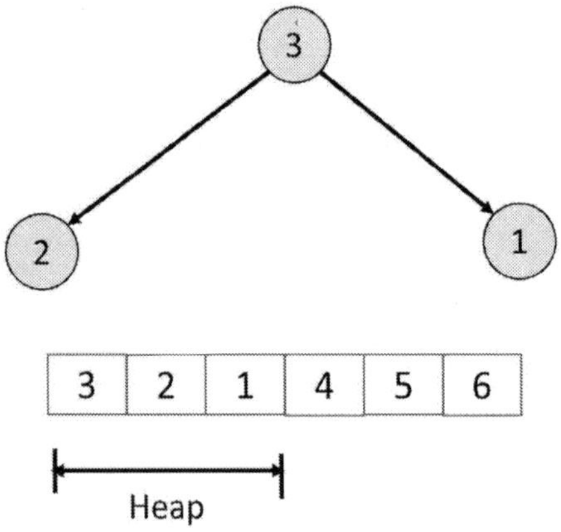


Heap property regained.

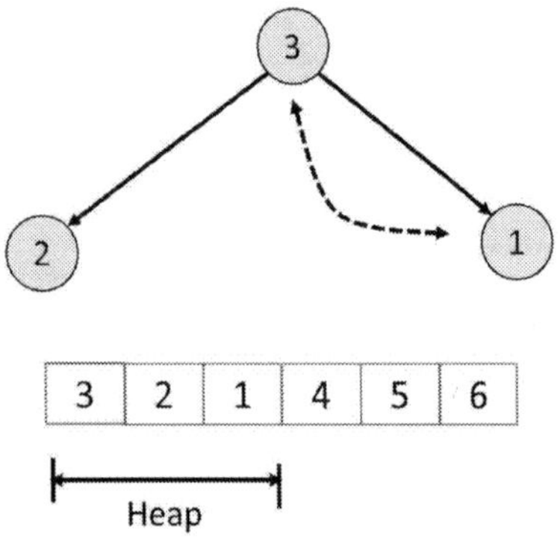


Swap the first and last element of the heap array. Reduce the size of the heap by one.

| | |
|---|---|
| 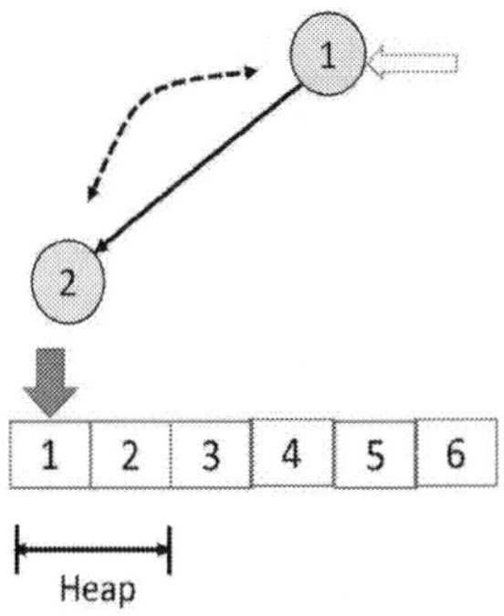 | Heap property lost so Percolate down. |
| 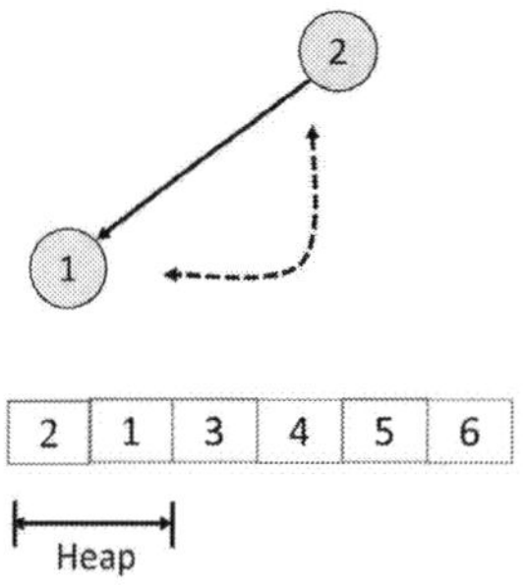 | Swap the first and last value stored in the Heap array. Reduce the size of the heap by one. |
|  | End |

**Example 10.10:**

```
public static void heapSort(int[] array, boolean inc) {
    // Create max heap for increasing order sorting.
    Heap hp = new Heap(array, !inc);
    for (int i = 0; i < array.length; i++) {
        array[array.length - i - 1] = hp.remove();
    }
}

// Testing code.
public static void main(String[] args)  {
    int[] a2 = { 1, 9, 6, 7, 8, 2, 4, 5, 3 };
    Heap.heapSort(a2, true);
    for (int i = 0; i < a2.length; i++) {
        System.out.print(a2[i] + " ");
    }
    System.out.println();

    int[] a3 = { 1, 9, 6, 7, 8, 2, 4, 5, 3 };
    Heap.heapSort(a3, false);
    for (int i = 0; i < a3.length; i++) {
        System.out.print(a3[i] + " ");
    }
}
```

**Output:**

```
1 2 3 4 5 6 7 8 9
9 8 7 6 5 4 3 2 1
```

| | |
|---|---|
| Data structure | List |
| Worst-case time complexity | O(n.log(n)) |
| Best-Case time complexity | O(n.log(n)) |
| Average-Case time complexity | O(n.log(n)) |
| Space Complexity | O(1) |

Time complexity analysis: Building the heap of the input array takes O(n) time and each element removal and adding to the end of the heap takes O(log(n)). So, the total time complexity will be O(n) + O(n.log(n)). The final time complexity of this sorting is O(n.log(n))

**Note**: Heap-Sort is not a Stable sort and does not require any extra space for sorting an array.

## Problems in Heap

### Kth Smallest

**Problem:** Given an unsorted array, find the kth smallest value.

**First Solution:** Sort the given array and then give the value at index K-1. Time complexity is O(n.log(n)).

**Example 10.11:**

```
public static int kthSmallest(int[] arr, int size, int k) {
    Arrays.sort(arr);
    return arr[k - 1];
}

// Testing code.
public static void main(String[] args)  {
    int arr[] = { 8, 7, 6, 5, 7, 5, 2, 1 };
    System.out.println("Kth Smallest :: " + kthSmallest(arr, arr.length, 3));
}
```

**Output:**

```
Kth Smallest :: 5
```

**Second solution:** Create a min-heap from the array, call DeleteMin() operation K times and the last operation will give Kth smallest value. Time Complexity O(n.log(n))

**Example 10.12:**

```
public static int kthSmallest2(int[] arr, int size, int k) {
    PriorityQueue<Integer> pq = new PriorityQueue<Integer>();
    for (int i = 0; i < size; i++)
        pq.add(arr[i]);
    for (int i = 0; i < k - 1; i++)
        pq.remove();
    return pq.peek();
}
```

**Third Solution**: Max-Heap, Create Max-Heap from the first k elements of the array. Traverse the rest of the elements of the array. If the top value of the heap is greater than the array element, then remove the top value and add the array element to the heap. If the top value is less than the array element, then ignore the array element. Perform this step till all the elements are traversed. Kth smallest element is at the top of the heap. Total time complexity is O(n.logk).

**Example 10.13:**
```
public static int kthSmallest3(int[] arr, int size, int k) {
    PriorityQueue<Integer> pq = new
PriorityQueue<Integer>(Collections.reverseOrder());
    for (int i = 0; i < size; i++) {
        if (i < k)
            pq.add(arr[i]);
        else {
            if (pq.peek() > arr[i]) {
                pq.add(arr[i]);
                pq.remove();
            }
        }
    }
    return pq.peek();
}
```

## Product of K smallest elements

**Problem:** Given an array of positive elements. Find products of k minimum elements in an array.

**First solution:** Sorting, Sort the array and find products of first K elements. Sorting will take O(n.log(n)) time. And then finding the product will take O(n) time, so total time complexity is O(n.log(n)).

**Example 10.14:**
```
public static int kSmallestProduct(int[] arr, int size, int k) {
    Arrays.sort(arr);
    int product = 1;
    for (int i = 0; i < k; i++)
        product *= arr[i];

    return product;
}

// Testing code.
public static void main(String[] args)  {
    int arr[] = { 8, 7, 6, 5, 7, 5, 2, 1 };
    System.out.println("Kth Smallest product:: " + kSmallestProduct(arr, 8, 3));
}
```

**Output:**
```
Kth Smallest product:: 10
```

**Second solution:** Min-Heap, Create min-heap from the array. Then pop K elements from the heap and find their product. Heapify will take O(n) time. Pop elements from the heap take O(log(n)) time. K elements are popped from the heap. So total time complexity is O(k.log(n))

**Example 10.15:**
```
public static int kSmallestProduct2(int[] arr, int size, int k) {
    PriorityQueue<Integer> pq = new PriorityQueue<Integer>();
    int i = 0;
    int product = 1;
    for (i = 0; i < size; i++) {
        pq.add(arr[i]);
    }
    i = 0;
    while (i < size && i < k) {
        product *= pq.remove();
        i += 1;
    }
    return product;
}
```

**Third solution:** Max-Heap, Max-Heap of size K can be created from the first K elements. Then traverse the rest of the array if the value at the top of the array is greater than the current value traversed. Then pop from the heap and then add the current value to the heap. Repeat this process till all the elements of the array are traversed. In the end, the heap contains the K minimum values, then finds their product.

**Example 10.16:**
```
public static int kSmallestProduct4(int[] arr, int size, int k) {
    PriorityQueue<Integer> pq =
                        new PriorityQueue<Integer>(Collections.reverseOrder());
    for (int i = 0; i < size; i++) {
        if (i < k)
            pq.add(arr[i]);
        else {
            if (pq.peek() > arr[i]) {
                pq.add(arr[i]);
                pq.remove();
            }
        }
    }
    int product = 1;
    for (int i = 0; i < k; i++) {
        product *= pq.remove();
    }
    return product;
}
```

**Fourth solution:** Quick select method, this method is the bi-product of the quick select method to find the kth element of an array. Run the quick select method to find the kth element of an array. The value at the left of the kth index is less than the value at the kth index. Find the product of the first k element. Average-Case time complexity of this solution is O(n).

**Example 10.17:**
```
public static int kSmallestProduct3(int[] arr, int size, int k) {
    quickSelectUtil(arr, 0, size - 1, k);
    int product = 1;
    for (int i = 0; i < k; i++)
        product *= arr[i];
```

```
    return product;
}
```

## K Largest in a Stream

**Problem:** There are billions of integers coming out of a stream. How would you determine the largest k numbers?

**Solution:** Large K numbers can be found by using a Heap. In this case, we will create a min-heap.

1. First, from the first k integers of the input stream, build a min-heap.
2. Then for each coming integer, compare if it is greater than the top of the min-heap.
3. If not greater than the top of the heap, then look for the next integer.
4. If greater than the top of the heap, then remove the top min value from the min-heap, insert the new value to the heap.
5. Repeat the process for all the elements of the stream. At any time you have the largest k values in your heap.
6. This solution will take O(logk) time for every insert operation. If in total n elements are observed then Time-complexity will be O(nlogk)

## Is Min-Heap

**Problem:** In the given list, find if it represents a Binary Min-Heap

**Solution:** The Min-Heap property we are going to check is that the value of the parent index is always less than or equal to its children index. Time-complexity O(n)

**Example 10.18:**

```
public static boolean isMinHeap(int[] arr, int size) {
    int lchild, rchild;

    // last element index size - 1
    for (int parent = 0; parent < (size / 2 + 1); parent++) {
        lchild = parent * 2 + 1;
        rchild = parent * 2 + 2;

        // heap property check.
        if (((lchild < size) && (arr[parent] > arr[lchild])) || ((rchild < size) &&
(arr[parent] > arr[rchild])))
            return false;
    }

    return true;
}

// Testing code.
public static void main(String[] args)  {
    int arr4[] = { 1, 2, 3, 4, 5, 6, 7, 8 };
    System.out.println("isMinHeap :: " + isMinHeap(arr4, arr4.length));
}
```

**Output:**

```
isMinHeap :: true
```

## Is Max-Heap

**Problem:** In the given list, find if it represents a binary Max-Heap

**Solution:** The Max-Heap property we are going to check is that the value of the parent index is always greater than or equal to its children index. Time-complexity O(n)

**Example 10.19**
```
public static boolean isMaxHeap(int[] arr, int size) {
    int lchild, rchild;
    // last element index size - 1
    for (int parent = 0; parent < (size / 2 + 1); parent++) {
        lchild = parent * 2 + 1;
        rchild = lchild + 1;
        // heap property check.
        if (((lchild < size) && (arr[parent] < arr[lchild])) || ((rchild < size) &&
(arr[parent] < arr[rchild])))
            return false;
    }
    return true;
}

// Testing code.
public static void main(String[] args)  {
    int arr3[] = { 8, 7, 6, 5, 7, 5, 2, 1 };
    System.out.println("isMaxHeap :: " + isMaxHeap(arr3, arr3.length));
}
```

**Output:**
```
isMaxHeap :: true
```

**Analysis:** If each parent value is greater than its children value, then heap property is true. We will traverse from the start to half of the array and compare the value of the index node with its left child and right child node.

## Nearly sorted array

**Problem:** Given a nearly sorted array, in which an element is at max k units away from its sorted position.

**First solution:** If you use sorting, then it will take O(n.log(n)) time
```
Arrays.sort(arr);
```

**Second solution:** There is one algorithm by which it can be done in O(NlogK) time.

- You can create a Min-Heap of size K+1 from the first K+1 elements of the input array.
- Create an empty output array.
- Pop an element from the heap and store it into an output array.
- Push the next element from the array to the heap.
- Repeat these processes 3 and 4 till all the elements of the array are consumed, and the heap is empty.
- In the end, you have sorted the array.

**Example 10.20:**
```
public static void sortK(int[] arr, int size, int k) {
    PriorityQueue<Integer> pq = new PriorityQueue<Integer>();

    int i = 0;
    for (i = 0; i < k; i++) {
        pq.add(arr[i]);
    }

    int index = 0;
    for (i = k; i < size; i++) {
        arr[index++] = pq.remove();
        pq.add(arr[i]);
    }

    while (pq.size() > 0)
        arr[index++] = pq.remove();
}

// Testing code.
public static void main(String[] args)  {
    int k = 3;
    int[] arr = { 1, 5, 4, 10, 50, 9 };
    int size = arr.length;

    sortK(arr, size, k);

    for (int i = 0; i < size; i++)
        System.out.print(arr[i] + " ");
}
```

**Output:**
```
1 4 5 9 10 50
```

## Get Median function

**Problem:** Give a data structure that will provide a median of given values in constant time.

**Solution:** We will use two heaps, one Min-Heap and another Max-Heap. Max-Heap will contain the first half of the data and Min-Heap will contain the second half of the data. Max-Heap will contain the smaller half of the data and its max value that is at the top of the heap will be the median contender. Similarly, the Min-Heap will contain the larger values of the data and its min value that is at its top will contain the median contender. We will keep track of the size of heaps. Whenever we insert a value to the heap, we will make sure that the size of two heaps differs by max one element, otherwise, we will pop one element from one and insert it into another to keep them balanced.

**Example 10.21**
```
public class MedianHeap {
    PriorityQueue<Integer> minHeap;
    PriorityQueue<Integer> maxHeap;

    public MedianHeap() {
        minHeap = new PriorityQueue<Integer>();
        maxHeap = new PriorityQueue<Integer>(Collections.reverseOrder());
    }
```

```
    public void add(int value) {
        if (maxHeap.size() == 0 || maxHeap.peek() >= value) {
            maxHeap.add(value);
        } else {
            minHeap.add(value);
        }

        // size balancing
        if (maxHeap.size() > minHeap.size() + 1) {
            value = maxHeap.remove();
            minHeap.add(value);
        }

        if (minHeap.size() > maxHeap.size() + 1) {
            value = minHeap.remove();
            maxHeap.add(value);
        }
    }

    public int getMedian() {
        if (maxHeap.size() == 0 && minHeap.size() == 0)
            return Integer.MAX_VALUE;

        if (maxHeap.size() == minHeap.size())
            return (maxHeap.peek() + minHeap.peek()) / 2;
        else if (maxHeap.size() > minHeap.size())
            return maxHeap.peek();
        else
            return minHeap.peek();
    }

    // Testing code.
    public static void main(String[] args) {
        int arr[] = { 1, 9, 2, 8, 3, 7 };
        MedianHeap hp = new MedianHeap();

        for (int i = 0; i < 6; i++) {
            hp.add(arr[i]);
            System.out.println("Median after addition of " + arr[i] + " is  " +
hp.getMedian());
        }
    }
}
```

**Output:**

```
Median after addition of 1 is 1
Median after addition of 9 is 5
Median after addition of 2 is 2
Median after addition of 8 is 5
Median after addition of 3 is 3
Median after addition of 7 is 5
```

**Time-complexity**:
Add() operation takes O(log(n)) time. GetMedian() operation takes O(1) constant time.

## Binomial Heap

A binomial heap is a specific implementation of the heap data structure. Binomial heap is a collection of binomial trees that are linked together where each tree follows the heap property. In a binomial heap, there are either one or zero binomial trees of order k. A binomial tree of order k has 2^k elements.

A Binary Heap merge() operation requires adding both the heap in a single array and then performing heapify() operation over them which takes linear time or O(n). Binomial heaps allow efficient merging of heaps which takes O(log(n)) time.

Comparison of Efficiency

| | Binary | Binomial |
|---|---|---|
| Insert | O(lg n) | O(lg n) |
| Minimum | Θ(1) | O(lg n) |
| Extract-Min | Θ(lg n) | O(lg n) |
| Union | Θ(n) | O(lg n) |
| Decrease-Key | Θ(lg n) | O(lg n) |
| Delete | Θ(lg n) | O(lg n) |

### Binomial Tree

A binomial tree Bk is an ordered tree defined recursively.

1 B0 consists of a single node.
2 For k ≥ 1, Bk is a pair of Bk−1 trees, where the root of one Bk−1 becomes the leftmost child of the other.

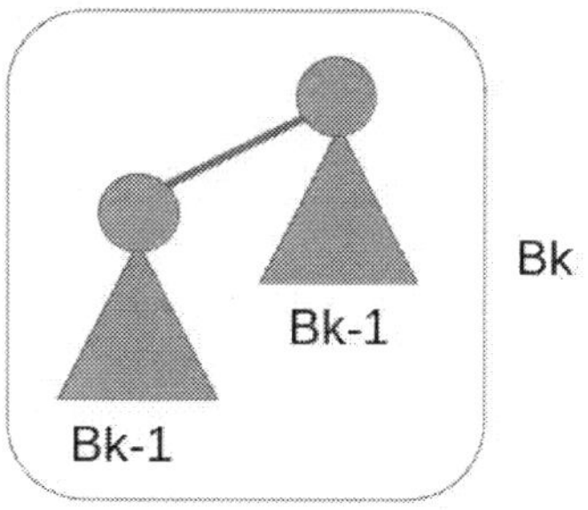


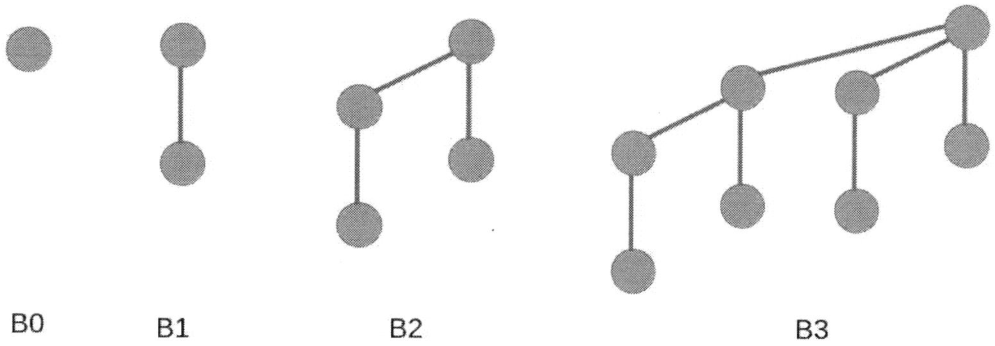


3

Properties of Binomial Trees Bk for all integers k ≥ 0 :

1. Bk has 2^k nodes.
2. Bk has height k.
3. For i = 0, . . . , k, Bk has exactly kCi = k! / ( i! * (k-i)! ) nodes at depth i.
4. The children of the root of binomial tree Bk of degree k are Bk−1, Bk−2, · · · , B0 from left to right.

## Min-Heap Binomial Tree or Max-Heap Binomial Tree

A Min-Heap Binomial Tree is a Binomial Tree that obeys the Min-Heap property. i.e. the parent node is smaller than or equal to its children nodes. Similarly, a Max-Heap Binomial Tree is a Binomial Tree that obeys the max-heap property i.e. the parent node is larger than or equal to its children nodes.

## Binomial Tree Node

| | |
|---|---|
| 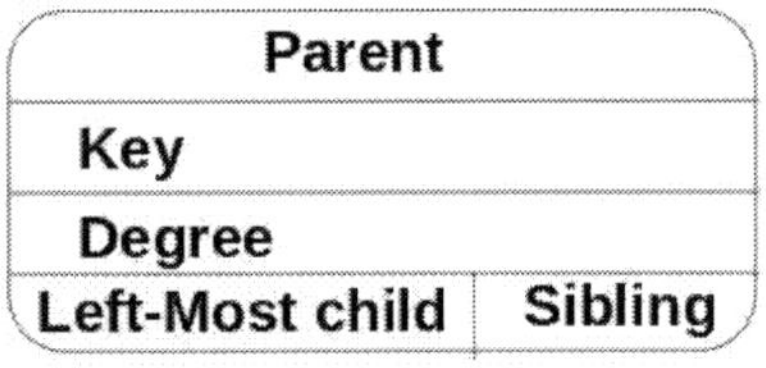  | Information stored in each node are following:<br>1 **Key** field to store key.<br>2 **Degree** field to store degree of the binomial tree. Which is also the number of children.<br>3 **Parent** pointer which points to the parent of the node.<br>4 **Child** pointer which points to the leftmost child node.<br>5 **Sibling** pointer which points to the right-sibling node. |

## Binomial Heap Implementation

A Binomial Heap is a set of Binomial Trees where each Binomial Tree follows the Min Heap property. And there can be at most one Binomial Tree of any degree.

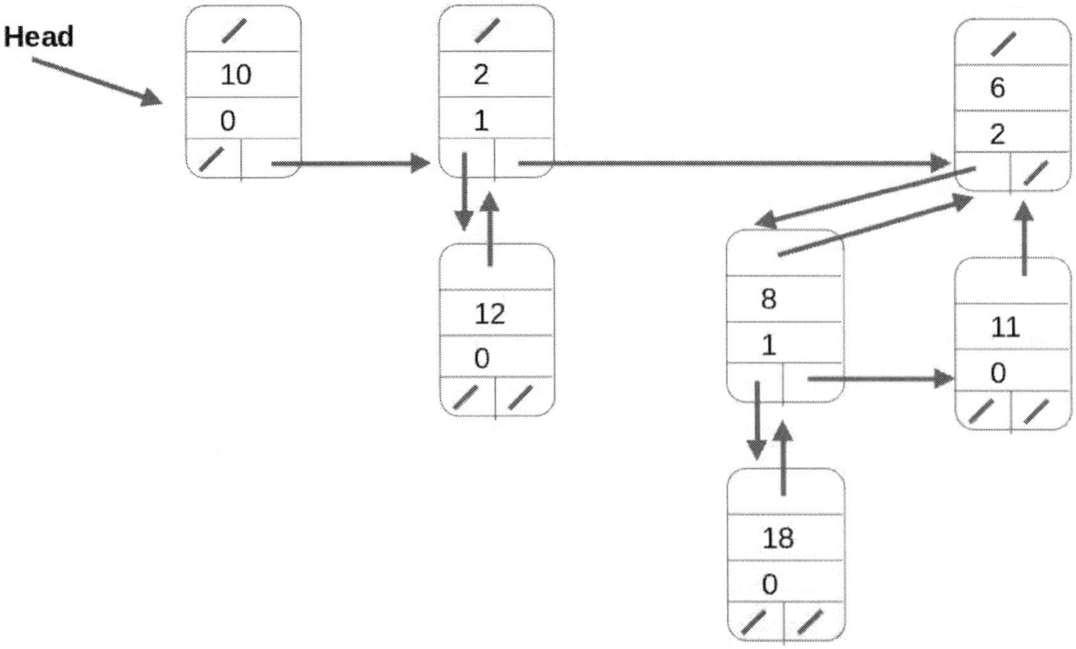

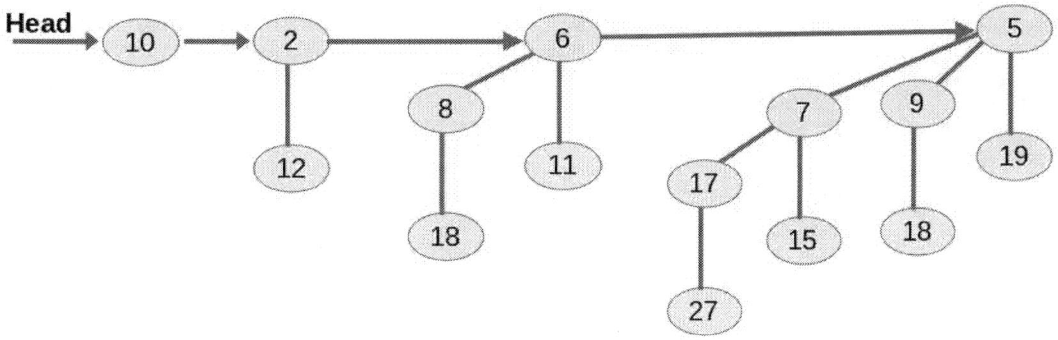


Binomial heaps can be implemented by using linked lists to store the root nodes of binomial trees. Each node stores information about the parent pointer, right sibling pointers, leftmost child pointer, the number of children it has(degree) , and its key.

A binomial heap H is a set of binomial trees that satisfies the following binomial-heap properties:

1 Each binomial tree in H is min-heap-ordered (or max-heap ordered) such that the key of a node is less than or equal to the key of its children.
2 For any non-negative integer k, there is at most one (either 0 or 1) binomial tree in H whose root has degree k.
3 The number of trees in in binomial heap are less then ⌊log2n⌋+1.
4 The height of binomial heap is less than ⌊log2n⌋.

Operations on Binomial Heaps

1. **Creation of a new Binomial Heap**: We create a heap object H with H.head = null.
2. **Search for the minimum key**: Iterate the root list and find the minimum key root node. The cost is O(log(n)) because there are O(log(n)) heaps, in each tree the minimum is located at the root.

```
function BinomialHeapMinimum(H)
    y = null
    x = H.head
    min = ∞
    while x != null
        do if x.key < min
        then min = x.key
        y = x
        x = x.sibling
    return y
```

3. **Uniting two Binomial Heaps**: BinomailHeapUnion(H1, H2 ) creates and returns a new heap that contains all the nodes of heaps H1 and H2. BinomailHeapUnion() procedure has two steps:
   - In the first step, simply merge two binomial heaps H1 and H2 into a single heap H in non-decreasing order of degree of binomial trees. Step 1 in the below diagram shows this step. There might be multiple binomial trees of the same degree.
   - In the second step, we need to make sure that at most one binomial tree of any order. If two binomial trees are of the same degree then merge them to create a higher degree tree. We traverse the list of merged roots, we keep track of three-pointers, previous, current and sibling of current. There can be the following 4 cases when we traverse the list of roots.

- Case 1: Orders of current and it's sibling are not same, we simply move ahead.
- Case 2: Order of current, its sibling and its sibling's sibling are same then also move ahead.
- Case 3: Order of current is same as sibling and the key of current is **smaller** than or equal to the key of it's sibling, then make sibling as a leftmost child of current.
- Case 4: Order of current is same as sibling and the key of current is **greater** than the key of it's sibling, then make current node as a leftmost child of sibling.

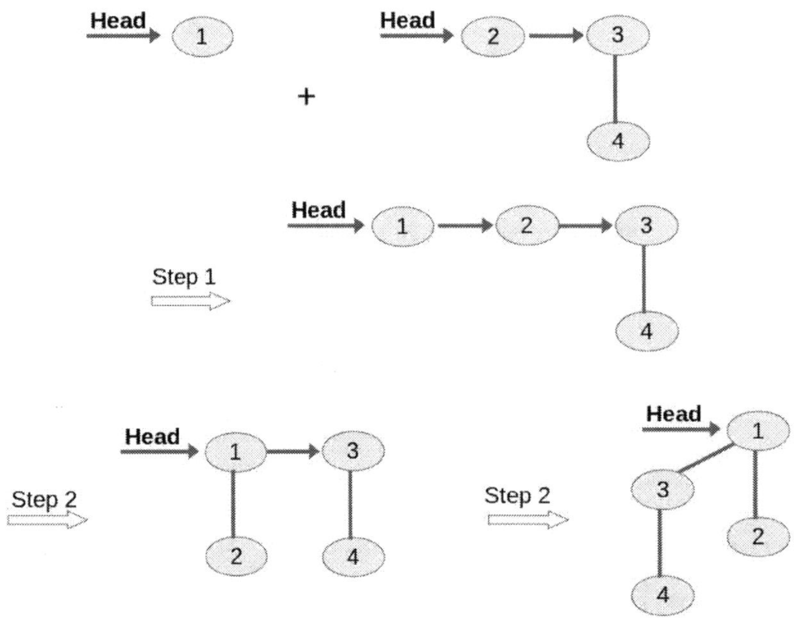


**Union of Binomial Heaps**

```
function BinomailHeapUnion(H1, H2):
    H = CreateBinomialHeap()
    H.head = BinomailHeapmerge(H1, H2)
    if H.head == null:
        return H

    prev = null
    curr = H.head
    sibling = curr.sibling

    while sibling != null:
        # Case 1 and 2
        if curr.degree != sibling.degree or
            ( sibling.next != null and sibling.next.degree == curr.degree ):
            prev = curr
            curr = sibling
        else :
            if curr.key <= sibling.key: #Case 3:sibling becomes child of
curr.
                curr.sibling = sibling.sibling
                left = curr.leftchild
                curr.leftchild = sibling
```

```
            sibling.sibling = left
            sibling.parent = curr

        else : # Case 4: curr becomes a child of a sibling.
            if prev == null:
                H.head = sibling
            else:
                prev.sibling = sibling

            left = sibling.leftchild
            sibling.leftchild = curr
            curr.parent = sibling
            curr.sibling = left
            # Sibling became a new root.
            curr = sibling
    sibling = curr.sibling # propagation step.

return H
```

4. **Removal of the minimum value root of a tree**: Find the minimum value root node tree T in the heap and remove T from heap. Then Create another heap H0 consisting of the children of T. In the end uniter H0 to H.

5. **Insertion of a node**: Suppose we wish to insert a node x into a binomial heap H. We create a single node heap H0 consisting of single node x and unite H and H0 .

```
function BinomialHeapInsert(H, x)
    H2 = CreateBinomialHeap()
    x.parent = null
    x.leftchild = null
    x.sibling = null
    x.degree = 0
    H2.head = x
    H = BinomailHeapUnion(H, H2)
```

6. **Decreasing value of a key**: We decrease the key and then keep exchanging the keys upward until the heap property is restored.

| Operation | Running Time |
|---|---|
| Insert | O(1) |
| Remove | O(log(n)) |
| Find Min | O(1) |
| Extract Min | O(log(n)) |
| Decrease Key | O(log(n)) |
| Merge | O(log(n)) |

## Fibonacci Heap

A fibonacci heap is a data structure that consists of a collection of trees which follow min heap property. All tree roots are connected using a doubly circular linked list. Fibonacci Heap maintains a pointer to the minimum value root node. All tree roots are connected so all of them can be accessed using single linked list traversal.

Fibonacci heap is similar to the binomial heap but has a faster amortized running time than binomial heap. Binomial heaps merge heaps immediately but Fibonacci heaps wait to merge until the ExtractMin() function is called.

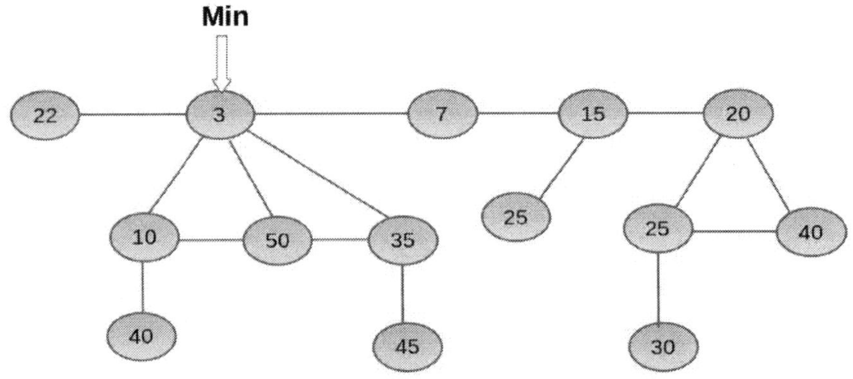


Properties of fibonacci heap:

- All trees in the fibonacci heap follow min heap property.
- Trees do not have strict requirements of 2^k nodes as in binomial heap.
- Roots of the tree in the fibonacci heap are unordered but are connected by a doubly circular list.
- Each node has a degree which is the number of children of that node.
- Nodes have a mark element which indicates whether their child has been removed or not.
- Nodes can have zero or any number of children.

Pointers representation of fibonacci heap.

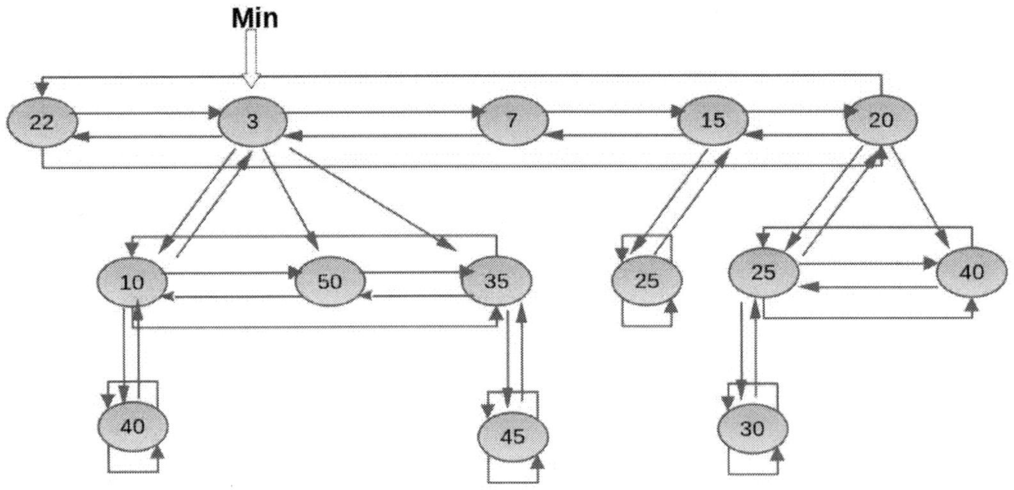


Operations on Fibonacci Heap:

1. **Creating Empty Heap**: Empty heap is created. Number of elements is set to 0 and min is set to null.

```
function MakeFibonacciHeap()
    H = CreateFibonnacciHeap()
    H.n = 0
    H.min = Null
     return H
```

2. **Find Minimum**: Min pointer points to the minimum value node, so finding the minimum is simple and can be done in O(1) time.

```
function FibonacciHeapMinimum(H)
    return H.min
```

3. **Merge Heaps**: Merging is performed by concatenating root lists of the two heaps. Min value of both the heaps are compared and whichever is small will be made min of the combined heap. Merge operation takes O(1) time.

```
function FibonacciHeapUnion(H1,H2)
    Concatenate the root list of H2 into H1

    if (H1.min = Null) or (H2.min != Null and H2.min.key < H1.min.key)
        H1.min = H2.min
    H1.n = H1.n + H2.n
    free H2
    return H1
```

4. **Insert Node**: Inserting node into an already existing heap. Create a new node for the element. If the heap is empty or the value of the new node is smaller than the min then set min of the heap to the new node.

```
function FibonacciHeapInsert(H, x)
    x.degree = 0
    x.parent = Null
    x.child = Null
    x.left = x
    x.right = x
    mark = FALSE

    concatenate the root x into root list of H
    if H.min = Null or x.key < H.min.key
        H.min = x
    H.n = H.n + 1
```

5. **Extract Min**: This is one of the most important of Fibonacci Heap. Heap rearranging (consolidate) is delayed until extract min. Consolidation occurs when heap properties are violated, for example, if two heaps have the same order, the heaps must be adjusted to prevent this.
   Deleting the minimum element is done in three steps. The node is removed from the root list and min points to the next root in the root list. The min node's children are added to the root list. Finally, consolidate the trees so that there are no trees with the same orders. Delaying consolidation saves time.

```
function FibonacciHeapExtractMin(H)
    z = H.min
    if z != Null
        for each child x of z
            x.parent = Null
            add x to the root list of H
        remove z from the root list of H
```

```
        if z = z.right
            H.min = Null
        else
            H.min = z.right

        Consolidate(H)
        H.n = H.n - 1
    return z

function FibonacciHeapLink(H, y, x)
    remove y from the root list of H
    make y a child of x
    x.degree = x.degree + 1
    y.mark = FALSE

function Consolidate(H)
    for i=0 to MaxDegree(H)
        A[i] = Null

    for each root w in the root list of H
        x = w
        d = x.degree

        while A[d] != Null
            y = A[d]
            if x.key > y.key
                swap x & y
            FibonacciHeapLink(H, y, x)
            A[d] = Null
            d = d+1
        A[d] = x

        if (H.min = Null) or (H.min.key > x.key)
            H.min = x
```

6. **Decreasing a Key** : The key value of the desired node is decreased. Following operations are performed.

DecreaseKey() Operation

- The node x be the node whose value is decreased and its new value will be k.
- The parent y of x. If y is not null and the key of parent is greater then key of x. Then call Cut(x) and CascadingCut(y) functions are called subsequently.
- If the key of x is smaller than the key of min, then mark x as min.

```
function FibonacciHeapDecreaseKey(H, x, k)
    if k > x.key
        error "new key is greater than current key"

    x.key = k
    y = x.parent

    if y  != Null and x.key < y.key
        Cut(H, x, y)
        CascadingCut(H,y)
```

```
    if x.key < H.min.key
        H.min = x
```

Cut(x,y) operation

- Remove x from its parent y. And add x to the root list.
- Mark x as false.

```
function Cut(H,x,y)
    Remove x from the child list of y, decrementing y.degree
    Add x to the root list of H
    x.parent = Null
    x.mark = FALSE
```

CascadingCut(y) operation

- If the parent z of y is not null then follow the following steps.
- If y is unmarked, then mark y.
- Else, call Cut(y, z), to cut y from its parent z. And CascadingCut(z) cascades z, which is the parent of y.

```
function CascadingCut(H,y)
    z =   y.parent
    if z   != Null
        if y.mark = FALSE
            y.mark = TRUE
        else
            Cut(H, y, z)
            CascadingCut(H, z)
```

7. **Delete a Key** : The key value of the desired node is decreased to minus infinity. Followed with extract min which is removing the node with minus infinity.

```
function FibonacciHeapDelete(H,x)
    FibonacciHeapDecreaseKey(H,x,-infinity)
    FibonacciHeapExtractMin(H)
```

| Operation | Amortized Running Time |
|---|---|
| Insert | O(1) |
| Remove | O(log(n)) |
| Find Min | O(1) |
| Extract Min | O(log(n)) |
| Decrease Key | O(1) |
| Merge | O(1) |

## Uses of Heap

1. **Heapsort**: One of the best sorting methods is in-place and log(N) time complexity in all scenarios.

2. **Selection algorithms**: Finding the min, max, both the min and max, median, or even the kth largest element can be done in linear time (often constant time) using heaps.

3. **Priority Queues**: Heap Implemented priority queues are used in graph algorithms like Prim's Algorithm and Dijkstra's algorithm. A heap is a useful data structure when you need to remove the object with the highest (or lowest) priority. Schedulers, timers

4. **Graph algorithms (BFS)**: By using heaps as internal traversal data structures, the run time will be reduced by polynomial order. Examples of such problems are Prim's minimal

5. Because of the lack of pointers, the operations are faster than a binary tree. In addition, some more complicated heaps (such as binomial) can be merged efficiently, which is not easy to do for a binary tree.

## Exercise

1. What is the worst-case runtime Complexity of finding the smallest item in a min-heap?

2. Find max in a min-heap.

   **Hint**: normal search in the complete list. There is one more optimization, you can search from the mid of the array at index N/2

3. What is the worst-case time complexity of finding the largest item in a min-heap?

4. What is the worst-case time complexity of deleteMin in a min-heap?

5. What is the worst-case time complexity of building a heap by insertion?

6. Is a heap, a full or complete binary tree?

7. What is the worst time runtime Complexity of sorting an array of N elements using heapsort?

8. In given sequence of numbers: 1, 2, 3, 4, 5, 6, 7, 8, 9
   - Draw a binary Min-heap by inserting the above numbers one by one
   - Also, draw the tree that will be formed after calling Dequeue() on this heap

9. In given sequence of numbers: 1, 2, 3, 4, 5, 6, 7, 8, 9
   - Draw a binary Max-heap by inserting the above numbers one by one
   - Also, draw the tree that will be formed after calling Dequeue() on this heap

10. In a given sequence of numbers: 3, 9, 5, 4, 8, 1, 5, 2, 7, 6. Construct a Min-heap by calling the CreateHeap function.

11. Show an array that would be the result after the call to deleteMin() on this heap

12. In the given list: [3, 9, 5, 4, 8, 1, 5, 2, 7, 6]. Apply heapify over this to make a min-heap and sort the elements in decreasing order?

13. In Heap-Sort once a root element has been put in its final position, how much time does it take to reheapify the array so that the next removal can take place? In other words, what is the Time Complexity of a single element removal from the heap of size N?

14. What do you think the overall Time Complexity for heapsort is? Why do you feel this way?

15. Find Kth largest in an unsorted array using Max-Heap.

    **Hint**: Create a Max-Heap from the input array. Then we call remove() operation K-1 times, and the element at the top of the heap is kth largest. Time Complexity O(n.log(n))

16. Find Kth largest in an unsorted array using Min-Heap.

    **Hint**: Create a Min-Heap from the first K elements of the input array. Then for the rest of the elements of the array. Compare array elements with the top of the heap. If the top value is less than the array element, then remove the top value and add the array element to the heap. If the top value is greater than the array element, then ignore the array element. Perform these steps till all the array elements are traversed. Time Complexity O(NlogK)

17. Given an array, print the larger half of the array when it will be sorted.

    **Hint:-**

    - **First solution:** Sorting, Sort the array and then print the larger half of the array. Sorting will take O(n.log(n)) time. And then printing the larger half will take O(n) time, so total time complexity is O(n.log(n)).
    - **Second solution:** Min-Heap, Create min-heap from the array. Then pop the first half n/2 elements from the heap and find the rest part. Pop elements from the heap take O(log(n)) time. Elements are popped n/2 times from the heap. So the total time complexity is O(n.log(n)).
    - **Third solution:** Min-Heap, Create min-heap from the first n/2 elements of the array. Traverse the rest of the elements of the array. If the top value of the heap is less than the array element, then remove the top value and add the array element to the heap. If the top value is greater than the array element, then ignore the array element. Perform this step till all the elements are traversed. Total time complexity is O(n.log(n)).
    - **Fourth solution:** Quick select method, run quick select method to find the middle element of the array. The values at the right half of the array will be greater than the middle element's value. Finally, print the value at the middle and right of it. The Average-Case time complexity of this solution is O(n).

18. Given two heaps, you need to merge them to create a single heap.

    **Hint:** There is no single solution for this. Let us suppose the size of the bigger heap is N and the size of the smaller heap is M.

    If both heaps are comparable in size, then put both heap arrays in the same bigger List. Alternatively, in one of the arrays if they are big enough, then apply CreateHeap() function which will take theta(N+M) time.

    If M is much smaller than N then add() each element of M list one by one to the N heap. This will take O(Mlog(n)) time in the worst case and O(M) in the Best-Case.

# CHAPTER 11: HASH TABLE

## Introduction

In the searching chapter, we have gone through various searching techniques. Consider the problem of searching for a value in an array. If the array is not sorted then we have no other option, but to look into each element one by one, so the searching time complexity will be O(n). If the array is sorted, then we can search the value in O(log(n)) logarithmic time using binary search.

What if it is possible to get the location/index of the value we are looking for in the array by a magic function that returns the index in constant time? We can directly go into that location and see whether the value we are searching for is present or not in O(1) constant time. The hash function works just like that, of course, there is no magic involved.

## Hash-Table

A Hash-Table is a data structure that maps keys to values. Each position of the Hash-Table is called a slot. The Hash-Table uses a hash function to calculate an index of an array. We use the Hash-Table when the number of keys is small relative to the number of possible keys.

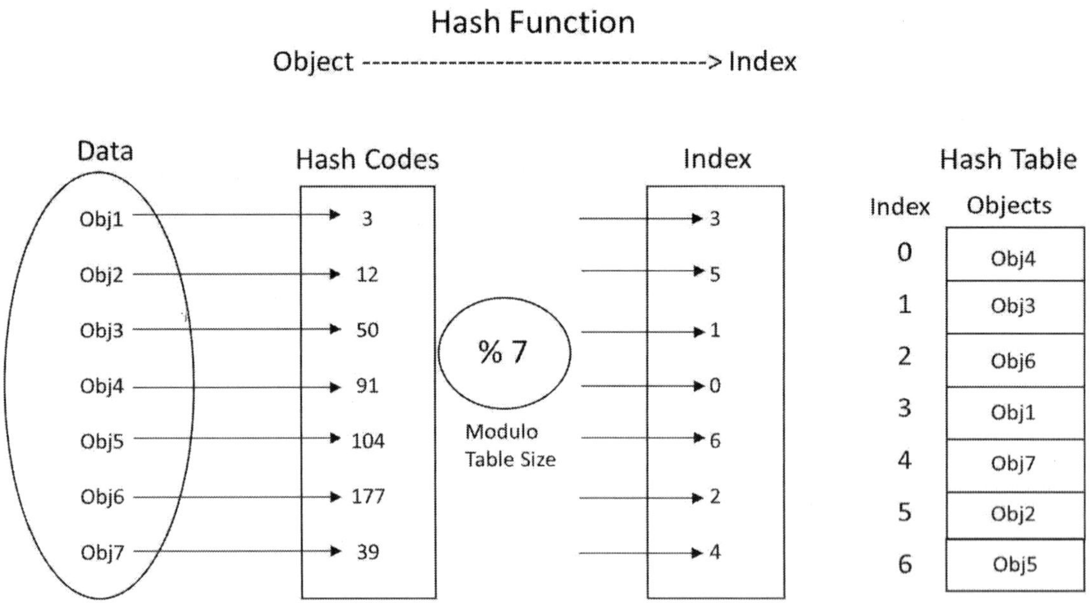


The process of storing data using a hash table is as follows:

1. Create an array of size M to store data; this array is called a Hash-Table.
2. Find a hash code of data by passing it through the hash function.
3. Take a module of hashcode by the size of Hashtable to get the index of the table where data will be stored.
4. Finally, store this data in the designated index.

The process of searching a value in Hash-Table using a hash function is as follows:

1. Find a hash code of the key we are searching for by passing it through the hash function.
2. Take a module of hashcode by the size of Hashtable to get the index of the table where the value is stored.
3. Finally, retrieve the value from the designated index.

## Hash-Table Abstract Data Type (ADT)

ADT of Hash-Table contains the following functions:

1 Insert(x), add x to the data set.

2 Delete(x), delete x from the data set.

3 Search(x), search x in the data set.

## Hash Function

A hash function is a function that generates an index in a table for a given key. An ideal hash function that generates a unique index for every key is called the perfect hash function.

**Example 11.1:** Most simple hash function

```
int computeHash(int key) {
    return key % tableSize;
}
```

There are many hash functions. The above function is a very simple hash function. Various hash generation logic will be added to this function to generate a better hash.

## Collisions

When a hash function generates the same index for the two or more different keys, the problem is known as the collision. Ideally, a hash function should return a unique address for each key, but practically it is not possible.

## Properties of a good hash function

1 It should provide a uniform distribution of hash values. A non-uniform distribution increases the number of collisions and the cost of resolving them.

2 Choose a hash function, which can be computed quickly and returns values within the range of the Hash-Table.

3 Choose a hash function with a good collision resolution algorithm that can be used to compute alternative indexes if the collision occurs.

4 Choose a hash function, which uses the necessary information provided in the key.

5 It should have a high load factor for a given set of keys.

## Load Factor

Load factor = (Maximum Allowed Number of elements in Hash-Table) / Hash-Table size

Based on the above definition, the Load factor is a measure of how many elements a hash table can contain before its capacity is increased. When the number of elements exceeds the product of load factor and current capacity, the hash table is rehashed. Normally the hash table size is doubled in this case. For example, if the load factor is 0.8 and hash table capacity is 1000 then we can add 800 elements to Hashtable without rehashing it.

## Collision Resolution Techniques

Hash collisions are practically unavoidable when hashing a large number of keys. Techniques that are used to find the alternate location in the Hash-Table is called collision resolution. There are several collision resolution techniques to handle the collision in hashing.

The most common and widely used techniques are:

1 Open addressing

2 Separate chaining

# Hashing with Open Addressing

When using linear open addressing, the Hash-Table is represented by a one-dimensional array with indices that range from 0 to the table size-1.

One method of resolving collisions is to look into a Hash-Table and find another free slot to hold the value that has caused the collision. A simple way is to move from one slot to another in some sequential order until we find a free space. This collision resolution process is called Open Addressing.

## Linear Probing

In Linear Probing, we try to resolve the collision of an index of a Hash-Table by sequentially searching the Hash-Table free location. Let us assume if k is the index retrieved from the hash function. If the kth index is already filled, then we will look for (k+1) %M, then (k+2) %M and so on. When we get a free slot, we will insert the data into that free slot.

**Example 11.2**: The resolver function of linear probing

```
int resolverFun(int index) {
    return index;
}
```

## Quadratic Probing

In Quadratic Probing, we try to resolve the collision of the index of a Hash-Table by quadratic increasing the search index of free location. Let us assume if k is the index retrieved from the hash function. If the kth index is already filled, then we will look for (k+1^2) %M, then (k+2^2) %M and so on. When we get a free slot, we will insert the data into that free slot.

**Example 11.3**: The resolver function of quadratic probing

```
int resolverFun2(int index) {
    return index * index;
}
```

**Note**: Table size should be a prime number to prevent early looping it should not be too close to 2powN

## Linear Probing implementation

The Hash table struct consists of an array that is used to store data and another array flag that is used to track if some slot is occupied or not. It also contains the size of the array.

**Example 11.4**: Below is Hash-Table class and its constructor function.

```
public class HashTableLP {
    private static int EMPTY_VALUE = -1;
    private static int DELETED_VALUE = -2;
    private static int FILLED_VALUE = 0;

    private int tableSize;
    int[] Key;
    int[] Value;
    int[] Flag;

    public HashTableLP(int tSize) {
        tableSize = tSize;
        Key = new int[tSize + 1];
        Value = new int[tSize + 1];
        Flag = new int[tSize + 1];
        Arrays.fill(Flag, EMPTY_VALUE);
    }

    /* Other Methods */
}
```

**Example 11.5:** Below is hash code generation and collision resolution function.

```
int computeHash(int key) {
    return key % tableSize;
}

int resolverFun(int index) {
    return index;
}
```

When the hash index is already occupied, the resolver function is used to get a new index.

**Example 11.6**

```
boolean add(int key, int value) {
    int hashValue = computeHash(key);
```

```
    for (int i = 0; i < tableSize; i++) {
        if (Flag[hashValue] == EMPTY_VALUE || Flag[hashValue] == DELETED_VALUE) {
            Key[hashValue] = key;
            Value[hashValue] = value;
            Flag[hashValue] = FILLED_VALUE;
            return true;
        }
        hashValue += resolverFun(i);
        hashValue %= tableSize;
    }
    return false;
}

boolean add(int value) {
    return add(value, value);
}
```

add() function is used to add values to the hash table. The first hash is calculated. Then we try to place that value in the Hash-Table. We look for empty nodes or lazy deleted nodes to insert values. In case the insert did not succeed, we try a new location using a resolver function.

**Example 11.7:**

```
boolean find(int key) {
    int hashValue = computeHash(key);
    for (int i = 0; i < tableSize; i++) {
        if (Flag[hashValue] == EMPTY_VALUE) {
            return false;
        }

        if (Flag[hashValue] == FILLED_VALUE && Key[hashValue] == key) {
            return true;
        }
        hashValue += resolverFun(i);
        hashValue %= tableSize;
    }
    return false;
}

int get(int key) {
    int hashValue = computeHash(key);
    for (int i = 0; i < tableSize; i++) {
        if (Flag[hashValue] == EMPTY_VALUE) {
            return -1;
        }

        if (Flag[hashValue] == FILLED_VALUE && Key[hashValue] == key) {
            return Value[hashValue];
        }

        hashValue += resolverFun(i);
        hashValue %= tableSize;
    }
    return -1;
}
```

find() function is used to search key in the hash table. And get() is used to find the value corresponding to the given key. The first hash is calculated. Then we try to find that value in the Hash-Table. We look for over desired values or empty nodes. In case we find the value that we are looking for, then we return that value or in case it is not found we return -1. We use a resolver function to find the next probable index to search.

**Example 11.8:**
```
boolean remove(int key) {
    int hashValue = computeHash(key);
    for (int i = 0; i < tableSize; i++) {
        if (Flag[hashValue] == EMPTY_VALUE) {
            return false;
        }

        if (Flag[hashValue] == FILLED_VALUE && Key[hashValue] == key) {
            Flag[hashValue] = DELETED_VALUE;
            return true;
        }
        hashValue += resolverFun(i);
        hashValue %= tableSize;
    }
    return false;
}
```

remove() function is used to delete values from a Hashtable. We do not delete the value, we just mark that value as DELETED_NODE. Same as the insert and search, we use resolverFun to find the next probable location of the key.

**Example 11.9:**
```
void print() {
    System.out.print("Hash Table contains ::");
    for (int i = 0; i < tableSize; i++) {
        if (Flag[i] == FILLED_VALUE) {
            System.out.print("(" + Key[i] + "=>"  + Value[i] + ") ");
        }
    }
    System.out.println();
}

// Testing code.
public static void main(String[] args) {
    HashTableLP ht = new HashTableLP(1000);
    ht.add(1, 10);
    ht.add(2, 20);
    ht.add(3, 30);
    ht.print();
    System.out.println("Find key 2 : " + ht.find(2));
    System.out.println("Value at  key 2 : " + ht.get(2));
    ht.remove(2);
    System.out.println("Find key 2 : " + ht.find(2));
}
```

**Output:**
```
Hash Table contains ::(1=>10) (2=>20) (3=>30)
Find key 2 : true
```

```
Value at  key 2 : 20
Find key 2 : false
```

Print function prints the content of the hash table. The main function demonstrates how to use a hash table.

## Hashing with separate chaining

Another method for collision resolution is based on the idea of putting the keys that collide in a linked list. This method is called separate chaining. To speed up the search we keep the linked list sorted.

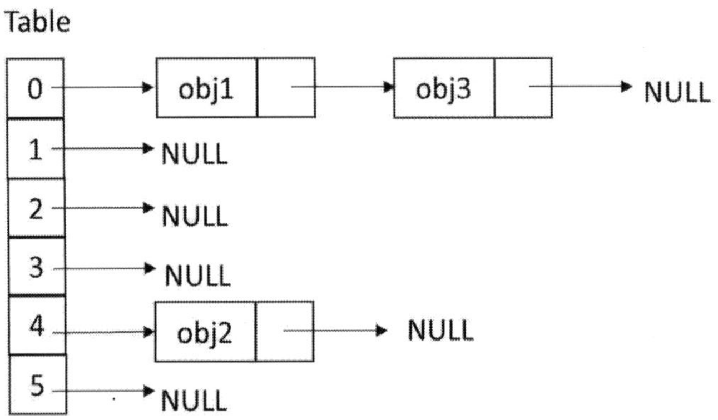


### Separate Chaining implementation

**Example 11.10:** Below is a separate chaining implementation of hash tables.

```
public class HashTableSC {
    private int tableSize;
    Node[] listArray;

    private class Node {
        private int key;
        private int value;
        private Node next;

        public Node(int k, int v, Node n) {
            key = k;
            value = v;
            next = n;
        }
    };

    public HashTableSC() {
        tableSize = 512;
        listArray = new Node[tableSize];
        Arrays.fill(listArray, null);
    }

    private int computeHash(int key) { // division method
        int hashValue = key;
        return hashValue % tableSize;
    }
```

```
public void add(int key, int value) {
    int index = computeHash(key);
    listArray[index] = new Node(key, value, listArray[index]);
}
public void add(int value) {
    add(value, value);
}

public boolean remove(int key) {
    int index = computeHash(key);
    Node nextNode, head = listArray[index];
    if (head != null && head.key == key) {
        listArray[index] = head.next;
        return true;
    }
    while (head != null) {
        nextNode = head.next;
        if (nextNode != null && nextNode.key == key) {
            head.next = nextNode.next;
            return true;
        } else {
            head = nextNode;
        }
    }
    return false;
}

public void print() {
    System.out.print("Hash Table contains :: ");
    for (int i = 0; i < tableSize; i++) {
        Node head = listArray[i];
        while (head != null) {
            System.out.print("(" + head.key + "=>" +head.value + ") ");
            head = head.next;
        }
    }
    System.out.println();
}

public boolean find(int key) {
    int index = computeHash(key);
    Node head = listArray[index];
    while (head != null) {
        if (head.key == key) {
            return true;
        }
        head = head.next;
    }
    return false;
}

public int get(int key) {
    int index = computeHash(key);
    Node head = listArray[index];
    while (head != null) {
        if (head.key == key) {
            return head.value;
        }
```

```
            head = head.next;
        }
        return -1;
    }

    // Testing code.
    public static void main(String[] args) {
        HashTableSC ht = new HashTableSC();
        ht.add(1, 10);
        ht.add(2, 20);
        ht.add(3, 30);
        ht.print();
        System.out.println("Find key 2 : " + ht.find(2));
        System.out.println("Value at  key 2 : " + ht.get(2));
        ht.remove(2);
        System.out.println("Find key 2 : " + ht.find(2));
    }
}
```

**Output:**

```
Hash Table contains :: (1=>10) (2=>20) (3=>30)
Find key 2 : true
Value at  key 2 : 20
Find key 2 : false
```

**Note**: It is important to note that the size of the table should be such that all the slots in the table will eventually be occupied. Otherwise, part of the table will be unused. It is suggested that the table size should be a prime number for better distribution of keys.

## Set implementation of Java Collections

Set is used to store unique elements. Set is implemented using a hash table. Set class **HashSet<>** is implemented using a hash table, its elements are not stored in sequential order.

**Example 11.11:**

```
import java.util.HashSet;

public class HashSetDemo {
    public static void main(String[] args) {
        // Create a hash set.
        HashSet<String> hs = new HashSet<String>();
        // Add elements to the hash set.
        hs.add("Banana");
        hs.add("Apple");
        hs.add("Mango");
        System.out.println(hs);
        System.out.println("Apple present : " + hs.contains("Apple"));
        System.out.println("Grapes present : " + hs.contains("Grapes"));
        hs.remove("Apple");
        System.out.println(hs);
        System.out.println("Apple present : " + hs.contains("Apple"));
    }
}
```

**Output**

```
[Apple, Mango, Banana]
Apple present : true
Grapes present : false
[Mango, Banana]
Apple present : false
```

## Dictionary implementation in Java Collection

A HashMap<> is a data structure that maps keys to values. It uses a hash table, so the key-value pairs are not stored in sorted order. Dictionaries do not allow duplicate keys, but values can be duplicated.

**Example 11.12:**

```
import java.util.HashMap;

public class HashMapDemo {
    public static void main(String[] args) {
        // Create a hash map.
        HashMap<String, Integer> hm = new HashMap<String, Integer>();

        // Put elements into the map
        hm.put("Apple", 40);
        hm.put("Banana", 10);
        hm.put("Mango", 20);

        System.out.println("Size :: " + hm.size());
        for (String key : hm.keySet())
            System.out.println(key + " cost :" + hm.get(key));

        System.out.println("Apple present ::" + hm.containsKey("Apple"));
        System.out.println("Grapes present :: " + hm.containsKey("Grapes"));
    }
}
```

**Output**

```
Size :: 3
Apple cost :40
Mango cost :20
Banana cost :10
Apple present ::true
Grapes present :: false
```

## Problems in Hashing

### Anagram solver

**Problem:** Find if two strings are anagrams, an anagram is a word or phrase formed by reordering the letters of another word or phrase.

**Solution**: Two words are anagrams if they are of the same size and their characters are the same. First, check if both are of the same size. Then traverse the first string and add the character count to the hashtable. Then traverse the second string and subtract the character count in the hashtable. If traversing the second string, if we don't find the character in the hashtable or if the count is zero we don't have an anagram. If the second string is traversed completely but still no mismatch is found, then we have an anagram. Time-complexity O(n), n is the size of the string.

**Example 11.13:**
```
public static boolean isAnagram(char[] str1, char[] str2) {
    int size1 = str1.length;
    int size2 = str2.length;
    if (size1 != size2)
        return false;

    HashMap<Character, Integer> hm = new HashMap<Character, Integer>();
    for (char ch : str1) {
        if (hm.containsKey(ch))
            hm.put(ch, hm.get(ch) + 1);
        else
            hm.put(ch, 1);
    }

    for (char ch : str2) {
        if (hm.containsKey(ch) == false || hm.get(ch) == 0)
            return false;
        else
            hm.put(ch, hm.get(ch) - 1);
    }

    return true;
}

// Testing code.
public static void main(String[] args)  {
    char[] first = "hello".toCharArray();
    char[] second = "elloh".toCharArray();
    char[] third = "world".toCharArray();

    System.out.println("isAnagram : " + isAnagram(first, second));
    System.out.println("isAnagram : " + isAnagram(first, third));
}
```

**Output:**
```
isAnagram : true
isAnagram : false
```

## Remove Duplicate

**Problem:** Remove duplicates in an array of numbers.

**Solution:** A new output string is created. The input string is traversed and its characters are added to the hashtable. If some character is not in the hashtable then it is added to the hashtable and the output string. If some character is already in the hashtable then it is ignored. Time-complexity O(n)

**Example 11.14:**

```
public static String removeDuplicate(char[] str) {
    HashSet<Character> hs = new HashSet<Character>();
    String out = new String();

    for (char ch : str) {
        if (hs.contains(ch) == false) {
            out += ch;
            hs.add(ch);
        }
    }
    return out;
}

// Testing code.
public static void main(String[] args)  {
    char[] first = "hello".toCharArray();
    System.out.println(removeDuplicate(first));
}
```

**Output:**

```
helo
```

## Find Missing

**Problem:** Given an array of integers, you need to find the missing number in the array.

**Solution**: All the elements in the array are added to a HashTable. All the integers from start to end of the given range are searched in a hashtable. If a missing element is found, then its value is returned. Time-complexity O(n)

**Example 11.15:**

```
public static int findMissing(int[] arr, int start, int end) {
    HashSet<Integer> hs = new HashSet<Integer>();
    for (int i : arr) {
        hs.add(i);
    }

    for (int curr = start; curr <= end; curr++) {
        if (hs.contains(curr) == false)
            return curr;
    }
    return Integer.MAX_VALUE;
}

// Testing code.
public static void main(String[] args)  {
    int arr[] = { 1, 2, 3, 5, 6, 7, 8, 9, 10 };
    System.out.println(findMissing(arr, 1, 10));
}
```

**Output:**

```
4
```

## Print Repeating

**Problem:** Given an array of integers, print the repeating integers in the array.

**Analysis:** All the values are added to the hash table. If we find some value that is already in the hash table, then that is the repeated value. Time-complexity O(n)

**Example 11.16:**

```
public static void printRepeating(int[] arr) {
    HashSet<Integer> hs = new HashSet<Integer>();

    System.out.print("Repeating elements are:");
    for (int val : arr) {
        if (hs.contains(val))
            System.out.print(" " + val);
        else
            hs.add(val);
    }
}

// Testing code.
public static void main(String[] args)  {
    int arr1[] = { 1, 2, 3, 4, 4, 5, 6, 7, 8, 9, 1 };
    printRepeating(arr1);
}
```

**Output:**

```
Repeating elements are: 4 1
```

## Print First Repeating

**Problem:** It is the same as the above problem in that we need to print the first repeating number. Care should be taken to find the first repeating number. It should be the one number that is repeating. For example, 1, 2, 3, 2, 1. The answer should be 1 as it is the first number, which is repeated.

**Solution:** The hashtable will keep a count of the values in the array. Now traverse the array again and see if the count is more than one. The first value whose count is more than 1 is the first repeating value.
Time-complexity O(n)

**Example 11.17:**

```
public static void printFirstRepeating(int[] arr) {
    int i;
    int size = arr.length;
    HashSet<Integer> hs = new HashSet<Integer>();
    int firstRepeating = Integer.MAX_VALUE;
    for (i = size - 1; i >= 0; i--) {
        if (hs.contains(arr[i])) {
            firstRepeating = arr[i];
        }
        hs.add(arr[i]);
    }
    System.out.println("First Repeating number is:" + firstRepeating);
}
```

```
//Testing code.
public static void main(String[] args)  {
    int arr1[] = { 1, 2, 3, 4, 4, 5, 6, 7, 8, 9, 1 };
    printFirstRepeating(arr1);
}
```

**Output:**

```
First Repeating number is : 1
```

## Uses of Hash-Table

Applications of Hash Table are:

1. Hash tables are commonly used in algorithms where fast data lookup is required.
2. HashTables are used in symbol trees for compilers
3. In some databases, data is stored in hash tables as key-value pairs.

## Exercise

1. Design a number (ID) generator system that generates numbers between 0-99999999 (8-digits). The system should support two functions:
   - int getNumber();
   - boolean requestNumber();

   getNumber() function should find out a number that is not assigned, then mark it as assigned and return that number. requestNumber() function checks the number if it is assigned or not. If it is assigned returns false, else marks it as assigned and returns true.

2. In a given large string, find the most occurring words in the string. What is the Time Complexity of the above solution?

   **Hint**:-
   - Create a Hashtable which will keep track of <word, frequency>
   - Iterate through the string and keep track of word frequency by inserting into Hash-Table.
   - When we have a new word, we will insert it into the Hashtable with frequency 1. For all repetitions of the word, we will increase the frequency.
   - We can keep track of the most occurring words whenever we are increasing the frequency we can see if this is the most occurring word or not.

   Time Complexity is **O(n)** where n is the number of words in the string and Space Complexity is the O(m) where m is the unique word in the string.

3. In the above question, what if you are given the whole work of OSCAR WILDE, the most popular playwrights in the early 1890s.

   **Hint**:-
   - Who knows how many books are there, let us assume there are a lot and we cannot put everything in memory. First, we need a Streaming Library so that we can read section by

section in each document. Then we need a tokenizer that will give words to our program. In addition, we need some sort of dictionary. Let us say we will use HashTable.

- What you need is - 1. A streaming library tokenizer, 2. A tokenizer 3. A hashmap
  Method:
  1. Use streamers to find a stream of the given words
  2. Tokenize the input text
  3. If the stemmed word is in a hash map, increment its frequency count else add a word to hash map with frequency 1
- We can improve the performance by looking into parallel computing. We can use map-reduce to solve this problem. Multiple nodes will read and process multiple documents. Once they are done with their processing, then we can do the reduced operation by merging them.

4. In the above question, what if we want to find the most common PHRASE in his writings.

   **Hint**: - We can keep <phrase, frequency> Hash-Table and do the same process of the 2nd and 3rd problems.

5. Write a hashing algorithm for strings.

   **Hint**: Use Horner's method

```
int hornerHash(char[] key, int tableSize) {
    int size = key.length;
    int h = 0;
    int i;
    for (i = 0; i < size; i++) {
        h = (32 * h + key[i]) % tableSize;
    }
    return h;
}
```

6. Pick two data structures to use in implementing a Map. Describe lookup, insert, & delete operations. Give time & Space Complexity for each. Give pros & cons for each.

   **Hint:-**

| **Linked List** | **Balanced Search Tree (RB Tree)** |
|---|---|
| Insert is O(1) | Insert is **O(log(n))** |
| Delete is O(1) | Delete is **O(log(n))** |
| Lookup is O(1) auxiliary and O(N) worst case. | Lookup is **O(log(n))** |
| Pros: Fast inserts and deletes, can be used for any data type. | Pros: Reasonably fast inserts/deletes and lookups. |
| Cons: Slow lookups. | Cons: Data needs to have order defined on it. |

# CHAPTER 12: GRAPHS

## Introduction

A **Graph** is represented by ordered pair G where G = (V, E), where V is a finite set of points called **Vertices** and E is a finite set of **Edges**. Each **edge** is a pair (u, v) where u, v $\in$ V.

The graph data structure consists of the following two components:

1. A finite set of nodes is called **vertices**.
2. A finite set of pairs of vertices called **edges**. Edges are connected between two vertices.

Some real-world examples of graphs are:

1. Google Maps: Various locations can be represented as Vertices of Graph and paths between them are represented by Edges of Graph. Graph theory algorithms are used to suggest the shortest and quickest path between two locations.
2. Facebook Friend Suggestion: Each user profile is represented as vertices of graphs and their friend relationship is represented by the edges of the Graph. In graph theory, algorithms are used for friend suggestions.
3. Topology Sorting: Topology sorting is a method to find sequences in which some events need to be performed to complete some task by looking into the dependency of various events on each other. For example, a sequence of classes that we take to become a graduate in computer science. Or a sequence of steps that we take to become ready for jobs daily
4. Transportation Network: The map of airlines is represented as a Graph. Various airports are represented as nodes of the graph and if there is a non-stop flight from airport u and airport v then in the graph there is an edge from node u to node v. You may want to go from one location to another, through graph theory algorithms we can compute a shortest, quickest or cheapest path from source to destination.

The flight connection between major cities of India can also be represented by the graph given below. Each city is represented as vertices, and flight between cities is represented as edges.

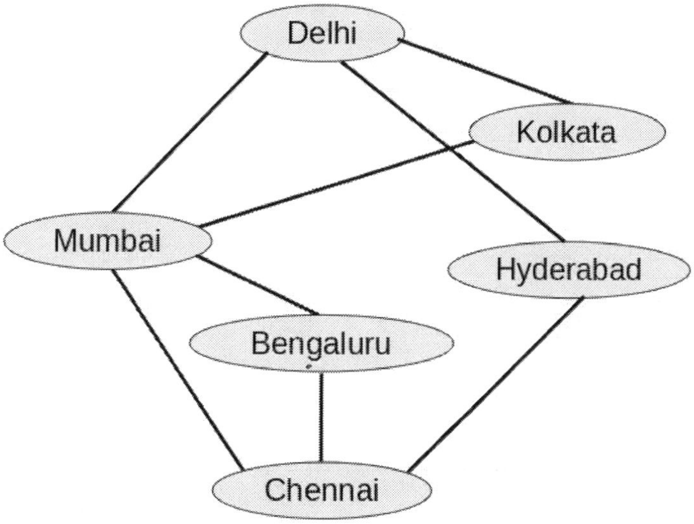

## Graph Terminology

**Undirected Graph**: An Undirected Graph is a graph in which edges have no directions. Here the edges of the graph are two ways. An edge (x, y) is identical to an edge (y, x).

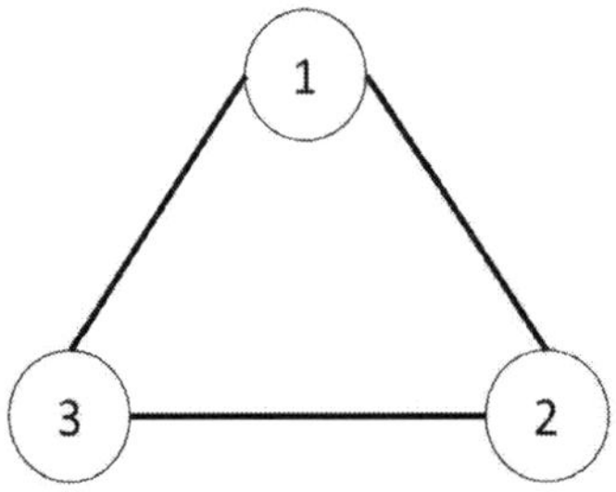


Undirected Graph

**Directed Graph or Digraph**: A Directed Graph is a graph in which edges have a direction. Here the edges of the graph are one way. An edge (x, y) is not identical to an edge (y, x).

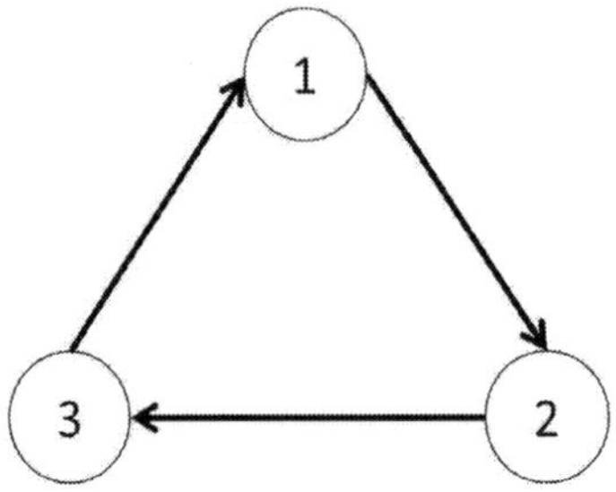


Directed Graph

**Weighted Graph**: A Graph is weighted if its edges have some value or weight associated with them.

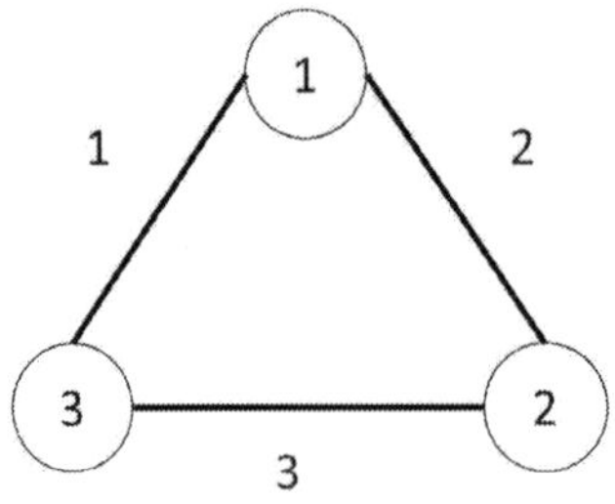


Weighted Graph

**Unweighted Graph**: A Graph in which edges do not have any weight associated with them.

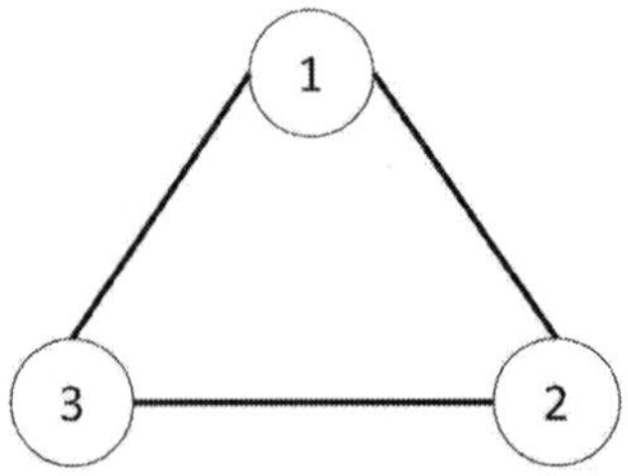


Unweighted Graph

**Path:** A Path is a sequence of edges between two vertices. The length of a path is defined as the sum of the weight of all the edges in the path.

**Simple Path:** A path with distinct vertices is called a simple path.

**Adjacent Vertex**: Two vertices u and v are **adjacent** if there is an edge whose endpoints are u and v.

In the below graph: V = {V1, V2, V3, V4, V5, V6, V7, V8, V9}
E = ( (v1, v0, 1), (v2, v1, 2), (v3, v2, 3), (v3, v4, 4), (v5, v4, 5), (v1, v5, 6), (v2, v5, 7), (v3, v5, 8), (v4, v5, 9) )

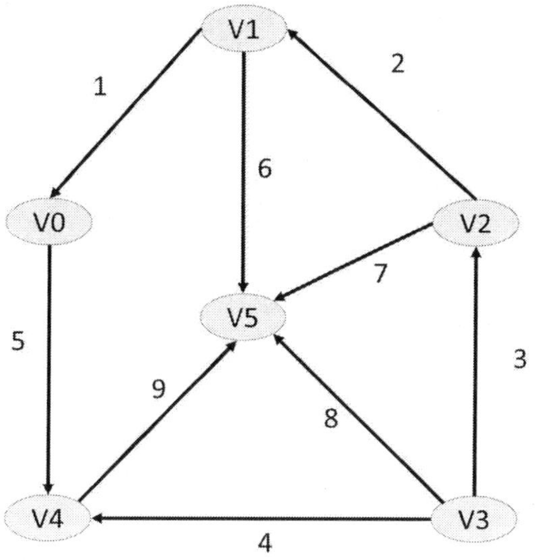


The **in-degree** of a vertex v, denoted by indeg(v) is the number of incoming edges to the vertex v.

The **out-degree** of a vertex v, denoted by outdeg(v) is the number of outgoing edges of a vertex v.

The **degree** of a vertex v, denoted by deg(v) is the total number of edges whose one endpoint is v.
deg(v) = Indeg (v) + outdeg (v)

In the above graph: deg(V4) =3, indeg(V4) =2 and outdeg(V4) =1

A **Cycle** is a path that starts and ends at the same vertex and includes at least one vertex.
An edge is a **Self-Loop** if two if its two endpoints coincide. This is a form of a cycle.

**Cyclic Graph**: A Graph that has one or more cycles is called a Cyclic Graph.

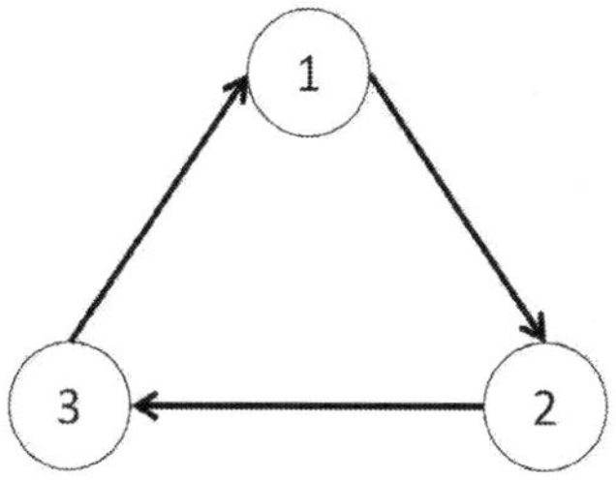


Cyclic Graph

**Acyclic Graph**: A Graph that has no cycle is called an Acyclic Graph.

**Directed Acyclic Graph / DAG**: A directed graph that does not have any cycle is called Directed Acyclic Graph.

**Reachable**: A vertex v is **Reachable** from vertex u or u reaches v, if there is a path from u to v. In an undirected graph if v is reachable from u then u is reachable from v. However, in a directed graph it is possible that u reaches v but there is no path from v to u.

**Connected Graph**: A graph is **Connected** if for any two vertices there is a path between them.
**Strongly Connected Graph**: A directed graph is strongly connected if each pair of vertices u and v, there is a path from u to v and a path from v to u.

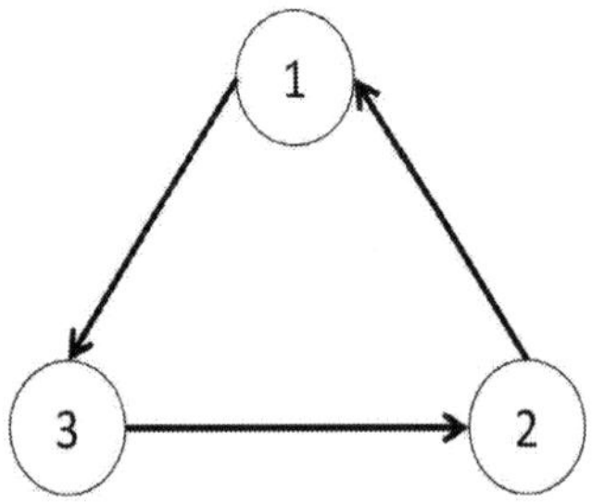


Strongly Connected Graph

**Strongly Connected Components**: A directed graph may have different sub-graphs that are strongly connected. These sub-graphs are called strongly connected components.

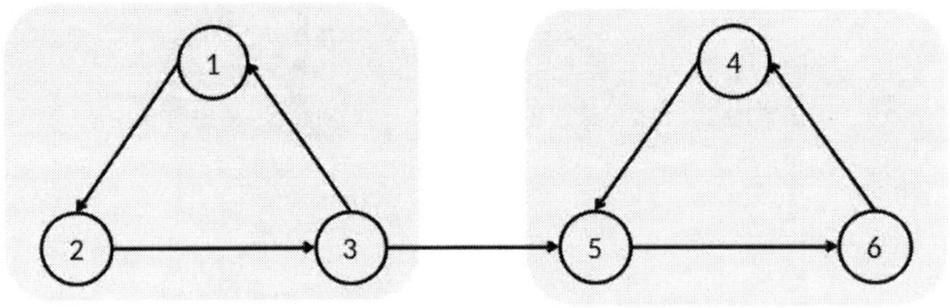


Strongly Connected Component

**Weakly Connected Graph**: A directed graph is weakly connected if each pair of vertices u and v, there is a path from u to v or a path from v to u.

**Complete Graph**: A graph is complete if any vertex is connected by an edge to all the other vertices of the graph. A complete graph has a maximum number of edges. For an undirected graph of n vertices, the total number of edges will be n(n-1)/2 and for a directed graph the total number of edges will be n(n-1).

A **Sub-Graph** of a graph G is a graph whose vertices and edges are a subset of the vertices and edges of G.

A **Spanning Sub-Graph** of G is a graph that connects all the vertices of G.

A **Forest** is a graph without cycles.

A **Tree** is a connected graph with no cycles. There is only one simple path between any two vertices u and v. If we remove any edge of a tree, it becomes a forest.

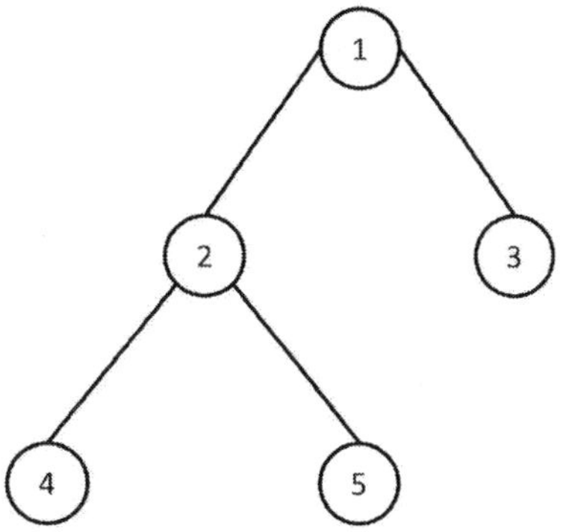


Tree

A **Spanning tree** of a graph is a tree that connects all the vertices of the graph. Since a Spanning-Tree is a tree, it should not have any cycle.

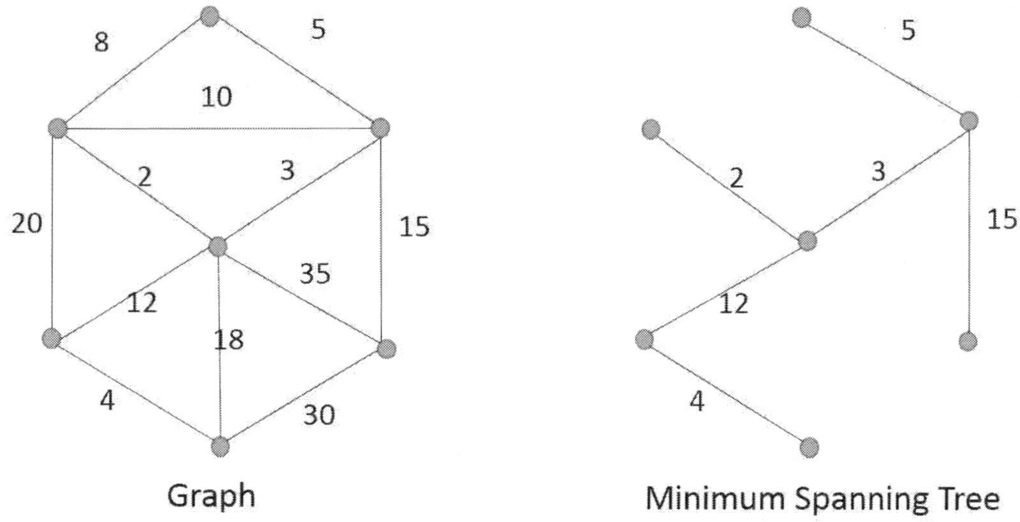


A **Hamiltonian path** is a path in which every vertex is visited exactly once with no repeats, it does not have to start and end at the same vertex.

A **Hamiltonian circuit** is a Hamiltonian Path such that there is an edge from its last vertex to its first vertex. A **Hamiltonian circuit** is a circuit that visits every vertex exactly once, and it must start and end at the same vertex.

**An Eulerian Path** is a path in the graph that visits every edge exactly once.

**An Eulerian Circuit** is an Eulerian Path, which starts and ends on the same vertex. Or the Eulerian **Circuit** is a path in the graph that visits every edge exactly once, and it starts and ends on the same vertex.

## Graph Representation

The two are the most common way of representing a graph are:

1 Adjacency Matrix

2 Adjacency List

## Adjacency Matrix

Adjacency Matrix is a two-dimensional matrix of size V rows and V columns, where V is the number of vertices in a graph. An adjacency matrix is represented using a V x V size two-dimensional array.

Let us suppose the array is "adj", so the node adj[i][j] corresponds to the edge from vertex i to vertex j. If adj[i][j] is not zero, then it means that there is a path from vertex i to vertex j. For an unweighted graph, the values in the array are either 0 for no path or 1 for a path. But in the case of a weighted graph, the value in the matrix indicates the cost/weight of a path from vertex i to j.

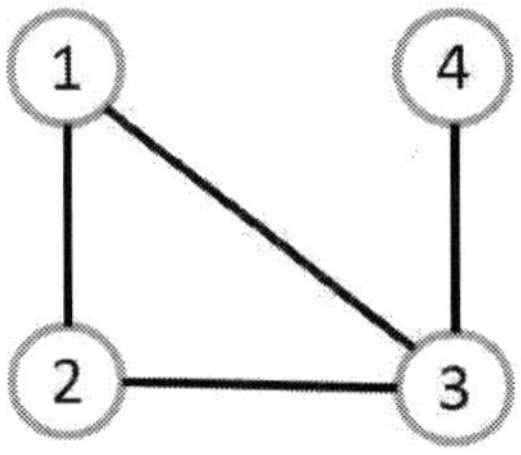


$$\begin{bmatrix} 0 & 1 & 1 & 0 \\ 1 & 0 & 1 & 0 \\ 1 & 1 & 0 & 1 \\ 0 & 0 & 1 & 0 \end{bmatrix}$$

In the above graph, each node has a weight of 1, so the adjacency matrix has just 1s or 0s. If the edges are of different weights, then that weight will be filled in the matrix.

**Example 12.1**: adjacency matrix representation of a graph

```
public class GraphAM {
    int count;
    int[][] adj;

    GraphAM(int cnt) {
        count = cnt;
        adj = new int[count][count];
    }

    public void addDirectedEdge(int src, int dst, int cost) {
        adj[src][dst] = cost;
    }

    public void addDirectedEdge(int src, int dst) {
        addDirectedEdge(src, dst, 1);
    }
```

```
    public void addUndirectedEdge(int src, int dst, int cost) {
        addDirectedEdge(src, dst, cost);
        addDirectedEdge(dst, src, cost);
    }

    public void addUndirectedEdge(int src, int dst) {
        addDirectedEdge(src, dst, 1);
        addDirectedEdge(dst, src, 1);
    }

    public void print() {
        for (int i = 0; i < count; i++) {
            System.out.print("Vertex " + i + " is connected to : ");
            for (int j = 0; j < count; j++) {
                if (adj[i][j] != 0)
                    System.out.print( j + "(cost: " + adj[i][j] + ") ");
            }
            System.out.println();
        }
    }

    // Testing code.
    public static void main(String[] args)  {
        GraphAM gph = new GraphAM(4);
        gph.addUndirectedEdge(0, 1);
        gph.addUndirectedEdge(0, 2);
        gph.addUndirectedEdge(1, 2);
        gph.addUndirectedEdge(2, 3);
        gph.print();
    }
}
```

**Output**:

```
Vertex 0 is connected to : 1(cost: 1) 2(cost: 1)
Vertex 1 is connected to : 0(cost: 1) 2(cost: 1)
Vertex 2 is connected to : 0(cost: 1) 1(cost: 1) 3(cost: 1)
Vertex 3 is connected to : 2(cost: 1)
```

**Analysis:**

1. In the constructor of graphs of N vertices, a NxN size of two-dimensional array adj is created.
2. The AddDirectedEdge function is used to add a directed edge from source to destination by setting the adj[source][destination] field of the adj array as one.
3. The AddUndirectedEdge function is used to add an undirected edge. It calls the AddDirectedEdge function twice to join source and destination both ways.

**Complexity Analysis:**

1. The space complexity of Adjacency Matrix representation is O(n^2) because a two-dimensional array is created.
2. The time complexity of the search is O(1). To find if there is an edge from vertex u to vertex v can be done in constant time.

## Pros and cons of the adjacency matrix

Pros of adjacency matrix:

- Queries if there is an edge from vertex 'u' to vertex 'v' it takes O(1) time.
- Removing an edge takes O(1) time.

Cons of adjacency matrix:

- Space complexity is O(n^2).
- Even if the graph is sparse (with few edges), space complexity remains the same.
- Adding a new vertex takes O(n^2) time.

**Sparse Matrix**: In a huge graph, each node is connected to a few nodes. So most of the places in the adjacency matrix remain empty. Such a matrix is called a sparse matrix. In most real-world problem's adjacency matrix is not a good choice for sore graph data.

## Adjacency List

A more space-efficient way of storing graphs is an adjacency list. **An adjacency list is an array of linked lists. Each list element corresponds to an edge of the Graph.** The size of the array is equal to the number of vertices in the graph. Let the array be Arr[]. An entry Arr[k] corresponds to the Kth vertex and is a list of vertices directly connected to the kth vertex. The weights of edges can be stored in nodes of linked lists.

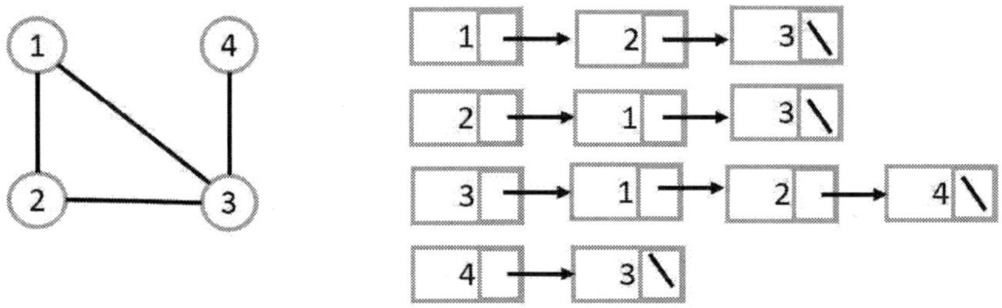


The adjacency list helps us to represent a sparse graph. An adjacency list representation also allows us to find all the vertices that are directly connected to any vertex by just one link list scan. In all our programs, we are going to use the adjacency list to store the graph.

**Example 12.2**: adjacency list representation of a graph

```
public class Graph {
    int count;
    private LinkedList<LinkedList<Edge>> Adj;
    int INF = 9999;

    private static class Edge implements Comparable<Edge> {
        int src, dest, cost;
        public Edge(int s, int d, int c) {
            src = s;
            dest = d;
            cost = c;
        }
        public int compareTo(Edge compareEdge) {
            return this.cost - compareEdge.cost;
        }
    }
```

```
    public Graph(int cnt) {
        count = cnt;
        Adj = new LinkedList<LinkedList<Edge>>();
        for (int i = 0; i < cnt; i++) {
            Adj.add(new LinkedList<Edge>());
        }
    }

    private void addDirectedEdge(int source, int dest, int cost) {
        Edge edge = new Edge(source, dest, cost);
        Adj.get(source).add(edge);
    }

    public void addDirectedEdge(int source, int dest) {
        addDirectedEdge(source, dest, 1);
    }

    public void addUndirectedEdge(int source, int dest, int cost) {
        addDirectedEdge(source, dest, cost);
        addDirectedEdge(dest, source, cost);
    }

    public void addUndirectedEdge(int source, int dest) {
        addUndirectedEdge(source, dest, 1);
    }

    public void print() {
        for (int i = 0; i < count; i++) {
            LinkedList<Edge> ad = Adj.get(i);
            System.out.print("Vertex " + i + " is connected to : ");
            for (Edge adn : ad) {
                System.out.print(adn.dest + "(cost: " + adn.cost + ") ");
            }
            System.out.println();
        }
    }

    // Testing code.
    public static void main(String[] args)  {
        Graph gph = new Graph(4);
        gph.addUndirectedEdge(0, 1);
        gph.addUndirectedEdge(0, 2);
        gph.addUndirectedEdge(1, 2);
        gph.addUndirectedEdge(2, 3);
        gph.print();
    }
}
```

**Output**:

```
Vertex 0 is connected to : 1(cost: 1) 2(cost: 1)
Vertex 1 is connected to : 0(cost: 1) 2(cost: 1)
Vertex 2 is connected to : 0(cost: 1) 1(cost: 1) 3(cost: 1)
Vertex 3 is connected to : 2(cost: 1)
```

**Analysis**:

1. In the constructor of graphs of N vertices, an array of lists of size N is created.

2. addDirectedEdge() function is used to add a directed edge from source to destination by adding a tuple (destination, cost) to the corresponding vertex list.
3. addUndirectedEdge() function is used to add an undirected edge. It calls addDirectedEdge() function twice to join source and destination both ways.

**Complexity Analysis**:
The space Complexity of Adjacency list is O(E+V), to create a vertex array and to store edges from each vertex. The time complexity of search if there is an edge from vertex u to vertex v is done in outdegree(u). We need to traverse the neighbours list of vertex u. In the worst case, it can be O(E)

## Graph traversals

**Traversal** is the process of exploring a graph by examining all its edges and vertices. The **Depth-first search (DFS**) and **Breadth-first search (BFS**) are the two algorithms used to traverse a graph. These same algorithms can also be used to find some node in the graph, find if a node is reachable etc.

A list of some of the problems that are solved using graph traversal are:
1. Determining a path from vertex u to vertex v, or report an error if there is no such path.
2. Given a starting vertex s, find the minimum number of edges from vertex s to all the other vertices of the graph.
3. Testing if a graph G is connected.
4. Finding a spanning tree of a Graph.
5. Find if there is some cycle in the graph.

## Depth First Traversal

We start the DFS algorithm from the starting point and go into the depth of the graph until we reach a dead-end and then move up to the parent node (Backtrack). In DFS, we use stack to get the next vertex to start a search. Alternatively, we can use recursion (system stack) to do the same.

The Depth First Traversal of a graph is like the Depth First Traversal of a tree. The only difference is that graphs may contain cycles (trees do not have cycles). So, while traversing, we may come back to the same node again. To avoid processing the same node again, we use a Boolean visited array.

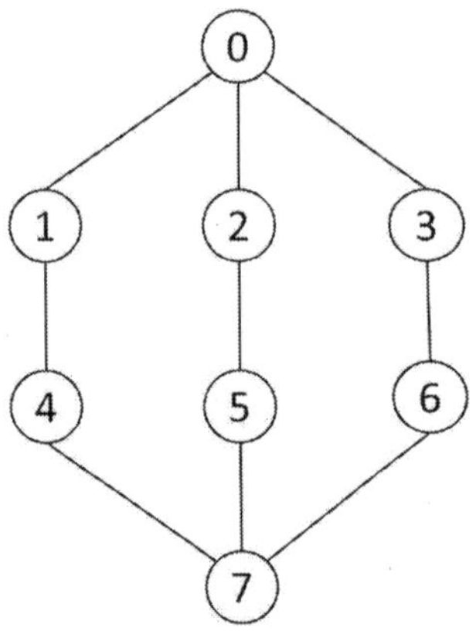


(0,1)
(0,2)
(0,3)
(1,4)
(2,5)
(3,6)
(4,7)
(5,7)
(6,7)

Below diagram demonstrates DFS traversal.

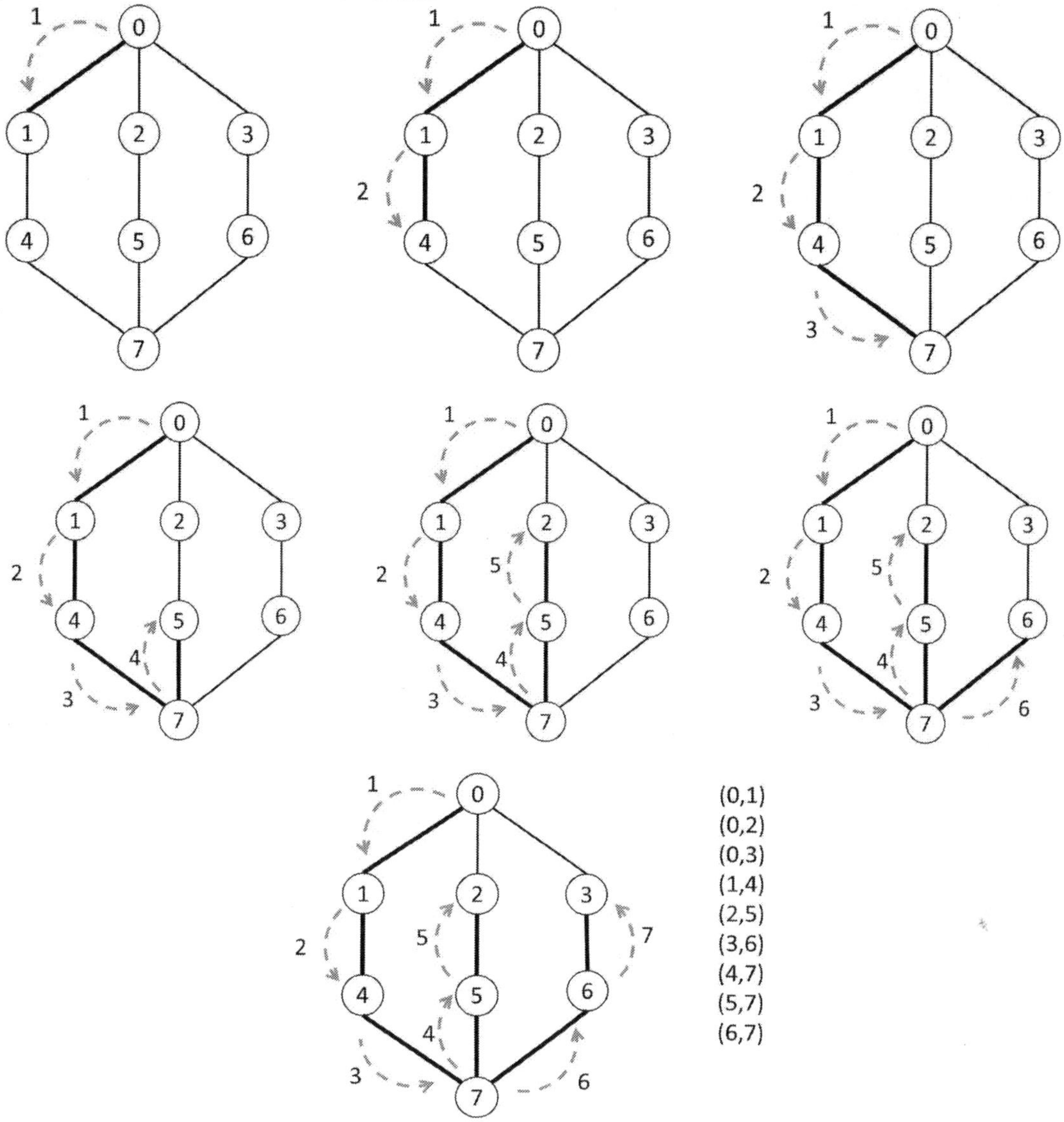


Depth First Traversal
0, 1, 4, 7 , 5, 2, 6, 3

## Stack-based implementation of DFS

Algorithm steps for DFS:

1. Push the starting node in the stack.
2. Loop until the stack is empty.
3. Pop node from the stack call this node current.
4. Process the current node. //Print, etc.
5. Traverse all the child nodes of the current node and push them into the stack.
6. Repeat steps 3 to 5 until the stack is empty.

**Example 12.3:** Stack based implementation of DFS.

```
public boolean dfsStack(int source, int target) {
    boolean[] visited = new boolean[count];
    Stack<Integer> stk = new Stack<Integer>();
```

```
    stk.push(source);
    visited[source] = true;

    while (stk.isEmpty() == false) {
        int curr = stk.pop();
        LinkedList<Edge> adl = Adj.get(curr);
        for (Edge adn : adl) {
            if (visited[adn.dest] == false) {
                visited[adn.dest] = true;
                stk.push(adn.dest);
            }
        }
    }
    return visited[target];
}

// Testing code.
public static void main(String[] args)  {
    Graph gph = new Graph(8);
    gph.addUndirectedEdge(0, 3);
    gph.addUndirectedEdge(0, 2);
    gph.addUndirectedEdge(0, 1);
    gph.addUndirectedEdge(1, 4);
    gph.addUndirectedEdge(2, 5);
    gph.addUndirectedEdge(3, 6);
    gph.addUndirectedEdge(6, 7);
    gph.addUndirectedEdge(5, 7);
    gph.addUndirectedEdge(4, 7);
    System.out.println("Path between 0 & 6 : " + gph.dfsStack(0, 6));
}
```

**Output:**

```
Path between 0 & 6 : true
```

**Complexity Analysis**:

1. The time complexity of the DFS algorithm when the graph is represented as an adjacency list is O(V+E) where V is the total number of vertices and E is the total number of edges in the graph.
2. When the graph is represented as an adjacency matrix the time complexity of algorithms is $O(V^2)$. We need to traverse adjacent vertices of a vertex, which is efficient in the graph when it is represented by an adjacency list.

## Recursion based implementation of DFS

Algorithm steps for DFS

1. In the DFS() function, create a visited array to keep track of visited nodes.
2. In the DFS() function, the source node is passed as the current node to the DFSRec() recursion function.
3. All the nodes which are visited from index nodes are further passed to DFSRec() function as recursion.
4. This recursion will return to the DFS() function when all the nodes which are visited from the source are visited. Finally, we can find if the target is visited or not by looking into the visited array.

**Example 12.4**
```
public boolean dfs(int source, int target) {
    boolean[] visited = new boolean[count];
    dfsUtil(source, visited);
    return visited[target];
}

public void dfsUtil(int index, boolean[] visited) {
    visited[index] = true;
    LinkedList<Edge> adl = Adj.get(index);
    for (Edge adn : adl) {
        if (visited[adn.dest] == false)
            dfsUtil(adn.dest, visited);
    }
}
```

**Complexity Analysis:**

1. The time complexity of the DFS algorithm when the graph is represented as an adjacency list is O(V+E) where V is the total number of vertices and E is the total number of edges in the graph.
2. When the graph is represented as an adjacency matrix the time complexity of algorithms becomes $O(V^2)$.

## Breadth First Traversal

In the BFS algorithm, a graph is traversed in a layer-by-layer fashion. The graph is traversed, closer to the starting point. The queue is used to implement BFS.

Breadth-First Traversal of a graph is like Breadth-First Traversal of a tree. The only difference is that graphs may contain cycles (trees do not have cycles). So, while traversing, we may come back to the same node again. To avoid processing the same node again, we use a Boolean visited array.

Algorithm steps for BFS

1. Push the starting node into the Queue.
2. Loop until the Queue is empty.
3. Remove a node from the queue inside a loop, and call this node current.
4. Process the current node. Like print, search etc.
5. Traverse all the child nodes of the current node and push them into the Queue.
6. Repeat steps 3 to 5 until the Queue is empty.

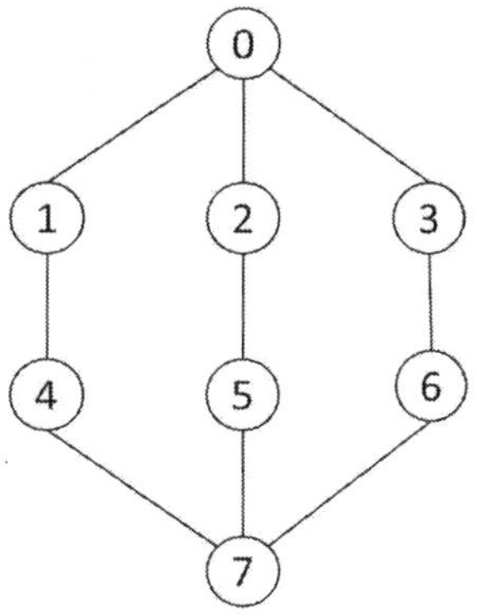


(0,1)
(0,2)
(0,3)
(1,4)
(2,5)
(3,6)
(4,7)
(5,7)
(6,7)

The below diagram demonstrates Graph Breadth First Traversal.

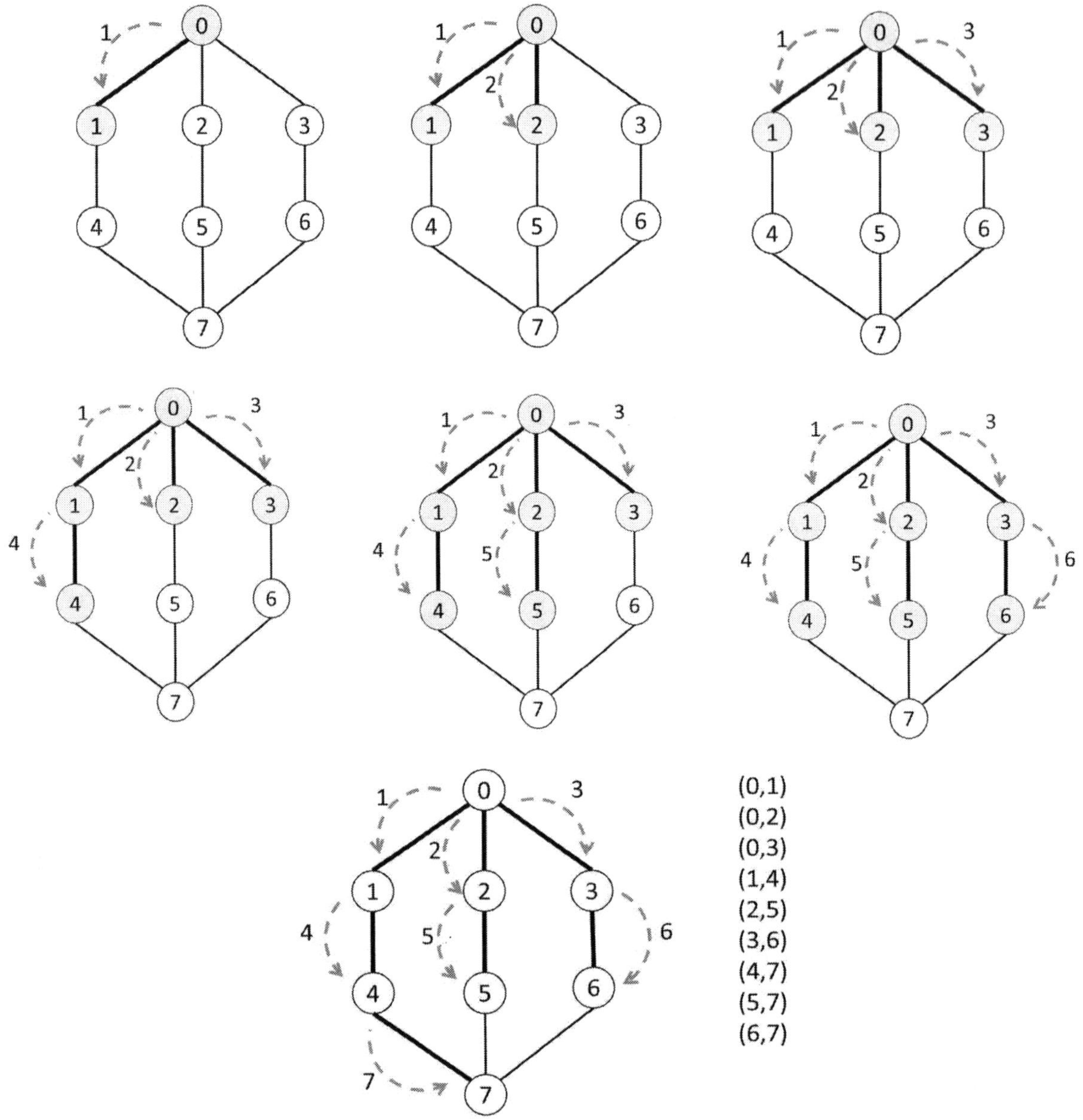


Breadth First Traversal
0, 1, 2, 3, 4, 5, 6, 7

**Example 12.5:**

```
public boolean bfs(int source, int target) {
    boolean[] visited = new boolean[count];
    LinkedList<Integer> que = new LinkedList<Integer>();
    que.add(source);
    visited[source] = true;

    while (que.isEmpty() == false) {
        int curr = que.remove();
        LinkedList<Edge> adl = Adj.get(curr);
        for (Edge adn : adl) {
            if (visited[adn.dest] == false) {
                visited[adn.dest] = true;
                que.add(adn.dest);
```

```
                }
            }
        }
        return visited[target];
    }

// Testing code.
public static void main(String[] args)  {
    Graph gph = new Graph(8);
    gph.addUndirectedEdge(0, 3);
    gph.addUndirectedEdge(0, 2);
    gph.addUndirectedEdge(0, 1);
    gph.addUndirectedEdge(1, 4);
    gph.addUndirectedEdge(2, 5);
    gph.addUndirectedEdge(3, 6);
    gph.addUndirectedEdge(6, 7);
    gph.addUndirectedEdge(5, 7);
    gph.addUndirectedEdge(4, 7);

    System.out.println("Path between 0 & 6 : " + gph.bfs(0, 6));
}
```

**Output:**

```
Path between 0 & 6 : true
```

**Complexity Analysis**: A runtime analysis of DFS and BFS traversal is O(V+E) time, where V is the number of edges reachable from the source node and E is the number of edges in the graph.

# DFS & BFS based problems

## Directed Acyclic Graph and Topological Sort

A Directed Acyclic Graph (DAG) is a directed graph with no cycle. A DAG represents a relationship, which is more general than a tree. Below is an example of DAG, this is how someone becomes ready for work. There are N other real-life examples of DAG such as courses selection to be a graduate from college.

A topological sort is a method of ordering the nodes of a directed graph in which nodes represent activities and the edges represent dependency among those tasks. For topological sorting to work it is required that the graph should be a DAG which means it should not have any cycle. Just use DFS to get topological sorting.

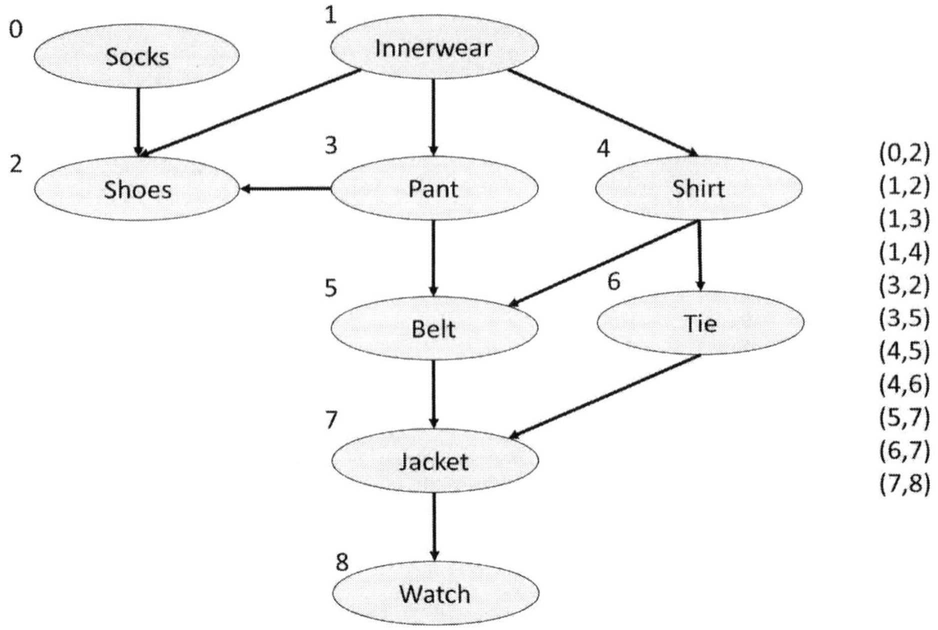


**Solution**: Topology sort uses DFS traversal of a topology graph. We use stack to store topology sort. In the topology graph, children nodes are dependent on the parent node. So first all the children of a node are added to the stack, then only the parent node is added to the stack. By doing this the parent node is above the child node. Or dependent nodes are lower in stack than the parent nodes. Run the above example to understand this algorithm.

**Example 12.6:**

```
public void dfsUtil2(int index, boolean[] visited, Stack<Integer> stk) {
    visited[index] = true;
    LinkedList<Edge> adl = Adj.get(index);
    for (Edge adn : adl) {
        if (visited[adn.dest] == false)
            dfsUtil2(adn.dest, visited, stk);
    }
    stk.push(index);
}

public void topologicalSort() {
    Stack<Integer> stk = new Stack<Integer>();
    boolean[] visited = new boolean[count];

    for (int i = 0; i < count; i++) {
        if (visited[i] == false) {
            dfsUtil2(i, visited, stk);
        }
    }

    System.out.print("Topological Sort::");
    while (stk.isEmpty() != true) {
        System.out.print(" " + stk.pop());
    }
}
```

```
// Testing code.
public static void main(String[] args)  {
    Graph gph = new Graph(9);
    gph.addDirectedEdge(0, 2);
    gph.addDirectedEdge(1, 2);
    gph.addDirectedEdge(1, 3);
    gph.addDirectedEdge(1, 4);
    gph.addDirectedEdge(3, 2);
    gph.addDirectedEdge(3, 5);
    gph.addDirectedEdge(4, 5);
    gph.addDirectedEdge(4, 6);
    gph.addDirectedEdge(5, 7);
    gph.addDirectedEdge(6, 7);
    gph.addDirectedEdge(7, 8);
    gph.topologicalSort();
}
```

**Output:**

```
Topological Sort:: 1 4 6 3 5 7 8 0 2
```

**Time-Complexity**: O(V+E), V is the number of vertices and E is the number of edges.
The topology sort algorithm is a DFS algorithm with a stack. So time complexity is the same as DFS.

## Determining a path from vertex u to vertex v

**Problem:** Find if there is a path from vertex u to vertex v.

**Solution:** If there is a path from vertex u to vertex v then when we perform DFS from vertex u we will visit vertex v.

**Example 12.7:**

```
public boolean pathExist(int source, int dest) {
    boolean[] visited = new boolean[count];
    dfsUtil(source, visited);
    return visited[dest];
}

// Testing code.
public static void main(String[] args)  {
    Graph gph = new Graph(5);
    gph.addDirectedEdge(0, 1);
    gph.addDirectedEdge(0, 2);
    gph.addDirectedEdge(2, 3);
    gph.addDirectedEdge(1, 3);
    gph.addDirectedEdge(3, 4);
    gph.addDirectedEdge(1, 4);
    System.out.println("PathExist :: " + gph.pathExist(0, 4));
}
```

**Output:**

```
PathExist :: true
```

**Complexity Analysis**: Time Complexity same as DFS for adjacency list implementation of the graph it is O(V+E) and for adjacency matrix implementation it is $O(V^2)$

## Count All Path DFS

**Problem:** Given a source vertex and a destination vertex, find all the possible paths from source to destination.

**Solution:** Perform DFS traversal of a graph starting from source vertex and count all the paths to reach the destination. We will keep a visited[] array to make sure that in a path, the same node is not considered twice.

**Example 12.8:**
```
public int countAllPathDFS(boolean[] visited, int source, int dest) {
    if (source == dest) {
        return 1;
    }
    int count = 0;
    visited[source] = true;
    LinkedList<Edge> adl = Adj.get(source);
    for (Edge adn : adl) {
        if (visited[adn.dest] == false) {
            count += countAllPathDFS(visited, adn.dest, dest);
        }
    }
    visited[source] = false;
    return count;
}

public int countAllPath(int src, int dest) {
    boolean[] visited = new boolean[count];
    return countAllPathDFS(visited, src, dest);
}

// Testing code.
public static void main(String[] args)  {
    Graph gph = new Graph(5);
    gph.addDirectedEdge(0, 1);
    gph.addDirectedEdge(0, 2);
    gph.addDirectedEdge(2, 3);
    gph.addDirectedEdge(1, 3);
    gph.addDirectedEdge(3, 4);
    gph.addDirectedEdge(1, 4);
    System.out.println("Path Count :: " + gph.countAllPath(0, 4));
}
```

**Output:**
```
Path Count : 3
```

**Complexity Analysis**: If the graph is completely connected, then in that case N! different paths are possible and traversed in DFS. So time complexity will be O(N!).

## Print All Path

**Problem:** Print all the paths from a source vertex to the destination vertex.

**Solution:** Perform DFS traversal of a graph starting from source vertex and count all the paths to reach destination vertex. We will keep a visited[] array to make sure that in a path, the same node is not considered twice. The path is stored in the stack path. When the destination is found, then the path is printed.

**Example 12.9:**
```
public void printAllPathDFS(boolean[] visited, int source, int dest, Stack<Integer> path) {
    path.push(source);
    if (source == dest) {
        System.out.println(path);
        path.pop();
        return;
    }
    visited[source] = true;
    LinkedList<Edge> adl = Adj.get(source);
    for (Edge adn : adl) {
        if (visited[adn.dest] == false)
            printAllPathDFS(visited, adn.dest, dest, path);
    }
    visited[source] = false;
    path.pop();
}

public void printAllPath(int src, int dest) {
    boolean[] visited = new boolean[count];
    Stack<Integer> path = new Stack<Integer>();
    printAllPathDFS(visited, src, dest, path);
}

// Testing code.
public static void main(String[] args)  {
    Graph gph = new Graph(5);
    gph.addDirectedEdge(0, 1);
    gph.addDirectedEdge(0, 2);
    gph.addDirectedEdge(2, 3);
    gph.addDirectedEdge(1, 3);
    gph.addDirectedEdge(3, 4);
    gph.addDirectedEdge(1, 4);
    gph.printAllPath(0, 4);
}
```

**Output:**
```
[0, 1, 3, 4]
[0, 1, 4]
[0, 2, 3, 4]
```

## Root Vertex

**Problem:** Find Root vertex in a graph. The root vertex is the vertex, which has a path to all the other vertices in a graph. If there are multiple root vertices, then return any one of them.

**Solution**: You need to return the top node of the stack in topology sort. When DFS traversal is called for some node, then this node visited index will be set and all the other nodes which are dependent on it or have path from current node will also be marked as their visited index set. If we find some nodes whose visited index is not set means the previous node is not the root vertex and this new node may be the root vertex. We traverse through the nodes and try to find the root vertex.

**Example 12.10:**
```
public int rootVertex() {
    boolean[] visited = new boolean[count];
    int retVal = -1;
    for (int i = 0; i < count; i++) {
        if (visited[i] == false) {
            dfsUtil(i, visited);
            retVal = i;
        }
    }
    System.out.print("Root vertex is :: " + retVal);
    return retVal;
}

// Testing code.
public static void main(String[] args)  {
    Graph gph = new Graph(7);
    gph.addDirectedEdge(0, 1);
    gph.addDirectedEdge(0, 2);
    gph.addDirectedEdge(1, 3);
    gph.addDirectedEdge(4, 1);
    gph.addDirectedEdge(6, 4);
    gph.addDirectedEdge(5, 6);
    gph.addDirectedEdge(5, 2);
    gph.addDirectedEdge(6, 0);
    gph.rootVertex();
}
```

**Output:**
```
Root vertex is :: 5
```

**Time-Complexity**: O(V+E), V is the number of vertices and E is the number of edges. Once a vertex is traversed, it is not traversed again.

## Transitive Closure

**Problem:** Given a directed graph, construct a transitive closure matrix or reachability matrix. Vertex v is reachable from vertex u if there is a path from u to v. The transitive closure of a graph G is a graph G', which contains the same set of vertices as G and whenever there is a path from vertex u to vertex v in G there is an edge from u to v in G'.

**Solution:** We create a two-dimensional array tc[][] and assign all it to zero. Perform DFS traversal of the graph for all the vertices as source vertex. If there is a path from source u to some vertex v, we will mark tc[u][v] as 1. The constraint in this problem is that if we had considered some destination vertex v then we will not consider it again. Further DFS traversal of some nodes is done only when tc[u][v] is 0.

**Example 12.11:**
```
public void transitiveClosureUtil(int source, int dest, int[][] tc) {
    tc[source][dest] = 1;
```

```
    LinkedList<Edge> adl = Adj.get(dest);
    for (Edge adn : adl) {
        if (tc[source][adn.dest] == 0)
            transitiveClosureUtil(source, adn.dest, tc);
    }
}

public int[][] transitiveClosure() {
    int tc[][] = new int[count][count];
    for (int i = 0; i < count; i++) {
        transitiveClosureUtil(i, i, tc);
    }
    return tc;
}

// Testing code.
public static void main(String[] args)  {
    Graph gph = new Graph(4);
    gph.addDirectedEdge(0, 1);
    gph.addDirectedEdge(0, 2);
    gph.addDirectedEdge(1, 2);
    gph.addDirectedEdge(2, 0);
    gph.addDirectedEdge(2, 3);
    gph.addDirectedEdge(3, 3);
    int[][] tc = gph.transitiveClosure();
    for (int i = 0; i < 4; i++) {
        for (int j = 0; j < 4; j++) {
            System.out.print(tc[i][j] + " ");
        }
        System.out.println();
    }
}
```

**Output:**

```
1 1 1 1
1 1 1 1
1 1 1 1
0 0 0 1
```

**Complexity Analysis**: DFS traversal is called for all the V vertices. In this DFS a node is processed only once when tc[u][v] is 0. So the total time complexity will be O(V*(V+E)).

## BFS Level Node

**Problem:** Perform BFS traversal of the graph. Along with the nodes, also print their distance from the starting source vertex.

**Solution**: We want to find the distance from the source vertex, so BFS is used as near nodes are traversed first, then far nodes. We create a queue and store the source vertex into it. We also want to keep track of the distance, so we can keep distance in the queue. Or we can keep a level[] array which will keep track of the distance from the source vertex. Perform BFS traversal, those nodes which are not traversed will only be added to the queue. Whenever a node is added to the queue, its corresponding distance from the source node is also updated in the level[] array. Time-Complexity will be O(V+E).

**Example 12.12:**
```
public void bfsLevelNode(int source) {
    boolean[] visited = new boolean[count];
    int[] level = new int[count];
    visited[source] = true;
    LinkedList<Integer> que = new LinkedList<Integer>();
    que.add(source);
    level[source] = 0;
    System.out.println("Node  - Level");

    while (que.isEmpty() == false) {
        int curr = que.remove();
        int depth = level[curr];
        LinkedList<Edge> adl = Adj.get(curr);
        System.out.println(curr + " - " + depth);
        for (Edge adn : adl) {
            if (visited[adn.dest] == false) {
                visited[adn.dest] = true;
                que.add(adn.dest);
                level[adn.dest] = depth + 1;
            }
        }
    }
}

// Testing code.
public static void main(String[] args)  {
    Graph gph = new Graph(7);
    gph.addUndirectedEdge(0, 1);
    gph.addUndirectedEdge(0, 2);
    gph.addUndirectedEdge(0, 4);
    gph.addUndirectedEdge(1, 2);
    gph.addUndirectedEdge(2, 5);
    gph.addUndirectedEdge(3, 4);
    gph.addUndirectedEdge(4, 5);
    gph.addUndirectedEdge(4, 6);
    gph.bfsLevelNode(1);
}
```

**Output:**
```
Node  - Level
1 - 0
0 - 1
2 - 1
4 - 2
5 - 2
3 - 3
6 - 3
```

## BFS Distance

**Problem:** Find the distance between source and destination vertex in a Graph.

**Solution**: We want to find the distance from the source vertex, so BFS is used as near nodes are traversed first, then far nodes. Perform BFS traversal of the graph starting from source vertex and keep track of distance of adjacent nodes before adding them to the queue. If we find the destination vertex, then return its distance from the source vertex. And if the destination vertex is not reachable, then return -1. Time-Complexity will be O(V+E).

**Example 12.13:**
```
public int bfsDistance(int source, int dest) {
    boolean[] visited = new boolean[count];
    LinkedList<Integer> que = new LinkedList<Integer>();
    que.add(source);
    visited[source] = true;
    int[] level = new int[count];
    level[source] = 0;

    while (que.isEmpty() == false) {
        int curr = que.remove();
        int depth = level[curr];
        LinkedList<Edge> adl = Adj.get(curr);
        for (Edge adn : adl) {
            if (adn.dest == dest) {
                return depth + 1;
            }
            if (visited[adn.dest] == false) {
                visited[adn.dest] = true;
                que.add(adn.dest);
                level[adn.dest] = depth + 1;
            }
        }
    }
    return -1;
}

// Testing code.
public static void main(String[] args)  {
    Graph gph = new Graph(7);
    gph.addUndirectedEdge(0, 1);
    gph.addUndirectedEdge(0, 2);
    gph.addUndirectedEdge(0, 4);
    gph.addUndirectedEdge(1, 2);
    gph.addUndirectedEdge(2, 5);
    gph.addUndirectedEdge(3, 4);
    gph.addUndirectedEdge(4, 5);
    gph.addUndirectedEdge(4, 6);
    System.out.println("BfsDistance(1, 6) : " + gph.bfsDistance(1, 6));
}
```

**Output:**
```
BFSDistance(1, 6) : 3
```

## Find cycles in a Directed Graph.

**Problem:** Given a directed graph, find if there is a cycle in the Graph. In a single traversal, if some node is traversed twice, then there is a cycle.

**First Solution:** We need to perform DFS traversal for all the nodes. Those nodes which are traversed should not be traversed again. Keeping track of visited vertices is enough to find cycles in directed graphs.

**Example 12.14:**
```
public boolean isCyclePresentDFS(int index, boolean[] visited, int[] marked) {
    visited[index] = true;
    marked[index] = 1;
    LinkedList<Edge> adl = Adj.get(index);
    for (Edge adn : adl) {
        int dest = adn.dest;
        if (marked[dest] == 1)
            return true;

        if (visited[dest] == false)
            if (isCyclePresentDFS(dest, visited, marked))
                return true;
    }
    marked[index] = 0;
    return false;
}

public boolean isCyclePresent() {
    boolean[] visited = new boolean[count];
    int[] marked = new int[count];
    for (int index = 0; index < count; index++) {
        if (!visited[index])
            if (isCyclePresentDFS(index, visited, marked))
                return true;
    }
    return false;
}

// Testing code.
public static void main(String[] args)  {
    Graph gph = new Graph(5);
    gph.addDirectedEdge(0, 1);
    gph.addDirectedEdge(0, 2);
    gph.addDirectedEdge(2, 3);
    gph.addDirectedEdge(1, 3);
    gph.addDirectedEdge(3, 4);
    System.out.println("isCyclePresent : " + gph.isCyclePresent());
    gph.addDirectedEdge(4, 1);
    System.out.println("isCyclePresent : " + gph.isCyclePresent());
}
```

**Output:**
```
isCyclePresent : false
isCyclePresent : true
```

**Complexity Analysis**: Time Complexity same as DFS for adjacency list implementation of the graph it is O(V+E) and for adjacency matrix implementation it is $O(V^2)$

**Second Solution:** Find if there is a cycle in a graph using the colour method.
In the colour method, the initially visited array is assigned the value "white" which means that nodes are not visited. When we visit a node, we mark its colour as "Grey". Nodes that are currently in the visited path remain "Grey" when all the connected nodes are traversed, and then the colour is changed to "Black". If a node that is marked "Grey" is visited again, then there is a cycle in that path.

**Example 12.15:** Cycle detection using colouring method.

```
public boolean isCyclePresentDFSColour(int index, int[] visited) {
    visited[index] = 1; // 1 = grey
    int dest;
    LinkedList<Edge> adl = Adj.get(index);
    for (Edge adn : adl) {
        dest = adn.dest;
        if (visited[dest] == 1) // "Grey":
            return true;

        if (visited[dest] == 0) // "White":
            if (isCyclePresentDFSColour(dest, visited))
                return true;
    }
    visited[index] = 2; // "Black"
    return false;
}

public boolean isCyclePresentColour() {
    int[] visited = new int[count];
    for (int i = 0; i < count; i++) {
        if (visited[i] == 0) // "White"
            if (isCyclePresentDFSColour(i, visited))
                return true;
    }
    return false;
}
```

**Complexity Analysis**: Time Complexity same as DFS for adjacency list implementation of the graph it is O(V+E) and for adjacency matrix implementation it is $O(V^2)$

## Find the cycle in an Undirected Graph.

**Problem:** Find if there is a cycle in an undirected graph.

**First Solution:** We need to perform DFS traversal for all the nodes. Those nodes which are traversed should not be traversed again. But keeping track of visited vertices is enough to find cycles in a directed graph. But in an undirected graph, the edges are bidirectional, so there is always a reverse path from child to the parent node. So this reverse path also needs to be ignored.

**Example 12.16:**

```
public boolean isCyclePresentUndirectedDFS(int index, int parentIndex, boolean[]
visited) {
    visited[index] = true;
    int dest;
    LinkedList<Edge> adl = Adj.get(index);

    for (Edge adn : adl) {
        dest = adn.dest;
        if (visited[dest] == false) {
            if (isCyclePresentUndirectedDFS(dest, index, visited))
                return true;
        } else if (parentIndex != dest)
            return true;
```

```
    }
    return false;
}

public boolean isCyclePresentUndirected() {
    boolean[] visited = new boolean[count];
    for (int i = 0; i < count; i++) {
        if (visited[i] == false && isCyclePresentUndirectedDFS(i, -1, visited))
            return true;
    }
    return false;
}

// Testing code.
public static void main(String[] args)  {
    Graph gph = new Graph(6);
    gph.addUndirectedEdge(0, 1);
    gph.addUndirectedEdge(1, 2);
    gph.addUndirectedEdge(3, 4);
    gph.addUndirectedEdge(4, 2);
    gph.addUndirectedEdge(2, 5);
    System.out.println("Cycle Present : " + gph.isCyclePresentUndirected());
    gph.addUndirectedEdge(4, 1);
    System.out.println("Cycle Present : " + gph.isCyclePresentUndirected());
}
```

**Output:**

```
Cycle Present : false
Cycle Present : true
```

**Complexity Analysis**: Time Complexity same as DFS for adjacency list implementation of the graph it is O(V+E) and for adjacency matrix implementation it is $O(V^2)$

**Second Solution:** A Disjoint-Set Data Structure is a data structure that keeps track of a number of disjoint or non-overlapping sets.

In a union-find algorithm, we have two operations to maintain disjoint sets:

1. Find: To find the set in which a particular element is present. This can be used to find if elements are in the same set.
2. Union: To join two sets into a single set.

Create a list of edges of the input graph. Traverse the edges and find if the two endpoints of edges are in the same or different set. If they are in the different set, then this edge does not create a cycle and then those sets should be merged (which is analogous to the two different groups of vertices are joined using this current edge.). If we find that both the two ends of the edge are in the same set then this means that if this edge is included then it will create a cycle.

Find() function will find the root node or first element of a set in which a particular element is present.
Union() function will merge roots of two sets to make a single set by making one parent of another.

Time-complexity: O(VE), find() function can take linear time.

**Example 12.17:**

```
public int find(int[] parent, int index) {
    int p = parent[index];
    while (p != -1) {
        index = p;
        p = parent[index];
    }
    return index;
}

public void union(int[] parent, int x, int y) {
    parent[y] = x;
}

public boolean isCyclePresentUndirected2() {
    int[] parent = new int[count];
    Arrays.fill(parent, -1);
    LinkedList<Edge> edge = new LinkedList<Edge>();

    boolean[][] flags = new boolean[count][count];
    for (int i = 0; i < count; i++) {
        LinkedList<Edge> ad = Adj.get(i);
        for (Edge adn : ad) {
            // Using flags[][] array, if considered edge x to y,
            // then ignore edge y to x.
            if (flags[adn.dest][adn.src] == false) {
                edge.add(adn);
                flags[adn.src][adn.dest] = true;
            }
        }
    }

    for (Edge e : edge) {
        int x = find(parent, e.src);
        int y = find(parent, e.dest);
        if (x == y) {
            return true;
        }
        union(parent, x, y);
    }
    return false;
}
```

**Third Solution**: This solution is also based on Disjoint-Set Data Structure. In the previous solution, the sets which are created may be of disproportionate size. Some sets are very big and others are too small because of which a find() operation takes place in linear time. But if we can make this set reference as a balanced tree, then find() operation will be efficient.

A Sets data structure is defined with elements parent and rank. Where the parent is used to refer to the parent of a node in sets and rank is used to represent hierarchy.

Union() function is used to join sets, such that the child is the parent of the set with higher rank. If the parent rank is less than the child, then promote the parent rank. This function takes the root node of two sets as input and combines them.

Create a list of edges of the input graph. Traverse the edges and find if the two endpoints of edges are in the same or different set. If they are in a different set, then this edge does not create a cycle and then those sets should be merged (which is analogues to the two different groups of vertices that are joined using this current edge.). If we find that both the two ends of the edge are in the same set then this means that if this edge is included then it will create a cycle.

Time-complexity: O(E*logV), find() function will take logV time as the tree of V will be balanced.

**Example 12.18**
```
public boolean isCyclePresentUndirected3() {
    //Different subsets are created.
    Sets[] sets = new Sets[count];
    for (int i = 0; i < count; i++)
        sets[i] = new Sets(i, 0);

    LinkedList<Edge> edge = new LinkedList<Edge>();
    boolean[][] flags = new boolean[count][count];
    for (int i = 0; i < count; i++) {
        LinkedList<Edge> ad = Adj.get(i);
        for (Edge adn : ad) {
            // Using flags[][] array, if considered edge x to y,
            // then ignore edge y to x.
            if (flags[adn.dest][adn.src] == false) {
                edge.add(adn);
                flags[adn.src][adn.dest] = true;
            }
        }
    }

    for (Edge e : edge) {
        int x = find(sets, e.src);
        int y = find(sets, e.dest);
        if (x == y) {
            return true;
        }
        union(sets, x, y);
    }
    return false;
}
```

## Transpose Graph

**Problem:** Transpose of a Graph G is a graph G' that has the same set of vertices, but the direction of edges is reversed.

**Solution**: Create an empty graph G' with the same number of nodes as the input graph G. Traverse the various nodes of the input graph G. If there is an edge v to u in input graph G then add an edge u to v in the new graph G'. Return new graph G'.

**Example 12.19:**
```
public Graph transposeGraph() {
    Graph g = new Graph(count);
```

```
    for (int i = 0; i < count; i++) {
        LinkedList<Edge> adl = Adj.get(i);
        for (Edge adn : adl) {
            int dest = adn.dest;
            g.addDirectedEdge(dest, i);
        }
    }
    return g;
}

// Testing code.
public static void main(String[] args)  {
    Graph gph = new Graph(5);
    gph.addDirectedEdge(0, 1);
    gph.addDirectedEdge(0, 2);
    gph.addDirectedEdge(2, 3);
    gph.addDirectedEdge(1, 3);
    gph.addDirectedEdge(3, 4);
    gph.addDirectedEdge(4, 1);
    Graph gReversed = gph.transposeGraph();
    gReversed.print();
}
```

**Output:**

```
Vertex 0 is connected to :
Vertex 1 is connected to : 0(cost: 1) 4(cost: 1)
Vertex 2 is connected to : 0(cost: 1)
Vertex 3 is connected to : 1(cost: 1) 2(cost: 1)
Vertex 4 is connected to : 3(cost: 1)
```

**Complexity Analysis**: Time Complexity for adjacency list implementation of the graph is O(V+E) and for adjacency matrix implementation it is $O(V^2)$

## Test if an undirected graph is connected.

**Problem:** Given an undirected graph, find if it is a connected graph.

**Solution:** Start from any vertex if we can visit all the other vertices using DFS or BFS then the graph is connected.

**Example 12.20:**

```
public boolean isConnectedUndirected() {
    boolean[] visited = new boolean[count];

    dfsUtil(0, visited);
    for (int i = 0; i < count; i++) {
        if (visited[i] == false) {
            return false;
        }
    }
    return true;
}

//Testing Code
public static void main(String[] args)  {
    Graph gph = new Graph(6);
```

```
    gph.addUndirectedEdge(0, 1);
    gph.addUndirectedEdge(1, 2);
    gph.addUndirectedEdge(3, 4);
    gph.addUndirectedEdge(4, 2);
    gph.addUndirectedEdge(2, 5);
    System.out.println("isConnectedUndirected:: " + gph.isConnectedUndirected());
}
```

**Output:**

```
isConnectedUndirected:: true
```

**Complexity Analysis**: Time Complexity same as DFS for adjacency list implementation of the graph it is O(V+E) and for adjacency matrix implementation it is $O(V^2)$

## Strongly Connected Graph

A directed graph is strongly connected if for each pair of vertices u and v, there is a path from u to v and a path from v to u.

To prove that the graph is a connected graph, we need to prove two conditions as true for anyone vertex:

1. The first condition, that every vertex can be visited from some vertex u. Or every vertex is reachable from vertex u.
2. The second condition, that vertex u is reachable from every other vertex.

First conditions can be verified by doing a DFS from some vertex u. We need to check that all the vertices of the graph are visited. The second condition can be verified by first creating a transpose graph G'. Then perform DFS over G' from vertex u. If all other vertices are visited from vertex u in graph G'. It means that vertex u is reachable from all the vertices of the original graph G.

**Kosaraju's Algorithm** to find if the graph is connected based on DFS:

1. Create a visited array of size V, and Initialise all vertices in the visited array as False.
2. Choose any vertex and perform a DFS traversal of the graph. For all visited vertices, mark them visited by setting their values as True in the visited array.
3. If DFS traversal does not mark all vertices as True, then return false.
4. Find transpose or reverse of the graph
5. Repeat steps 1, 2 and 3 for the reversed graph.
6. If DFS traversal marks all the vertices as True, then return true.

**Example 12.21:**

```
public boolean isStronglyConnected() {
    boolean visited[] = new boolean[count];
    dfsUtil(0, visited);
    for (int i = 0; i < count; i++) {
        if (visited[i] == false) {
            return false;
        }
    }
    Graph gReversed = transposeGraph();
    for (int i = 0; i < count; i++) {
        visited[i] = false;
    }
```

```
    gReversed.dfsUtil(0, visited);
    for (int i = 0; i < count; i++) {
        if (visited[i] == false) {
            return false;
        }
    }
    return true;
}

// Testing code.
public static void main(String[] args)  {
    Graph gph = new Graph(5);
    gph.addDirectedEdge(0, 1);
    gph.addDirectedEdge(1, 2);
    gph.addDirectedEdge(2, 3);
    gph.addDirectedEdge(3, 0);
    gph.addDirectedEdge(2, 4);
    gph.addDirectedEdge(4, 2);
    System.out.println("IsStronglyConnected:: " + gph.isStronglyConnected());
}
```

**Output:**

```
IsStronglyConnected:: true
```

**Time Complexity:** O(V+E), for two times doing DFS traversal.

## Strongly Connected Components

**Strongly Connected Components**: A directed graph may have different sub-graphs that are strongly connected. These sub-graphs are called strongly connected components. In the below graph the whole graph is not strongly connected but its two sub-graphs are strongly connected components.

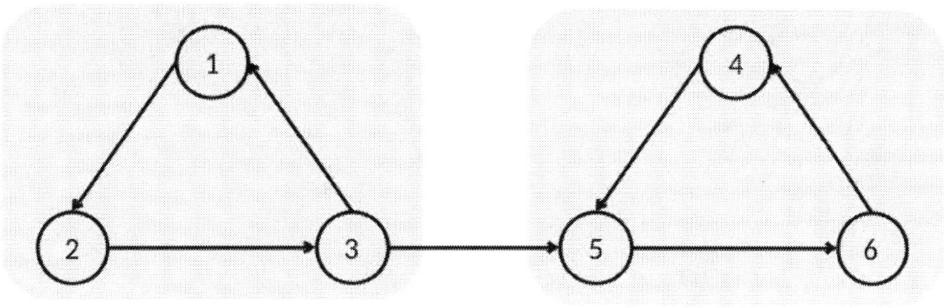


Strongly Connected Component

Algorithm to find Strongly Connected Component

- Create an empty stack, do DFS traversal on graph G. Call DFS for adjacent vertices, and push them into the stack.
- Reverse the graph G to get a new graph G'
- Perform the DFS traversal on the graph G' by picking vertices from the top of the stack.
- Each strongly connected component is traversed in one single iteration.

**Example 12.22:**
```
public void stronglyConnectedComponent() {
    boolean[] visited = new boolean[count];
    Stack<Integer> stk = new Stack<Integer>();
    for (int i = 0; i < count; i++) {
        if (visited[i] == false)
            dfsUtil2(i, visited, stk);
    }

    Graph gReversed = transposeGraph();
    Arrays.fill(visited, false);

    Stack<Integer> stk2 = new Stack<Integer>();
    while (stk.isEmpty() == false) {
        int index = stk.pop();
        if (visited[index] == false) {
            stk2.clear();
            gReversed.dfsUtil2(index, visited, stk2);
            System.out.println(stk2);
        }
    }
}

// Testing code.
public static void main(String[] args)  {
    Graph gph = new Graph(7);
    gph.addDirectedEdge(0, 1);
    gph.addDirectedEdge(1, 2);
    gph.addDirectedEdge(2, 0);
    gph.addDirectedEdge(2, 3);
    gph.addDirectedEdge(3, 4);
    gph.addDirectedEdge(4, 5);
    gph.addDirectedEdge(5, 3);
    gph.addDirectedEdge(5, 6);
    gph.stronglyConnectedComponent();
}
```

**Output:**
```
[1, 2, 0]
[4, 5, 3]
[6]
```

**Time Complexity:** O(V+E), for two times doing DFS traversal.

## Minimum Spanning Tree (MST)

A **Spanning Tree** of a graph G is a tree that contains all the vertices of the Graph.
A **Minimum Spanning Tree** is a spanning tree whose sum of length/weight of edges is as minimal as possible.

For example, if you want to set up communication between a set of cities, then you may want to use the least amount of wire possible. MST can be used to find the network path and wire cost estimate.

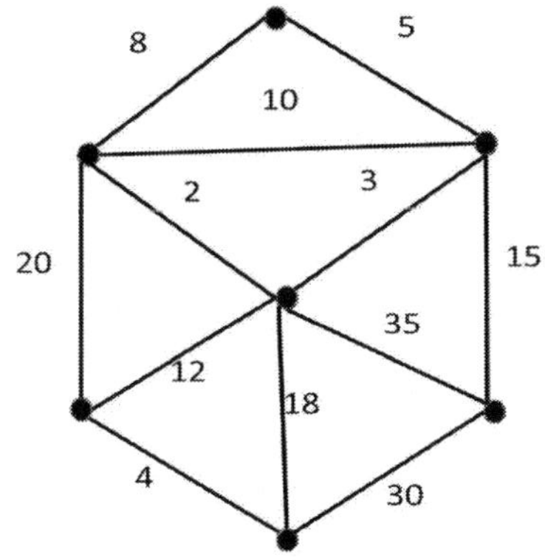


Graph

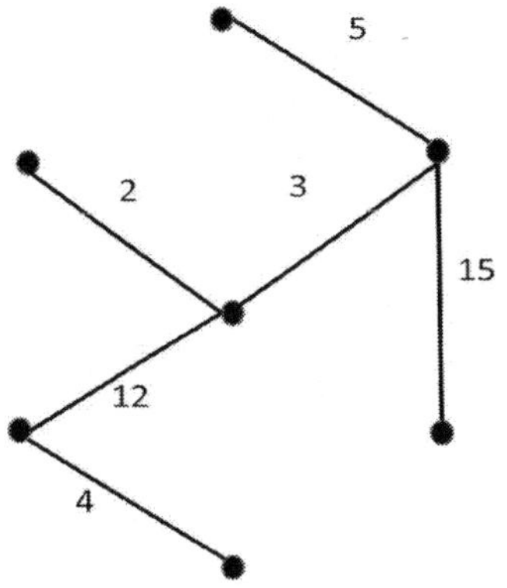


Minimum Spanning Tree

## Prim's Algorithm for MST

Prim's algorithm grows a single tree T, one edge at a time, until it becomes a spanning tree.
We Initialise T with zero edges and U with a single node. Where T is spanning tree edges set and U is spanning tree vertex set.

At each step, Prim's algorithm adds the smallest value edge with one endpoint in U and the other not in us. Since each edge adds one new vertex to U, after n − 1 additions, U contains all the vertices of the spanning tree and T becomes a spanning tree.

```
// Returns the MST by Prim's Algorithm
// Input: A weighted connected graph G = (V, E)
// Output: Set of edges comprising a MST

function Prim(G)
    T = {}
    Let r be any vertex in G
    U = {r}

    for i = 1 to |V| - 1 do
        e = minimum-weight edge (u, v)
            With u in U and v in V-U
        U = U + {v}
        T = T + {e}
    return T
```

Prim's Algorithm uses a priority queue to get the closest next vertex, The algorithm starts with adding a dummy node source to the source to the queue. The nodes of the queue are taken one at a time. Then that node is processed and the nodes that are visited by it are added to the queue. The queue is a priority queue, so it will always give a node with the least weight. If the node that is popped out of the queue includes some new node, then that node is marked as visited, else that edge is ignored.

**Example 12.23:** Prims algorithm implementation for adjacency list representation of graph.

```
public void primsMST() {
    int[] previous = new int[count];
    int[] dist = new int[count];
    boolean[] visited = new boolean[count];
    Arrays.fill(previous, -1);
    Arrays.fill(dist, Integer.MAX_VALUE);// infinite
```

```
    int source = 0;
    dist[source] = 0;
    previous[source] = source;
    PriorityQueue<Edge> queue = new PriorityQueue<Edge>(100);
    Edge node = new Edge(source, source, 0);
    queue.add(node);

    while (queue.isEmpty() != true) {
        node = queue.peek();
        queue.remove();
        visited[source] = true;
        source = node.dest;
        LinkedList<Edge> adl = Adj.get(source);
        for (Edge adn : adl) {
            int dest = adn.dest;
            int alt = adn.cost;
            if (dist[dest] > alt && visited[dest] == false) {
                dist[dest] = alt;
                previous[dest] = source;
                node = new Edge(source, dest, alt);
                queue.add(node);
            }
        }
    }

    // printing result.
    int sum = 0;
    boolean isMst = true;
    String output = "Edges are ";
    for (int i = 0; i < count; i++) {
        if (dist[i] == Integer.MAX_VALUE) {
            output += ("(" + i + ", Unreachable) ");
            isMst = false;
        } else if (previous[i] != i) {
            output += ("(" + previous[i] + "->" + i + " @ " + dist[i] + ") ");
            sum += dist[i];
        }
    }

    if (isMst) {
        System.out.println(output);
        System.out.println("Total MST cost: " + sum);
    } else
        System.out.println("Can't get a Spanning Tree");
}

// Testing code.
public static void main(String[] args)  {
    Graph gph = new Graph(9);
    gph.addUndirectedEdge(0, 1, 4);
    gph.addUndirectedEdge(0, 7, 8);
    gph.addUndirectedEdge(1, 2, 8);
    gph.addUndirectedEdge(1, 7, 11);
    gph.addUndirectedEdge(2, 3, 7);
    gph.addUndirectedEdge(2, 8, 2);
    gph.addUndirectedEdge(2, 5, 4);
    gph.addUndirectedEdge(3, 4, 9);
    gph.addUndirectedEdge(3, 5, 14);
```

```
    gph.addUndirectedEdge(4, 5, 10);
    gph.addUndirectedEdge(5, 6, 2);
    gph.addUndirectedEdge(6, 7, 1);
    gph.addUndirectedEdge(6, 8, 6);
    gph.addUndirectedEdge(7, 8, 7);
    System.out.println();
    gph.primsMST();
}
```

**Output:**

```
Edges are : (0->1 @ 4) (5->2 @ 4) (2->3 @ 7) (3->4 @ 9) (6->5 @ 2)
            (7->6 @ 1) (0->7 @ 8) (2->8 @ 2)
Total MST cost: 37
```

**Time complexity** is O((E + V) log V) where V vertices and E edges of the graph.

**Example 12.24:** Prims algorithm implementation for adjacency matrix representation of graph.

```
public void primsMST() {
    int[] previous = new int[count];
    int[] dist = new int[count];

    boolean[] visited = new boolean[count];
    Arrays.fill(previous, -1);
    Arrays.fill(dist, Integer.MAX_VALUE); // infinite

    int source = 0;
    dist[source] = 0;
    previous[source] = source;

    PriorityQueue<Edge> queue = new PriorityQueue<Edge>(100);
    Edge node = new Edge(source, source, 0);
    queue.add(node);

    while (queue.isEmpty() != true) {
        node = queue.peek();
        queue.remove();
        source = node.dest;
        visited[source] = true;
        for (int dest = 0; dest < count; dest++) {
            int cost = adj[source][dest];
            if (cost != 0) {
                if (dist[dest] > cost && visited[dest] == false) {
                    dist[dest] = cost;
                    previous[dest] = source;
                    node = new Edge(source, dest, cost);
                    queue.add(node);
                }
            }
        }
    }

    // printing result.
    int sum = 0;
    boolean isMst = true;
    String output = "Edges are ";

    for (int i = 0; i < count; i++) {
```

```
        if (dist[i] == Integer.MAX_VALUE) {
            output += ("(" + i + ", Unreachable) ");
            isMst = false;
        } else if (previous[i] != i) {
            output += ("(" + previous[i] + "->" + i + " @ " + dist[i] + ") ");
            sum += dist[i];
        }
    }

    if (isMst) {
        System.out.println(output);
        System.out.println("Total MST cost: " + sum);
    } else
        System.out.println("Can't get a Spanning Tree");
}
```

**Time complexity** is O(V^2) where V vertices of the graph.

## Kruskal's Algorithm

Kruskal's Algorithm repeatedly chooses the smallest-weight edge that does not form a cycle.

Sort the edges in non-decreasing order of cost: c (e1) ≤ c (e2) ≤ · · · ≤ c (em).

Set T to be the empty tree. Add edges to the tree one by one, if it does not create a cycle.

```
// Returns the MST by Kruskal's Algorithm
// Input: A weighted connected graph G = (V, E)
// Output: Set of edges comprising a MST
function Kruskal(G)
    Sort the edges E by their weights
    T = { }
    while |T | + 1 < |V | do
        e = next edge in E
        if T + {e} does not have a cycle then
            T = T + {e}
    return T
```

A **Disjoint-Set data structure** is a data structure that keeps track of a number of disjoint or non-overlapping sets.

In a union-find algorithm, we have two operations to maintain disjoint sets:

1. Find: To find the set in which a particular element is present. This can be used to find if elements are in the same set.
2. Union: To join two sets into a single set.

Create a list of edges of the input graph. Traverse the edges and find if the two endpoints of edges are in the same or different set. If they are in the different set, then this edge does not create a cycle and then those sets should be merged (which is analogous to the two different groups of vertices are joined using this current edge.). If we find that both the two ends of the edge are in the same set then this means that if this edge is included then it will create a cycle.

Find() function will find the root or first element of a set in which a particular element is present.

Union() function will merge the roots of two sets to make a single set.

**Example 12.25:**

```
public static class Sets {
    int parent;
    int rank;

    Sets(int p, int r) {
        parent = p;
        rank = r;
    }
}

// root element of set
public int find(Sets[] sets, int index) {
    int p = sets[index].parent;
    while (p != index) {
        index = p;
        p = sets[index].parent;
    }
    return index;
}

// consider x and y are roots of sets.
public void union(Sets[] sets, int x, int y) {
    if (sets[x].rank < sets[y].rank)
        sets[x].parent = y;
    else if (sets[y].rank < sets[x].rank)
        sets[y].parent = x;
    else {
        sets[x].parent = y;
        sets[y].rank++;
    }
}

public void kruskalMST() {
    //Different subsets are created.
    Sets[] sets = new Sets[count];
    for (int i = 0; i < count; i++)
        sets[i] = new Sets(i, 0);

    // Edges are added to array and sorted.
    int E = 0;
    Edge edge[] = new Edge[100];

    for (int i = 0; i < count; i++) {
        LinkedList<Edge> ad = Adj.get(i);
        for (Edge adn : ad) {
            edge[E++] = adn;
        }
    }
    Arrays.sort(edge, 0, E - 1);

    int sum = 0;
    String output = "Edges are ";

    for (int i = 0; i < E; i++) {
        int x = find(sets, edge[i].src);
        int y = find(sets, edge[i].dest);
```

```
        if (x != y) {
            output += ("(" + edge[i].src + "->" + edge[i].dest + " @ " +
edge[i].cost + ") ");
            sum += edge[i].cost;
            union(sets, x, y);
        }
    }
    System.out.println(output);
    System.out.println("Total MST cost: " + sum);
}
```

**Time-complexity**: The time complexity of the above program is O(ElogV). E times loop is executed and find() takes logV time for V number of vertices.

## Euler path and Euler Circuit

**Eulerian Path** is a path in the graph that visits every edge exactly once.
**Eulerian Circuit** is an Eulerian Path, which starts and ends on the same vertex. Or **Eulerian Circuit** is a path in the graph that visits every edge exactly once, and it starts and ends on the same vertex.

**Problem**: A graph is called Eulerian if there is an Euler circuit in it. A graph is called Semi-Eulerian if there is an Euler Path in the graph. If there is no Euler path possible in the graph, then it is called Non-Eulerian. Check if the graph is Eulerian, Semi-Eulerian or Non-Eulerian.

**Solution**: A graph is Eulerian if all the edges have an even number of edges in it. A graph is Semi-Eulerian if it has exactly two vertices with an odd number of edges or an odd degree. In all other cases, the graph is Non-Eulerian.

**Example 12.26:**

```
public int isEulerian() {
    // Check if all non - zero degree nodes are connected
    if (isConnected() == false) {
        System.out.println("graph is not Eulerian");
        return 0;
    }

    // Count odd degree
    int odd = 0;
    int[] inDegree = new int[count];
    int[] outDegree = new int[count];
    LinkedList<Edge> adl;

    for (int i = 0; i < count; i++) {
        adl = Adj.get(i);
        for (Edge adn : adl) {
            outDegree[i] += 1;
            inDegree[adn.dest] += 1;
        }
    }
    for (int i = 0; i < count; i++) {
        if ((inDegree[i] + outDegree[i]) % 2 != 0) {
            odd += 1;
        }
```

```
    }

    if (odd == 0) {
        System.out.println("graph is Eulerian");
        return 2;
    } else if (odd == 2) {
        System.out.println("graph is Semi-Eulerian");
        return 1;
    } else {
        System.out.println("graph is not Eulerian");
        return 0;
    }
}

// Testing code.
public static void main(String[] args)  {
    Graph gph = new Graph(5);
    gph.addDirectedEdge(1, 0);
    gph.addDirectedEdge(0, 2);
    gph.addDirectedEdge(2, 1);
    gph.addDirectedEdge(0, 3);
    gph.addDirectedEdge(3, 4);
    gph.isEulerian();
    gph.addDirectedEdge(4, 0);
    gph.isEulerian();
}
```

**Output:**

```
graph is Semi-Eulerian
graph is Eulerian
```

# Shortest Path Algorithms in Graph

## Single-Source Shortest Path for an unweighted Graph.

**Problem**: Given an unweighted graph G= (V, E), where V is the set of vertices and E is the set of edges. Find the shortest path from a given source vertex 's' to all the vertices of V.

**Solution:**

1. First, the starting point source is added to a queue.
2. Breadth-first traversal is performed
3. Nodes that are closer to the source are traversed first and processed.
4. Time-complexity will be O(V+E), the total number of times the inner loop will be executed will be E which is the total number of edges in the graph.

**Example 12.27:**

```
public void shortestPath(int source) {
    int curr;
    int[] distance = new int[count];
    int[] path = new int[count];
    for (int i = 0; i < count; i++) {
        distance[i] = -1;
        path[i] = -1;
```

```
    }

    Queue<Integer> que = new LinkedList<Integer>();
    que.add(source);
    distance[source] = 0;
    path[source] = source;

    while (que.isEmpty() == false) {
        curr = que.remove();
        LinkedList<Edge> adl = Adj.get(curr);
        for (Edge adn : adl) {
            if (distance[adn.dest] == -1) {
                distance[adn.dest] = distance[curr] + 1;
                path[adn.dest] = curr;
                que.add(adn.dest);
            }
        }
    }
    printPath(path, distance, count, source);
}

String printPathUtil(int[] previous, int source, int dest) {
    String path = "";
    if (dest == source)
        path += source;
    else {
        path += printPathUtil(previous, source, previous[dest]);
        path += ("->" + dest);
    }

    return path;
}

public void printPath(int[] previous, int[] dist, int count, int source) {
    String output = "Shortest Paths: ";
    for (int i = 0; i < count; i++) {
        if (dist[i] == 99999)
            output += ("(" + source + "->" + i + " @ Unreachable) ");
        else if (i != previous[i]) {
            output += "(";
            output += printPathUtil(previous, source, i);
            output += (" @ " + dist[i] + ") ");
        }
    }
    System.out.println(output);
}

// Testing Code
public static void main(String[] args)  {
    Graph gph = new Graph(9);
    gph.addUndirectedEdge(0, 1);
    gph.addUndirectedEdge(0, 7);
    gph.addUndirectedEdge(1, 2);
    gph.addUndirectedEdge(1, 7);
    gph.addUndirectedEdge(2, 3);
    gph.addUndirectedEdge(2, 8);
    gph.addUndirectedEdge(2, 5);
    gph.addUndirectedEdge(3, 4);
```

```
        gph.addUndirectedEdge(3, 5);
        gph.addUndirectedEdge(4, 5);
        gph.addUndirectedEdge(5, 6);
        gph.addUndirectedEdge(6, 7);
        gph.addUndirectedEdge(6, 8);
        gph.addUndirectedEdge(7, 8);
        gph.shortestPath(0);
}
```

**Output:**

```
Shortest Paths: (0->1 @ 1) (0->1->2 @ 2) (0->1->2->3 @ 3) (0->7->6->5->4 @ 4)
                (0->7->6->5 @ 3) (0->7->6 @ 2) (0->7 @ 1) (0->7->8 @ 2)
```

## Dijkstra's algorithm / Single Source Shortest path with positive weighted graph

**Problem**: Given a weighted graph G= (V, E), where V is the set of vertices and E is the set of edges. Where all the edges E of the graph are non-negative. Find the shortest path from a given source vertex 's' to all the vertices of V.

**Solution**: Dijkstra's algorithm is used for a single-source shortest path problem for weighted edges with no negative weight. Dijkstra's algorithm is like a prim's algorithm. It maintains a set of nodes for which the shortest path is known.

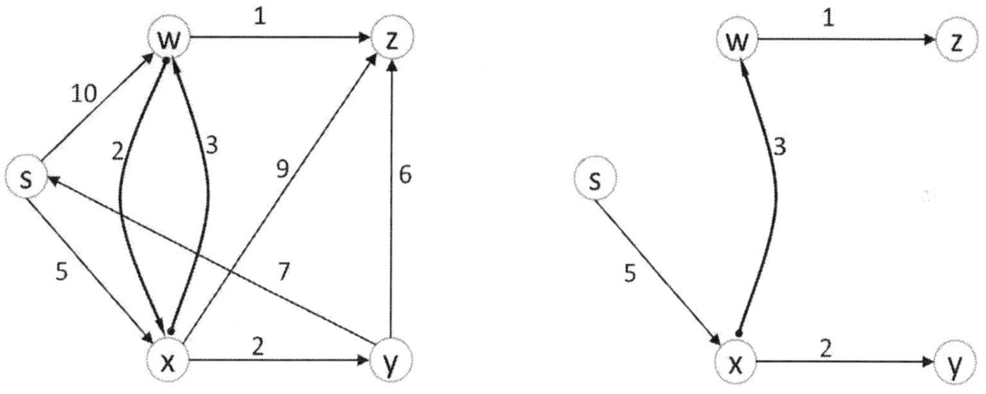


Single-Source shortest path

The algorithm starts by keeping track of the distance of each node and its parents. All the distance is set to infinite in the beginning as we do not know the actual path to the nodes and parents of all the vertices are set to null. All the vertices are added to a priority queue (min-heap implementation)
Each step algorithm takes one vertex from the priority queue (which will be the source vertex in the beginning). Then update the distance list corresponding to all the adjacent vertices. When the queue is empty, then we will have the distance and a parent list fully populated.

```
// Solves SSSP by Dijkstra's Algorithm
// Input: A weighted connected graph G = (V, E)
// with no negative weights, and source vertex v
// Output: The length and path from s to every v

function Dijkstra(G, s)
    for each v in V do
       D[v] = infinite    // Unknown distance
       P[v] = null    //unknown previous node
```

```
        add v to PQ    //adding all nodes to priority queue

    D[source] = 0 // Distance from source to source

    while (PQ is not empty)
        u = vertex from PQ with smallest D[u]
        remove u from PQ
        for each v adjacent from u do
            alt = D[u] + length (u, v)
            if alt < D[v] then
                D[v] = alt
                P[v] = u

    return D[], P[]
```

**Note:** Dijkstra's algorithm does not work for graphs with negative edge weight.
**Note:** Dijkstra's algorithm applies to both undirected and directed graphs.

**Example 12.28:** Dijkstra's algorithm for adjacency list implementation of graph.

```
public void dijkstra(int source) {
    int[] previous = new int[count];
    int[] dist = new int[count];
    boolean[] visited = new boolean[count];

    Arrays.fill(previous, -1);
    Arrays.fill(dist, 99999); // infinite

    dist[source] = 0;
    previous[source] = source;

    PriorityQueue<Edge> queue = new PriorityQueue<Edge>(100);
    Edge edge = new Edge(source, source, 0);
    queue.add(edge);
    int curr;

    while (queue.isEmpty() != true) {
        edge = queue.peek();
        queue.remove();
        curr = edge.dest;
        visited[curr] = true;
        LinkedList<Edge> adl = Adj.get(curr);

        for (Edge adn : adl) {
            int dest = adn.dest;
            int alt = adn.cost + dist[curr];

            if (alt < dist[dest] && visited[dest] == false) {
                dist[dest] = alt;
                previous[dest] = curr;
                edge = new Edge(curr, dest, alt);
                queue.add(edge);
            }
        }
    }

    printPath(previous, dist, count, source);
}
```

```
// Testing Code
public static void main(String[] args)  {
    Graph gph = new Graph(9);
    gph.addUndirectedEdge(0, 1, 4);
    gph.addUndirectedEdge(0, 7, 8);
    gph.addUndirectedEdge(1, 2, 8);
    gph.addUndirectedEdge(1, 7, 11);
    gph.addUndirectedEdge(2, 3, 7);
    gph.addUndirectedEdge(2, 8, 2);
    gph.addUndirectedEdge(2, 5, 4);
    gph.addUndirectedEdge(3, 4, 9);
    gph.addUndirectedEdge(3, 5, 14);
    gph.addUndirectedEdge(4, 5, 10);
    gph.addUndirectedEdge(5, 6, 2);
    gph.addUndirectedEdge(6, 7, 1);
    gph.addUndirectedEdge(6, 8, 6);
    gph.addUndirectedEdge(7, 8, 7);
    gph.dijkstra(0);
}
```

**Output:**
```
Shortest Paths: (0->1 @ 4) (0->1->2 @ 12) (0->1->2->3 @ 19) (0->7->6->5->4 @ 21)
                (0->7->6->5 @ 11) (0->7->6 @ 9) (0->7 @ 8) (0->1->2->8 @ 14)
```

**Time complexity** is O((E + V) log V) where V vertices and E edges of the graph.

**Example 12.29:** Dijkstra's algorithm for adjacency matrix implementation of graph.
```
public void dijkstra(int source) {
    int[] previous = new int[count];
    int[] dist = new int[count];
    boolean[] visited = new boolean[count];

    Arrays.fill(previous, -1);
    Arrays.fill(dist, Integer.MAX_VALUE); // infinite

    dist[source] = 0;
    previous[source] = source;

    PriorityQueue<Edge> queue = new PriorityQueue<Edge>(100);
    Edge node = new Edge(source, source, 0);
    queue.add(node);

    while (queue.isEmpty() != true) {
        node = queue.peek();
        queue.remove();
        int src = node.dest;
        visited[src] = true;
        for (int dest = 0; dest < count; dest++) {
            int cost = adj[src][dest];
            if (cost != 0) {
                int alt = cost + dist[src];
                if (dist[dest] > alt && visited[dest] == false) {

                    dist[dest] = alt;
                    previous[dest] = src;
                    node = new Edge(src, dest, alt);
```

```
                    queue.add(node);
                }
            }
        }
    }
    printPath(previous, dist, count, source);
}
```

**Time complexity** is O(V^2) where V vertices of the graph.

## Bellman Ford Algorithm / Single source shortest path with negative weights graph

**Problem**: Given a weighted graph G= (V, E), where V is the set of vertices and E is the set of edges. Where the edges E of the graph can be negative but no negative weight cycle. Find the shortest path from a given source vertex 's' to all the vertices of V.

**Solution**: Bellman Ford algorithm is used to find a single source shortest path to all the other vertices in a graph with a negative edge but no negative weight cycle. A negative weight cycle is a cycle whose total weight is negative. In this algorithm, the distance of all the vertices is assigned to ∞ and the source vertex distance is assigned as 0. Then V-1 passes (passes also called relaxation) over all the edges and the distance to the destination is updated for each vertex. We can stop the algorithm if a pass / relaxation does not modify the distance to any of the vertices.

If there is a change in weight of the distance after the V-1 pass (relaxation) then we have a negative cycle in the graph.

Time complexity is O(V.E), where V is the number of vertices and E is the total number of edges.

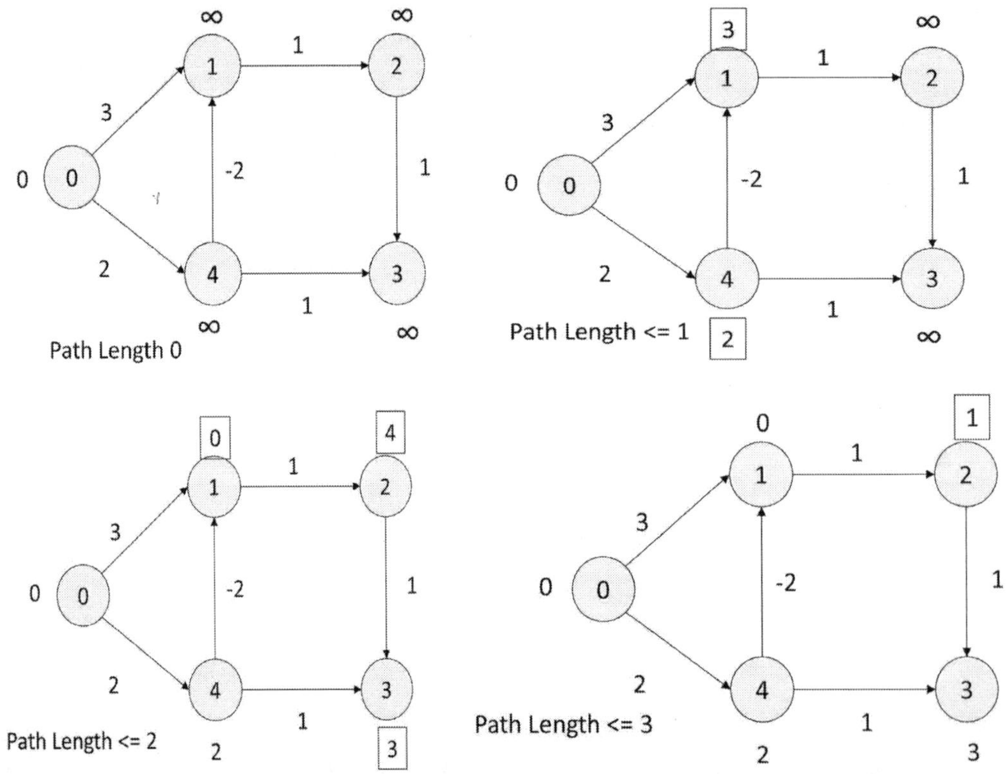

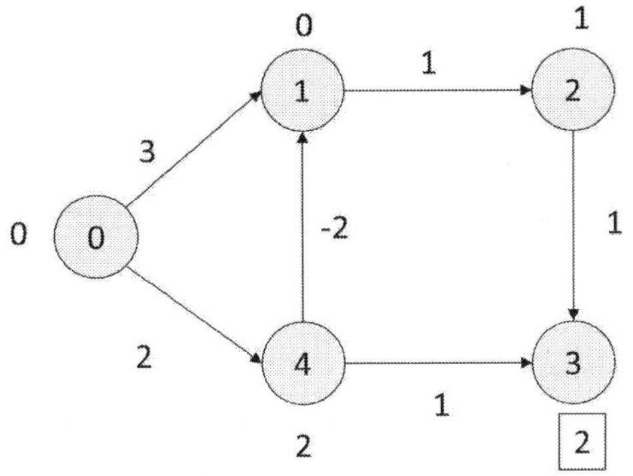


Path Length <= 4

**Example 12.30:**
```
public void bellmanFordShortestPath(int source) {
    int[] distance = new int[count];
    Arrays.fill(distance, 99999); // infinite
    int[] path = new int[count];
    Arrays.fill(path, -1);

    distance[source] = 0;
    path[source] = source;
    // Outer loop will run (V-1) number of times.
    // Inner for loop and while loop runs combined will
    // run for Edges number of times.
    // Which make the total complexity as O(V*E)

    for (int i = 0; i < count - 1; i++) {
        for (int j = 0; j < count; j++) {
            LinkedList<Edge> adl = Adj.get(j);
            for (Edge adn : adl) {
                int newDistance = distance[j] + adn.cost;
                if (distance[adn.dest] > newDistance) {
                    distance[adn.dest] = newDistance;
                    path[adn.dest] = j;
                }
            }
        }
    }
    printPath(path, distance, count, source);

}

// Testing code.
public static void main(String[] args)  {
    Graph gph = new Graph(5);
    gph.addDirectedEdge(0, 1, 3);
    gph.addDirectedEdge(0, 4, 2);
    gph.addDirectedEdge(1, 2, 1);
    gph.addDirectedEdge(2, 3, 1);
    gph.addDirectedEdge(4, 1, -2);
    gph.addDirectedEdge(4, 3, 1);
    gph.bellmanFordShortestPath(0);
}
```

**Output:**
```
Shortest Paths: (0->4->1 @ 0) (0->4->1->2 @ 1) (0->4->1->2->3 @ 2) (0->4 @ 2)
```

## All Pairs Shortest Paths / Floyd Warshall Algorithm

**Problem**: Given a weighted graph G= (V, E), where V is the set of vertices and E is the set of edges. Where the edges E of the graph can be negative. Find the shortest path between all the pairs of vertices u, v ϵ V.

**Solution**: Floyd Warshall Algorithm can be used to find the shortest path between all the pairs of vertices in a graph if the graph does not contain a negative weight cycle. If the graph contains a negative-weight cycle, then it reports a negative cycle too. It compares all the possible paths between each pair of vertices in the graph.

Create an output matrix same as the given cost matrix of the graph. After that, the output matrix will be updated with all vertices as the intermediate vertex. When we had selected vertex k as intermediate vertex, then we had already selected all the previous vertices from 0 to k-1 as intermediate vertices.

$Dist^{K}$ [i, j] = minimum ( $Dist^{K-1}$[i, j] , $Dist^{K-1}$ [i, k] + $Dist^{K-1}$ [k, j] )
All the diagonals of the distance matrix dist[i][i] are set to 0 in the start. If we find a better path from i to i. Which means two things: that there is a cycle and the cycle has a negative weight.

The time complexity of this algorithm is O(V^3), where V is the number of vertices in the graph.

**Example 12.31:**
```
void floydWarshall() {
    int V = count;
    int dist[][] = new int[V][V];
    int path[][] = new int[V][V];
    final int INF = 99999;

    for (int i = 0; i < V; i++) {
        for (int j = 0; j < V; j++) {
            dist[i][j] = INF;
            if (i == j)
                path[i][j] = 0;
            else
                path[i][j] = -1;
        }
    }

    for (int i = 0; i < V; i++) {
        LinkedList<Edge> adl = Adj.get(i);
        for (Edge adn : adl) {
            path[adn.src][adn.dest] = adn.src;
            dist[adn.src][adn.dest] = adn.cost;
        }
    }

    // Pick intermediate vertices.
    for (int k = 0; k < V; k++) {
        // Pick source vertices one by one.
        for (int i = 0; i < V; i++) {
            // Pick destination vertices.
            for (int j = 0; j < V; j++) {
                // If we have a shorter path from i to j via k.
```

```
                // then update dist[i][j] and  and path[i][j]
                if (dist[i][k] + dist[k][j] < dist[i][j]) {
                    dist[i][j] = dist[i][k] + dist[k][j];
                    path[i][j] = path[k][j];
                }
            }
            // dist[i][i] is 0 in the start.
            // If there is a better path from i to i and is better path then we
have -ve cycle.                //
            if (dist[i][i] < 0) {
                System.out.println("Negative-weight cycle found.");
                return;
            }
        }
    }
    printSolution(dist, path, V);
}

private void printSolution(int[][] cost, int[][] path, int V) {
    System.out.print("Shortest Paths : ");
    for (int u = 0; u < V; u++) {
        for (int v = 0; v < V; v++) {
            if (u != v && path[u][v] != -1) {
                System.out.print("(");
                printPath2(path, u, v);
                System.out.print(" @ " + cost[u][v] + ") ");
            }
        }
    }
    System.out.println();
}

private void printPath2(int[][] path, int u, int v) {
    if (path[u][v] == u) {
        System.out.print(u + "->" + v);
        return;
    }
    printPath2(path, u, path[u][v]);
    System.out.print("->" + v);
}

// Testing code.
public static void main(String[] args)  {
    Graph gph = new Graph(4);
    gph.addDirectedEdge(0, 0, 0);
    gph.addDirectedEdge(1, 1, 0);
    gph.addDirectedEdge(2, 2, 0);
    gph.addDirectedEdge(3, 3, 0);
    gph.addDirectedEdge(0, 1, 5);
    gph.addDirectedEdge(0, 3, 10);
    gph.addDirectedEdge(1, 2, 3);
    gph.addDirectedEdge(2, 3, 1);
    gph.floydWarshall();
}
```

**Output**:

```
Shortest Paths : (0->1 @ 5) (0->1->2 @ 8) (0->1->2->3 @ 9) (1->2 @ 3) (1->2->3 @ 4)
(2->3 @ 1)
```

## Hamiltonian Path

A **Hamiltonian path** is a path in which every vertex is visited exactly once with no repeats, it does not have to start and end at the same vertex.

The **Hamiltonian path** is a Np-Complete problem, so the only solution is possible using backtracking, which starts from a vertex s and tries all adjacent vertices recursively. If we do not find the path, then we backtrack and try other vertices.

**Solution**: Backtracking Approach, finding all the possible paths is the graph that satisfies the hamiltonian path conditions. In a hamiltonian path, the node which is added should not be added again. A path[] array will be created to store path[]. And an added[] array is used to keep track of the elements already added to the path. If we find a path that is of length equal to the number of vertices, we have our solution.

**Time-complexity**: O(N!), All possible paths are traversed, so the total number of paths will be N!.

**Example 12.32:**
```
public boolean hamiltonianPathUtil(int path[], int pSize, int added[]) {
    // Base case full length path is found
    if (pSize == count) {
        return true;
    }
    for (int vertex = 0; vertex < count; vertex++) {
        // There is an edge from last element of path and next vertex
        // and the next vertex is not already included in the path.
        if (pSize == 0 || (adj[path[pSize - 1]][vertex] == 1 && added[vertex] ==
0)) {
            path[pSize++] = vertex;
            added[vertex] = 1;
            if (hamiltonianPathUtil(path, pSize, added))
                return true;
            // backtracking
            pSize--;
            added[vertex] = 0;
        }
    }
    return false;
}

public boolean hamiltonianPath() {
    int[] path = new int[count];
    int[] added = new int[count];

    if (hamiltonianPathUtil(path, 0, added)) {
        System.out.print("Hamiltonian Path found :: ");
        for (int i = 0; i < count; i++)
            System.out.print(" " + path[i]);
        System.out.println("");
        return true;
    }
```

```
    System.out.println("Hamiltonian Path not found");
    return false;
}

// Testing code.
public static void main(String[] args)  {
    int count = 5;
    GraphAM gph = new GraphAM(count);
    int[][] adj = { { 0, 1, 0, 1, 0 }, { 1, 0, 1, 1, 0 }, { 0, 1, 0, 0, 1 },
                    { 1, 1, 0, 0, 1 }, { 0, 1, 1, 1, 0 } };

    for (int i = 0; i < count; i++)
        for (int j = 0; j < count; j++)
            if (adj[i][j] == 1)
                gph.addDirectedEdge(i, j, 1);
    System.out.println("hamiltonianPath : " + gph.hamiltonianPath());

    GraphAM gph2 = new GraphAM(count);
    int[][] adj2 = { { 0, 1, 0, 1, 0 }, { 1, 0, 1, 1, 0 }, { 0, 1, 0, 0, 1 }, { 1,
1, 0, 0, 0 },
            { 0, 1, 1, 0, 0 } };
    for (int i = 0; i < count; i++)
        for (int j = 0; j < count; j++)
            if (adj2[i][j] == 1)
                gph2.addDirectedEdge(i, j, 1);

    System.out.println("hamiltonianPath :  " + gph2.hamiltonianPath());
}
```

**Output:**

```
Hamiltonian Path found ::  0 1 2 4 3
hamiltonianPath : true
Hamiltonian Path found ::  0 3 1 2 4
hamiltonianPath :  true
```

## Hamiltonian Circuit

A **Hamiltonian circuit** is a Hamiltonian Path such that there is an edge from its last vertex to its first vertex. A **Hamiltonian circuit** is a circuit that visits every vertex exactly once and it must start and end at the same vertex.

**Solution**: Backtracking Approach, find all the possible paths that satisfy the hamiltonian path conditions and the path should also satisfy one more condition that there should be a path from the last node of the Hamiltonian path to the first element.. In a hamiltonian path, the node which is added should not be added again. A path[] array will be created to store path[]. And an added[] array is used to keep track of the elements already added to the path. If we find a path that is of length equal to the number of vertices and there is a path from the last node to the first, then we have our solution.

**Time-complexity**: O(n!)

**Example 12.33:**

```
public boolean hamiltonianCycleUtil(int path[], int pSize, int added[]) {
    // Base case full length path is found
```

```
    // this last check can be modified to make it a path.
    if (pSize == count) {
        if (adj[path[pSize - 1]][path[0]] == 1) {
            path[pSize] = path[0];
            return true;
        } else
            return false;
    }
    for (int vertex = 0; vertex < count; vertex++) {
        // there is a path from last element and next vertex
        if (pSize == 0 || (adj[path[pSize - 1]][vertex] == 1 && added[vertex] ==
0)) {
            path[pSize++] = vertex;
            added[vertex] = 1;
            if (hamiltonianCycleUtil(path, pSize, added))
                return true;
            // backtracking
            pSize--;
            added[vertex] = 0;
        }
    }
    return false;
}

public boolean hamiltonianCycle() {
    int[] path = new int[count + 1];
    int[] added = new int[count];
    if (hamiltonianCycleUtil(path, 0, added)) {
        System.out.print("Hamiltonian Cycle found :: ");
        for (int i = 0; i <= count; i++)
            System.out.print(" " + path[i]);
        System.out.println("");
        return true;
    }
    System.out.println("Hamiltonian Cycle not found");
    return false;
}

// Testing code.
public static void main(String[] args)  {
    int count = 5;
    GraphAM gph = new GraphAM(count);
    int[][] adj = { { 0, 1, 0, 1, 0 }, { 1, 0, 1, 1, 0 }, { 0, 1, 0, 0, 1 },
                    { 1, 1, 0, 0, 1 }, { 0, 1, 1, 1, 0 } };

    for (int i = 0; i < count; i++)
        for (int j = 0; j < count; j++)
            if (adj[i][j] == 1)
                gph.addDirectedEdge(i, j, 1);
    System.out.println("hamiltonianCycle : " + gph.hamiltonianCycle());

    GraphAM gph2 = new GraphAM(count);
    int[][] adj2 = { { 0, 1, 0, 1, 0 }, { 1, 0, 1, 1, 0 }, { 0, 1, 0, 0, 1 },
                     { 1, 1, 0, 0, 0 }, { 0, 1, 1, 0, 0 } };
    for (int i = 0; i < count; i++)
        for (int j = 0; j < count; j++)
            if (adj2[i][j] == 1)
                gph2.addDirectedEdge(i, j, 1);
```

```
    System.out.println("hamiltonianCycle :  " + gph2.hamiltonianCycle());
}
```

**Output:**
```
Hamiltonian Cycle found ::  0 1 2 4 3 0
hamiltonianCycle : true
Hamiltonian Cycle not found
hamiltonianCycle :  false
```

## Travelling Salesman Problem (TSP)

**Problem:** The travelling salesman problem tries to find the shortest tour through a given set of n cities that visits each city exactly once before returning to the city where it started.

Or

Given a weighted connected graph G= (V, E) where V are the vertices and E are the edges. Since the graph is fully connected, there are multiple hamiltonian circuits. We need to find the shortest Hamiltonian Circuit in a graph. A cycle that passes through all the vertices of the graph exactly once.

```
function TSP
    Select a city
    MinTourCost = infinite
    for (All permutations of cities) do
        if(LengthOfPathSinglePermutation < MinTourCost)
            MinTourCost = LengthOfPath
```

Total number of possible combinations = (n-1)!, Cost for calculating the path: Θ(n)
So the total time complexity finding the shortest path: **Θ(n!)**

It is an NP-Hard problem and there is no efficient algorithm to find its solution. Even if some path is given as a solution, it is equally hard to verify that this is a correct solution or not.

**Example 12.34:**
```
public class TSP {
    // Function to find the minimum weight Hamiltonian Cycle
    static int tsp(int[][] graph, int n, int[] path, int pSize, int pCost,
boolean[] visited, int ans, int[] ansPath) {
        if (pCost > ans)
            return ans;

        int curr = path[pSize - 1];
        if (pSize == n) {
            if (graph[curr][0] > 0 && ans > pCost + graph[curr][0]) {
                ans = pCost + graph[curr][0];
                for(int i = 0; i<=n; i++)
                    ansPath[i] = path[i%n];
            }
            return ans;
        }

        for (int i = 0; i < n; i++) {
            if (visited[i] == false && graph[curr][i] > 0) {
                visited[i] = true;
```

```
                path[pSize] = i;
                ans = tsp(graph, n, path, pSize + 1, pCost + graph[curr][i],
visited, ans, ansPath);
                visited[i] = false;
            }
        }
        return ans;
    }

    static int tsp(int[][] graph, int n) {
        boolean[] visited = new boolean[n];
        int[] path = new int[n];
        int[] ansPath = new int[n+1];
        path[0] = 0;
        visited[0] = true;
        int ans = Integer.MAX_VALUE;
        ans = tsp(graph, n, path, 1, 0, visited, ans, ansPath);
        System.out.println("Path length : " + ans);
        System.out.print("Path : ");
        for(int i = 0; i<=n; i++)
            System.out.print(ansPath[i] + " ");
        return ans;
    }

    // Testing code.
    public static void main(String[] args) {
        int n = 4;
        int[][] graph = { { 0, 10, 15, 20 },
                          { 10, 0, 35, 25 },
                          { 15, 35, 0, 30 },
                          { 20, 25, 30, 0 } };
        tsp(graph, n);
    }
}
```

**Output**:

```
Shortest Path weight: 80
Shortest Path: 0 1 3 2 0
```

## Uses of Graph algorithms

Applications of Graph algorithms are:

1. Maps are represented by Graph.
2. GPS navigation uses shortest path algorithms like Dijstra algorithm.
3. Social networks like Facebook, Instagram etc. used graphs to represent connections between profiles.
4. Path finding algorithms are used in Robotics, Video Games etc.
5. Spanning Tree algorithms are used to set up communication networks in graphs of nodes.
6. Finding if a path exists between two vertices can be done using BFS or DFS.
7. Given a starting vertex u, finding the minimum number of edges from vertex s to all the other vertices of the graph is done using BFS.

8. Testing if a graph G is connected can be done using BFS or DFS.
9. Finding if there is a cycle in the graph or checking if a given graph is a tree is done using DFS.
10. Topological Sorting is done using DFS.
11. Strongly connected components or graphs in directed graphs are done using DFS.

## Exercise

1. In the various path-finding algorithms, we have created a path array that just stores the immediate parent of a node, and prints the complete path for it.

2. All the functions are implemented as if the graph is represented by an adjacency list. Write all those functions for graph representation as adjacency matrices.

3. In a given start string, end string and a set of strings, find if there exists a path between the start string and end string via the set of strings.

4. A path exists if we can get from the start string to end the string by changing (no addition/removal) only one character at a time. The restriction is that the new string generated after changing one character has to be in the set.
   Start: "cog"      End: "bad"
   Set: ["bag", "cag", "cat", "fag", "con", "rat", "sat", "fog"]
   One of the paths: "cog" -> "fog" -> "fag" -> "bag" -> "bad"

# Chapter 13: String Algorithms

## Introduction

String in C language is an array of characters. We use string algorithms in so many tasks, when we are using some copy-paste, some string replacement, and some string search. When we are using some dictionary program, we are using string algorithms. When we are searching something in google, we are passing some information that is also a string and that will be further converted and processed by google.

Note: This chapter is very important for the interview point of view as many interview problems are from this chapter.

## String Matching

Every word-processing program has a search function in which you can search all occurrences of any word in a long text file. For this, we need string-matching algorithms.

**Problem:** Search a pattern of length m in a given text of length n. Where m < n.

**Approach 1: Brute Force Search**

The brute force search algorithm will check the pattern at all possible values of "i" in the text where the value of "i" ranges from 0 to n-m. The pattern is compared with the text, character by character from left to right. When a mismatch is detected, then the pattern is compared by shifting the compare window by one character.

**Example 13.1:**

```
public static int bruteForceSearch(String textIn, String patternIn) {
    char[] text = textIn.toCharArray();
    char[] pattern = patternIn.toCharArray();
    final int n = text.length;
    final int m = pattern.length;
    int i = 0, j = 0;

    while (i <= n - m) {
        j = 0;
        while (j < m && pattern[j] == text[i + j]) {
            j++;
        }

        if (j == m) {
            return (i);
        }
        i++;
    }

    return -1;
}
```

```
// Testing code.
public static void main(String[] args) {
    String st1 = "hello, world!";
    String st2 = "world";
    System.out.println("Using BruteForceSearch pattern found at index : " +
bruteForceSearch(st1, st2));
}
```

**Output:**

```
Using BruteForceSearch pattern found at index : 7
```

The time complexity of the algorithm is **O(m*n)**, we get the pattern at the end of the text or we do not get the pattern at all**.**

**Approach 2: Robin Karp Algorithm**

The Robin-Karp algorithm is somewhat like the brute force algorithm, in which the pattern is compared to each portion of the text of length m. Instead of comparing patterns, character by character its hash code is compared. The hash code of the pattern is compared with the hash code of the text window. We try to keep the hash code as unique as possible. So that when hashcode matches, then the text should also match.

The two features of a good hash code are:

1. The collision should be excluded as much as possible. A collision occurs when the hashcode matches, but the pattern does not.
2. The hash code of text must be calculated in constant time.

In this algorithm, the hash code of some window is calculated from the hash code of the previous window in constant time. At the start, the hash value of the text of length m is calculated. We compare its hash code with the hash code of the pattern string. To get the hash code of the next window, we exclude one character and include the next character. The portion of text that needs to be compared moves as a window of characters. For each window, calculation of hash is done in constant time, one member leaves the window and a new number enters the window.

Multiplication by 2 is the same as left shift operation. Multiplication by $2^{m-1}$ is the same as left shift m-1 times. If the pattern is "m" character long. Then, when we want to remove the leftmost character from the hash, we will subtract its ASCII value multiplied by $2^{m-1}$. We shift the whole hash calculation by multiplying it by 2. Finally, the hash value of the new window is calculated by adding the ASCII value of the rightmost element of this window. We do not want to do large multiplication operations, so modular operations with a prime number are used.

**Example 13.2:**

```
public static int robinKarp(String textIn, String patternIn) {
    char[] text = textIn.toCharArray();
    char[] pattern = patternIn.toCharArray();
    int n = text.length;
    int m = pattern.length;
    int i, j;
    int prime = 101;
    int powm = 1;
    int TextHash = 0, PatternHash = 0;
```

```
    if (m == 0 || m > n) {
        return -1;
    }

    for (i = 0; i < m - 1; i++) {
        powm = (powm << 1) % prime;
    }

    for (i = 0; i < m; i++) {
        PatternHash = ((PatternHash << 1) + pattern[i]) % prime;
        TextHash = ((TextHash << 1) + text[i]) % prime;
    }

    for (i = 0; i <= (n - m); i++) {
        if (TextHash == PatternHash) {
            for (j = 0; j < m; j++) {
                if (text[i + j] != pattern[j]) {
                    break;
                }
            }
            if (j == m)
                return i;
        }

        if (i < n - m)
            TextHash = (((TextHash - text[i] * powm) << 1) + text[i + m]) % prime;

        if (TextHash < 0) {
            TextHash = (TextHash + prime);
        }
    }
    return -1;
}
```

The time complexity of the algorithm is **O(n).**

**Approach 3: Knuth Morris Pratt Algorithm**

There is an inefficiency in the brute force method of string matching. After a shift of the pattern, the brute force algorithm forgot all the information about the previously matched symbols. This is because of which its worst-case time complexity is O(mn).

The Knuth-Morris-Pratt algorithm makes use of this information that is computed in the previous comparison. It never compares the whole text. It uses preprocessing of the pattern. The preprocessing takes O(m) time and the whole algorithm time-complexity is **O(n)**

Preprocessing step: we try to find the border of the pattern at a different prefix of the pattern.

A **prefix** is a string that comes at the beginning of a string.
A **proper prefix** is a prefix that is not the complete string. Its length is less than the length of the string.
A **suffix** is a string that comes at the end of a string.
A **proper suffix** is a suffix that is not a complete string. Its length is less than the length of the string.
A **border** is a string that is both a proper prefix and a proper suffix.

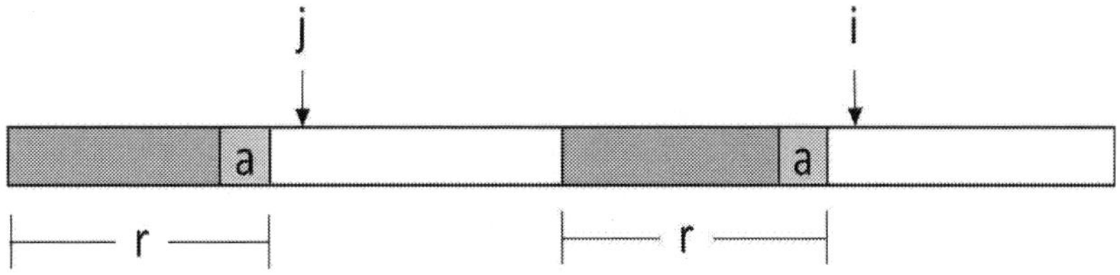


**Example 13.3:**
```
public static void KMPPreprocess(char[] pattern, int[] ShiftArr) {
    final int m = pattern.length;
    int i = 0, j = -1;
    ShiftArr[i] = -1;

    while (i < m) {
        while (j >= 0 && pattern[i] != pattern[j]) {
            j = ShiftArr[j];
        }
        i++;
        j++;
        ShiftArr[i] = j;
    }
}
```

We have two, loop outer loop for the text and inner loop for the pattern when we have matched the text and pattern mismatch, we shift the text such that the widest border is considered and then the rest of the pattern matching is resumed after this shift. If again a mismatch happens then the next mismatch is taken.

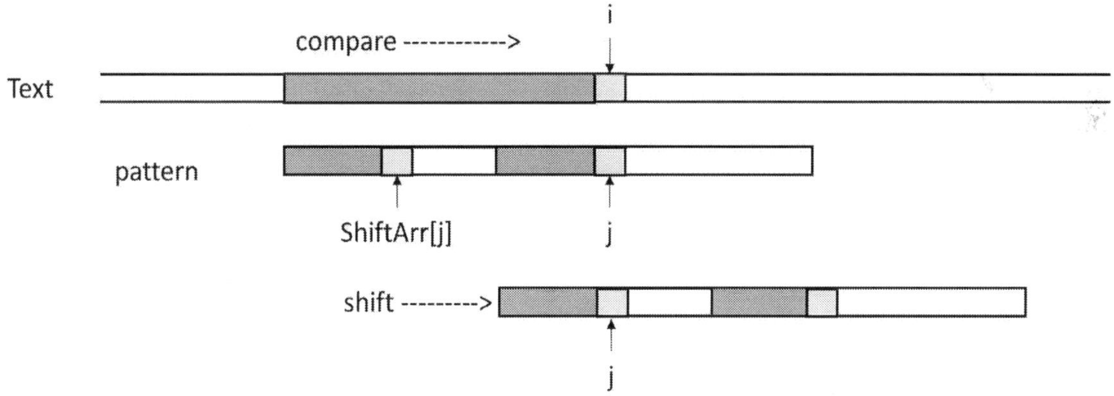


**Example 13.4:**
```
public static int KMP(String textIn, String patternIn) {
    char[] text = textIn.toCharArray();
    char[] pattern = patternIn.toCharArray();
    final int n = text.length;
    final int m = pattern.length;
    int[] ShiftArr = new int[m + 1];
    KMPPreprocess(pattern, ShiftArr);
    int i = 0, j = 0;

    while (i < n) {
        while (j >= 0 && text[i] != pattern[j])
            j = ShiftArr[j];

        i++;
        j++;
```

```
        if (j == m) {
            return (i - m);
        }
    }
    return -1;
}
```

**Problem:** Use the same KMP algorithm to find the number of occurrences of the pattern in a text.

**Example 13.5:**

```
public static int KMPFindCount(String textIn, String patternIn) {
    char[] text = textIn.toCharArray();
    char[] pattern = patternIn.toCharArray();
    final int n = text.length;
    final int m = pattern.length;
    int[] ShiftArr = new int[m + 1];
    KMPPreprocess(pattern, ShiftArr);
    int i = 0, j = 0, count = 0;
    while (i < n) {
        while (j >= 0 && text[i] != pattern[j]) {
            j = ShiftArr[j];
        }
        i++;
        j++;
        if (j == m) {
            count++;
            j = ShiftArr[j];
        }
    }
    return count;
}

// Testing code.
public static void main(String[] args) {
    String str3 = "Only time will tell if we stand the test of time";
    System.out.println("Frequency of 'time' is : " + KMPFindCount(str3, "time"));
}
```

**Output:**

```
Frequency of 'time' is : 2
```

## Dictionary / Symbol Table

A symbol table is a mapping between a string (key) and a value that can be of any type. A value can be an integer such as occurrence count, dictionary meaning of a word and so on. Dictionaries can be implemented in various ways. We will be studying the Binary Search Tree of strings, Hash-Table, Tries and Ternary Search Tree.

### Binary Search Tree (BST) for Strings

Binary Search Tree (BST) is the simplest way to implement a symbol table. A simple strcmp() function can be used to compare two strings. If all the keys are random and the tree is balanced, then an average key lookup can be done in O(log(n)) time. Below is an implementation of a binary search tree to store a string as a key. This will keep track of the occurrence count of words in a text.

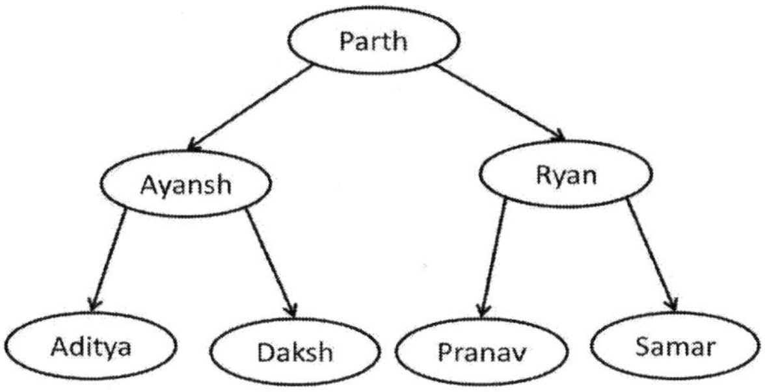


Binary Search Tree as Dictionary

**Example 13.6:**

```
public class StringTree {
    Node root = null;

    class Node {
        String value;
        int count;
        Node lChild;
        Node rChild;
    };

    public void print() {
        print(root);
    }

    public void print(Node curr) { /* pre order */
        if (curr != null) {
            System.out.print(" value is ::" + curr.value);
            System.out.println(" count is :: " + curr.count);
            print(curr.lChild);
            print(curr.rChild);
        }
    }

    public void add(String value) {
        root = add(value, root);
    }

    Node add(String value, Node curr) {
        if (curr == null) {
            curr = new Node();
            curr.value = value;
            curr.lChild = curr.rChild = null;
            curr.count = 1;
        } else {
            int compare = curr.value.compareTo(value);
            if (compare == 0)
                curr.count++;
            else if (compare == 1)
                curr.lChild = add(value, curr.lChild);
            else
                curr.rChild = add(value, curr.rChild);
        }
        return curr;
    }
```

```
    boolean find(String value) {
        boolean ret = find(root, value);
        return ret;
    }

    boolean find(Node curr, String value) {
        if (curr == null)
            return false;
        int compare = curr.value.compareTo(value);
        if (compare == 0)
            return true;
        else {
            if (compare == 1)
                return find(curr.lChild, value);
            else
                return find(curr.rChild, value);
        }
    }

    int frequency(String value) {
        return frequency(root, value);
    }

    int frequency(Node curr, String value) {
        if (curr == null)
            return 0;

        int compare = curr.value.compareTo(value);
        if (compare == 0)
            return curr.count;
        else {
            if (compare > 0)
                return frequency(curr.lChild, value);
            else
                return frequency(curr.rChild, value);
        }
    }

    void freeTree() {
        root = null;
    }

    // Testing code.
    public static void main(String[] args) {
        StringTree tt = new StringTree();
        tt.add("banana");
        tt.add("apple");
        tt.add("mango");
        System.out.println("Apple Found : " + tt.find("apple"));
        System.out.println("Banana Found : " + tt.find("banana"));
        System.out.println("Grapes Found : " + tt.find("grapes"));
    }
}
```

**Output:**

```
Apple Found : true
Banana Found : true
Grapes Found : false
```

## Hash Table

The Hash-Table is another data structure that can be used for symbol table implementation. Below the Hash-Table diagram, we can see the name of that person is taken as key, and their meaning is the value of the search. The first key is converted into a hash code by passing it to the appropriate hash function. Inside the hash function, the size of the Hash-Table is also passed, which is used to find the actual index where values will be stored. Finally, the value, which is the meaning of the name, is stored in the Hash-Table. Hash-Table has an excellent lookup of **O(1)**.

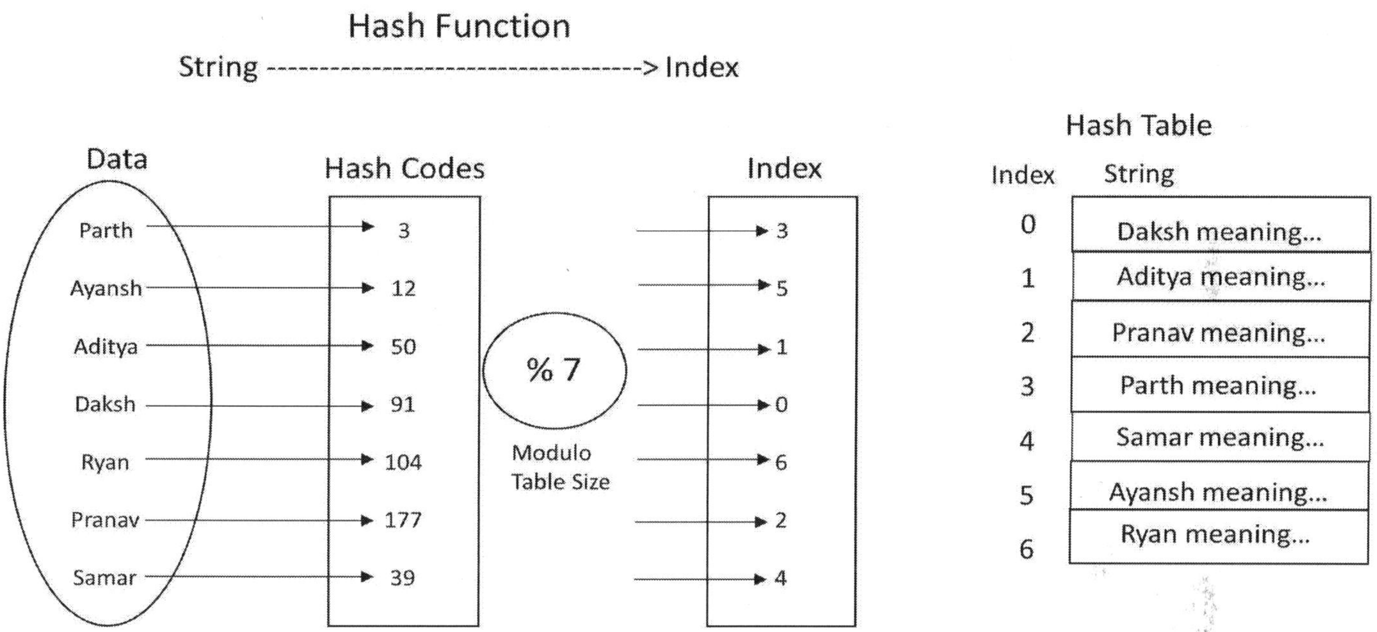


**Note**: Implementation of hashtable in hashtable chapter.

Let us suppose we want to implement auto-complete the box feature of Google search. When you type some string to search in google search, it proposes some complete string even before you have done typing. BST cannot solve this problem, as related strings can be in both the right and left subtree.

The Hash-Table is also not suited for this job. One cannot perform a partial match or range query on a Hash-Table. The hash function transforms a string into a number. Moreover, a good hash function will give a distributed hash code even for partial strings and there is no way to relate two strings in a Hash-Table.

Trie and Ternary Search tree are a special kind of tree that solves partial match and range query problems efficiently.

## Trie

**Trie** is a tree, in which we store only one character at each node. The final key-value pair is stored in the leaves. Each node has R children, one for each possible character. For simplicity purposes, let us consider that the character set is 26, corresponding to different characters of English alphabets.

Trie is an efficient data structure. Using Trie, we can search the key in O(M) time. Where M is the maximum string length. Trie is also suitable for solving partial match and range query problems.

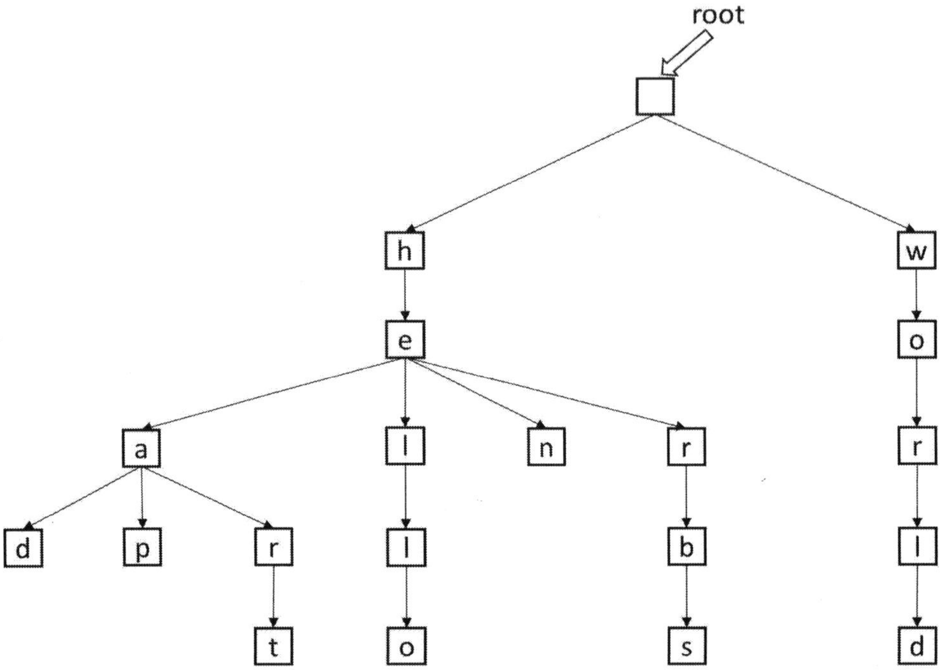


TRIE DICTIONARY

**Example 13.7:**
```
public class Trie {
    private static final int CharCount = 26;
    Node root = null;

    private class Node {
        boolean isLastChar;
        Node[] child;

        public Node(char c) {
            child = new Node[CharCount];
            for (int i = 0; i < CharCount; i++) {
                child[i] = null;
            }
            isLastChar = false;
        }
    };

    public Trie() {
        root = new Node(' ');
    }

    Node add(String str) {
        if (str == null) {
            return root;
        }
        return add(root, str.toLowerCase(), 0);
    }
```

```
    Node add(Node curr, String str, int index) {
        if (curr == null) {
            curr = new Node(str.charAt(index - 1));
        }
        if (str.length() == index) {
            curr.isLastChar = true;
        } else {
            curr.child[str.charAt(index) - 'a'] = add(curr.child[str.charAt(index)
- 'a'], str, index + 1);
        }
        return curr;
    }

    void remove(String str) {
        if (str == null) {
            return;
        }
        str = str.toLowerCase();
        remove(root, str, 0);
    }

    void remove(Node curr, String str, int index) {
        if (curr == null) {
            return;
        }
        if (str.length() == index) {
            if (curr.isLastChar) {
                curr.isLastChar = false;
            }
            return;
        }
        remove(curr.child[str.charAt(index) - 'a'], str, index + 1);
    }

    boolean find(String str) {
        if (str == null) {
            return false;
        }
        str = str.toLowerCase();
        return find(root, str, 0);
    }

    boolean find(Node curr, String str, int index) {
        if (curr == null) {
            return false;
        }
        if (str.length() == index) {
            return curr.isLastChar;
        }
        return find(curr.child[str.charAt(index) - 'a'], str, index + 1);
    }

    // Testing code.
    public static void main(String[] args) {
        Trie tt = new Trie();
        tt.add("banana");
        tt.add("apple");
        tt.add("mango");
```

```
        System.out.println("Apple Found : " + tt.find("apple"));
        System.out.println("Banana Found : " + tt.find("banana"));
        System.out.println("Grapes Found : " + tt.find("grapes"));
    }
}
```

**Output:**

```
Apple Found : true
Banana Found : true
Grapes Found : false
```

## Ternary Search Tree

Tries have a very good search performance of O(M) where M is the maximum size of the search string. However, tries have a very high space requirement. In every node, Trie contains pointers to multiple nodes, which are pointers corresponding to possible characters of the key. To avoid this high space requirement, Ternary Search Trie (TST) is used.

A TST avoids the heavy space requirement of traditional Trie, keeping many of its advantages. In a TST, each node contains a character, an end of the key indicator and three pointers. The three pointers are corresponding to the current char held by the node(equal), characters less than and characters greater than.

The Time Complexity of the ternary search tree operation is proportional to the height of the ternary search tree. In the worst case, we need to traverse up to 3 times the length of the largest string. However, this case is rare. Therefore, TST is a very good solution for implementing Symbol Table, Partial match and range query.

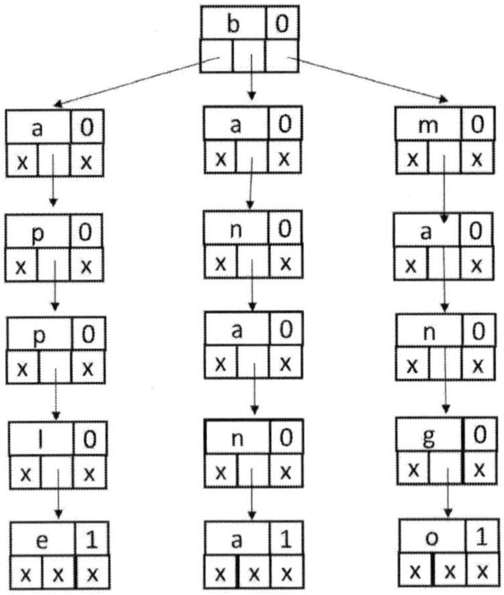


Ternary Search Tree

**Example 13.8:**

```
public class TST {
    Node root  = null;
```

```
    private class Node {
        char data;
        boolean isLastChar;
        Node left, equal, right;

        private Node(char d) {
            data = d;
            isLastChar = false;
            left = equal = right = null;
        }
    };

    public void add(String word) {
        root = add(root, word, 0);
    }

    private Node add(Node curr, String word, int wordIndex) {
        if (curr == null)
            curr = new Node(word.charAt(wordIndex));
        if (word.charAt(wordIndex) < curr.data)
            curr.left = add(curr.left, word, wordIndex);
        else if (word.charAt(wordIndex) > curr.data)
            curr.right = add(curr.right, word, wordIndex);
        else {
            if (wordIndex < word.length() - 1)
                curr.equal = add(curr.equal, word, wordIndex + 1);
            else
                curr.isLastChar = true;
        }
        return curr;
    }

    private boolean find(Node curr, String word, int wordIndex) {
        if (curr == null)
            return false;
        if (word.charAt(wordIndex) < curr.data)
            return find(curr.left, word, wordIndex);
        else if (word.charAt(wordIndex) > curr.data)
            return find(curr.right, word, wordIndex);
        else {
            if (wordIndex == word.length() - 1)
                return curr.isLastChar;
            return find(curr.equal, word, wordIndex + 1);
        }
    }

    public boolean find(String word) {
        boolean ret = find(root, word, 0);
        return ret;
    }

    // Testing code.
    public static void main(String[] args) {
        TST tt = new TST();
        tt.add("banana");
        tt.add("apple");
        tt.add("mango");
```

```
        System.out.println("Apple Found : " + tt.find("apple"));
        System.out.println("Banana Found : " + tt.find("banana"));
        System.out.println("Grapes Found : " + tt.find("grapes"));
    }
}
```

**Output:**

```
Apple Found : true
Banana Found : true
Grapes Found : false
```

# Problems in String

## Order Matching

**Problem:** In a given long text string and a pattern string, find if the characters of the pattern string are in the same order in the text string. E.g. Text String: ABCDEFGHIJKLMNOPQRSTUVWXYZ Pattern string: JOST

**Solution**: Traverse through the text string, keep a pattern index. If we find a character of pattern same as the text string, then increment the pattern index. Pattern index is equal to the pattern length, then returns true. If the text string is completely traversed and the pattern is not found completely, then return false.

**Example 13.9:**

```
public static boolean matchPattern(String src, String ptn) {
    char[] source = src.toCharArray();
    char[] pattern = ptn.toCharArray();
    int iSource = 0;, iPattern = 0;
    int sourceLen = source.length;
    int patternLen = pattern.length;

    for (iSource = 0; iSource < sourceLen; iSource++) {
        if (source[iSource] == pattern[iPattern]) {
            iPattern++;
        }
        if (iPattern == patternLen) {
            return true;
        }
    }
    return false;
}

// Testing code.
public static void main(String[] args)  {
    System.out.println(matchPattern("harrypottermustnotgotoschool",
"potterschool"));
}
```

**Output:**

```
true
```

**Time complexity:** O(n), where n is the length of a text string.

## ASCII to Integer Conversion

**Problem:** Write a function that takes an integer as an ASCII char list and converts it into an int.

**Solution**: Characters of the input string are traversed, and their ASCII value is subtracted by the ASCII value of 0. The value needs to be multiplied by 10 each time we want to include one more digit.

**Example 13.10:**
```
public static int myAtoi(String str) {
    int value = 0;
    int size = str.length();
    for (int i = 0; i < size; i++) {
        char ch = str.charAt(i);
        value = (value << 3) + (value << 1) + (ch - '0');
    }
    return value;
}

// Testing code.
public static void main(String[] args)  {
    System.out.println(myAtoi("100"));
}
```

**Output:**
```
100
```

**Time complexity:** O(n), where n is the length of an ASCII string.

## Unique Characters

**Problem:** Write a function that will take a string as input and return true if it contains all unique characters, else returns false.

**Solution**: An array bitArray[] to mark if some character is traversed. Traversed the input string if some character is traversed, then mark it in bitArray[]. If some character came a second time, then return false. If not repetition of character happened then return true.

**Example 13.11:**
```
public static boolean isUniqueChar(String str) {
    boolean[] bitarr = new boolean[26];
    int index;

    int size = str.length();
    for (int i = 0; i < size; i++) {
        char c = str.charAt(i);
        if ('A' <= c && 'Z' >= c) {
            index = (c - 'A');
        } else if ('a' <= c && 'z' >= c) {
            index = (c - 'a');
        } else {
            System.out.println("Unknown Char!\n");
            return false;
        }
```

```
        if (!bitarr[index]) {
            System.out.println("Duplicate detected!");
            return false;
        }
        bitarr[index] = true;
    }
    System.out.println("No duplicate detected!");
    return true;
}

// Testing code.
public static void main(String[] args)  {
    isUniqueChar("aple");
    isUniqueChar("apple");
}
```

**Output:**

```
No duplicate detected!
Duplicate detected!
```

**Time complexity:** O(n), where n is the number of characters in the input text.

## ToUpper

**Problem:** Write a function to convert small case characters of English alphabets to large case characters.

**Solution**: If the character is a lower case character, then subtract 32 from its ASCII value to get its corresponding upper case.

**Example 13.12:**

```
public static char toUpper(char s) {
    if (s >= 97 && s <= (97 + 25)) {
        s = (char) (s - 32);
    }
    return s;
}
```

**Time complexity:** O(1).

## ToLower

**Problem:** Write a function to convert large case characters of English alphabets to small case characters.

**Solution**: If the character is an upper case character, then add 32 to its ASCII value to get its corresponding lower case.

**Example 13.13:**

```
public static char toLower(char s) {
    if (s >= 65 && s <= (65 + 25)) {
        s = (char) (s + 32);
    }
```

```
    return s;
}
```

**Time complexity:** O(1).

## Palindrome Check

**Problem:** Find if the string is a palindrome or not

**Solution**: Index i is used to traverse the string forward. Index j is used to traverse the string backwards from the end. If j is less than i which means we found the corresponding characters and string is a palindrome.

**Example 13.14:**

```
public static boolean isPalindrome(String str) {
    int i = 0, j = str.length() - 1;
    while (i < j && str.charAt(i) == str.charAt(j)) {
        i++;
        j--;
    }

    if (i < j) {
        System.out.println("String is not a Palindrome");
        return false;
    } else {
        System.out.println("String is a Palindrome");
        return true;
    }
}

// Testing code.
public static void main(String[] args)  {
    isPalindrome("hello");
    isPalindrome("oyo");
}
```

**Output:**

```
String is not a Palindrome
String is a Palindrome
```

Time Complexity is **O(n)** and Space Complexity is **O(1)**

## String Compare function

**Problem:** Write a function strcmp() to compare two strings. The function return values should be:

- The return value is 0 indicates that both first and second strings are equal.
- The return value is negative; it indicates that the first string is less than the second string.
- The return value is positive; it indicates that the first string is greater than the second string.

**Solution**: Traverse both the strings till both the characters of the string are the same or one is traversed completely. If both strings are completely traversed, then return 0. If string one is ended, then return -1. If string two is ended, then return 1. Else, return the difference of the ASCII value of the character of both the strings.

**Example 13.15:**

```
public static int myStrcmp(String a, String b) {
    int index = 0;
    int len1 = a.length();
    int len2 = b.length();
    int minlen = (len1 < len2)? len1 : len2;

    while (index < minlen && a.charAt(index) == b.charAt(index)) {
        index++;
    }

    if (index == len1 && index == len2) {
        return 0;
    } else if (len1 == index) {
        return -1;
    } else if (len2 == index) {
        return 1;
    } else {
        return a.charAt(index) - b.charAt(index);
    }
}

// Testing code.
public static void main(String[] args)  {
    System.out.println(myStrcmp("apple", "appke"));
    System.out.println(myStrcmp("apple", "apple"));
    System.out.println(myStrcmp("apple", "appme"));
}
```

**Output:**

```
1
0
-1
```

**Time complexity:** O(n), where n is the length of a smaller string.

## Reverse String

**Problem:** Reverse all the characters of a string.

**Solution**: Traverse from forward and backward and keep on swapping the characters. In the end, the string is reversed.

**Example 13.16:**

```
public static String reverseString(String str) {
    char[] a = str.toCharArray();
    reverseStringUtil(a);
    String expn = new String(a);
    return expn;
}

public static void reverseStringUtil(char[] a) {
    int lower = 0;
    int upper = a.length - 1;
    char tempChar;
```

```
    while (lower < upper) {
        tempChar = a[lower];
        a[lower] = a[upper];
        a[upper] = tempChar;
        lower++;
        upper--;
    }
}

// Testing code.
public static void main(String[] args)  {
    System.out.println(reverseString("apple"));
}
```

**Output:**

```
elppa
```

**Time complexity:** O(n), where n is the number of characters in the input string.

## Reverse Words

**Problem:** Reverse order of words in a sentence.

**Solution**: Call reverse string on each of the words in the string. Then call the reverse string on the complete string.

**Example 13.17:**

```
public static void reverseStringUtil(char[] a, int lower, int upper) {
    char tempChar;
    while (lower < upper) {
        tempChar = a[lower];
        a[lower] = a[upper];
        a[upper] = tempChar;
        lower++;
        upper--;
    }
}

public static String reverseWords(String str) {
    char[] a = str.toCharArray();
    int length = a.length;
    int lower = 0, upper = -1;
    for (int i = 0; i <= length; i++) {
        if (i == length || a[i] == ' ') {
            reverseStringUtil(a, lower, upper);
            lower = i + 1;
            upper = i;
        } else {
            upper++;
        }
    }
    reverseStringUtil(a, 0, length - 1);
    String expn = new String(a);
    return expn;
}
```

```
// Testing code.
public static void main(String[] args)  {
    System.out.println(reverseWords("hello world"));
}
```

**Output:**

```
world hello
```

**Time complexity:** O(n), where n is the number of characters in the input string.

## Print Anagram

**Problem:** Given a string as a character list, print all the anagrams of the string.

**Solution**: At each level of recursion, every element is positioned at the first position and the rest of the array is passed recursively to produce permutation of the rest part. When one element is completely processed, then put it back to its original position.

**Example 13.18:**

```
public static void printAnagram(String str) {
    printAnagram(str.toCharArray(), 0, str.length());
}

public static void printAnagram(char[] arr, int i, int length) {
    if (length == i) {
        printArray(arr, length);
        return;
    }

    for (int j = i; j < length; j++) {
        swap(arr, i, j);
        printAnagram(arr, i + 1, length);
        swap(arr, i, j);
    }
    return;
}

private static void printArray(char[] arr, int n) {
    for (int i = 0; i < n; i++)
        System.out.print(arr[i]);
    System.out.println();
}

private static void swap(char[] arr, int i, int j) {
    char temp = arr[i];
    arr[i] = arr[j];
    arr[j] = temp;
}

// Testing code.
public static void main(String[] args)  {
    printAnagram("123");
}
```

**Output:**

```
123
132
213
231
321
312
```

**Time complexity:** O(n!), where n is the number of characters in the input string.

## Exercise

1. In a given string, find the longest substring without repeating characters.

2. The function memset() copies ch into the first 'n' characters of the string

3. Serialise a collection of strings into a single string, and deSerialise the string into that collection of strings.

4. Write a smart input function, which takes 20 characters as input from the user. Without cutting some words.
   User input: “Harry Potter must not go”
   First 20 chars: “Harry Potter must no”
   Smart input: “Harry Potter must”

5. Write a code that finds if a string is a palindrome, and it should return true for the below inputs too.
   Stella won no wallets.
   No, it is open in one position.
   Rise to vote, Sir.
   Won't lovers revolt now?

6. Write an ASCII to integer function, which ignores the non-integral character and gives the integer. For example, if the input is “12AS5” it should return 125.

7. Write code that would parse a Bash brace expansion.
   Example: the expression "(a, b, c) d, e" and would give output all the possible strings: ad, bd, cd, e

8. In a given string, write a function to return the length of the longest substring with unique characters

9. Replace all occurrences of "a" with "the"

10. Replace all occurrences of %20 with ' '.
    E.g. **Input**: www.Hello%20World.com **Output**: www.Hello World.com

11. Write an expansion function that will take an input string like "1..5,8,11..14,18,20,26..30" and will print "1,2,3,4,5,8,11,12,13,14,18,20,26,27,28,29,30"

12. Suppose you have a string like "Thisisasentence". Write a function that would separate these words. Moreover, will print the whole sentence with spaces.

13. Given three strings str1, str2 and str3. Write a complement function to find the smallest sub-sequence in str1 which contains all the characters in str2 but not those in str3.

14. In given two strings A and B, find whether any anagram of string A is a substring of string B. For eg: If A = xyz and B = afdgzyxksldfm then the program should return true.

15. In a given string, find whether it contains any permutation of another string. For example, given "abcdefgh" and "ba", the function should return true, because "abcdefgh" has substring "ab", which is a permutation of the given string "ba".

16. In a given algorithm that removes the occurrence of “a” by “bc” from a string? The algorithm must be in place.

17. In the given string "1010101010" in base2 convert it into a string with base4. Do not use any extra space.

18. In the Binary Search tree to store strings, the delete() function is not implemented, implement it.

19. If you implement the delete() function, then you need to make changes in the find() function. Do the needful.

# CHAPTER 14: ALGORITHM DESIGN TECHNIQUES

## Introduction

In real life, when we are asked to do some work, we try to correlate it with our experience and then try to solve it. Similarly, when we get a new problem to solve. We first try to find the similarity of the current problem with some problems for which we already know the solution. Then solve the current problem and get our desired result.

This method provides the following benefits:

1. It provides a template for solving a wide range of problems.
2. It provides us with an idea of the suitable data structure for the problem.
3. It helps us in analysing the space and Time Complexity of algorithms.

In the previous chapters, we have used various algorithms to solve different kinds of problems. In this chapter, we will read about various techniques for solving algorithmic problems.

Various Algorithm design techniques are:

1. Brute Force
2. Greedy Algorithms
3. Divide-and-Conquer
4. Dynamic Programming
5. Backtracking

## Brute Force Algorithm

In the Brute-Force approach, while solving any problem, all the possible solutions are generated. From these solutions, we pick the best and feasible solution which satisfies the given requirements. These methods are time-consuming and slow as we are generating various solutions which do not satisfy the requirements.

Brute Force is a straightforward approach to solving a problem based on the problem statement. It is one of the easiest approaches to solve a problem. It is useful for solving small size dataset problems.

Some examples of brute force algorithms are:

1 Bubble-Sort

2 Selection-Sort

3 Sequential search in an array

4 Computing pow(a, n) by multiplying a, n times.

5 String matching

## Greedy Algorithm

In the **Greedy Algorithm** approach, the problem is solved through a sequence of steps. At each step, a choice is made which is locally optimal. Greedy algorithms are generally used to solve optimization problems.

**Note:** Greedy algorithms do not always give optimal solutions.

Some examples of greedy algorithms are:

1 Minimal spanning tree: Prim's algorithm, Kruskal's algorithm
2 Dijkstra's algorithm for single-source shortest path problem
3 A greedy algorithm for the Knapsack problem
4 The coin exchange problem
5 Huffman trees for optimal encoding

## Divide and Conquer

The Divide-and-Conquer algorithm approach involves three steps. First, the given problem is divided into various smaller sub-problems. Second, these smaller sub-problems are solved independently. Finally, the result of these sub-problems is combined to get the final result.

Examples of divide-and-conquer algorithms:

1. Merge-Sort algorithm (using recursion)
2. quickSort algorithm (using recursion)
3. Computing the length of the longest path in a binary tree (using recursion)
4. Computing Fibonacci numbers (using recursion)
5. Closest Pair between a given list of 2d points.
6. Quick-hull
7. Computing pow(a, n) by calculating pow(a, n/2) using recursion.
8. Searching in BST
9. Graph traversal algorithms (DFS and BFS)

## Dynamic Programming

While solving problems using the Divide-and-Conquer method, there may be a case when recursively sub-problems can result in the same computation being performed multiple times. In other words, when there are identical subproblems that arise repeatedly in a recursion.

Dynamic programming is used to avoid the requirement of repeated calculation of the same sub-problem in a recurrence relation. In this method, we usually store the result of sub-problems in a table and refer to that table to find if we have already calculated the solution of sub-problems before calculating it again.

Examples:

1. Fibonacci numbers are computed by iteration.
2. Warshall's algorithm for transitive closure, implemented by iterations
3. Floyd's algorithms for all-pairs shortest paths

## Backtracking

In the **Backtracking** approach, In each step of creating an answer, it is checked if this step satisfies the given conditions. If it does satisfy constraints, then continue generating subsequent solutions.
If constraints are not satisfied, then we backtrack one step to check for another solution. The way backtracking works is that we build up a solution step-by-step. Sometimes we realise that our current state isn't going to get us to the desired solution, in which case we 'backtrack' by going back a few steps. So we just undo the last few steps until our desired criteria are again met, and continue building our solution by making different choices this time.

## Conclusion

Usually, a given problem can be solved using several methods; however, it is not wise to settle for the first method that comes to our mind. Some methods result in a much more efficient solution than others do.

For example, the Fibonacci numbers are calculated recursively (decrease-and-conquer approach) and computed by iterations (dynamic programming). In the first case, the complexity is **O(2^n),** and in the other case, the complexity is **O(n)**.

Another example, consider sorting based on the Insertion-Sort and basic bubble sort. For almost sorted files, Insertion-Sort will give almost linear complexity, while bubble sort sorting algorithms have quadratic complexity.

So, the most important question is how to choose the best method?
First, you should understand the problem statement.
Second, by knowing various problems and their solutions.

# CHAPTER 15: BRUTE FORCE ALGORITHM

## Introduction

In the **Brute-Force** approach, while solving any problem, all the possible solutions are generated. From these solutions, we pick the best and feasible solution which satisfies the given requirements. These methods are time-consuming and slow as we are generating various solutions which do not satisfy the requirements.

Brute Force is a straightforward approach to solving a problem based on the problem statement. The algorithm relies completely on computation power and tries each and every combination. It is one of the easiest approaches to solve a problem. It is useful for solving small size dataset problems. In most cases, other algorithm techniques can be used to get a better solution to the same problem.

For example, imagine you have a 3-digit number lock. You forgot its combination now you will try each and every combination from 000 to 999. One of the combinations will open the lock. Here you had used a brute force method to open your lock. In the worst case, 1000 combinations need to be tested.

Some examples of brute force algorithms are:

1. Bubble-Sort
2. Selection-Sort
3. Sequential search in an array
4. Computing pow (a, n) by multiplying a, n times.
5. String matching
6. Exhaustive search
7. Knapsack
8. Assignment problems

## Problems in Brute Force Algorithm

### Bubble Sort

Given an array, we need to sort the elements of the array in ascending order. In Bubble-Sort, adjacent elements of the array are compared and are exchanged if they are out of order. This scanning is performed n number of times to make the whole array sorted.

```
// Problem: Sorts a given list using Bubble Sort Algorithm
// Input: An array A[0..n-1] of order-able elements
// Output: The array A[0..n-1] sorted in ascending order

function BubbleSort(A[0..n-1])
    sorted = false
    while sorted is false do
        sorted = true
        for j = 0 to n-2 do
            if A[j] > A[j + 1] then
                swap A[j] and A[j + 1]
                sorted = false
```

Time Complexity is Θ(n^2)

***Note:*** *Executable code is given in the Sorting chapter.*

## Selection Sort

The entire given list of N elements is traversed to find its smallest element and exchange it with the first element. Then, the array is traversed again to find the second element and exchange it with the second element. After N-1 passes, the array will be completely sorted.

```
//Problem: Sorts a given list using Selection Sort Algorithm
//Input: An array A[0..n-1] of order-able elements
//Output: The array A[0..n-1] sorted in ascending order

function SelectionSort (A[0..n-1])
    for i = 0 to n-2 do
        min = i
        for j = i+1 to n-1 do
            if A[j] < A[min] then
                min = j
        swap A[i] and A[min]
```

Time Complexity is Θ(n^2)
***Note:*** *Executable code is given in the Sorting chapter.*

## Sequential Search

Given an unsorted array, you need to find some value in it. The algorithm compares consecutive elements of a given list with a given search keyword until either a match is found or the array is exhausted.

```
//Problem: Find a particular value in an array.
//Input: An array A[0..n-1] and value K
//Output: Index of the K in array or -1

function SequentialSearch (A[0..n], K)
    i = 0
    While A[i] not equal K do
        i = i + 1

    if i < n then
        return i
    else
        return -1
```

Worst-case time complexity is Θ(n).

**Note:** Executable code is given in the Searching chapter.

## Computing pow (a, n)

Computing $a^n$ (a > 0, and n is a non-negative integer) based on the definition of exponentiation. N-1 multiplications are required in the brute force method.

```
// Problem: Find A Power N.
// Input: A real number A and an integer N = 0
// Output: A^N

function pow(A, N)
    result = 1
    for i = 1 to N do
        result = result * A

    return result
```

The algorithm requires Θ(n)

## String Matching

Given a string T and another string P, you need to find if T contains P. A brute force string matching algorithm takes two inputs, the first text T consists of n characters and a pattern P consists of m characters (m<=n). The algorithm starts by comparing the pattern with the beginning of the text. Each character of the pattern is compared to the corresponding character of the text. The comparison starts from left to right until all the characters are matched, or a mismatch is found. The same process is repeated until a match is found. Each time the comparison starts from one position to the right.

```
//Input: An array T[0..n-1] of n characters representing a text
// an array P[0..m-1] of m characters representing a pattern
//Output: The position of the first character in the text that starts the
// first matching substring if the search is successful and -1 otherwise.

function BruteForceStringMatch (T[0..n-1], P[0..m-1])
    for i = 0 to n-m do
        j = 0
        while j < m and P[j] = T[i + j] do
            j = j + 1

        if j = m then
            return I

    return -1
```

In the worst case, the algorithm is O(mn).

**Note:** Executable code is given in the String chapter.

## Closest Pair Brute Force Algorithm

The closest-pair problem is to find the two closest points in a set of n points in a 2-dimensional space.

A brute force implementation of this problem computes the distance between each pair of distinct points and finds the smallest distance pair.

```
// Find the closest points using brute force approach
// Input: An array P of n >= 2 points
// Output: The closest pair

function BruteForceClosestPair(P)
    dmin = infinite

    for i = 1 to n-1 do
        for j = i + 1 to n do
            d = (xi - xj)² + (yi - yj)²
            if d < dmin then
                dmin = d
                imin = i
                jmin = j

    return imin, jmin
```

**Example 15.01:**

```
public double closestPairBF(int[][] arr) {
    int n = arr.length;
    double dmin = Double.MAX_VALUE, d;
    for (int i = 0; i < n - 1; i++) {
        for (int j = i + 1; j < n; j++) {
            d = Math.sqrt((arr[i][0] - arr[j][0]) * (arr[i][0] - arr[j][0])
                    + (arr[i][1] - arr[j][1]) * (arr[i][1] - arr[j][1]));
            if (d < dmin) {
                dmin = d;
            }
        }
    }
    return dmin;
}

// Testing code.
public static void main(String[] args) {
    int[][] arr = { { 648, 896 }, { 269, 879 }, { 250, 922 }, { 453, 347 }, { 213,
17 } };
    ClosestPair cp = new ClosestPair();
    System.out.println("Smallest distance is:" + cp.closestPairBF(arr));
}
```

**Output:**

```
Smallest distance is: 47.010637
```

Time Complexity is Θ(n^2)

**Note**:- We will look for a more efficient solution using the divide-and-conquer method in the coming chapter.

## Exhaustive Search

Exhaustive search is a brute force approach applied to combination problems.
In an exhaustive search, we generate all the possible combinations. At each step, we try to find if the combinations satisfy the problem constraints. Either, we get the desired solution, which satisfies the problem constraint, or there is no solution.

Examples of exhaustive search are:

- Knapsack problem
- Assignment problem

## 0/1 Knapsack Problem

Given an item with cost C1, C2,..., Cn, and volume V1, V2,..., Vn and knapsack of capacity Vmax, find the most valuable (max ∑Cj) that fits in the knapsack (∑Vj ≤ Vmax).

The solution is one of the subsets of the set of objects taking 1 to n objects at a time, so the Time complexity is O(2^n).

```
function KnapsackBruteForce(objects)
    MaxProfit = 0
    for (All permutations of objects) do
        CurrProfit = sum of cost of objects selected
        if(MaxProfit < CurrProfit)
            MaxProfit = CurrProfit
            Store the current set of objects selected
    print the max profit objects selected
    return MaxProfit
```

**Note:** Executable code is in the Dynamic Programming Chapter where we will further discuss this problem in more details.

## Conclusion

Brute force is the first algorithm that comes to mind when we see some problem. They are the simplest algorithms that are very easy to understand. However, these algorithms rarely provide an optimum solution. In many cases, we will find other effective algorithms that are more efficient than the brute force method.

# CHAPTER 16: GREEDY ALGORITHM

## Introduction

Greedy algorithms are generally used to solve optimization problems. To find the solution that minimises or maximises some value (cost/profit/count etc.). In greedy algorithms, solutions are constructed through a sequence of steps. At each step, a choice is made which is locally optimal. Greedy algorithms do not always give optimal solutions. For some problems, greedy algorithms give an optimal solution. For others, they are useful for fast approximations.

Some examples of greedy algorithms are:

Optimal solutions:

1. Minimal spanning tree:
   - Prim's algorithm,
   - Kruskal's algorithm
2. Dijkstra's algorithm for single-source shortest path
3. Huffman trees for optimal encoding
4. Scheduling problems

Approximate solutions:

1. A greedy algorithm for the Knapsack problem
2. Coin exchange problem

## Problems on Greedy Algorithm

### Coin Exchange Problem

How can a given amount of money N be made with the least number of coins of given denominations D= {d1… dn}?

For example, the Indian coin system {5, 10, 20, 25, 50,100}. Suppose we want to give a change of a certain amount of 40 paise.

**Solution**: We can make a solution by repeatedly choosing a coin ≤ to the current amount, resulting in a new amount. In the greedy algorithm, we always choose the largest coin value possible without exceeding the total amount. For 40 paisa: our algorithm will give {25, 10, and 5} but the optimal solution will be {20, 20}.

This greedy algorithm did not always give us an optimal solution, but it gave us a fair approximation.

```
function MAKE-CHANGE (N)
    C = {5, 20, 25, 50, 100}    // constant denominations.
    S = {}            // set that will hold the solution set.
    Value = N
    while Value != 0
        x = largest item in set C such that x < Value
        if no such item THEN
            return  "No Solution"

        S = S + x
        Value = Value - x
    return S
```

**Example 16.1:**

```
static int minCoins(int[] coins, int n, int val) { // Greedy may be wrong.
    if (val <= 0)
        return 0;

    int count = 0;
    Arrays.sort(coins);

    for (int i = n - 1; i >= 0 && val > 0;) {
        if (coins[i] <= val) {
            count++;
            val -= coins[i];
        } else {
            i--;
        }
    }
    return (val == 0) ? count : -1;
}
```

Time-Complexity: O(n.log(n))

## Minimum Spanning Tree

A spanning tree of a connected graph is a tree containing all the vertices.

A minimum spanning tree of a weighted graph is a spanning tree with the smallest sum of the edge weights.

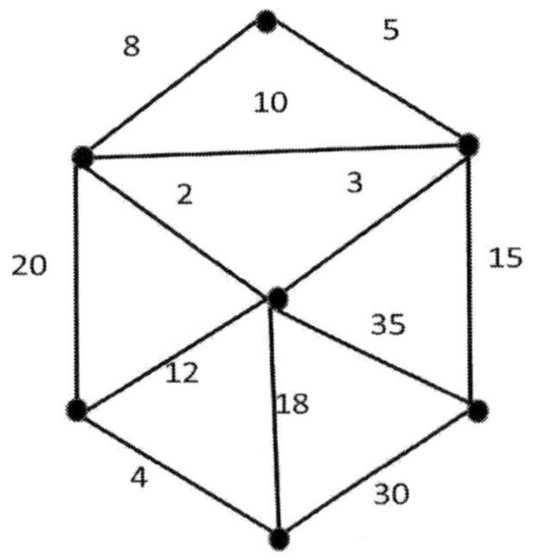

Graph

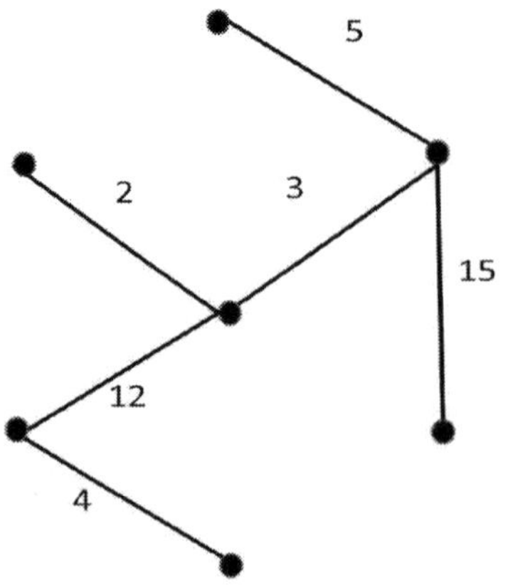

Minimum Spanning Tree

## Prim's Algorithm

Prim's algorithm grows a single tree T, one edge at a time until it becomes a spanning tree.
We Initialise T with zero edges and U with a single node. Where T is a spanning tree, edges set and U is a spanning tree vertex set.

At each step, Prim's algorithm adds the smallest value edge with one endpoint in U and the other not in U. Since each edge adds one new vertex to U, after n − 1 addition, U contains all the vertices of the spanning tree and T becomes a spanning tree.

```
// Returns the MST by Prim's Algorithm
// Input: A weighted connected graph G = (V, E)
// Output: Set of edges comprising a MST

function Prim(G)
    T = {}
    Let r be any vertex in G
    U = {r}
    for i = 1 to |V| - 1 do
        e = minimum-weight edge (u, v)
            With u in U and v in V-U
        U = U + {v}
        T = T + {e}
    return T
```

Prim's Algorithm uses a priority queue (min-heap) to get the closest fringe vertex

Time complexity is O(m log n) where n vertices and m edges of the MST.

**Note**: Executable code is given in the Graph chapter.

## Kruskal's Algorithm

Kruskal's Algorithm is used to create a minimum spanning tree. Spanning trees are created by choosing the smallest weight edge that does not form a cycle. And repeat this process until all the edges from the original set are exhausted.

Sort the edges in non-decreasing order of cost: c (e1) ≤ c (e2) ≤ · · · ≤ c (em).

Set T to be the empty tree. Add edges to the tree one by one, if it does not create a cycle. (If the new edge forms a cycle then it ignores that edge.)

```
// Returns the MST by Kruskal's Algorithm
// Input: A weighted connected graph G = (V, E)
// Output: Set of edges comprising a MST

function Kruskal(G)
    Sort the edges E by their weights
    T = {}
    while |T | + 1 < |V | do
        e = next edge in E
        if T + {e} does not have a cycle then
            T = T + {e}
    return T
```

Kruskal's Algorithm is O(E log V) using efficient cycle detection.

**Note**: Executable code is given in the Graph chapter.

## Dijkstra's algorithm

Dijkstra's algorithm is used for a single-source shortest path problem for weighted edges with no negative weight. It determines the length of the shortest path from the source to each of the other nodes of the graph. In a given weighted graph G, we need to find the shortest paths from the source vertex s to each of the other vertices.

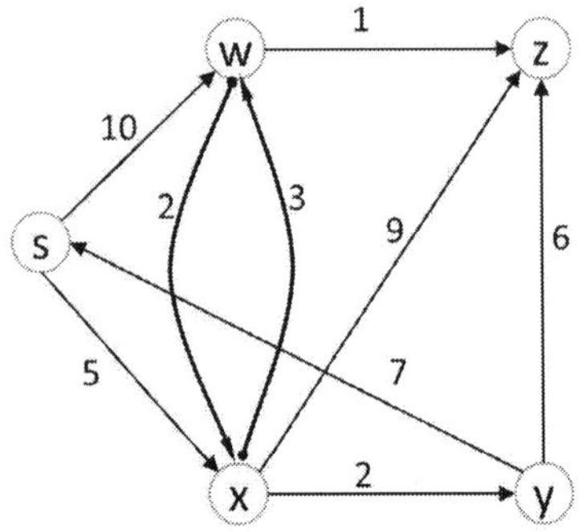


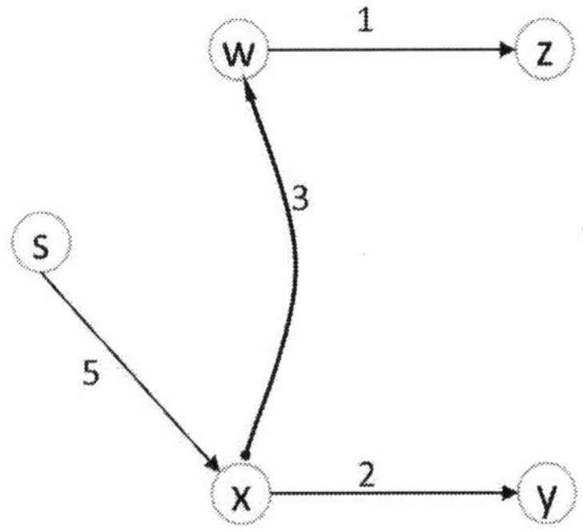


Single-Source shortest path

The algorithm starts by keeping track of the distance of each node and its parents. All the distance is set to infinite in the beginning, as we do not know the actual path to the nodes and the parent of all the vertices are set to null. All the vertices are added to a priority queue (min-heap implementation)

Each step algorithm takes one vertex from the priority queue (which will be the source vertex in the beginning). Then, update the distance list corresponding to all the adjacent vertices. When the queue is empty, then we will have the distance and parent list fully populated.

```
// Solves SSSP by Dijkstra's Algorithm
// Input: A weighted connected graph G = (V, E)
// with no negative weights, and source vertex v
// Output: The length and path from s to every v

function Dijkstra(G, s)
    for each v in V do
        D[v] = infinite    // Unknown distance
        P[v] = null    // Unknown previous node
        add v to PQ    // Adding all nodes to priority queue
    D[source] = 0 // Distance from source to source
    while (PQ is not empty)
        u = vertex from PQ with smallest D[u]
        remove u from PQ
        for each v adjacent from u do
            alt = D[u] + length (u, v)
            if alt < D[v] then
                D[v] = alt
                P[v] = u
    return D[], P[]
```

Time complexity is O(|E|log|V|).

Note: Executable code is given in the Graph chapter.

Note: Dijkstra's algorithm does not work for graphs with negative edge weight.

Note: Dijkstra's algorithm applies to both undirected and directed graphs.

## Huffman trees for optimal encoding

Encoding is an assignment of bit strings of alphabet characters.

There are two types of encoding:

- Fixed-length encoding (e.g., ASCII)
- Variable-length encoding (e.g., Huffman code)

Variable length encoding can only work on prefix-free encoding. This means that no codeword is a prefix of another codeword.

Huffman codes are the best prefix-free code. Any binary tree with edges labelled as 0 and 1 will produce a prefix-free code of characters assigned to its leaf nodes. Huffman's algorithm is used to construct a binary tree whose leaf value is assigned a code, which is optimal for the compression of the whole text that needs to be processed. For example, the most frequently occurring words will get the smallest code so that the final encoded text is compressed.

Initialise n one-node trees with words and the tree weights with their frequencies. Join the two-binary tree with the smallest weight into one, and the weight of the newly formed tree as the sum of the weight of the two small trees. Repeat the above process N-1 times and when there is just one big tree left you are done. Mark edges leading to the left and right subtrees with 0's and 1's, respectively.

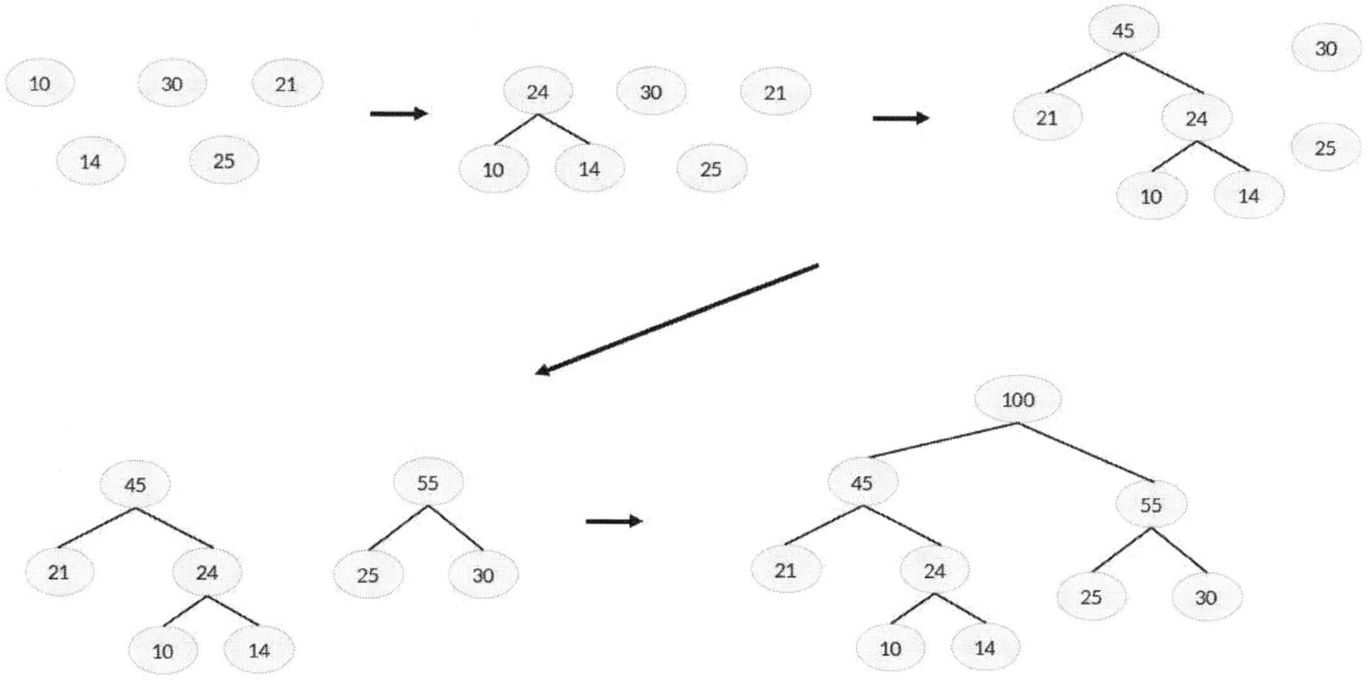

| Character | Frequency |
|---|---|
| A | 30 |
| B | 25 |
| C | 21 |
| D | 14 |
| E | 10 |

| Character | Frequency | Code |
|---|---|---|
| A | 30 | 11 |
| B | 25 | 10 |
| C | 21 | 00 |
| D | 14 | 011 |
| E | 10 | 010 |

```
// Computes optimal prefix code.
// Input: List W of character probabilities
// Output: The Huffman tree.

function Huffman(C[0..n-1], W[0..n-1])
    PQ = {} // priority queue
    for i = 0 to n-1 do
        T.char = C[i]
        T.weight = W[i]
        add T to priority queue PQ

    for i = 0 to n-2 do
        L = remove min from PQ
        R = remove min from PQ
        T = node with children L and R
        T.weight = L.weight + R.weight
        add T to priority queue PQ
    return T
```

**Example 16.2:**

```
public class HuffmanTree {
    Node root = null;

    class Node implements Comparable<Node> {
        char c;
        int freq;
        Node left;
        Node right;

        Node(char ch, int fr, Node l, Node r) {
            c = ch;
            freq = fr;
            left = l;
```

```
            right = r;
        }

        public int compareTo(Node n2) {
            return this.freq - n2.freq;
        }
    }

    HuffmanTree(char[] arr, int[] freq) {
        int n = arr.length;
        PriorityQueue<Node> que = new PriorityQueue<Node>(n);

        for (int i = 0; i < n; i++) {
            Node node = new Node(arr[i], freq[i], null, null);
            que.add(node);
        }

        while (que.size() > 1) {
            Node lt = que.peek();
            que.poll();
            Node rt = que.peek();
            que.poll();

            Node nd = new Node('+', lt.freq + rt.freq, lt, rt);
            que.add(nd);
        }
        root = que.peek();
    }

    private void print(Node root, String s) {
        if (root.left == null && root.right == null && root.c != '+') {
            System.out.println(root.c + " = " + s);
            return;
        }
        print(root.left, s + "0");
        print(root.right, s + "1");
    }

    public void print() {
        System.out.println("Char = Huffman code");
        print(root, "");
    }

    // Testing code.
    public static void main(String[] args) {
        char[] ar = { 'A', 'B', 'C', 'D', 'E' };
        int[] fr = { 30, 25, 21, 14, 10 };
        HuffmanTree hf = new HuffmanTree(ar, fr);
        hf.print();
    }
}
```

Output:

```
Char = Huffman code
C = 00
E = 010
D = 011
```

```
B = 10
A = 11
```

Time Complexity is **O(n.log(n)),** a heap is created and elements are removed from the heap one by one.

## Activity Selection Problem

Suppose that activities require exclusive use of common resources, and you want to schedule as many activities as possible.

Let S = {a1,..., an} be a set of n activities. Each activity ai needs the resource during a time period starting at si and finishing before fi, i.e., during [si, fi).

Example: Consider these activities:

| I | 1 | 2 | 3 | 4 | 5 | 6 | 7 | 8 | 9 | 10 | 11 |
|---|---|---|---|---|---|---|---|---|---|---|---|
| S[i] | 1 | 3 | 0 | 5 | 3 | 5 | 6 | 8 | 8 | 2 | 11 |
| F[i] | 4 | 5 | 6 | 7 | 8 | 9 | 10 | 11 | 12 | 13 | 14 |

The optimization problem is to select the non-overlapping largest set of activities from S. We assume that activities S = {a1,..., an} are sorted in finish time f1 ≤ f2 ≤ ... fn-1 ≤ fn (this can be done in Θ(n lg n)).

We choose an activity that starts first and then looks for the next activity that starts after it is finished. This could result in {a4, a7, a8}, but this solution is not optimal.

An optimal solution is {a1, a3, a6, a8}. (It maximises the objective of the largest number of activities scheduled.). Another one is {a2, a5, a7, a9}. (Optimal solutions are not necessarily unique.)

How do we find (one of) these optimal solutions?

We are trying to optimise the number of activities:

1. The time left after running the activity can be used to run subsequent activities.
2. If we choose the first activity to finish, more time will be left.
3. Since activities are sorted by finish time, we will always start with a1.
4. Then we can solve the single subproblem of activity scheduling in the remaining time.

```
function ActivitySelection(S[], F[], N)
    Sort S[] and F [] in increasing order of finishing time
    A = {a1}
    K = 1
    for m = 2 to N do
        if S[m] >= F[k]
            A = A + {am}
            K = m
    return A
```

**Example 16.3:**

```
class ActivitySelection {
    class Activity implements Comparable<Activity> {
        int start, stop;

        Activity(int s, int f) {
            start = s;
            stop = f;
        }

        public int compareTo(Activity s2) {
            return this.stop - s2.stop;
        }
    }

    public void maxActivities(int s[], int f[], int n) {
        Activity[] act = new Activity[n];
        for (int i = 0; i < n; i++)
            act[i] = new Activity(s[i], f[i]);
        Arrays.sort(act); // sort according to finish time.

        int i = 0; // The first activity at index 0 is always gets selected.
        System.out.print("Activities are : (" + act[i].start + "," + act[i].stop +
")");

        for (int j = 1; j < n; j++) {
            // Find next activity whose start time is greater than or equal
            // to the finish time of previous activity.
            if (act[j].start >= act[i].stop) {
                System.out.print(", (" + act[j].start + "," + act[j].stop + ")");
                i = j;
            }
        }
    }

    // Testing code.
    public static void main(String[] args) {
        int s[] = { 1, 5, 0, 3, 5, 6, 8 };
        int f[] = { 2, 6, 5, 4, 9, 7, 9 };
        int n = s.length;
        ActivitySelection as = new ActivitySelection();
        as.maxActivities(s, f, n);
    }
}
```

**Output:**

```
Activities are : (1,2), (3,4), (5,6), (6,7), (8,9)
```

**Time-Complexity**: O(n.log(n))

## Fractional Knapsack Problem

A thief enters a store and sees several items with their mentioned cost and weight. His Knapsack can hold a max weight. What should he steal to maximise profit? A thief can take a fraction of an item (they are divisible substances, like gold powder).

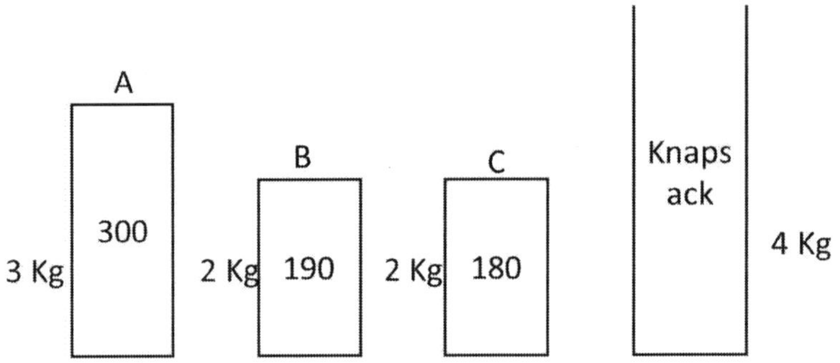


| Item | A | B | C |
|---|---|---|---|
| Cost | 300 | 190 | 180 |
| Weight | 3 | 2 | 2 |
| Cost/weight | 100 | 95 | 9 |

For a knapsack of the capacity of 4 kg. The optimum solution of the above will take 3kg of A and 1 kg of B.

**Solution**: The fractional knapsack problem has a greedy solution: one should first sort the items in terms of cost density against weight. Then fill up as much of the most valuable substance by weight as one can hold, then as much of the next most valuable substance, etc. Until W is reached.

```
function FractionalKnapsack(W[], C[], Wk)
    for i = 1 to n do
        X[i] = 0
    Weight = 0
    H = BuildMaxHeap(C/W)    //Use Max heap
    while Weight < Wk do
        i = H.GetMax()
        if(Weight + W[i] <= Wk) do
            X[i] = 1
            Weight = Weight + W[i]
        else
            X[i] = (Wk - Weight)/W[i]
            Weight = Wk
    return X
```

**Example 16.4:**
```
public class FractionalKnapsack {
    private class Items implements Comparable<Items> {
        int wt;
        int cost;
        double density;

        Items(int w, int v) {
            wt = w;
            cost = v;
            density = (double) cost / wt;
        }

        public int compareTo(Items s2) { // decreasing order.
            return (int) (s2.density - this.density);
```

```
        }
    }

    public double getMaxCostFractional(int[] wt, int[] cost, int capacity) {
        double totalCost = 0;
        int n = wt.length;
        Items[] itemList = new Items[n];
        for (int i = 0; i < n; i++)
            itemList[i] = new Items(wt[i], cost[i]);

        Arrays.sort(itemList);
        for (int i = 0; i < n; i++) {
            if (capacity - itemList[i].wt >= 0) {
                capacity -= itemList[i].wt;
                totalCost += itemList[i].cost;
            } else {
                totalCost += (itemList[i].density * capacity);
                break;
            }
        }
        return totalCost;
    }

    // Testing code.
    public static void main(String[] args) {
        int[] wt = { 10, 40, 20, 30 };
        int[] cost = { 60, 40, 90, 120 };
        int capacity = 50;

        FractionalKnapsack kp = new FractionalKnapsack();
        double maxCost = kp.getMaxCostFractional(wt, cost, capacity);
        System.out.println("Maximum cost obtained = " + maxCost);
    }
}
```

**Output:**

```
Maximum cost obtained = 230.0
```

**Time-Complexity**: O(n.log(n))

## 0/1 Knapsack Problem

In this Knapsack problem, a thief can only take or leave the item. He cannot take a fraction.

**Solution**: A greedy strategy same as above could result in empty space, reducing the knapsack with a non-optimal solution.

**Example 16.5:**

```
public class Knapsack {
    private class Items {
        int wt;
        int cost;
        double density;

        Items(int w, int v) {
            wt = w;
            cost = v;
```

```
            density = (double) cost / wt;
        }
    }

    class decDensity implements Comparator<Items> {
        @Override
        public int compare(Items a, Items b) {
            return (int) (b.density - a.density);
        }
    }

    // Approximate solution.
    public int getMaxCostGreedy(int[] wt, int[] cost, int capacity) {
        int totalCost = 0;
        int n = wt.length;
        Items[] itemList = new Items[n];
        for (int i = 0; i < n; i++)
            itemList[i] = new Items(wt[i], cost[i]);

        Arrays.sort(itemList, new decDensity());
        for (int i = 0; i < n && capacity > 0; i++) {
            if (capacity - itemList[i].wt >= 0) {
                capacity -= itemList[i].wt;
                totalCost += itemList[i].cost;
            }
        }
        return totalCost;
    }

    // Testing code.
    public static void main(String[] args) {
        int[] wt = { 10, 40, 20, 30 };
        int[] cost = { 60, 40, 90, 120 };
        int capacity = 50;

        Knapsack kp = new Knapsack();
        int maxCost = kp.getMaxCostGreedy(wt, cost, capacity);
        System.out.println("Maximum cost obtained = " + maxCost);
    }
}
```

**Output:**

Maximum cost obtained = 150

Moreover, the result of the greedy solution is not optimal or we can say it gives the wrong answer. The optimal

**Time-Complexity**: O(n.log(n))

## Chota Bhim

**Problem**: A boy named Chota Bhim had visited his grandfather Takshak. Takshak had offered Chota Bhim to drink an elixir of power. He had offered several cups filled with different quantities of elixir. Chota Bhim is instructed to drink a maximum quantity of elixir from the cups one by one. The cups are magical when Chota Bhim empties a cup, it refills itself with half the previous quantity it uses ceil [previous amount / 2] function to fill itself. Chota Bhim is given 1 minute. He is efficient, in each second, he drinks from one cup and puts it back. Chota Bhim had consumed a lot of elixirs by always picking the cup with maximum elixir. Now Takshak had called you to find how much he had consumed.

Example: 5 Cups

| | |
|---|---|
| Minute 1 Cups: 2, 1, 7, 4, 2 | 7 is selected |
| Minute 2 Cups: 2, 1, 4, 4, 2 | 4 is selected |
| Minute 3 Cups: 2, 1, 2, 4, 2 | 4 is selected |
| Minute 4 to 7 Cups 2, 1, 2, 2, 2 | 2 is selected four times |
| Minute 8 and rest of days Cups: 1, 1, 1, 1, 1 | 1 is selected for rest all |

Total: 7+4+4+2+2+2+2+(60 - 7) = 76 units of elixir

**First Solution**: Sorted list method, First sort the ropes list. The minimum two will be at the start of the array. We remove the first two and then join them and add them to the sorted list in such a way that it remains sorted. Now repeat this process till all the arrays are added.

Each insertion into a proper position such that the array remains sorted takes linear time so the total time complexity is O(n^2).

**Example 16.6:**

```
public class ChotaBhim {
    public static int chotaBhim(int cups[]) {
        int size = cups.length;
        int time = 60;
        Arrays.sort(cups);
        reverse(cups, size);
        int total = 0;
        int index, temp;

        while (time > 0) {
            total += cups[0];
            cups[0] = (int) Math.ceil(cups[0] / 2.0);
            index = 0;
            temp = cups[0];
            while (index < size - 1 && temp < cups[index + 1]) {
                cups[index] = cups[index + 1];
                index += 1;
            }
            cups[index] = temp;
            time -= 1;
        }
        System.out.println("Total : " + total);
        return total;
    }
```

```
    public static void reverse(int cups[], int size) {
        int temp = 0;
        for (int i = 0, j = size - 1; i < j; i++, j--) {
            temp = cups[i];
            cups[i] = cups[j];
            cups[j] = temp;
        }
    }

    // Testing code.
    public static void main(String[] args) {
        int cups[] = { 2, 1, 7, 4, 2 };
        chotaBhim(cups);
    }
}
```

**Output:**

```
Total : 76
```

**Second Solution:** Greedy Algorithm, Performance can be improved by using a heap to store values. Create a min-heap of all the ropes. Then remove the lowest two values from the heap. Add these two values and then insert them into the heap. Deletion and Insertion will take O(log(n)) time, so the total time complexity of this algorithm will be O(n.log(n)).

**Example 16.7:**

```
public static int chotaBhim2(int cups[]) {
    int size = cups.length;
    int time = 60;
    PriorityQueue<Integer> pq =
                    new PriorityQueue<Integer>(Collections.reverseOrder());
    int i = 0;
    for (i = 0; i < size; i++) {
        pq.add(cups[i]);
    }

    int total = 0;
    int value;
    while (time > 0) {
        value = pq.remove();
        total += value;
        value = (int) Math.ceil(value / 2.0);
        pq.add(value);
        time -= 1;
    }
    System.out.println("Total : " + total);
    return total;
}
```

## Join Rope

**Problem:** Given N number of ropes of various lengths. You need to join these ropes to make a single rope. The cost of joining two ropes of length X and Y is (X+Y) which is their combined length. You need to find the minimum cost of joining all the ropes. The minimum cost of joining rope is obtained when we always join the two smallest ropes.

**First Solution:** Sorted list method, First sort the rope's list. The minimum two will be at the start of the array. We remove the first two and then join them and add them to the sorted list in such a way that it remains sorted. Now repeat this process till all the arrays are added.

Each insertion into a proper position such that the array remains sorted takes linear time, so the total time complexity is O(n^2).

**Example 16.8:**
```
public class JoinRopes {
    public static int joinRopes(int ropes[], int size) {
        Arrays.sort(ropes);
        for (int i = 0, j = size - 1; i < j; i++, j--) {
            int temp = ropes[i];
            ropes[i] = ropes[j];
            ropes[j] = temp;
        }
        int total = 0, value = 0;
        int index, length = size;

        while (length >= 2) {
            value = ropes[length - 1] + ropes[length - 2];
            total += value;
            index = length - 2;
            while (index > 0 && ropes[index - 1] < value) {
                ropes[index] = ropes[index - 1];
                index -= 1;
            }
            ropes[index] = value;
            length--;
        }
        System.out.println("Total : " + total);
        return total;
    }

    // Testing code.
    public static void main(String[] args) {
        int ropes[] = { 4, 3, 2, 6 };
        joinRopes(ropes, ropes.length);
    }
}
```

**Output:**
```
Total : 29
```

**Second Solution:** Greedy Algorithm, Performance can be improved by using a heap to store values. Create a min-heap of all the ropes. Then remove the lowest two values from the heap. Add these two values and then insert them into the heap. Deletion and Insertion will take O(log(n)) time, so the total time complexity of this algorithm will be O(n.log(n)).

**Example 16.9:**
```
public static int joinRopes2(int ropes[], int size) {
    PriorityQueue<Integer> pq = new PriorityQueue<Integer>();
    for ( int i = 0; i < size; i++) {
        pq.add(ropes[i]);
    }
```

```
    int total = 0;
    int value = 0;
    while (pq.size() > 1) {
        value = pq.remove();
        value += pq.remove();
        pq.add(value);
        total += value;
    }
    System.out.println("Total : " + total);
    return total;
}
```

## Convex-Hull Problem

**Problem:** Convex-hull of a set of points is the smallest convex polygon that contains all the points. All the points of the set will lie on the convex hull or inside the convex hull. The convex-hull of a set of points is a subset of points in the given sets.

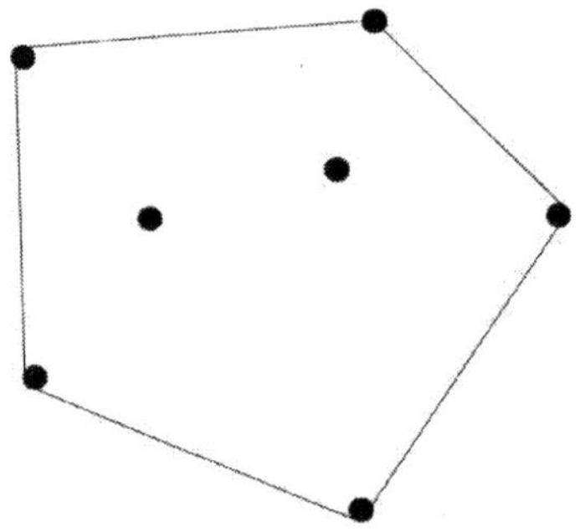

### Graham Scan Algorithm

Graham Scan Algorithm:

- Find the bottom most point with least value of y-coordinate. If there are two points with the same y coordinate value then take the point with the smaller x-coordinate. Let the bottom most point be P0. This point P0 is the point in the output convex hull.
- Sort the rest of the n-1 points of the P[] array according to the polar angle in anti-clockwise order around the point P0. If the angle of the two points are the same then remove the nearer point as this will not be part of the output convex hull.
- If the number of points are less than 3 then a convex hull is not possible and returns false.
- Add the first 3 points P[0], P[1] and P[2] to an empty stack 'S'.
- Loop through all the remaining points P[i] from array P[].
    - Keep popping the top of the stack 'S', till the top two points from stack 'S' and P[i] make clockwise angles.
    - Add point P[i] to the stack 'S'
- Print content of stack 'S'.

Time Complexity of this algorithm will be O(n.log(n)), which is the time taken in the sorting step.

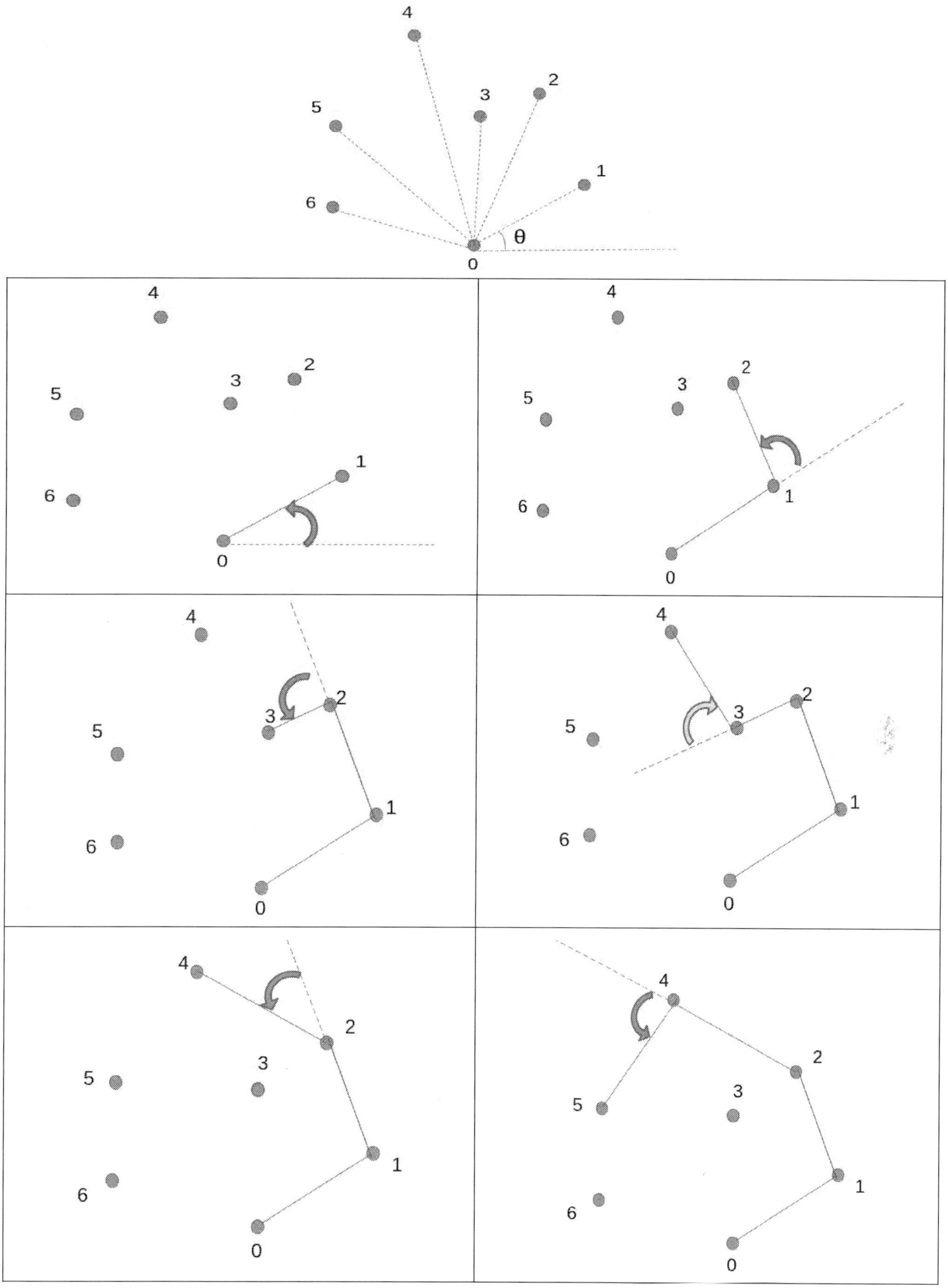
4
5
3
2
1
6
θ
0

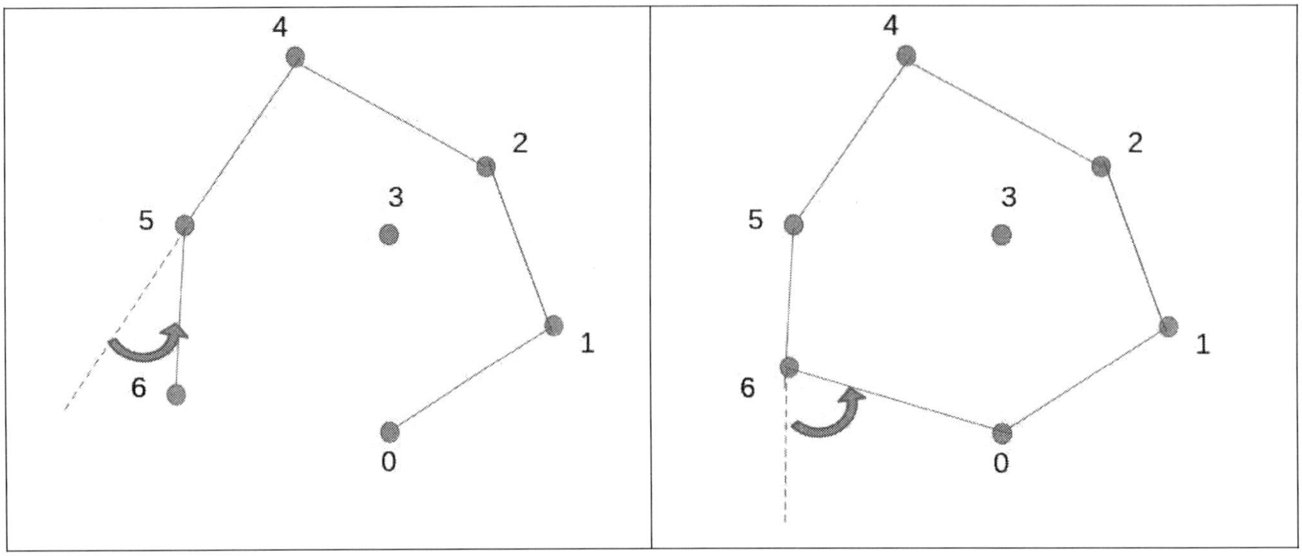


## Jarvis's March algorithm

In Jarvis's March algorithm we start from the leftmost point and we keep wrapping points in an anti-clockwise direction.

Jarvis's March Algorithm:

- From the given set of points array P[], we find the leftmost point P0 with minimum x-coordinates. This point is guaranteed to be in the convex hull, we add this point P0 to the convex hull list. Initialise variable p by P0.
- While we don't come back to the first point p0.
    - From the list of vertices we choose a vertice q such that all other vertices r make an anticlockwise angle with triplate (p, q, r). We traverse for all the vertices r in p[] such that If angle with triplate (p,q,r) is clockwise then we Initialise variable q as r.
    - Now add q to the convex hull. Assign variable p as q.

Time Complexity: For every vertice in the convex hull we examine all the other points to determine the next point. Time complexity is O(m * n)

## Conclusion

Greedy algorithms are generally used to solve optimization problems. In greedy algorithms, solutions are constructed through a sequence of steps. At each step, a choice is made which is locally optimal. Not always greedy algorithms give optimal solutions. Sometimes greedy algorithms give wrong answers too.

# CHAPTER 17: DIVIDE AND CONQUER

## Introduction

Divide-and-Conquer algorithms work by recursively breaking down a problem into two or more subproblems (divide step) of the same type, until these sub-problems become simple enough so that they can be solved directly. The solution of these sub-problems is then combined (conquer step) to give a solution to the original problem.

Divide-and-Conquer algorithms involve basic three steps

1. Divide the problem into smaller problems.
2. Conquer by solving these problems.
3. Combine these results.

In divide-and-conquer, the size of the problem is reduced by a factor (half, one-third etc.), while in decrease-and-conquer the size of the problem is reduced by a constant.

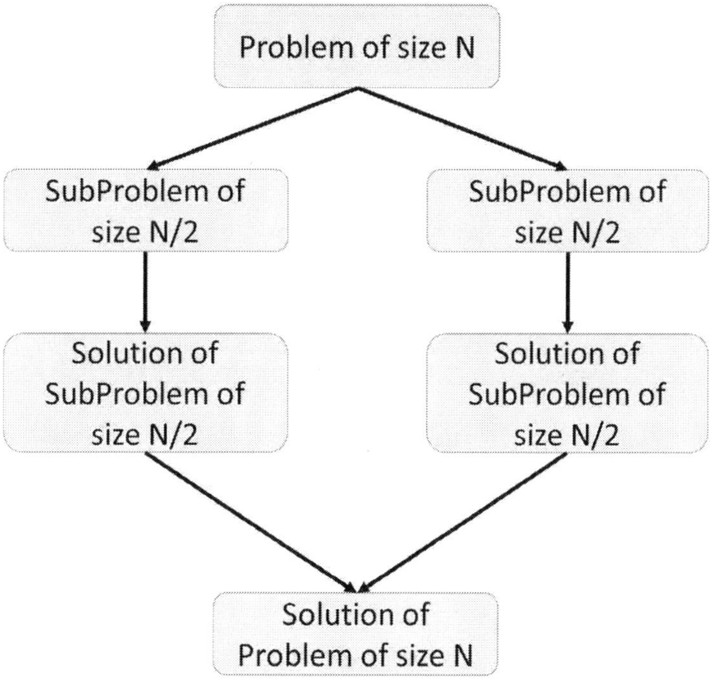


Divide-and-Conquer algorithms

```
function Divide&Conquer(P)
    if (P is small)
        // Base Case: P is very small so the solution of P is obvious.
        return Solution of P

    Divide problem P into K sub-problems P1, P2, P3 and so on.
    Return Combine ( Divide&Conquer(P1) , Divide&Conquer(P2), ..... so on)
```

Examples of divide-and-conquer algorithms:

1. Merge-Sort algorithm (recursion)
2. Quick-Sort algorithm (recursion)
3. Computing the length of the longest path in a binary tree (recursion)
4. Computing Fibonacci numbers (recursion)
5. Searching in BST
6. Computing POW (a, n) by calculating POW (a, n/2) using recursion

## General Divide & Conquer Recurrence

$T(n) = aT(n/b) + f(n)$

1. Where $a \geq 1$ and $b > 1$.
2. "n" is the size of a problem.
3. "a" is the number of subproblems in the recursion.
4. "n/b" is the size of each sub-problem.
5. "f(n)" is the cost of the division of the problem into subproblems or merge of the results of the sub-problem to get the final result.

## Problems on Divide & Conquer Algorithm

### Merge Sort Algorithm

A merge-sort algorithm is used to sort an array of integers using the divide-and-conquer technique.

For Merge-sort explanation and executable code, please refer to the Sorting chapter.

### Quick Sort Algorithm

A quick-sort algorithm is used to sort an array of integers using the divide-and-conquer technique.

For Quick-sort explanation and executable code, please refer to the Sorting chapter.

### Binary Search Algorithm

Binary-search is used to search a key in a sorted array.

For Binary-search explanation and executable code, please refer to the Searching chapter.

### Power function

**Problem**: Write a function that will calculate xn, taking x and n as arguments.

**Example 17.1:**

```
int power(int x, int n) {
    int value;
```

```
    if (n == 0) {
        return (1);
    } else if (n % 2 == 0) {
        value = power(x, n / 2);
        return (value * value);
    } else {
        value = power(x, n / 2);
        return (x * value * value);
    }
}
```

**Time complexity:** O(log(n)), where N is an exponent in the desired value.

## Nuts & Bolts

**Problem**: Given an array of nuts and bolts of different sizes. There is a one-one mapping between nuts and bolts. You need to arrange nuts and bolts in increasing order of size. Given the constraint that a nut cannot be compared with another nut. And a bolt cannot be compared with another bolt. In other words, nuts can be compared with bolts.

**Solution**: Take the first element of the bolts[] array, call it bolt1 and use bolt1 to do partition of the nuts[] array. Now, this partition array will return the index of the nut corresponding to bolt1, call it nut1. Now use nut1 to partition the bolt[] array. By doing this, we had to partition both the arrays. Do this for all the elements. (same as quick sort)

**Example 17.2:**

```
public class NutsAndBolts {
    public static void makePairs(int[] nuts, int[] bolts) {
        makePairs(nuts, bolts, 0, nuts.length - 1);
        System.out.println("Matched nuts and bolts are : ");
        printArray(nuts);
        printArray(bolts);
    }

    // Quick sort kind of approach.
    private static void makePairs(int[] nuts, int[] bolts, int low, int high) {
        if (low < high) {
            // Choose first element of bolts array as pivot to partition nuts.
            int pivot = partition(nuts, low, high, bolts[low]);

            // Using nuts[pivot] as pivot to partition bolts.
            partition(bolts, low, high, nuts[pivot]);

            // Recursively lower and upper half of nuts and bolts are matched.
            makePairs(nuts, bolts, low, pivot - 1);
            makePairs(nuts, bolts, pivot + 1, high);
        }
    }

    private static void swap(int[] arr, int first, int second) {
        int temp = arr[first];
        arr[first] = arr[second];
        arr[second] = temp;
    }
```

```
    // Partition method similar to quick sort algorithm.
    private static int partition(int[] arr, int low, int high, int pivot) {
        int i = low;
        for (int j = low; j < high; j++) {
            if (arr[j] < pivot) {
                swap(arr, i, j);
                i++;
            } else if (arr[j] == pivot) {
                swap(arr, high, j);
                j--;
            }
        }
        swap(arr, i, high);
        return i;
    }

    private static void printArray(int[] arr) {
        for (int i : arr)
            System.out.print(i + " ");
        System.out.println();
    }

    // Testing code.
    public static void main(String[] args) {
        int nuts[] = { 1, 2, 6, 5, 4, 3 };
        int bolts[] = { 6, 4, 5, 1, 3, 2 };
        makePairs(nuts, bolts);
    }
}
```

**Output:**

```
Matched nuts and bolts are :
1 2 3 4 5 6
1 2 3 4 5 6
```

## Closest Pair Problem

Given N points in a 2-dimensional plane, find two points whose mutual distance is the smallest.

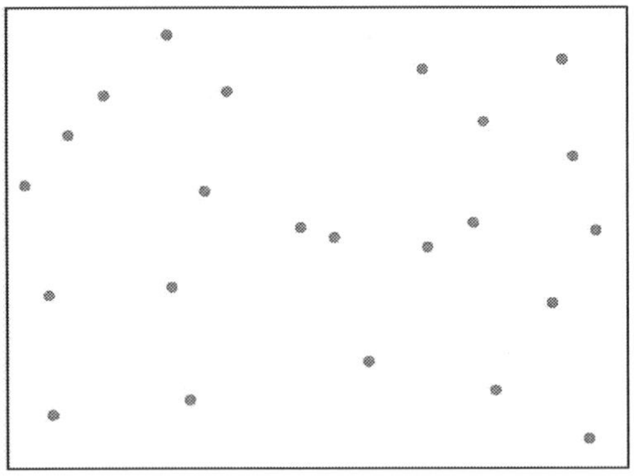

A brute force algorithm takes every point and finds its distance from all the other points in the plane. In addition, keep track of the minimum distance points and minimum distance. The closest pair will be found in O(n^2) time.

Let us suppose that there is a vertical line, which divides the graph into two separate parts (let us call it the left and right parts). In the brute force algorithm, we will notice that we are comparing all the points in the left half with the points in the right half. This is the point where we are doing some extra work.

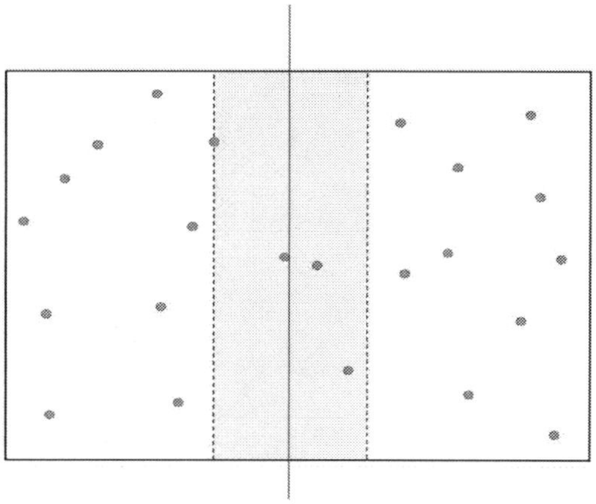

To find the minimum we need to consider only three cases:

1. The Closest pair in the right half
2. The Closest pair in the left half.
3. The Closest pair in the boundary region of the two halves. (Grey)

Every time we will divide the space S into two parts S1 and S2 by a vertical line. Recursively, we will compute the closest pair in both S1 and S2. Let us call minimum distance in space S1 as δ1 and minimum distance in space S2 as δ2.

We will find δ = min (δ1, δ2)

Now we will find the closest pair in the boundary region. By taking one point each from S1 and S2 in the boundary range of δ width on both sides.

The candidate pair of points (p, q) where p Є S1 and q Є S2.

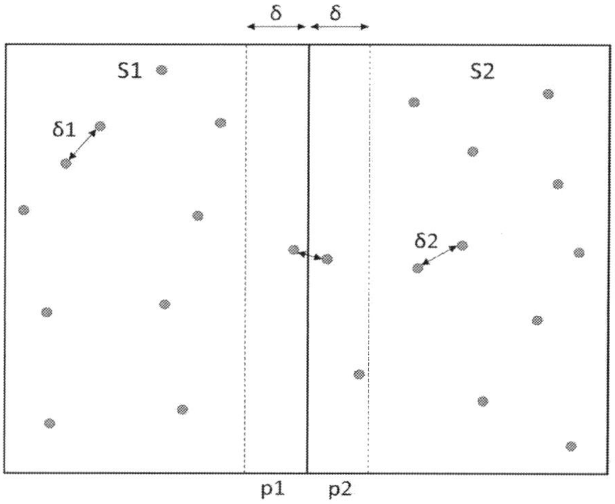


We can find the points that lie in this region in linear time O(N) by just scanning through all the points and finding that all points lie in this region.

Now we can sort them in increasing order in the Y-axis in just O(n.log(n)) time. Then scan through them and get the minimum in just one linear pass. The closest pair cannot be far apart from each other.

Let us look into the next figure.

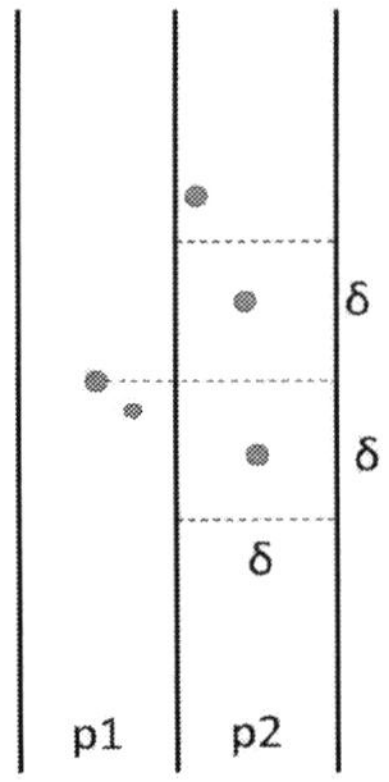


Then the question is how many points we need to compare. We need to compare the points sorted in the Y-axis only in the range of δ. Therefore, the number of points will come down to only 6 points.

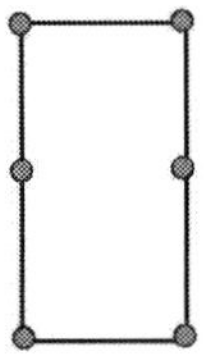

By doing this, we are getting an equation.

T(N) = 2T(N/2) + N + n.log(n) + 6N = O(n(log(n))2)

Can we optimise this further?

Yes

Initially, when we are sorting the points in X coordinate, we are sorting them in Y coordinate too.

When we divide the problem, then we traverse through the Y coordinate list too and construct the corresponding Y coordinate list for both S1 and S2. And pass that list to them. Since we have the Y coordinate list passed to a function the δ region points can be found sorted in the Y coordinates in just one single pass in just O(N) time.

T(N) = 2T(N/2) + N + N + 6N = O(n.log(n))

```
// Finds closest pair of points
// Input: A set of n points sorted by coordinates
// Output: Distance between closest pair

function ClosestPair(P)
    if n < 2 then
        return ∞
    else if n = 2 then
         return distance between pair
    else
        m = median value for x coordinate
        δ1 = ClosestPair(points with x < m)
        δ2 = ClosestPair(points with x > m)
```

```
        δ = min(δ1, δ2)
        δ3 = process points with m –δ < x < m + δ
        return min(δ, δ3)
```

First pre-process the points by sorting them in X and Y coordinates. Use two separate lists to keep these sorted points. Before recursively solving a sub-problem, pass the sorted list for that sub-problem.

**Example 17.3:**

```
public class ClosestPair {
    public static class Point {
        int x, y;

        Point(int a, int b) {
            x = a;
            y = b;
        }
    }

    private static double distance(Point a, Point b) {
        return Math.sqrt((a.x - b.x) * (a.x - b.x) + (a.y - b.y) * (a.y - b.y));
    }

    class xComp implements Comparator<Point> {
        public int compare(Point s1, Point s2) {
            return (s1.x - s2.x);
        }
    }

    class yComp implements Comparator<Point> {
        public int compare(Point s1, Point s2) {
            return (s1.y - s2.y);
        }
    }

    private static double stripMin(Point q[], int n, double d) {
        double min = d;

        // Find the distance between all the points in the strip.
        // Array q is sorted according to the y axis coordinate.
        // The inner loop will run at most 6 times for each point.
        for (int i = 0; i < n; ++i)
            for (int j = i + 1; j < n && (q[j].y - q[i].y) < min; ++j) {
                d = distance(q[i], q[j]);
                if (d < min)
                    min = d;
            }
        return min;
    }

   private double closestPairUtil(Point p[], int start, int stop, Point q[], int n)
{
        if (stop - start < 1)
            return Double.MAX_VALUE;

        if (stop - start == 1)
            return distance(p[start], p[stop]);

        // Find the middle point
```

```
        int mid = (start + stop) / 2;

        double dl = closestPairUtil(p, start, mid, q, n);
        double dr = closestPairUtil(p, mid + 1, stop, q, n);
        double d = Math.min(dl, dr);

        // Build an array strip[] that contains points whose x axis coordinate
        // in the range p[mid]-d and p[mid]+d
        // Points are already sorted according to y axis.
        Point[] strip = new Point[n];
        int j = 0;
        for (int i = 0; i < n; i++) {
            if (Math.abs(q[i].x - p[mid].x) < d) {
                strip[j] = q[i];
                j++;
            }
        }
        // Find the closest points in strip and compare with d.
        return Math.min(d, stripMin(strip, j, d));
    }

    public double closestPairDC(int[][] arr) {
        int n = arr.length;
        Point[] p = new Point[n];
        for (int i = 0; i < n; i++) {
            p[i] = new Point(arr[i][0], arr[i][1]);
        }
        // Sort according to x axis.
        Arrays.sort(p, new xComp());

        Point q[] = p.clone();
        // Sort according to y axis.
        Arrays.sort(q, new yComp());
        return closestPairUtil(p, 0, n - 1, q, n);
    }

    // Testing code.
    public static void main(String[] args) {
        int[][] arr = { { 648, 896 }, { 269, 879 }, { 250, 922 }, { 453, 347 },
{ 213, 17 } };
        ClosestPair cp = new ClosestPair();
        System.out.println("Smallest distance is:" + cp.closestPairDC(arr));
    }
}
```

**Output:**
```
Smallest distance is:47.01063709417264
```

## Strassen's Matrix Multiplication

**Problem**: Given two square matrices A and B of size n x n each, find their multiplication matrix.

**Solution 1**: Naive Method, multiply two matrices using three for loop.
```
function multiply(a, b):
    for i=0 to N-1
```

```
        for j=0 to N-1
            c[i, j] = 0
            for k=0 to N
                c[i, j] += a[i, k]*b[k, j]
    return c
```

**Solution 2**: Divide and Conquer
Following is a simple Divide and Conquer method to multiply two square matrices.
1) Divide matrices A and B in 4 sub-matrices of size N/2 x N/2.
2) Calculate the product recursively for all the subproblems and combine the result to get the final output. Output = (ae + bg), (af + bh), (ce + dg) and (cf + dh).

In the above method, we do 8 multiplications for matrices of size N/2 x N/2 and 4 additions. Addition of two matrices takes O(N^2) time. So the time complexity can be written as
T(N) = 8T(N/2) + O(N^2)

From Master's Theorem, time complexity of above method is O(n^3)
which is unfortunately the same as the above naive method.

```
function multiply(x, y)
    // Base case when size of matrices is 1x1
    if Size(x) = 1
        return x * y

    // Splitting the matrices into 4 quadrants.
    // This will be done recursively until the base case is reached.
    a, b, c, d = Split(x)
    e, f, g, h = Split(y)


    A = multiply(a)
    B = multiply(b)
    C = multiply(c)
    D = multiply(d)
    E = multiply(e)
    F = multiply(f)
    G = multiply(g)
    H = multiply(h)

    // Computing the values of the 4 quadrants of the output matrix c
    c11 = A*E + B*G
    c12 = A*F + B*H
    c21 = C*E + D*G
    c22 = C*F + D*H

    // Combining the 4 quadrants into a single output matrix.
    c = Combine(c11, c12, c21, c22)
    return c
```

**Solution 3**: Strassen's method, the strassen's method is similar to the divide-&-conquer method described above. In this method the matrix is divided into sub matrices of size N/2 x N/2. The idea of this method is to reduce the number of recursive calls to 7.

T(N) = 7T(N/2) + O(N^2)

From Master's Theorem, time complexity of above method is
O(N^Log7) which is approximately O(N^2.8074)

```
function StrassenMultiply (x, y)
    // Base case when size of matrices is 1x1
    if Size(x) = 1
        return x * y

    // Splitting the matrices into 4 quadrants.
    // This will be done recursively until the base case is reached.
    a, b, c, d = Split(x)
    e, f, g, h = Split(y)

    // Computing the 7 sub-problems, recursively.
    m1 = StrassenMultiply(a, f - h)
    m2 = StrassenMultiply(a + b, h)
    m3 = StrassenMultiply(c + d, e)
    m4 = StrassenMultiply(d, g - e)
    m5 = StrassenMultiply(a + d, e + h)
    m6 = StrassenMultiply(b - d, g + h)
    m7 = StrassenMultiply(a - c, e + f)

    // Computing the values of the 4 quadrants of the output matrix c
    c11 = m5 + m4 - m2 + m6
    c12 = m1 + m2
    c21 = m3 + m4
    c22 = m1 + m5 - m3 - m7
    // Combining the 4 quadrants into a single output matrix.
    c = Combine(c11, c12, c21, c22)
    return c
```

## Exercise

1. Problem: Given a sorted array of integers, find the index of the first and last occurrence of a given value.

   Hint: Using binary search, find the element smaller than the searched key. Again, find the element greater than the given value.

2. Problem: Given a sorted array of integers, find the number of occurrences of a given value.

   Hint: Binary search based. Same as above, just find the difference of index and report count.

3. Problem: Given a sorted array of distinct non-negative whole numbers, find the smallest missing number.

   Hint: Binary search based. Whole numbers are considered. If the number at some index is greater than the index value, then something is missing in the left portion else right portion. Narrow down your search and reach the solution.

4. Problem: Given a sorted array of integers and a key. Find the floor and ceiling of the key in the given array.

   Hint: Binary search based. Like in binary search, we compare our key with value at index i = n/2. In this algorithm, we will have to consider index (i-1) and (i+1) before ignoring half part of the search space, the same as Binary Search.

5. Problem: Given a sorted array that is further rotated in a clockwise direction. You need to find the number of rotations.

   Hint: Using a binary search kind of technique, find the point when the next value is smaller than the previous value.

6. Problem: Given a sorted array that is further rotated. Find a given key-value inside this given array.

   Hint: Binary search based. Consider rotated segments and continuous segments. The rotated segment value at the end is smaller than the beginning. And the other segment will have the last value greater than the first value.

7. Problem: Given a box with locks and keys, where one lock can be opened by one key in the box. We need to match the pairs.

   Hint: Same problem as Nuts and Bolts.

# Chapter 18: Dynamic Programming

## Introduction

Dynamic programming algorithms are used to solve optimization problems by breaking them into smaller sub-problems. The optimal solution of the sub-problems is used to construct optimal solutions to the overall problems. Dynamic programming is applied to solve problems that have properties of Optimal Substructure and Overlapping Sub-Problems.

**Optimal Substructure**: The optimization problem is divided into simpler sub-problems. The optimal solution of the overall problem is constructed from optimal solutions of its sub-problems.

**Overlapping subproblems**: While calculating the optimal solution of sub-problems, the same computation is performed multiple times.

If the problems with overlapping subproblems are solved using recursion. Then because the sub-problems are overlapping, it results in the same computation being performed multiple times. This repeated computation gives less efficient solutions. Dynamic programming is used to avoid repeated calculation of the same sub-problem. In this method, we usually store the result of sub-problems in some data structure (like an array) and refer to it to find if we have already calculated the solution of sub-problems before calculating it again.

Let's take an example of the Fibonacci Series. Few elements of the Fibonacci series are 0, 1, 1, 2, 3, 5 and so on. Fibonacci numbers are a series of numbers in which each number is the sum of the two preceding numbers. The Fibonacci number is represented by the below formula.

```
Fibonacci(n) = Fibonacci(n-1) + Fibonacci(n-2) where n > 1
Fibonacci(0) = 0
Fibonacci(1) = 1
```

**Example 18.01:** Recursive solution of fibonacci number.

```
public static int fibonacci(int n) {
    if (n < 2) {
        return n;
    }
    return fibonacci(n - 1) + fibonacci(n - 2);
}
```

The problem is to divide into sub-problems. These subproblems are overlapping, so the same calculations are performed again and again, which reduces the performance of this solution. This algorithm has an exponential time complexity of O(2^n).

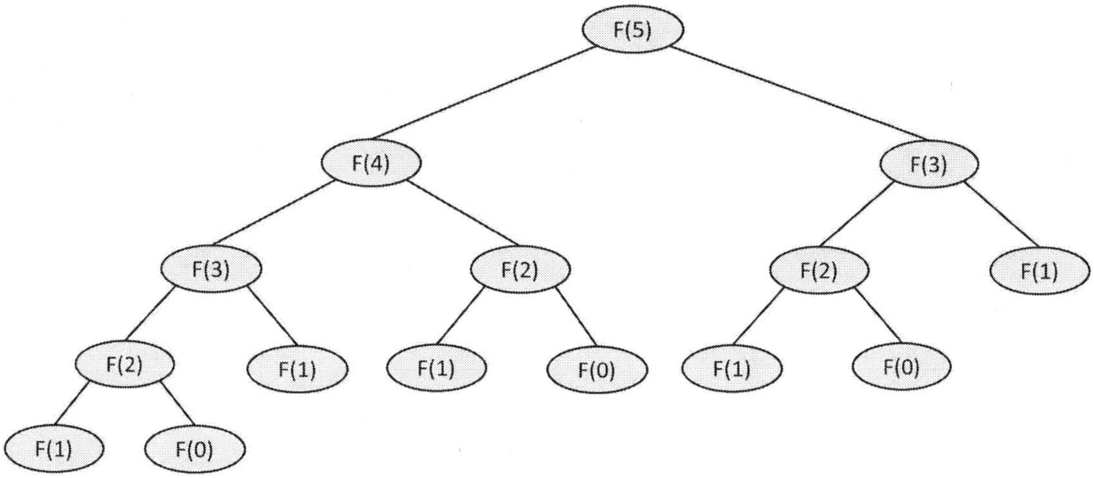


From the above diagram it is clear that to calculate fibonacci(5), fibonacci(2) is calculated 3 times. Further, if we want to find the complete Fibonacci series then the number of times these sub-problems are calculated is increases further.

## Dynamic Programming Methods

DP offers two methods to solve a problem2:

1. Tabulation (Bottom-Up)
2. Memoization (Top-Down)

## Tabulation (Bottom-Up)

**Bottom-up with Tabulation** is the approach in which smaller subproblems are solved first, and their solution is stored in a table. Bigger problems are calculated by using solutions to these sub-problems. Below is the Bottom-up calculation of the Fibonacci Number. Array dp[ ] is created to store the result of sub-problems.

**Example 18.02** : Bottom-up solution of fibonacci problem

```
public static int fibonacciBU(int n) {
    if (n < 2)
        return n;

    int[] dp = new int[n + 1];
    dp[0] = 0;
    dp[1] = 1;

    for (int i = 2; i <= n; i++) {
        dp[i] = dp[i - 2] + dp[i - 1];
    }

    return dp[n];
}
```

**Analysis:**

1 In this, the array dp[] is created, which is used to store the sub-problems and used in further calculation of bigger problems.

2 This solution is efficient and takes linear time O(n) to compute the Fibonacci series.

## Memoization (Top-Down)

**Top-down with Memoization** is the approach in which a bigger problem is recursively divided into smaller sub-problems. These sub-problems are solved, and their result is stored in a table / an array. So that we do not solve the same sub-problem again when it is called again. Instead, we just use the saved result. This approach is called Top-down with Memoization.

**Example 18.03:** Top down solution of fibonacci problem

```
public static int fibonacciTD(int n) {
    int[] dp = new int[n + 1];
    fibonacciTD(n, dp);
    return dp[n];
}

public static int fibonacciTD(int n, int[] dp) {
    if (n < 2)
        return dp[n] = n;

    if (dp[n] != 0)
        return dp[n];

    dp[n] = fibonacciTD(n - 1, dp) + fibonacciTD(n - 2, dp);
    return dp[n];
}
```

**Analysis**:

1 This is a top-down approach to solving the problem.

2 First, we had created an array dp[] to store intermediate states.

3 If some calculations are already done, then they will not be performed again.

4 Again this solution time complexity is O(n)

Steps for Solving Dynamic Programming problem :

1. **Optimal Substructure**: Try to find if there is a recursive relation between problem and sub-problem.
2. Write a recursive relation of the problem. Observe **Overlapping subproblems** at this step.
3. **Bottom-up approach**:
   - The bottom-up approach uses loops.
   - Compute the value of sub-problems in a bottom-up fashion and store this value in some table.
   - Construct the optimal solution from the value stored in the above step.
4. **Top-Down approach**:
   - The top-down approach uses recursion.
   - Identify the base case of recursion.
   - Create a recursive solution.

- Store results of sub-problems in some tables.
- Check for overlapping subproblems solutions in the table before recalculating them.

## Dynamic Programming Patterns

Optimal Substructure and Overlapping subproblems is the core of Dynamic programming. But we can group similar dynamic programming questions to make it easy to understand which all types of problems can be solved with dynamic programming. Learning one problem can help you solve many more that resemble it. The solution to those problems had the same approach.

Below are some types of problems for which solutions can be obtained using a Dynamic Programming approach:

**Type 1 : Maximum or Minimum cost to reach some state.**

- **Climbing Stairs with a minimum cost**: Given a list cost[] representing the cost of climbing from any step in the stair. From each step, you can climb 1 or 2 steps. You need to **minimise** the **cost** of reaching the **top** of the stairs. Can start from $0^{th}$ or $1^{st}$ stair.
- **Coin Change**: Given a list of coins[] representing various denominations of coins and an amount total representing the total amount of money. Return the **least number of coins** needed to make the total amount. If coins can't make the required total, then return -1.
- **Grid Min Value Path**: Given a grid of dimension m x n filled with positive numbers. Find the **minimum cost** path from **bottom-left (0, 0)** to **top-right(m-1,n-1)**. You can only move up or right.
- **Min Cost Travel**: Given a list of days[] which represent days in future. There are three different types of tickets: a 1 day ticket, 7 days ticket and a 30 days ticket, with their respective cost in costs[] array. 1 day ticket cost is costs[0], 7 days ticket cost is costs[1] and 30 days ticket cost is costs[2]. You want to **minimise** the **cost** of travel, but also have to travel in all the days in days[] array.

**Type 2 : Distinct ways to reach some state.**

- **Fibonacci sequence**: The Fibonacci sequence is a series of numbers, where a number is the addition of the previous two numbers. Starting numbers of the series are 0 and 1. Find the nth number in the Fibonacci numbers series.
- **Stair Climbing ways**: Given a stair of n steps. For each step, you can climb 1 or 2 steps. How many **distinct ways** can you climb to the **top** of the stairs?
- **Grid Unique Paths**: Given a grid of dimension m x n. Find the various unique paths from **bottom-left (0, 0)** to **top-right(m-1,n-1)**. You can only move up or right.
- **N Dice with Target Sum**: Given N dice with M faces. When all the dice are thrown together. Find the number of ways to get sum V.

**Type 3 : Merging intervals to get an Optimal solution.**

- **BST with minimum non-leaf nodes sum:** Given a list, arr[] of positive integers corresponds to the value of leaf node in a binary tree. The value of a non-leaf node is equal to the product of the largest leaf value of the left and right subtree. Among all the possible binary trees, return the smallest possible sum of the values of the non-leaf node.
- **Optimal Binary Search Tree:** Given a sorted array keys[] and a list freq[] both arrays of length n. keys[i] is searched freq[i] a number of times. Create a binary search tree of all the input keys such that the overall cost of all the searches is as small as possible. The cost of a BST node is the level of the node multiplied by its frequency.
- **Matrix Chain Multiplication**: Given a sequence of matrices, M = M1,..., Mn. The goal of this problem is to find the most efficient way to multiply these matrices. The goal is not to perform the actual multiplication, but to decide the sequence of the matrix multiplications, so that the result will be calculated in minimal operations. To compute the product of two matrices of dimensions pXq and qXr, p*q*r number of operations will be required. Matrix multiplication operations are associative. Therefore, n matrix multiplication can be done in many ways.

**Type 4 : Subsequence, Substrings and String Manipulation using Dynamic Programming**

- **Longest Common Subsequence**: Given X = {x1, x2,...., xm} is a sequence of characters and Y = {y1, y2,..., yn} is another sequence. Z is a subsequence of X if it can be driven by deleting some elements of X. Z is a subsequence of Y if it can be driven by deleting some elements from Y. Z is LCS of it is subsequence to both X and Y, and length of all the sub-sequences is less than Z. Find the longest common subsequence Z given X and Y.
- **Largest Increasing Subsequence**: Given a list of integers, you need to find the largest subsequence in increasing order. You need to find the largest increasing sequence by selecting the elements from the given array such that their relative order does not change.
- **Longest Bitonic Subsequence**: Given a list, you need to find the longest bitonic subsequence.
- **Longest Palindromic Subsequence**: Given a string s, find the longest palindromic subsequence length in s. A **Subsequence** is a sequence that can be derived from another sequence by deleting some or no elements without changing the order of the remaining elements.
- **Longest Palindromic Substring**: Given a string s, find the longest palindromic substring length in s. A **Substring** is a string that is part of a longer string.
- **Edit Distance**: Given two strings s1 and s2, find the minimum number of operations required to convert s1 to s2. The available operations are “Insert a character”, “Delete a character” or “Replace a character”.

**Type 5 : State Selection:** To reach the current state, you need to decide which previous state needs to be used.

- **Assembly Line Scheduling**: Calculate the least amount of time necessary to build a car when using a manufacturing chain with two assembly lines. The problem variables:
  - e[i]: entry time in assembly line i
  - x[i]: exit time from assembly line i

- a[i, j]: Time required at station S[i, j] (assembly line i, stage j)
- t[i, j]: Time required to transit from station S[i, j] to the other assembly line

➢ **House Robber**: A robber wants to rob houses along a certain street. He has a rule that he doesn't rob from adjacent houses. Given an integer array representing the amount of money in each house. You need to return the maximum amount of money the robber can rob without breaking his rule.

➢ **Job Scheduling**: Given N jobs, where every job has a start time, finish time and positive value associated with it. Find the maximum values of the jobs which can be scheduled, such that no two jobs overlap.

## Type 1 : Maximum / Minimum cost to reach some state problems

In this type of problem, it is asked to find the minimum / maximum cost to reach some state.

General **Top-Down** function to solve Min and Max problems:

```
int TopDownFunction(int[] dp, int[] ways, int target ) {
    // Base Case
    if(target == 0)
        return 0;

    if (dp[target] != INVALID) {
        return dp[target];
    }

    // Recursion
    for (int i = 0; i < ways.length; i++) {
        dp[target] = min(dp[target], TopDownFunction(dp, ways, target - ways[i])
                                                        + cost);
    }

    return dp[target];
}

int TopDownFunction(int[] ways, int target ) {
    int[] dp = new int[target];
    fill dp[] with INVALID value;
    return TopDownFunction(dp, ways, target);
}
```

General **Bottom-Up** function to solve Min-Max problems:

```
int BottomUpFunction( int[] ways, int target ) {
    int[] dp = new int[target];
    fill dp[] array with value INVALID;
    dp[0] = 0; // Base value.

    for (int i = 1; i <= target; i++) {
        for (int j = 0; j < ways.length; j++) {
            // For all fusible ways.
            dp[i] = min(dp[i], dp[i - ways[j]] + cost);
        }
    }

    return dp[target];
}
```

## Coin Change

**Problem:** Given an array of coins[] representing various denominations of coins and an amount total representing the total amount of money. Return the least number of coins needed to make the total amount. If coins can't make the required total then return -1.

For example, the Indian coin system {5, 10, 20, 25, 50,100}. Suppose we want to give a change of 40 paisa.

**Solution**: We can make a solution by repeatedly choosing a coin ≤ to the current amount, resulting in a new amount. The greedy solution always chooses the largest coin value possible. For 40 paisa: {25, 10, and 5}

This is how billions of people around the globe make changes every day. That is an approximate solution to the problem. But this is not the optimal way, the optimal solution for the above problem is {20, 20}

Step (I): Characterise the class of a coin-change solution.
Define C [j] to be the minimum number of coins we need to make a change for j cents. If we knew that an optimal solution for the problem of making change for j cents used a coin of denomination di, we would have:
C[j] = 1+C[j – di]

Strep (II): Recursively defines the value of an optimal solution. Where j is the total amount.

$$c[j] = \begin{cases} 0 & if\ j=0 \\ 1+min(c[j-di]) & 1 \le i \le k \,\&\, j \ge 1 \end{cases}$$

**Example 18.04:** Brute force solution
```
static int minCoins2(int[] coins, int n, int val) { // Brute force.
    if (val == 0)
        return 0;

    int count = Integer.MAX_VALUE;
    for (int i = 0; i < n; i++) {
        if (coins[i] <= val) {
            int subCount = minCoins2(coins, n, val - coins[i]);
            if (subCount >= 0)
                count = Math.min(count, subCount + 1);
        }
    }
    return (count != Integer.MAX_VALUE) ? count : -1;
}
```

**Analysis:** The above solution have overlapping subproblem so have exponential time complexity.

Step (III): Compute values using dynamic programming in a bottom-up fashion.

**Example 18.05:**
```
static int minCoinsBU(int[] coins, int n, int val) { // DP bottom up approach.
    int[] count = new int[val + 1];
    Arrays.fill(count, Integer.MAX_VALUE);
    count[0] = 0; // Base value.
```

```
    for (int i = 1; i <= val; i++) {
        for (int j = 0; j < n; j++) {
            // For all coins smaller than or equal to i.
            if (coins[j] <= i &&
                count[i - coins[j]] != Integer.MAX_VALUE &&
                count[i] > count[i - coins[j]] + 1)
            {
                count[i] = count[i - coins[j]] + 1;
            }
        }
    }
    return (count[val] != Integer.MAX_VALUE) ? count[val] : -1;
}
```

**Time-Complexity**: O(nk)

Step (iv): Construct an optimal solution. We use an additional list Deno[1.. n], where Deno[j] is the denomination of a coin used in an optimal solution.

**Example 18.06:**

```
static void printCoinsUtil(int[] cvalue, int val) {
    if (val > 0) {
        printCoinsUtil(cvalue, val - cvalue[val]);
        System.out.print(cvalue[val] + " ");
    }
}

static void printCoins(int[] cvalue, int val) {
    System.out.print("Coins are : ");
    printCoinsUtil(cvalue, val);
    System.out.println();
}

static int minCoinsBU2(int[] coins, int n, int val) { // DP bottom up approach.
    int[] count = new int[val + 1];
    int[] cvalue = new int[val + 1];

    Arrays.fill(count, Integer.MAX_VALUE);
    Arrays.fill(cvalue, Integer.MAX_VALUE);
    count[0] = 0; // Base value.

    for (int i = 1; i <= val; i++) {
        for (int j = 0; j < n; j++) {
            // For all coins smaller than or equal to i.
            if (coins[j] <= i &&
                count[i - coins[j]] != Integer.MAX_VALUE &&
                count[i] > count[i - coins[j]] + 1)
            {
                count[i] = count[i - coins[j]] + 1;
                cvalue[i] = coins[j];
            }
        }
    }
```

```
    if (count[val] == Integer.MAX_VALUE)
        return -1;

    printCoins(cvalue, val);
    return  count[val];
}

// Testing code.
public static void main(String[] args) {
    int[] coins = { 5, 6 };
    int value = 16;
    int n = coins.length;
    System.out.println("Count is : " + minCoinsBU2(coins, n, value));
}
```

**Output:**

```
Coins are : 6 5 5
Count is : 3
```

The same problem can be solved using a top-down approach.

**Example 18.07:**

```
static int minCoinsTD(int[] coins, int n, int val) {
    int[] count = new int[val + 1];
    Arrays.fill(count, Integer.MAX_VALUE);
    count[0] = 0; // zero val need zero coins.
    return minCoinsTD(count, coins, n, val);
}

static int minCoinsTD(int[] count, int[] coins, int n, int val) {
    // Base Case
    if (count[val] != Integer.MAX_VALUE) {
        return count[val];
    }

    // Recursion
    for (int i = 0; i < n; i++) {  // For all possible coins
        if (coins[i] <= val) { // check validity of a sub-problem
            int subCount = minCoinsTD(count, coins, n, val - coins[i]);
            if (subCount != Integer.MAX_VALUE && count[val] > (subCount + 1))
                count[val] = subCount + 1;
        }
    }
    return count[val];
}
```

**Time-Complexity**: O(nk)

## Climbing Stairs with minimum cost

**Problem:** Given an array cost[] representing the cost of climbing from any step in the stair. From each step, you can climb 1 or 2 steps. You need to minimise the cost of reaching the top of the stairs. Can start from 0th or 1st stair.

**Solution:** Recurrence Relation is MinCost(n) = min( MinCost(n-1) + MinCost(n-2)) + Cost[n]
Using a bottom-up approach, an array dp[] is used to store the total cost of climbing from each stair. After populating this array, dp[]. In the end, the n-1th and nth stair minimum are returned, after which we will reach the top.

**Example 18.08:**
```
static int minStairCost(int cost[], int n) {
    // base case
    if (n == 1)
        return cost[0];

    int dp[] = new int[n];
    dp[0] = cost[0];
    dp[1] = cost[1];

    for (int i = 2; i < n; i++) {
        dp[i] = Math.min(dp[i - 1], dp[i - 2]) + cost[i];
    }

    return Math.min(dp[n - 2], dp[n - 1]);
}

// Testing code.
public static void main(String[] args) {
    int a[] = { 1, 5, 6, 3, 4, 7, 9, 1, 2, 11 };
    int n = a.length;
    System.out.print("minStairCost : " + minStairCost(a, n));
}
```

**Output:**
```
minStairCost : 18
```

**Time-Complexity**: O(n)

## Grid Min Value Path

**Problem:** Given a grid of dimension m x n filled with positive numbers. Find the **minimum cost** path from **bottom-left (0, 0)** to **top-right(m-1,n-1)**. You can only move up or right.

**Solution**:
1. minCost(cost, m, n) = cost[m-1][n-1] + min( minCost(cost, m-1, n), minCost(cost, m, n-1) )
2. Each cell in the grid can be reached from at most 2 paths- bottom or left.
3. The bottom-up approach is used to populate dynamic programming array dp[].

**Example 18.09:**
```
private static int minCostBU(int[][] cost, int m, int n) {
    int tc[][] = new int[m][n];
    tc[0][0] = cost[0][0];

    // Initialize first column.
    for (int i = 1; i < m; i++) {
        tc[i][0] = tc[i - 1][0] + cost[i][0];
    }
```

```
    // Initialize first row.
    for (int j = 1; j < n; j++) {
        tc[0][j] = tc[0][j - 1] + cost[0][j];
    }

    for (int i = 1; i < m; i++) {
        for (int j = 1; j < n; j++) {
            tc[i][j] = cost[i][j] + min(tc[i-1][j-1],tc[i-1][j],tc[i][j-1]);
        }
    }
    return tc[m - 1][n - 1];
}

// Testing code.
public static void main(String[] args) {
    int[][] cost = { { 1, 3, 4 }, { 4, 7, 5 }, { 1, 5, 3 } };
    System.out.println(minCostBU(cost, 3, 3));
}
```

**Output:**

```
11
```

**Time-Complexity**: O(mn)

## Min Cost Travel

**Problem:** Given an array of days[] which represent days in future. There are three different types of tickets: a 1 day ticket, 7 days ticket and a 30 days ticket, with their respective cost in costs[] array. 1 day ticket cost is costs[0], 7 days ticket cost is costs[1] and 30 days ticket cost is costs[2]. You want to **minimise** the **cost** of travel but also have to travel in all the days in days[] array.

**Solution:**

Recurrence Relation is minCost(i) = min (minCost(i-1) + costs[0], minCost(i-7) + costs[1], minCost(i-30) + costs[2]) where "i" is travel days.

The bottom-up approach is used to solve this problem.

**Example 18.10:**

```
public static int minCostTravel(int[] days, int[] costs) {
    int n = days.length;
    int max = days[n - 1];
    int[] dp = new int[max + 1];

    int j = 0;
    for (int i = 1; i <= max; i++) {
        if (days[j] == i) {// That days is definitely travelled.
            j++;
            dp[i] = dp[i - 1] + costs[0];
            dp[i] = Math.min(dp[i], dp[Math.max(0, i - 7)] + costs[1]);
            dp[i] = Math.min(dp[i], dp[Math.max(0, i - 30)] + costs[2]);
        } else
            dp[i] = dp[i - 1]; // day may be ignored.
    }
    return dp[max];
}
```

```
// Testing code.
public static void main(String[] args) {
    int[] days = { 1, 3, 5, 7, 12, 20, 30 };
    int[] costs = { 2, 7, 20 };
    System.out.println("Min cost is:" + minCostTravel(days, costs));
}
```

**Output:**

```
Min cost is:13
```

**Time-Complexity**: O(n)

## Type 2 : Distinct ways to reach some state problems

In this type of problem, it is asked to find the total number of distinct ways to reach some state.

All possible ways to reach the target state are stored in the dp[] array.

General **Top-Down** function to solve Distinct-Way problems:

```
int TopDownFunction(int[] dp, int[] ways, int target ) {
    // Base Case
    if(target == 0)
        return 0;

    if (dp[target] != 0) {
        return dp[target];
    }

    // Recursion
    for (int i = 0; i < ways.length && ways[i] <= i; i++) {
        // For all fusible ways.
        dp[target] += TopDownFunction(dp, ways, target - ways[i]);
    }
    return dp[target];
}

int TopDownFunction(int[] ways, int target ) {
    int[] dp = new int[target];
    return TopDownFunction(dp, ways, target);
}
```

General **Bottom-Up** function to solve Distinct-Way problems:

```
int BottomUpFunction( int[] ways, int target ) {
    int[] dp = new int[target];

    for (int i = 1; i <= target; i++) {
        for (int j = 0; j < ways.length && ways[i] <= i ; j++) {
            // For all fusible ways.
            dp[i] += dp[i - ways[j]];
        }
    }
    return dp[target];
}
```

## Stair Climbing Ways

**Problem:** Given a stair of n steps. For each step, you can climb 1 or 2 steps. How many **distinct ways** can you climb at the **top** of the stairs?

**Solution:** The Recurrence Relation is ways(i) = ways(i-1) + ways(i-2). Bottom up approach is used to solve this problem.

**Example 18.11:**
```
public static int stairUniqueWaysBU2(int n) {
    if (n < 2)
        return n;

    int[] ways = new int[n];
    ways[0] = 1;
    ways[1] = 2;

    for (int i = 2; i < n; i++)
        ways[i] = ways[i - 1] + ways[i - 2];

    return ways[n - 1];
}

// Testing code.
public static void main(String[] args) {
    System.out.println("Unique way to reach top:: " + stairUniqueWaysBU2(4));
}
```

**Output**:
```
Unique way to reach top:: 5
```

**Time-Complexity**: O(n)

## Grid Unique Paths

**Problem:** Given a grid of dimension m x n. Find the various unique paths from **bottom-left (0, 0)** to **top-right(m-1,n-1)**. You can only move up or right.

**Solution:** The Recurrence Relation is uniqueWays(m, n) = uniqueWays(m-1, n) + uniqueWays(m, n-1) dp[][] array is used to store unique ways to reach some cells. Index dp[0][0] is 1 as there is only one way to reach (0,0). The first column and first row cells are also populated by 1 as there is only one way to reach them. Which is the direct path from (0,0). The bottom-up approach is used to populate the dp[][] array.

**Example 18.12:**
```
private static int gridUniqueWays(int m, int n) {
    int[][] dp = new int[m][n];
    dp[0][0] = 1;
    // Initialize first column.
    for (int i = 1; i < m; i++) {
        dp[i][0] = dp[i - 1][0];
    }
```

```
    // Initialize first row.
    for (int j = 1; j < n; j++) {
        dp[0][j] = dp[0][j - 1];
    }

    for (int i = 1; i < m; i++) {
        for (int j = 1; j < n; j++)
            dp[i][j] = dp[i - 1][j] + dp[i][j - 1];
    }
    return dp[m - 1][n - 1];
}

// Testing code.
public static void main(String[] args) {
    System.out.println(gridUniqueWays(3, 3));
}
```

**Output**:

```
6
```

**Time-Complexity**: O(mn)

**Problem**: Given a grid of dimension m x n. Find the various unique paths from **bottom-left (0, 0)** to **top-right(m-1,n-1)**. You can only move up, right or diagonally up-right.

**Solution**:

```
dp[i][j] = dp[i-1][j-1] + dp[i-1][j] + dp[i][j-1];
```

## N Dice with Target Sum

**Problem:** Given N dice with M faces. When all the dice are thrown together. Find the number of ways to get sum V.

**Solution:** The Recurrence Relation for this problem:

findWays(N, V) = ΣfindWays(N-1, V-k), where k = 1 to M, N total number of dice.

Populate dp[x][y] array which will store the number of ways to reach value y by x number of dices.

**Example 18.13:**

```
public static int findWays(int n, int m, int V) {
    int[][] dp = new int[n + 1][V + 1];

    // Table entries for only one dice.
    for (int j = 1; j <= m && j <= V; j++)
        dp[1][j] = 1;

    // i is number of dice, j is Value, k value of dice.
    for (int i = 2; i <= n; i++) {
        for (int j = 1; j <= V; j++) {
            for (int k = 1; k <= j && k <= m; k++)
                dp[i][j] += dp[i - 1][j - k];
        }
    }

    return dp[n][V];
}
```

```
// Testing code.
public static void main(String[] args) {
    for (int i = 1; i <= 6; i++) {
        System.out.print(findWays(i, 6, 6) + " ");
    }
}
```

**Output:**

```
1 5 10 10 5 1
```

**Time-Complexity**: O(n*m*V), n is the number of dice, m is the different faces of one dice and V is the input value.

## Fibonacci Sequence

**Problem:** The Fibonacci sequence is a series of numbers where a number is the addition of the previous two numbers. Starting numbers of the series are 0 and 1. Find the nth number in the Fibonacci numbers series.

**Note**: This problem is solved at the start of this chapter.

# Type 3 : Merging intervals to get optimal solution problems

**Problem**: Given a list of values, find an optimal solution for a problem using the current value and optimal solution of the left and right sub-problem.

**Solution**: Find all optimal solutions in the interval and return the best optimal solution.
Recurrence Relation of the problem is:
optimalSolution(i, j) = optimalSolution(i, k-1) + cost[k] + optimalSolution(k+1, j) for k in range "i" to "j".

General **Top-Down** function to solve Merging-Interval problems:

```
int TopDownFunction(int[] costs) {
    int n = costs.length;
    int[][] dp = new int[n][n];

    for (int[] row : dp)
        fill row[] array with value INVALID;

    return TopDownFunction(dp, costs, 0, n-1);
}

int TopDownFunction(int[][] dp, int[] costs, int i, int j ) {
    // Base Case
    if(i == j)
        return 0;

    if (dp[i][j] != INVALID) {
        return dp[i][j];
    }
```

```
    // Recursion
    for (int k = i; k < j; k++) {
        dp[i][j] = Min (dp[i][j], TopDownFunction(dp, costs, i, k) + costs[k] +
TopDownFunction(dp, costs, k+1, j));
    }

    return dp[i][j];
}
```

General **Bottom-Up** function to solve Merging-Interval problems:

```
int BottomUpFunction(int[] costs) {
    int n = costs.length;
    int[][] dp = new int[n][n];
    for (int row : dp)
        fill array row[] with value INVALID;

    for(int l = 1; l<n; l++) { // l is length of range.
        for(int i = 1, j = i+l; j<n; i++,j++) {
            for(int k = i; k<j; k++) {
                dp[i][j] = min(dp[i][j], dp[i][k] + costs[k] + dp[k+1][j]);
            }
        }
    }

     return dp[1][n-1];
}
```

## Matrix Chain Multiplication

**Problem:** Given a sequence of matrices, M = M1,…, Mn. The goal of this problem is to find the most efficient way to multiply these matrices. The goal is not to perform the actual multiplication, but to decide the sequence of the matrix multiplications, so that the result will be calculated in minimal operations. To compute the product of two matrices of dimensions pXq and qXr, p*q*r number of operations will be required. Matrix multiplication operations are associative. Therefore, n matrix multiplication can be done in many ways.

For example, M1, M2, M3 and M4, can be fully parenthesized as:
(M1·(M2·(M3·M4)))
(M1·((M2·M3)·M4))
((M1·M2)·(M3·M4))
(((M1·M2)·M3)·M4)
((M1·(M2·M3))·M4)

For example,
Let M1 dimensions be 10 × 100, M2 dimensions are 100 × 10, and M3 dimensions are 10 × 50.
((M1·M2)· M3) = (10*100*10) + (10*10*50) = 15000
(M1· (M2·M3) = (100*10*50) + (10*100*50) = 100000

Therefore, in this problem, we need to parenthesize the matrix chain so that the total multiplication cost is minimised.

**Solution**: Given a sequence of n matrices M1, M2,… Mn. And their dimensions are p0, p1, p2,…, pn. Where matrix Ai has dimension pi − 1 × pi for 1 ≤ i ≤ n. Determine the order of multiplication that minimises the total number of multiplications.

p[0] = row of the M1
p[i-1] = row of the Mi 1<=i<=N
p[1] = column of the M1
p[i] = column of Mi 1<=i<=N

M(1,N) = min( M(1, K) + M(K+1, N) + p0*pk*pn ) where 1<= K <=N
If M (1, N) is minimal, then both M (1, K) & M (K+1, N) are minimal. Otherwise, if there is some M'(1, K) is there whose cost is less than M (1.. K), then M (1.. N) can't be minimal, and there is a more optimal solution possible.

**Recurrence relation:**

$$M(i,\ j) = \begin{cases} 0 & if\, i=j \\ min\{M(i,k)+M(k,j) \ + \ pi-1*pk*pj\} & i\leq k<j \end{cases}$$

If you try to solve this problem using the brute-force method, then you will find all possible parenthesization. Then you will compute the cost of multiplications. Thereafter you will pick the best solution. This approach will be exponential.

**Example 18.14:** Brute-force approach to solve matrix chain multiplication problem.
```
static int MatrixChainMulBruteForce(int[] p, int i, int j) {
    if (i == j)
        return 0;

    int min = Integer.MAX_VALUE;

    // place parenthesis at different places between
    // first and last matrix, recursively calculate
    // count of multiplications for each parenthesis
    // placement and return the minimum count
    for (int k = i; k < j; k++) {
        int count = MatrixChainMulBruteForce(p, i, k) +
                MatrixChainMulBruteForce(p, k+1, j) +
                p[i-1]*p[k]*p[j];

        if (count < min)
            min = count;
    }

    // Return minimum count
    return min;
}

static int MatrixChainMulBruteForce(int[] p, int n) {
    int i = 1, j = n - 1;
    return MatrixChainMulBruteForce(p, i, j);
}
```

The brute force approach is insufficient. Take an example of M1, M2,..., Mn. When you have calculated that ((M1·M2) · M3) is better than (M1· (M2·M3) so there is no point of calculating then combinations of (M1· (M2·M3) with (M4, M5.... Mn).

Directly calling a recursive function will lead to the calculation of the same sub-problem multiple times. This will lead to an exponential solution. So dynamic programming is used to prevent recalculation of already calculated values.

Overlapping subproblems:

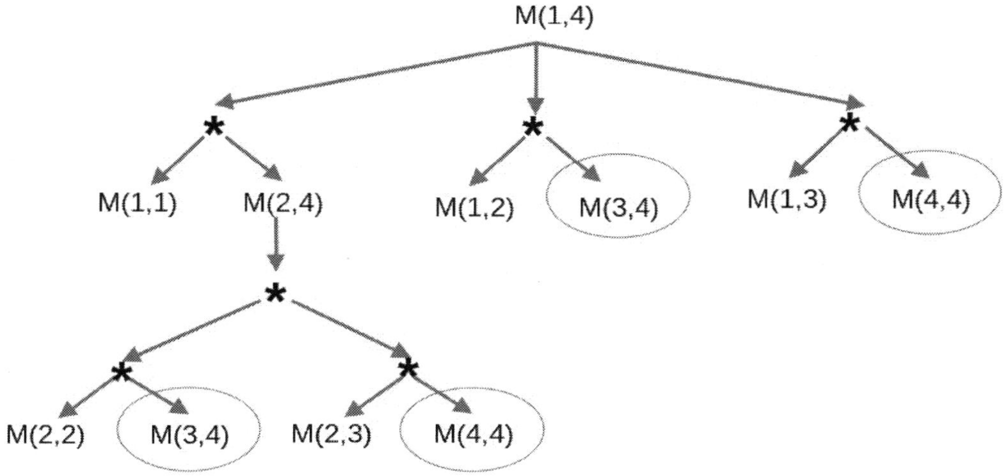


**Example 18.15**: Top-down Dynamic programming Implementation

```
static int MatrixChainMulTD(int[] p, int n) {
    int[][] dp = new int[n][n];
    for (int[] row : dp)
        Arrays.fill(row, Integer.MAX_VALUE);

    for (int i = 1; i < n; i++)
        dp[i][i] = 0;

    return MatrixChainMulTD(dp, p, 1, n - 1);
}

static int MatrixChainMulTD(int[][] dp, int[] p, int i, int j) {
    // Base Case
    if (dp[i][j] != Integer.MAX_VALUE) {
        return dp[i][j];
    }

    for (int k = i; k < j; k++) {
        dp[i][j] = Math.min(dp[i][j], MatrixChainMulTD(dp, p, i, k) +
            MatrixChainMulTD(dp, p, k+1, j) + p[i-1]*p[k]*p[j]);
    }

    return dp[i][j];
}
```

Time Complexity will O(n^3)

**Example 18.16**: Bottom-Up dynamic programming Implementation

```
static int MatrixChainMulBU(int[] p, int n) {
    int[][] dp = new int[n][n];
    for (int[] row : dp)
        Arrays.fill(row, Integer.MAX_VALUE);

    for (int i = 1; i < n; i++)
        dp[i][i] = 0;

    for (int l = 1; l < n; l++) { // l is length of range.
        for (int i = 1, j = i + l; j < n; i++, j++) {
            for (int k = i; k < j; k++) {
                dp[i][j] = Math.min(dp[i][j], dp[i][k] + p[i - 1] * p[k] * p[j] +
dp[k + 1][j]);
            }
        }
    }
    return dp[1][n - 1];
}
```

`Time Complexity: O(n^3)`

**Example 18.17**: Testing code

```
public static void main(String[] args) {
    int arr[] = { 1, 2, 3, 4 };
    int n = arr.length;
    System.out.println("Matrix Chain Mul is: " + MatrixChainMulBU(arr, n));
}
```

**Output**:

```
Matrix Chain Multiplication is: 18
```

Printing brackets in Matrix Chain Multiplication. Another table pos[n][n] is used to keep track of the position where the product is split. Each entry pos[i][j] records the value of k such that the optimal parenthesization of Mi to Mj splits the product into ( M1 to Mk ) and ( Mk+1 to Mj).

**Example 18.18**: Bottom-Up dynamic programming Implementation

```
static void PrintOptPar(int n, int[][] pos, int i, int j) {
    if (i == j)
        System.out.print("M" + pos[i][i] + " ");
    else {
        System.out.print("( ");
        PrintOptPar(n, pos, i, pos[i][j]);
        PrintOptPar(n, pos, pos[i][j]+1, j);
        System.out.print(") ");
    }
}

static void PrintOptimalParenthesis(int n, int[][] pos) {
    System.out.print("OptimalParenthesis : ");
    PrintOptPar(n, pos, 1, n-1);
    System.out.println("");
}
```

```
static int MatrixChainMulBU2(int[] p, int n) {
    int[][] dp = new int[n][n];
    int[][] pos = new int[n][n];

    for (int[] row : dp)
        Arrays.fill(row, Integer.MAX_VALUE);

    for (int i = 1; i < n; i++){
        dp[i][i] = 0;
        pos[i][i] = i;
    }

    for (int l = 1; l < n; l++) { // l is length of range.
        for (int i = 1, j = i + l; j < n; i++, j++) {
            for (int k = i; k < j; k++) {
                dp[i][j] = Math.min(dp[i][j], dp[i][k] + p[i - 1] * p[k] * p[j] +
dp[k + 1][j]);
                pos[i][j] = k;
            }
        }
    }
    PrintOptimalParenthesis(n, pos);
    return dp[1][n - 1];
}

// Testing code.
public static void main(String[] args) {
    int arr[] = { 1, 2, 3, 4 };
    int n = arr.length;
    System.out.println("Matrix Chain Mul is: " + MatrixChainMulBU2(arr, n));
}
```

**Output**:

```
OptimalParenthesis : ( ( M1 M2 ) M3 )
Matrix Chain Multiplication is: 18
```

## Optimal Binary Search Tree

**Problem:** Given a sorted array keys[] and an array freq[] both arrays of length n. keys[i] is searched freq[i] a number of times. Create a binary search tree of all the input keys such that the overall cost of all the searches is as small as possible. The cost of a BST node is the level of the node multiplied by its frequency.

**Solution**: Recurrence Relation:
**optCost(i, j) = min(optCost(i, r-1) + optCost(r+1, j)) + Σkey[r]** where r is from i to j .

When the tree from 'i' to 'r-1' & tree form 'r+1' to 'j' is added by the node at 'r' then both of the trees will go one level down and then node 'r' is added. Change in cost will be the sum of all the nodes from 'i' to 'r-1' & cost of all the nodes from 'r+1' to 'j' & cost of node 'r'. These all three parts sum up to Σkey[r] in the recurrence relation.

This recurrence relation has overlapping solutions, so dynamic programming is applied. Top-down and bottom-up approaches are used to create solutions for this problem.

**Example 18.19: Top-down** Implementation
```
static int optBstCostTD(int[] keys, int[] freq) {
    int n = freq.length;
    int[][] cost = new int[n][n];
    for (int[] row : cost)
        Arrays.fill(row, Integer.MAX_VALUE);

    for (int i = 0; i < n; i++)
        cost[i][i] = freq[i];

    return optBstCostTD(freq, cost, 0, n - 1);
}

static int optBstCostTD(int[] freq, int[][] cost, int i, int j) {
    if (i > j)
        return 0;

    if (cost[i][j] != Integer.MAX_VALUE)
        return cost[i][j];

    int s = sum(freq, i, j);
    for (int r = i; r <= j; r++) {
        cost[i][j] = Math.min(cost[i][j], optBstCostTD(freq, cost, i, r - 1) +
optBstCostTD(freq, cost, r + 1, j) + s);
    }
    return cost[i][j];
}

// Code to find sum in range i to j.
static int sum(int[] freq, int i, int j) {
    int s = 0;
    for (int k = i; k <= j; k++)
        s += freq[k];
    return s;
}

// Testing code
public static void main(String[] args) {
    int keys[] = { 9, 15, 25 };
    int[] freq = { 30, 10, 40 };
    System.out.println("OBST cost:" + optBstCostTD(keys, freq));
}
```

**Output**:
```
OBST cost:130
```

**Example 18.20: Bottom-Up** implementation:
```
static int optBstCostBU(int[] keys, int[] freq) {
    int n = freq.length;
    int[][] cost = new int[n][n];
    for (int[] row : cost)
        Arrays.fill(row, Integer.MAX_VALUE);

    for (int i = 0; i < n; i++)
        cost[i][i] = freq[i];
```

```
    int sm = 0;

    for (int l = 1; l < n; l++) { // l is length of range.
        for (int i = 0, j = i + l; j < n; i++, j++) {
            sm = sum(freq, i, j);
            for (int r = i; r <= j; r++) {
                cost[i][j] = Math.min(cost[i][j], sm + ((r-1 >= i)?cost[i][r-1]:0)
                                            + ((r+1 <= j) ? cost[r+1][j] : 0));
            }
        }
    }

    return cost[0][n - 1];
}
```

**Time-complexity**: O(n^3)

## BST with minimum non-leaf nodes sum

**Problem:** Given an array of positive integers corresponds to the value of leaf node in a binary tree. The value of a non-leaf node is equal to the product of the largest leaf value of the left and right subtree. Among all the possible binary trees, return the smallest possible sum of the values of the non-leaf node.

**Solution:** The recurrence relation for the problem is:
findSum(i,j)= Min( findSum(i,k) + findSum(k+1,j) + maxVal(i,k)* maxVal(k+1,j))
We need to create two arrays, the first dp[][] array to keep the value of the various nodes of the tree. Along with this, we need another array max[][] which will store the max of the left of that subtree.

**Example 18.21: Top-Down** approach to solve the problem

```
static int minCostBstTD(int[][] dp, int[][] max, int i, int j, int[] arr) {
    if (j <= i)
        return 0;

    if (dp[i][j] != Integer.MAX_VALUE)
        return dp[i][j];

    for (int k = i; k < j; k++) {
        dp[i][j] = Math.min(dp[i][j], minCostBstTD(dp, max, i, k, arr) +
minCostBstTD(dp, max, k + 1, j, arr) + maxVal(max, i, k) * maxVal(max, k + 1, j));
    }

    return dp[i][j];
}

static int minCostBstTD(int[] arr) {
    int n = arr.length;
    int[][] dp = new int[n][n];
    for (int[] row : dp)
        Arrays.fill(row, Integer.MAX_VALUE);

    int[][] max = new int[n][n];
    for (int[] row : max)
        Arrays.fill(row, Integer.MIN_VALUE);
```

```
    for (int i = 0; i < n; i++)
        max[i][i] = arr[i];

    return minCostBstTD(dp, max, 0, n - 1, arr);
}

static int maxVal(int[][] max, int i, int j) {
    if (max[i][j] != Integer.MIN_VALUE)
        return max[i][j];

    for (int k = i; k < j; k++) {
        max[i][j] = Integer.max(max[i][j], Integer.max(maxVal(max, i, k),
maxVal(max, k + 1, j)));
    }
    return max[i][j];
}
```

**Example 18.22: Bottom-Up** approach to solve problem:

```
static int minCostBstBU(int[] arr) {
    int n = arr.length;
    int[][] dp = new int[n][n];
    int[][] max = new int[n][n];

    for (int i = 0; i < n; i++)
        max[i][i] = arr[i];

    for (int l = 1; l < n; l++) { // l is length of range.
        for (int i = 0, j = i + l; j < n; i++, j++) {
            dp[i][j] = Integer.MAX_VALUE;
            for (int k = i; k < j; k++) {
                dp[i][j] = Math.min(dp[i][j], dp[i][k] + dp[k + 1][j] + max[i][k] *
max[k + 1][j]);
                max[i][j] = Math.max(max[i][k], max[k + 1][j]);
            }
        }
    }

    return dp[0][n - 1];
}

// Testing code.
public static void main(String[] args) {
    int arr[] = { 6, 2, 4 };
    System.out.println("Total cost: " + minCostBstTD(arr));
    System.out.println("Total cost: " + minCostBstBU(arr));
}
```

**Output**:

```
Total cost: 32
Total cost: 32
```

**Time Complexity:** O(n^3)

## Type 4 : Subsequence, Substrings and String Manipulation problems

In this type of problem, sometimes a single string or array is given, and you need to find some pattern inside it. Or you may be given two strings or arrays, and you need to get some pattern out of it.

Type1 : Increasing or decreasing subsequence or substring in a given string.

```
for (int i = 0; i < n; i++) {
    for (int j = 0; j < i; j++) {
        // incremental found pattern of sub-problem.
    }
}
```

Type2 : Largest substring or subsequence in a given string.

```
for (int l = 1; l < n; l++) {  // Range.
    for (int i = 0, j = i+l; j < n; i++, j++) {
        // incremental calculation of sub-problem
        // with increasing range.
    }
}
```

Type3 : Comparison of two different strings.

```
for (int i = 1; i <= m; i++) { // First string index.
    for (int j = 1; j <= n; j++) { // Second string index.
            // Comparison of two strings.
    }
}
```

### Largest Increasing Subsequence

**Problem:** Given an array of integers, you need to find the largest subsequence in increasing order. You need to find the largest increasing sequence by selecting the elements from the given array such that their relative order does not change.

Input V = [10, 12, 9, 23, 25, 55, 49, 70]
Output will be 6 corresponds to [10, 12, 23, 25, 49, 70]

**Solution:** Optimal Substructure for this problem:
LIS(k) = max (LIS(k), LIS(j) + 1, where 0<j<k & v[j]<v[k]) where 0 < k < n
Keep populating the LIS[] array to create the Largest Increasing Subsequence.

```
function LIS(v[], n)
    for i ← 1 to n do
        lis[i] ← 1
        for j ← 1 to i do
            if v[j] < v[i] and lis[i] < lis[j]+1 then
                lis[i] ← lis[j] +1
    return max (length[i] where 1≤i≤n)
```

**Time Complexity:** O(n^2), **Space Complexity:** O(n).

**Example 18.23:**
```
static int lis(int[] arr) {
    int n = arr.length;
    int[] lis = new int[n];
    int max = 0;

    // Populating LIS values in bottom up manner.
    for (int i = 0; i < n; i++) {
        lis[i] = 1; // Initialize LIS values for all indexes as 1.
        for (int j = 0; j < i; j++) {
            if (arr[j] < arr[i] && lis[i] < lis[j] + 1)
                lis[i] = lis[j] + 1;
        }
        if (max < lis[i]) // Max LIS values.
            max = lis[i];
    }
    return max;
}

// Testing code.
public static void main(String[] args) {
    int arr[] = { 10, 12, 9, 23, 25, 55, 49, 70 };
    System.out.println("Length of lis is " + lis(arr));
}
```

**Output:**
```
Length of lis is 6
```

## Longest Bitonic Subsequence

**Problem:** Given an array, you need to find the longest bitonic subsequence.

**Solution:** Largest bitonic subsequence is the addition of the longest increasing subsequence and longest decreasing subsequence.

Optimal Substructure is
```
LBS = Max( LIS(i) + LDS(i) - 1 ) where i range from 0 to n.
LIS( Largest increasing subsequence) and LDS(Largest decreasing subsequence) are created.
```

```
function LBS(arr )
    maxValue = 0
    size = len(arr)
    lis = [1]*size
    lds = [1]*size
    for i in range(size)
        for j in range(i)
            if arr[j] < arr[i] and lis[i] < lis[j] + 1
                lis[i] = lis[j] + 1

    for i in reversed(range(size))
        for j in reversed(range(i, size))
            if arr[j] < arr[i] and lds[i] < lds[j] + 1
                lds[i] = lds[j] + 1
```

```
    for i in range(size)
        maxValue = max((lis[i] + lds[i] - 1), maxValue)

    return maxValue
```

**Example 18.24:**

```
static int lbs(int[] arr) {
    int n = arr.length;
    int[] lis = new int[n];
    Arrays.fill(lis, 1); // Initialize LIS values for all indexes as 1.
    int[] lds = new int[n];
    Arrays.fill(lds, 1); // Initialize LDS values for all indexes as 1.
    int max = 0;

    // Populating LIS values in bottom up manner.
    for (int i = 0; i < n; i++) {
        for (int j = 0; j < i; j++) {
            if (arr[j] < arr[i] && lis[i] < lis[j] + 1)
                lis[i] = lis[j] + 1;
        }
    }

    // Populating LDS values in bottom up manner.
    for (int i = n - 1; i > 0; i--) {
        for (int j = n - 1; j > i; j--) {
            if (arr[j] < arr[i] && lds[i] < lds[j] + 1)
                lds[i] = lds[j] + 1;
        }
    }
    for (int i = 0; i < n; i++) {
        max = Math.max(max, lis[i] + lds[i] - 1);
    }

    return max;
}

// Testing code.
public static void main(String[] args) {
    int arr[] = { 1, 6, 3, 11, 1, 9, 5, 12, 3, 14, 6, 17, 3, 19, 2, 19 };
    System.out.println("Length of lbs is " + lbs(arr));
}
```

**Output:**

```
Length of lbs is 8
```

**Time Complexity:** O(n^2)

## Longest Palindromic Subsequence

**Problem**: Given a string s, find the longest palindromic subsequence length in s. A Subsequence is a sequence that can be derived from another sequence by deleting some or no elements without changing the order of the remaining elements.

**Solution:** Recurrence Relation of the problem is:

$$\text{PalindromicSubSeq(i,j)} = \begin{cases} \text{PalindromicSubSeq(i-1, j-1) + 2} & \text{if char(i) == char(j)} \\ \text{max(PalindromicSubSeq(i+1, j), PalindromicSubSeq(i, j-1))} \end{cases}$$

Where i = 0 to n, and i<j<n.

**Example 18.25:**
```
static int largestPalindromicSubseq(String str) {
    int n = str.length();
    int[][] dp = new int[n][n];

    for (int i = 0; i < n; i++) // each char is itself palindromic with length 1
        dp[i][i] = 1;

    for (int l = 1; l < n; l++) {
        for (int i = 0, j = l; j < n; i++, j++) {
            if (str.charAt(i) == str.charAt(j))
                dp[i][j] = dp[i + 1][j - 1] + 2;
            else
                dp[i][j] = Math.max(dp[i + 1][j], dp[i][j - 1]);
        }
    }
    return dp[0][n - 1];
}

// Testing code.
public static void main(String[] args) {
    String str = "ABCAUCBCxxCBA";
    System.out.println("Largest Palindromic 
Subseq:"+largestPalindromicSubseq(str));
}
```

**Output:**
```
Largest Palindromic Subseq: 9
```

**Time Complexity:** O(n^2)

## Longest Palindromic Substring

**Problem**: Given a string s, find the longest palindromic substring length in s. A Substring is a string that is part of a longer string.

**Solution:** Recurrence Relation of the problem is:

$$\text{PalSubStr(i,j)} = \begin{cases} \text{PalSubStr}(i-1, j-1)+2 \text{ where char(i)=char(j) \& length(substring}(i-1, j-1)) \text{ is } i+j-1 \\ 0 \in \text{ all other case} \end{cases}$$

where i = 0 to n, and i<j<n.

**Example 18.26:**
```
static int largestPalinSubstr(String str) {
    int n = str.length();
    int[][] dp = new int[n][n];
    for (int i = 0; i < n; i++)
        dp[i][i] = 1;
```

```
    int max = 1;
    int start = 0;

    for (int l = 1; l < n; l++) {
        for (int i = 0, j = i + l; j < n; i++, j++) {
            if (str.charAt(i) == str.charAt(j) && dp[i + 1][j - 1] == j - i - 1) {
                dp[i][j] = dp[i + 1][j - 1] + 2;
                if (dp[i][j] > max) {
                    max = dp[i][j]; // Keeping track of max length and
                    start = i; // starting position of sub-string.
                }
            } else {
                dp[i][j] = 0;
            }
        }
    }
    System.out.println("Max Length Palindromic Substrings : " +
str.substring(start, start + max));
    return max;
}

// Testing code.
public static void main(String[] args) {
    String str = "ABCAUCBCxxCBA";
    System.out.println("Max Palindromic Substrings len: " +
largestPalinSubstr(str));
}
```

**Output:**

```
Max Length Palindromic Substrings : BCxxCB
Max Palindromic Substrings len: 6
```

**Time Complexity:** O(n^2)

## Longest Common Subsequence

**Problem**: Given X = {x1, x2,…., xm} is a sequence of characters and Y = {y1, y2,…, yn} is another sequence. Z is a subsequence of X if it can be driven by deleting some elements of X. Z is a subsequence of Y if it can be driven by deleting some elements from Y. Z is the Longest Common Subsequence, if it is subsequence to both X and Y, and length of all the subsequences is less than Z. Find the longest common subsequence Z given X and Y.

**Solution**: Optimal Substructure of the problem
Let X = < x1, x2, ..., xm > and Y = < y1, y2, ..., yn > be two sequences, and let Z = < z1, z2, ..., zk > be a LCS of X and Y.

- If xm = yn, then zk = xm = yn ⇒ Zk−1 is a LCS of Xm−1 and Yn−1
- If xm != yn, then:
    - zk != xm ⇒ Z is an LCS of Xm−1 and Y.
    - zk != yn ⇒ Z is an LCS of X and Yn−1.

Recurrence relation, Let c[i, j] be the length of the longest common subsequence between X = {x1, x2, …., xi} and Y = {y1, y2,…, yj}. Then c[n, m] contains the length of an LCS of X and Y

$$c[i][j] = \begin{cases} 0 & \text{if } i = 0 \text{ or } j = 0 \\ c[i-1][j-1] + 1 & \text{if } i, j > 0 \text{ and } xi = yi \\ \max(c[i-1][j],\ c[i][j-1]) & \text{otherwise} \end{cases}$$

```
function LCS(X[], m, Y[], n)
    Initialise dp[m][n]
    for i = 1 to m
        dp[i][0] = 0

    for j = 1 to n
        dp[0][j] = 0;

    for i = 1 to m
        for j = 1 to n
            if X[i] == Y[j]
                dp[i][j] = dp[i-1][j-1] + 1
                p[i][j] = ↖
            else
                if dp[i-1][j] ≥ dp[i][j-1]
                    dp[i][j] = dp[i-1][j]
                    p[i][j] = ↑
                else
                    dp[i][j] = dp[i][j-1]
                    p[i][j] = ←
```

```
function printLCS(p[],X[], i, j)
    if i = 0 or j = 0
        return

    if p[i][j] = ↖
        printLCS (p[],X[], i - 1, j - 1)
        print X[i]
    else if p[i][j] = ↑
        printLCS (p[],X[], i - 1, j)
    else
        printLCS (p[],X[], i, j - 1)
```

**Example 18.27:**

```
static int LCSubSeq(String st1, String st2) {
    char X[] = st1.toCharArray();
    char Y[] = st2.toCharArray();
    int m = st1.length();
    int n = st2.length();

    int dp[][] = new int[m + 1][n + 1]; // Dynamic programming array.
    int p[][] = new int[m + 1][n + 1]; // For printing the substring.

    // Fill dp array in bottom up fashion.
    for (int i = 1; i <= m; i++) {
        for (int j = 1; j <= n; j++) {
```

```
            if (X[i - 1] == Y[j - 1]) {
                dp[i][j] = dp[i - 1][j - 1] + 1;
                p[i][j] = 0;
            } else {
                dp[i][j] = (dp[i-1][j] > dp[i][j-1]) ? dp[i-1][j] : dp[i][j-1];
                p[i][j] = (dp[i-1][j] > dp[i][j-1]) ? 1 : 2;
            }
        }
    }

    PrintLCS(p, X, m, n);
    return dp[m][n];
}

static void PrintLCS(int[][] p, char[] X, int i, int j) {
    if (i == 0 || j == 0)
        return;

    if (p[i][j] == 0) {
        PrintLCS(p, X, i - 1, j - 1);
        System.out.print(X[i - 1]);
    } else if (p[i][j] == 1)
        PrintLCS(p, X, i - 1, j);
    else
        PrintLCS(p, X, i, j - 1);
}

// Testing code.
public static void main(String[] args) {
    String X = "carpenter";
    String Y = "sharpener";
    System.out.println(LCSubSeq(X, Y));
}
```

**Output:**

```
arpener
7
```

**Time Complexity:** O(n^2)

## Edit Distance

**Problem:** Given two strings s1 and s2, find the minimum number of operations required to convert s1 to s2. The available operations are “Insert a character”, “Delete a character” or “Replace a character”.

**Solution**: To convert one string to another, there are a few cases to consider:

1 If any string is empty, then empty the other string.
2 If the last characters of both strings are the same, ignore the last characters.
3 If the last characters are not the same, consider all three operations:
  - Insert the last char of second into first.
  - Remove the last char of the first.
  - Replace the last char of the first with the second.

Recurrence Relation is

$$
editDist(str1,str2,m,n) = \begin{cases} n & \text{if } m = 0 \\ m & \text{if } n = 0 \\ editDist(str1, str2, m-1, n-1) & \text{if } char(m) == char(n) \\ 1 + \min(editDist(str1, str2, m, n-1), editDist(str1, str2, m-1, n), \\ \quad editDist(str1, str2, m-1, n-1)) & \text{otherwise} \end{cases}
$$

where m is index of str1 and n is index of str2

**Example 18.28**

```
static int editDistDP(String str1, String str2) {
    int m = str1.length();
    int n = str2.length();
    int[][] dp = new int[m + 1][n + 1];

    // Fill dp[][] in bottom up manner.
    for (int i = 0; i <= m; i++) {
        for (int j = 0; j <= n; j++) {
            // If any one string is empty, then empty the other string.
            if (i == 0 || j == 0)
                dp[i][j] = (i + j);
            // If last characters of both strings are same, ignore last characters.
            else if (str1.charAt(i - 1) == str2.charAt(j - 1))
                dp[i][j] = dp[i - 1][j - 1];
            // If last characters are not same, consider all three operations:
            // (1) Insert last char of second into first.
            // (2) Remove last char of first.
            // (3) Replace last char of first with second.
            else
                dp[i][j] = 1 + min(dp[i][j - 1], // Insert
                        dp[i - 1][j], // Remove
                        dp[i - 1][j - 1]); // Replace
        }
    }
    return dp[m][n];
}

// Testing code.
public static void main(String[] args) {
    String str1 = "sunday";
    String str2 = "saturday";
    System.out.println(editDistDP(str1, str2));
}
```

**Output:**

```
3
```

**Time Complexity:** O(n^2)

## Regular Expression Matching

**Problem:** Implement regular expression matching with the support of '?' and '*' special characters.
'?' Matches any single character.
'*' Matches zero or more of the preceding elements.

**First Solution**: Backtracking approach, traverse both the pattern and input string.

- If we see a '?' in pattern, then it can match with any character of the input string. To traverse the next characters of both pattern and input string.
- If we see a '*' in pattern, then there are two cases
  - We ignore the '*' character and consider the next character in the pattern.
  - We ignore one character in the input str and consider the next character.
- If both the pattern and input string are traversed to the end, then return match.
- If one of the patterns or input strings is reached to end and other not then return unmatched.

**Example 18.29:**

```
public static boolean matchExp(String exp, String str) {
    return matchExpUtil(exp.toCharArray(), str.toCharArray(), 0, 0);
}

public static boolean matchExpUtil(char[] exp, char[] str, int m, int n) {
    if (m == exp.length && (n == str.length || exp[m - 1] == '*')) {
        return true;
    }

    if ((m == exp.length && n != str.length) || (m != exp.length && n ==
str.length)) {
        return false;
    }

    if (exp[m] == '?' || exp[m] == str[n]) {
        return matchExpUtil(exp, str, m + 1, n + 1);
    }

    if (exp[m] == '*') {
        return matchExpUtil(exp, str, m + 1, n) || matchExpUtil(exp, str, m, n +
1);
    }

    return false;
}

// Testing code.
public static void main(String[] args)  {
    System.out.println("matchExp :: " + matchExp("*llo,?World?", "Hello, World!"));
}
```

**Output:**

```
matchExp ::true
```

**Time complexity:** O(2^n) since T(n) ≈ 2T(n-1) + 1, where n is the number of elements in str.

**Second Solution**: Dynamic Programming, Let T[i][j] be true if the first i characters in a given pattern matches the first j characters of the input string.

1. The 0th row will always be false, as empty expressions can't match with any input string.
2. * can match with an empty input string, so column 0 is updated accordingly.
3. Now process and fill the rest of the dynamic programming array.

4. If we see a '?' in pattern, then it can match with any character of the input string. To traverse the next characters of both pattern and input string.
5. If we see a '*' in pattern, then there are two cases
   - o We ignore the '*' character and consider the next character in the pattern.
   - o We ignore one character in the input str and consider the next character.
6. If both the pattern and input string are traversed to the end, then return match.
7. If one of the pattern or input string is reached to end and other not then return unmatched.

**Example 18.30:**
```
public static boolean matchExpDP(String exp, String str) {
    return matchExpUtilDP(exp.toCharArray(), str.toCharArray(), exp.length(),
str.length());
}

public static boolean matchExpUtilDP(char[] exp, char[] str, int m, int n) {
    boolean[][] lookup = new boolean[m + 1][n + 1];
    lookup[0][0] = true; // empty exp and empty str match.

    // 0 row will remain all false. empty exp can't match any str.
    // '*' can match with empty string, column 0 update.
    for (int i = 1; i <= m; i++) {
        if (exp[i - 1] == '*')
            lookup[i][0] = lookup[i - 1][0];
        else
            break;
    }

    // Fill the table in bottom-up fashion
    for (int i = 1; i <= m; i++) {
        for (int j = 1; j <= n; j++) {
            // If we see a '*' in pattern:
            // 1)We ignore '*' character and consider next character in the
pattern.
            // 2) We ignore one character in the input str and consider next
character.
            if (exp[i - 1] == '*') {
                lookup[i][j] = lookup[i - 1][j] || lookup[i][j - 1];
            }
            // Condition when both the pattern and input string
            // have same character. Also '?' match with all the
            // characters.
            else if (exp[i - 1] == '?' || str[j - 1] == exp[i - 1]) {
                lookup[i][j] = lookup[i - 1][j - 1];
            }
            // If characters don't match
            else {
                lookup[i][j] = false;
            }
        }
    }
    return lookup[m][n];
}
```

**Time complexity:** T(n)=O(m*n), where n is the length of a text string and m is the length of the pattern.

## Type 5 : State Selection kind of problems

We need to reach at some final state. To create a current state you need to decide which previous state needs to be used. We need to choose the previous states which gives the best result.

Solution of State-Selection problems will look something like this:
```
int BottomUpFunction(int[] costs) {
    int n = costs.length;
    int[][] dp = new int[n][2];
    /* Initialization of 0th state of various types.*/
    dp[0][1] = /* Initialization value */
    dp[0][0] = /* Initialization value */

    for (int i = 1; i < n; ++i) {
        dp[i][1] = /*Max values based on previous states.*/
        dp[i][0] = /*Max values based on previous states.*/
    }
    return Math.max(dp[n-1][1] , dp[n-1][0]);
}
```

### Assembly Line Scheduling

**Problem**: Calculate the least amount of time necessary to build a car when using a manufacturing chain with two assembly lines. The problem variables:

1. e[i]: entry time in assembly line i
2. x[i]: exit time from assembly line i
3. a[i, j]: Time required at station S[i, j] (assembly line i, stage j)
4. t[i, j]: Time required to transit from station S[i, j] to the other assembly line

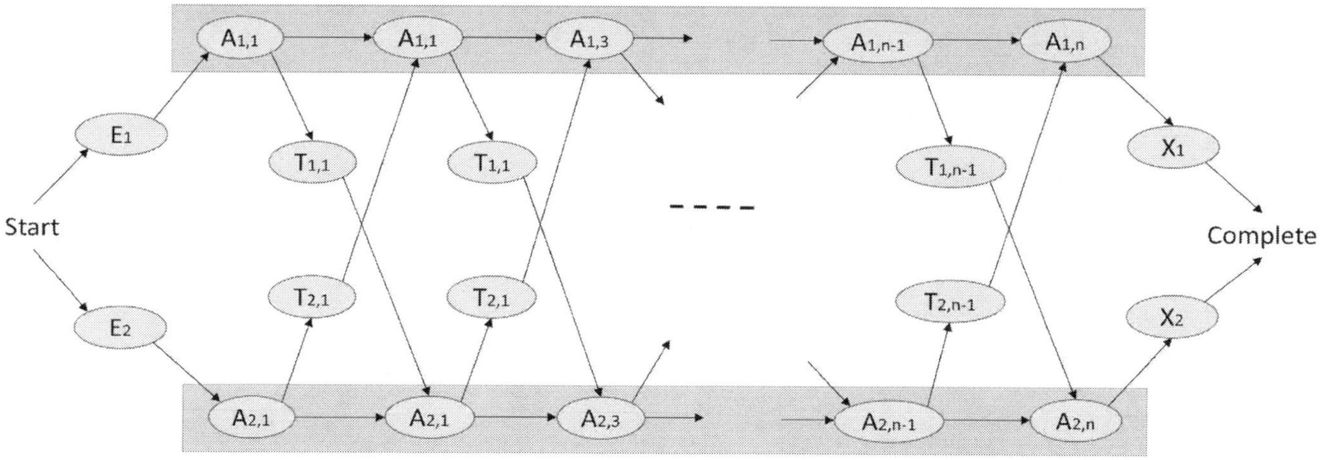


**Solution**: This program must calculate:

1. The least amount of time needed to build a car
2. The array of stations to traverse to assemble a car as fast as possible.

The manufacturing chain will have no more than 50 stations.

If we want to solve this problem in the brute force approach, there will be in total $2^n$ Different combinations, so the Time complexity is $O(2^n)$

Step 1: Characterising the class of the optimal solution
To calculate the fastest assembly time, we only need to know the fastest time to $S1_n$ and the fastest time to $S2_n$, including the assembly time for the nth part. Then we choose between the two exit points by taking into consideration the extra time required, x1 and x2. To compute the fastest time to $S1_n$ we only need to know the fastest time to $S1_{n-1}$ and to $S2_{n-1}$. Then there are only two choices.

Step 2: A recursive definition of the values to be computed

$$f1[j] = \begin{cases} e1 + a1[1] & if\ j=1 \\ min(f1[j-1] + a1[j],\ f2[j-1] + t2[j-1] + a1[j]) \end{cases}$$

$$f2[j] = \begin{cases} e2 + a2[1] & if\ j=1 \\ min(f2[j-1] + a2[j],\ f1[j-1] + t1[j-1] + a2[j]) \end{cases}$$

Step 3: Computing the fastest time finally, compute f* as
Step 4: Computing the fastest path computes li[j] as the choice made for fi[j] (whether the first or the second term gives the minimum). Also, compute the choice for f* as l*.

```
function FASTESTWAY(a, t, e, x, n)
    f1[1] ← e1 + a1[1]
    f2[1] ← e2 + a2[1]

    for j ← 2 to n do
        f1[j] ← min( f1[j-1] + a1[j], f2[j-1] + t2[j-1] + a1[j])
        f2[j] ← min( f2[j-1] + a2[j], f1[j-1] + t1[j-1] + a2[j])

    return min(f1[n] + x1, f2[n] + x2)
```

**Example 18.31:**

```
static int fastestWayBU(int a[][], int t[][], int e[], int x[], int n) {
    int[][] f = new int[2][n];

    // Time taken to leave first station.
    f[0][0] = e[0] + a[0][0];
    f[1][0] = e[1] + a[1][0];

    // Fill the tables f1[] and f2[] using
    // bottom up approach.
    for (int i = 1; i < n; ++i) {
        f[0][i] = Math.min(f[0][i - 1] + a[0][i], f[1][i - 1] + t[1][i - 1] + a[0]
[i]);
        f[1][i] = Math.min(f[1][i - 1] + a[1][i], f[0][i - 1] + t[0][i - 1] + a[1]
[i]);
    }

    // Consider exit times and return minimum.
    return Math.min(f[0][n - 1] + x[0], f[1][n - 1] + x[1]);
}
```

```
// Testing code.
public static void main(String[] args) {
    int a[][] = { { 7, 9, 3, 4, 8, 4 }, { 8, 5, 6, 4, 5, 7 } };
    int t[][] = { { 2, 3, 1, 3, 4 }, { 2, 1, 2, 2, 1 } };
    int e[] = { 2, 4 };
    int x[] = { 3, 2 };
    int n = 6;
    System.out.println(fastestWayBU(a, t, e, x, n));
}
```

**Output:**

```
38
```

**Time Complexity:** O(n)

## 0/1 Knapsack

Problem: Given an item with cost C1, C2,..., Cn, and volume V1, V2,..., Vn and knapsack of capacity Vmax, find the most valuable (max ∑Cj) that fits in the knapsack (∑Vj ≤ Vmax).

**Solution 1**: Brute-force algorithm, In this approach, we will consider all the combinations for which each element is included or not included.

**Example 18.32:** Brute-force algorithm to solve 0/1 knapsack problem.

```
int maxCost01Knapsack(int[] wt, int[] cost, int capacity) {
    int n = wt.length;
    return maxCost01KnapsackUtil(wt, cost, n, capacity);
}

int maxCost01KnapsackUtil(int[] wt, int[] cost, int n, int capacity) {
    // Base Case
    if (n == 0 || capacity == 0)
        return 0;

    // Return the maximum of two cases:
    // (1) nth item is included
    // (2) nth item is not included
    int first = 0;
    if (wt[n - 1] <= capacity)
        first = cost[n - 1] + maxCost01KnapsackUtil(wt, cost, n - 1, capacity -
wt[n - 1]);

    int second = maxCost01KnapsackUtil(wt, cost, n - 1, capacity);
    return Math.max(first, second);
}

// Testing code.
public static void main(String[] args) {
    int[] wt = { 10, 40, 20, 30 };
    int[] cost = { 60, 40, 90, 120 };
    int capacity = 50;
    double maxCost = maxCost01Knapsack(wt, cost, capacity);
    System.out.println("Maximum cost obtained = " + maxCost);
}
```

**Output**:

```
Maximum cost obtained = 210.0
```

**Time complexity:** T(n) ≈ 2T(n-1) + 1. the time complexity will be O(2^n)

**Solution 2**: Dynamic Programming Approach, In this approach, we will create a dp array dp[][] with the size of capacity x item index. We will maximise the cost that can be generated in a given weight capacity with the first i elements.

**Example 18.33: Top-down** dynamic programming approach to solve 0/1 knapsack problem.

```
int maxCost01KnapsackTD(int[] wt, int[] cost, int capacity) {
    int n = wt.length;
    int[][] dp = new int[capacity + 1][n + 1];
    return maxCost01KnapsackTD(dp, wt, cost, n, capacity);
}

int maxCost01KnapsackTD(int[][] dp, int[] wt, int[] cost, int i, int w) {
    if (w == 0 || i == 0)
        return 0;

    if (dp[w][i] != 0)
        return dp[w][i];

    // Their are two cases:
    // (1) ith item is included
    // (2) ith item is not included
    int first = 0;
    if (wt[i - 1] <= w)
        first = maxCost01KnapsackTD(dp, wt, cost, i - 1, w - wt[i - 1]) + cost[i -
1];

    int second = maxCost01KnapsackTD(dp, wt, cost, i - 1, w);
    return dp[w][i] = Math.max(first, second);
}
```

**Example 18.34: Bottom-Up** dynamic programming approach to solve 0/1 knapsack problem.

```
int maxCost01KnapsackBU(int[] wt, int[] cost, int capacity) {
    int n = wt.length;
    int[][] dp = new int[capacity + 1][n + 1];

    // Build table dp[][] in bottom up approach.
    // Weights considered against capacity.
    for (int w = 1; w <= capacity; w++) {
        for (int i = 1; i <= n; i++) {
            // Their are two cases:
            // (1) ith item is included
            // (2) ith item is not included
            int first = 0;
            if (wt[i - 1] <= w)
                first = dp[w - wt[i - 1]][i - 1] + cost[i - 1];

            int second = dp[w][i - 1];
            dp[w][i] = Math.max(first, second);
        }
    }
```

```
    printItems(dp, wt, cost, n, capacity);
    return dp[capacity][n]; // Number of weights considered and final capacity.
}

void printItems(int[][] dp, int[] wt, int[] cost, int n, int capacity) {
    int totalCost = dp[capacity][n];
    System.out.print("Selected items are:");
    for (int i = n - 1; i > 0; i--) {
        if (totalCost != dp[capacity][i - 1]) {
            System.out.print(" (wt:" + wt[i] + ", cost:" + cost[i] + ")");
            capacity -= wt[i];
            totalCost -= cost[i];
        }
    }
}

// Testing code.
public static void main(String[] args) {
    int[] wt = { 10, 40, 20, 30 };
    int[] cost = { 60, 40, 90, 120 };
    int capacity = 50;
    double maxCost = maxCost01KnapsackBU(wt, cost, capacity);
    System.out.println("Maximum cost obtained = " + maxCost);
}
```

**Output:**

```
Selected items are: (wt:30, cost:120) (wt:20, cost:90)
Maximum cost obtained = 210.0
```

**Time complexity**: O(W*N), where w is the weight capacity and N is the number of objects.

## House Robber

**Problem:** A robber wants to rob houses along a certain street. He has a rule that he doesn't rob from adjacent houses. Given an integer array representing the amount of money in each house. You need to return the maximum amount of money the robber can rob without breaking his rule.

**Solution:** We can have two kinds of states in which ith house is not included and the ith house is included.
If the ith house is included then (i-1)th house cannot be included.
If the ith house is not included then (i-1)th house can be included / it's optional.

**Example 18.35:**

```
public static int maxRobbery2(int[] house) {
    int n = house.length;
    int[][] dp = new int[n][2];

    dp[0][1] = house[0];
    dp[0][0] = 0;

    for (int i = 1; i < n; ++i) {
        dp[i][1] = Math.max(dp[i - 1][0] + house[i], dp[i - 1][1]);
        dp[i][0] = dp[i - 1][1];
    }
```

```
    return Math.max(dp[n - 1][1], dp[n - 1][0]);
}

// Testing code.
public static void main(String[] args) {
    int arr[] = { 10, 12, 9, 23, 25, 55, 49, 70 };
    System.out.println("Total cash: " + maxRobbery2(arr));
}
```

**Output:**

```
Total cash: 160
```

**Time Complexity:** O(n)

## Exercise

1. Given number of elements n, display the fibonacci series with n elements. Create a linear time algorithm using both top-down and bottom-up approaches.
2. In the 0/1 knapsack problem, repetition of objects is allowed to solve the unbounded 0/1 knapsack problem.
3. In the coin change problem discussed before, write the code of printing coins selected.

   Take help from algorithms given with coin selection problems.
4. Similarly in climbing stairs, the problem is finding which all stairs are used.
5. In the Grid min value path problem, modify the solution such that diagonal movement is also allowed.
6. Generalised the min-cost travel problem such that the costs[] can take another array numDays[] which are the number of days corresponding to the ticket cost.
7. Implement printing Fibonacci series with the help of a few variables. Don't use arrays to store Fibonacci numbers.
8. In the Optimal Binary Search tree problem, write a function to print OBST.
9. In the Matrix Chain Multiplication problem, print the Matrix parenthesized.
10. In BST with minimum non-leaf node problems, print the tree.
11. Implement the Largest Increasing Substring. Also, implement The Largest Bitonic Substring.

# CHAPTER 19: BACKTRACKING

## Introduction

In the **Backtracking** approach, In each step of creating an answer, it is checked if this step satisfies the given conditions. If it does satisfy constraints, then continue generating the rest of the solution. If constraints are not satisfied, then we backtrack one step to check for another solution.

The way backtracking works is that we build up a solution step-by-step. Sometimes we realise that our current state isn't going to get us to the desired solution, in which case we 'backtrack' by going back a few steps. So we just undo the last few steps until our desired criteria are again met, and continue building our solution by making different choices this time.

Backtracking problems have the following components:

1. Initial state
2. Target / Goal state
3. Intermediate states
4. The path from the initial state to the target/goal state
5. Operators to get from one state to another
6. Pruning function

The solving process of the backtracking algorithm starts with the construction of a state's tree, whose nodes represent the states. The root node is the initial state and one or more leaf nodes will be our target state. Each edge of the tree represents some operation. The solution is obtained by searching the tree until a Target state is found.

Backtracking uses depth-first search:

1. Store the initial state in a stack
2. While the stack is not empty, repeat:
3. Read a node from the stack.
4. While there are available operators, do:
    - Apply an operator to generate a child
    - If the child is a goal state – return solution
    - If it is a new state and the pruning function does not discard it, then push the child into the stack.

# Problems on Backtracking Algorithm

## All permutations of an integer list

**Problem:** Generate all permutations of an integer array.

**Solution:** At each level of recursion, every element is positioned at the first position and the rest of the array is passed recursively to produce permutation of the rest part. When one element is completely processed then put it back to its original position. This solution is both brute-force and backtracking as a constraint is not there.

**Example 19.01:**
```
public static void permutation(int[] arr, int i, int length) {
    if (length == i) {
        printArray(arr, length);
        return;
    }

    for (int j = i; j < length; j++) {
        swap(arr, i, j);
        permutation(arr, i + 1, length);
        swap(arr, i, j);
    }
    return;
}

// Testing code.
public static void main(String[] args) {
    int[] arr = {1, 2, 3, 4};
    permutation(arr, 0, 4);
}
```

**Output:**
```
1 2 3 4
1 2 4 3
....
4 1 3 2
4 1 2 3
```

**Analysis**: In the permutation method, at each recursive call number at index, "i" is swapped with all the numbers that are right of it. Since the number is swapped with all the numbers in its right one by one, it will produce all the permutations possible.

**Time Complexity**: O(n!), where n is the number of integers.

## All permutations with constraints

**Problem:** Generate all permutations of an integer array. Such that no two consecutive digits have an absolute difference less than 2.

**Hint:** This is the same as the previous problem, but we have an extra constraint that the absolute difference of two consecutive digits should be greater than or equal to 2.

**Brute-force Solution:** All the different permutations are created and at the end, before printing them, it is checked that they satisfy the given constraint.

**Example 19.02:**
```
private static boolean isValid(int[] arr, int n) {
    for (int j = 1; j < n; j++) {
        if (Math.abs(arr[j] - arr[j - 1]) < 2)
            return false;
    }
    return true;
}

public static void permutation2(int[] arr, int i, int length) {
    if (length == i) {
        if (isValid(arr, length))
            printArray(arr, length);
        return;
    }

    for (int j = i; j < length; j++) {
        swap(arr, i, j);
        permutation2(arr, i + 1, length);
        swap(arr, i, j);
    }
    return;
}

// Testing code.
public static void main(String[] args) {
    int[] arr = {1, 2, 3, 4};
    permutation2(arr, 0, 4);
}
```

**Output:**
```
2 4 1 3
3 1 4 2
```

**Analysis**: All permutations are created and before printing the constraint is checked.
**Time Complexity**: O(n!), where n is the number of integers.

**Backtracking Solution:** While creating various solutions at each step, constraint is checked and further state space is traversed only if the constraint is met.

**Example 19.03:**
```
private static boolean isValid2(int[] arr, int i) {
    if (i < 1 || Math.abs(arr[i] - arr[i - 1]) >= 2)
        return true;
    return false;
}

public static void permutation3(int[] arr, int i, int length) {
    if (length == i) {
        printArray(arr, length);
        return;
    }
```

```
    for (int j = i; j < length; j++) {
        swap(arr, i, j);
        if (isValid2(arr, i))
            permutation3(arr, i + 1, length);
        swap(arr, i, j);
    }
    return;
}
```

**Analysis**: All permutations are created step-by-step and before adding any number to the permutation it is checked if it results in a valid permutation satisfying the constraint. While creating a solution, if an invalid condition is found then it is reverted.

**Time Complexity**: O(n!), where n is the number of integers.

## N Queens Problem

**Problem:** There are N queens given, you need to arrange them in a chessboard on NxN such that no queen should attack each other.

**Solution:** Since the queen can attach horizontally, diagonally. Queens are added one by one, for horizontally we can make sure that no two queens are in the same row. The conditions that need to be made sure that the new queen added are in different columns and not diagonally attacking.

**Example 19.04:**

```
public static boolean feasible(int[] Q, int k) {
    for (int i = 0; i < k; i++) {
        if (Q[k] == Q[i] || Math.abs(Q[i] - Q[k]) == Math.abs(i - k)) {
            return false;
        }
    }
    return true;
}

public static void nQueens(int[] Q, int k, int n) {
    if (k == n) {
        print(Q, n);
        return;
    }
    for (int i = 0; i < n; i++) {
        Q[k] = i;
        if (feasible(Q, k)) {
            nQueens(Q, k + 1, n);
        }
    }
}

// Testing code.
public static void main(String[] args) {
    int[] Q = new int[8];
    nQueens(Q, 0, 8);
}
```

**Output:**

```
0 4 7 5 2 6 1 3
0 5 7 2 6 3 1 4
....
7 2 0 5 1 4 6 3
7 3 0 2 5 1 6 4
```

**Analysis**: The recurrence relation is T(n) = n*T(n-1) + O(n^2). Time complexity will be O(n^n)

## Tower of Hanoi

**Problem:** In the **Tower of Hanoi**, we are given three rods and N number of disks, initially all the disks are added to the first rod (the leftmost one) such that no smaller disk is under the larger one. The objective is to transfer the entire stack of disks from the first tower to the third tower (the rightmost one), moving only one disk at a time. Moving a larger disk onto a smaller one is not allowed.

**Solution:** If we want to transfer N disks from source to destination tower. Let's consider the bottom-most disk, it is the largest disk so can not be placed to any other tower except the destination tower. Also, all the disks above the largest disk need to be placed in the temporary tower then only the largest disk can be moved to the destination tower. So we move N-1 disks from source to temporary tower and then move the lowest Nth disk from source to destination. Then we will move N-1 disks from the temporary tower to the destination tower.

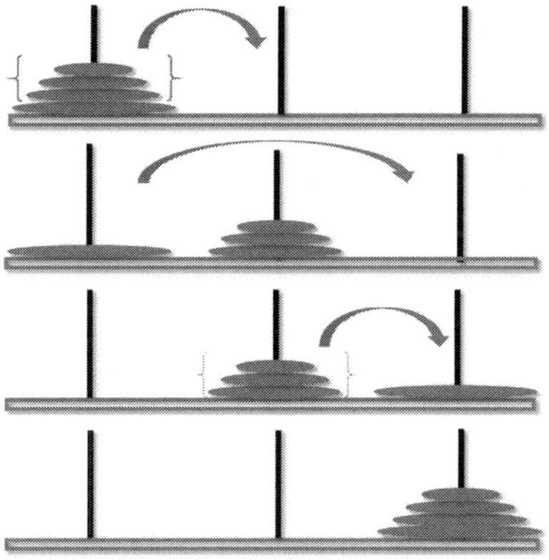

**Example 19.05:**

```
public static void tohUtil(int num, char from, char to, char temp) {
    if (num < 1) {
        return;
    }

    tohUtil(num - 1, from, temp, to);
    System.out.println("Move disk " + num + " from peg " + from + " to peg " + to);
    tohUtil(num - 1, temp, to, from);
}

public static void toh(int num) {
    System.out.println("Moves involved in the Tower of Hanoi are :");
    tohUtil(num, 'A', 'C', 'B');
}
```

```
// Testing code.
public static void main(String[] args) {
    toh(3);
}
```

**Output:**

```
Moves involved in the Tower of Hanoi are :
Move disk 1 from peg A to peg C
Move disk 2 from peg A to peg B
Move disk 1 from peg C to peg B
Move disk 3 from peg A to peg C
Move disk 1 from peg B to peg A
Move disk 2 from peg B to peg C
Move disk 1 from peg A to peg C
```

**Analysis**: Recurrence Relation will be T(n) = 2*T(n-1) + 1. So the final time complexity will be O(2^n).

## Graph Colouring Problem

**Problem**: Graph colouring is the procedure of assignment of colours to each vertex of a graph G such that no adjacent vertices get the same colour. The objective is to minimise the number of colours while colouring a graph.

**Brute-force solution**: Various colours are assigned to all the nodes one by one. When all the nodes are coloured, then the constraint checking function isSafe2() is used to check if a colour assignment is correct or not. This is the brute force approach as various permutations of colours are assigned, and then it is checked if criteria are fulfilled or not.

**Example 19.06:**

```
static void printSolution(int[] colour, int V) {
    System.out.print("Assigned colours are::");
    for (int i = 0; i < V; i++)
        System.out.print(" " + colour[i]);
    System.out.println();
}

// Check if the whole graph is coloured properly.
static boolean isSafe2(boolean[][] graph, int[] colour, int V) {
    for (int i = 0; i < V; i++)
        for (int j = i + 1; j < V; j++)
            if (graph[i][j] && colour[j] == colour[i])
                return false;
    return true;
}

static boolean graphColouring2(boolean[][] graph, int V, int m, int[] colour, int
i) {
    if (i == V) {
        if (isSafe2(graph, colour, V)) {
            printSolution(colour, V);
            return true;
        }
        return false;
    }
```

```
    // Assign each colour from 1 to m
    for (int j = 1; j <= m; j++) {
        colour[i] = j;
        if (graphColouring2(graph, V, m, colour, i + 1))
            return true;
    }
    return false;
}

static boolean graphColouring2(boolean[][] graph, int V, int m) {
    int[] colour = new int[V];
    if (graphColouring2(graph, V, m, colour, 0))
        return true;
    return false;
}

// Testing code.
public static void main(String[] args) {
    boolean[][] graph = {{ false, true, false, false, true },
                         { true, false, true, false, true },
                         { false, true, false, true, true },
                         { false, false, true, false, true },
                         { true, true, true, true, false }};
    int V = 5; // Number of vertices
    int m = 4; // Number of colours
    if (!graphColouring2(graph, V, m))
        System.out.println("Solution does not exist");
}
```

**Output:**

```
Assigned colours are:: 1 2 1 2 3
```

**Analysis**: Since various colouring permutations are created and at the end, it is checked if the generated colouring is valid. This solution is inefficient. There is a total O(m^V) combination of colours. So the time complexity is O(m^V).

**Backtracking Solution:** In the backtracking solution colour is assigned to the nodes one by one and at each assignment isSafe() function is called to check if the assignment will produce a legal graph colouring.

**Example 19.07:**

```
static boolean isSafe(boolean graph[][], int V, int colour[], int v, int c) {
    for (int i = 0; i < V; i++)
        if (graph[v][i] == true && c == colour[i])
            return false;
    return true;
}

static boolean graphColouringUtil(boolean graph[][], int V, int m, int colour[],
int i) {
    if (i == V) {
        printSolution(colour, V);
        return true;
    }
```

```
    for (int j = 1; j <= m; j++) {
        if (isSafe(graph, V, colour, i, j)) {
            colour[i] = j;
            if (graphColouringUtil(graph, V, m, colour, i + 1))
                return true;
        }
    }
    return false;
}

static boolean graphColouring(boolean[][] graph, int V, int m) {
    int[] colour = new int[V];
    if (graphColouringUtil(graph, V, m, colour, 0)) {
        return true;
    }
    return false;
}
```

**Analysis**: Since a lot of invalid colouring combinations are discarded in between, this backtracking approach gives a more efficient solution. There is a total O(m^V) combination of colours. So the time complexity is O(m^V).

## Subset Sum Problem

**Problem**: Given a set of integers, find a subset of elements such that their sum adds up to a given target value T.

**Backtracking Solution**: For each element, there are two cases: it is included in the subset or not included. So the total state space is created with these two choices. If the partial sum is greater than the target value, then that combination cast produces the desired subset, so we need to backtrack in that case.

**Example 19.08:**

```
static void printSubset(boolean flags[], int arr[], int size) {
    for (int i = 0; i < size; i++) {
        if (flags[i])
            System.out.print(arr[i] + " ");
    }
    System.out.println();
}

static void subsetSum(int arr[], int n, int target) {
    boolean[] flags = new boolean[n];
    subsetSum(arr, n, flags, 0, 0, target);
}

static void subsetSum(int arr[], int n, boolean flags[], int sum, int curr, int
target) {
    if (target == sum) {
        printSubset(flags, arr, n); // Solution found.
        return;
    }
```

```
    if (curr >= n || sum > target) { // constraint check and Backtracking.
        return;
    }

    flags[curr] = true; // Current element included.
    subsetSum(arr, n, flags, sum + arr[curr], curr + 1, target);
    flags[curr] = false; // Current element excluded.
    subsetSum(arr, n, flags, sum, curr + 1, target);
}

// Testing code.
public static void main(String[] args) {
    int arr[] = { 15, 22, 14, 26, 32, 9, 16, 8 };
    int target = 53;
    int n = arr.length;
    subsetSum(arr, n, target);
}
```

**Output**:

```
15 22 16
15 14 16 8
22 14 9 8
```

**Analysis**: Flag array is used to create state space of the various elements of the input array. The flag value at ith index is true, then the ith element of the input array is considered in the subset. If the flag value of the ith index is false, then the ith element of the input array is not considered in the subset. Those subsets which do not fulfil the required criteria are ignored and backtracked.

**Time-complexity**: O(2^n)

## Exercise

1. Monks and Demons: There are three monks and three demons on one side of a river. We want to move all of them to the other side using a small boat. The boat can carry only two persons at a time. Given if on any shore the number of demons will be more than monks then they will eat the monks. How can we move all these people to the other side of the river safely? Provide bounding function, initial state and final state of these problems.

   Hint: In this problem, the bounding function is that all the monks are safe. The initial state is all the monks and demons on one side. The final state is that all the monks and demons are on the other side of the bridge.

2. Farmers Problem: Same as the above problem, there is a farmer who has a goat, a cabbage, and a wolf. If the farmer leaves the goat with cabbage, the goat will eat the cabbage. If the farmer leaves the wolf alone with the goat, the wolf will kill the goat. How can the farmer move all his belongings to the other side of the river?

   Hint: The bounding function is to discard all the states in which the goat and cabbage or goat and wolf are alone. The initial state is all the belongings of the farmer on one side. The final state is all the belongings of the farmer on the other side of the river.

# CHAPTER 20: COMPLEXITY THEORY

## Introduction

Computational complexity theory focuses on classifying solvable problems according to the amount of resources required to solve them using some algorithm.

There are two types of resources:
1. Time: Number of steps required to solve a problem.
2. Space: Amount of memory required to solve a problem.

## Decision Problem

Much of Complexity theory deals with decision problems. A decision problem always has a yes or no answer.

Travelling Salesman Problem as optimization and decision problem:

**Optimization Problem:** Given a graph G and vertices v1 and vn in that graph, what is the minimum weight of the path from v1 to vn that visits every vertex exactly once?

**Decision Problem:** Given a graph G, a cost C and vertices v1 and vn in the graph, is there a path from v1 to vn which visits each vertex exactly once and has cost less than C?

Many other problems can be converted to a decision problem that has answers as yes or no. For example:
1. Searching: Find if a particular number is there in the array?.
2. Graph Colouring: Can we perform the graph colouring using X number of colours, such that no adjacent nodes have the same colour?
3. Hamiltonian Path: Given a graph G and vertices v1 and vn in that graph, is there a path from v1 to vn such that it visits every vertex exactly once?
4. Hamiltonian Cycle: Given a graph G with vertices v1 to vn, is there a path through all the nodes such that each node is visited exactly once and comes back to the starting node without breaking?
5. Substring: Given a Text string T and pattern string P, find if P appears inside T?
6. Minimal Spanning Tree: Given a graph G with integral weights of its edges, Given some value K, find if the weight of minimal spanning tree is less than k?

## Complexity Classes

Depending upon time-complexities (Big-O notation) and some other properties, various solvable problems are classified into the following classes: P, NP, NP-Complete and NP-Hard.

The time complexities of various algorithms are used to divide problems into two categories, depending upon their growth rate.

| Name | Time Complexities | Category |
|---|---|---|
| Constant | O(1) | Polynomial Time Complexities (Clever algorithms with fast solutions) |
| Logarithmic | O(log(n)) | |
| Linear | O(n) | |
| N-log(n) | O(n.log(n)) | |
| Quadratic | O(n^2) | |
| Polynomial | O(n^c) c is a constant & c>1 | |
| Exponential | O(c^m) c is a constant & c>1 | Exponential Time complexities (Slow solutions which try all possibilities ) |
| Factorial | O(n!) | |
| N-Power-N | O(n^n) | |

## Class P Problems

Class P consists of a set of problems that can be solved in polynomial time by modern computers. The Big-O notation of a Class P problem is always polynomial. For example, O(1), O(log(n)), O(n), O(n.log(n)), O(n^2), O(n^c), where n is input size and k is some constant (k is independent of n).

Class P Definition: Class P contains all decision problems which can be solved into "yes/no" answers by a Deterministic Turing Machine (Modern Computers) in polynomial time.

A Deterministic Turing machine is a theoretical machine that manipulates symbols on a strip of tape according to a table of rules. Given the current state of the Deterministic Turing Machine, it can manipulate symbols on tape, then produce only one next state. A Turing machine can be used to simulate any algorithm and is particularly useful in explaining the functions of a CPU inside a computer.

Deterministic Algorithms: The algorithms in which we know every step of how they work, and conventional computers can perform them are called deterministic algorithms.

For example: Given a sequence a1, a2, a3…. an. Find if a number X is there in this list.
We can traverse the list and answer if the number X in this list in linear time (polynomial time)

Another example: Given a sequence a1, a2, a3…. an. Do you need to find if this sequence is sorted in increasing order?
We can again traverse the list and see if all the elements are sorted in linear time (polynomial time).

Some problem of P class is:

1. Stack insertion and deletion with time complexity, O(1).
2. Binary Search in a sorted array with time complexity, O(log(n)).

3. Linear Search in an unsorted array with time complexity, O(n).
4. Sorting using bubble sort with time complexity, O(n^2).
5. Sorting using merge sort with time complexity, O(n.log(n)).
6. Shortest path in an unweighted graph, O(n).
7. Minimum Spanning Tree using Kruskal's Algorithm with time complexity, O(E log V).
8. Closest Pair divide-and-conquer algorithm with time complexity, O(n.log(n)).
9. Matrix Multiplication Problem, O(n^3)

Trackable Problems: Problems that can be solvable in a polynomial time.

In-trackable Problems: Problems that cannot be solved in polynomial time. Or which have exponential solutions only.

## Class NP Problems

The Class NP consists of a set of problems that cannot be solved in polynomial time by conventional computers. But given a solution, we can verify the solution in a polynomial time.

Class NP Definition: Class NP means "Non-Deterministic Polynomial" class. They are kind of problems that can be solved in polynomial time by a Non-Deterministic Turing Machine (No such computer exists till now). The class NP contains all decision problems for which, given a solution, it can be verified if the solution is correct or not by a Deterministic Turing Machine in polynomial time. A problem Q ϵ NP if it can be verified in polynomial time.

A Non-deterministic Turing machine for some state and symbol pair, the non-deterministic machine makes an arbitrary choice between a finite number of states. At each point, all the possibilities are executed in parallel. If there are n possible choices, then all n cases will be executed in parallel. We do not have non-deterministic computers. Do not be confused with parallel computing because the number of CPUs is limited in parallel computing. In parallel computing, it may be 16 core or 32 cores, but it cannot be N-Core. In short, NP problems are those problems for which, if a solution is given, we can verify that solution (if it is correct or not) in polynomial time.

Non-Deterministic Algorithms: The algorithms in which some steps are not solvable in polynomial time by conventional computers. These steps can be solved by a Non-deterministic Turing machine in polynomial time, and so such a computer exists.

Now let's understand what a Non-deterministic algorithm looks like for a 0/1 Knapsack problem, which is an NP Problem.

```
// 0/1 Knapsack problem finds the set of objects that a thief can carry.
// Input: List of object weights & cost and capacity of the knapsack.
// Output: Set of objects that the thief can carry.

function NonDeterministic01Knapsack(Weight[], Cost[], Capacity)
    S = GetObjectSet()           // This is a nondeterministic step. Will give
                                 // a list of binary numbers each value of this
                                 // list corresponds to object in the input
```

```
                                  // list of which 0 means ignore and 1 means
                                  // take objects.
NetWeight = GetNetWeight(S)       // Linear time step.

if NetWeight < Capacity than      // Constant time step.
    Sum = SumAll(S)               // Linear time step.
    return Sum                    // Constant time step

return -1                         // Constant time step.
```

Since for a nondeterministic Turing machine, the non-deterministic step will take polynomial time. But we don't have non-deterministic computers, so this algorithm will not work in realistic computers.

P is a subset of NP ($P \subseteq NP$), any problem that can be solved by a deterministic machine in polynomial time can also be solved by a non-deterministic machine in polynomial time.

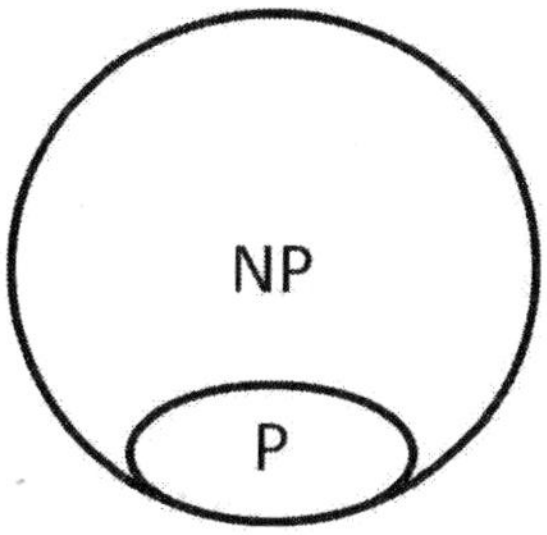


## Reduction

Given two problems A and B, we say that problem A is reducible to problem B if there exists a polynomial algorithm to transform A to B. If we have an algorithm to solve problem B, then this same algorithm can be used as a subroutine to solve problem A.

SolutionA = TransformAtoB + SolutionB

When this condition is true, solving A cannot be harder than solving B.

First Example: Quadratic Equation Solver: We have a Quadratic Equation Solver, which solves equations of the form ax2 + bx + c = 0. It takes input a, b, c and generates output r1, r2.
Now try to solve a linear equation 2x+4=0. Using reduction, the second equation can be transformed into the first equation.
2x+4 = 0
0x2 + 2x + 4 = 0

Second Example: ATLAS, We have an atlas, and we need to colour maps so that no two countries have the same colour. Let us suppose below are the various countries. Moreover, different patterns represent different colours.

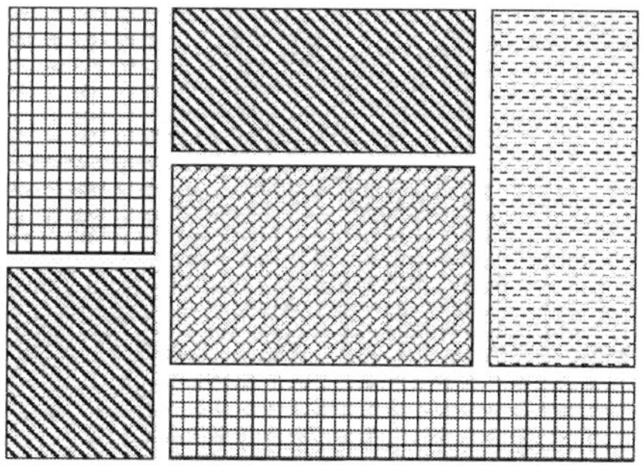

We can see that the same problem of atlas colouring can be reduced to graph colouring and if we know the solution of graph colouring then the same solution can work for atlas colouring too. Where each node of the graph represents one country, and the adjacent country relation is represented by the edges between nodes.

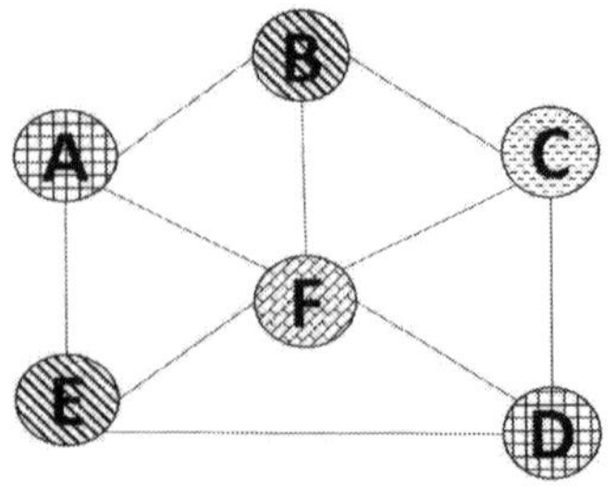


## NP Hard Problems

A problem is in Class NP-Hard if every problem in NP can be polynomially reduced to it. Because of this, NP-Hard problems are at least as hard as NP problems, but could be much harder or more complex.

The Class NP-Hard are a set of problems that are not only hard to solve but may be hard to verify as well. NP-Complete is a subset of NP-Hard and is verifiable, the rest of the problems of NP-Hard are non-verifiable.

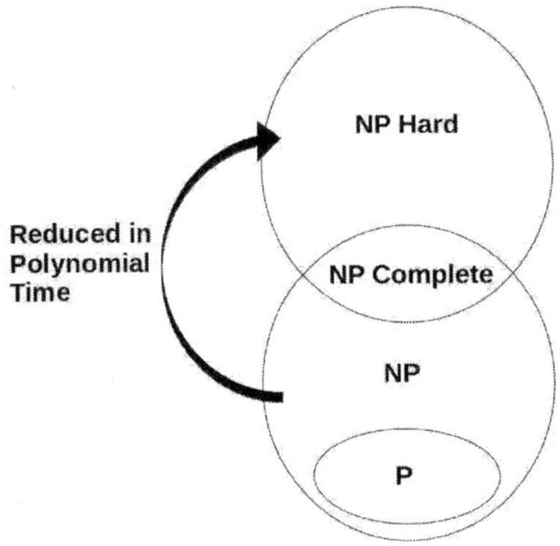


Note: If we find a polynomial-time solution to any problem in the NP-Hard set then since all the NP problem reduces to it, we will find a solution to all the NP problems in polynomial time.

## NP-Complete Problems

The Class NP-Complete includes all the problems in class NP and also in class NP-Hard. These are the hardest kind of problems in NP since all NP problems are reduced to it.

Properties of NP-Complete class are:

1. Its solutions can be verified in polynomial time.
2. All problems of NP are reduced to NP-complete problems in polynomial time.

**Note**: NP-Complete is a subset of NP-Hard so, If we find a polynomial-time solution to any problem in the NP-Complete set then since all the NP problems reduce to it, we will find a solution to all the NP problems in polynomial time. However, so far no one has found any solution to the NP-Complete problem in polynomial time.

For the question "Is P = NP" the solution is No-till now. If P=NP becomes true, then factoring of a number will become P and then various cryptography algorithms which depend on prime factoring become solvable in polynomial time.

Some NP-Complete problems are:

1. **Boolean Satisfiability Problem (SAT)**: Given a Boolean expression (i.e. (x1 V x2) Λ (x3 V x4) ....Λ (.. V xn) , is there an assignment of true or false to the variables xi so that the expression is true?
2. **3-CNF**: A Boolean expression in 3-CNF is an AND OPERATOR of Boolean clauses, where each clause has exactly 3 literals. (x1 V x3 V x4) Λ (x2 V x3 V x4) Λ (x1 V x3 V x4), is there an assignment of true or false to the variables xi so that the expression is true?
3. **Independent Set**: Given a graph G and an integer K, is there a set S of K vertices in G such that no two vertices in S are connected by an edge?
4. **Clique**: Given a graph G and an integer K, is there a set S of K vertices in G such that every pair of vertices in S are connected by an edge?
5. **Vertex Cover**: An vertex cover is a subset V' of the vertices of graph G = (V, E) such that for every edge (u, v) ϵ E, either u ϵ V' or v ϵ V'.
6. **Travelling Salesman Problem**: Given a graph G, a cost C. and vertices v1 to vn, is there a path from v1 to vn which visits each vertex exactly once and has cost less than C?
7. **Hamiltonian Path**: Given a graph G and vertices v1 to vn, is there a path from v1 to vn which visits each vertex exactly once?
8. **Graph-Colouring**: Given a graph G and K colours, is there a colouring of the vertices with K colours so that no two adjacent vertices have the same colour?
9. **Subset Sum**: Given a set of positive integers S = {x1, x2, . . , xn} and an integer K, is there a subset of S' whose sum equals K?
10. **Sub-graph Isomorphism**: Given two graphs G1 and G2, is G2 a sub-graph of G1?
11. **Quadratic Equations**: Given integers, a, b, and c, are there positive integers x and y which satisfies the equation ax + by =c?

How to prove some problem is an NP-Complete problem?

To prove NP-Complete, we need to prove both the properties.

- Its solutions can be verified in polynomial time. This property shows that if we have a solution to the problem, then we can verify that it is a correct solution in polynomial time.
- All problems of NP are reduced to NP-complete problems in polynomial time. This is a tricky thing to prove. What we need to do in this step is to prove that there is some known NP-Complete problem P' that reduces to this given problem P in polynomial time. Since all the NP problems reduce to P', which in turn reduces to P. So all the NP problems reduce to P in polynomial time.

## Boolean Satisfiability problem (SAT)

Given a Boolean expression, is there an assignment of true and false to the variables xi, so that the expression is true?
For example, (x1 V x2) Λ (x2 V x3 V x4) Λ … Λ (xn)

Cook's Theorem (1971) proves that the Boolean satisfiability problem (SAT) is an NP-Complete problem. The proof of this theorem is beyond the scope of this book.

There are in total, “n” Different Boolean Variables x1, x2… xn. There is an “m” number of clauses. At max, there are “k” variables in a single clause.
There are“n” variables, so the number of solutions will be 2n.
To find the solution for this equation, the total time complexity will be O(2n * km).
NP property: If a solution is given, then it can be verified in O(km) time.

## 3-CNF

A Boolean expression in 3-CNF is an AND of Boolean clauses, where each clause has exactly 3 variables. Is there an assignment of true and false to the variables xi, so that the expression is true?
For example, (x1 V x3 V x4) Λ (x2 V x3 V x4) Λ (x1 V x3 V x4)

NP property: A truth assignment is an assignment of true (T) or false (F) to each variable that can be verified by assigning these values in an expression in polynomial time.

We can convert any length clause to 3CNF with three variables.
(a V b V c V d) == (a V b V x) ∧ (¬x V c V d) // Converting 4 cnf to 3 cnf.
(a V b V c V d V e ) == (a V b V x1) ∧ (¬x1 V c V x2) ∧ (¬x2 V d V e) // Converting 5 cnf to 3 cnf.
(a V b) == (a V b V b ) // Converting 2 cnf to 3 cnf.
(a) == (a V a V a ) // Converting 1 cnf to 3 cnf.

All NP problems can be reduced to SAT and SAT reduces to 3SAT, so 3SAT is NP-complete.

## Independent Set

Given a graph G = (V, E), an independent set is a subset V' of the vertices of a graph such that if u & v ϵ V' then there is no edge (u, v) or (u, v) ∉ E.

Problem: Given a graph G = (V, E) and an integer K, does G contain an independent set of size K?

NP problem condition: Given an independent subset V' of the vertices of graph G with “n” number of vertices and “m” number of edges.

1. We first verify if subset V’ contains K elements.
2. For each pair u, v ∈V’ we check that (u,v) ∉ E.

There are O(n^2) pairs of vertices in V', so time complexity will be O(m.n^2) which is polynomial.

Now, to prove the Independent Set problem as NP-Complete, we need to reduce some known NP-Complete problems into Independent Set problems.

We will try to reduce 3-SAT to the Independent Set Problem in polynomial time. Let Q be a Boolean expression in 3-CNF. We want to express Q as a graph G so that if graph G has an independent set, then expression Q is satisfiable.

Steps to convert the 3-SET expression to the graph.

- Create a vertex for each variable.
- Connect each variable to the other two variables in the same clause.
- Connect each variable with its negation.

In the expression Q, "n" is the number of variables and "m" is the number of clauses. Q can be satisfied if and only if the graph has an independent set of size "m". This graph G is constructed in polynomial time O(m*n) so the reduction time complexity will be O(m*n).

## Clique Problem

Given a graph G = (V, E), a clique V' is a subset of the vertices V of G, such that if u, v ϵ V' then (u, v) ϵ E. That means all the vertices in the subset V' are is completely connected.

Clique Problem: Given a graph G and an integer M, does G contain a clique of size M?

For example: {A, B, E, D } is a clique of the given graph.

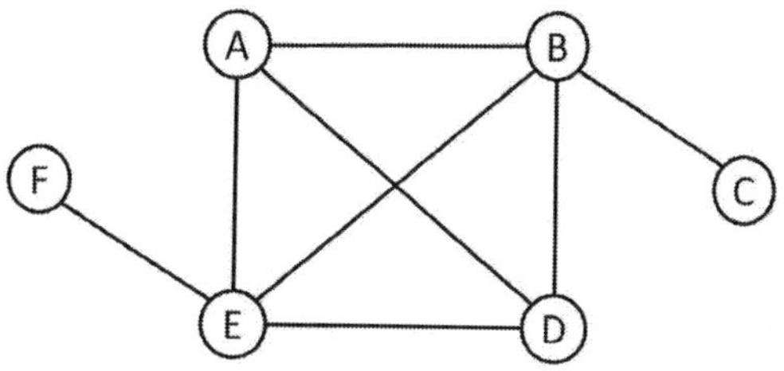


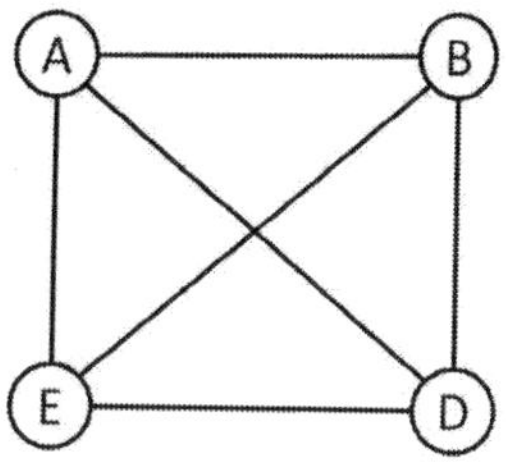


Clique of size 4

NP problem property: Given a solution to the clique problem is a subset V'. Let n be the number of vertices of graph G = (V, E) and m be the number of edges.

1. Check if V' contains M elements.
2. For each pair u, v ϵ V', check that (u, v) ϵ E. There are O(n^2) pairs of vertices in V', so time complexity will be O(n^2) time which is a polynomial in n.

NP-Complete property:
The Independent Set Problem reduces to the Clique Problem in polynomial time.
Independent Set Problem: Given a graph G and an integer K, does G contain an independent set of size K?

Note: In Independent Set the vertices of the set have no connectivity on the other hand in a Clique problem the vertices of the set have complete connectivity.

Complement of Graph: The complement of a graph G = (V, E) is a graph G' with the same vertices as G such that (u, v) is an edge of G' if and only if (u, v) is not an edge of G.

If V' is an independent set of G, then V' is a clique of G':

1. V' be an independent set of G = (V, E). such that every pair of vertices u,v ∈ V', (u,v) ∉ E.
2. G' be the complement of graph G.
3. By complement property, If (u,v) ∉ E. then (u, v) is an edge of G'.
4. That is. for every pair of vertices u,v ϵ V', (u, v) is an edge of G'. So, V' is a clique of G'.

Creating a complement of a graph takes O(n^2) time which is polynomial time.

## Vertex Cover

An vertex cover is a subset V' of the vertices V of graph G = (V, E) such that for every edge (u, v) ϵ E, either u ϵ V' or v ϵ V'.
The Independent Set Problem can be reduced to the Vertex Cover problem in polynomial time.

V' is an independent set of G = (V E), then V -V' is a vertex cover of G.

1. V' be an independent set of G = (V, E)
2. V'' =V - V'.
3. (u,v) ϵ E, since V' is an independent set either u or v are not in V'.
4. (u,v) ϵ E, at least one of the edge u or v is in V'' = V -V'. So V'' is a vertex cover of G.

The number of vertices in set V'' is equal to the number of vertices V of graph G minus the number of vertices in the independent set V'.

Vertex Cover Problem: Given a graph G, does it have a vertex cover of size M?
Independent Set Problem: Given a graph G, does it contain an independent set of size N-M? Where N is the number of vertices in the graph G.
Time complexity of reduction is O(n).

## Class Co-NP Problems

Given a solution, if we can check in a polynomial time if that solution is incorrect, the problem is a co-NP problem.

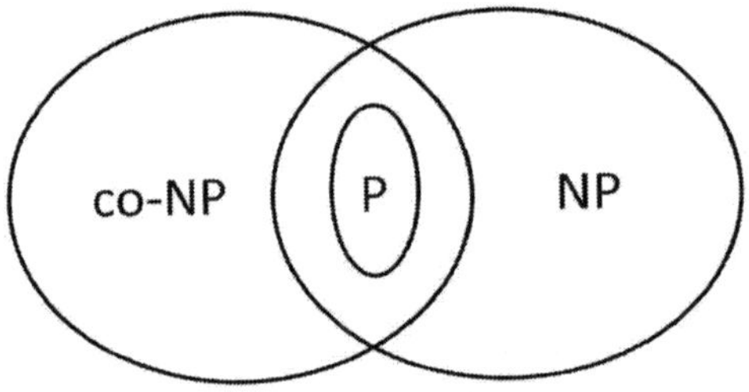


Relationship between P, NP and co-NP

## End Note

Solvable problems are classified into following groups based on time-complexities:

1 Class P problems are quick to solve.
2 Class NP problems are slow to solve but quick to verify.
3 Class NP-Complete problems are also slow to solve but quick to verify. Each NP-Complete problem can be reduced to any other NP-Complete problem.
4 NP-Hard problems are both slow to verify and slow to solve. Each NP-Hard problem can be reduced to any other NP problem.

Till now, nobody has come up with a polynomial-time algorithm to solve a NP-Complete problem. Many important algorithms depend upon it. However, at the same time, nobody has proven that no polynomial-time algorithm is possible. There is a million US dollars for anyone who can solve any NP-Complete problem in polynomial time. The whole economy of the world will fall as most of the banks depend on public-key encryption, which will be easy to break if a polynomial-time solution is found for any NP-Complete problem.

# APPENDIX

## Appendix A

| No. | Algorithms | Time Complexity |
|---|---|---|
| 1. | Binary Search in a sorted array of N elements | O(log(N)) |
| 2. | Compare two strings with lengths L1 and L2 | O(min(L1, L2)) |
| 3. | Reversing a string of N elements | O(N) |
| 4. | Linear search in an unsorted array of N elements | O(N) |
| 5. | Computing the Nth Fibonacci number using dynamic programming | O(N) |
| 6. | Checking if a string of N characters is a palindrome | O(N) |
| 7. | Finding a string in another string using the Aho-Corasick algorithm | O(N) |
| 8. | Computing the Nth Fibonacci number using dynamic programming | O(N) |
| 9. | Sorting an array of N elements using Merge-Sort/Quick-Sort/Heap-Sort | O(N.Log(N)) |
| 10. | The Knapsack problem of N elements with capacity M | O(N * M) |
| 11. | Finding a string in another string – the naive approach | O(L1 * L2) |
| 12. | Sorting an array of N elements using Bubble-Sort | O(n^2) |
| 13. | Two nested loops from 1 to N | O(n^2) |
| 14. | Three nested loops from 1 to N | O(n^3) |
| 15. | Twenty-eight nested loops … you get the idea | O(N^28) |
| | **Stack** | |
| 16. | Adding a value to the top of a stack | O(1) |
| 17. | Removing the value at the top of a stack | O(1) |
| 18. | Reversing a stack | O(N) |
| | **Queue** | |
| 19. | Adding a value to end of the queue | O(1) |
| 20. | Removing the value at the front of the queue | O(1) |
| 21. | Reversing a queue | O(N) |
| | **Heap** | |
| 22. | Adding a value to the heap | O(log(N)) |
| 23. | Removing the value at the top of the heap | O(log(N)) |
| | **Hash Table** | |
| 24. | Adding a value to a hash table | O(1) |
| 25. | Checking if a value is in a hash tabke | O(1) |

# Index

Made in United States
Orlando, FL
05 November 2026

90229888R00321